Love, Honor, Obey

Never let anyone know our relationship is anything but perfect;
Always smile when you're with Paul;
Be a perfect girlfriend for Paul;
Remember you're stupid;
Remember you're ugly;
Remember you're fat . . .
— From Karla Homolka's "self-improvement" list

She was a vibrant, spirited young woman who suddenly became a deranged man's plaything. He was the child of an upwardly mobile family, whose father cut the lawn in dress clothes and whose mother was obese and unkempt. They came together in a night of furious, passionate sex, and from there began a journey into terror . . .

A Main Selection of True Crime Book Club®

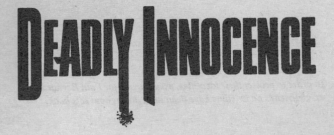

DEADLY INNOCENCE

SCOTT BURNSIDE AND ALAN CAIRNS

WARNER BOOKS

A Time Warner Company

In order to protect their identities, pseudonyms for Paul Bernardo's ex-girlfriends and victims have been used throughout this book.

WARNER BOOKS EDITION

Cover design by Tony Russo
Cover photo by Canada Wide Feature Service

Warner Books, Inc.
1271 Avenue of the Americas
New York, NY 10020

W A Time Warner Company

Printed in the United States of America

First Printing: November, 1995

10 9 8 7 6 5 4 3 2 1

Acknowledgements

If this book has merit, it is entirely the result of the people who have chosen to tell us their story. For many, talking about this was a painful process. But, put simply, they felt the telling of the truth was worth the pain. Dozens of people whose lives have been touched by this strange and tragic tale have chosen to trust us to tell that story. For that act of trust, we are humbly grateful.

Some of these people we can thank openly: Van Smirnis, Alex and Kathy Ford, Lisa Stanton, and Patty Seger. Others, whose jobs and careers depend on anonymity, were no less helpful in sorting through the rumor, the innuendo, the false-hoods. We thank you, too.

We are, by trade, journalists. We are not book writers. No one knows this better than Warner Books editor, Jeanne Tiedge, who bravely waded through some three thousand pages of manuscript, guiding the mass of information that follows to its final form. Thank you.

Our agent, Helen Heller, is also acutely aware of our short-comings as authors and our stubbornness as journalists. She, too, deserves a vote of thanks for her unflagging support.

As journalists, we ply our trade at the *Toronto Sun*. "The Little Paper That Grew," is one of the largest daily newspapers in Canada and one of the great success stories in print journalism anywhere.

From top to bottom, from publishers to senior manage-ment, through to the general assignment reporter on the street, there has only been support from the *Toronto Sun* for us and this project. Our colleagues and superiors have endured two trials, secret meetings, coded telephone calls and just plain cantankerousness from the authors. Thank you one and all.

On a personal note, Mr. Burnside would like to thank his spouse and best friend, Colleen McEdwards: You were always there when I needed a hug or a gentle nudge. Always. Thank you.

Alan Cairns would like to thank his dear son, Robbie, who did without his father so many nights and weekends: Don't ever forget I love you. I would also like to thank Jennifer Beale without whose inspiration and support none of this would have been possible; Lahring Tribe, for teaching me wisdom; my late grandparents, George and Mary Cairns, who raised, fed, and clothed me and taught me wrong from right by their own example.

Alan Cairns and Scott Burnside
Toronto
September 1995

DEADLY INNOCENCE

CHAPTER

1

To the south of St. Catharines, Ontario, between it and the neighboring city of Thorold, lies a serpentine-shaped stretch of water called Lake Gibson. Not far from two of the Great Lakes and the tourist attraction of Niagara Falls, this smaller lake is part of a man-managed water area that feeds the Ontario Hydro power-generating station at nearby DeCew Falls, which in turn feeds electricity to Canadians in the region. The scenic area has a long-standing history as a perfect getaway spot for country driving, picnics, skimming stones, canoeing, and fishing; a few secluded places serve as destinations for lovers—usually teens—seeking privacy; if luck is on their side, anglers can net relatively pollution-free pickerel, lake trout, speckled trout, and, on a good day, salmon. Of all the people who visit Lake Gibson, perhaps only the fishermen, those who watch the waters most, would be aware of the water fluctuations in this tranquil lake. While the average water level is 556 to 557 feet above sea level, it can drop three or more feet during peak times of power usage.

On Saturday, June 29, 1991 at approximately 5:30 P.M., William Grekul and his wife decided to launch their canoe into the fast-flowing waters not far from a dirt path off a gravel shoulder on Beaverdams Road. It was a perfect site because immediately to the right of the land protrusion, a small back eddy, perhaps thirty meters across, provided calm waters. But upon reaching the water's edge, Grekul was dis-

mayed to see that the water level had dropped about two feet.
He would have to stand in the muddy bank to launch his
canoe. It was then he noticed five blocks of concrete half buried in the slimy mud. With his wife waiting for him to push
off, Grekul used a paddle and his foot to dislodge what he
thought was a discarded patio slab from another block of cement. The concrete block tipped into the mud. To Grekul's
bewilderment, the bottom part contained what appeared to be
part of a human body. Refusing to believe his own eyes,
Grekul turned around, climbed into the canoe, and pushed
away from the blocks. Unsure of what he had seen and anxious to escape the hot summer day, Grekul shouted his apparent find to a couple of fishermen on a nearby bridge and then
paddled off for two hours. Upon their return to shore, the
Grekuls noted two fishermen standing a dozen or so feet from
the slabs, completely oblivious to them.

"Hey, you should look at those blocks. It looks like there's
part of a body in there," Grekul called to Reverend Michael
Doucette, thirty-eight, and his son, Michael Jr., nineteen. The
elder Doucette assumed that the canoeist was pulling his leg,
but he felt obliged to check out his find. Doucette trudged
through the slime to the blocks and turned another one over
with his foot. There, encased in the concrete block, was a
human thigh and a human shin and foot. A thigh lay in the
block Grekul had uncovered. He looked at the other blocks
and it appeared they were leaking blood or fluids of some
kind. The Doucettes ran out to Beaverdams Road and flagged
down a passing fire truck that was searching for teens reported to have been starting brush fires.

Within an hour a dozen Niagara Regional Police officers
from the force's Welland branch were at the scene. Two more
concrete blocks were discovered nearby. As uniformed officers scoured the surrounding area for fringe evidence, detectives took a cursory look at the slabs. In just over six years as
a police forensic investigator Terry Smith had seen enough
blood and guts to last him a lifetime. Having attended the
major crime scenes, he was used to photographing, taking
fingerprints and plaster prints of footprints, preparing suspect
facial composites of crime suspects, and taking weights and

measurements of evidence. But never had he videotaped a scene as eerie as the one before him. When darkness fell, he elected to secure the area overnight and start afresh the following morning.

Tipped to something newsworthy happening at Lake Gibson, reporters and photographers swooped to the area. Later that night, police wouldn't say much about the find. The body was so crudely dismembered that they couldn't ascertain even a tentative cause of death; nor was there any suspected identification because there were no recent disappearances of young women in the St. Catharines area. Staff Sergeant Ed Tronko told reporters: "I've never seen anything like this before. I've seen some pretty morbid stuff in my time, but never have I seen anything quite like this."

The next morning at about 8 A.M., fisherman Randy Zdrobov, his sister Karen, and Zdrobov's friend Randy Corman pulled their vehicle up to the Beaverdams Road spot to see numerous police cruisers parked there. Behind the cruisers, a length of yellow tape stretched from shore to shore of the tiny peninsula fishing spot. A Niagara police officer told them a better fishing spot would be the secluded bridge over Faywell Rd., a narrow lane off DeCew Road, which, of course, led to the DeCew Falls generating station. Reaching the idyllic fishing spot, Zdrobov and his sister put lures on their lines as Randy Corman fished from one of the steel bridge's concrete support posts.

"Hey, Randy, come here!" shouted Corman. "Look at that, man."

From atop the bridge, Zdrobov's eyes looked down; about five feet below him, a blackened human torso floated atop the murky water. To keep the torso from floating under the bridge and away in the current, Zdrobov held it in place with the tip of his fishing rod. Judging from the breast development, the body was clearly that of a female. The torso's limbs and the head had been crudely removed, perhaps cut by a saw or hacked with an ax.

As he was about to examine the seven blocks at Beaverdams Road, forensic investigator Smith was called to the find at the Faywell Road bridge. When he arrived, Zdrobov stood on the bridge, still using the tip of his rod to prevent the torso from floating away in the current. Smith realized immediately that the dismembered trunk was that of a female. He noted the absence of any penetrating injuries such as a knife wound. Thorold firefighters launched a rescue boat and cradled the torso in a metal basket with handles at the ends. Smith returned to the initial site as scuba divers continued to probe the lake in the area of the blocks for more evidence. The blocks were removed and placed in polyethylene bags and, along with the torso, were driven to the regional forensic pathology unit at Hamilton General Hospital and sealed in a refrigerated vault at the morgue.

That night, Debbie Mahaffy watched televised reports about a dismembered female body that had been found in Lake Gibson. Initial reports estimated her age at mid-teens to mid-twenties, five feet five, and about 110 pounds. Nobody, least of all Debbie Mahaffy, wanted to believe it was her missing fourteen-year-old daughter, Leslie.

Smith returned to the morgue the next day, July 1, 1991, to measure and weigh the blocks on an electronic scale. The three smallest blocks, which contained the right upper arm, right forearm and hand, and the left upper arm, weighed 39.8 pounds, 48.2 pounds, and 50.8 pounds, respectively. The next-heaviest block was one foot by one foot by eight inches and carried the severed head. The right thigh was encased in a block weighing a total of 106.6 pounds; the left lower forearm and hand and the lower left leg and foot were in a slab weighing 104 pounds; and the right lower leg and foot and the left thigh were in a slab weighing 126.6 pounds. As Smith, a short and lean man, struggled to lift the blocks and their grisly contents onto an examination table, he concluded that whoever threw the blocks into the lake must have been fairly strong. The torso itself weighed 53 pounds.

Smith and pathologist Dr. David King set about removing the body parts by delicately chipping away at the interior concrete borders with small chisels and hammers. Police were still baffled over the body's identification: there was no clothing, the ears were pierced, there was no nail polish, the hair was blond but had the appearance of having been dyed brown, and the eyes were apparently brown. Because of the hair and the eyes, police initially ruled out the body as that of Leslie Mahaffy despite the fact there were braces on the upper and lower teeth—just like those of the missing teen. Because of the dismemberment and the adherence of the concrete to the skin, the remnants were not easy to examine.

At 1:35 P.M., July 2, 1991, while Smith was again examining the body parts with Dr. King, he was told Niagara police divers had recovered a broken concrete block that had once contained the torso from under the Faywell Road bridge. The concrete casket was brought to Hamilton and weighed. The implication was enormous. It appeared the total weight of the casket and the torso was 200 pounds, meaning that whoever had tossed it over the bridge would have to have been extremely strong. More likely, two people had thrown the blocks into the lake. That day, X rays were taken of the body parts and Dr. King, in the presence of Smith, King's assistant Paul Swioklo, and resident medical student Robert Chen, commenced his medical examination of the remains and handed Smith various samples, including hair, splenic blood, bile samples, a hair from the anal cavity, brain tissue, swabs from the cuts to the limbs, and a vaginal wash.

As the days passed, police in Niagara and the adjacent Hamilton-Wentworth and Halton Regions, pored over missing-persons' reports and decided that no other teenage girl had gone missing within the short time frame that the person whose dismembered corpse was found in the lake could have been killed. Halton detectives still feared it might be Leslie Mahaffy, even though the Niagara detectives had ruled Leslie out because of the brown eyes and dyed-blond hair. Police took fingerprints and decided they would compare the teeth with Mahaffy's dental records.

On July 4, 1991, Ivan Severinsky took delivery of some concrete samples at his office, McGlone and Associates Ltd., in the St. Catharines area. A concrete expert, Severinsky was asked by Niagara police to determine what kind of concrete had been used to encase the young girl's corpse. Starting with the basic questions, Severinsky would, through a process of elimination, figure out the concrete type. He figured that whoever made the blocks must have used at least nine bags of Kwik Mix concrete. Police would ask local hardware stores to track down their sales of the cement.

Despite assurances from police, her husband, and other family members that the dismembered corpse could not be Leslie's, Debbie Mahaffy sensed the worst. Any doubts she had were eliminated when July 5, 1991, Leslie's birthday, passed without Leslie telephoning either home or a friend, which Leslie had done almost daily when she had run away from home before. When Robert ''Dan'' Mahaffy returned to Midland for work the week of July 8, 1991, Debbie went with him out of fear and loneliness. Together they stayed at his hotel room and awaited any news.

Meanwhile, Niagara detectives were cautioned by pathologists that the corrosive lime in the cement would have eaten through the eye skin and the cornea within hours and would have ultimately destroyed the colored iris, making it impossible to judge eye color. Leslie's dentist was on vacation in early July at his summer residence in northern Ontario. But he agreed to compare the jaw of the deceased girl with Leslie's dental records. On July 9, 1991, the dentist examined the charts and the dismembered girl's teeth and solved the mystery.

As the Mahaffys' watched Cal Ripken Jr. hit a three-run homer and the American League take the National League 4–2, in the televised All-Star Game at Toronto's SkyDome that night, Debbie Mahaffy heard footsteps approaching the hotel room's open door from the parking lot. She knew her worst fears were about to be confirmed even before Halton Regional Police Detective Sergeant Bob Waller, staff inspector Kent Laidlaw, and a victims' specialist arrived at the door. They knocked.

''You found her, you found her in the lake, didn't you?'' cried Mahaffy.

Then Waller told her the hardest news he'd ever had to deliver in his career as a police officer.

It was the day before Debbie Mahaffy's birthday.

CHAPTER
2

At the same time that William Grekul canoed along Lake Gibson, a young couple was married in a carefully orchestrated ceremony and reception many compared to a fairy tale. St. Mark's church, a magnificent stone building in the picturesque tourist village of Niagara-on-the-Lake, was the perfect and preferred setting for many brides-to-be in this quaint town not far from Niagara Falls and the New York–Ontario border.

But as the groom's mother struggled to her feet and began lumbering toward the head table at the Queen's Landing Inn, it looked decidedly more like a Monty Python script than a Brothers Grimm fantasy.

Marilyn Bernardo's ill-fitting mauve dress stuck to her lumpy body in an unflattering manner, leaving the distinct impression that she wasn't wearing a slip underneath. Her dark, short hair was slick, matted to the side of her head; from early in the wedding day there had been speculation about whether she had washed it at all, or had simply left it to dry haphazardly in the humidity. One couple, friends of the bride, suggested unkindly that Marilyn looked as if she'd been dragged through a hedge backwards. On her left leg was a white cast, which clomped noisily as she drew closer to the head table.

Alex and Kathy Ford glanced at each other from opposite ends of the head table and held their collective breaths. Married five months, they were close friends of Marilyn's son, Paul Bernardo, and his honey-haired bride, Karla Homolka.

Kathy fiddled absently with the puffy sleeves of the satiny, peach bridesmaid dress. Alex adjusted his bow tie. They were not quite sure why the sight of Marilyn ambling toward them filled them with such nervous anticipation, but the feeling grew nonetheless. Although they were separated by other members of the wedding party and couldn't share their thoughts, both recalled Marilyn's earlier entrance at historic St. Mark's. Refusing to wait for her traditional escort down the aisle to the front of the church, Marilyn had chosen to make her own way to her assigned seat, the echoes of her cast drifting into the wooden rafters on this hot, sticky June day in 1991.

Other guests waited patiently, fanning themselves with the wedding program Paul had produced on his computer and commissioned friends to tie with a pink satin ribbon. They watched Marilyn as she plunked herself down next to her wheelchair-bound mother at the front of the church. The conversation between the two women was loud, swirling uncomfortably around the rest of the pews, stiff competition for the soothing baroque music playing in the church.

From their seats in the designated bride's section of the church, Kathy Ford's parents, Stan and Lynda Wilson, tried to watch the mother of the groom without being too obvious. But it was painfully clear to them that Marilyn was giving a giant wad of gum a ferocious working-over.

"There's only one word to describe that woman," Lynda Wilson whispered to her husband, a math teacher at the St. Catharines High School, attended by both his daughter and Karla.

"Yeah," her husband answered, "cow!"

Outside the church, a magnificent horse-drawn landau rolled gently to a stop. Bells on the dun animal's harness jingled merrily. Cars full of tourists had slowed along the tree-lined streets of Niagara-on-the-Lake, beeping their horns in congratulations at the quaint sight on this fine Saturday morning. Tourists in sun hats and T-shirts motioned to each other to watch as the landau passed on its way to St. Mark's. A man on a bicycle paused to consider the spectacle.

Karla Homolka, resplendent in her white flowing gown, smiled slightly from the back of the landau. She sat facing her father, Karel, who was grinning self-consciously at the attention, a little stiff in his black tuxedo and black bow tie. Even the driver of the landau was dressed regally in a formal black jacket and à top hat.

"Smile, Karla!" someone yelled from the steps of the church while a video camera held by Karla's uncle followed the bride's every move. And, always obliging, the diminutive twenty-one-year-old grinned.

Minutes later the tall, striking figure of Alex Ford appeared in the doorway. One of four ushers, he escorted Karla's mother, Dorothy, down the aisle while the matronly strawberry blonde looked around nervously. Dorothy's entrance was the signal for the gathered guests that the time was near. Programs rustled and cameras were unholstered in anticipation.

Alex and the rest of the ushers stood in a line next to the groom, who was shuffling from foot to foot. The service had been delayed, and Alex couldn't help but think that Paul and Karla deserved this. Habitually late, their big day was also marked by delays.

Still, Paul Bernardo gave no indication of any nervousness or even mild concern about the delay in his wedding ceremony. His blue eyes were alert as he gazed toward the rear of the church watching for his bride.

The guests, who numbered more than 150, restlessly shifted in the wooden pews, as the church's grand organ released the first notes of the Bridal Chorus, follwed by "Here Comes the Bride" from Wagner's *Lohengrin*. As the bridal party appeared in the doorway, the sun framed their entrance, surrounding them with a soft glow as the bridesmaids walked down the aisle.

Paul's sister, Debbie, older than the groom by two years, appeared first, a tall woman teetering unsteadily on her heels. There were smiles and discreet waves to guests as the procession, in matching peach, made its way forward. Kathy Wilson

Ford and Debbie Purdie, both high-school friends of Karla, walked down the aisle as well as Karla's younger sister, Lori, and another childhood friend.

Finally the bride appeared, her father gently holding his eldest daughter's elbow. They passed Marilyn Bernardo, whose obvious chewing continued uninterrupted, and arrived at the front of the church. Paul smiled even more broadly as he nodded and accepted Karel Homolka's gift of his daughter in the traditional handing over of the bride.

Karel, a small wiry man with a pleasant disarming grin, bowed ever so slightly and smiled self-consciously as he retreated to his seat next to his wife, Dorothy.

Karla handed a garland of roses to her maid of honor, Debbie Purdie, and with both hands gently lifted the delicate veil from her face. Paul's head was slightly bowed, his hands clasped, and it seemed as though all of Karla's nervous attention was focused on her soon-to-be husband.

"Dear friends, we have come together in the presence of God to witness the marriage of Paul Bernardo and Karla Homolka, and to rejoice with them," the minister announced, his salt-and-pepper beard and flowing white gowns giving him a distinguished look. "Marriage is the gift of God and the means of displaying which man and woman become one flesh. It is God's purpose that a husband and wife become compelled to each other in love."

Somewhere, a child let out a screech that, picked up by the microphone, reverberated through the church. The child belonged to one of Paul's ushers and childhood friends, Steve Smirnis, and although the groom betrayed no emotion, he later gave Steve a dressing-down for having brought his baby boy to the church.

To Paul's right, the men of his wedding party were smiling and appearing attentive. They looked comfortable, but they were not. Most, with the possible exception of Alex, were suffering debilitating hangovers. Although the wedding pictures didn't show it, several of the guests remarked quietly that it looked as though the men of the wedding party had slept in their tuxedos. Earlier, most of the group of young men in their mid-twenties had been wearing sunglasses until the last possible moment in a not-so-subtle attempt to shield their bloodshot eyes from the unyielding sunlight or the judgmental inspection of the guests. Their boutonnieres which had arrived late, were jammed onto their lapels haphazardly.

Karla's bridesmaids were all smiles as well, beaming despite the heat, their bulky dresses, and the uncomfortable heels.

When the minister asked if anyone knew any reason why Paul and Karla shouldn't be married, Karla's younger sister Lori whispered aloud, "Is jealousy a good reason?" Kathy Wilson Ford thought she must have been hearing things. The words were spoken quietly by the slight, blond-haired girl, a year younger than Karla, and without a hint of irony or humor. But the moment passed and Kathy shook her head almost subconsciously: another surreal element to a wedding and relationship full of oddities.

After the exchange of vows and rings and readings from the Bible, Paul and Karla faced each other for the first time as man and wife. They smiled and embraced, Karla's tiny hands on Paul's biceps.

There was polite applause as the traditional signing of the register ensued. Karla's longtime friend and neighbor, Sarah Anderson, moved to the front of the church, where, accompanied by the organist, she provided a haunting version of the hymn "O Perfect Love."

Once the ceremony was over and everyone had left the stifling heat of the church, the official wedding photographer, a fastidious man named Haig Semerjian, competed with assorted handheld cameras as Paul and Karla posed inside the landau carriage. Behind the carriage, a Cadillac limousine was waiting to transport the bridesmaids while a black limousine waited for the ushers.

A second wedding group, thrown off schedule by the delay in the Bernardo/Homolka service, waited patiently in the parking lot of the historic church. They didn't have to worry about taking down bows and flowers from the sides of the pews from the earlier service, since someone had forgotten to bring them.

A friend suggested to Marilyn Bernardo that perhaps they

should move out of the way so the next group could make its way inside.

"Fuck 'em," Marilyn said without missing a beat, still rolling her gum around inside her mouth.

Finally, the landau moved on, bells jingling, bride and groom toasting each other with champagne, grinning and waving like characters on a parade float.

Behind, on the cobbled lane, the horse had deposited a great pile. No one bothered to clean it up.

At the reception several hours later, as the mother of the groom thumped toward the head table, Alex and Kathy Ford had a pretty fair idea of what was on Marilyn Bernardo's mind. Pheasant.

The entrée, pheasant stuffed with veal, was Paul's idea. In fact, the entire wedding was pretty much his creation although as Kathy and Alex couldn't help but notice, he'd borrowed ideas liberally from their recent wedding. Paul had picked out Karla's outrageously expensive dress—more than $2,000 U.S. for the stunning Demetrios number; a figure that continued to fluctuate depending on whom Paul was trying to impress. Karla's high-school friends who were in the wedding party or who'd gone to help her get fitted for her big day thought the Cinderella-style gown, festooned with heavy beads and sequins, was too imposing for Karla's tiny frame. Still, Paul was not to be denied. He'd supervised the purchase of the dress in Niagara Falls, New York, and had smuggled it back into Canada folded under the back tarp of his shiny gold Nissan 240SX sports car. The booze for the postwedding party had also been smuggled in from the States.

Even the bride's hairdo was dictated by the groom. Kathy and Debbie had lobbied unsuccessfully to have Karla's long, golden locks put up. It would look regal, stunning, they reasoned. How could she get her veil to stay in place with her hair down? They even tried to subvert Paul's decree by appealing directly to Karla's hairdresser. But Paul wanted Karla's hair down, and down it would be.

Paul had also dictated the tone of the vows, describing to Alex and Kathy how he wanted a traditional service and especially wanted the line "to love, honor, and obey" included.

DEADLY INNOCENCE 13

He also insisted that the minister pronounce them man and wife as opposed to husband and wife. This drove Kathy crazy, but Karla either didn't care or wouldn't risk opposing her husband on those details.

"It should be man and slave," Alex joked to Kathy, although neither found the comment funny.

The meal, too, was Paul's domain. It wasn't necessarily that he had strong feelings about pheasant, but Paul figured pheasant was the type of entrée befitting the grand scale of the wedding. And if it was to be a grand wedding with a grand entrée, then people could be expected to donate money and gifts on a similarly grand scale. Paul confided to Alex and Kathy beforehand that he viewed the entire process as a great business opportunity. "If I spend fifty dollars a plate, I expect to get a hundred dollars per person," the junior accountant proclaimed. He told them he'd set a goal of realizing $50,000 from the wedding.

Marilyn Bernardo, however, was not a big fan of pheasant. And she'd made that abundantly clear. At the rehearsal party the night before, after screeching about some artwork hanging in her son's fashionable Cape Code–style home that she felt belonged to her, she'd complained about the menu. At the photo session after the service in the sweltering Royal Botanical Gardens near the roar of Niagara Falls, she'd taken another run at her youngest child. And now, as she set her sights on the head table, it was clear that pheasant, again, was giving Marilyn Bernardo grief.

"I can't believe you got pheasant," she squawked. "I can't eat bird. I can only eat meat! You got this just to bother me!"

At several of the closest tables, guests raised their eyes from the offending bird, which some had muttered was only just lukewarm, or their leek-and-Stilton soup to watch the unfolding sound and fury.

Blond hair stylishly cut short, already on his way to a pretty good drunk, the groom looked up from his red wine, fixing his million-dollar grin on his mother. Pausing for a moment, he examined the odd-looking creature in front of him.

"Fuck you, Mom," his voice sounded out calmly. "Fuck you! Sit down and eat your fucking meal!"

A brief moment of surprised silence enveloped mother and son before Marilyn turned and thumped her way back to her seat. Not another word was spoken between the two. Paul, still smiling, gave his mother the finger and turned to Alex. In unison they shrugged their shoulders. Alex recalled a number of conversations he and Paul had had regarding Paul's mother, almost all of which degenerated into expletive-filled rants. Lately, he'd complained that his parents had ungraciously opted not to lend financial support for the wedding, a decision Paul believed had been solely his mother's.

At the other end of the table, Kathy turned to the best man and Paul's childhood friend, Van Smirnis. They, too, shrugged their shoulders. And soon the unpleasant exchange was swallowed by the muted clamor of dinner chatter and comfortable clinking of cutlery.

Periodically, the festivities were interrupted by the tinkling of knives and spoons on wineglasses, in the age-old tradition that signals the groom to kiss his bride. Paul needed little prompting, rising several times to embrace his new wife, much to the delight of the guests. At one point, he thrust his arm triumphantly in the air as they kissed, to enthusiastic cheers and hoots.

Paul's best man nervously watched the couple. Van Smirnis, born less than a year after Paul in June 1965, was about to give the speech he had been agonizing about for days. He had scribbled down notes, made periodic calls on his cellular phone to his old pal, and checked dates and details in an effort to compose a memorable toast. Sometimes Van was frustrated by the answering machine at Paul and Karla's immaculate new home in the St. Catharines suburb of Port Dalhousie. The sound of the beep annoyed Van, who suspected Paul was just sitting there, screening his calls as if he were a business tycoon or a Hollywood mogul.

He had helped Paul with the arrangements. He had held the ring and guided Paul through the dicey moments of the rehearsal and the postrehearsal party that threatened to get out of hand the night before. All of that had been easy. But speaking in front of everyone about his childhood friend seemed daunting to Van. He knew Paul better than anyone.

The wedding plans reflected exactly how Paul felt he should be perceived. The opulent, even excessive garnishes were an extension of his personality. The limousine fit the image to which he aspired perfectly.

This was Paul's big day, and Van knew it. A fastidious planner, Paul had everything organized for his day. Duties had been detailed and delegated to various friends. They were chores Paul expected to be taken seriously. At the Royal Botanical Gardens, where the wedding party endured a lengthy picture-taking session, Paul became enraged when he discovered that Lori Homolka had forgotten her bouquet of flowers at the church. And when the wedding party became a bit unruly, wilting in the heat, and the photographer threatened to pack up his equipment and go home, a clearly agitated Paul demanded that everyone shape up, or else.

On the ride to the church, Paul's back was to the limousine driver. He appeared distracted, fidgeting, looking out the windows, playing with the mini-bar and stereo and other gadgets. So Van began to discuss a business venture they were involved in, trying to confirm that Paul wasn't going to back out because of his marriage.

"Oh yeah, I'm in," Paul assured his best man. "I just wanted to think about it. I had a lot to think about. As soon as Karla and I get back from Hawaii, we'll get right back to work. Promise."

The great car was rolling quietly from Karla's hometown of St. Catharines through the countryside toward Niagara-on-the-Lake, past lush vineyards and fruit groves en route to the church.

"If you want, we'll just split and get out of here. You don't feel like getting married. . . . You want to go to Florida, we'll go to Florida," Van offered.

"Don't worry, buddy, I'm still going to be the same guy. The same nice guy," Paul answered, the grin that had broken a hundred hearts creasing his face.

"Hey, wouldn't it be funny if Alyson and Kim showed up?" Van asked, referring straight-faced to two young women the boys had met on Paul's wild bachelor-party trip to Florida three months earlier, and with whom they'd maintained steady contact.

"Oh shit, man, don't even talk about it. Don't even talk like that," Paul said, dismissing the subject.

"Oh, I don't know, she might surprise you," Van joked.

Standing at the microphone in the basement banquet hall of the elegant waterfront Queen's Landing Inn, Van began describing the night Paul and Karla met. This was a good topic for him. He had been there.

"Rockets were flying that night, believe me," the husky, good-looking Greek began. "I knew that my brotherly love would have to be shared with Karla. But I'm willing to share that with such a beautiful person as her."

The sharing suggestion drew a number of derisive catcalls from the audience, which made Van blush, but he continued, ultimately mumbling his last few words as he toasted the bride and groom.

Van's older brother, Steve, was the master of ceremonies. The publisher of a builder and architect magazine, he and his wife, Bev, lived across the border in Youngstown, New York. He was doing his best to regulate the flow of speakers to the microphone amid the dinner clatter.

The next speaker Steve Smirnis called to the microphone was Karel Homolka. There was a visible change in the dinner guests' demeanor: more attention, louder applause, and then more-pronounced silence. People seemed to be on edge as Karel made his way somewhat unsteadily to the microphone.

"To my daughter and son . . . I wish I had a drink with me right now," he said absently, and magically a glass of red wine was produced from the audience to a ripple of hoots and hollers. There was reason for his uneasiness. Karel, his reading glasses perched unsteadily on the end of his nose, was about to make a toast at his oldest daughter's wedding, while he and the rest of the family were still dealing with the sudden death six months earlier of his youngest daughter, Tammy Lyn. Two weeks shy of her sixteenth birthday, Tammy Lyn had asphyxiated and died in the family home on Christmas Eve. Both Paul and Karla had been with the young girl at the time; Paul had tried in vain to revive his future sister-in-law with mouth-to-mouth resuscitation.

"To all my friends here. Paul now is officially in Karla's hands. I want to make a toast to my daughter and my son. I also want to thank our friends and relatives for their love and support over the past six months. Please join me in a special toast to honor our angel, Tammy Lyn." Karel raised his glass and looked heavenward.

Behind him came the sound of glasses chinking and subdued whispers of "To Tammy. To Tammy Lyn." Throughout the reception hall, guests dabbed their eyes and reached out to touch Karel as he made his way back to his table near the front of the hall.

The specter of Tammy's sudden death loomed large over the wedding. There had been much debate about whether the wedding should even go ahead. Karla's parents, who were footing the bill for much of the extravagant affair, made it clear to friends that the unexpected burden of having to bury their youngest daughter, coupled with the wedding, was breaking them. But Karla and Paul were determined that the wedding they'd imagined and planned for would go ahead according to script, and in fact suggested that Karel and Dorothy mortgage their house in order to fulfill their promise to the bride and groom. There was also discussion about the appropriate way to recognize Tammy without destroying Paul and Karla's special day.

Initially, Karla had wanted to leave an empty space for her as the bridesmaids made their way to the front of the church, or to leave an empty place setting at the head table. But Kathy Wilson Ford and others convinced her that such a tribute might be too morbid for a wedding-day celebration. So it was left to Karel to remember the buoyant, happy teen, painfully absent on that day. The family's loss was made abundantly clear during dinner as friends of Paul and Karla unveiled a slide presentation showing both as children, as youngsters growing up, and young adults dating one another. Among the pictures were several showing Tammy frolicking around the Homolka family pool.

For a few moments after Karel's toast an uncomfortable

silence gripped the hall as Paul's father and then the couple's many friends made their way to the microphone. Once the party atmosphere resumed, the guests danced in the elegant reception hall. When Paul approached Karla's childhood friend, Lisa Stanton, she agreed to dance with the drunken groom.

Lisa looked into Paul's blue eyes and at his huge grin.

"You'd better take care of her," she warned, an edge to her voice that she couldn't or wouldn't control.

"Oh, I will, don't worry," he said, still smiling.

But somehow Lisa couldn't help but recall the scene in Niagara Falls, New York, about a month before the big day, during one of the final fittings for Karla's wedding dress. Dorothy, Kathy, Lori, and Lisa were waiting in a large fitting room as Karla deliberated over what kind of veil to wear. As she changed, Lisa found herself staring at her childhood friend's gaunt frame. Her ribs were plainly visible and there were angry bruises down her left side, as though someone had grabbed her roughly. Lisa had looked at Kathy and they had both shaken their heads.

Afterward, in a corner of the reception hall, someone had set up a video camera. The guests, some of whom appeared to have ingested vast quantities of alcohol, stopped by and sent best wishes to the happy couple.

Paul's sister Debbie Bernardo, cigarette smoke wafting around her, set herself in front of the camera. "Paul, Karla, the wedding was fabulous. Karla, you're a great sister-in-law. Paul, well, what can I say, you're my brother. Have a good life. I hope you guys are very happy together."

"Hello, brother," Paul's older sibling, Dave Bernardo began. "By the time you see this video, you will probably be already married. I wish you the best and take it easy on all the women." With a big, goofy grin and then a laugh, he added, "That is, ex-women, Karla, in case you're listening. Anyways, you know my feelings. Give me a shout sometimes, whenever you get in trouble or anything like that, which I don't think you will. Anyway, all the best."

Steve Smirnis followed. "Buddy, I wish you the best, I love you guys no matter what, good times, bad times, call me, anytime, and I'll be there. I'll be at your beck and call, whenever you want, just call me. Like I said, you're the cutest couple in the world. I'm happy to be your designated driver for your wedding weekend. I'll look after your friends and family. I love being with them all.''

Van also added his wishes. ''I wish you all the best. Karla, keep an eye on him. I love you guys. I can't wait till you guys get back.''

Andy Douglas, a friend of Paul's, had earlier toasted the couple saying, ''Karla, you're an animal lover. Paul, you're an animal.'' Now he followed the parade to the camera. ''Good luck. I know you're great for each other. I've never seen animal lovers so good together. I love both of you. It's the only wedding I've ever been to where, when they said pray for their happiness, I really prayed for you guys. I really want it to work. I know you guys are committed.''

The sounds of the party winding down floated across the water behind the reception hall. Steve Smirnis decided to stay with the rest of the guys from the wedding party, so his wife, Bev, hitched a ride with a friend, who was also a coworker of Dorothy Homolka at Shaver Hospital in St. Catharines.

As they chatted about the wedding, a news report from a local radio station interrupted the women's conversation. They listened to details of a grisly find in nearby Lake Gibson. Fishermen there had apparently discovered parts of a human body encased in cement.

''God, we get our water from that lake! Turn that off, who wants to hear such horrible things on such a beautiful day?'' the driver moaned. And the station was changed.

CHAPTER
3

The free spirited teenager had been nothing short of a miracle for Debbie and Robert—a.k.a. Dan—Mahaffy. Debbie had had a bout with ovarian cancer in her teens, and doctors had told her that the radiation treatments she'd received would permanently impair her ability to have children. Yet, on July 5, 1976, Leslie Erin Mahaffy was born. Debbie Mahaffy brought baby Leslie home from the hospital on July 10, 1976—her birthday. Seven years later, Debbie Mahaffy gave birth to Ryan. The age spread between the two ensured that the two children didn't compete or fight. Their roles in the family were clearly defined. Each thought the other was just the greatest thing in the world.

From her earliest days, Leslie had been a bright, articulate, and pleasant child. But almost overnight, the obedient, eager-to-please girl had turned into a headstrong, passionate, and spontaneous young woman. The emerging adult in her sought control of her own comings and goings, her own growth, her destiny. Although she tended to run with the crowd, she fought hard for her independence and even harder to keep it. Leslie sometimes acted out her wildness whenever her father worked out of town in the summer months, sometimes for weeks at a time as an oceanographer for the federal government's Fisheries and Oceans branch. Her mother attributed Leslie's mysterious ways to youth. Like so many women across North America, Debbie found her energies split between her kids at home and her work. Debbie was employed as a contract teacher at the Halton Board of Education.

The Mahaffy's knew their situation was far short of perfect, but it wasn't bad. They had chosen to live in a spacious home on Keller Court, a small, out-of-the-way cul-de-sac in Burlington's north end.

Debbie was most proud of her daughter's personality. She was pleased her daughter wasn't being sucked into the female trappings of image and clothing. She always kept her flowing straw-blond hair natural and never overdid the perfume or makeup. The unsightly braces she wore on her teeth interfered with her natural attractiveness, but Leslie knew she had to wear them if she wanted good teeth and just shrugged it off with an easy acceptance. Leslie not only returned her mom's love but also reciprocated her friendship. But in the weeks before her fifteenth birthday Leslie's raw emotions exploded like a volcano over what she saw as Debbie's harsh application of the house rules.

One of the main issues was Leslie's habit of staying out beyond her parent-imposed curfew. On Monday, April 1, 1991, shortly after she had been caught shoplifting at the Price Chopper in Burlington, she pouted out of her parent's home and made off with her girlfriends, Nikki Eisbrenner and Christian Fee. Her parents signed a warrant of apprehension, which allowed police to take Leslie in and send her home. They found her Saturday, April 13, 1991, staying with an older teen, David Scott, in a room at the Crestwood Motel on Plains Road East in Burlington. Three days later, she went missing again and was on the run with friends for six more days before police brought her home.

The Mahaffys told police Leslie's problems emanated from peer pressure from friends who were older and more street-wise than she. But while Leslie sought her independence by staying away from home, they noted, she routinely called them to tell them she was okay. And she would never miss an opportunity to chat with Ryan. Debbie and Dan never really considered Leslie a runaway. It was more like a phase she was going through as part of those typically troubled teenage years.

For her part, Debbie Mahaffy, who had long felt some rejection at her husband's lengthy work absences, was being threatened by Leslie's sense of independence. Mother and daughter had numerous discussions on their problems; they even attended joint counseling sessions at the high school. Through that spring, the relationship between mother and daughter improved. For a while, whenever Leslie wanted to stay out late she called her parents to see if they would extend her curfew.

At 7 P.M. on Friday, June 14, 1991, Leslie dressed in a pair of beige shorts, a white silk blouse, and tan leather dock shoes and joined her ninth-grade friends for the trip to the Smith Funeral Home in Burlington for the wake of Chris Evans, a schoolmate who died in a car crash along with three other teens. As she went out the door, she promised Debbie Mahaffy she would return before her 11 P.M. curfew. Evans's mother, Helen, gave Leslie a heartfelt hug as the shy teen took her turn in the lineup. Chris had often told his mom about Leslie, but this was the first time the woman had laid eyes on her. They cried together. Staying at the sorrowful visitation only a short time, Leslie and some friends walked to the Supercentre store in a nearby mall off the Guelph Line. There, she linked up with Martin McSweeney, a quiet and rugged fifteen-year-old student from Notre Dame High School. McSweeney was more retiring than usual: he had lost his best friend when Chris Evans died.

After the visitation, students at M. M. Robinson High School and Evans's friends had arranged to meet in a wooded area near Upper Middle Road and Centennial Road. Dubbed "The Rock," the clearing was popular with teens, especially those from nearby M. M. Robinson, because it was well hidden from the main track and they could smoke cigarettes and drink booze. Evans had been a regular at The Rock; it was his favorite party spot. In his memory, the mourners would meet there and talk and hug and laugh and cry and at the same time try to numb their sorrows with various libations.

After a short time at the Supercentre, McSweeney and Leslie and others headed for The Rock; they were among about a hundred teens who partied there that late-spring night. Leslie flitted in and out of the throng, consoling Evans's friends and those who knew the others, hugging them with the kind of exaggerated emotion that could only come from a teenage girl. One friend recalled Leslie scrawling an epitaph to Evans on the rock: "To Chris: I'll never forget you, love forever, Leslie."

On this night she quietly sipped on one beer. Her friend Paul Bernier would later say: "If she ever drank it would be one, maybe two beers, maybe every other party. . . . She didn't need to be drunk or to dress up . . . she was who she was and everyone liked her for that." McSweeney and a buddy had convinced an older friend to buy them a twelve-pack and a six-pack. They brought the eighteen bottles of beer to The Rock and set out to reach oblivion. McSweeney systematically downed eight bottles. As he stood there, beer bottle in hand, contemplating how the world would be without his buddy, Leslie put on her trademark smile and tried to cheer him up. Mostly, Leslie talked with her best girlfriend, Amanda Carpino, about her memories of Evans, about her falling-out that day with her boyfriend Grant Vanderveen, and about her curfew. Amanda Carpino didn't know Chris Evans as well as Leslie did, but she was still sad about Chris and the other dead teens. She left for home at 10:30 P.M., Leslie giving her a warm embrace as she did.

An hour later, McSweeney took the five-minute walk to the beer-store parking lot, where Leslie and a dozen kids had congregated.

"Which way are you going home, Martin?" Leslie asked.

McSweeney agreed to walk along Upper Middle Road and walk her safely to her home. But there was no rush: Leslie had already missed her curfew, and in the eyes of her parents, being late three hours was as offensive as being late one hour. Together they walked back to The Rock. The wake had dwindled to about twenty mourners as midnight approached. McSweeney, a friend and Leslie caught a ride to St. Mark's School with another teen and then walked the rest of the way along Upper Middle Road to a tiny strip plaza at the Brant Street Mall, only a few hundred yards from Leslie's home. The plaza boasted only a twenty-four-hour Mac's Milk convenience store, a neighborhood pub called the Carrigan Arms, and a couple of other stores.

At 12:30 A.M., McSweeney's friend cried out in alarm at his sudden realization of the time. He ran off up Duncaster Street and into the darkness. McSweeney asked Leslie to wait while he called his own parents from the telephone in the Mac's Milk store. He called. Everything was cool. The only other people in the store were the overnight salesclerk and a couple of customers at the counter. He and Leslie set off for her house. They stopped by a ravine and sat on the curb. They stayed forty-five minutes, maybe less. Talking, maybe smoking a cigarette, maybe sneaking a kiss. At about 1:50 A.M., they walked through the unfenced lots and approached the rear of 2015 Keller Court, Leslie's parents' house. The house was in total darkness. Leslie tried the side door. It was locked. They moved to the front of the house and stood outside the garage. Leslie assured McSweeney the front door would be open and bade him good night.

"Don't worry, they'll just yell at me. Call me in the morning and we'll go to the funeral together," she said.

He agreed to call at 8 A.M. and take her to Evans's funeral. With that, he stole into the night through the same backyards they had traveled. As he trotted along he saw nothing unusual.

Leslie turned, strode the few steps to the raised porch, and tried the front door. It, too, was locked. In a show of toughness, her mom had locked the door. Debbie Mahaffy had wanted to make a point to her daughter: If she wanted access to the house she would have to ring the front doorbell and rouse the sleeping family. Instead, Leslie wandered back to Upper Middle Road intent on calling Amanda Carpino to see if Amanda would let her sleep over. Amanda's mom, Jacqueline Carpino, was one of those cool parents who would do anything for their daughters, and, if needed, anything for their friends. Amanda's mom had picked her up from the Mac's Milk store when she was having all those troubles a month earlier; that act, of course, had annoyed Debbie Mahaffy and a chill had set in between the two women. For some reason, Leslie didn't return to Mac's Milk to use the telephone, but instead called Amanda from a pay-phone booth, likely the one in a strip mall a short distance to the south on Brant Street.

Awakened by the telephone ringing in Amanda's room, Jacqueline Carpino slipped out of bed, strode into her eldest daughter's bedroom, and answered it. She noted the time to be about 2 A.M. Her youngest daughter, Sarah, was at a girl-friend's sleepover but wasn't feeling well. Jacqueline wondered if she might be calling for reassurance.

"Hello?"

"Hi, Mrs. Carpino. It's Leslie. Is Amanda there?"

Jacqueline calmly passed the telephone to the waking Amanda. She knew something was wrong with Leslie, but she felt it was best to let the friends talk it over. She went back to bed.

Leslie immediately asked Amanda if she could stay over, but Amanda didn't feel comfortable asking her mother for that favor after the lecture Debbie Mahaffy had given her mother the month before. Leslie told Amanda her parents had put out all the lights and locked the doors and she was out in the cold without any money. Leslie was talking faster than she normally spoke. She seemed anxious, confused, very unlike herself. Twice during the thirty minutes Amanda and Leslie spoke, Sarah came through on call waiting to tell her mom she wasn't feeling well and wanted to come home. After the second call, at around 2:30 A.M., Jacqueline Carpino dressed and set out in the family car to pick up Sarah. Amanda was still on the telephone to Leslie when she left. Driving west on Upper Middle Road, Jacqueline peered into the brightly lit Mac's Milk windows to see if Leslie was using the wall-mounted telephone next to the door. There was no sign of anyone in the store. Leslie confided to Amanda that she and Martin McSweeney had kissed. Leslie finally hung up, saying she was going home to ring the doorbell and face her parents' wrath.

Debbie Mahaffy wasn't immediately beside herself with a mother's worse fear when she awoke Saturday morning to find Leslie hadn't come home. True, there was no sign of Leslie, but despite her daughter's ongoing defiance, Debbie reasoned that she was likely upset and staying at a friend's house.

But later that day, while Chris Evans and the other three crash victims were being buried in separate funeral services across Burlington that drew more than a thousand mourners, Leslie was nowhere to be seen. Debbie Mahaffy suddenly panicked. She knew something awful was wrong; Leslie would have moved heaven and earth to be at Chris Evans's funeral. At 4:30 P.M., answering Debbie's call, a Halton police officer entered the Mahaffy home and took Leslie's description for a missing-person's report. The alert was broadcast throughout the Halton Region and the information was placed on the Canadian Police Information Computer data bank, which is accessible by police forces across Canada. Debbie became frustrated at the police's apparent lack of action in the case, but from a police point of view, all they had was a missing teenage girl who only two months earlier had twice been reported missing and had twice shown up safe and sound with her friends.

That Sunday, Debbie called long-distance to Leslie's friends, Nikki Eisbrenner and Christian Fee, who were working as chambermaids at a hotel in the picturesque Rocky Mountain hot springs tourist town of Banff, Alberta. They told her they hadn't seen or heard from Leslie and they didn't have a clue where she could be. Meanwhile, Mac's Milk employee Mike Haaman told police he had seen Leslie at 2:15 A.M. Saturday morning with three other people. She was in the store five minutes, made a telephone call, then left, he told police.

On Tuesday, June 18, 1991, Debbie Mahaffy called Constable Lyle Parker about the probe into her daughter's disappearance. Parker spoke with Mahaffy in her home, and she told him everything that Leslie's friends had told her, including the fact that none of them had seen or heard from Leslie, which was most unusual. Parker advised her to sign a warrant of apprehension. On that day, Leslie was supposed to take a final exam at M. M. Robinson. She didn't show up. The school guidance counselor told Parker that the entire school, not just Leslie, was devastated by the four teen deaths. Parker tracked down David Scott, who'd been with Leslie at the Crestwood Motel in April. He hadn't seen her since April. Then he interviewed most of Leslie's friends, including Martin McSweeney, Monika Hubner, and Amanda Carpino. Still, there was no sign or word of Leslie. The next day, Debbie Mahaffy signed another apprehension warrant for police and it was placed on CPIC.

While Parker and other officers were at work, Debbie and Robert Mahaffy, Leslie's grandmother, and her school chums pinned about five hundred missing person posters of Leslie in hotels, doughnut shops, bars, and convenience stores and Laundromats across Burlington. Parker saw the posters himself on Friday, June 21, 1991, when he checked out the city's west-end motels to see if any staff members recalled seeing Leslie. Nobody had. Parker checked out reported sightings at a Tim Horton's coffee shop and at a strip bar in nearby Brampton, all to no avail.

On Sunday, Anthony Caputo, a 14-year-old friend of Leslie's, walked into the Halton Region 3 District police station and told Parker he saw Leslie two days earlier at the corner of James and Martha St. She was dressed in blue denim jean cutoff shorts and white top, he said. Although Debbie Mahaffy would later look back on the police effort and charge that the force didn't do enough, Det. Sgt. Bob Waller of Halton Region Police would review Parker's efforts and conclude that Parker did everything he should have done.

On June 29, 1991, Leslie's body was found in Lake Gibson, in circumstances that suggested a particularly brutal sex murder. As her parents had insisted, she was no runaway. She was dead. Niagara police began the depressing and terrifying search for a deranged killer.

The people of the area were horrified and upset. But, some of them reckoned, Leslie had been out by herself at all hours of the night. Perhaps that had contributed in some way to her own demise.

The implications of the teenager's death weren't immediately clear, but ten months later, the people of the Niagara region would be devastated when another teenager was reported missing. And this child would be no rebellious kid fighting a curfew battle with her mother. This child was bright, beautiful, and dutiful, and she was snatched in broad daylight as she walked home from parochial school.

CHAPTER
4

On April 16, 1992, rain poured steadily all morning, its gusting winds blowing an intrusive wetness under umbrellas and into faces and onto clothes. It fell with an enduring intensity from low-lying, dark-gray clouds, blotting out almost any evidence of sunlight. It was as if the Earth had been thrown into a shadowy eclipse. It was as if the season had missed the wake-up call for its rebirth. It was, for the most part, rather typical of rainy days in the Great Lakes region during early spring.

On this, the day before Good Friday, the time-cherished Easter weekend had begun. Early business closings combined with the weather ushered in the rush-hour traffic jams between Niagara Falls and Oshawa two hours earlier than usual. At 2:30 P.M. Ontario's inadequate throughways were already congested with bumper-to-bumper traffic. In downtown St. Catharines, the rain bounced and splashed off hurried pedestrians as they banked and shopped and set about doing last-minute preparations.

On the north side of town, dry and safe within the walls of Holy Cross High School, teenage students ended classes at 2:45 P.M. and made their way to their lockers to a chorus of spirited and carefree laughter and excited chatter. The four-day holiday was finally here, and the kids talked about their weekend plans for hockey tournaments, family get-togethers, romance, and even, for some, a weekend of religious observance. Corridor joy and energy wasn't unusual to the modest but cozy Roman Catholic school. Holy Cross staff had tried hard to engender an atmosphere of mutual trust, respect for self and others, and a comfortable interdependency among their student wards. Emotional needs were given high priority, along with academics and sports. At Holy Cross, kids knew they weren't just kids, but individuals with as much importance as anyone else. As dreamy or utopian as it may have seemed to the outside world, Holy Cross teachers never lost sight of the belief that whenever a child's emotional needs were addressed their performance in other areas improved.

Kristen Dawn French was one of the Holy Cross flock who embodied the warmth and spirit Holy Cross staff had tried to nurture. Almost every student who knew Kristen treated her with the utmost respect, not because of her attractiveness, her place on the school honor role, or because she was a team player in various athletic pursuits. Nor was there spillover popularity from her older brother, Darren, a recent graduate of the school. Kids and teachers alike were drawn to Kristen because of her personality, her intelligence, and her genuine warmth. In a world too often trapped in image and make-believe, Kristen French was a very real person.

She loved people and always wanted to help the distressed feel happy. If one of the girls fell out of place in skating practice with the Marathon Precision Skating Team, for example, Kristen would be the first to skate over and, with her contagious ear-to-ear smile, offer a helping hand. Her favorite words, it seemed, were "don't worry." A member of the school's rowing team, Kristen always encouraged and urged her teammates to go further, to exert and stretch their bodies and minds to the maximum. When Kristen's friend Tara Wilson broke her ankle in 1991 and hobbled around the school on crutches, it was Kristen who offered to carry her books from class to class.

Her admirers recognized that the self-confident and satisfied, yet still-humble, person was the product of stable and modest parents, Doug and Donna French, who embraced religious, moral, and ethical values and applied them with love and tenderness to nurture the closeness of family.

As she closed her school locker for the weekend, Kristen looked forward to this Easter as never before. Her doting boyfriend Elton Wade would be at her house, along with her brothers and sisters. Elton was so in love with Kristen that he'd even show up at her 7 A.M. skating practices, cracking as many smiles as he would yawns. And she loved him, in the way only a fifteen-year-old can love. Around her neck she wore a gold charm he had given her, inscribed with the words "Yesterday, Today and Forever." On a finger she wore his signet ring, which bore the letter E for Elton. Kristen's family enjoyed his company; her mom and dad were keenly aware of their daughter's youth, but they were quite respectful of their daughter's desire to be with this young man. They trusted Kristen to make responsible choices. It was her life. Christmas had been very special with Elton around, and Kristen was sure Easter would be the same.

As Kristen walked through the school's front doors toward Lake Street, Tara Wilson shouted out her good-bye and wished her a nice weekend. The rain poured down as Kristen walked alongside the tarmac driveway that led to and from the school, passing other students as they escaped the soaking by boarding bright yellow school buses or jumping into the cars of waiting parents. Kristen's mom always drove her to school in the morning, but both her parents worked in the afternoon and she had to walk the 1.2 miles home by herself. Kristen crossed Lake Road and walked a couple hundred yards on residential side streets that brought her to Linwell Road. Waiting in the backyard, as always, would be her precious white husky-Samoyed cross Sasha. The dog's bright blue eyes would sparkle and its tail would wag furiously when Kristen rounded the corner of the house each day. To Sasha, Kristen meant freedom from the restrictive backyard pen, a full belly, and lots of hugs and kisses.

Kristen was only a few dozen yards short of Linwell Road when Holy Cross student Andy Morin passed her in his van. The gregarious Morin waved in acknowledgment. Kristen looked damp but content as she walked through the rain.

When Morin waved his greeting, she saluted in return. As he drove on, she kept walking.

In her Holy Cross school uniform of green plaid skirt, green tights, green V-neck sweater, white shirt, and oxblood Bass loafers, Kristen was a familiar site to Linwell Road residents as she walked along the concrete sidewalk. Most didn't know her name, but they'd often admired her undeniable beauty. She was only five feet five, 110 pounds, and her walk bounced with vitality, her long, dark-brown hair flowing freely behind her. As always, she carried her Kettle Creek gym bag, a typical choice of the more traditional preppies at Holy Cross. In it she carried her pencil case, calculator, her math set, the remains of the day's lunch, and homework. Kristen was lost in her own thoughts as student Mark Lobsinger, a friend of her brother Darren, drove by her on Linwell Road at about 2:55 P.M. He noted she was wearing a black suede leather jacket, but other than that nothing was different from the norm. She was alone.

The pouring rain had subsided to an uncomfortable and steady drizzle as Kristen passed in front of the Giles Presbyterian Church and approached the north entrance to the asphalt parking lot of Grace Luthern Church. Numerous cars were passing by, their wipers fighting to clear windshields, their drivers staring straight ahead in single-minded concentration to get from one place to the next. Those people who were in their homes busied themselves with chores or hobbies on this dreary day. Whatever they were doing, everybody was too busy to notice the beautiful girl in green as she walked down Linwell Road. There was no reason for Kristen to feel worried or in any way vulnerable as she approached the church. She was only a few hundred yards away from home and standing right out in the open on one of St. Catharines' busier streets.

At about 2:55 P.M., Barbara Joan Packham dropped off a box of papers and receipts at her accountant's office at the corner of Linwell Road and Lake Street, then turned south on Linwell Road on her way to pick up her daughter, Wendy, at a nail boutique in downtown St. Catharines. As she drove through the rain, her eyes mesmerized by the wipers that swished back and forth across the windshield, Packham saw a person leaning into a car in the Grace Lutheran Church parking lot, apparently struggling with someone inside the car. She could see from her rear view of the person's pants that the individual was tall, though not heavily built. The two-door car was close to the front of the church, back from the sidewalk. She thought it unusual, but she had seen so many people coming out of Holy Cross school earlier that she thought it was just teenagers fooling around, perhaps a boyfriend and girlfriend having a tiff. Packham met Wendy at 3:15 P.M. and they met Wendy's boyfriend at a local strip mall to get food and groceries for the weekend. She put the car incident out of her mind.

At about 3 P.M., Doug French entered his modestly furnished home and eased into the holiday weekend. He'd come home early from his salesman's job at Wegu Canada knowing this would be a busy but beautiful weekend. His older children were coming to visit. What more could a father want during the holiday? But by 3:15 P.M. he wondered what was keeping Kristie. She was always home on time. She never went anywhere without telling her parents where she was going and whom she was with. Even in the screwed-up world that was out there, Doug and his wife Donna trusted her judgment implicitly. He decided she would be home soon.

At age sixty, Doug knew life was starting to wind down, but he felt like a man who not only had everything but still had everything to live for. Still a close father to his four children—Brad, Brian, Pam and Dwayne—from his previous marriage to his first wife, Joan, Doug was blessed with his second wife, Donna, eighteen years his junior, their son Darren, seventeen, and his beloved fifteen-year-old daughter Kristie. Doug loved all of his kids, but his relationship with Kristie, the youngest of his six children, was special. She was the apple of his eye, as he was hers. Whenever Doug looked into Kristie's lovely brown eyes, his heart melted. She was the embodiment of love, of feeling.

Similarly, the little frame house at 495 Geneva Street symbolized the happiness Doug and Donna French had created together. They could have moved to a larger, much grander abode, but all their happy memories were here: memories of young Kristie jumping through the lawn sprinkler in her bathing suit, as Sasha, a puppy then, bounded after her with unflagging enthusiasm; memories of decorating the Christmas tree with Kristie and Darren, Kristie always placing the angel at the top.

Doug had doted on Kristie ever since he'd cradled her in his arms at the hospital. He often recalled how he and Donna had laid the tiny and fragile babe, a "gift from God" as they'd called her, in her crib for the first time. He'd laughed as she rolled over, watched proudly as she took her first tentative steps. He'd chuckled at her first words and at the question that Kristen had asked again and again and again: "Why?" As a teenager, Kristen was armed with enough personality, character, confidence, knowledge, and moral backbone that the normal teenage peer-pressure lures of sex, booze, and drugs had passed her by.

Doug wasn't much of a romantic really, but whenever Christmas came around, he'd buy Donna a dozen red roses. He'd get a single red rose for Kristen and put it in a vase in her bedroom. She was always thrilled. On November weekends, she'd grab his arm and drag him out to the stores. They'd look at gifts she'd earmarked for her mom way back in September and October. She was always so alive, always so excited.

"Oh look, Dad, Mom would really like this," she'd offer, pulling gifts from the shelves as if there were no tomorrow, her big brown eyes quizzing his own for approval. Doug would express some practical thought, like "It's far too expensive." "Dad!" Kristen would exclaim with agitated bemusement. "Just pay for it. Mom is worth it, no matter what the price tag." He couldn't resist her. Kristen knew, and loved, her father's soft spot, but she never took advantage of it. He found it hard to believe Kristen's sixteenth birthday was just around the corner, on May 10.

At 3:40 P.M. Doug knew it was highly unlikely that Kristie had been detained at school for some kind of punishment, because she never got into trouble at school. Besides, it was the night before the Easter weekend and even the teachers would want to get away early. Doug's rationalizing turned to agitation and worry when Elton telephoned to ask if he could speak to Kristie.

Dogs and cats can't tell time by the clock, but they have a knack of knowing—perhaps by the position of the sun or the predictable sounds of city life—when their masters should return home. Sasha, too, as if sensing something was wrong, gave gentle whines of impatience. Doug couldn't stand it any longer. He called Donna at Wayside Parole Centre, where she worked as a secretary. Donna had no idea where Kristen could be. But surely nothing could be wrong. She assured Doug that everything was okay. Doug called Donna back shortly after 4 P.M.; Kristie was still not home. Doug had to leave the house to run an errand, but he left a note for Kristie telling her to telephone her mother when she returned.

At 4:50 P.M., after a brief stop at the bank, Donna came home and noticed that Sasha was still in her pen. Kristen would never forget Sasha. Donna began calling everyone who knew Kristen, starting with Holy Cross principal Maurice Charbonneau. He told the Frenches he'd talked with Kristen in the hall the previous day and she appeared positive and upbeat, as always. Nothing unusual. Nothing wrong. Charbonneau, puzzled himself, promised to question other teachers about Kristen's whereabouts. Donna then made calls to Kristen's friends from school and the rowing club.

At 5:50 P.M. she called Niagara Regional Police headquarters and reported her daughter missing.

As Hildegard Vollmer's husband pulled their car up to the Grace Lutheran Church parking lot's west entrance at 6:45 P.M. she looked to see if anyone else in the congregation's choir had arrived before them. The Vollmers, proud and methodical German immigrants, had been members of the church for its entire forty years of existence and took their worship obligations seriously on what they referred to simply as "the Holy Weekend." As the car turned right into the rain-soaked parking lot next to the church's main doors, Hildegard scanned the lot and saw no other cars, but she did notice a brown shoe in the outer corner of the parking lot, back from the sidewalk and a few feet in front of the lawn.

"Look at that shoe; that kid walked away without one shoe today," Hildegard noted to her husband. Since kids routinely played on the church lawn, she didn't think further about the shoe.

That night, while their family members and friends continued calling Kristen's friends to see if anyone had seen her, Doug and Donna French were interviewed at length by detectives about their daughter, her habits, her friends, what she wore, items she may have had on her person, and about her movements and activities in the weeks leading up to her disappearance. Donna told them Kristen rarely took money to school, except for those times when she didn't take a packed lunch and had to purchase one; nor did she carry identification. She gave a detailed description of Kristen's school uniform but couldn't say what underwear she had worn to school that day. She told them about the oxblood Bass loafers, and how they had arch supports to help Kristen over the back injury that had kept her out of figure skating and rowing for the past few months. Donna described her jewelry: the diamond stud earrings; the gold chain with two charms, the "Yesterday, Today and Forever" charm Elton had given her and another with two hands clasped together; the signet ring with Elton's initial on it; the Mickey Mouse watch she had bought a month earlier while in Florida with her parents and her schoolfriend Tara Wilson. That night, Doug and Donna and their family stayed up almost all night and prayed to God for Kristen's safe return.

At 8:25 A.M. on a dreary and drizzly gray Good Friday morning, retired General Motors worker Horst Keuhn and his wife Heidi pulled into the west side of the parking lot on their way to the Grace Lutheran Church's early-morning German-language service. When Keuhn noticed the shoe lying on the pavement he picked it up and an orthopedic arch support fell out onto the asphalt. Keuhn's first instinct was to throw the soaking shoe in the garbage, but he decided to hang it on the one-way sign that directed cars into the west side of the parking lot. He left it there.

Michelle Tousignant had skated with Kristen at the St. Catharines Winter Club for ten years. She had been one of the first schoolgirls contacted by Kristen's parents the previous evening. On Good Friday, as Michelle and her parents drove along Linwell Road doing their part in the impromptu search for Kristen, Michelle's eyes caught sight of the shoe perched on the one-way sign at Grace Lutheran Church. She shouted for her parents to stop the car and picked up the shoe. It was an oxblood Bass loafer—the same type Kristen owned—and it had an arch support. Michelle had seen Kristen and noted the loafers the previous afternoon, and there was no doubt in her mind about the importance of the find. Only two houses away, she noted that two police officers had started their house-to-house canvass along the route Kristen was known to take home. She raced up to them, waving the shoe in her hand.

Detective Ken Mitchell—the same Niagara police officer who had investigated Tammy Homolka's sudden death—watched as the young girl handed over the loafer to his partner. After taking a statement from Michelle, the officers took the shoe back to the Frenches's home and Donna identified the loafer as her daughter's. At 10:32 A.M., police sealed off the west entrance of the church parking lot. Suddenly, the disappearance of Kristen French had become a broad-daylight abduction. Police returned to the lot to find a soaked part of a map of Canada on the asphalt. The map was folded over onto itself, but when opened it revealed a portion of Scarborough. There were tears in the well-used map and pen markings under a reference to Toronto.

At 2:55 P.M., Constable Paul Grantham and identification officer Constable Richard Ciszek found a tiny lock of curled hair on the fast-drying asphalt of the parking lot. The hair had apparently been invisible on the wet black asphalt, but now it had dried, and it fluttered in the breeze. Police measured its distance from the sidewalk at just under six feet and its dis-

tance from the lawn at fourteen feet. The hair looked like
Kristen's, but they wouldn't be sure until it was tested.

A sizable crowd gathered at the scene as the forensic team
painstakingly searched the lawn, peering through blades of
grass and scooping up trace evidence into plastic bags. It was
soon apparent to everyone that Kristen had been snatched
right off the street. Veteran detectives who feared the items
were left behind by a deranged killer announcing his presence, immediately realized the need for action. More police
officers were put on the door-to-door search and tracker dogs
were brought in.

At Holy Cross High School a score or more students were
keeping silent vigil, waiting for the latest word from police
teams as they returned to the makeshift headquarters. Janet
Bertrand and Cheryl Neethling, who had skated with Kristen
on the Marathon Precision Skating Team, were outwardly dis-
traught as they tried to process the bizarre situation. The two
girls wondered aloud how anyone could have forced their athletic friend into a car. "She's not the type to go with a
stranger or anything. If they wanted any help or anything,
maybe she would try," said Bertrand. Another friend of Kristen, Mandy Gerrie, bowed her head in dismay. "She would
never have taken a ride with a stranger," Mandy said. "I
don't get it."

The more enterprising in the reporter corps were quick to
draw potential links between Kristen's disappearance and the
horrible sex slaying of Leslie Mahaffy the summer before.
Although Leslie Mahaffy was from Burlington and was last
seen in that city, her concrete-encased body parts were found
in Lake Gibson on the outskirts of St. Catharines, just a few
miles from where Kristen was apparently abducted.

A mile or so down Linwell Road, *Toronto Sun* reporter Alan
Cairns sat across the kitchen table from a man who'd lived
through hell for five months. Terry Anderson's fifteen-year-
old daughter, Terri, had been missing since the previous November 30. Terri, a student and cheerleader at Lakeport Secondary School, had disappeared from her Linwell Road town

house after coming home from a party at which she'd taken LSD for the first time. She had apparently left the home at about 2 A.M. Police thought the tiny schoolgirl might have chosen to run away from home, but her dad didn't believe it for a second. If Terri was still alive, he reasoned, she'd have telephoned home for some money, or at the very least would have telephoned her close friends to talk. "It was as if a UFO had sucked her up," her dad said. "If there is some weirdo out there, the police should put twice as much effort into it. . . . I hate to see this happen to this girl. I hated it to happen to Terri, but it would be worse if it happens to someone else. We don't need a serial killer in St. Catharines."

Inspector Robert Clarkson criticized "inaccurate" newspaper accounts that suggested links between Kristen and the two other girls. He said the stories confused the facts and put undue stress on the investigators. "But I won't be stupid enough to say it hasn't crossed my mind," he added. "Theory is fine, but there is not one shred of evidence to support a link at this moment," said Detective Sergeant Murray MacLeod.

Word of Kristen's abduction spread throughout the Golden Horseshoe on the radio news. Toronto and the scores of Ontario communities bounded by Niagara Falls to the south, London to the west, Barrie to the north, and Oshawa to the east were gripped with fear. Denizens of doughnut shops and bars couldn't resist the temptation to link the Kristen French case with a dozen other cases of missing girls or unsolved murders. One unsolved murder stood out in particular: University of Western Ontario student Lynda Shaw, twenty-one, was bludgeoned to death and her body set on fire after she was abducted late at night on Highway 401 while returning from her home in Brampton to her student residence. Her abandoned car was found on the highway shoulder with an emergency tire. One theory was that someone had tampered with the tire's air valve when Lynda stopped at a service center just west of the town of Woodstock. The date was startling: Lynda Shaw was killed on April 16, 1990.

As the news from St. Catharines filtered down to the general public, tipsters called police with reports of suspicious vehicles. Apparently a brown van had slowly followed a girl on Cecil Drive; its driver had been looking at the girl the entire time. Police were most interested in reports of a blue van with white wing mirrors that had been spotted three times that afternoon, once at Holy Cross High School, once at Orchard Park School, and another time between the two schools. Other rumors had linked Terri Anderson's disappearance with a blue van as well.

At suppertime that night, Barbara Joan Packham was at home watching the Global-TV news when a report of a missing schoolgirl was aired and footage of Grace Lutheran Church and Linwell Road was shown. She flipped quickly to CHCH-TV, the local station, to see if there had been more comprehensive coverage on that station's news show. She recoiled in horror as she realized the scene she had witnessed in the parking lot was probably the abduction. She called a police officer friend in the nearby town of Grimsby, and he called St. Catharines. That night, the Niagara detective team of Sergeant Brian Nesbitt and Constable Scott Kenney met Packham and drove her over the route she had taken the day before. The officers didn't tell Packham where they suspected the abduction had taken place, but as they drove along Linwell Road she could see the yellow police tape outside the Grace Lutheran Church. She explained that she hadn't paid much attention as she drove along Linwell Road but that she had seen a person struggling at the car in the church parking lot. She thought the car was a plain-looking two-door sports model, very sloped at the front, a cream color without any spoilers or chrome. To Packham, the car seemed similar to one owned by an employee in the municipal office, so she said a Camaro, but she wasn't certain it was that type of car. Police revealed publicly late Friday night that more than one witness had seen a light-colored Firebird or Camaro in that area. Police now felt they had to go with the belief that Kristen had been abducted in a Camaro or Firebird. The only other choice was to say nothing. Inspector Peter Gill told reporters that the car was cream or ivory, 1982 or newer, with no chrome on the bumper. Police wouldn't say if there were one or two suspects. A Canada-wide alert was issued for the vehicle, and Canadian and U.S. border crossings were alerted, especially the three on the Niagara River.

Detective Sergeant Murray MacLeod said a public search for clues would be postponed for a couple of days to avoid trampling potential evidence. Police drew up plans for a huge door-to-door campaign over the next few days.

Back at the French house, the family huddled and shared their misery and their fears. All of Doug's children and their spouses were there: Brad, thirty-seven, and his wife Rita; Brian, thirty-one; Pam, thirty-nine, and her husband Bill Radinsky, who'd come from Capreol, up north near Sudbury, to share Easter with their kin; Dwayne, thirty-four, from California, had come when he heard the bad news. The relatives—Talin and her mom and many others—were all there. Everybody except Kristen.

Media representatives from across southern Ontario and upstate New York descended on St. Catharines to report on the missing-schoolgirl case. After the initial interviews with friends and neighbors of the Frenches, the news crews targeted police for more information on Kristen's abductors.

Was there any similarity with the abduction and the death of Leslie Mahaffy? Could there be a serial killer on the loose? The case's head investigator, Inspector Vince Bevan, had always played his cards close to his chest, even with some of his own detectives. The son of a former Niagara Regional Police superintendent, Bevan didn't have any time for the interfering media. Whether it was planned or not, in the early days of the probe, Niagara police simply ignored the reality of media interests and deadlines. As the case wore on, the media would similarly ignore police concerns.

Toronto Sun reporter Tom Godfrey recalls standing in the lobby of the police station with dozens of other journalists waiting to "scrum" Bevan and others as he came out. The alternative, it seemed, was to be happy with the two-sentence media release police offered every day. The release normally said little more than "the investigation is continuing" and police are "searching for witnesses." This went on day after day. Godfrey became impatient at Bevan's inability to work with the media.

On the morning of Sunday, April 19, the *Toronto Sun* ran a thirty-point front-page headline that screamed: "Serial killer feared loose." Inside the paper was Godfrey's story that police had only one piece of evidence, the shoe, and the nagging fear that a serial killer was loose. Godfrey quoted Inspector Robert Clarkson as saying, "We're not discounting it."

On Easter Monday morning, Godfrey was standing in the lobby awaiting any tidbit of information when Bevan came out of the locked door to the police department's inner sanctum. He pointed directly to Godfrey with a rude finger. "You. I want to talk with you." Godfrey followed him into an interview room, where Bevan, in the company of another police officer, ranted and raved at Godfrey for half an hour, calling him irresponsible for writing an article about a potential serial killer. Bevan, it seemed to Godfrey, didn't want the words "serial killer" to appear in print. The officer scolded Godfrey, saying the news piece could only generate havoc, panic, and hysteria. Godfrey couldn't believe Bevan was getting so red in the face, "freaking out, blowing a fuse," as he put it. "You might not be sayin' it, but people out there are thinking it," said Godfrey. The police seemed to dread the presence of the Toronto media: the *Sun*, *Star*, and *Globe* newspapers; CFTO, CITY, Global, and CBC television; and a half-dozen radio stations.

Later that same day, as twenty-five hundred civilian volunteers searched parking lots, garbage bins, doorways, swimming pools, drains, ditches, and anywhere else they could imagine, Doug French spoke to an assembled crowd of media people in the Holy Cross school library. He made an emotional appeal for his daughter's safety, often breaking into tears. "Kristen, if you hear or read this, we'd like you to know that we're thinking of you, and that everything that can be done is being done. We'll bring you back real quick," he said.

After the news conference, Doug French told reporters that he and Donna had "great vibes" that Kristen would be returned alive. "As the investigation continues, we hope that anyone in a position to help will come forward," he said.

Tuesday came. "We're on really dangerous ground saying there's a serial killer out there," said Murray MacLeod. At the same time, the detective teams from Niagara and Halton were given mandates to probe Kristen's disappearance and simultaneously check potential links with Mahaffy and Anderson.

As Holy Cross students returned to school and prayed for Kristen, two airplanes scoured the countryside between Third Street and Sixteen Mile Creek to the Lake Ontario shoreline, as well as Lake Gibson, Martindale Pool, and the Niagara River. Police and foot searches continued, with ninety on-duty Niagara officers, forty off-duty, twelve auxiliaries, and hundreds of civilians involved. But nothing turned up.

Two days later, Holy Cross staff and students pinned on ribbons—green, in keeping with the school uniform—as a symbol of hope.

On Friday, April 24, reporters, frustrated with the endless replies of "No comment" from the police, began to question Bevan about his aloofness. "I'm not at issue here. This case and Kristen, that's what is at issue, not me," he retorted. "I know how all the guys here feel. Let's get this job done."

At first, Bevan's team of Niagara detectives and a corresponding squad of Halton regional detectives under Det. Sgt. Bob Waller focused on a Camaro, based mainly on Packham's sighting. It was a good lead, but because of the holiday weekend many St. Catharines people didn't hear about Kristen's Thursday abduction and the ramifications of it until they read the Tuesday newspapers. It was widely broadcast and reported that a Camaro had snatched Kristen from Linwell Road. Scores of people called police about seeing a Camaro in that area. They were right, of course. The boyfriend of a local resident drove a Camaro almost identical to the one being sought by police. But his alibi was solid. The suspicious car was likely unconsciously stamped on local minds because General Motors products were part and parcel of the blue-collar city: GM had three motor plants in St. Catharines and employed 7,628 workers. The phantom Camaro started to take on a life of its own.

Doug and Donna French returned to their home, once a comfortable sanctuary, now a kind of prison. Every day, reporters tramped up to the door looking for another interview, another quote, or some more footage. Police officers were back each day, asking question after question but never giving any answers. Cards and letters arrived from villages, towns, and cities across Canada. A handful came from the United States and Great Britain. For whatever reason, Kristen had become a symbol of goodness and innocence in the fight against a frightening and growing evil that, it was perceived, threatened everything good in Canada's social fabric. An entire nation kept a hopeful vigil.

CHAPTER
5

Roger Boyer adjusted his scruffy Canada Iron Metal base-ball cap, quietly closed the door to his modest home, and walked to the GMC half-ton pickup truck he'd parked on the narrow one-way street that was so typical of old residential Toronto. The truck had seen better days, but then again, so had Roger. He'd worked for years trying to make a better life for himself and his family. He'd succeeded somewhat, getting together a down payment on the tiny house on Morse Street. But the recession that hit Ontario in the late 1980s had been pretty tough on ironworkers. There just wasn't much work around anymore, and Roger found it hard to get enough cash to make the mortgage payments. Only a year away from his fiftieth birthday, Roger worried what the future would bring for him and his wife Carroll, their son Ronald, and their daughter Geraldine.

As he piled his slight, still half-slumbering body into his old truck, Roger felt a few aches and pains. His head still hadn't cleared, probably from drinking beer the previous night. It was about 6:30 A.M. and the sky was overcast and the roads damp from overnight rain when Roger stopped for breakfast—a couple of large takeout coffees—at a doughnut shop at Queen and Carol streets. Returning to the truck, he turned on an oldies radio station, lit himself an Export A cigarette, and chugged away to make some extra cash by hunting industrial sites, Dumpsters, and rural roads for scrap metal.

He'd been doing this for twenty-five years in his attempts to make ends meet. Roger's tiny backyard was cluttered with all kinds of junk and scrap. From it he'd scavenge and salvage copper or aluminum parts, and when he'd get a truckload together he'd visit a local scrap dealer. The useless stuff went to the dump.

Roger's biggest handicap in life was his inability to read or write. Scrap metal would motivate him to drive all over southern Ontario, but because of his illiteracy he simply followed roadways and watched the position of the sun in order to retrace his steps to familiar territory and home. Sometimes he would get lost, but he enjoyed the sense of freedom he got driving around, not knowing what would come up next.

It had rained all night and the sun still hadn't appeared from behind the heavy clouds and mist, but Roger knew vaguely where he wanted to start looking this spring morning. On his way to a temporary job near Sixteen Mile Creek in Oakville earlier that week, he'd seen an old car sitting in the brush north of the Queen Elizabeth Way highway at the Ford of Canada plant. He figured he'd check out a few other places in the area at the same time. The car yielded a radiator, an aluminum bumper, and some other smaller pieces. Not a bad scoop. He threw them into the back of the truck and moved on. Finding himself on old Highway 2 in the built-up sections of Oakville, and realizing this would be a bust on scrap, he turned north, above Burlington, and pulled off on a couple of barely traveled back roads, eventually coming out on the Guelph Line. He grabbed a couple of batteries and some tin sheets he'd seen in the bush.

As he drove south on the Guelph Line, back toward Burlington, he took the last sips from his can of ginger ale and threw the can out the window. It was about 9 A.M. or so. Time to head home. He turned left onto the paved asphalt of the No. 1 Sideroad and noticed cars parked along the side of the road. As his truck crested a couple of hills and dips, Boyer casually peered off to the right and through the still-leafless trees his eyes spotted a rusted conveyor system, the kind used by farmers to send hay bales to the top of the barn. It was barely a couple of hundred feet from the road. He screeched the truck to a halt and reversed a few score yards onto the shoulder, then took a muddy roadway back into the woods. The grass had dried a little, enough so his pants and boots wouldn't be wet from walking around. Roger could hear birds singing here and there, but he couldn't see them; he wouldn't really have known what they were if he could have seen them.

Roger's mind was firmly set on the conveyor belt. As he walked, he glanced around at other garbage that was strewn around: old tires, cast carelessly into the little stream created by a nearby draining culvert; old car seats, the discolored vinyl ripped and torn; pieces of rusted tin or sheet metal; to his left, something bright pink, like a carpet or something, partially hidden by some brush placed over it. His mind was still on the machinery, but for some reason his eyes remained focused on the pink thing. He walked toward it to get a closer look, down a slight slope and through some trees and tangled bush.

First he saw a pair of tiny feet, raised slightly on one of the branches, then the left arm, hanging from the limp body. The body was lying almost in a fetal position, its other hand bent under the chin as if it were asleep. It looked as if someone had made a quick but unsuccessful attempt to cover its nakedness with handfuls of bushes and sticks. Roger was shocked at how pink the body appeared. As he stepped closer, he saw black hair on the head, cut short like a boy's, but due to the size of the feet and the hands and the general shape of the body he felt it had to be the body of a young woman.

Roger suddenly felt the urge to vomit and began shaking. He wanted to escape. He fled, stumbling and falling as much as he was running, back to his truck. He drove a hundred yards or so and turned left into the driveway of an elegant country property that boasted nice, tidy white fences, a sprawling new-age farmhouse, and a satellite dish. It was intimidating for a simple guy like Roger to knock on the door of such a nice home, but he had an important mission. He beeped the horn and got out of the truck. A teenage boy answered the door.

"I'd like you to phone the police, I just found a body down the road."

"You're kidding," the teen said.

"No."

A woman came to the door.

"What's the matter? You're shaking, you're pale. Are you feeling okay?"

"No, I just found a body down the road."

"What, by my house?"

The kid, Greg Hughes, called police and agreed to meet them at the spot where the guy in the truck had found the body. Roger, Greg, and Greg's dog were on the scene only a matter of minutes when a Halton Regional Police cruiser pulled up. The tall, blond cop told them to stand on the other side of the truck, and, if they were going to smoke, to put their butts in the ashtray so they would not contaminate the scene.

Constable Ken DeBoer arrived at 9:51 A.M. Roger led him to the side of the road opposite the body and pointed to where it lay about sixteen feet off the roadway. DeBoer estimated that the body was that of a female in her thirties, with short hair and weighing about 150 to 160 pounds. DeBoer radioed for help and for detectives, and about half an hour later a dozen police officers were on the scene. Roger's body still trembled from shock when a detective approached him. He'd hunted and fished for years and he'd often killed and skinned animals and drained their blood. But this was different. There had once been a real, living human being in the body he had just discovered.

At 10:20 A.M., during a break in questioning, Roger Boyer figured he'd better check in with Carroll. If nothing else it would soothe his nerves. He borrowed the teen's cellular telephone and, with a little help, dialed his home.

"Carroll, it's Rog. I'm in Burlington. I just found a body and the cops are here."

Carroll, who can read and makes it a point of keeping up on the news, let out a gasp, then asked in her shrill and anxious voice, "Do you think it could be Kristen French? Burlington is so close to St. Catharines."

"I don't know, it could be. If it is, her hair's all cut off. It could be a boy, for all I know. I didn't look to find out. Jesus

. . . but it has to be a girl, she's . . . she's so pretty and well manicured and tiny. Such tiny feet.''

A voice bellowed out: ''Get the fuck off the phone. You're busy here.'' It was the detective. His agitation was obvious.

''It's just my wife . . .'' countered Roger.

''Tell her you're tied up,'' retorted the officer.

Roger obediently told Carroll he was tied up and gave the cell phone back to Greg Hughes. The cop continued to ask Roger questions about how he'd shown up at this site. He really didn't have any answers. Couldn't really say which roads he'd been on. Once again, Roger found, his illiteracy was making life difficult. Police asked him to leave his boots behind so they could take a print mold and match it with any found at the scene. The questioning was pretty intense, and suddenly Roger realized that in the absence of anybody else even he was a suspect.

By this time, news of the macabre find had spread like wildfire through the newspaper, TV, and radio news offices from Toronto to Niagara Falls. Initial reports said the body was that of a 30- to 40-year-old woman. About fifty media types swarmed about the police roadblocks that barred off the crime scene. After they finished their interviews with Boyer, detectives suggested he take a back way out. He was so scared that he did.

At 10:56 A.M., Detective Sergeant Bob Waller took control. A perimeter was set up, and shortly thereafter detectives huddled in the mobile command post vehicle. Waller, believing the body was most likely Kristen's, called Bevan at Niagara Region.

''Is it Kristen?'' Bevan asked Waller.

''I don't know, Vince, the hair is short. I really don't know.''

''Who's in charge of the scene?'' asked Bevan.

''I am.''

''Okay, we're on our way.''

As soon as Waller hung up, he called both the Halton coroner and Dr. David King, chief pathologist at Hamilton General Hospital. Waller wanted King on the site because of the likely link with Leslie Mahaffy and King's previous experience with her case.

As the Niagara detective group headed north toward Burlington, Detective Sergeant Murray MacLeod choked back emotion. It had to be Kristen. There were no other missing girls. He and the others had tried their hardest and had given their all to find her while she was still alive. They'd followed all kinds of leads and worked all kinds of overtime in an effort to find Kristen. He'd been involved in this case since the telephone's ring interrupted his slumber at 2:30 A.M. April 17. And he'd hardly had a sound night's sleep since then.

At 12:31 P.M., Halton Detective Leonard Shaw, joined by Niagara Inspector Vince Bevan and coroners Dr. King and Dr. Brannon, entered the woods from a back route Shaw had set up so any potential evidence would not be disturbed. They found the body in a three-quarters prone position, the right arm across and under the body, the left arm hanging down to the left. The face was down, below the head. The legs were slightly tucked. It was as if the arms had been thrown down but the feet placed. The corpse, purple in color but very clean, had been covered with armfuls of dried brush and twigs. Within seconds, Shaw confirmed the worst: He lifted the left hand and saw that the tip of the little finger was missing—a disfigurement Kristen had suffered as a child. Bevan looked up and nodded to Waller.

With the assistance of the coroners, police pulled the brush off the body, photographing and videotaping as they went. Shaw noted discolorations on the back, one dark mark on the right buttock, and another on the shoulder blade; there were dark stains on the left side of the face and what appeared to be a bruise on the right temple. When the team turned the body over they immediately noticed a dark horizontal mark across the front of the throat, a sign of ligature strangulation. In addition, Kristen's face was bruised and blood was coming from her nose. Paper bags were wrapped around the head, feet, and hands to protect any evidence during transportation. At 4:20 P.M., the body was rolled onto a white transfer bag and carried out to the roadway on a stretcher. Subsequent searches around the body, on the dirt road, and on the shoulder of No. 1 Sideroad revealed nothing.

The nightmare wasn't lost on anybody in the detective ranks. They'd hoped against hope that Kristen was still alive. But here she was, naked, cold, dead; her body dumped pathetically into a drainage ditch. But beyond the immediate horror were the awful ramifications: Her hair had been cut off, which likely meant it had been taken as a trophy or a souvenir; the freshness of the body gave the initial indication she had been kept alive for perhaps ten, maybe as long as thirteen days; her body lay less than a mile away from Leslie Mahaffy's grave in the adjoining cemetery, which amounted either to a serial killer's taunt or an attempt by Kristen's killer to make police think the two slayings were linked when they weren't. At that moment, detectives at the scene had no trouble believing that a crazed sex killer had murdered Kristen, but as yet there was no real link with Leslie Mahaffy.

Sgt. Murray MacLeod had been on the Niagara police force twenty years and had worked on some bizarre and horrific cases, but after accompanying Kristen's body to the morgue and staying with it through the autopsy he was more emotionally drained than he had ever been before. While on the job, his emotions had fought to get out, but he'd denied them and had set about to do what had to be done. But when he reached home that week and found himself alone after his family had retired for bed, he thought about how he would react if anything remotely similar had ever happened to his own children.

Reporters seeking official confirmation that the body was Kristen French's descended on the Niagara Regional Police's Church Street headquarters throughout the morning and afternoon. But there was no press release, no spokesman, no advisement of a press conference. Nothing. Veteran news reporters had never witnessed what they felt was total disrespect for reporters and indirectly, such a disregard for the public. In this vacume, dozens of reporters realized that their only hope lay inside the little bungalow on Geneva Street. And there they stood, on the concrete pavement only twenty yards or so from the Frenches' front window, waiting.

In the late afternoon, an unmarked car carrying Inspector Vince Bevan, a couple of detectives, and Niagara Regional Police Deputy Chief Frank Parkhouse pulled into the Frenches' driveway. They avoided the throng of reporters and entered the home. They came out about thirty minutes later under the same cloak of silence. Two detectives asked reporters to leave, saying the French family was "very upset" and wanted privacy, but they refused to say anything more. The news hounds, under direction from their editors, had no option but to remain at the home until either a family member or police confirmed that the newly discovered body was Kristen's.

Just after Bevan and the others pulled away, a woman ran from the house's back door, screaming in a shrill voice that reporters were "driving us crazy." Talin French, the woman's daughter, ran after her, grabbed her and spun her around, and took an angry slap to the face for her trouble. The two embraced tightly, the mother in tears. Then, still hugging, they returned to the house.

Amazingly, it was left to Doug French to tell the world that his daughter was dead. At about 7 P.M., word filtered through the news ranks that a Toronto radio station had talked with Doug by telephone and he'd confirmed the body was Kristen's. The reporters returned to their stations and homes. It wasn't until 9 or 10 P.M. that night, in a terse announcement delivered to newsrooms by facsimile, that Niagara Regional Police officially declared the body to be Kristen's.

Over the next couple of days, an intensive police search for clues in the wooded area yielded nothing.

Massive newspaper coverage of the slaying included a photograph of Roger Boyer, complete with his basecall cap. *Toronto Sun* reporters who picked up the May 2 copy of the paper were quick to point out to editors the startling similarity between Boyer and a composite released by police in connection with the Lynda Shaw slaying. The two images, facing each other across the pages of the *Sun*, were almost identical. Readers called the newspaper with the same message. The theory circulating around the newspaper was that Boyer had killed both Shaw and Kristen and was trying to dump and burn Kristen's body as he'd done with Shaw's. But when he tried to dump Kristen's body he'd run into a problem because someone saw his truck. His only hope, the far-fetched rumor went, was for him to say he found the body.

One of Boyer's neighbors also called police, recalling overhearing Boyer boasting to a friend how he'd once "shot a pig," which they thought was a slang term for a police officer. Yes, Roger had shot a pig, but one of the domestic animal variety. It had gone wild and so Roger shot it, then turned it into sausage. No big deal.

Still, police took Roger for a drive, asking him to retrace his route. During several subsequent visits to Halton police he was bombarded with more questions.

Later, someone called a police 1-800 number saying a member of Roger's family had a Camaro and it was sitting with all the other junk in Roger's backyard. On another occasion, police asked him about his brother in the Tillsonburg area and some long-forgotten and unproven sexual assault charges against him.

Roger realized at this time that the questions had gone beyond the merely routine. Obviously, police didn't believe his story and thought he was the one who'd killed Kristen French. As late as November, they asked Roger to do a series of polygraph tests, which he passed with flying colors. The bottom line was that Boyer had worked April 16, 1992, the day Kristen was reported missing. He wasn't the killer.

Results of the autopsy on Kristen came back as expected: Kristen had been brutally sexually assaulted and beaten and had likely died within a twenty-four-hour period prior to her body being found. This meant she'd died at the hands of a sexual sadist who could strike again at any time.

Debate raged among Niagara and Halton detectives as to whether even basic autopsy information should be shared with the public. Halton had a long-standing policy of informing the public; Niagara, on the other hand, with a history of internal political turmoil, had long shut the public out of its affairs. Sergeant Carey Smith, the popular media officer for Halton, had been asked to speak on behalf of the task force. He advised Bevan and others to divulge as much information as possible. Smith had been around the media long enough to know that if the police didn't control the flow of information to the competitive reporters, the media would ferret out its own information and create its own stories. That would ultimately control the police agenda.

When no news was forthcoming, the media seized the offensive, just as Smith had predicted. One story announced that Kristen was sexually assaulted and may have been alive thirteen days. It said detectives had a working theory that a serial killer was responsible for the French and Mahaffy slayings and Terri Anderson's disappearance.

On Saturday, May 2, Smith announced that a lengthy autopsy at the Centre for Forensic Sciences revealed that Kristen had been sexually assaulted before she was asphyxiated. He told a throng of reporters that detectives didn't want to reveal details of the autopsy to protect evidence. He said laser tests didn't reveal any fingerprints but exposed other evidence, suggesting it was fibers. Smith denounced the news report, but in his heart he knew it was partially correct. Within a week he had resigned as the task force spokesman. Murray MacLeod told reporters on Sunday, May 3, that there was "no hard evidence" to link the three cases. He told the truth.

On May 4, about 4,000 mourners trekked to St. Alfred's Church in St. Catharines for Kristen's funeral service. The church was awash with a sea of tears that day. There was barely a dry eye among the 2,800 people who packed into the brick church's massive hall or the 1,200 mourners who stood outside. Among them students from Holy Cross, older students from St. Catharines' other high schools, family friends, teachers, acquaintances, and gawkers. The media weren't invited to the funeral, but in an unsettling trend that was developing, nobody had bothered to tell the media.

As the hearse drove off for the Pleasantview Cemetery, where Kristen was to be buried in a family plot alongside her grandparents, a former neighbor of the Frenches spoke angrily: "I shouldn't say this in front of the church, Dear Christ, but when they catch this man they should hang him. It's unfair for good people to die at the hands of a monster like this . . . they can't redeem these animals."

The autopsy results were officially released May 5. Inspector Vince Bevan said a "cruel, sadistic, and dangerous" murderer had held Kristen for thirteen days before she was killed. The autopsy revealed that Kristen was killed only twelve to twenty-four hours before her naked body was found. Bevan told the *Toronto Sun*'s Alan Cairns in an interview in his office in the Niagara Regional Police headquarters that the worst scenario for police would be that not one killer but three killers were responsible for the French, Mahaffy, and Anderson cases. Cairns, who had hoped to patch up the ever-widening chasm between the media and police, pleaded with Bevan to release more information to help protect the public. He asked if Leslie's hair had been cut. He asked if Leslie had died from asphyxia. Were there any other marks on Kristen? What else happened to the girls? But Bevan was unyielding. He said the tests didn't tell police that much. "Al, you give us too much credit."

Cairns lambasted him: "Vince, do you realize that if another dead girl shows up the media is going to come down here and shit on your head—and I'll be the first one! Are you prepared to accept that?"

Bevan's fiery eyes shot back at Cairns as if to say, "You do your job, I'll do mine." The interview was obviously over. The division was obvious. The chasm was widening by the minute and there was no stopping it.

Within a month of discovering Kristen's body, police had checked a thousand Camaros and had interviewed or reviewed hundreds of potential suspects. Through it all, reporters with the bigger media outlets in Toronto found themselves in a bizarre war with the Niagara Regional Police in general and Vince Bevan in particular.

Facing an immovable brick wall when trying to get information, reporters sought, and found, their own stories. In a *Toronto Sun* story of May 10, 1992, serial-killer expert Professor Jack Levin of Boston's Northeastern University said that there was only a "minuscule" chance that the brutal killings of Mahaffy and French and the Terri Anderson disappearance were not linked. "It's almost conclusive. If another body shows up . . . I'd say 1,000-to-1 in favour." Although Anderson's body turned up in Lake Ontario on May 23, 1992, her death was subsequently ruled accidental. Levin's opinion, however, didn't change. Based on police reports that French was held for up to thirteen days, Levin suggested she was raped, tortured, and killed by a sexual sadist "who just wants to see his victims scream and beg for mercy."

The fruitless police search and the hounding media articles—some of questionable truth and value—continued through the early summer. Then, on July 21, 1992, Niagara police stunned a huge television audience in a CHCH-TV special when they revealed that two men—not one, as had been assumed and widely reported but never denied—were seen abducting Kristen. Again, the main focus of the show was an off-white Camaro, an older model, perhaps from the late 1970s. It was revealed that the Camaro had a patch of gray primer on the driver's door.

A psychological profile by agent Gregg McCrary of the FBI's Behavioral Sciences Unit in Quantico, Virginia, suggested that the two offenders had a "very rich fantasy life." One was dominant, McCrary said, "better described as a true predator." It was he who fantasized about the abduction and rape, he who probably stalked Kristen's school and other areas where teenagers hang out. He was "a manipulator, a cold-blooded killer. He has no guilt or remorse for Kristen, for Kristen's family or her community. He is impulsive, volatile and unpredictable, especially under stress."

There may have been a stressful event in his life prior to Kristen's abduction, said McCrary, perhaps with "a wife, girlfriend, or he may have been fired from work. If he has a consensual relationship, he is the boss. He does not have to answer questions or explain himself. His wife, girlfriend, or children will be submissive to him and perhaps abused by him. He harbors a great deal of hatred towards women."

McCrary said the dominant killer worked with his hands, perhaps with power tools in a metal shop, and was likely to have a home workshop and access to power tools and equipment. "He has a record, which probably includes sexual assault, and he probably was in jail at one time."

The accomplice, McCrary said, was a follower who may not have become a sex killer if it weren't for his association with the dominant partner. "He now regrets his involvement and is suffering some remorse and guilt and is having trouble coping with the crime," he said. "These coping troubles may manifest themselves in a problem with sleeping, eating or such things as increased use of alcohol or drugs."

McCrary said the two offenders had a close bond: "If they're not related, it's almost like they are brothers. They are together all the time."

Appearing in a question-and-answer session on CHML radio with talk-show host Roy Green the next day, Inspector Vince Bevan said the "odds are good" that the killers watched the TV show on which the two-abductors theory was announced. Bevan said police would not answer some questions because they didn't want to say anything that might fuel the killer, but he added that "one person is likely concerned about their own safety, very concerned." Bevan ended the show by saying the dominant one, aged twenty-four to thirty, would be putting a lot of pressure on the passive one, who was "maybe in for the abduction but not for the murder as well." He appealed to the passive partner: "If you're listening, please, for your own good, give us a call!"

When told about the killing duo by the *Toronto Sun*, Northeastern's Levin said leader-and-follower serial-killing teams were nothing new. He noted Ken Bianchi and his cousin Angelo Bueno, who together were the so-called Hillside Stranglers in Los Angeles in the 1980s. Together they were successful in L.A., strangling numerous women and dumping their corpses on a hill, but when Bianchi moved to Washington State he screwed up on a double murder and left evidence at the scene. A similarly bizarre killing team existed in Charles Ng and Leonard Lake, who allegedly tortured, raped and killed entire families in Calaveros County, California, around 1985.

"They are caught when they make a mistake or one is apprehended and snitches on the other," said Levin. "It is usually a plea bargain . . . a lot of times people do things as a team. There is something crazy about their relationship; they feel one another's sadistic impulses. They are very weak in the sense of what is right and wrong. They don't have the normal constraints.''

The television program served the dual purpose of not only putting psychological pressure on the killer but also encouraging tips from the public. From a tip standpoint, it worked. Too well. Police later estimated that the show generated 44,000 telephone calls from across Canada. One or two tips focused on a strip-bar disk jockey named Paul McIntyre who, like an estimated 127,000 people in the province of Ontario alone, happened to own a Camaro-style vehicle. McIntyre's name was phoned in because people were suspicious of his long hair, bedraggled beard, backwards baseball cap, and the yellow Firebird he drove. Interviewed by the *Toronto Sun* in a seedy St. Catharines strip bar called Dimensions of Pleasure, McIntyre said detectives had ''hounded'' him because of his car, his appearance, and the fact that his ex-girlfriend, a stripper with the stage names of Crazy Chrisy and Justin Lust, lived down the street from where Kristen French was kidnapped. Another article told how St. Catharines flower vendor Amanda Ballantyne was ogled April 15, 1992, by two men in an off-white Camaro only blocks away from where Kristen was taken. Ballantyne said she had twice called police but nobody had interviewed her. Psychics came out of the woodwork, with some seventy-five offering help to police and dozens calling the media.

Whenever tipsters didn't get satisfaction or were given the cold shoulder, they called the newspapers. Soon the media, not the police, were setting the public agenda. The tight-lipped Green Ribbon Task Force was losing by default. Every day, it seemed, the *Toronto Sun* received calls from disenfranchised tipsters from Niagara Falls to Scarborough. Alan Cairns took one anonymous telephone call from a male who asked him what had become of the Scarborough Rapist, a brutal blitz rapist who terrorized the Toronto suburb for two years in the late 1980s.

''I hear one of the prime suspects is living up in Kitchener, Ontario. You should check it out,'' said the caller, one of hundreds.

"Yeah, but there are two of these guys," Cairns responded. "And the MOs are different. The Scarborough Rapist hit women coming off the transit system; this guy snatches young girls right off the street."

As the hot days of summer turned into fall and then to winter, police had exhausted the strongest tips. At a media conference, Bevan revealed that between five and ten callers had, for some reason, confessed to Kristen French's murder. As Christmas of 1992 approached, it looked rather dismal. In the words of one police detective: "We're essentially just waiting for another body to show up."

Wednesday, February 17, 1993, was just another workday at the *Toronto Sun* for reporters Scott Burnside and Alan Cairns. Through Christmas, the telephone tips on the Kristen French murder had subsided to a trickle and the two were busily involved in a myriad of other stories. On this day, Cairns had something else on his mind: He was leaving on a golf trip to Myrtle Beach, South Carolina, in only two days. Cairns and Burnside had talked briefly about keeping tabs on the case during that vacation because a reliable police source hadn't answered their pages in the last two weeks. Something was up, but what? At about 1 P.M., a tip came through the *Sun*'s police desk chief, Lee Lamothe, that an arrest had been made in the Kristen French murder and Global-TV crime reporter Sue Sgambatti was already in St. Catharines. Frantic telephone calls were placed by Cairns and Burnside and tense pleas for information passed on. At about 2 P.M., while a clutch of editors stood around Cairns and Burnside seeking answers, Cairns answered his telephone and heard a familiar voice:

"It's me. Listen, I only have a few seconds. Pull your Scarborough Rapist files."

"What?"

"Pull your Scarborough Rapist files. It's the same guy! See ya, I have to go. Call you later."

Cairns put down the phone and whirled around to see Burnside and a half-dozen editors staring at him.

"It's the Scarborough Rapist!" said an astouned Cairns.

"No, Al, it's an arrest in the Kristen French murder," reminded city editor Jane Van der Voort.

"It's the same fucking guy!" said Cairns.

Jaws dropped in collective disbelief. The Niagara serial killer and the Scarborough Rapist were one and the same. Impossible.

At about 2:30 P.M., the familiar voice came on the telephone again.

"Got a pen?"

"Yep."

"Okay, Paul Kenneth Bernardo, age twenty-eight, 57 Bayview Drive, Port Dalhousie. You should get down there right away. I have to go."

"Hey, hold on . . . hold on," pleaded Cairns, trying to remain calm.

"Tell me something about him. Does he work?"

"He's an accountant, I believe."

"Okay, uhmm, is he married?" asked Cairns.

"Yes," the voice said. "We're still investigating that part."

CHAPTER
6

Paul is remembered as an adorable baby. Piercing, bright blue eyes, wavy blond hair, and a delightful smile that lit his cherubic little face like the sun itself had Ken and Marilyn Bernardo's new neighbors wanting to whisk away the babe as their own. It was summer 1965 and the mothers and kids on newly built Sir Raymond Drive in suburban Scarborough were out in their yards both enjoying the sun and trying to strike up conversations with others on the street. Marilyn Bernardo, a stout woman in her thirties with an obvious lack of dress sense, joyously wheeled Paul's stroller outside her new home at number 21, beside her the older kids: David, three, and Debbie, two. Sensing that an opportunity to meet Marilyn lay with the fair babe in the stroller, some other moms smiled and waved at little Paul, lightly pinching his glowing chubby cheeks and rubbing his baby-smooth arms and legs. Paul cooed and grinned at his audience.

"Isn't he a doll!"

"What a gorgeous baby!"

"He looks just like his dad!"

The moms chatted the typical suburban-housewife small talk about the kids, where they lived before, and the schools and stores closest to Sir Raymond Drive. After only a few minutes with Marilyn, the other women realized that she was somehow different from them. She was pleasant enough. Intelligent, too. Although they found her loud voice and its neurotic tone unattractive, they forgave her because there was genuine friendliness in the words it spoke. But she had a strange demeanor. It was as if she was holding back; they sensed she was hiding something. And Marilyn was hiding many personal details from her neighbors, especially one secret she had shared with only her husband. She had vowed that secret would not be revealed until the kids, especially Paul, were much older.

Marilyn Bernardo was raised as Marilyn Eastman in Kitchener, Ontario, about seventy-five kilometers west of Toronto in the comfortable, Christian home of relatively well-to-do lawyer, Gerald Eastman, and his wife. Marilyn, one of three girls born to her blood mother, was adopted by the Eastmans at an early age and raised as if she were their own daughter. Throughout her teenage years and adult life, Marilyn had often told friends she "thanked God" she was nurtured by "good people" and did not suffer the unpleasantness of being cast adrift like some abandoned children. In the Eastman home, Marilyn received what she called "a proper upbringing" and a "good education." On Sundays and special occasions, the Eastmans brought out their sterling-silver cutlery and their expensive china; she was taught table manners, social protocol, and politeness. She would be forever thankful to the Eastmans for what they gave and taught her.

Toward the end of high school in the mid-1950s, Marilyn, who had blossomed into a very attractive and curvaceous young woman, developed a soft spot for a robust, vital, and wild young man. He became her sweetheart. Marilyn had a direct fondness for the boy and at one point would have gladly married him, but her suitor soon developed a taste for alcohol and other women. The boyfriend shunned college and university in order to start work and get some money. Marilyn felt he had no potential and would ultimately turn into a rogue and a wastrel. She wrote him off as marriage material, following her adoptive parents' advice to be practical in her selection of a husband. As they saw it, Marilyn should marry a man who could adequately support her.

Through the Eastmans, Marilyn was introduced to Ken Bernardo, the son of their friends. The Eastmans encouraged

Marilyn to first date and then marry Ken. He always dressed so neatly; he was always so well groomed; he came from good stock, and, besides, he had a degree in business and was well on his way to becoming an accountant, a respected and lucrative profession. Like many women of her generation, Marilyn saw marriage as a way of jumping into higher classes; she saw Ken Bernardo, his education and his money-making potential, as her ticket to happiness and prosperity.

In the early 1960s, Marilyn and Ken married and moved to Scarborough, living in a rented room. Within a few months she became pregnant with David. She would later recall to friends that she and Ken went through tough times in that little room, with Ken frequently losing his temper and getting downright "nasty" over their situation. But Marilyn kept her faith in her marriage to Ken; she always felt thankful that Ken loved her enough to marry her. Friends concluded that Marilyn lacked self-confidence and lived with the belief that nobody could love her.

David was born in 1962 and Debbie in 1963. Ken became a full-fledged chartered accountant that year, and together he and Marilyn tried to pursue the middle-class dream of affluence, property, and family. Both Marilyn and Ken stayed in close contact with their parents and drove to Kitchener on many occasions. Sometimes, while Ken stayed behind in Scarborough working at his job, Marilyn traveled to Kitchener alone to visit her parents. Infrequently, she bumped into her old sweetheart, who since their breakup had done well for himself in business and was on the verge of becoming a very wealthy man.

On August 27, 1964, Paul Bernardo was born.

A year later, with some financial help from their parents, Marilyn and Ken bought their first home, a new house on Sir Raymond Drive in a spacious subdivision of Scarborough in an area known as the Guildwood.

At first glance, the women on Sir Raymond Drive thought the Bernardos were well on the way to achieving the suburban dream. Ken was doing well at work and drove a relatively plush car. Within a few years he would have a company car. Each day, Ken went back and forth to work dressed immaculately in a pinstripe wool suit, a pressed shirt, and a dapper tie, his black leather shoes shined brightly and not a hair was ever out of place. Ken even dressed in walking shorts and a dress shirt to cut the lawn. There was even money left over to get Marilyn a Volkswagen "Beetle," which she drove back and forth to the grocery store and on the nights she led the local Girl Guide troop. They owned inexpensive but adequate furnishings, and the Bernardos were the first family on Sir Raymond Drive to install a pool. While Ken worked, Marilyn did the home chores: the laundry, the cleaning, the cooking, here and there a bit of gardening, and, as best she could, the nurturing. The kids were always reasonably well dressed and appeared clean. It was easy to look at Paul's smiling face, Debbie's curly brown locks, and, despite his apparent strangeness, David, and believe that the Bernardos and their kids had it all. But behind the front door of 21 Sir Raymond Drive, behind the carefully arranged facade, was a bizarre family life very few would get to see.

It quickly became apparent to the neighbors from cursory peeks of the Bernardo driveway that Ken and Marilyn did not have many old friends; from the way they hid from everyone, it was clear they weren't looking for new ones. Some women tried to reach Marilyn and found themselves invited over for a cup of tea, but curiously there was never any socializing as couples. The women on the street didn't warm up to Ken; it was as if his eyes were ice, as if he looked straight through them. He would never talk and would not give them as much as a polite smile. As odd as Marilyn seemed to be, she was nonetheless harmless. Ken, however, always made them feel uncomfortable, but nobody could put her finger on exactly why.

In contrast to Ken's dapper image, Marilyn was, quite bluntly, a mess. Neighbors sometimes ridiculed her lack of dress sense, wondering why she could not find a more aesthetic way of covering her stout, flabby body than with the well-worn T-shirts, unfashionable blouses, and baggy shorts she seemed to choose. As Marilyn put on more weight and verged on obese, she wore an oversize caftan-styled dress. The garment was usually a drab, dull, uninspiring color and it hung loosly off her flabby body, giving her the appearance of a center-pole tent that had lost its ground pegs. This seemed so out of character for a woman who had talked about her classy and distinguished upbringing and the way she would display the sterling silver on the table for Sunday dinner. But, then again, it was Marilyn's voice that had boomed out: "People should like a person for the way they are, not for how they look." Marilyn, however, stretched that philosophy to the extreme.

Marilyn acted as if her status as a housewife made her inferior to her husband. While she felt it was her duty to stay home with the kids, she felt awkward and guilty about spending money on anything but the barest of necessities. Her chosen thriftiness and a complementing reluctance to spend cash showed through in almost every domestic situation. While other wives made their families pork chops, chicken breast, or steak for supper on weeknights, Marilyn opted to stretch the budget, offering spaghetti and meat loaf. Sometimes she would simply open cans of spaghetti or soup for the children. At Christmas, the couples on the street would feel guilty about spending so much money on their own kids, until they looked across at the Bernardo home. There were no Christmas lights at 21 Sir Raymond Drive, and all the Bernardo kids received practical gifts like sweaters, shirts, and winter jackets. If the other moms talked about going swimming together, Mrs. Bernardo asked, "How much does that cost?"

Even though Ken was a chartered accountant and likely making good money, Marilyn acted as though she had to scrimp and save every penny. The reality was that Ken Bernardo was socking money into his mortgage and investments and he had set up a rigorous budget routine for his wife. Each year they set financial goals, such as the swimming pool or Marilyn's car, and each year those goals were accomplished. Marilyn never questioned Ken's leadership.

While Marilyn and Ken Bernardo kept to themselves, their youngest child, Paul, spent as little time as possible inside his parents' home. He forged an early friendship with two neighborhood boys—the Smirnis brothers—that would last well into his teen years and throughout his married life.

During the summer of 1968 little Van Smirnis hadn't any conscious knowledge of the blond boy who lived across the street. Van was a tiny baby when Gina Smirnis and the other mothers had admired baby Paul that first year. But suddenly the face of a blond boy, poking his head over the fence railings with an expression of haughty arrogance, taunted young Van.

"Fatty, fatty, two-by-eight, can't get through the garden gate," mocked Paul. He giggled, then chirped the hurtful little rhyme a second time. The blond boy's heartless ridicule hurt Van's feelings. The boy would return several times, often with his older sister, and the two of them would chant the derisive verse. Even at that tender age, Van was self-conscious of his pudginess and felt like crying. He would not have imagined this young bully would soon become his best friend.

It wasn't long before the Smirnises allowed Van to leave the safety of his front yard to join his older brother, Steve, and the freedom of the yards and lawns of Sir Raymond Drive. He knew Paul also had a brother, Dave, who was three years older than Paul. Dave didn't show his face much, and even when he did come out he tended to keep to himself.

In those early days, Gina Smirnis was among the moms who chatted as their kids played during the humid summer days. She and her husband had both immigrated to Canada from Greece as children, and Bill worked at his father's restaurant in a strip mall. They were a friendly, family-oriented couple, but neither was close to either of the Bernardo adults. Like everyone else on the street, Bill and Gina felt Marilyn was odd and Ken was simply boring—all image, no substance. As the years progressed, the families sent each other Christmas cards and exchanged birthday gifts for the kids, but otherwise their relationship was always arm's length.

The bonds between the Smirnis and the Bernardo children grew stronger as the children approached school age. Steve and Paul started school together, and due to part puppy fat and his naturally large physical frame, Van was always the same size as the older boys, both of whom were scrawny in comparison. The boys socialized back and forth between the two yards and houses, playing with trains and dinky toys and toy soldiers; playing war games, hide-and-seek, and tag. Van's earliest memories are of Paul always being at the Smirnis home rather than the other way round. It was as if, for some reason, he didn't find his own home comfortable. Van recalls that Paul readily gave up his toys to the other kids in the neighborhood, almost as if he craved the attention and friendship and was willing to give up almost anything to get it.

When Van did gain access to the mostly off-limits Bernardo home, he found it cold, almost uncaring. It seemed Paul received sparse attention and affection and found little comfort there; Van didn't witness a warm embrace or a parting "I love you" whenever Paul left the house to play or go to school. Given this apparent coldness, the Smirnis boys naturally stayed close to their own home. Paul, too, was always at the Smirnis house, timidly knocking on the side door before he wandered into the hallway. This was so unlike the Smirnis boys, who typically burst into their friends' houses without giving a hint of their arrival. Bill and Gina Smirnis felt sorry for Paul. He clearly wasn't a homeless waif or a bedraggled orphan, but nevertheless his situation was lacking in spirit and heart; they were quite willing to have him play in their house or sleep over for the night with Steve, Van, and little baby Alex, all three of whom were overjoyed to have an unofficial brother around.

Being both Greek and restaurateurs, the Smirnises always had an abundance of food in their home, and young Paul eagerly seized the chance at any home-cooked meal Gina Smirnis would offer him, diving into the food as soon as the plate hit the table. The Smirnis boys realized the root of Paul's insatiable appetite for their mom's culinary delights; Marilyn Bernardo's idea of cooking for her children, it seemed, was to open cans of beans, soup or spaghetti and heat them in a saucepan.

One day, at about the age of five, Van entered the Bernardo home without knocking or announcing his presence, went up the stairs, and wandered down the hall toward Paul's bedroom. He almost ran into Paul's startled father, Ken, as Ken came out of Debbie's bedroom.

"What the hell are you doing?" Marilyn Bernardo

shrieked at Van. "Why did you walk right in! You're supposed to knock." Paul's dad just stood and looked at Van with a blank expression as his wife continued her fuming.

At home, Marilyn was emotional, moody, and high-strung. She often embarked on accusatory fits, shouting at her kids to clean up their rooms or do this thing or that thing. Marilyn kept a minor pharmacy in her medicine cabinet. She seemed to be a hypochondriac, always taking some pill for a variety of minor ailments, including colds, a sore back, and high blood pressure. On the surface, Ken was introverted, almost docile, but at times his anger would flare up and the couple would get into raging shouting matches. Mostly, he seemed oblivious to the emotional wants and needs of his kids. Sometimes he didn't even respond to comments or questions from Paul; it seemed as if his mind was miles away from Paul's reality. Van was puzzled one day when Ken Bernardo was chasing the kids out of the house because they were underfoot. "Come on, you little bastard, get out of here," he said to Paul, then gave him a parting kick on the behind as Paul went outside.

Neighbors, too, noticed the strange way in which the Bernardos treated their children. Almost like clockwork, Marilyn would appear outside 21 Sir Raymond Drive after Ken returned home from work and shout her kids in for supper. It didn't matter if they were playing several houses down the block or just across the street; Marilyn yelled at the top of her lungs: "Get in the goddamn house, right now!" On at least one occasion, a neighbor heard her call: "Get in the fucking house, right now!"

Despite her scolding and her lack of public affection, Marilyn was never seen to hit her children. Ken, on the other hand, seemed to have that capacity, especially when it came to his dealings with Debbie. One day, the three kids were playing quietly in the yard when Marilyn told them to get inside for a meal. Nobody budged. Without warning, Ken came outside, grabbed Debbie by the scruff of her neck, and threw her through the open doorway.

"You heard your mother calling. Now get in here, right now!" he yelled.

This was followed by Debbie screaming inside the house. The boys walked slowly in behind their father without saying a word.

The next day, Marilyn probed neighbors to see if their husbands ever hit their kids. "I think sometimes Ken doesn't have enough control over his temper," she conceded.

When Debbie was about ten years old, Marilyn complained to one of her friends that she thought Ken was far too hard on their daughter. But in almost the same breath she reconsidered her position and suggested that maybe Debbie "deserves all she gets because she is such a tease to her dad." She became visibly upset as she related how Debbie would sit on Ken's knee and hug him and kiss him and rub up against him. Marilyn called her daughter "a troublemaker" and "her own worst enemy." To the friend Debbie's actions sounded like those of a typical preadolescent girl testing her emerging sexuality with the safest possible mate in her life, her father. It didn't seem that Marilyn understood this and instead was defending Ken for something that had occurred during Debbie's attempts at attention.

Ken and Marilyn Bernardo were only in their mid-thirties when their sex life essentially came to an end and they stopped sleeping together. The double bed they once had in the master bedroom was replaced by two single beds that were placed apart in hotel-room style. Later, Marilyn would sleep in the basement, leaving Ken alone in the upstairs bedroom. She admitted openly to one friend that she and Ken did not have a good sex life. This struck the neighbors as strange, because Ken had the best dress sense and style of any man on the street; the women had often talked with each other about how they would like their husbands to dress as tastefully as Ken did. How could this same man be a dud in bed?

"Anything Ken knows about sex I taught him," Marilyn said, laughing. "Ken has never been a sexy man and doesn't have much interest in making love. Ken says sex should not be the most important thing in everyone's life."

People living on the street cannot ever remember Ken and Marilyn showing any affection toward each other, yet they never put each other down. Marilyn seemed genuinely grateful that Ken was able to put up with her. Ken, for his part, was happy that Marilyn could put up with his temper tantrums. It was as if two dysfunctional people without adequate confidence in themselves were trapped in a prison from which there was no escape.

At one point in the early 1970s, perhaps 1971 or 1972, Marilyn located her two blood sisters who had been adopted by other families and traveled back and forth to Kitchener in her efforts to renew her relationship with them after so many years. She rented an apartment and furnished it only with a mattress and nothing else. When relatives asked her why she was being so bohemian, Marilyn said, "All I do is sleep there, so what's the difference?" She spent many weekends in Kitchener.

Around this time Marilyn began seeing a psychiatrist for her various personal problems. Sometimes, when Ken was at work and the women on the street had an informal social or a baby shower, Marilyn would talk incessantly, her loud voice carrying across the room. She talked about issues that most people would keep to themselves, including her visits to the psychiatrist, telling everyone what the doctor thought of her problems. "Even the poor shrink is confused when he meets ol' Marilyn," she blurted out once.

Life for the three kids appeared to go on as normal. By the time he reached puberty, David, always a little odd, was polite and pleasant but also in his own odd world. It was as if David thrived on being by himself, as if he didn't miss the love from his mother and father because he didn't really need it. Debbie, despite her gorgeous curly hair, was a tomboy. She played road hockey with the boys and joined a girls' baseball team. The odd blaze of femininity shone through, such as when she dressed in her blue uniform and followed her mom to the Girl Guide meetings at Elizabeth Simcoe School. Apart from the odd road hockey game, Paul, who as the smallest boy on the street often found himself garbed in protective gear and put in net as goalie, wasn't that interested in sports. While David had difficulty in school, Paul and Debbie excelled.

In their pre-teen years, Steve, Van and Paul became constant companions: walking to and from school; seeking each other out at recess; running cross-country after school at Heron Park and Morningside Park; ice skating at the rink in front of Sir Wilfrid Laurier High School; or playing road hockey on Sir Raymond Drive with rickety nets, tennis balls and battered hockey sticks. Van and Paul received bronze swimming medallions at the high school pool on the same day. Paul also joined the scouts with Steve and Van and at age 11 or 12, he won the coveted chief scout award. As part of their scouting duties they put in 120 hours of volunteer work at the Canadian National Exhibition in Toronto during the summer, pushing seniors around in their wheelchairs and escorting the elderly to the various displays and events. In scouting as in other facets of life, Paul was always the innovative and imaginative one, amazing his friends with his skills at starting fires with a magnifying glass and some twigs and kindling.

It was in the Smirnis backyard that Van and Paul, assisted by Steve, pulled their first scam, the first of many to come in the years ahead. The three boys had been watching kids' TV hero Commander Tom on a Buffalo TV station. One day, he described the fun kids would have with their own carnival kit and how the proceeds would help sick kids—for example, muscular dystrophy patients. The kids thought it was a great idea. They set up coin tosses, horseshoe pitching, and a petting zoo featuring the Smirnises' cat Jean Tom, their German shepherds Prince and Chief, and Paul's dog Libby. In all they raised thirty dollars for muscular dystrophy and Van was all set to send it away to Commander Tom's charity. But once the cash was in his hands, Paul demanded they keep the money. "Look at all the time we spent on this thing and look at how little we got," said Paul. At Paul's urging, the trio opted to divert the money to their own charity—themselves. M.D., they resolved, stood for My Dad. The trio laughed as they went off to the local stores to spend their charity cash.

In the mid-1970s, Paul joined a judo club and quickly established himself as an orange belt. Steve and Van had started karate at a local club, but then switched to taking judo lessons with Paul's instructor. The three pals spent hours together practicing their judo holds. Paul had an affinity for the choke hold and for some reason liked to apply it in an unrelenting fashion to his friends' necks. Sometimes Van or Steve would have to interject on the other's behalf as Paul pressed his arm tight against his opponent's windpipe. It seemed Paul could easily get carried away, out of control; he would choke until his opponent was wheezing.

"Relax, man, relax," Van or Steve would pant, barely able to regain his breath.

"Sorry, I didn't know it was that hard," Paul would explain.

The brothers put it down to natural boyish exuberance. No big deal.

During high school, whatever closeness Paul had lacked at home he'd seem to find with his pals across the street. He was intelligent and analytical and seemed full of energy and vigor. The Smirnises and other neighbors on Sir Raymond Drive thought Paul had a bright and prosperous future. They believed that of all three Bernardo siblings, Paul was the most normal, especially since Debbie, during her early teen years, had lost her vitality and turned into a withdrawn, introspective, and deeply bothered young woman. It was as if she was tormented with unseen demons. Dave seemed as self-indulgent, detached, and just plain weird as ever.

Paul sailed through Sir Wilfrid Laurier Secondary School with ease. He was a bright student and achieved high marks without pushing himself to the limit. At times, he astounded his friends with his ability to analyze a complex situation and dissect it into understandable components. If he didn't have a photographic memory, he had an amazing ability to recall details. Van and the others would kid him that he was going to be an accountant, just like his father.

"I'll never be an accountant," he'd swear. "Never!"

Still, his academic successes were never enough for Ken and Marilyn.

"I got ninety-three and they're asking where the other seven percent is," he confided to Van.

Paul saw his sixteenth birthday as his ticket out of the house. He wanted to make more money than a humble paperboy could make with the *Toronto Star*. But at age fourteen and fifteen, opportunities for him were few. When Bill Smirnis opened the Silver Nugget restaurant in 1977, Van was up at 6 A.M. and took a city bus along Kingston Road to help open the restaurant for the early-morning rush. Paul still made pocket money by working a newspaper route with the *Toronto Star*, but he would frequently help out at the Smirnises' restaurant weekends and nights for a few extra bucks and some extra food. Compared to the hulking Van, Paul was a scrawny pipsqueak. Every time he saw Paul, Bill Smirnis would remind him: "Paul, you gotta eat, man." And Paul did. By the time he was fifteen, the slender boy had filled out into a sturdy young man.

Paul and Steve decided to make some extra cash by worm picking and subsequently joined a nocturnal crew that was driven across Scarborough in the dark hours and dropped off at parks, sports fields, and golf courses. They would strap a pail to each hip and gather up earthworms by flashlight. They were paid by the bucketful. Van later joined them.

Building on their earlier experiences with the My Dad charity, Paul and the Smirnis boys began talking about similar scams and schemes. It didn't take long for Steve and Paul to realize they could make worm picking pay even more. When Steve turned sixteen and had passed his driving test, he told the other boys they should start their own worm-picking operation. Steve bought an aging Chrysler van using worm-picking proceeds and a loan from his parents. Paul agreed to pay back his share of the van from the money he planned to make. Using a pay-telephone number outside the Silver Nugget restaurant, the boys put advertisements in local newspapers asking for worm pickers. The young entrepreneurs then hung around the telephone all day waiting for telephone calls. A pickup spot would be arranged and Steve would drive the van. The pals would pay $9 to $10 per thousand worms to the workers, then sell the haul to bait operators for three times that much. On good wet nights, when the earthworms would come to the surface to avoid the seeping water, the trio could make $1,000 profit between them.

Sometimes, at Paul's suggestion, they wouldn't pay some

of the workers, especially those who, for one reason or another, didn't work out. It was Paul who suggested they should avoid detection by simply changing the name of the unregistered company and keeping the same pay-phone number. "Who will know?" he reasoned. Paul laughed at some of the workers, saying they were brainless immigrants who deserved to be stiffed because they didn't know their rights. Although it wasn't enjoyable work, the worm picking paid well. Paul not only organized the operation but picked worms himself. He had no patience for workers who didn't want to do their best. One cold and rainy night, one of Paul's friends who'd joined the worm-picking crew to make some extra pocket money made his way back to the van to keep warm and dry. Paul became angry and concerned about his profit margin: "Get the fuck out of the van. Get out of here; get out there and pick." The nocturnal operation was pursued off and on until the end of high school.

In addition to worm picking and the odd shifts at the Smirnises' restaurant, Paul made cash as a waiter at the Crock and Block restaurant on Markham Road. Work was necessary for Paul because he was spending money as fast as he made it. After he turned sixteen he became obsessed with his image, buying expensive clothes and seeking that perfect look. He openly sought the affection of girls. Around the same time Steve bought the van, Paul passed his driving test and put a deposit on a white Mustang with the intent of being not only mobile but also hip. Not long after buying the car he totaled it in an accident and was without his own means of transportation. Neither David, Debbie, nor Paul liked driving the family car because Ken and Marilyn made each kid responsible for their own insurance and recorded the mileage on the car so that they could charge the kids a mileage rate. Marilyn often jotted down the mileage as the kids were about to drive the car away. This caused Paul great embarrassment.

David moved out of the house at age eighteen to a tiny apartment in the Victoria Park area of Scarborough, telling neighbors he simply couldn't stand being around his mom and dad any longer. David went to his apartment with hardly any furniture or the other accoutrements of everyday life.

While other mothers on the street wondered aloud how David would make out without any financial help, Marilyn didn't seem to be worried. She was happy, however, that when she and Ken visited David he brought a set of fine crystal glasses out of the closet and offered a toast to his home. Because they did not care for alcohol, Marilyn drank milk and Ken water from the crystal glasses.

"At least it shows his upbringing," a proud Marilyn told Ken on the way home.

Although he joined Sir Wilfrid's football team, Paul was never a football star. While Van played offensive guard and defensive tackle, Paul mostly warmed the bench. But despite his lack of athletic status, many of the girls who lived on Sir Raymond Drive had a silent crush on Paul Bernardo. As he walked to school with the Smirnises and others, the unassuming Paul would give a friendly smile to the prettier girls who came his way. When the girls got together and giggled and tittered over the guys they'd like to date, kiss, and even go further with, Paul's name was always brought up. Unlike some of the guys, he didn't come on to a girl with typical hormonal or chauvinistic ignorance. At parties he stood in the corner, shy and retiring. And yet he still had a physical presence. The girls placed him squarely in the cute category. From his earliest dating days, Paul fell hard for pretty girls. Sometimes the girls reciprocated his interests, but it was Paul who seemed to crave strong, intimate relationships.

His first love was Nadine Brammer, a diminutive and attractive blonde who, most students felt, could have had almost any guy she desired. Nadine shared an apartment with her older sister, and Van was there the night Paul and Nadine had sex for possibly the first time.

Soon after this, Paul and Nadine began dating exclusively. Paul bought her red roses and diamond earrings. They exchanged love letters. They swapped T-shirts and other gifts. She affectionately called him Scoundrel and he romantically called her Princess. They fell deeply in love with each other. As far as sex was concerned, Paul was the least pushy guy she'd ever encountered. Nadine was filled with respect for Paul because they'd chatted at length about having sex and they had taken precautions to avoid pregnancy. Paul wore condoms. As far as Nadine was concerned, she couldn't have had a more caring and kind lover to take her virginity. In one love letter, Paul wrote: "Made for loving each other. Princess and Scoundrel, together for eternity." The two even drew up a phony marriage license in which Bernardo, or the husband, agreed to turn over to his wife Nadine all money and dispose of his little black book of numbers. In return, Nadine was to give him car fare and "any other favours that he might find appropriate."

Van recalls Paul saying he wanted to move in with Nadine, but she already had the security her sister's apartment offered. Nadine's friends weren't surprised by her close attachment to Paul; she was a needy, insecure young girl who didn't want to be alone. And yet she would complain about Paul trying to dominate and rule her. She often complained about how demanding he was and that Paul didn't want her to do anything without his giving his approval first. She didn't say it publicly, but Nadine's friends knew she was fed up, if not downright scared of what Paul might do in the wrong circumstances.

Their love affair lasted from June 1980 to the spring of 1981. Nadine told friends they'd split up by mutual consent because they were worried about the strong feelings they had for each other at such a young age. But it was more profound than that. Nadine and Paul were not seeing eye to eye about a visit Steve Smirnis paid her. Nadine was fond of Steve, and the two were drawn into necking on the couch. Suddenly Steve saw Paul's framed photograph on the table and asked Nadine if they were still an item. When Nadine said yes, Steve pulled away from her and left. Steve couldn't believe his ears that night when Paul stood outside the Smirnis home shouting and screaming at him; in an effort to make Paul jealous, Nadine had called him and told him about her short tryst with Steve. Steve wouldn't go outside because he knew Paul was crazed and he didn't want to start a fight. After he kicked in the taillights of Steve's car, Paul gathered up all the presents and knickknacks Nadine had given him, piled them into a steel barrel on his parents' front lawn, and set fire to them. In the weeks after this explosive fit, Paul apologized to Steve and the two renewed their friendship, but it was never the same. From then on, Van became Paul's closest friend.

The love affair with Nadine, his many jobs, and his efforts to gain strong marks at school didn't give Paul much time to do chores around the home. Shortly after his sixteenth birthday, Paul and his mother were getting into some hectic and regular shouting matches during which Marilyn would berate Paul for his lack of consideration. Paul would either turn a deaf ear or tell his mom to get lost.

Then, one day, during a typical emotional tirade, Marilyn's temper exploded and she shouted at Paul: "You're just a bastard!"

"What do you mean by that?" Paul asked.

"Do you think that's your real father?" she said in a snide tone, pointing to a photograph of Ken. "Look, he doesn't even look like you."

She paused to seek out a photograph of her old sweetheart. "This is your real father."

She then related to Paul the story of how she had dated a boy through high school but had dumped him for Ken Bernardo after he had thrown the towel in on a college or university career. After she and Ken were married, Paul heard, she gave birth to David and Debbie, but then in the early 1960s she returned to Kitchener and had a brief affair with her former lover. Marilyn then told Paul the shocking news that she'd become pregnant and Ken had reluctantly taken her and her illegitimate baby back into his life.

Marilyn related to Paul how, when he was a small child, she would drive up to Kitchener, ostensibly to see her sisters. After a visit, she would take Paul to McDonald's for a hamburger or a milk shake. Unknown to Paul, his biological father—who was himself married with a family—would be sitting off in a corner somewhere, as arranged. The man had begged Marilyn for the clandestine appointment so he could set eyes on his son, the fruit of their illicit lovemaking. When Marilyn told Ken in 1964 that she had become pregnant by another man, Ken told her matter-of-factly that the baby needed a home and parents and he would endeavor to raise the child as his own.

Upon hearing this, Paul stormed out of the house and made a beeline for the Smirnis home, where he found Van. Paul was obviously upset, almost in tears. "I don't believe this— you're not going to believe this," he told Van.

Van knew something was wrong and listened intently as Paul asked if his facial looks resembled his father, Ken. He noted the physical similarities between Ken and Dave, then pointed out to Van that his own face was different from them both. He finally told Van that he considered himself a bastard, and began weeping uncontrollably as he revealed to Van what his mother had told him. "That explains my father's resentment towards me over all these years," Paul said, his voice quivering and his eyes blank.

Marilyn's revelation clawed at Paul's soul. The feeling of betrayal by the woman who should have loved him more than anyone else in his life would not leave him, ever. Tensions rose dramatically in the Bernardo house. Paul became less obedient and openly ridiculed his mother. Whenever her name came up in conversations, he mocked her, calling her a "slob," a "big fat cow," a "fucking cunt," and a "whore." Whenever she shouted at him to tidy up his room he shrugged it off and told her to "fuck off," whether his friends were present or not.

Clearly Paul and Marilyn's relationship was deeply troubled. His relationship with his father was also less than idyllic. Soon Ken Bernardo became the topic of neighborhood gossip. The skeletons of the Bernardo household would become increasingly public, further alienating Paul from the parents he had come to loathe.

"Are you sure? Ken Bernardo? No way!" was one woman's response to the shocking teapot gossip that dapper-dressed chartered accountant Ken Bernardo was the Peeping Tom who had been active in the Guildwood neighborhood for some time. It was the summer of 1985 or 1986 and many women and girls who had heard eerie noises outside their ground-floor bedroom windows after nightfall found the Peeping Tom's telltale footprints in the soil or grass the following morning. One teenage girl who lived on Sir Raymond Drive saw the silhouette of a man outside her friend's basement bedroom window, peering into the window and the tiny crack between the curtains. The man was partially hidden by a clump of decorative cedars and the girl could not get an age, height, or description. But sure enough, a man's footprints were there the next day.

One woman who was leaving the neighborhood and didn't mind breaking her silence warned another woman with a teenage daughter that Ken was a peeper. She explained that Ken frequently came out of the side door after dark and took cover behind the carport at 21 Sir Raymond Drive. From there, he could see directly across the street to his neighbor's house, specifically their daughter's basement window. On one occasion, the woman and her husband had also watched him cross the street to their lot and walk around in their yard. On many occasions, mysterious footprints were discovered outside their daughter's window. When the husband confronted Ken, he denied the accusation.

One night, a girl who lived on Sir Raymond Drive was being dropped off at her home by her girlfriend. Wanting to chat for a while, the friend shut off the car and the two sat quietly in the dark, talking about their lives and loves and dreams. It was around midnight when suddenly the side door to 21 Sir Raymond Drive creaked open and out came Ken, dressed only in his pajamas. Failing to see the girls in the car, he walked down the driveway and out onto the street.

"My Lord, that's Ken Bernardo! What's he doing out at this time . . . in his pajamas?" said the girl who lived on Sir Raymond Drive.

The girls, frightened because they didn't have a clue what Ken was going to do, clung tightly to the bucket seats so he wouldn't notice their presence. Ken walked behind the car and down the street. The girls strained their necks to see him walk behind some trucks that were parked in a neighbor's driveway. Then they saw him looking inside a basement window where a young woman had her bedroom. The girls started up the car and drove away without bothering to look back for Ken Bernardo's response. A few minutes later they called police from a public telephone and gave them the number of the house where it had happened. When they returned with police, Ken was nowhere in sight.

The homeowners returned to find police chatting with their frightened daughter and a witness. They were stunned when told about the Peeping Tom, but floored when told it was Ken Bernardo. At first, the adults didn't want to believe their neighbor could be involved in such a sick act, but two girls had witnessed it happen. Neither girl had any reason to lie. The couple asked police what could be done.

"Peeping Toms are harmless," the male officer replied.

Ken's would-be victim was livid at this response.

"What about my privacy?"

In an effort to soothe her, the officers spoke with Ken in an unofficial effort to scare him into stopping his habitual night prowling. After they spoke with Ken, in front of Marilyn and David, they returned to the victim's house. Ken, they said, had checked out the trucks because he heard some noises, knew the homeowners were not at home, and thought there was a break-in.

The officers noted that Ken's statement was odd—how would he know the adults were out unless he had been watching the house for the night?

The next day, Marilyn approached the homeowners and asked if they had called police, and if it wasn't them, then who was it? She wanted to track down the person who was spreading incorrect rumors about her husband.

"This damned Neighborhood Watch is causing nothing but trouble for me . . . why is everybody picking on us?" she said.

Obviously eager to leave this troubled home, Debbie Bernardo chucked in the nursing career her parents had chosen for her, and in 1981 met and married Glen Yandeau. She then moved to northern Ontario. The Smirnises held the reception for Debbie at the restaurant they had bought some years earlier, the Silver Nugget. Debbie's wedding plans were executed with haste. When asked by her closest friends if she was sure she was doing the right thing, she replied that Glen loved her for who she was and that he "knows all about me." Paul told Van that Debbie didn't want to live with her parents for one day longer than was necessary, but he didn't give any details as to why.

In order to live the lifestyle he assumed was rightfully his, Paul began to cast around for ways to make easy money. When he left 21 Sir Raymond Drive, he wanted to be driving a fancy car with a beautiful girl at his side and a wad of cash in his wallet.

CHAPTER
7

Two good-looking and fast-talking men in business suits finished their meal, paid their bill, and were just about to leave the Silver Nugget when the one with the laminated smile handed their waiter, Van Smirnis, an Amway business card. Paul, who had been sitting off to the side in a corner, rose to his feet and sauntered over to the crowd of three to take a card as well. As soon as the customers were out the door, Van and Paul looked at the cards, then at each other, and wondered about the possibilities of making real cash through Amway. Sure, Van had the restaurant job, and the pair still had the ongoing worm-picking enterprise with Steve, but maybe there was potential for a big-bucks yield with Amway. They later talked it over with Steve, who was just as curious as they were. They called their Amway contacts, and within a few weeks the three were attending courses at the Howard Johnson's hotel on Markham Road, just south of Highway 401 in Scarborough. The courses taught them the concepts of networking, bringing others into the direct selling fold, and maximizing earning potential. The Amway instructors pumped up their new recruits, promising that such a strategy would provide a healthy income for whoever sat at the top, for whoever was the *king*, a term Paul Bernardo would later ascribe to himself.

During the recession of the early 1980s, Paul and the Smirnis brothers lived the Amway philosophy, going as far as inviting Amway officials to the Silver Nugget to give their follow-the-yellow-brick-road presentations to the latest recruits. They learned how to sell the new arrivals their own aspirations and dreams, how to appeal to and manipulate their emotions so at the end of the show they would see Amway as a vehicle to achieving that new car, their own house, and a college education for the kids. Paul and Van learned how to paint an ugly picture of what can happen to people if they miss the boat, then show them how to make sure they were on the boat, the Amway boat.

Unfortunately, many people seem incapable of digging deeper than the immediate physical image before assessing a situation, an item, or another person. Advertising and beauty products thrive on this human failing, selling an image to people while at the same time feeding their deepest fears and insecurities. Not surprisingly, image is everything in sales, and Amway was no exception. The corporation's tutors pumped the message into their eager young salesmen over and over again. In order to be the part, the boys had to look the part. Appearance was extremely important, they reasoned, because in order to sell your ideas, your philosophies, and your plans, you first have to sell yourself, and that meant you had to sell yourself through your image.

Already preoccupied with his image, this philosophy made sense to Paul. So the boys dressed in natty suits with trendy ties; their previously unkempt teenage locks were clipped tight behind the ears. For the first time, Paul looked down at the tops of his black leather shoes and could see his young, handsome face beaming back at him.

After the twice-weekly Amway sales meetings at Howard Johnson's or the Silver Nugget, Steve, Van, and Paul would sit up into the early hours, excitedly discussing how they could manipulate the Amway model to meet their own ends, how they could engineer a business based on the Amway concept that would stop the big money from going into someone else's pocket and into their own. They had done it with worm picking, but that was schoolboy stuff. They came up with the idea of a discount card that could be offered to Amway distributors, featuring cost-saving offers from rental-car companies, grocery-store chains, service stations, and the like. Paul was the armchair architect, pitching Steve and Van his notions on how it could all work. There was no doubt they had the ambition and their dreams were quite feasible, but Paul and his sidekicks were short on basic street experience and lacked the essential business smarts to set the plan into motion.

Paul came into his element during his years with Amway. He loved the idea of selling himself to strangers; he loved the jargon. Paul clung to oft-repeated sales-pitch phrases such as "fake it 'til you make it"; he learned to use any means at his disposal to get what he wanted. Always eager to duplicate a working system to fit his own peculiar circumstances, Paul used Amway techniques in many facets of his life, not only in sales and business but also in personal relationships. He bought the books and tapes of famous motivational get-rich-and-famous experts, like Tommy Vu. Friends began to comment on how Paul had learned to be charming and was now skillful at striking up conversations with complete strangers.

In order to better realize his ambitions, Paul became obsessed with learning how to instantly win friends and influence people. He enlisted in Dale Carnegie courses, taking to heart his tutor's initial advice that in order to attain personal growth it is almost a prerequisite to believe in a greater being, a God.

Paul conveniently and expediently set out to embrace the Christian God, but the religion's traditions, contradictions, and naive dogma didn't set well with the bastard boy who had learned some harsh realities at home with his atheist and loveless family. Instead, he found his answer in television religion, a calling of image over substance, and thereafter he became infatuated with televangelist Reverend Jim Bakker and his Praise the Lord Club. He adored Bakker's style, and he loved the idea of wrapping religion and business into one. He quickly realized that a good-looking, presentable young man like himself could do well if he moved his image among the vulnerable who got their spiritual comfort from sitting both in the pews of organized church religion and in the armchairs of televised faith. Paul joined the PTL Club and carried its prestigious black plastic card with him wherever he went, flashing its impressive gold-embossed introduction with a view to gaining instant credibility and trustworthiness. If nothing else, he reasoned, his membership in the PTL Club was a surefire way to strike up a conversation. All the while Paul didn't get any closer to any god. Like many things in his life, his newfound spirituality was a lie. In reality, Paul believed he was his own God.

Although Paul didn't make much money from Amway, the philosophy he embraced from it and other motivational mavericks justified his own crude and selfish longings. Armed with an entire arsenal of predatory talents and strategies, Paul formed a formidable team with Steve when the troupe routinely trolled the local bars for girls after they reached nineteen, the legal drinking age in Ontario. Steve, a self-confident, silver-tongued fox if there ever was one, appealed to girls because he had a knack for encouraging women to talk about themselves; once Steve had set the scene, Paul moved in and spun his charismatic web. Van, still eighteen years old and the youngest and most reserved, stuck around to see what came his way. Because of his huge size and friendly manner, his share of the action was usually worthwhile. Typically, they picked up women much older than themselves. Paul often expressed his preference for women with long, blond hair and tight, firm bodies, but ultimately sex was sex, and if he needed it, any willing woman would be worthy of his consideration.

They spun lies about their ages, their identities, and about their status in life. The lies were fabricated early in the evening, over supper at the Silver Nugget or in the car on the way to the bar. Sometimes they posed as the whiz-kid owners of a major restaurant chain, with Paul telling the girls his father was the president of a large multinational corporation. Sometimes they posed as professional hockey players, drafted by the Toronto Maple Leafs and playing at one of the organization's farm teams, only one more season away from making it to the Big Time, fame, money, and, of course, beautiful women. Other times they were business entrepreneurs. The strategies had roots in the lessons of Amway; it was "The Bigger Better Deal." It was mostly Paul's idea.

During his last years at Sir Wilfrid Laurier High School, Paul put only as much effort into studying as he had to, yet he still managed to pull mostly good marks. According to the 1982 school yearbook, his nickname was "Stud" and he spent most of his time picking up girls: "Stud will remember Laurier, where he pursued his favourite pastime—meeting girls. He plans to become rich and famous so he can go to California and 'check out the girls on the beach.' Paul says the only way to go through life is to 'go for it.' "

After the Smirnises had moved to Markham in 1981, Van and Steve gave their school officials the Silver Nugget restaurant as their mailing address so they wouldn't have to leave Sir Wilfrid Laurier or the Scarborough school district.

In 1983, however, Van, Steve, and Paul ended their high-school years at Albert Campbell High School, where Van and Steve upgraded various marks and Paul, who graduated from Laurier, took a six-month calculus course.

The 1983 Laurier yearbook, showing a photograph of Paul with his dirty-blond and wavy hair touching the back of his neck and covering his ears, stated: "P.B.'s activities are swimming, working late nights and, staying out even later. He plans to go into commerce, probably at the U of T. Paul's favourite person is a certain A.K. Good Luck Guy. (Sorry we couldn't swing a licensed cafeteria while you were here.)"

It was in 1983 that Paul made his first of what would become many raucous trips to Florida with some male friends. When Paul and the gang returned to Toronto, he anxiously related to Van how the rowdy group had been kicked out of their hotel but ended up staying with some girls at another hotel. Paul told Van about a girl he met, Tammy, from Dearborn, Michigan, and, as he always did, proceeded to relate how they had engaged in healthy doses of sex. Paul described Tammy as skinny, blond, and a "nymphomaniac." Paul was infatuated with her.

One weekend Paul and Van, accompanied by Steve and two other friends, drove to the Detroit area. Tammy's parents weren't home and the gang stayed there the first night. After this weekend, Tammy broke off her relationship with Paul, saying the distance between Dearborn and Toronto was just too great. Paul's ego was shattered. Because he had billed Tammy as a sex fiend and painted himself as a stud, Paul now seemed genuinely worried that his friends would think Tammy had dumped him because he wasn't man enough to satisfy her endless libido. "She's a slut," he told Van in passing.

That same year, Steve, Van, Paul, and a friend named Chris drove to Rochester, New York, for a weekend for the purpose of attending a Tommy Vu motivational seminar and visiting a couple of women Steve and Van had met the previous year. One of the women agreed to let the foursome stay both Friday and Saturday nights. After Vu performed Saturday night, the guys drove back to the woman's home. Paul was ecstatic with Vu's talk, mimicking for his friends Vu's promise of "wotta money and bootifool gall." Paul, Van, and Chris played cards in the woman's basement as Steve slept with the woman in her upstairs bedroom. At about 2 A.M., Paul excused himself for a washroom visit and went upstairs. Minutes later he came downstairs with the woman's purse, pulling it open and showing his friends a wad of American money, about five hundred dollars in all.

"Hey, look at this! Look at this! This girl's got money. Chris, you take this . . . Van you take this," he said as he handed bills to his buddies.

"No, Paul," Van protested. "Steve knows this girl. She is a nice person. Shit, she's letting us stay here. You can't take her money."

"I need this money, man. I need it." With these words, he folded the bills up and put them in his pocket.

They left early on Sunday, stopping in Rochester at a McDonald's restaurant to eat before they made the long trip west along Interstate 90, through Lewiston, and across the bridge at Queenston, before taking Highway 405 to the Queen Elizabeth Way and home.

Van told Steve about Paul's theft.

"You have to give it back, Paul," said Steve.

Paul handed the money over to Steve, short the five dollars

or so he had used to buy the McDonald's food. Once home, Steve wrote out a money order and mailed it to the Rochester woman.

Paul began his business and commerce studies at the University of Toronto's Scarborough campus in the fall of 1983. His first goal was to become a chartered accountant, but his dream was to become a partner or an executive in a large corporation. Marilyn Bernardo was ecstatic that Paul was going to the University of Toronto. Where David and Debbie had failed, perhaps Paul would succeed.

Some friends who couldn't continue their education because of finances or circumstances felt Paul used his student status and his future dreams to humiliate them. It was quite evident to many that Paul had developed a problematic superiority complex. Van, too, noticed this emerging character flaw in Paul, but he overlooked it because of their history and their friendship. And besides, Paul was still fun to be around, still a good partner for girl hunting.

One night in the fall, as Van and Paul were having one of their usual conversations about money and girls, an impudent grin crossed Paul Bernardo's face as he probed Van's face. They'd been talking about sex, and Paul had told Van how he preferred obedient virgins over any other kind of girl. Think about it, mused Paul, how fulfilling and satisfying it would be to have a stable of girls, a Virgin Farm, stocked with beautiful virgins with only one purpose in life: to do your exclusive bidding. Paul was serious, his words measured, precise: "Think about it, Van, about a farm full of women, all mine, with the only purpose of having sex with me."

Van had heard Paul talk about his Virgin Farm before. It had been an adolescent fantasy that he had assumed would likely pass from Paul's thoughts with time. But Paul was now an adult still thinking about this fantasy with unguarded candor. He told Van regularly about his fantasy of having young virgin schoolgirls, all around eleven or twelve years old and dressed in school uniforms with their hair in pigtails, perform fellatio on him as he sat in his business suit at his executive's desk. He fantasized that the schoolgirls would perform whatever he asked of them. The fantasy culminated with the schoolgirls licking his spent semen from their baby-smooth faces.

While it was true that Van and Paul had talked themselves blue in the face about what they liked and didn't like in girls, Van's idea of love, as crudely physical and juvenile as it might have been, was to have a beautiful girl who enjoyed sex with him as much as he liked sex with her. Paul clearly viewed women as something to be used, dominated, manipulated, and controlled. Paul also announced his philosophy that it was a cruel dog-eat-dog world and that vulnerable humans, especially women, existed to be consumed and used by the more powerful of the species. To Paul, a woman was merely another creature living in the jungle, a creature who could be exploited.

The younger, impressionable girls on Paul's street, however, knew nothing of his bizarre daydreams. To them he was the quintessential "boy next door." They all had a crush on the smiley, friendly blond guy who gushed personality and dressed like a store-catalogue model. Most of the girls within a two-block radius of Sir Raymond Drive would have dated Paul in a second but were either too shy or afraid of rejection to approach him. In the summertime, several girls from the neighborhood would hang out in their bathing suits around the pool in a yard that adjoined Paul's backyard. He was often in his parents' backyard in his swimsuit or shorts, by himself, listening to music. The girls would giggle among themselves whenever Paul would look up.

In 1984, Van and Steve were outside the movie theaters at the Scarborough Town Centre shopping mall when they met a girl named Carol and a friend. Van had been dating a girl named Marie for almost three years and he wasn't too interested in either of the new girls. But the quicksilver Steve edged in on Carol and dated her for a short time. One day he called Paul and asked if he wanted to double-date with Carol and her friend. They went to a drive-in movie in an old Ford Fairlane convertible the Smirnises had borrowed while the family car was being fixed. Steve had a fetish for blondes, and on this night he overlooked Carol's brunette allure and fixated on her friend. When the four walked to get popcorn, Steve suggested that he and Paul switch partners. Steve and Paul were both shocked at how quickly the girls agreed. Paul and Carol began making out in the front seat while Steve and his swap went at it in the backseat. Paul and Carol became an item.

A short time into Paul's relationship with Carol, Paul and Van were enjoying the sex-fantasy talk when, without warning, Paul bragged that he'd had such forceful intercourse with Carol in his dad's Capri that the front seat broke. Van laughed. Sure, Paul. But then, for the first time in his life, he was shocked by something Paul told him.

"You know, Carol and me . . . she likes to be tied up and then I fuck her in the ass," said Paul with a mischievous grin.

Paul went on to describe how he would tie Carol to the bed and play sadomasochistic games with her. The sexual escapades almost always ended in anal sex, and Paul admitted to getting immense pleasure and satisfaction at the power and authority he had over Carol. Furthermore, Paul related, he derived intense sexual excitement from the pain he inflicted during the anal-sex sessions. Van had tried anal sex once and wasn't thrilled at all. He was incredulous not only that his buddy would like it but that he'd found a girl who would actually go along with it.

"And she likes you doing this to her?" Van asked, hardly believing his ears.

"Yeah, she loves it. And I really get off on it," he replied.

Paul's relationship with Carol lasted several years, and at first it offered Van a unique glimpse into the two-sided emotional psyche of Paul: On the one hand there was the kinky, seemingly masochistic side that Paul occasionally revealed when he bragged about his sexual prowess; but then, there were times, albeit infrequently, when he confessed a great affection for Carol, even suggesting that one day he might marry her.

Affection was certainly lacking one night in 1984, when Paul and Carol came to the Smirnises' new house in Markham with Carol's girlfriend, Janet, in tow. While Van and Janet watched a hockey game upstairs, Paul led Carol to the basement recreation room. Van chuckled aloud, thinking he knew what Paul was after. But Paul and Carol were having their problems that night. Unknown to Van, Carol and Janet had gone out to a bar earlier and Carol had made the terrible mistake of not telling Paul.

Some time passed and Van and Janet were absorbed in the hockey game when all hell broke loose downstairs. They heard a muffled thumping and banging and then a piercing scream coming from the basement. Van rushed downstairs and rounded the corner of the wall to see Paul straddled over Carol on the couch, his fist viciously pounding her face with the speed of a jackhammer. Van froze in horror for a moment as Paul hit her again and again. Van jumped across the room and hauled his friend off the girl.

"Come on, relax, Paul . . . Paul . . . come on, man. That's it. Quit," Van said, grabbing both Paul's arms tightly to prevent any more violence and looking him straight in the eyes. But Paul's eyes never met his; they were still fixed on Carol, staring right at her, gleaming with anger.

Carol was curled up in a fetal position, holding her hands above her head in a pathetic attempt to both quell her weeping and hide her battered face, reddened and swollen and already showing the first signs of bruises from Paul's punches.

"She's just a fucking whore. A fucking bitch. She deserves no respect," said Paul, now free of Van's large hands. With this he turned and spat on her.

"Give up, Paul," shouted Van as he moved toward Carol to ask if she was okay.

Carol was crying and moaning, in serious pain.

"He's going to kill me; he's going to kill me," she shouted.

While tending to her stricken friend, Janet got into the act. "Quit hitting her; quit beating her!" she yelled at Paul.

Van felt terrible about what had happened. He asked Carol if she wanted to go to a hospital.

At this, Paul ranted and raged at his friend. "Just leave the fucking bitch. Fuck her. Just fucking leave her."

The embarrassment was so great for Van and Janet that the

foursome never reunited again. But incredibly, Paul and Carol remained an item.

Through 1986 and 1987, Van witnessed some strange incidents involving Paul. They involved Van's on-again-off-again girlfriend of about five years, Marie, and Carol. Van had met Marie when he was only fifteen years old. After they broke up, Marie started getting weird phone calls from an anonymous man who whispered things like "There's buggery going on" and "I'd like to fuck you in the ass." Van's aunt told him Marie believed Paul was making these telephone calls. Later in 1986, Metro Police traced these telephone calls to Sir Raymond Drive. In September 1986, a court restraining order was placed on Paul.

Despite Paul's various one-night stands and sexual relationships here and there, he still kept dating Carol. One night, Van had invited Paul and Carol to his parents house and they were sitting in the living room when out of the blue Paul casually mentioned to Carol that Van had set him up with a girl a few nights before.

"Van's been trying to make me cheat on you," he explained to Carol. It was true, Van thought, but why would Paul want to tell Carol about it?

Carol looked at Van with a violent rage in her eyes. "You bastard. You fucker!" she screamed, then launched herself at him with her fists flying.

Paul laughed at the entertainment, then called her off in an instant. She immediately returned to his lap, as if he had rung a bell, as if he had trained her for a conditioned response, as if she unquestionably accepted his orders even amid terrible emotional turmoil. Van felt uncomfortable after the incident, wondering why Paul would get such strange delight in this simple demonstration of the wide-ranging powers he had over Carol.

Around the same time Paul started dating Suzie, a beautiful student he had met while they were both at the University of Toronto's Scarborough campus. She fell completely head over heels in love with Paul and was extremely jealous of the attention Paul received from other women. She often followed him around to see what he was doing when he wasn't with her. One night, when Paul was making out with Carol at his parents' home, Suzie passed by Sir Raymond Drive and knocked on the door. Nobody answered the door, but she knew Paul was inside with Carol.

"You bastard," she screamed as she pounded on the door. In a rage, she walked around the house kicking in basement windows, and as a coup de grâce she smashed her hand through a fashionable lead-glass window opposite the front door. The window had been installed four months earlier after Marilyn bought it as a keepsake with money her parents had given her, telling neighbors it was her favorite piece in the house because it was not only beautiful but the money that bought it was hers.

Neighbors who heard the commotion came out of their houses to see a young girl with a bloodied hand screaming at the top of her lungs in the direction of the house.

"You better let me in, you bastard. I know you're in there. Let me in or I'll pull the fucking house down.

Paul reluctantly called the police, but when they arrived Suzie had already left. A police offficer called Suzie at her home and she explained she didn't realize Paul was screwing around behind her back. Carol also told police in a doleful statement she was madly in love with Paul and didn't know about Suzie.

Ultimately, the case ended without any charges. The police officer gave Paul a resigned look, saying, "I don't know what you got, buddy, but whatever it is I wish I had some."

For whatever reason, the women drawn into Paul's life fell deeply in love with him and were willing to forsake their own dignity to keep his love. Initially, Paul would use his charm, good looks, and sex to draw a woman into his web, but inevitably it would end up as a violent struggle for control and power. "Bullshit baffles brains," Paul would say about his magnetic control over women.

Paul's behavior toward women reminded Van of a dog salivating at finding a bitch in heat. As they cruised the streets on summer nights in the mid-1980s in Paul's Ford Capri, Paul would often remark as they passed some woman: "Wouldn't you want to knock her down and rape her?"

Van would give him a puzzled look and the conversation would abruptly change to something else.

One day, as they watched two young girls on McCowan Road, Paul spurted out suddenly, "Wouldn't you want to jump her and fuck her in the ass?"

Van looked over to see a gleam in Paul's eyes. He seemed enthralled at the possibility. "Rape, no. Fuck up the ass, no. Screw, yes," replied Van.

"Oh well, that's what I meant," said Paul.

Paul was clearly becoming obsessed with women and addicted to sex. To those outside the inner circle, it seemed as though these obsessions were surpassing his greed for material things and his lust for power. But his friends knew that to Paul, sex and power were one and the same thing.

Money paved the way to both sex and power. Paul didn't have enough, but he was determined to get it.

While most people are acutely aware of the sometimes thin line between legal and illegal and moral and immoral activities, Paul denied its existence. He believed nothing mattered except supply and demand. When Paul and Van, now in their early twenties, met Gord, who promised to make them rich selling goods he received through a pipeline into the "gray market" they eagerly embarked on another get-rich-quick scheme.

Van and Paul soon learned that Gord made a full-time living selling goods and products that were stolen, smuggled, or obtained in some other questionable way. In reality, Gord's gray market was perhaps just a lighter shade of black.

Gord and the young men were first involved with selling pay-TV satellite decoders to the Bahamas, where there was no cable television and a great market for the devices, which unscramble the pay-for-view transmissions. What they were doing wasn't illegal, but then they started moving computer hardware and software.

Over business beers, Gord and his understudies would often discuss the world of easy money. Gord, his streetwise brain experienced in such matters, announced one night a plan to make big bucks. Thanks to a friend in a bank, he could get his hands on certified-check and specialized date stampers that could produce illegitimate checks. So the trio set up a fake company using a pseudonym with a voice mailbox number. They ran advertisements in the newspaper looking for office staff and hired two men without their ever knowing for whom they were working. One man was used merely to set up a bank account; the other was used to set up a voice telephone mailbox for the phony company. The bank account and the telephone line were in their names. A month later, the checks were mailed to the anonymous mailbox by the duped employee and they ordered goods from numerous computer companies in Toronto and Markham, netting themselves three top-of-the-line Toshiba laptops and other computer equipment, as well as $30,000 in gold coins. Taxi drivers were hired to take the certified checks to the unwitting retail companies. Van would order the equipment on a Thursday, then on late Friday pay a cabdriver $65 if he would drop off the check, pick up the equipment, and return within the hour. This way, neither Gord, Van, nor Paul had any contact with the store, which usually didn't realize the check was bad until the next Monday at the earliest.

Van and Paul looked up to Gord for his simple genius. This was the perfect crime. They left no stone unturned in covering their tracks. Immediately after they received the computers, for example, Van drove to Price Waterhouse, where Paul began working as a junior accountant after his graduation from the University of Toronto in 1987. There they would transfer the defrauded goods to Paul's car. That weekend, the buddies took the computers apart and sanded off any identification numbers so they couldn't be traced. Then it was up to Gord to find buyers in the thriving Oriental underground market. In all, the trio wrote about a dozen checks worth $100,000.

A few weeks after the scam, Van was contacted by someone identifying himself as a detective with the Metro Police fraud squad. Van was told Gord was being busted or had been questioned about some computer frauds and he had mentioned Van's name and an accomplice.

"You are up to your eyeballs in this," the officer pressed.

"I don't know what you are talking about," said Van. Gord later told Van the cops hadn't even called him, but it was obvious they were trying to play each of the threesome off against the other. Van hired a lawyer named Barry Fox. They heard nothing more from Toronto police.

Paul seemed thrilled with the checks adventure. It was quick, easy money and it was exciting.

He looked at Van one night and said, "That's the biggest scam I've ever seen. You are really bad, Van. You're worse than any of us."

Van took it as a compliment. He believed Paul was attracted to these quick-hit, shady moneymaking schemes because of his disdain for his parents' conservative, passionless, and boring lifestyle. Although Ken Bernardo had made a decent living for his family, Paul didn't experience the expensive vacations he saw his friends and their families enjoying. Paul often compared himself to the Kennedys and other upstanding families of contemporary North America who made their initial money from shady dealings such as booze smuggling during the Prohibition years. Paul said he respected the Kennedys and others for the way they made their cash.

Paul did, however, become nervous when Van told him about the telephone call from the fraud squad. Van thought Paul's reaction to the police had always been odd. Whenever police came near, Paul would flee, as if for his life. He seemed terrified of any contact with them. Van recalled the night, a few years earlier, when they had been out drinking in bars and both of them had drunk so much that they were hammered. On the way home, Paul weaved past a parked Metro Police cruiser, which then pulled out some distance behind them. Its roof lights were on. But Paul ducked right, into a residential section. He threw the lights off, then turned quickly, again and again, then pulled sharply into a driveway. The pair got out of the car and walked off. The cruiser sped past. About ten minutes later Van and Paul returned to the car and made their way home through the side streets.

On another night Van, Paul, Van's cousin, and another friend used the cover of darkness to sneak into a trout-fishing farm near Stouffville intending to bag a few buckets of fish.

Paul threw fish pellets into the water and when the fish surfaced to feed, Van and the others scooped them in a net. They had three buckets of fish when a neighbor who had seen them drove up in a car. Simultaneously, the trout-farm owner approached them with a shotgun and trained it on Van's cousin and the friend.

"Stop, or I'll shoot 'em, I'll shoot 'em," theatened the owner.

Van stopped in his tracks; he didn't want anything to happen to the others. But Paul took off into the fields like a deer and wasn't seen again that night. Police came and asked Van about the guy who ran away.

"I don't know who it is; he's just some guy I met in a doughnut shop," Van said.

The three remaining suspects, hoping to avoid any criminal charges, agreed to pay for their illegal catch; the owner, hoping to avoid the unpleasantness of a court appearance, didn't press for charges. Van couldn't figure out why Paul would run away and leave his friends over three buckets of fish.

CHAPTER
8

Van had met Kevin at the Smirnis' Pizza Stop, where the two often talked while Kevin waited for his order. Van would listen to him describing his work, repulsed yet at the same time fascinated by what he did at a local crematorium. One night, Kevin told Van that he didn't have any money but needed some food for him and his family to eat. Kevin offered Van a deal: if Van could give him two large pizzas Van could visit the crematorium and fill his car with gas at one of the on-site pumps and grab himself a few cans of engine oil at the same time. It was a deal Van couldn't refuse.

After Kevin had filled up Van's car he asked if Van wanted to watch him work, maybe even help him do a few nightly chores. Van was uncertain at first, but his curiosity gained the better of him and he agreed. Van was so disturbed by what Kevin showed him that he didn't sleep a wink that night. The next day Van related his bizarre experience to Paul. He was shocked at his friend's response.

"I want to go . . . I want to see," said Paul, his eyes wide with excitement and anticipation.

Over the next few weeks, Kevin appeared at the Pizza Stop for his free food and Van arranged a time to fill up the Mercedes. At that time, Kevin had no objection if Paul tagged along. Paul's eyes widened when he saw the bodies in cardboard coffins waiting to be burned.

He turned to Van. "Ooh boy, this is awesome. This is neat."

Paul left no stone unturned as Kevin gave him the tour through the crematorium, gawking at the lineup of cadavers in the freezer, asking questions about this body and that body. On Paul's behalf, Kevin went through the same spiel he had given Van on his initial visit. While doing so, he pulled three bodies out of the walk-in freezer for cremation, then wheeled a fourth body to the table for pre-cremation preparation, a macabre task that Kevin hadn't shown Van on his first visit. When they came to Kevin, most bodies had already been given formal funeral services and were already prepared, but some corpses, those of derelicts and paupers, came directly to the crematorium without being touched. Kevin led Van and Paul to the table, deftly inserted a needle-tipped clear plastic tube into a main artery, and began to pump a formaldehyde solution into the jugular to simultaneously pump out blood through another plastic tube he had inserted. As the formaldehyde was pumped into the neck, Van and Paul watched the blood push out, along the tube and into the bucket. As the flow became more steady, Kevin raised the table with a hand crank, lifting the feet to increase the flow of blood through gravity.

Paul was awestruck.

"This is amazing. It is fascinating," he commented, asking Kevin to explain each maneuver in intricate detail.

So enthralled was Paul with the process that he talked about Kevin's job almost nonstop over the next week and arranged with Van to take a second visit. He came away from his second visit as captivated as he was following the first.

"That guy could have anybody killed and no one would ever know," he said to Van, a tone of admiration in his voice.

Van didn't pay attention to this raw comment; he put it down to Paul's watching too many gangster movies. On the way home, Paul even made jokes about the bodies' being cooked for dinner. Van felt vomit welling up in him.

In October of 1987 Paul was working as a junior accountant at Price Waterhouse but he seemed depressed. His love life was in a shambles. His two girlfriends, Carol and Suzie, were in the process of kissing him off. Neither had been the same since Suzie kicked in the basement windows at 21 Sir Raymond Drive when she discovered Paul with Carol. Van realized that Paul, like all the boys, enjoyed the reckless fun with the one-night stands, but for some reason he didn't seem content without having a permanent girlfriend in his life. And he preferred that one girl, it seemed, to be an "unspoiled" virgin. Even one former lover was one too many for Paul. Spending a Saturday night at the Pizza Stop without a sexy girl at his beck and call was hardly Paul's idea of fun. His dejection had infected Van; he knew that this October night could be a long one.

Van remembered what Paul had said about the good times with Suzie, and how he wanted so much to win her love back. He would even forgive her for kicking in the basement windows. Van wasn't surprised to hear Paul wanting Suzie back: not only was she extraordinarily beautiful, her face exquisite and her dark-skinned body the stuff of fantasies, but, according to Paul, she was also fantastic in bed, both dominant and adventurous. Her enjoyment of sex made her, from Paul's perspective, a real catch. And Van recalled Paul's past whisperings about how Suzie liked to "take it up the ass." Her apparent enjoyment of anal sex seemed to bring great pleasure to Paul, who had on many occasions expressed his love of anal sex. He'd often chided his buddies that screwing a girl anally was "the way of getting respect from them." Earlier that night, Paul had persuaded Van to call Suzie and ask her to return the wristwatch Paul had bought her. It was an excuse to contact her, really, but Van had dutifully called from his brother Alex's bedroom.

"No, I love that watch. It brings back memories," Suzie had said, and without much further ado had hung up. Paul was furious. He raged about Suzie, shouting at Van that he'd paid almost $800 for the watch. After a while, even Paul became sick of wallowing in his own sorrow at the Pizza Stop. He suggested that a change of scenery and some food would do him good. They made for the restaurant at Howard Johnson's, the same place where Paul, Van, and Steve would huddle to chew the fat after their Amway meetings.

Van parked outside the restaurant's front door, only fifteen yards or so from the front windows. It was October 17, 1987. Summer's warmth was fading fast with fall's arrival, and an almost brumal nip was permeating the night air. With no plans for the night, the pals had opted for casual clothing: Van was in a sweatshirt and casual cotton pants; Paul had pulled a Nautica windbreaker over his blue Ralph Lauren button-down Oxford shirt, which he tucked into black pants.

Paul was first out of the car, then Van, locking the door behind him, as had become the habit in Scarborough. As they strode slowly toward the coffee shop's front door, Paul glanced at the front windows to their right. He let out a curious chuckle. "Van," he mused, "take a look at those chicks." Van's head turned to see a blond girl's cute face smiling at them through the unclosed vertical fabric blinds from a bench seat at the front windows. Opposite her was another girl, her face partially hidden but seemingly attractive. At the blond girl's behest, she turned to look. The blond girl then gave what Van recognized as a come-and-get-me smile. Paul seemed to cheer up immediately. The two buddies had been through this before.

The restaurant—or Bluffer's Atrium Lounge, as it was labeled throughout the hotel—had a reputation for good service and staff were hired with a view to maintaining this reputation. Paul and Van were met at the front door by an amicable Oriental guy whom Van recalls having a "Wok-with-Yan" smile and "Lee" on his name tag.

"Hi, how are you?" asked Lee. "Table for two?"

Van and Paul looked to their right, down the row of bench seats and tables at the window. The blond girl had her head tilted out into the aisle and gave another inviting smile. Van, with Paul following, walked right by Lee and toward the girls. The two strutted up to the table. "Mind if we join you girls?" asked Van. "Sure, sit down," said the blonde, simultaneously moving toward the window and making more room. Paul had moved to Van's left and quickly bunked onto the bench seat with the blonde. Van moved alongside the blonde's friend.

There wasn't much room, because the bench seats were squat and short. Van and Paul found their thighs and shoulders scrunched against the girls. Perfect.

First came the introductions. The blonde said her name was Karla; her friend called herself Debbie. Paul didn't waste a second. He moved in on Karla like a starving raptor. "So, are you from around here?" he asked her. She replied that they were from St. Catharines. Paul smiled and shook his head. "Well, how am I going to see you, if you live down there and I live here?" This brought a schoolgirl giggle from the girls. As they picked away at the remains of their salads and sipped at their glasses of house wine, Van and Paul ordered all-you-can-eat chicken wings.

Karla Homolka and one of her best friends, Debbie Purdie, explained that they were in Scarborough for the weekend at a pet convention for their employer, Number One Pet Store. As the blonde told how they both worked at a branch in St. Catharines and how they were really excited about the convention, Van studied her face. She wasn't wearing makeup, but she had a natural beauty. Her dirty-blond hair was long and curly, framing a pleasant face. She looked about sixteen, perhaps younger. Her lips were gorgeous, her smile cute. As Karla spoke, she looked right into Paul's eyes. Van immediately sensed the animal magnetism between Paul and this girl. For a few seconds, jealousy wandered through Van's mind.

"Where are you staying? asked Paul.

"Here at the hotel," responded Karla.

Paul gave his friend a sly grin. Van believed both girls were excited at being away from home and fancy-free in the city. It was evident to him that both girls wanted to have some fun. The plan Paul and Van had developed years ago was put into action again: separate, divide, and conquer. It was clear Paul wanted Karla for his girlfriend, at least for the evening.

The foursome continued their idle chitchat, during which Paul slipped in some subtle compliments about Karla's appearance, praising her eyes, her hair, and how he wanted to see her again. With supper done and the wine all gone, Debbie announced suddenly, "Hey, you guys want to come up to our room for a drink?" They didn't need a second invitation.

Van didn't find Debbie that attractive, but he wasn't going to ruin the evening for his friend, who had obviously targeted Karla for the night.

When the girls went to the washroom, Van couldn't help but telling Paul, "She's nice, man."

Paul's eyes surveyed the washroom door for Karla's return. "Yes, and I've got her tonight," came his gloating reply. And then, almost as an afterthought, he told Van, "Hey, as soon as I'm done with her, you can have her, if she wants you."

Van laughed. They'd done plenty of crazy things together, but having sex with a girl that Paul had had only minutes earlier was not something he'd seriously consider.

The girls returned from the washroom and the foursome made for the elevator. Karla pushed the button for the third floor and stood facing outward. No sooner had the steel doors closed than Paul slipped his arms around Karla's waist and began to rub his face in her hair and kiss her neck. As if she was powerless to resist him, she turned her body and stood up on her toes to kiss him. Van watched as their lips met and ground together. The instant passion between her and Paul was like a chemical reaction, he thought. She saw him and she responded; he touched her, she responded. Van was leaning against the wall at the rear of the elevator. He felt obliged to hold Debbie so she wouldn't feel out of place. Picking up girls and having sex with them was like one hand washing the other for Paul and Van. The aim was to give your buddy any opportunity he needed so he could make the move.

As Karla opened the hotel-room door, the girls walked in first and Karla put the light on. "This could get ugly," Paul whispered to him, "so don't look." Van wondered what the hell he was talking about. Tonight, Paul seemed very much in control of the situation. They stood in the hallway for a second and surveyed the room: To the left, about four paces away, was a queen-size bed; straight ahead, in front of a window, was a pullout sofa. About seven feet separated the bed and the sofa.

With no hesitation, Paul pounced on Karla and the two were on the bed, their bodies writhing in unison. Karla's sneakers were off and Paul tugged at her sweatshirt. Debbie and Van pulled the couch bed out. Although reluctant, Van had to go along with the mood; he wondered if Debbie was doing the same thing to ensure that Karla got her man. Van and Debbie made a tentative kiss, but their hearts weren't in it. Van looked over toward Paul and Karla, watching them kissing frantically in the illumination of the bedside light, Karla's clothes in a state of disarray. Paul caught Van looking. He turned off the light and chuckled. Van laughed and called Paul "an asshole."

After a few minutes of unsatisfactory kissing on the pullout sofa, Van and Debbie cooled off and made do with holding each other. At first, it was too dark for them to see what was going on between Paul and Karla on the bed; all they could hear was heavy breathing and jerky movements under the sheets. Before long Van's eyes became accustomed to the dark. The sheets were moving crazily, as if they were a wind-whipped ocean. All at once the sheets were pushed aside and he saw Karla's body, as clear as day, writhing and squirming atop Paul's body, her hips grinding into his midriff and her breasts hanging down in Paul's face. She was naked, quite beautiful, as he had imagined she would be.

Van and Debbie looked at each other, and although shocked, Van just chuckled.

"Oh my God, they're having sex," Debbie said, exasperated. Horrified. Suddenly Paul pushed Karla back onto the bottom. It was as if the two were fighting for who would be on top, who would dominate the other. Clearly Karla was trying to lead, but Paul would have none of it. The two of them were locked in animal passion, totally oblivious to their friends. It was as if Van and Debbie didn't exist. Paul held Karla's hands above her head in mock confinement. The sex went on almost nonstop for four hours. Amid the fury Van heard Karla's voice calling out between moans: "You're beautiful; I love you." Van couldn't believe his ears; this Karla chick had just met Paul only half an hour earlier and already she was in love with him.

Sleep finally overcame Debbie's shock at what was happening. After she drifted off, Van, envious of his friend's luck at bedding a highly sexed woman, figured it was time to cash in on Paul's earlier promise. This girl was obviously no shrinking violet, and he didn't want to miss out.

"Hey, Paul, can I get in, man?"

"No!"

"Psst, Paul. Come on, man. Give me a go."

"No, man, I've got feelings for her."

Van looked over at the sleeping Debbie, her light snores proof of his own dreamy reality. Within a few minutes he had joined her in slumber.

It was 8 a.m. when the room came alive the next day. Karla and Debbie had a bus to catch back to St. Catharines, but Karla wanted to take a shower with Paul. They were already like lovebirds, cooing at each other's every move. Karla dressed in the bathroom, out of sight of Van. She appeared wearing the same clothes as the night before.

"What was going on over there last night?" he chided. "I heard a lot of noise."

Karla snickered, her face radiant. She looked to Paul to give the answer.

"Don't ask that stupid question," he said, then put his arms around her.

Paul was intent on making a final impression, telling Karla how beautiful she was, getting her telephone number and her address. Van was puzzled at his friend's apparent interest. This wasn't like the one-night stands in Florida hotel rooms, where Paul's interest ended with his first orgasm. A few hours of slumber hadn't changed Van's impression of Debbie, nor, apparently, her feelings for him. They were civil, but telephone numbers weren't swapped. At about 9 a.m., Van led them to their car and drove the girls to the bus. As the car left Paul let out an ecstatic war whoop.

"I'm gonna call her, man. That was great last night. Fuck! I've never had anything that good."

Late that night, Van tried to telephone Paul to touch base. The line was busy for hours. This was odd, thought Van, because Paul didn't like using the telephone that much. He thought that perhaps Karla had called. Finally, after dozens of attempts, Van reached his buddy. Paul told him he'd called

Karla and she'd told him she already started writing a letter to him.

"She really likes me and she wants to go out with me. She really likes me. God, she was fantastic," cried Paul.

Suddenly, Paul had another babe who was fantastic in bed. And it was Van who was down in the dumps and single.

"Hey, Paul," he interrupted. "Ask her if she has another friend."

Scott Burnside and Alan Cairns

CHAPTER
9

Lisa Stanton had never met anyone like Karla Homolka. She was the first girl she knew at Ferndale Public School that yelled at the top of her lungs, just for the sake of yelling. She was also the first girl Lisa knew who occasionally shook the neighborhood by yelling "Fuck Off!" Karla was the first girl Lisa knew who talked back to her parents, sometimes abruptly ending arguments by storming into her downstairs bedroom and slamming the door for emphasis. She was the first girl she knew who dyed her hair.

For Lisa, almost painfully shy, her skin perpetually a pale Victorian hue, Karla and her robust European family represented uncharted territory, a brand-new world she was happy to explore. Lisa doesn't remember exactly when the blond-haired imp showed up at school. It was either grade four or grade five, but she definitely recalls sitting in the tiny desks arranged in perfect rows looking at the new girl. It wasn't long before Lisa and Karla discovered that their comfortable suburban homes were only a few blocks apart and they began walking to the one-story, redbrick school that occupied a half city block with its soccer fields, baseball diamonds, and myriad playground equipment. It was, and still is, a white, middle-class school serving up a white, middle-class education.

Karla Leanne Homolka was born on May 4, 1970. Her parents moved to St. Catharines four years later. The streets in this 1960s subdivision are winding and tree lined. The

houses, distinct and tidy, are arranged without the jam-packed
cookie-cutter feel of newer housing developments. Karel,
Karla's father, a Czech immigrant, was a salesman, selling
various lighting products, a job that frequently took him on
the road. He was a slight man, about five feet seven, with a
ready grin and the kind of skin that seemed almost permanently tanned, even in the dead of winter. Her mother, Dorothy, was a stockier woman who worked at St. Catharines'
Shaver Hospital. Karla had two sisters: Tammy, just a baby
when Karla and Lisa met, and Lori, a year younger than
Karla. The family was a handsome one, with their defined
cheekbones and ruddy complexions, and their house on Dundonald Street was often abuzz with the sound of visiting family from southern Ontario and neighbors with whom the
Homolkas struck up lasting friendships.

In the backyard of the semidetached brick home was a
swimming pool, and it was there, over the ensuing years, that
Lisa and the cadre of close-knit friends that she and Karla
shared would spend a great deal of time.

Dorothy always seemed to have a ball of dough in the refrigerator that could quickly be turned into a mini-pizza, and
Karla and Lisa took delight in creating their own pizza creations. For Lisa, whose parents came from strict British stock,
and who were conservative in most things, trips to the
Homolka house were initially considered with a mixture of
enjoyment and awe.

Especially incredible to young Lisa was Karla herself.
Loud and stubborn, Karla displayed behavior well beyond the
bounds of anything Lisa had ever imagined. One day as they
walked along the placid streets Karla began screaming
"Fuck!" at the top of her lungs. She wasn't mad, she wasn't
upset, merely releasing some sort of hidden wellspring of energy, kind of like a geyser in a park releasing steam and pressure.

"Fuck! Fuck! Fuck!"

Lisa's eyes bulged with amazement. *Oh, my God!* she
thought to herself.

As for Karla's relationship with her parents, Lisa often became confused as to who was master and who was child. Ar-

guments about chores or cleaning her room or homework or other matters sometimes ended with Karla screaming an emphatic ''No!'' and equally emphatically slamming a door in case anyone wasn't sure whether the conversation was over.

When this happened, Lisa always waited breathlessly for Karel to burst through the door and tan his oldest daughter's behind, but it never happened, at least not in her presence.

''She had better control over her parents compared to what the rest of us did,'' Lisa recalls. ''She was quite stubborn and willful. And I think her parents got used to that.''

Lisa recalls that from a young age Karla was loath to ever admit she was wrong; she flatly refused to back down even if the argument was clearly lost. And arguments certainly weren't limited to weighty or controversial topics. If it could be talked about, Karla could argue about it.

''You couldn't push her on anything. Forget it.'' says Lisa.

Karla, always a talker and outgoing, made friends easily. But accepting her stubbornness was a prerequisite for those who were to remain within Karla's sphere of friends for any length of time.

Arguments with Karla sometimes ended with the challenge ''Well, are you my friend or not?''

And as with all youngsters who need to constantly define and redefine who is their friend and who likes whom, there were those who moved quickly through Karla's sphere, either banished or fleeing.

''If she was mad about something, she'd let you know about it,'' says Lisa.

It didn't matter if you were a parent, a teacher, a friend, or a stranger, Karla always spoke her mind. And yet Karla wasn't a malcontent or a troublemaker.

''The only thing Karla probably ever got in trouble for at school was talking,'' says Lisa. ''I can remember a few times when Karla actually lost her voice from talking,'' she continues, laughing. ''She never shut up.''

Karla, then, was the perfect foil for Lisa, who was especially quiet and given to long periods of silence, especially around a group of people.

As many shy people realize at an early age, they are often

the targets of insensitive peers who interpret silence as a sign of weakness or disability that they can manipulate in order to elevate their own childhood status.

Karla, however gregarious, was never mean. It is one reason she and Lisa became such fast friends.

While Karla demanded much of her friends and certainly liked to be heard, she never sought to lead her social group. She never demanded that she be in charge of things, or that she organize and dictate who was in and who was excluded.

"She didn't look to anyone for anything. That's how I remember her," says Lisa. "She was a friendly, outgoing person. But if you didn't like her, she didn't care. She wasn't a person who got all hung up on 'Oh, gee! What can I do to be your friend?' She'd say, 'Oh well, big deal.'"

During the summer between grade seven and grade eight, the final year of elementary school, Karla dyed her hair from blond to brunette. She was the first person Lisa had known who willingly changed the color of her hair.

Karla phoned Lisa and told her she had made the switch.

"What color did you do it?" Lisa asked, still having trouble accepting the fact that Karla would even attempt such a dramatic change.

It was not the last time Karla asserted her independence through hair color. In fact, as high school approached and began, there was to be an almost weekly experiment carried out on the top of Karla's head.

For Lisa, these experiments were amazing not only for their colorful results but for the actual act of change. In the Stanton home, by contrast, Lisa wasn't even allowed to wear makeup until later in her teen years. Karla had none of those restrictions.

"If I ever dyed my hair, I'd get killed," Lisa would moan to Karla, although if the truth were told, Lisa wasn't absolutely sure that even if she'd been given carte blanche to have green and purple locks, she'd have exercised that right. Still, it was fun to watch Karla.

Although Karla's parents were tolerant of their oldest daughter's mood swings and sometimes nuclear stubbornness, there seemed to be little friction with respect to Karla's performance at school. A bright, inquisitive girl, Karla always did well and had developed a level of competitiveness that was reflected in her marks. Even in the summer months, Karla and Lisa would write and then swap short stories or poetry they'd written.

"She was actually quite good at it," recalls Lisa.

Both Lisa and Karla enjoyed French class in elementary school and joined the French Club, which meant spending lunch hours several times a week with other club members trying to speak French.

Karla, Lisa, and the girls that populated their social sphere had limited contact with members of the opposite sex. Conversations about boys were basically relegated to hushed cafeteria conversations, or hurried notes written in class and passed surreptitiously under desks and in books.

At their eighth-grade graduation, special permission had to be obtained for the girls to attend an after-dance pizza party at a local pizzeria, Julio's. It was the first time for many that they got to stay out late with a group of peers. Curfew was 12:30 a.m. If there was any drinking or smoking, even at this celebration, it wasn't being done by Lisa, Karla, or anyone in their crowd.

Still, fascination with boys began to intrude on daily life during this time. And as high school approached, the prospect of a seemingly endless array of boys, many older and seemingly more worldly was both chilling and exhilarating.

During the summer between grade eight and the commencement of high school, Karla began phoning Lisa and Mandy Whatling, another close friend, and suggesting they go for walks in the neighborhood. These walks Karla dubbed SOGGings—Searching Out Gorgeous Guys. And as the girls wandered through the quiet residential streets and over into the more commercial areas of north St. Catharines, Karla would wave at cars bearing guys she felt were attractive.

Sometimes, much to the horror of the girls, who never expected any kind of acknowledgment beyond perhaps a quick beep of the car horn, the cars would stop. On those rare occasions, the girls would try to give the impression that they were older than their thirteen or fourteen years. Mandy and Lisa were both painfully shy and offered little or nothing to these roadside conversations. Karla, however, seemed quite at ease chatting with perfect strangers, and her friends looked to her to carry the conversation and to set the tone.

Only occasionally, and after repeated goading from Karla, would either Mandy or Lisa even wave at passing cars. But sometimes, buoyed by their fearless friend, they would take up the challenge and the three of them would wave wildly at passing traffic.

Ontario's education system is based on the feeder system, which funnels students from elementary schools in a defined geographic area into specific secondary schools. Had Lisa and Karla followed the designed plan, they would have, along with the bulk of their classmates, attended Collegiate Secondary School, or Merritton, the closest high schools to their neighborhood.

Instead, Karla and Lisa travelled the extra distance to Sir Winston Churchill Secondary School, hoping to take advantage of its superior academic, arts and music programs. Sir Winston, as it was more commonly called, was smaller than most of the city's high schools, and serviced some of its most affluent subdivisions. Students at Sir Winston liked to fancy themselves a cut above their peers. And conversely, there was a general disdain for SWC among other schools, kind of a reverse discrimination.

"It was regarded as the snob school. It didn't matter that you got the best education there. It was a rich kid's school," recalls Lisa.

One of the first things Lisa and Karla did as members of the Sir Winston school community in the fall of 1984 was buy a fancy school jacket. It was one of the last acts of conformity for both girls for a long time. Although Lisa and Karla rode the bus to school together and joined the vocal ensemble, the girls' interests diverged after Lisa and her family journeyed to England to visit relatives. There, she discovered and developed a significant affection for new-wave and underground music when it was still new and underground and not merely trendy.

Karla and Mandy, however, were into a definite Prince phase. While Lisa explored the alternative-music scene and its corresponding dress code—black, black, black—Karla was experimenting on her own. Entirely in keeping with her robust character, it was not a subtle period of experimentation for the young teen.

For Karla, her stamp of independence was triumphantly displayed on her head, in her ears, and even on her shoes. A kaleidoscope of colors—greens, blues, and reds—appeared on a regular basis in Karla's hair. Long, jangly, overpowering earrings appeared in her ears in often painful numbers. Bracelets and bangles decorated her wrists, and there were even bells in her shoes that announced Karla's movements with each bouncy step. The hair designs and jangling accessories were all complemented by Karla's favorite outfit: white long underwear over which she wore flashy boxer shorts and ballet slippers, either white or black.

Given that SWC was a school that didn't take kindly to free spirits and those who bucked the school's demanding, if unwritten, fashion code, Karla was clearly different. Despite being rather small and academically sophisticated, Sir Winston had a definite way of doing things, and it wasn't to show up at school with green hair. Up and down the halls of the brick building the uniform was obvious: penny loafers, Lacoste sweaters, button-down shirts, Polo, Ralph Lauren. At SWC in the mid-1980s, prep was the style, and if you weren't prep, you were out of the loop.

"Karla wasn't cool. People thought she was weird. But people who knew her didn't care. It was part of her strange charm," says Lisa. "She disliked preppies. And diehard preppies disliked her. But she didn't care what anybody thought of her."

The vocal class was held in the special-education classroom near the guidance counselors' office. The few desks in the classroom would be pushed against the wall and chairs arranged in a loose semicircle around the upright piano. There were a couple of armchairs and a sofa on which Karla and Lisa most often sought space.

Although the class was held at lunchtime and students

would munch sandwiches and cookies while poring over sheet music and listening to Mr. Gunther Loffleman's instructions as he sat perched on the piano stool, it was no easy course. The dozen or so students were required to learn various parts and to sing solo and as part of the chorale.

Kevin Jacoby loved to sing. A large, intensely bright boy, he'd been singing in his Lutheran church choir for years. He was, despite the stigma that singing and the choir weren't particularly manly pursuits, an eager member of Loffleman's class. He quickly asserted himself as a strong singer despite the presence of more senior members of the vocal class who liked to leave the impression that they were the resident divas. For Kevin, being in the vocal class gave him a sense of belonging.

Several weeks into the course, Loffleman decided that each student would perform in front of the class a section of a simple, German Renaissance piece, "The Trout." Kevin volunteered to go first. He felt confident of his clear, tenor voice and he figured that by going first, Mr. L might cut him a break on the marks.

The news of performing solo came as unpleasant news to many of the students, especially the handful of ninth-grade students who feared performing alone. One of those especially unnerved by Mr. L's request was an alto named Karla Homolka. On the second of the two-day tests Karla began to sing her part in a sweet, faltering voice. She stopped after a few notes.

"I can't do this," she said nervously.

Mr. L tried to comfort her, encourage her, but she'd have none of it.

"But they'll be watching," she complained, jiggling around nervously in front of the other vocal classmates. Finally, Karla made an announcement: "Everyone either leave the room or turn your chair around," she commanded.

Mr. L smiled, and since he wasn't about to kick the rest of his class into the hallway, humored his new vocal student and asked if everyone wouldn't mind turning their chairs to the back of the class to Karla could complete her test.

Although Kevin and Karla shared geography and English

classes, it wasn't until the following year that they became close friends.

"No one really dressed like Karla," Kevin recalls. "At least in our grade or any grade above us. She was a different girl."

Painfully shy, Kevin would occasionally offer some comment to his classmate about a particular outfit or look she might be trying out. "This is interesting. Where's the bottom half?"

Karla would laugh and give him a shot back about Kevin's preoccupation with conformity in clothing. But Kevin was a conformist and proud of it. Karla admired his honesty and liked to tease him about being part of the herd of teenage cattle at Sir Winston, driven by trends and a fear of individuality. But the kidding was always good-natured, unlike some of the snide comments other students made about Karla behind her back. And as the teasing progressed, so too did their friendship. For Kevin, who was a large young man, weighing about 270 pounds, the relationship was purely platonic.

"I saw someone who was open and honest. She just said what was on her mind and it didn't bother her how it might be taken. She never got along with any of the popular people, to be honest. She was seen as something weird or different. She helped that image along an awful lot."

One day in Karla's ninth-grade English class, the teacher launched into a discussion of career goals. One young girl, Kathy Wilson, announced she'd like to be a television broadcaster. Like most freshmen, Kathy was less sure about her role in a new high school than she was about a job ten years down the line.

Her father, Stan Wilson, a teacher at Sir Winston, was a warm, teddy bear of a man who taught the most difficult subjects: calculus, physics, computer sciences. Although the family had lived for years in Niagara-on-the-Lake, the tourist and fruit-growing hub of the region, it was decided that Kathy should travel with her father into Sir Winston as her older brother had done two years earlier.

She met new people flitting from niche to niche, exploring new friendships. One of the first people she noticed, if not met outright, was the young girl with the snappy long johns, boxer shorts, and kaleidoscope hair designs.

Although an admitted prep—Lacoste, Polo, and Tretorn were brands Kathy was intimately familiar with—she was intrigued by her new classmate. "She stood out," the attractive foster-child worker says now. On the day in question, Karla announced that she was determined to become a police officer, likely a plainclothes or undercover detective. Either that or a veterinarian, she added.

Kathy and Karla debated what kind of life being a police officer would entail and how hard it would be, but Karla remained steadfast that she could handle it.

At this stage, sixteen or seventeen years old, Karla, like many teenage girls, was given to fits of melodrama. Several times she purposely cut her wrist with a knife or some other instrument. Once she cut herself with a steak knife. The cut was not terribly deep and it was horizontal (as opposed to vertical, which is the method that actually endangers life through loss of blood). But when Lisa questioned her about the marks and the bandages, Karla couldn't tell her what prompted her depression or anxiety. In fact, Lisa couldn't think of a particular event, a boy, or traumatic episode that sparked these moods. Now she says it may simply have been the tumultuous adolescent changes Karla was going through. Too young to experience the adult domain, but having left childhood behind, these are for many young women periods of great angst. Simply being a teenager sometimes means viewing the most mundane events as cataclysmic happenings, and perhaps the cuttings were a way of expressing freedom or power or the frustration of being neither adult nor child.

Kathy's concern over Karla's behavior and periods of depression were real enough for Lisa and Mandy to discuss it one day in geography after phys ed class. In the time-honored way of communicating between girls, Karla, Lisa and Mandy discussed this and other teen situations via notes passed in class, or in the case of science class, simply left in an unused drawer in the lab desks, since Karla and Lisa didn't share the same class.

"Karla, this isn't normal," Lisa would write.

"Yeah, I know, I'm just depressed." But there was no elaboration. It was a phase, like many teenage phases, that lasted a short period of time, and as quickly as it began, Karla seemed to snap out of it. Whether she was merely acting out for attention or was abusing herself as a way of dealing with the anger she felt to someone close to her but whom she couldn't deal with, remained unknown.

It was also during Karla's first year in high school that she found herself at the heart of the great dissection controversy. Part of the science class involved dissecting a worm. But Karla refused to take part, wearing an SPCA button to class. It wasn't that she was squeamish, but she said that she couldn't understand why they needed to cut up more worms. The textbooks already showed what was inside, so why did more worms have to be sacrificed to teenage scientists? she asked pointedly.

A breathtaking variety of hair colors wasn't the only form of experimenting Karla discovered in her early high-school career. Like thousands of teenagers, Karla and her friends discovered the heady, often painful mixture of high-school dances and alcohol.

Karla was no stranger to alcohol, having watched her parents, especially Karel, drink on a regular basis for years. Still, the rite of passage was no different for Karla as she explored the sometimes tenuous relationship between quantity and control.

Later, in eleventh grade, Karla would become extremely popular with her friends when she sent away for a piece of laminated identification from an American magazine. The blue identification card bearing Karla's picture had no official purpose in Ontario, but thanks to a creative application by Karla, indicated she was nineteen or twenty. When the card came, lo and behold, workers at the government-run liquor store accepted the ID without question.

Kathy, Lisa, and some others were discussing the dilemma of how to obtain alcohol one day when Karla piped up nonchalantly, "I can go, I've got ID."

"Where'd you get it?" was the incredulous reply.

"Oh, I sent away for it."

"Wow! I wish I'd done that."

Karla was thus designated the liquor gofer.

Karla's sixteenth birthday coincided with her first real job at the Pen Centre shopping mall pet store, a short walk from SWC. Always a great lover of animals, Karla saw a Help Wanted sign in the store window and, clad in her usual uniform of long johns and boxer shorts, explained to the manager that she did, indeed, love animals and would like nothing better than to work with them. It was good enough, and Karla began spending after-school hours and weekends in the store.

Shortly after she started working at Pen Centre pet store, Karla and Lori threw money together to pay for a second phone line, which lessened the telephone wars in the Homolka house that had begun when the girls entered their midteen years.

Although Karla had little but her love of animals to recommend her for the job at the pet store, she devoted herself to learning about animals and what made them tick. She read up on various animal diseases, information that was often passed on to a less-than-thrilled Kevin. "Oh great, I really want to know about yak cysts," he would say when informed of the various and sundry afflictions in the animal world.

Karla's duties included feeding and watering the various animals on display in the pet store, and she took great care to make them as comfortable as possible. The puppies, for instance, were sure to get their daily run in the outside paddock because Karla worried about the damage to their paws if they simply stood in the wire cages all day.

It was her first job, and she tackled it with her unique brand of gusto.

"Karla doesn't do anything halfway. Karla was the kind of person who would get upset if you swatted a fly. She never wanted harm to come to an animal," Kevin recalls.

It wasn't long after Karla started working that a steady stream of animal friends began making their way into the Homolka household and specifically Karla's basement bedroom, a room marked by a distinctly feminine quality. Although the room would never be described as pristine, it certainly wasn't messy. At least until furry friends began calling the room their home.

Along with the invincible gray, black, and orange striped tabby named Shadow, which seemed to have outlived its nine lives and more, Karla soon had several rats (including one that belonged to a student coworker, Debbie Purdie, who was forbidden from bringing the rodents into the Purdie home), some hamsters, a fuzzy angora rabbit, and a long-eared French lop rabbit. There was also another cat, Ariel—named after the Shakespearean character from *The Tempest*—which Mandy had a half-share in.

The French lop rabbit, named Rebel Bunny, with its long floppy ears, lived in a cage on the floor, but Karla would often bring it to bed to cuddle with. Along with the ubiquitous raisinlike droppings that rabbits are famous for, there were numerous accidents that stained the pale carpet, prompting frequent spot bleach jobs to erase the mark and the pungent smell of urine.

As Kevin and Karla grew even closer in grade eleven, he began to see the Homolka home as beset with almost constant tension. Even during periods of relative calm, there seemed to be a caldron bubbling beneath, threatening to erupt at any time into a shouting match or drinking binge. While others described the Homolkas as a happy-go-lucky, liberal clan, Kevin recalls tearful phone calls from Karla following blow-ups with her mother or raucous arguments between her parents.

"There were many times she just got so upset, she just wanted to leave the house," says Kevin.

As is often the case when mother and daughter are at loggerheads, it's the father who finds himself in the middle. A heavy drinker, Karel was often the target if Karla needed a favor or some money or a reversal of a decision made earlier by Dorothy. She was, after all, Daddy's little girl, his first-born.

Although Kevin never saw Karel upset, Karla would often relate stories about his anger. Usually the big family disputes came when Karel was drinking. "When he was drinking, it was hell for her," says Kevin. "Everything she did or said would be taken in the worst possible way. But then, when he wasn't drinking, Karla was his little girl and that's when she'd get what she wanted.''

Often there were tearful calls to Kevin, late at night after serious family blow-ups.

"I can't handle this anymore" was a familiar refrain.

Sometime toward the end of grade eleven and into the summer of 1987, after Karla turned seventeen, she began a long-distance phone friendship with a classmate who'd moved south to Kansas with his family.

Doug was part of SWC's hip crowd in his early high-school years. Well-to-do, he wore the obligatory preppie uniform and hung out with football players and other high-profile students at the school. He was attractive in that preppy sort of way, with stylishly short, dark hair and a pleasant, disarming grin.

One day shortly after starting high school, Karla, Mandy, and Lisa were walking home and a group of boys including Doug drove up in someone's father's car. They were all drunk. The car, which had a standard transmission, was lurching along because whoever was driving was unfamiliar with a gearshift, or was simply too drunk to know it.

"I just thought, that kind of stuff is out of hand," Lisa recalls. "He's driving around in a car he doesn't know how to drive. He's not licensed to drive, and he's drunk out of his face. I just didn't want to have anything to do with it."

Still, on that occasion, Lisa recalls Karla and Mandy getting in the car with the boys and driving around. That was Karla, too. "She was up for anything," Lisa remembers.

Still, there was no discussion of Doug either before he moved to Kansas, or after. Karla never said she missed him, whether she thought he was cute, whether she was even vaguely interested in him. Nothing.

Which was why it seemed unusual that one day late in the summer Lisa and Karla were talking on the phone and Karla announced that she was going to Kansas.

"What the heck are you going to Kansas for?" Lisa asked.

Well, Karla explained, she had been talking on the phone a

few times to Doug and he'd invited her down for a visit and she was going to go.

What about her mother and father? What did they think of this rather unusual journey? Lisa wanted to know.

Well, Karla told her close friend, her parents weren't exactly thrilled about the trip. But Karla said she was going anyway. This in itself wasn't that unusual, as Karla would sometimes ask Lisa or other friends to indicate she was at one location when in fact she was in another, presumably somewhere her parents wouldn't approve of or one that she'd decided her parents didn't need to know about.

Still, cruising around in St. Catharines or going to a bush party was a world away from hopping on a bus or train and heading off to Kansas. For Lisa, the situation was perplexing. Karla, who had never had a boyfriend to speak of and certainly didn't seem to be the worse for it, was flitting off to Kansas on a whim to visit a boy she didn't particularly know but who seemed, suddenly, to be a boyfriend of sorts.

Several weeks later the gang was gathered at Karla's house, sitting around gabbing. The girls were having a few drinks late in the evening. At some point the conversation turned to sex and drugs and Karla announced nonchalantly that she'd tried cocaine. Lisa and Kathy looked at their friend in disbelief. Karla then went on to describe how, during her visit with Doug, she had tried cocaine.

"That sort of set me panicking," Lisa recalls. "Like, if you're going to try drugs, why don't you stick to the stuff that's not addictive? I've seen people who are on coke and they are way out of control. Why are you just starting with that, you know?"

Except for her experimentation with eating catnip in elementary school, this was to Lisa's knowledge Karla's first experimentation with drugs of any kind, let alone a heavy scene like cocaine.

"Why would you try it?" Lisa asked, unable to hide the shock.

"Oh, I just wanted to try it," Karla responded. "It was okay, but I don't think I'll do it again."

But that wasn't all Karla revealed about her recent clandestine trip to the States. The two had experimented with a strange drink involving straight grain alcohol and grape juice—a favorite of college/university parties and affectionately known as Purple Jesus.

"That stuff can make you go blind!" exclaimed Lisa.

But there was more. Karla had also had sex with Doug.

If it was possible, the girls' eyes bulged even further out of their heads. Talk about a lost weekend! At seventeen or eighteen years of age, the girls had begun to experiment sexually, but by no means were they experienced. Like all teenage girls they talked about "doing it" and who they'd consider "doing it" with or under which conditions they imagined "doing it." But for the most part, the girls were sexually naive.

"Well, tell us about it," someone said, intrigued by their friend's newfound sexual liberation.

But the story horrified rather than titillated.

In a matter-of-fact tone, Karla described how Doug had tied her up with his belt and slapped her around during sex. Later, he called her names and berated her for allowing him to behave so roughly.

"How could you let me do that!" Doug reportedly screamed. "I don't respect you because you let me do that to you!"

Much later, Doug would deny that there was anything but a casual friendship between him and Karla, but at the time there was nothing in Karla's story to indicate she was not telling the truth. The girls were speechless.

"Karla, that's not normal!" Lisa finally said. "Don't put up with that! Don't let him do that!"

While Lisa, Kathy, and Debbie were deeply troubled by the story, and talked often of it in the following weeks, what struck Lisa was Karla's complete lack of emotion of any kind in regard to the event. There was no crying, no indication of regret, no sense of shame, no sense of enjoyment. Nothing.

"There was absolutely no resolution to the situation," recalls Lisa. "I never got the impression that she liked it." But neither did Karla describe it as a horrible, unpleasant experience. "It was more like, 'Well, this is what happened to me.' A very detached kind of thing."

Never promiscuous, at least not to her friends' knowledge, Karla was the last person Kathy and Lisa could imagine being involved in kinky, bondage sex. Karla was outspoken on issues of animal rights, feminism, and any kind of injustice, real or perceived, and this seemed entirely out of character for her.

She emerged from the experience at least outwardly unscathed. Back at school, her demeanor changed little. She was, it appeared to her close friends, who now paid special attention to her behavior, the same carefree, free-spirited young woman she'd always been.

But the girls never quite forgot the peculiar behavior of their close friend. "It really bothered me for a long time. I was worried about who she was going to get involved with next," says Lisa.

CHAPTER
10

It was the fall of 1987. Labor Day weekend came and went, the traditional signaling of the end of summer and the beginning of school. The girls, now in grade twelve, were beginning to explore career opportunities, thinking of college.

Kathy still contemplated a career in broadcast journalism. Karla thought out loud about going on to the University of Guelph to study veterinary sciences if she could save up enough money.

Toward the end of September, Lisa stopped by the pet store, where Karla and Debbie Purdie announced exciting news. Karla and Debbie and their store manager, Kristy Maan, were going to go to Toronto to a pet-store suppliers and merchants convention. They were going to take the bus up and stay in a hotel room on their own. The girls were flushed with excitement. The thought of going to a convention and staying in a hotel in the big city, even if it was only a suburb on the edge of a big city, gave them a welcome sense of independence and maturity.

"They were really looking forward to it," Lisa recalls. "It was a pretty big deal."

The story of Paul and Karla's steamy first night was spread initially, not only through Karla, but through Debbie as well. Not surprisingly, the tone and texture of the recounting depended on who was actually providing the information.

Debbie, for instance, was still ticked off at the scene that had unfolded before her eyes. She and Lisa met on the following Monday morning and Debbie told Lisa to skip music so she could recount the weekend's events. And while she didn't go into graphic detail, she did suggest that Karla and this older man they'd met in the dining room of Howard Johnson's had become quite friendly quite quickly.

From Debbie's perspective, there were two main themes: Karla's physical attachment to the blond-haired man, and Debbie's great discomfort at being stuck in a hotel room with another guy while her friend made out a few feet away. Gross!

"Oh, my God! That's really smart!" Lisa said when Debbie described the scenario. "Here's a guy, you don't even know who he is, and you just jump right into bed with him. Besides, that is really rude to do to you, Debbie. It's extremely rude."

Unspoken, but certainly among their thoughts, were questions about potential pregnancy or sexually transmitted diseases (AIDS was still on the periphery of public consciousness at this point). It was a stupid thing to have done, the girls conceded.

"Well, she's gone and done it now. There's no point in lecturing her, it's over and done with. Let's see what happens now," said Lisa.

Still, rude or not, Lisa and the other girls pumped Debbie for details. What did he look like? How did they meet? What kind of car does he drive? What were they doing on the bed? What's he like?

When it came time for Karla's retelling of the story, not surprisingly her version was significantly more romantic and significantly less ribald than Debbie's version.

"I met the perfect guy! He's great! He's wonderful!" Karla gushed that same week. Karla, in a rare display of reticence, downplayed the physical element of the weekend, saying they'd "fooled around," and it wasn't until several months later that Karla confessed that they'd "gone at it" for three hours or more on the first night she and Paul met.

"She was really excited that she met him," recalls Kathy Wilson.

They talked about the new boy much of that first week. Kathy expressed amazement that Karla's mother had let her go to Toronto at all. And had she told her mom about Paul? No. But he was coming down to visit on the weekend, and Karla insisted that Lisa and Kathy and the rest of the girls come by and meet him.

Karla talked of little else during the week but the return meeting with the mysterious stranger from Scarborough. She was, it appeared, in heaven.

When Karla told her friends that her new boyfriend was twenty-three, six years older than she, they were astounded.

"Oh, my God!" Kathy blurted out, thinking to herself what her parents would say if she brought home some strange man in his mid-twenties. That they'd kill her wasn't a question; only in which manner they might choose would be up for debate.

"We were happy for her because she was so happy, but I think we wondered what the guy's intentions were because he was older. And we thought, Oh, she's going to get taken here," recalls Kathy.

The next weekend, Paul and his best friend, Van Smirnis, made the trip to St. Catharines in Paul's white Capri. They got lost and eventually Karla, Kathy, Lisa, Lianne McCabe, and some others caught up with them at the Q-Way Inn just off the four-lane Queen Elizabeth Way that dissects the city as it winds its way to the American border about twenty miles away.

As soon as he got out of the car, Paul gave Karla a nice hug and kiss, an open display of affection that seemed a bit strange to Lisa until she considered their advanced physical relationship.

Lisa and Karla got in the backseat of Paul's car and the little convoy headed off to the Homolkas'. As the evening progressed Lisa found Paul extremely cocky. And while maybe they expected too much, he just didn't exactly act the way Lisa and Kathy thought a twenty-three-year-old accountant should act. He told a couple of goofy jokes and in fact acted in an all-around goofy manner. Kathy said later she felt Paul was "haughty" and that perhaps he had a big-city attitude. All in all, he seemed quite immature, the girls agreed after meeting Karla's new mystery man.

Still, he was quite cute and he seemed genuinely interested in Karla, kissing her and being very affectionate. Karla, for her part, seemed in awe of the well-dressed, well-mannered young man from Toronto.

"I could see how other people would find him attractive," says Lisa. "But I wasn't attracted to him. He's not my type at all. Like, if it had been me there [at the hotel] instead of Karla, no chance."

Apart from the obvious questions about why Karla would simply jump into bed with a perfect stranger, there was also the outstanding issue of Doug. Even though Karla's stories of her relationship with Doug left her friends cold, one question still begged an answer: What was to become of Doug now that Paul was on the scene and seemed as smitten with Karla as she was with him?

The general consensus was that despite the age difference—which also produced nagging questions about why a twenty-three-year-old accountant from far away in Toronto would want to date a seventeen-year-old high-school student—Paul seemed like a better match. The girls wondered, at least initially, whether Karla had lied about her true age and was concealing the fact she was still attending high school.

Whatever loose ends there were dangling about Karla, it became clear from the way she talked about Paul and how often she spoke to him that she was interested in pursuing this relationship.

Still, there was the issue of Doug, and it was Lisa who broached the subject in the delicate way that good friends have.

"So, what are you going to do about Doug? You've got to call him!"

"I know, I know," Karla would say, pulling on her lip, clearly troubled by the proposition of dumping the man who for all intents and purposes was her first boyfriend.

It was not the decision that was so hard, Karla explained to Lisa. She clearly wanted to be with Paul, and dumping Doug was an obvious prerequisite for carrying on. There were obvious benefits to being with Paul, not the least of which was that he treated her like a queen. But it was telling Doug that she didn't relish.

For a strong young woman, the task seemed surprisingly daunting.

"What do you think I should say to him?" Karla asked, knowing it was a problem her friend really couldn't help her with.

"I'm going to call him and tell him," Karla announced several days later. And as far as Lisa knew, that was it. Whether Karla actually told Doug about her burgeoning relationship with Paul or simply begged off, citing the long distance separating them, is unclear, but Karla seemed to feel better about it.

After that, Doug was persona non grata. He was not to be mentioned, Karla instructed her friends. And he was especially not to be mentioned around Paul, who hated talk of other men, even past men, in Karla's life.

This curious demand later gave rise to Karla's ascension to Born Again Virgin status, a label the girls attached after Karla confessed that Paul didn't like the idea that she'd been with anyone else before he arrived on the scene. In fact, Karla confessed, he was downright disgusted at the thought, and the girls were reminded many times that other boys were not part of the acceptable conversation playlist when Paul was around. Kathy and Lisa and the rest didn't bother to mention that at age twenty-three, Paul was almost certainly a man of much greater experience than his new girlfriend and that didn't seem to be a problem.

Nevertheless, those first few months of Paul and Karla's relationship seemed to have been touched by magic.

Although the girls speculated in Karla's absence that Paul's interest in their friend wasn't based solely on her great mind, his interest never seemed to wane.

The weeks passed and Paul's name appeared prominently on Karla's notebooks and she often doodled his name in her loopy script. Occasionally she'd doodle things like "Karla Bernardo," much to the alarm of her young friends.

Paul would sometimes drive down twice in one weekend to see Karla because he wasn't comfortable asking if he could stay over, and likely wasn't being offered much positive reinforcement from Dorothy and Karel at that stage. He sent flowers. He called daily. He took Karla to expensive, trendy restaurants.

Karla's friends, who were still skeptical of Paul's intentions, had to admit to themselves that he was treating her like a princess. And clearly Karla, a seventeen-year-old with a limited romantic history, was being swept off her feet by this Prince Charming from Scarborough.

Eventually Dorothy and Karel Homolka agreed that it was silly for Paul to be driving back and forth like a crazy man, so he began sleeping on the upstairs couch. At least that was the official plan. The reality was that he spent most of his nights in Karla's room in the basement and then snuck upstairs in the morning to escape the wrath of Karel.

Sometimes, Paul told his friends, Dorothy, or "Mrs. H," as he affectionately dubbed Karla's mother, would give a polite rap on the door to let the two lovebirds know it was time to move to separate quarters.

Although Karla had her own phone line, she didn't have an inexhaustible flow of cash, so it didn't take long before the relationship had a price, a real, financial one. Her parents chastised her for being irresponsible and talking so long and so frequently, but she remained undaunted. Paul initially was paying for most of Karla's share of the bill, sometimes $200 a month, not to mention his own hefty payments for Scarborough–to–St. Catharines communications.

Karla's conversations with her friends at school and work became dominated by the goings-on in her new relationship. Paul this. Paul that. Paul, Paul, Paul.

Cafeteria conversations, which had traditionally featured hypothetical questions about which classmates might be the best kissers, et cetera, soon lost their spontaneity, because Karla always answered "Paul" even though he didn't go to school at Sir Winston and wasn't around to hear the sickening adoration.

"He was the best at everything," says Kathy.

"What do you think of Ice-T?" Karla asked Lisa one day.

The rapper/actor didn't quite fit into Lisa's personal play-list, and as far as she knew her friend had never shown any affection for the rap genre. Lisa made some disparaging re-mark about rap music in general. But Karla remained non-plussed.

"Oh, well, Paul really likes it."

A few months after the fateful weekend at the Howard Johnson's, Kathy was visiting and Karla had just had her hair permed. Kathy commented on how nice the short, bouncy curl looked on her friend. "I think it looks like shit," offered Paul. "I think she'd look much better with it out."

A short time later, Lisa was visiting and Karla was brush-ing her hair, which had grown quite long.

"Ugh! I want to perm my hair! I hate it!" Karla moaned, throwing her brush down.

"So? Why don't you?" Lisa asked, surprised.

"Paul won't let me," Karla answered.

"So! Big deal!" said Lisa, incredulous.

"No, he likes it. I'll leave it."

And that was that. Paul wanted long hair and he was going to get it. The situation stunned Lisa, who had always consid-ered her friend a strong, independent woman. In fact, it might have been more in character for the Karla Lisa knew to cut her hair short just to assert herself. Still, it was early in the relationship, and Lisa accepted that her friend was determined to make things work. If she wanted to wear her hair long even though she hated it, well, that was one price for love Karla seemed prepared to pay.

On the surface, Paul and Karla seemed ill-matched. He was an immaculate dresser who seemed to delight in wearing the trendiest of clothes. Sweaters, button-down collars, designer logos. Ralph Lauren, Polo. That was Paul. Karla's feelings about preppiness and conformity, of course, were well known to friends and foe alike.

So the day Karla appeared in the Pen Centre sporting a

brand-new, pink Beaver Canoe sweatshirt, her friends could have been excused for performing a Marx Brothers movie double take and maybe even a triple take.

Her outfit, which still included the boxer shorts and long johns, gave her a strange look, like a generic experiment half finished. She seemed oblivious to the contradictions and gushed to her friends about her new shirt, which, of course, had been given to her by Paul.

"Can you believe I'm wearing this?" she said with a giggle.

Lisa nearly fell over. All she could think of were the countless rants of "I hate preppies, I hate preppies," and here was Karla showing off the same uniform, pleased as punch.

For Lisa, the change in wardrobe brought a faint gnawing of unease. One of the reasons she and Karla had remained such good friends was their individuality and their respect for freethinking. Karla had blazed her own fashion trail, as had Lisa, at the risk of being ridiculed and shunned by their classmates. But here she was throwing those principles out the window after a few months of dating some guy. Although she still considered Karla a close friend, Lisa couldn't help but feel a twinge of disgust.

The night happened to be Lisa's seventeenth birthday. Kathy Wilson and Lianne McCabe met Lisa at the London Arms. They bought Lisa a couple of drinks to celebrate and then headed to the Pen Centre to meet Debbie and Karla when they got off work. The gang was to go to Lianne's house, but at the mall there was a small complication. Karla hadn't received what she felt was a proper invitation to Lianne's and so announced she wouldn't be going. Debbie at one point sided with Karla and announced that she wouldn't be joining the party either.

After a minor scene erupted in the middle of the mall, the girls turned to Lisa and demanded that she resolve the issue. Lisa, angry that her friends' stubbornness was threatening to ruin her birthday, burst into tears.

"You guys! What am I supposed to do? One of you wants to come, one doesn't want to! What am I supposed to do?"

Finally everyone apologized to one another once they realized Lisa was upset and it was, after all, her night. And off they went, the evening saved.

Karla's dresser and mirror were festooned with pictures of Paul: Paul skiing, Paul mugging for the camera in macho poses, Paul's high-school yearbook picture with long hair almost to his shoulders, which the girls secretly thought was the goofiest thing they'd ever seen.

Soon Karla began talking not only about loving Paul, but that she was going to marry him and spend the rest of her life with him. Her friends smiled and resisted the impulse to stick their fingers down their throats in mock vomiting motions.

"Paul this and Paul that. Paul's so wonderful. I love Paul. Paul, Paul, Paul," recalls Lisa. "After a while it stopped being Me, or Us, it was just Paul."

Lisa and Kathy and the other girls also noticed subtle changes in Karla's diet. Once an aficionado of Burger King and McDonald's fare, Karla now begged off eating at these places, saying it wasn't healthy. She began instead to crave salads. Her new favorite was an odd mixture of carrots, ham, and lettuce. Sometimes she'd add cheese to the mixture. But rarely would there be salad dressing to top off the salad.

As Paul and Karla's relationship evolved and solidified, it became clear to Karla's friends that this was not just a passing fancy. And while they never questioned Karla directly about concerns they had, they spent a great deal of time talking about Paul and Karla when Karla wasn't around. The conversations were more often than not fueled by comments or actions by Karla. The first discussion of the young couple's sex life, for instance, provided conversation fodder for weeks.

It was a weekend a few months after Paul and Karla met, likely early in 1988. Kathy and Lisa and a couple of friends were at Karla's house, as was Paul, who'd come down for the weekend.

They were having a few drinks, and as tradition dictated, ordered soupy pizza from Pizza Pizza or Domino's. Kathy was sitting on Karla's bed talking to Paul and Karla. As they chatted, Karla began fiddling with a pair of handcuffs. Kathy's eyes widened, but she didn't say anything.

The next morning, as they were cleaning up, Kathy noticed the handcuffs and two lengths of pink ribbon on the floor near the bed.

Paul had left to go back to Scarborough, so Kathy and Lisa began asking about their relationship.

"What do your parents think? My mom would never let me go out with somebody that old," Kathy said.

"Oh, they love Paul," Karla replied.

Then Kathy asked what the handcuffs and ribbon were for.

Kathy, Lisa, and Debbie listened wide-eyed as Karla explained.

"You guys are going to think I'm kinky," she warned.

Karla explained that Paul liked to play games during sex. In one game he was a successful businessman and she was the little girl who sexually pleased him when he came home from the office in his business suit, briefcase in hand. He liked Karla to wear her long, blond hair in ponytails, tied with ribbon to make her look even younger than she was. He liked to use the handcuffs during this game, Karla confided. And sometimes a dog chain was part of their sexual landscape.

"Karla, that's really weird. Why does he want to play that?" someone asked.

"Oh, I think it's fun," she said, quick to dispel any suggestion the sex play was anything other than mutual.

Lisa and Kathy recalled Karla's discussion of her sexual experiences with Doug and noted the same coldly detached tone as she described her latest sexual escapades. Again she did little to avoid the subject; in fact, the handcuffs were hung on the wall on the right side of the door near her bed. The dog's studded choke collar also hung in plain view.

But Karla was not interested in discussing her sexual life in any kind of introspective way.

But Lisa, Kathy and Debbie talked about Karla's sex life for days.

"Oh my God, that's disgusting!" seemed to be the general consensus.

If Karla's comments forced her friends to view her in a completely different light, then the discovery of The List took Karla to an entirely different planet. Kathy noticed the list in an open drawer of Karla's night table one time while visiting. Karla had left the room. It was entitled "Karla's Self-Improvement List."

Kathy glanced quickly but heard Karla returning to her room and turned away from the drawer. Later, Kathy called Lisa and described what she'd seen. Upset and unsure of the ramifications, Kathy wanted Lisa to see it as well. On their next visit, Kathy and Karla were either talking in the living room downstairs, or Karla had gone to the washroom, when Lisa read the list.

"Oh, my God! What is this?" Lisa asked, aghast.

Written in Karla's unmistakable script on lined school paper, the list contained innocuous references to having a healthy diet, exercising regularly, and the importance of good personal hygiene. But interspersed with these were disturbing requirements for self-improvement and comments or quotes on life ascribed to Paul:

Never let anyone know our relationship is anything but perfect;
Don't talk back to Paul;
Always smile when you're with Paul;
Be a perfect girlfriend for Paul;
If Paul asks for a drink, bring him one quickly and happily;
Remember you're stupid;
Remember you're ugly;
Remember you're fat;
I don't know why I tell you these things because you never change.

Although the list was written by Karla, it seemed clear to Lisa and Kathy that these measures for self-improvement came from one source—Paul.

If Karla saw these as ways to improve herself, at least in her boyfriend's eyes, Lisa and Kathy saw it as abuse that was being institutionalized by being made part of Karla's daily routine.

Paul may have explained this as a way that Karla could improve, that she could become a better person, but the cold

message it sent Lisa and Kathy was that of a carefully orchestrated attempt to break down and redefine their good
friend.

For Lisa and Kathy, who knew Karla as a tough-as-leather
young woman, the list was vexing. It reduced her to an insig-
nificant piece of sand but offered her redemption and rebirth
provided she followed Paul's carefully scripted plan to overcome her obvious shortcomings.

"I think she thought Paul was her way to make herself a
better person and improve herself," says Kathy. "She could
rise to the occasion with these quotes. And with this sheet in
her hand as her shield, it would help her grow."

Despite their concerns, Kathy and Lisa never mentioned
the list to Karla. Much later they would question themselves
over and over again about why they didn't. But hindsight ne-
glects the fact that they were eighteen years old and dealing
with a close friend who seemed very much in love. They
questioned, then, their own perceptions of what they'd seen
and believed was happening. Were they right? What did it
mean? Why would Karla put up with that kind of treatment?

Of course, another reason they didn't explore Karla's relationship in a meaningful way with Karla is that as time passed
they saw her less and less frequently. Sometimes Lisa would
get a call from Karla saying she was going to Scarborough
for the weekend and needed her to cover. "If anyone calls,
tell them I'm in the shower," Karla instructed. And Lisa
agreed.

On weekends that Paul and Karla didn't see one another,
Karla warned her friends that she couldn't talk because Paul
liked to call and didn't want to get a busy signal. And when
Paul came down for a visit, he liked to spend time alone with
Karla.

During the summer, Lisa, who worked across the street
from the Pen Centre, would sometimes join Karla for lunch,
but inevitably the conversation was dominated by how great
things were with Paul, what he was doing, saying, thinking
. . . blah, blah, blah.

The only complaint Karla ever verbally revealed in the first
year or so of their relationship was that one time she'd gone

to visit Paul in Scarborough and he and his friends had driven around in his car smoking dope. The scene confused Karla, who'd been instructed by Paul never to touch drugs of any kind. And in keeping with his edict, Karla declined the joint when it was passed her way. Later, Paul berated her for embarrassing him in front of his friends. Karla was confused, she told her friends later, about how she was supposed to act.

Beyond that, life seemed supernaturally wonderful.

One person who was aware of life on the other side of the storybook image Karla liked to portray was Kevin Jacoby. Although the two had spent less time together after Karla met Paul, they still talked occasionally, especially when Karla was upset.

One Sunday night after Karla returned from a weekend visit to Scarborough, she had a violent argument with Karel, who'd been drinking. Kevin was asleep when the call came. "I just can't take it anymore. I'm getting out of this fucking house now!" the tiny, shaky voice said across the phone line. "I just don't want anything to do with this crap. I don't need to take this garbage!"

Kevin recognized the voice as Karla's, but hadn't the faintest idea what she was talking about.

"What's wrong? What's going on? Tell me what happened."

So she told him. She'd returned from her trip to Toronto and Karel had been drinking. Karla began describing their weekend and how romantic and wonderful it was and what a wonderful guy Paul was. Paul, Paul, Paul. For some reason this set Karel off and the two got into an argument about her relationship with Paul.

He called her a whore, Karla told Kevin.

"If you want to do that kind of shit, you can get the hell out of the house!" Karel screamed. "Get out of my house!"

The first thing Kevin asked was whether Karla's dad had been drinking, because by this time he realized a lot of the Homolka family blowups occurred after Karel had been at the bottle.

"Yeah, he's been drinking all day."

"Okay, what's your mom have to say?"

"She just stood there and let him say these things to me."

"Great! All right, well what is going on? Is there anything to worry about? Are you being kicked out of your house? If so, I'll come and pick you up and you can stay here tonight and we'll figure things out tomorrow."

"No, everything's fine. I locked the door in my room."

From then on the conversation eased into how the weekend in Toronto had gone, how things were going in her relationship with Paul. Karla gushed about the wonderful dinner Paul had taken her to, the flowers, the dancing. It was a stark contrast to the reception she'd received at home. For hours the two talked, Karla becoming increasingly calm and relaxed.

It was, for Kevin, an odd situation. He had never particularly cared for Paul, and he, too, didn't think the idea of Karla going to spend weekends in the big city with him was a particularly good one. There was, he admits, an element of jealousy, too. He was seeing a close friend drift away to be with a new man without seeming to make any effort to maintain her old relationships. It was, in many ways, a painful situation for Kevin.

Karla had told Kevin about the new man in her life shortly after she returned from the pet convention in Scarborough that September. She sanitized this version of the historic meeting as well, saying she'd met Paul at a party. But when Kevin met him he wasn't impressed.

"He just wasn't fun. He was quiet. He was polite. But he wasn't swift. Sarcasm was just wasted on him. That also was kind of fun, because people would say, 'You just insult him and he doesn't notice.' "

Kevin, like some of Karla's girlfriends, secretly assumed that the relationship would have a short life span. It was too much, too soon. Karla was spending virtually all of her money on phone bills, traveling costs, presents for Paul. She never had time for old friends or school or even work. Kevin wondered if the relationship wasn't a way for Karla to break free from her home life, to exert her independence and defy her parents.

"I think Paul was a way out. I think that's the way she saw it," said Kevin.

This particular blowout at the Homolka house came after a month in which Karla incurred a $300 phone bill, almost all of which was from calls to Paul. Karla paid the bill, but her parents were furious.

By the time Kevin set the phone back in its cradle the bedside clock read 3 a.m. Neither he nor Karla went to school the next day.

The next afternoon, Kevin called to make sure everything was okay and Karla seemed fine. He father had left on a sales trip, so the tension in the house had been relieved.

When Kevin saw Karla next, at school on Tuesday, it was as though nothing had ever happened.

CHAPTER
11

Van listened intently as Paul excitedly related his first nervous meeting with Karla's parents. His concern that her parents would reject him as an appropriate suitor because their daughter was so young had been alleviated as soon as he walked through the door at 61 Dundonald Street. Karla's dad welcomed him into the home and immediately offered him a beer; her mom told Paul to make himself at home. He wasn't sure if Karel and Dorothy Homolka offered him alcohol because they noticed his discomfort and wanted to loosen him up, or whether his mere presence was as good an excuse as any to have a drink themselves. Whatever their motive, he liked them. "They're cool," he told Van, then shot his wolfish grin across the table. "Hey, she has two beautiful sisters." Paul went on to describe Lori, sixteen, petite, thin, with long, beautiful blond hair; and Tammy, only thirteen, virginal, with a gorgeous smile, golden hair, and an infectious personality.

In those first days, Van found himself hanging out alone as his girl-hunting pal made trips to St. Catharines each weekend and on some weeknights to spend time with his newfound love. After subsequent meetings with Karla's parents, whom he soon referred to as "Mr. H" and "Mrs. H," Paul was given their approval to stay over for the night rather than take the long, tiresome drive home to Scarborough. Only rarely did Karla come to Toronto, in part because she didn't have a

driver's license, but mostly because Paul liked to keep his
worlds distinctly separate. Paul derived great pleasure from
having Karla dangling on a string at St. Catharines, while at
the same time maintaining his bizarre on-again, off-again affair with Carol and playing the field with a seemingly endless
bevy of one-night stands. On those weekends that Karla came
to stay at Sir Raymond Drive, tension would build in the Bernardo home. Paul complained to Van that his parents frowned
on Karla's staying in their home; they especially disliked the
time the two would spend in Paul's bedroom. When Paul
would return from taking Karla home to St. Catharines, he
complained to Van that they would call her a tramp. This
annoyed Paul more than anything. He had never dated tramps,
he reminded Van, never. He was too worthy of a tramp. His
girls were beautiful, gorgeous. Paul's response to his family
was a terse "Fuck them."

Paul talked incessantly to Van about Karla and her quirks.
He confided to Van that Karla was not only beautiful but incredible malleable. "She will do anything I want, Van," he
said.

Paul described to Van how Karla would play a role in making his old fantasies become reality, how she was going to
dress as a schoolgirl in pigtails, get on her knees to give him
oral sex after he walked through the door after a day of high
finance in his top-flight accounting job. It was the ultimate
fantasy, said Paul, success at business and unbridled sexual
gratification.

But Paul also confided to Van that he was having difficulty
keeping the long-distance relationship going while working
as a junior accountant at Price Waterhouse and educating
himself for the Chartered Accountants of Ontario examination he would have to take in the future. Paul was highly
thought of at Price Waterhouse. He was seen as quite intelligent, and a few colleagues called him "The Ace" because of
his acumen with figures. He told friends he found the work
too easy, if not boring. By day he dressed in business suits,
spending up to $900 on Hugo Boss designs and outdoing the
more senior accountants in the image department; nights and

weekends he opted for the casual clothes by Ralph Lauren, Polo, and other designers.

In the summer of 1988, Paul became even more image conscious than before. He became more particular about his clothing, his shoes and his aftershave lotion. He still wasn't in a position to buy or lease his own car, but on July 29, 1988, he took ownership of Ken Bernardo's Mercury Capri hatchback and would drive it until later that year when the car no longer suited the image he was trying to cultivate at Price Waterhouse. He had told Van he intended to climb up the corporate ladder using not only his native intelligence but also his good looks, his dress sense, and whatever image-posting material goods he could lay his hands on. Late that year, he leased a spanking-new champagne-gold 1989 Nissan 240SX two-door hatchback. Although it didn't perform like a true sports car, the 240SX gave the look and feel of a sports car without the huge sticker price. Bernardo leased the $24,000 automobile, but the factory stereo wasn't good enough for the budding accountant; he replaced it with an enhanced system that included twelve-inch woofers and a 200-watt amplifier.

Paul strived for better physical health, opting for a high-fiber, low-fat diet. He wanted more strength. In weight-room workouts with Van, he constantly flexed his chest and his biceps, but for some reason he ignored his legs. He told Van he was trying for greater upper-body bulk to be more attractive to the women he would meet in the Toronto bar scene. Within a few months of lifting weights his own weight had increased to about 190 pounds, a good weight for his six-foot-one frame. Soon Paul was bench-pressing 225 pounds. Compared to the petite women he dated, he was incredibly strong.

One afternoon in August 1988, while Van was working as a manager at a Hilderbrandt Estate Winery retail store on Highway 48 in Markham, Paul highlighted his hair with streaks of blond. Impressed with the outcome on Paul, Van also began highlighting his hair. The two also began regular tanning sessions in an effort to capture what they called the total "California look." Paul became obsessed with the image of the all-American beach boy. Naturally Karla thought he looked great, a fact she would tell anyone who would listen.

Karla's wasn't the only head that turned in appreciation of Paul's new look. When Van's parents sold the Pizza Stop in 1988 and moved to the Greens of Markham, a voluptuous girl, Anna, began working at the restaurant. Although not immediately attracted to Anna, Paul did strike up a relationship with her. Soon, he began a double life, driving to St. Catharines on the weekends to stay with Karla, and returning to Scarborough to date Anna during the week.

Paul frequently discussed the Karla and Anna dilemma with Van, seeking his friend's advice. Paul wondered whether he should break it off with Karla, now that he had found a beautiful girlfriend and potential wife in Scarborough. And then, almost in the same breath, he wondered aloud if he should propose to Karla. He felt that Anna was bright, independent, and self-confident. She had a stable well-to-do family and he felt that there was therefore the guarantee of financial security in the years ahead. But much to Paul's chagrin, Anna could not be controlled and routinely caught Paul lying. Paul couldn't seem to pull the wool over Anna's eyes; she always wanted to know what Paul was doing and whom he was doing it with. On the other hand, Paul didn't find Karla that interesting and he sometimes resented what he felt was her stupidity. He felt she would drag him down in life; he felt he would forever be a breadwinner and Karla would be his dependent. And he couldn't expect any financial help from the humble Homolka family, who had three girls to marry off before they would have any access to cash. Yet Paul loved Karla's devotion and obedience, describing her in puppy dog—like terms.

"Karla listens to me. Karla doesn't second-guess my opinions," Paul explained.

Paul spent an inordinate amount of time comparing the two girls physically and sexually. Karla was better because she had a firmer body than Anna; Karla was better because she had less pubic hair than Anna; Anna was better because her vagina was tighter than Karla's; Anna was better because she had large breasts, and so on.

The biggest roadblock facing Paul in his life with Karla was the fact that another man had possessed her before he had. Paul was furious over Doug and the affair in Kansas. He often talked about Doug, calling him an idiot, and wondered aloud how Karla could have been so stupid to go to Kansas just to get laid. In contrast, Paul was Anna's first and only lover. This brought him great satisfaction. Van knew well that if Karla had had a promiscuous past or had even known multiple partners, perhaps three or four men, Paul would not have even entertained marriage or a long-term relationship with her. Ultimately, Paul would argue: "Me and Karla, we've been through a lot. Too much together . . . No, we've gone through too much together, we're going to make it work."

Van believed Paul was talking about the trials of the long-distance relationship between Scarborough and St. Catharines, the intrusions of his own family in their relationship, and the ongoing affair with Anna and various other women.

During several of Van and Paul's many discussions, Paul allowed Van to see the "wall of words" he was accumulating in his bedroom. The clipped motivational quotations were neatly stacked in columns of about five to ten words wide, stretching fifteen feet or so along the length of the room and eight feet high up to the ceiling.

One day, Van noticed how the sayings had multiplied and now dominated the room.

"Paul, what is this all about?"

"It's to get me motivated," he said. "I need something to get me going, something to focus on." It seemed to Van that Paul was programming himself rather than helping his mind to focus.

At first blush, the wall of words might have seemed like just a bunch of sayings that mean everything in general but nothing in specific. Their thrust, in essence, was a combination of capitalism, hedonism, and narcissism without any hint of a soul. They dwelt on money, strength of will, power, and machismo. Every day when Paul woke up, his eyes would feast on his wall of words, his own writings to himself of how to be a success in the world.

"Poverty sucks!" was a clipped headline atop a Porsche poster. "Time is money," read a clipping above a two-handed clock on a framed poster.

Other motivational sayings were borrowed from catchy statements he heard at the Amway meetings—words, of course, borrowed from someone else who said them somewhere else, or out of the mouths of capitalistic self-help gurus and entrepreneurial preachers: "Out of every adversity comes the seed of an equal or greater benefit"; "it's better to be a big fish in a little pond"; the facts don't count when you have a dream; "you must judge for yourself and you must act on that judgement whatever the costs"; "what is true is less important than what is believed."

Whether Paul knew it or not, one of his wall sayings is popularly attributed to American revolutionary John Paul Jones, who uttered the words as he stood aboard the *Bonhomme Richard* on September 23, 1779, midway through the War of Independence: "I have not yet begun to fight." Paul also borrowed a phrase from nightmarish rocker Alice Cooper—"No More Mr. Nice Guy"—and turned to Lisa Bonet's character in the movie *Angel Heart* for the line "a bad ass makes a woman's heart beat faster."

Another wall quote came from the German philosopher Friedrich Wilhelm Nietzsche, although it is likely Paul culled it from one of his favorite movies, *Criminal Law,* which uses the Nietzsche quotation to kick off the movie: "Whoever fights monsters should see to it that in the process they do not become a monster; when you look into the abyss, the abyss also looks into you."

Many quotes on his bedroom wall are followed by an attribution to Gordon Gekko, the unethical and immoral wheeler-dealer money magnate fictionalized in Oliver Stone's 1987 movie *Wall Street.* Played by Michael Douglas, Gekko is a cutthroat stock dealer who, in the words of one of his financial adversaries, would sell his mother to make a deal. In the movie, Gekko drags youngblood Wall Street broker Bud Fox, played by Charlie Sheen, into his heartless web with promises of fame and fortune and beautiful women; all Fox has to do in return is sell his soul. With raptorlike intensity, Gekko explains to Fox that he, the college-educated son of an Italian immigrant, beat the WASPs at their own game. For a short time, Fox gets to touch Gekko's ill-gotten possessions of gorgeous houses with butlers and kept wives, private jets, chauffeur-driven limousines, but when he realizes the inhumane shark that Gekko truly is, Fox turns him in to trade regulators.

When watching *Wall Street*, Paul must have stopped the video player numerous times to write down the Gekko quotes that ultimately made their way onto his beloved wall of inspiration. He gave special pride of place to two lengthy Gekko monologues, one of which is: "Greed is good. Greed is right. Greed works. Greed clarifies. Cuts through and captures the essence of the evolutionary spirit. Greed, in all of its forms. Greed for life, for money, for love and knowledge has marked the ground upsurge of mankind . . . and greed will do it for you." The last seven words were not Gekko's, but words that Paul himself added, seemingly for his own motivation.

The movie is about good and evil, right and wrong, playing by the rules and ignoring the rules. Paul chose to embrace Gekko's quotes even though the character in the movie takes a giant tumble at the end. It is interesting to note that two *Wall Street* characters act as a conscience: Fox's father, played by Martin Sheen, and a broker firm colleague named Lou. Paul does not use the following conscience quotes anywhere on his wall: "If a man looks in the abyss and there's nothing staring back at him, at that moment man finds his character, and that is what keeps him out of the abyss; remember there are no shortcuts, son; quick-buck artists come and go with any bull market, but the steady players make it through the bear markets; I don't go to sleep with no whore, I don't wake up with no whore—that's how I live with myself; it's yourself you've got to be proud of!"

In one *Wall Street* scene, Gekko points out a painting to Fox that he bought for $60,000 but sold for $600,000. "The illusion has become real," Gekko says. Paul started to use "the illusion is real" in his conversations. Gekko always resorted to using the word "pal" whenever emphasizing a point; Paul, too, started to refer to his girls, friends, and acquaintances as "pals."

On top of Paul's dresser was a small, framed picture of Karla beside twin photographs of his nephew David and his niece Samantha, Debbie's children. Located above it, on the wall, was a certificate in official-looking red and black colors that read: "This certificate hereby certifies that Karla Leanne Homolka loves Paul Kenneth Bernardo with all her heart and soul and will follow him wherever . . ."

Karla's devotion and malleability remained the qualities Paul Bernardo most appreciated. His ability to influence and manipulate her by using techniques culled from books, television and music was the feat of which he was most proud. For Van, his buddy's behavior was entirely consistent. But what struck Van about Paul's new love interest, was the bizarre relationship he forged with Karla's youngest sister, Tammy.

Paul talked incessantly to his childhood friend about Karla's young sister, Tammy Homolka. After a double date Karla and Paul had arranged early in their relationship with Van and Kathy Wilson, Paul related to his friend how Tammy had told him she thought Van was "mint." Van was flattered that such a beautiful girl would think of him in such glowing terms. He teased Paul about Tammy's availability, her interest in him, and the lure of young, virginal flesh.

At first, Paul brushed aside his remarks, but it soon became obvious to Van that Paul was extremely attracted to his girlfriend's youngest sister. He became animated and excited when he talked about Tammy, about her cuteness and about how she was growing up so quickly. It was as if he was watching out for her, almost like a father figure. He told Van he didn't want any roguish boys to have sex with Tammy; he didn't want *anyone* to have sex with Tammy. And yet, at the same time, his various comments about Tammy indicated to Van that he secretly fantasized about her. He often commented to Van about the lovely shape of her young breasts and the curves of her athletic body. Van sensed a definite sexual undertone to Paul's feelings.

Paul told Van how he would often flirt with Tammy and how she, clearly flattered by the attention she was taking away from her older sister, would often respond. She would ask Paul if he found her beautiful, even more beautiful than Karla.

Paul told Van about a day at the Homolka house when Karla was sitting on Paul's lap in the recreation room, fully clothed, but straddling him. Tammy was sitting across the room, trying her best not to notice her sister's dry humping of her boyfriend. Paul related that Karla's gyrations gave him an erection. When Karla stood up to get something, Paul's erection was evident through his cotton pants. He looked over to see Tammy staring at his penis. Paul had a glint in his eye when he told this story to Van.

Later, he told Van, Tammy would play-fight with Paul and would end up sitting on Paul's lap, pressing her body closely against him. Clearly, Tammy had developed affection for Paul, who, by this time, had been accepted as the son Dorothy and Karel Homolka never had and the brother Tammy and Lori had missed. Paul laughed about the time Karla came home from work to find Tammy sitting on Paul's lap, hugging and kissing him. Van couldn't figure out why Tammy would do this, other than to make her sister jealous in some form of competitive game that sisters play. There was, he noted, an obvious undercurrent of jealousy between the sisters.

Mike Donald, Lori Homolka's boyfriend in 1987 and 1988, also witnessed Tammy Homolka snuggling up with Paul, just as she had done with Mike when he dated Lori. It was as if Tammy looked up to Paul and Mike as the big brothers she never had. To Mike, it was innocent kid's stuff, the kind of thing a little girl does for attention.

"I'm more pretty than Karla, ain't I?" Tammy would ask Paul.

"Of course you are," Paul would answer.

Karla's eyes would burn with jealousy.

Sometimes when Tammy got a little too close, Paul would jokingly push her away and say, "What are you doin'? People can get arrested for that. It's not funny. The cops are after a rapist in Scarborough for that kind of thing!"

The Scarborough Rapist first struck at night on May 4, 1987, when a late-night bus roared away in a dense cloud of spent diesel fuel. A young woman was making her way home along the sidewalk when, yards away from her front yard, she was grabbed from behind, overpowered, and dragged between her parents' home and a neighbor's house. She was so terrified, so shocked, she could not manage a scream. After what seemed like an eternity, she broke free, yelled, and pounded on her door. Her father turned on the porch light and scared off the attacker. The frightened woman initially gave police the impression that the rape wasn't as bad as it could have been. Ten days later, a twenty-two-year-old woman was grabbed from behind after getting off a bus at the same inter- section. She was punched in the right eye and almost choked to death with an electrical cord as her attacker forced anal sex on her for twenty minutes. The rapist tied her to a fence with her own belt. These were the first assaults of a man who would terrorize the quiet Guildwood enclave of suburban Scarborough.

As the reports came over his tidy desk at Metropolitan Tor- onta Police 4 District Headquarters, Inspector Joe Wolfe could see the immediate similarities between the attacks: both were blitz attacks from the rear; in both cases the victims were confined; but even more revealing was that in both cases the attacker was a "talker," degrading both victims with statements like "I'm going to kill you. You slut. You cunt. You bitch. You whore." The rapist also demanded that both victims pay homage to him, forcing them to repeat over and over that he was the man they wanted, he was the best, and that she would do anything for him. The rapist also told his victims personal details about themselves. As if that wasn't conclusive enough, police further cemented the two cases when the first victim belatedly confessed that she, too, had been anally raped. Police initially theorized that the attacker must have previously stalked his prey on foot or by car from the bus stop to their home and knew where to lie in wait. Detectives began backtracking through the old sexual-assault files in an effort to find a similar modus operandi, but they came up empty-handed. Fortunately, these types of brutal blitz rapes were quite rare. Night patrols were beefed up in that area, but in the next seven months no rapes were re- ported.

Then, on a cold, early-winter night, December 16, 1987, a

fifteen-year-old girl who had just alighted from a bus was grabbed from behind, dragged by the hair and neck in between two homes, and raped for almost an hour. As he forcibly took his pleasure, the rapist held a knife to girl's head and forced her face into the ground to prevent her from seeing him. As he anally raped and forced the girl to perform fellatio, he asked the terrified teenager a series of questions about her home, her sex life; he also rubbed the knife blade on her face, her back, and her vagina. As in the other attacks, the girl didn't see the rapist's face. A homicide-style team of twelve detectives and uniformed officers was set up to track down the attacker, whom the media dubbed The Scarborough Rapist.

Within a few days of the third attack, police alerted the Guildwood area to the rapist and almost four hundred residents showed up at Jack Miner Public School to hear how they could best protect themselves from him. Women were told not to walk alone late at night, to avoid dimly lit areas, and to report any suspicious behavior.

On December 23, 1987, a woman in her early twenties was slammed into the freshly fallen snow just outside her house. She screamed and her attacker ran away. Police braced themselves for another attack, but nothing happened through the early part of the New Year. Then, on April 18, 1988, a late-night telephone caller to Wolfe's home announced "We've got another one." This time, the victim was nineteen years old. Like the others, she was attacked after getting off a bus. She was raped for more than thirty minutes. Again, the rapist talked, whispering in her ear: "Tell me you love me, tell me I'm the best." When she struggled, the rapist punched her in the face and violently subdued her. She suffered a broken arm, a broken collarbone, and other injuries. The rapist also ground soil into her face and hair. In March 1988, Metro Police formally set up the Scarborough Rapist Task Force, but, apart from a Scarborough Rapist–style attack in May 1988 some thirty miles away on Lakeshore Boulevard in Mississauga, the rapes stopped.

That November, an eighteen-year-old woman was attacked close to her Scarborough home, slashed on the calf with a serrated steak knife, then raped. The rapist warned this woman that if she told anyone he would return and kill her and her family. Before he left, as he had with his previous victims, he rummaged through her purse, taking either a driver's license, a transit pass, or some other souvenir.

After this attack, special agent Gregg McCrary of the FBI's Behavioral Sciences Unit visited Toronto and drew up a psychological profile on the attacker. McCrary told police that the Scarborough Rapist was an anger-retaliatory rapist, the most violent of all. The man likely had a history of rocky relationships with significant women in his life, McCrary offered, and he believed, correctly or incorrectly, that he had been wronged or slighted by a woman and as a consequence was angry at all women.

From vaginal swabs, police knew the rapist was a nonsecretor, which meant that when analyzed his saliva and sweat would not indicate a blood type. Only twenty percent of the population are nonsecretors. Task-force detectives jokingly referred to themselves as "The Spit Police" because any suspect was asked to give a saliva sample on a tissue to see if he was a secretor. If not, further investigations would be done. Through 1988 and 1989 hundreds of spit samples were sent to the understaffed Centre for Forensic Sciences in Toronto. Meanwhile, on the streets, undercover policewomen rode the transit systems as decoys in the attack area, but the rapist didn't take the bait.

On June 20, 1989, a nineteen-year-old girl was attacked in the Guildwood area as she crossed the road from a friend's house to her home in the pouring rain. Fortunately, her friend had watched her cross the street and raised the alarm when she saw the attacker. The girl told police he was five feet eight and wore jeans and a dark jacket. On August 15, 1989, a twenty-two-year-old woman was bound, beaten, and sexually assaulted in a 1 a.m. attack. The woman told of being followed the night before. Even after pooling all the information from all the victims, police could not glean enough details to put a solid composite drawing together. By this time, over a thousand suspects had been ruled out.

In an article written by *Toronto Sun* reporter James Wallace, Dr. John Bradford of the Royal Ottawa Hospital warned that the attacks indicated an escalation of violence that could ultimately lead to the Scarborough Rapist becoming a serial killer. Bradford, one of Canada's leading authorities on serial rapists, said the rapist was almost certainly a psychopath. Bradford said the rapist probably lived in the area and, from the outside, "blends into the background." That September, police tripled a $50,000 reward that had been offered for information leading to the conviction. Two months later, another woman was anally raped.

On December 19, 1989, a Christmas poster campaign was launched warning women to take care and urging friends and family of the rapist to come forward with details. The poster appeared on all buses and city works trucks in Scarborough. Three days later, at 2:45 a.m. in the freezing cold, a teenage girl was attacked in a stairwell after leaving her car in an underground parking lot. The victim was anally raped at knifepoint, but there was less dialogue. She described her attacker as nineteen, white, baby-faced, with sandy-blond curly hair. He was wearing a dark leather jacket, jeans, and running shoes. Early Christmas Eve morning a woman was accosted by a man with a knife when she stepped off a bus. She ran away and called police. The manhunt yielded nothing. Through most of May nothing happened, but on May 26, 1990, police got the break they needed. Unfortunately, it came at the expense of a nineteen-year-old woman who was attacked as she walked along Midland Avenue at about 1:40 a.m. It started when a man walked up to her from behind and began talking.

"Hi, how's it going? Nice night."

She gave a guarded reply, but kept walking.

The man backed off, but seconds later he charged her from behind. He literally picked her up off her feet and carried her to the deserted Agincourt Collegiate school grounds. She was tied with twine, cut with a knife, and sexually assaulted. The rapist fled. Police learned something they had not heard before: the rapist was eighteen to twenty-two years of age, six feet, with a muscular build and broad shoulders. He had a smooth, tanned complexion, light-colored eyes, and spoke without an accent; he had blondish hair, parted and feathered in the front and the sides and collar-length in the back; he wore a baby-blue shirt, khaki knee-length walking shorts, and running shoes. Police decided to release a composite, knowing that its public appearance would effectively create an entirely new probe, with people focusing on the composite to the exclusion of everything else.

The Scarborough Rapist Task Force, which had been renamed and broadened across Toronto under the name Sex Assault Squad, had set up five telephone lines to take tips. Within weeks thousands of suspects were identified and up to a hundred police officers were chasing suspects. Hundreds of saliva swabs were taken that summer, and later that year nonsecretors who were firm suspects were asked to give a sample for state-of-the-art DNA genetic fingerprint testing to be performed by the CFS, which had brought the DNA-testing status on-line in July of that year. The Centre, however, had only one qualified scientist and one technician on staff at the time. The Scarborough Rapist suspect samples were among up to sixteen hundred samples submitted from across the province of Ontario waiting for analysis.

After a busy Tuesday morning at the Brownhill restaurant, Bill Smirnis finally had a chance to sit down at the kitchen's staff table for a cup of coffee, a bite to eat, and his first look at the *Toronto Sun*. Only a few yards away, Van stood at the oven making a roast beef sandwich for a customer's lunch. As Van's hands worked the meat into a tidy pile atop a slice of bread, Bill's right hand raised the cup to his lips and he took a sip of coffee, simultaneously lifting the left corner of the tabloid with his spare hand to look at the front page.

"Have You Seen This Man?" the stark headline asked.

Then he glanced at the front-page artist's composite sketch of the Scarborough Rapist. The face looked familiar. He took a second look and his head jolted back in surprised recognition.

"Hey, Van, come here," he beckoned in his deep voice, waving his son over. "Who does this look like?"

Van walked to the table and looked over his father's shoulder. He was stunned. "Paul? Wow, that's Paul!"

Van poured himself a cup of coffee and sat down to read the newspaper.

The composite sketch released by Metro Police showed an attractive, boyish-faced male with stylish blond hair. Alongside the picture, police said the rapist suspect was about eighteen to twenty-two years old, five feet ten to six feet, had light-colored eyes, a medium but muscular build, was clean shaven, and had a tan complexion with blond hair parted on the left side and feathered just over the top of the right ear. He was wearing a baby-blue top, tan knee shorts, and running shoes.

"When you have finished reading today's *Sun*, please cut out this page and post it prominently in your workplace," the newspaper suggested.

The composite was produced only after the latest victim of the Scarborough Rapist was able to see his face and give a decent description to the police. It was drawn two years after the attacks had begun and was released to the media Monday, May 28, 1990, less than forty-eight hours after the nineteen-year-old Don Mills woman was raped at Agincourt Collegiate.

Van read on as *Sun* reporter Rob Lamberti described the breakthrough: "The Scarborough Rapist now has a face. And he looks like the boy next door. For the first time since the rapist's rampage of fear began in Scarborough in May 1987, a victim has been able to help police create a composite drawing of the man. . . ."

Paul had a baby-smooth bed-tanned face; Paul had a medium but muscular build; Paul had blond hair parted on the left side. And the age wasn't that far off. Although Paul was twenty-five, he could easily be mistaken for twenty or twenty-one. But Van couldn't believe his best buddy, the friend he'd known since he was a baby, could be the Scarborough Rapist. If Paul had been into this kind of thing he surely would have told Van about it. Later that day, Van picked up the restaurant telephone and called his buddy Gus Drakopoulous.

"Hey, Gus, check out *The Sun*. Paul's on the front page!"

"I haven't seen the paper," said Gus.

"Hey, you have to pick it up," Van continued. "It's Paul. There's a picture of the Scarborough Rapist on the front page and it looks like Paul, man."

Within minutes of Van's hanging up the telephone after the conversation with Gus, it rang.

"Hello?"

"Van, it's Paul!"

"Hi, Paul, how are you doing?"

Van swallowed. He hadn't expected Gus to call Paul with such haste.

"Listen, what the fuck's goin' on? What's this you're telling Gus?" Paul screamed into the phone.

"Why are you telling people I'm the Scarborough Rapist? This really fucking bothers me, Van. I'm really hurt. I don't need this shit!"

Van babbled out his explanation. "Um . . . em . . . sorry Paul. Listen buddy, I'm just joking."

"It's no fucking joke! Where's the fucking joke?" Paul was livid. Van had never heard Paul so mad.

"Don't fucking tell anybody else this bullshit. If you're my friend, Van, don't say any more. It hurts, get it!"

After Paul hung up, Van shook his head and wiped his eyes to help him think straight. *Paul is a dead ringer for the composite,* Van said to himself, *but surely he cannot be responsible for those terrible rapes. Paul could get almost any woman he wanted, and he already has Karla.*

When Van's brother, Alex Smirnis, arrived at the Brownhill around 2 P.M., Van showed him the newspaper. Some months later, Alex's wife, Tina, called Metro Police. Later, Alex told Van what Tina had done.

Not long after Van learned of Tina's phone call, he and Paul were drinking in a pub called Hannibal's when Paul leaned over, close to Van so nobody else in the bar could hear. He told Van that police had called him in for a DNA sample in the Scarborough Rapist case.

"It wasn't much fun," he said.

Paul reiterated his innocence to Van, but added that he

found the concept of DNA most interesting and he intended to study it, "find out what it is all about."

Van nodded.

Paul took another sip from his beer. He glanced around the North York pub again. Then his expression grew serious. His cold, blue eyes looked right into Van's.

"Did you fucking go to the cops to tip them off?"

Van was startled. Clearly, Paul had not forgiven the telephone call Van made to Gus after seeing the Scarborough Rapist composite in the *Toronto Sun*. But Van wasn't about to tell Paul that Tina was the one who called.

"Think, Paul! It must have been some girlfriend you pissed off or something. Carol might have done it, or maybe Janet. It wasn't me, buddy."

His answer seemed to make sense to Paul, who scratched his head and lamented: "Why is this happening to me?"

After that night of drinking, Paul didn't mention the issue again. In the following months, Van didn't see any police action against his friend. Whenever he asked Paul about it from then on, Paul brushed off the question and said they had checked it out but had cleared him.

Van had no reason to doubt he was telling the truth. After all, DNA was foolproof, wasn't it?

Meanwhile, on Sir Raymond Drive, Marilyn Bernardo had confided to a neighbor that "the police had knocked on the door and had asked Paul to go to the station for an interview" on the Scarborough rapes.

"Apparently somebody said Paul looks like the picture in the paper. Paul went down and they took some samples, but we haven't heard anything back," she said. "Well, I guess that's the end of that."

CHAPTER
12

Just as Paul tended to attract younger women and somehow cement them to his personality, he accomplished the same with teenage males who came into his sphere. During those first few months of his relationship with Karla, Paul did this with Mike Donald, who at the time was a naive and impressionable sixteen-year-old who was dating Lori. Paul knew Mike looked up to him, even if Lori didn't. According to Mike, Paul could do no wrong. Even after his relationship with Lori ended, Mike and Paul maintained a close friendship.

Lori, however, thought Paul was too old and overbearing for Karla; she had been appalled at Karla's confession to her that she had slept with Paul within hours of meeting him.

As Paul struggled with his accounting studies through 1988 and 1989, Lori told her friends that he was a loser because he didn't have his shit together and was still going through school at age twenty-six. She told friends of her hatred for Paul's domination over Karla, but then added, as if in justification, that at least he "gave her a life," taking her away from her pet-shop job, her animals, and some of the "geeky" friends she used to hang out with.

Paul's continued quest for self-improvement included his purchase of numerous self-help and motivational books, videotapes, and audiotapes. In March 1989, he ordered a replacement audiotape from Nightingale-Conant of Niles, Illinois, titled "Lead the Field." The tape was one of many goal-attainment lessons offered by Nightingale-Conant's founder, motivational specialist Earl Nightingale. Paul had bought the original tape but had either lost or destroyed it; hence his request for a $15 replacement tape.

Around her fourteenth birthday, Tammy confided to Paul that she had begun dating a teenage boy whom she liked. But she was put off by his constant attempts to coerce her into sex. Paul was so furious that he called Van at home to complain about the boy's antics. Paul didn't want Tammy having sex with anyone, and he suggested to Van that the two of them should scare him off. Van supported his buddy, because he truly believed Tammy was still a little young for sex, especially sex forced on her by some young punk with an attitude.

As Paul began spending more time in St. Catharines, he became increasingly good friends with a U.S. marine, Alex Ford, the then-boyfriend and soon-to-be-husband of Karla's friend Kathy Wilson.

Kathy met Alex during the long Victoria Day weekend of May 1988 on the Canadian side of Niagara Falls. Alex was a member of a prestigious drill team that performed twice-weekly in Washington, D.C., and was on the road virtually every weekend of the year, traveling to community events, inaugurations, and military celebrations. The team had even performed for Queen Elizabeth II while representing the United States Marine Corps.

Soon after a sudden and romantic meeting at the Falls, there were phone calls and visits to and from Washington, D.C., where Alex was based. Although Kathy was at first determined to prevent her parents from knowing of her relationship with the strapping marine, she immediately confided in her good friend Karla Homolka.

"Oh, Karla, I met the perfect guy too," she gushed as she discussed the marine and her affection for a young man who lived so far away. Karla nodded her head in excitement. With Paul in Scarborough, she of course knew the trials and tribulations of a long-distance relationship. It was a subject that would be discussed at great length over the following weeks as the two girls became increasingly close. The girls often talked of how they coped, sometimes joking about their long-distance love affairs, sometimes talking about the frustrations.

Schoolmates would often tease them mean-spiritedly about how their older men were off with other women in the big city while Karla and Kathy were foolishly pining away in tiny St. Catharines. It was a possibility that Karla and Kathy acknowledged to each other. But Karla insisted that Paul was too busy with school and driving back and forth to St. Catharines to be fooling around. "She didn't want to show that her relationship was anything less than perfect," Kathy recalls.

A by-product of maintaining these long-distance love affairs were the gargantuan monthly telephone bills, expensive but tangible signals of real commitment from their men.

Karla and Kathy were determined that Alex and Paul should meet as soon as possible.

Alex was admittedly a bit nervous about meeting Kathy's best friend and her boyfriend. After all, he'd heard a great deal about the accountant from Scarborough from Kathy and he was concerned that an enterprising, university-educated accountant wouldn't be interested in spending time with a simple "jarhead" marine from the United States.

"I thought, he's probably going to think I'm some moron. I didn't think he'd think much of me," Alex recalls.

Alex needn't have worried. On a lazy June weekend, Alex was up for a visit and Paul was, naturally, at 61 Dundonald when the two boyfriends first met. One of the first things Paul suggested was that he and Alex go to the liquor store so they could make some exotic drinks.

So, sporting shorts and T-shirts, the two young men piled into Paul's car. Since Paul was still driving his Capri at this time, he immediately began making excuses for it and described the sporty model he hoped to buy.

On the radio "Blister in the Sun," a song by the band, the Violent Femmes, was playing. The tune contained sexually provocative lyrics Alex was amazed could go over the air.

"I can't believe you can say that on the radio up here," he said.

Paul laughed. "Oh, you can say whatever you like up here," he said, ever the expert.

Back at the house, Paul made B-52s for everyone to drink.

Although Paul was always one to sell himself to people, he seemed entirely at ease with Alex.

"It wasn't like there were any barriers, and we just became really good friends right off the bat," Alex recalls. "I really liked him because I thought, I don't have to impress this guy."

The first weekend, the four new friends talked and joked and told stories about their lives and listened to music and drank exotic drinks.

For Karla and Kathy, things couldn't have worked out better. Dating older men in faraway cities had left them isolated in many ways from normal teen socializing. They still had friends, but their relationships required a lot more maintenance than most of their other peers', so it was gratifying, even relieving, to see that their boyfriends had hit it off so well. It was clear that they were going to spend a lot of time together.

Paul made it clear that he wanted to know whenever Alex was going to come north for a visit, because he'd make time from his accounting studies and work to come down. Alex thought that was a nice gesture, especially given the demands on Paul's time studying for the grueling provincial accounting exam.

Often the four young people would just drive around the peninsula or go out to eat at restaurants. More often than not, Paul picked up the tab.

Alex and Kathy were still struggling financially, she as a student and Alex as a marine making expensive trips to Canada, and Paul loved to enhance the image he'd created of himself as a young entrepreneur, a go-getting, suave businessman with unlimited potential.

"He was a wining and dining type of guy. You've got to understand that everything that Paul was depended upon how other people perceived him."

Late in the summer of 1988, Alex feared he might be transferred to a marine base at Seven Palms, California. He was determined to maintain his relationship with Kathy, so he bought her a promise ring. Not to misrepresent the significance of the gift, Alex presented it to Kathy in the parking lot of a McDonald's in Niagara Falls. Nonetheless, it was a bold step for Kathy, who was just finishing high school.

It was a significant event as far as her friends were concerned as well. Debbie Purdie was also dating a much older man and had discussed engagement, but this was a real ring, albeit with a fairly diminutive diamond. Karla was especially interested in the promise ring, and she oohed and aahed with great delight and more than a little longing.

One thing Kathy and Alex noticed about their friends was that they seemed to be in a continuous state of subtle competition with Alex and Kathy. Alex, for instance, drove a flashy Nissan Pathfinder, and Paul, when they first met, was driving a junky white Capri. Soon, Paul leased a Nissan 240SX.

Alex always had a top-notch stereo system in his Nissan. Paul installed a similar model in his own car, although he claimed to have gotten a deal on the equipment. Still, it never sounded quite as clear and crisp as Alex's stereo, a fact that always annoyed Paul.

So it wasn't too much of a surprise that on her birthday, May 4, 1989, Karla appeared with her own promise ring. Not surprisingly, the ring was significantly bigger than Kathy's.

"It was bigger than some of the engagement rings I've seen," recalls Lisa Stanton. "She was very proud of it. It was really noticeable on a girl that age, a ring that size."

People at school or in the Pen Centre would marvel at Karla's new possession. "Oh, is that an engagement ring?"

"No," Karla would reply. "It's a promise ring, but we're going to get married."

"That was her goal," says Lisa.

Later, the proliferation of promise rings would spark stories of some secret "diamond club" that legend has it was a cabal of young girls hunting down the wealthiest single men in southern Ontario (and beyond) with an eye to marrying as quickly as possible.

Kathy and Karla and the rest of the girls may have joked

about their little "diamond club," but they harbored no gold-digging agenda.

While some people recall the Homolka house as one dominated by tension and unhappiness, Alex and Kathy and Lisa recall only warmth and kindness.

Kathy, of course, had been a regular visitor to the semidetached home for a number of years. And it wasn't long after Alex began making regular visits to St. Catharines and eventually moved north that he was greeted at the door by Karel with a familiar and friendly "Hi, Alex, how's it going? Can I get you a beer?"

"You know, all in one breath," says Alex. "It was always a nice place to relax."

In the summer, neighbors and relatives and friends of all sorts would invariably be found lounging around the in-ground pool in the backyard, protected by a low fence. The small bar refrigerator would be moved from its winter position in the basement to the corner of the cement deck, and hot, sunny days would be passed in pleasant obliviousness to the troubles of the rest of the world.

If Paul and Karla and Alex and Kathy weren't hanging out around the pool, often they'd be found in the basement poolroom. This was Karel's domain, his kingdom.

One day not long after Alex had been embraced by Paul and the Homolkas, Paul and Alex were playing a game against Karel and a neighbor. Kathy may have been upstairs or out by the pool, but Karla was sitting watching the game and Paul looked over and yelled out, "Hey, bitch, get me a beer!"

Alex looked around, shocked, waiting for a reaction from Karel or the neighbors or even Karla herself. But there was none. Karla dutifully jumped up and retrieved a cold beer from the fridge.

"Nobody said a damn word," says Alex. "Without the blink of any eye, she got up and got him a beer."

Perhaps it was because Paul's tone was light enough to ignore. Perhaps it was that Karel had on occasion referred jokingly to Dorothy as "bitch" or "the old bitch." The moment passed without comment or notice, but it seemed to form a base of tacit approval that fueled Paul's continued use of "bitch" as a nickname for his girlfriend and later his fiancée and then his wife.

During one of Alex's first few visits to Canada the infamous Karla Self-Improvement List resurfaced. After Lisa and Kathy had first noticed the perplexing two-page letter, it had disappeared, or at least was more securely hidden from view. But one afternoon while the gang was watching TV or playing pool or sitting by the pool, Kathy noticed it attached to the bureau mirror amid a collage of Paul's pictures. This time there was an addendum, a third page, which seemed to more fully outline the kind of behavior that Paul demanded of his girlfriend.

"Oh, my God! There's that list again!" said a startled Kathy. She motioned for Alex to come in and inspect the document himself.

"Oh man, this is weird," Alex said, shaking his head.

It was the last time they would see the list.

Shortly after meeting Paul, Karla had taken the balance of the fall semester off to work full-time. She returned to classes in January 1988.

But after returning to school, despite getting decent marks, her interests and goals had been completely renovated by her relationship with Paul. Her friends noticed she'd even stopped offering personal opinions on things like music and the news of the day. Instead she parroted what Paul had told her or what she thought Paul would think about a given subject.

Her friends merely shook their heads.

In the spring, while high-school seniors everywhere bit their nails to the quick wondering if their applications to college would be accepted, Karla once again announced a significant altering of career choice.

Sitting by the Homolka pool, Karla told her friends that she'd been accepted at the University of Toronto. She'd applied, she told her friends earlier, so she could take business courses and eventually help Paul in his work.

"Well, are you going to go?" they asked excitedly. "Are you going to live on campus, or get an apartment?"

"Well, actually, I'm not going to go," Karla announced nonchalantly.

"Why?"

"Well, I'm going to be getting married and having babies soon, so Paul says it's a waste of money."

There was a stunned silence. Although they realized college wasn't for everybody, Karla had often talked about getting out of the house and being on her own.

"You know, an education is never a waste of money," Lisa offered. But Karla ignored the comment. The case was closed.

Early on in their socializing, Paul confided to Alex that he didn't get along with his parents at all and that, if the truth were told, he downright hated his mother. He described to his new friend how he was the product of an extramarital affair between his mother and an old sweetheart. The man, Paul proudly explained, was filthy rich. But things at home hadn't been particularly cozy, with his mother banished to a downstairs bedroom, apart from her husband.

Alex was sympathetic, and the two would often talk about their family relationships. But Paul would almost always lapse into an angry tirade about his parents, and specifically his mother. She'd been under psychiatric care a number of times, Paul also confided, and had blamed Paul for the disintegration of her relationship with her husband. It was usually at this point that Paul would launch into a venomous string of epithets about his mother that included "bitch," "slut," and much worse.

Through the rest of 1988 and into 1989, Alex visited as often as he could, given the drill team's hectic travel schedule. One of the team's trips during that period took him to England and Wales, where they performed a special routine for Queen Elizabeth II.

The team had flown on a special DC-9 similar to the U.S. president's aircraft, and after the performance, which had gone extremely well, the team was packing up when Queen Elizabeth herself strolled by with the head of the drill team.

The marines snapped to attention and stood board-straight as she passed. But as she passed Alex, he allowed himself a quick peek at one of the world's most famous personalities. The queen caught him and smiled, and she stopped and chatted about the weather and how "smart" the team looked.

Because she was a tiny woman and Alex is over six feet tall, he had to bend from the waist to hear her. A bit flustered, he called her "ma'am," a protocol no-no, although no one seemed to care much since she seemed to be enjoying herself.

Paul loved that story. He loved to hear Alex talk about the pomp and the ceremony, the royalty and the tradition. In fact, Paul loved to hear any details of Alex's life in the military. He was absolutely fascinated with Alex's knowledge of weapons, which came from his regular training with a variety of firearms, including semiautomatic weapons.

For instance, Alex recalls Paul's interest in a stun gun, which Alex recalled having read about in a military supply magazine. He loved to hear about the M-16s and the other famous guns that Alex not only knew about but had fired himself.

Once, while Alex was still stationed in Washington, he and Paul were talking about the violence in Washington and how Alex could walk down the street and buy anything, from crack to pot to guns to women. Hell, he could go into the corps barracks and get any kind of weapon he wanted, he said.

"I can just ask for any type of firearm and get it," Alex explained.

Paul's eyes lit up.

"You can get me a handgun?" he asked.

"Oh yeah, I can get you anything you want," Alex said.

"Hey, I got a great idea. Why don't you get me handguns. I'll pay you money and I'll bring them over the border in the car."

Alex looked at his new friend for a moment, waiting for the smile to come that would denote that the whole conversation was a joke. But it didn't come.

"I can sell them in Toronto for maybe five times what you pay for them in the States," Paul said, already figuring the profits and how he'd get the weapons across the border and through customs.

"I'm joking. I don't want to get a bad rep in my barracks," Alex explained patiently. "After all, I'm in the honor guard. It wouldn't look too honorable to be caught selling guns."

In many ways, Paul reminded Alex of his colleagues in the Marine Corps. Full of bravado, talk, and bluster, it was drilled into the young men of the Corps over and over that they were men and that men behaved in very defined ways, ways not dominated by introspection or sensitivity.

It wasn't unusual, therefore, to find the boys in the drill team discussing topics over a narrow range that included sex, war, death, and other "manly" things.

"We were airbags," says Alex candidly. "Paul struck me as the kind of guy who would do really well in this kind of environment."

If Alex joked about "kicking some ass," Paul joined in without hesitation. "Yeah, let's go do it!"

Alex described to Paul how someone always had a porno-movie cassette, which they'd pop into the VCR between parades or training sessions. Or how they'd sit around sometimes and try to gross each other out, telling the foulest stories, real or imagined, or coming up with the most disgusting images they could think of.

Alex noticed that Paul would pick up certain phrases or expressions that he'd described from his days with the marines. Terms like "skull-fucker" or "Suzy Rottencrotch" became part of his vocabulary.

"It sounds sick to most people. But you're a marine. You live with a bunch of guys for so long, you don't have normal conversations. It just becomes really bizarre. And when you get really drunk and you're with a bunch of people who are basically trained to go out and kill people, your conversations basically revolve around that whole instinct," Alex explains.

Still, there is one story Alex related to Paul about his time with the Marine Corps that continues to haunt him to this day. It was an incident that involved watching a snuff movie.

One day during infantry training school, a small group of
marines were sitting around chatting and a corpsman was
talking about a film he'd seen that showed a woman being
killed after orally gratifying a man.

"A lot of us, we didn't know what he was talking about.
So he asks, 'Have you guys ever heard of snuff films?' " Alex
recalls. "No, what the hell is a snuff film? I mean, the only
snuff I knew was from Copenhagen."

Alex and the others razzed the man after he explained just
what a snuff film was. They told him he was full of it and that
no such film existed.

The corpsman insisted that there was a film and he had a
copy and they should see it because there is a lot of sickness
in the world and it would make them tougher if they understood just what the world had to offer.

"Of course, we're all thinking, Yeah! Cool!"

That was the general sentiment until the guys in Alex's
unit watched the grainy, poor-quality video showing a woman
shot in the head with a revolver. Later the recruits confided to
each other that they'd been sickened by the film and disturbed
by its contents.

"This was the film I saw. So I told Paul about this. Paul
was really into it. He was like, Wow! Really? That's so cool!
He thought it was so cool how they could waste people on
movies."

CHAPTER
13

Through late 1989, Paul continued to commute from Scarborough where he was living with his parents, completing his university course while working at Price Waterhouse.

Karla, having graduated from high school, was working full-time at the Martindale Animal Clinic, while Kathy was going to college in St. Catharines, studying psychology. Alex was completing his final tour with the marines. By May 1990, he left the Corps and moved north, working at a variety of jobs before the Gulf War.

Paul had always talked about the accounting program and his internship at prestigious Price Waterhouse. He gave the impression that he was a young financial genius in the making, poised to be a great investment accountant with a salary and lifestyle commensurate with that position. He made sure Alex and Kathy knew that the provincially set Certified Accountancy (CA) accounting exam was one of the most rigorous tests facing any professional body. Those studying for the test are known to take weeks off from work and study round-the-clock in the days leading up to the exam. Anxiety is high and the pass rate is low.

Despite this, Paul never seemed to be too busy to see his new friends.

"Paul always made an attempt to see us. When he heard we were coming up, he was in his car, on his way down," says Alex. "It didn't matter if he had an exam to study for or not, he'd study on the way down. And the way he drove, I wouldn't doubt it.''

Some weekends, Paul spent the entire time studying and Karla sometimes complained to Kathy that she wouldn't see Paul for several weeks at a time because he was studying so hard. She in fact once wrote in her high-school yearbook that she was waiting for Paul to finish his exams so she could see him more than once a week.

Suddenly the talk about studying and exams and being a CA stopped. Alex and Kathy assumed Paul had failed to pass on his first try, a fate shared by thousands of would-be accountants. But he wouldn't discuss it other than to say he wasn't interested in being a CA and working for a large, impersonal corporation anymore. He told a shadowy story about how he'd left Price Waterhouse because of problems with an old girlfriend who worked at the firm and how he'd had to steal some of the keys to important files in order to get the back pay that was owed to him. He assured his friends that he'd make more money free-lancing anyway.

Once out of Price Waterhouse, Paul began to change radically. Gone was the superprep with the lucrative job and the bright future in business. Paul no longer aimed at the respectability of upper middle class. He became enamored of rap music and was forever quoting the lyrics of white rapper Vanilla Ice. His vision of Karla changed also. No longer the demure faux schoolgirl, Karla now went out to clubs in Paul's new favorite look: tight black spandex skirt, black shirt, and black high heels. Trashy was clearly in—and preppy was out. The pink Beaver Canoe sweatshirt Paul had bought Karla when they first started dating was consigned to the back of the closet.

Paul Bernardo committed to memory profane lyrics by the likes of Niggas With Attitudes (NWA), Public Enemy, Ice-T, and, the band that emerged as his favorite, 2 Live Crew. Friends say he thrived on the rawness and vulgarity of their lyrics; he liked the way the outlaw rappers thumbed their noses at authority and somehow managed not only to get away with it, but make themselves a fortune in the process.

As rebellious as Paul was becoming, he and Karla still remained friends with Alex and Kathy. And no one was more thrilled than Karla when Alex finally proposed to his girlfriend in the most romantic of circumstances atop a Ferris wheel in Niagara Falls. Karla couldn't take her eyes off Kathy's beautiful diamond ring: clearly she wanted to be engaged herself. Paul continued publicly to kiss and fondle Karla in the most intimate ways. He would shock his friends by grabbing Karla's head and forcing her to commit a kind of simulated fellatio in nightclubs, but he still wasn't interested in formally tying himself down. As much as she might want it, Karla was only Paul's girlfriend, not his fiancée.

One night the four were heading off to the same Niagara Falls club when Paul suggested they go in separate vehicles: he and Alex together, and the girls in the second car. He told Karla and Kathy to go in on their own and that he and Alex would follow a short time later and pretend not to know them and try to pick them up. It seemed like a harmless adventure, so they all agreed. But when the boys got to the bar, Paul began homing in on several other women, including a blond bombshell behind the bar.

"Man, we could really wreak some havoc in here, couldn't we?" said Paul, his eyes lighting up at the hint of the chase.

"Uh, Paul, aren't we supposed to look for two very specific women?" Alex asked, looking for their mates in the crowded bar.

"Yeah, but we got plenty of time," Paul said, dismissing his friend, his eyes never still as they probed and searched the bar. He was having a wonderful time. The last thing on his mind was establishing a permanent bond with any one woman in particular, a fact more clearly obvious when he and Van celebrated Paul's twenty-fifth birthday in Florida.

The trip to Florida in August 1989 would be a wild celebration of booze and girls for the two old friends. Van couldn't figure Paul out when it came to girls; at home he had Karla and was still making out with Anna, as well as enjoying the odd surreptitious tryst with Carol, but it still didn't seem to satisfy his appetite for different women. They were heading for Fort Lauderdale, where the more affluent among Ontario's high-school and college student population tend to head for

March break. August wasn't exactly prime time for picking up girls, Paul had conceded, but what the hell, if anybody could find girls, it was Paul and Van, and sometimes their friend Gus, who was also along for the ride.

On this trip, the first of what would be many to Florida together, Paul and Van had opted to drive Paul's Nissan 240SX, which was packed tightly with three duffel bags of designer-brand clothes and the half-dozen bottles of liquor they had bought weeks before at Supermarket Liquors in Niagra Falls, New York.

After two days in Fort Lauderdale, where they found the road to meeting party girls blocked because the city was jammed with U.S. Marines, Van, Paul, and Gus drove to Daytona Beach and booked into the Whitehall Hotel, an eleven-story white stucco building that had its narrow end to the ocean and its length running a hundred yards or so to the boulevard.

The day after his birthday, with his video camera in hand, Paul drove Van and Gus to the Publix store for food and to replenish their booze supply. As they drove into the parking lot, Paul's ever-functioning radar noticed two girls hanging out in front of the liquor store. He drove past, videotaping them as he did, then pulled the car into the parking lot. The threesome walked toward the store.

"Hi," Paul offered with his gushing smile, which he focused on a pretty, dark-haired girl who stood outside the liquor store with a slightly chubby girlfriend.

"Hi. Hey, would you guys buy us some liquor? We're not old enough . . . we'll give you the money," the dark-haired girl offered, pulling out some American bills.

The girls were obviously not twenty-one, the legal drinking age in Florida. The dark-haired girl looked about sixteen; her friend was perhaps eighteen or nineteen.

"Sure," said Paul. "We'll even buy the booze, as long as you come back to our hotel room and party with us!"

The girls were so happy to score booze that they agreed in a second.

Van had seen Paul use this technique many times with excellent results. Paul never asked a girl if she would like to join them, which opened the door to a negative answer, but effectively told them they were coming. And always, there was the lure of free booze.

Freshly armed with bottles of tequila, rum, and vodka, the group returned to the Whitehall. Gus took a liking to the attractive brunette, Michelle, but Van and Paul commented to each other on how Michelle's heavy friend, Karen, was "good from far but far from good."

The next night was more of the same, with Van inviting two New Jersey women up to the room for drinks. The women, one brunette and the other blond, were staying at the Whitehall and had been on a picnic with some other men earlier that day, but they quickly cast them aside when invited to spend time in room 201. The dark-haired woman was interested in Paul, while the blond took a liking to Gus. Early that night, Paul used his credit card to slip open the lock of the room next door and spirited himself away with his woman. Van did the brotherly thing and left Gus alone in room 201 with his date. He went to the bar. After a couple of beers, Van went back to room 201. Van was standing outside the room and about to knock for Gus when he heard some loud shouting from the next-door room where Paul had gone.

"Aah, aah."

Van pressed his ear to the door.

"Liar!" a woman's voice said.

"Aah."

Then he heard Paul: "My father is wealthy . . . he's rich!"

"Liar!"

"Aah. Don't do that!"

"Don't lie!"

"It's true; I can have anything I want."

"Liar! Liar! Liar!"

"Slut . . . you fucking bitch!"

Paul was clearly losing his temper.

"Liar!"

Suddenly, Paul burst from the room into the hallway in only a pair of shorts. He looked at Van with wild eyes and turned his back to him, turning his head and pointing his finger at the deep and bloody fingernail gouges down the length of his back.

"Bit of rough sex, Paul?" Van laughed.

"It isn't funny. Look at me, look at me; she's fucking made me bleed. She's a fucking bitch. Fucking whore. I'm going to take care of her."

Paul pounded his fist on the door where Gus and his friend were squirreled away. "Gus, Gus, let me in."

Gus's face was a study of puzzlement. "What the hell, Paul, what's going on . . ."

With a brash, "Let me in," Paul ducked past Gus's large hairy body and into the room. Seconds later he came out with an X-Acto knife in his right hand. His eyes were wide open and crazed, and he was breathing hard, gasping for air.

"That slut. I'm going to cut her. I've got to cut her. I've got to get her back; she's a fucking bitch."

Van grabbed Paul's forearms and looked him in the eyes.

"Relax. You're not going to cut her. Now give me the knife." Paul stared into Van's eyes for a moment, then reluctantly handed over the blade. Paul went back into room 201. Van walked into the room next door to find the woman sitting up in bed dressed only in her panties. She was half stoned from all the booze she had consumed.

"I think you'd better go. Paul doesn't want to see you anymore."

"Well, he was lying to me!" the girl shouted. She put on her bra.

After dressing, the girl returned to room 201, where she apologized to Paul for scratching his back and after a few drinks she left for her own room. Everyone had drunk so much that the situation was soon forgotten. Van passed off Paul's knifeplay as an attempt to get attention. Paul wouldn't really cut her, he thought.

Once he returned from Florida, Paul resumed his relationship with Karla. Clearly in awe of Kathy's engagement ring, Karla talked about little else; she was shameless in her desire to have one of her own. As fall gave way to the damp cold of November,

Paul began talking to Alex about shopping around for an engagement ring for Karla. He told Alex about his shopping expeditions and the fancy stores he'd been in searching for the perfect rock for his perfect girlfriend explaining that he was prepared to spend thousands of dollars. He described to Alex how he was going to take Karla to the Festival of Lights in Niagara Falls, New York, and in front of the manger scene, he was going to get down on one knee and propose.

And sure enough, when the pair finally announced their engagement at Christmas of 1989, the scenario had unfolded exactly as Paul had detailed weeks earlier. They both wept, Paul told Alex and Kathy, that's how poignant the moment was. One thing that did surprise Alex was how unimpressive Karla's diamond really was. Despite the fact that Paul insisted first the diamond cost $3,000 and then $5,000 and then had been appraised at the astronomical figure of $20,000, it was without a doubt a pretty ordinary ring, at least to Alex's untrained eye. The lower-grade gem had clear flaws even Alex could see.

But it was big. Karla clearly loved to show off her new trophy, wiggling her finger for all to see.

During the following spring, in May 1990, Alex left the marines and moved to the Niagara Falls area first living with Stan and Lynda Wilson in Niagara-on-the-Lake for a month or so before finding an apartment in Lewiston, New York, just across the border, about a fifteen-minute drive from Kathy, who was still going to university at the time.

"When I moved to Canada, I only had two friends, and that was Kathy's brother and Paul," Alex recalls. Soon after, Alex bought himself a shiny, black Nissan Pathfinder. Meticulous about his vehicles as well as his music systems, Alex made sure this machine had it all: oversized tires, fog lights and, inside one of the most powerful stereo systems Alex could find and afford.

Paul loved this vehicle. He was still making monthly payments on his Nissan 240SX, but he coveted Alex's new vehicle.

In January of 1990, Paul had accepted a job at Goldfarb,

but within two months he had quit. In April he failed his accounting examination for the third and final time.

Surviving on unemployment benefits was tough on Paul Bernardo, but it wasn't impossible. Even after paying the monthly lease payment on his car, Paul could have survived on the $1,216 he received each month from the generous Canadian government. He did not have any other significant debts to pay and was either living at home in Scarborough or bunking in at Karla's parent's house in St. Catharines. But Paul didn't have the fortitude to draw in his horns to match his jobless status: The dinner dates with Karla and numerous women continued; he still showered gifts on the new women who came into his life; he persisted in using the cellular phone Anna had bought him; he wore the best clothes; he journeyed to and from St. Catharines as he pleased.

Owning almost every credit card he could lay his hands on, he not only never left home without them but never went out without using them. He had three MasterCard accounts and four Visa accounts with seven separate financial institutions, and four gas cards. By the time his bills were going unpaid and debtors realized what was happening and begun to chase him for their money, he had sought the protection of the Bankruptcy Act. The only asset he listed was the $300 cellular telephone. Since it was leased, the Nissan was not his property and as such could not be touched. He owed a staggering $25,399 to his creditors.

Although Paul was granted bankruptcy in November 1990, he didn't stop spending money. Within weeks of the bankruptcy application, Paul and Karla were still shopping on credit cards obtained in Karla's name and using the address of her parents at 61 Dundonald Street, St. Catharines. Paul, of course, had signing privileges on Karla's cards. Any cross-referencing the financial institutions may have done didn't lead them to cancel Karla's card. Friends tell stories of Paul and Karla returning from lavish cross-border shopping trips to New York state, to stores in Williamsville, Niagara Falls, Lewiston, Amherst, and the other commerical places, dining out and buying shoes, clothes, liquor, cigarettes, and gas, this time running Karla's credit cards to the limit. And they weren't only using plastic; there always seemed to be cash, friends say, and lots of it, though no one could figure out how the couple had accumulated so much money.

In an apparent effort to turn around his desperate financial situation, Bernardo turned once again to the motivational tape business, this time placing a huge $515 US credit card order with Nightinale-Conant through one of its distributors. Although he would plan to expertly copy the tape's information and re-sell the same material, Paul eventually found a quicker, more lucrative money making scheme and never actually pirated the tape.

CHAPTER 14

During one of Paul's many shopping sprees in late 1990, Paul decided he needed a video camera and went out and bought one at an Eaton's department store. He then proceeded to film everything in sight.

He liked to videotape from the car, and he liked to videotape people walking around, all the while providing background commentary. He especially liked to videotape the Homolka clan, even though he knew it drove Dorothy up the wall. And since Paul had officially moved out of his parents' home in Scarborough and into the Homolka household, he had endless opportunities to film his future in-laws.

Two days before Christmas, in the tiny kitchen at the top of the stairs, Dorothy Homolka was dressed in her yellow terry-cloth bathrobe even though it was early in the evening. She wanted to relax. She'd been doing Christmas baking and the family, including Paul, were going to taste some of the treats throughout the evening. Out of the refrigerator freezer she pulled some chocolate ice cream with which to make chocolate parfaits. From the living room off the kitchen, the happy voices of Paul, Karla, Lori, and Tammy lit up the air. Paul once again had his video camera out. It seemed as though he never went anywhere without it.

The dining-room table was cluttered with liquor bottles: vodka, scotch, and rye. Tammy was slouched on the couch holding a large goblet filled with strawberry daiquiris. Paul turned the camera on his fiancée's youngest sister. "Are there supposed to be two of you?" Tammy asked, her voice already thick, even though the evening had barely begun.

"Why, what do you mean, Tammy?" Paul asked, the camera humming in his ear.

Tammy pointed toward Paul, her head slumped over her glass, as though she was having trouble focusing.

"What I want to know, Tammy, is are you in the Christmas cheer, or what?" Paul asked.

"Karla was at his side, prompting him to mimic one of her favorite parts of the movie *Wayne's World*.

"Extreme close-up!" they yelled together, zooming the camera in on Tammy and then pulling back quickly. "Whoa!" they cheered in unison.

The ritual was repeated several times and Lori, dressed in cutoff denim shorts and T-shirt, was close-upped as well. "Let's get Mom," Karla suggested, and it was off to the kitchen, where Paul trained the camera on Dorothy. "Extreme close-up! Whoaaa!" the pair hollered.

Dorothy, busy at the kitchen counter cluttered with dishes, ice cream, and bottles of vodka, grimaced and turned her back to the lens. She tried to shoo Paul and Karla away. She hated being photographed, and damn it if Paul wasn't determined to tape everything! "There goes Mrs. H, running away from the camera again," Paul joked before focusing on the ice cream on the counter. "Whoa! Parfait excellent!" Paul narrated with an exaggerated *Wayne's World* accent.

Then the couple was off to the basement in search of Karel. Shadow the cat greeted them at the bottom of the stairs and got the extreme close-up treatment.

"Extreme close-up! Whoaaaaa!" Paul and Karla howled.

In the basement rec room, the camera-toting couple found Karel sprawled on the couch in front of the television, naked from the waist up, covered only in a bath towel.

"Mr. H" Paul announced, "Extreme close-up! Whoa!"

Karel grimaced and waived his daughter and her fiancée away. "Go on," he moaned.

Dorothy came downstairs, plunked herself in an easy chair, smirked, and covered her face with a magazine to avoid the probing camera. Lori, too, joined the family, while Tammy spoke on the phone to a friend upstairs. Lori and Karla posed on their knees in front of the Christmas tree, smiling broadly.

Later that evening, the three Homolka sisters and Paul began watching a rented movie on the upstairs television. Paul cracked open some champagne. Everyone but Lori had a glass or two. Eventually, Lori bid good night, saying she was going to phone her boyfriend, then turn in. Tammy staggered to her feet to give her sister a hug. Lori could feel her wobbling in her arms. Lori looked at Paul and Karla and sternly warned them not to give Tammy any more to drink. Shortly after Lori's departure, Dorothy and Karel came up from the basement, announcing that they, too, were off to bed. Karla and Paul suggested they finish watching the movie in the basement and asked Tammy if she wanted to join them. Dorothy suggested that her youngest daughter turn in, but the teen, two weeks from her sixteenth birthday, said she wanted to watch the rest of the movie with her big sister and Paul.

That night it was snowing so hard, Constable David Weeks could barely see the ambulance crew in front of his cruiser. It was 1:20 A.M., early Christmas Eve Day, 1990. A trip that should have taken a couple of minutes at most, took five minutes through the blizzard. The Niagara Regional Police cruiser and ambulance crew pulled up in front of 61 Dundonald Street simultaneously. Firefighters, also alerted by a 911 call, were there as well. Constable Weeks, the ambulance crew, and firefighters entered the side door of the semi-detached brick home at the same time. As they did, they encountered Dorothy and Karel Homolka emerging from the upstairs bedroom. They looked confused, and Weeks wondered whether they even knew why a cop and ambulance crew were barging into their house in the middle of the night.

"What's going on?" Dorothy asked.

"I don't know," said Lori as she stood in the doorway of her bedroom, having been awakened by the sounds of static crackling from the emergency crew's two-way radio. She, too, shook her head uncomprehendingly.

David Weeks, tall and gangly with a thin black mustache and braces, had been with the Niagara Regional Police for only seven months. Three years before, Weeks was a security guard with the Ontario Housing Corporation in Toronto. He barely had his feet wet at his first police job, but Weeks was enthusiastic and bright. Having noticed that the parents were awake and on their feet, Weeks headed for the recreation room. As he reached the bottom of the stairs he noticed a flurry of activity in a small room off the main rec-room area. He entered the room he would come to know as Karla Homolka's bedroom. Weeks noted two bureaus and a single bed. In the corner was a video camera and a stand.

On the floor, lying parallel to the bed, was a young girl. The emergency crews were working furiously, performing CPR and other lifesaving techniques on her. Weeks noticed that the girl was an alarming shade of gray, and appeared not to be responding to treatment. He also noted an odd mark on her face. It appeared to him to be a burn of some kind. A young man and a woman were watching intently. Weeks later learned they were Paul Bernardo and Karla Homolka.

The room was crowded, the atmosphere one of panic, so Weeks suggested that the couple leave the room. Paul and Karla agreed, and Weeks led them back upstairs to the kitchen. Dorothy, Karel, and Lori were there, still not fully aware of what was going on in their basement. Paul and Karla held each other near the microwave oven as Paul moaned out loud. "No! No! he cried." "I should have been able to save her! She can't be gone!"

"What happened?" demanded Lori.

"Tammy stopped breathing," the couple responded.

"Oh, my God!"

Weeks began asking preliminary questions, jotting down notes in his black police notebook. The young constable quickly learned that Paul and Karla had been the only ones with Tammy and that they'd been in the basement of the house, so he began directing questions at them, trying to get an overview of what had happened.

Together, Paul and Karla explained that they'd been in the basement with Tammy watching a movie. They had been on the main, green couch while Tammy was on the smaller love seat next to the Christmas tree. At one point in the evening,

Tammy complained to Paul and Karla that she was having trouble seeing. Paul and Karla told Weeks that they assumed she was talking about the effects of having been drinking through the evening.

"Well, what had she had to drink?" Weeks asked, continuing to make notes.

Paul and Karla looked at each other and listed some of the beverages consumed: daiquiris, a glass and a half of champagne, some wine, as well as tastes of other drinks from other family members. They'd eaten early, about 5 P.M., at which time they had macaroni and cheese, Paul and Karla said. When Tammy made the comment about impaired vision, had Paul or Karla asked her to elaborate? But neither had. In fact, not long after that, they said, both dozed off on the couch while watching the movie. They said they awakened to the sound of wheezing and noticed Tammy in distress, still on the love seat.

As Paul and Karla continued their description of what had happened to Tammy, Weeks noticed the emergency crew at the bottom of the stairs. He interrupted Paul and Karla to make room so Tammy could be moved outside into the ambulance.

She was brought upstairs on a stretcher, feet first, a tube extending from her mouth. And whether it was merely the angle that allowed the blood to gather at Tammy's face, or whether she had been revived, Weeks noted that she looked less gray and more pink as they passed. Paul and Karla also noticed the change in color. The family seemed encouraged and talked optimistically about Tammy's recovery.

Weeks noticed the curious red mark that was still around Tammy's mouth and nostrils. It was a clearly defined mark, and it reminded Weeks of stains he'd seen on people emerging from burning buildings, the area below their nostrils blackened from having drawn in smoke. Later, an ambulance attendant would draw Weeks's attention to another curious aspect of Tammy's burns: the facial hair in the burned area was still intact. That would seem to indicate that she hadn't been burned by a flame or heat, which would have singed her facial hair along with her skin.

Tammy was loaded into the ambulance. Karel and Dorothy followed with a police officer to St. Catharines General Hospital. The firefighters also left at this time, leaving Weeks alone in the house with Paul, Karla, and Lori. Weeks left the house for a few minutes to gather a workbook and some report forms from his cruiser so he could complete the formal paperwork on the call. When he returned, Weeks guided Paul and the sisters to the basement, where they sat down to talk. Weeks carefully scanned the room, noticing its single entrance and single light switch, next to the doorway. It was a circular dimmer switch that Weeks had activated as he entered the room. He also noted the couch on which Tammy had been lying. It was draped with a white throw cover, and there appeared to be vomit on it. Weeks explained that he would be taking a formal statement from each of the three about what had happened during the evening. He began to ask Paul questions first, taking notes in his black book. It was 1:55 A.M.

Weeks wrote down Paul's name, address, and date of birth, and gave the statement a file number for future administrative reference. He also wrote down an opening administrative paragraph that included Paul's home address and phone number.

As Weeks continued to write the opening notes of the statement, Paul interjected, explaining he had something he wanted to say.

"There were absolutely no drugs involved in this incident," he said emphatically. Weeks thought the statement curious. At no point had anyone suggested drugs had been involved. He certainly hadn't broached the subject himself. Weeks explained that they would get to that information later in the statement. Paul nodded and Weeks continued to ask questions, writing the answers on the formal Niagara Regional Police statement form.

"On Sunday, December the twenty-third, I was at the house with the whole family. Tammy, sixteen years, Lori, nineteen, and Karla, twenty, and Mr. and Mrs. Homolka . . ."

Just then the phone rang and Weeks reached from his position in the chair to the small table next to him where the phone rested. As he did, he noted in his report that he'd been interrupted at 2:03 A.M.

The police officer who had escorted Karel and Dorothy to the hospital was on the other end of the line. He had devastating news. He told Weeks that efforts to revive Tammy Homolka had failed and that the teen was dead. Weeks shook his head gravely. He set the receiver down and turned to tell Lori, Karla, and Paul, who were seated across from him. They looked at Weeks with stunned disbelief. Karla and Lori began to cry quite softly, hugging each other on the couch. Paul, too, began to cry, but very loudly. He pulled his knees to his chest and began to rock back and forth. ''No!'' he screamed, throwing his head back, banging it against the wall, and pulling at his hair. ''No!'' Suddenly, Lori fled the rec room and tore upstairs.

''I'm going to check on Lori,'' Weeks told Paul and Karla before following her up. Hearing noises, the young officer poked his head into a bedroom he assumed was Lori's and found her talking on the phone, sobbing. Seeing that she was all right, Weeks returned to the basement. He'd been gone three or four minutes at the most. But when he returned, Weeks was surprised to see that only Paul remained in the rec room. ''Where is Karla?'' Weeks asked.

Paul motioned toward the lower level of the basement, where the pool table was located. Weeks went down a short set of stairs to the subbasement and walked along a hallway, toward the front of the house. As he continued he was surprised to hear what sounded like a washing machine running. He looked around the end of a partition wall into the cramped washing area and saw Karla standing in front of the machine, the lid open, a corner of the throw cover already in the filling washer. She held the balance of the blanket in her hand as though she were about to feed the rest in. Weeks rushed to stop her. Worried about further upsetting an already agitated woman, Weeks quietly explained that they would need to keep the items in their current condition, at least for the time being. Karla nodded and shut off the machine. Weeks took the cover from Karla but discovered that another article, a comforter, was already at the bottom of the washing machine and covered with water, ruining it as an evidence item.

Weeks led Karla back into the rec room and resumed questioning. They explained that when they heard Tammy's labored breathing, they put her on the floor in front of the love seat. They thought Tammy had vomited and was trying to vomit again, so they held her head to enable her to throw up. Paul and Karla said they were panicked and decided the lighting in the room wasn't adequate, so they moved her into Karla's room so they could see better in their attempts to revive her. Weeks noted that when he'd turned the rec-room light on it seemed to be very similar to the lighting in Karla's room. In addition, the only route Paul and Karla could have followed to move Tammy would have been directly past the light switch. But he didn't broach the subject.

Paul told Weeks that he began to perform CPR on Tammy and that he searched for a pulse but couldn't find one. A few seconds later he corrected himself, saying it wasn't formal CPR he was performing but rescue breathing, since he didn't know exactly how to do chest compressions. Karla called 911, Paul explained.

Weeks told them they would have to go to the police station to file a formal report, because Tammy's death had made the matter more serious than anyone had first anticipated, and the administrative duties would have to be handled by an officer of higher rank. Paul then stood up and went to the downstairs washroom at the bottom of the stairway leading to the kitchen. He was gone a few moments. Weeks heard the sound of the toilet flushing. When he returned, Paul asked if he could change his pants before leaving. Weeks quickly checked Paul's trousers and, seeing nothing unusual, nodded his okay. Paul went into Karla's room and closed the door, but Weeks quickly moved to open it, just a crack, so he could still hear and see. Later, Weeks saw Paul's pants on the floor and examined them again, checking the pockets. No burn marks, nothing in the pockets, nothing untoward.

Before they left for the police station, Weeks turned to Paul and Karla and asked if they had any idea what would have caused the burn marks on Tammy's face. Paul quickly responded, saying he thought it might have been a rug burn from when they moved Tammy into Karla's room. Weeks looked skeptical. He told Paul he found it hard to believe that they would have dragged Tammy from the rec room to the bedroom by her feet, upside down, on her face. Paul said nothing in response.

The senior officer who would be taking charge of this Christmas Eve case was Detective Ken Mitchell, a veteran of the Criminal Investigations Branch of the Niagara Regional Police force. He hauled himself out of bed and arrived at the Homolka home at 2:35 A.M. Weeks and a police officer who had returned from the hospital, brought Mitchell up to date. At some point, an officer pulled Paul aside and suggested that perhaps they had been using drugs and had, in fact, been free-basing cocaine, which might explain the odd discloration on Tammy's face. But Paul again denied there were any drugs involved.

At 2:50 A.M. the officer and the detective left for the police station with Paul, Karla, and Lori, leaving Weeks alone in the house. The young cop wandered through the basement, looking for anything that might help explain the curious events that had unfolded earlier. He entered the laundry area and noticed a hamper filled with clothes. Past the dryer there was a tall, narrow brown cabinet on top of which sat an old television. Although he took note of the shelf unit, Weeks did not search in any of the compartments. Soon, Dorothy and Karel returned home from the hospital, with a neighbor in tow. They remained upstairs when another police officer arrived and began taking a series of photographs of the downstairs area.

Detective Ken Mitchell made a visit to St. Catharines General Hospital, where he examined Tammy's body. The girl had been transported wearing a pair of track pants and a blouse. She was wearing no bra and no underwear, but a sanitary napkin had been fastened inside her track pants. Mitchell noticed the curious burnlike mark on the left side of Tammy's face. It extended from the side of her mouth and curved around to her left ear. There was a similar mark around her nostrils and even on her left shoulder.

Dr. Joseph Rosloski was the attending coroner. He asked Detective Mitchell if he thought the burn could have been caused by a botched attempt at freebasing cocaine, like the mishap that befell Richard Pryor. But Tammy's remaining facial hair seemed to rule out that possibility. They surmised that the burn might have been caused by some sort of caustic agent ingested by the teen, or by stomach acid that would have been present in her vomit. They decided that the unusual marks, coupled with Tammy's young age, necessitated a postmortem exam, which would include a standard drug screen and an examination of the contents of Tammy's stomach. That procedure would have to be done at the regional pathology department at Hamilton's General Hospital.

Mitchell traveled back to the downtown police station, where Paul, Karla, and Lori were waiting to give their statements. It was now about 4 A.M. The detective interviewed both Paul and Karla, taking them separately into an interview room and asking them to reiterate what they'd told Constable Weeks earlier. Mitchell wrote out Paul's statement as the young man spoke:

"I am twenty-six years of age and reside at 21 Sir Raymond Drive, West Hill, Scarborough, Ontario, with my parents. I have been dating Karla Homolka for the past three years and am currently engaged to her. On Sunday, the twenty-third of December, 1990, I was visiting at the Homolka home. I visit there every weekend. Karla and I had been over at the river for about 3–4 hrs on Sunday afternoon. We returned home at approximately 6:30–7:00 P.M. and had supper. After supper was finished we sat around and talked for awhile. Mr. and Mrs. Homolka went down to the rec room. Karla, Lori, Tammy and I stayed up in the living room and watched T.V. We watched a movie that we had rented. While we watched the movie Karla, Tammy and I had some drinks. I had one or two Caesars, maybe a rye and Coke, and a rusty nail, which is scotch and Drambuie.

Karla and Tammy were drinking pina coladas and strawberry daiquiris. Tammy had a couple of drinks of my rusty nail. We also opened a bottle of champagne. I don't know how much Karla or Tammy drank of the champagne. I think I had a half a glass. Around 11 P.M. Mr. and Mrs. Homolka came upstairs and went to bed. At this time, we went downstairs to the rec room and continued watching the movie. I was sitting on one couch with Karla, and Tammy was on the other by herself. Sometime I fell asleep. I was awakened and Tammy was choking. She was lying on her back with her head towards the Christmas tree. She was choking and vomiting. I tried to pick her up off the couch, but I was not too successful. I got her off onto the floor [this next part was later added by Paul in his own writing after he had scratched out three and a half lines written by Mitchell] *and administered mouth to mouth resuscitation 2 or 3 times*. I tried to pick her up and I moved her into Karla's bedroom on the floor and continued trying mouth to mouth. Karla called 911 [*immediately,* Paul wrote later]. I continued administering mouth to mouth till the fire dept. arrived. I asked the fireman if he would continue mouth to mouth and he said yes.

After making the minor corrections to the statement, Paul signed it and marked the time. It was 5 A.M. Mitchell then ushered Karla into the interview room, where she provided him with a five-page statement echoing what her fiancé had said. She, too, examined Mitchell's handwritten version of what Karla had told him, making a number of corrections in her own handwriting. While this process unfolded, Paul became quite agitated.

Finally, when Karla was finished, he announced angrily that the police had no right to hold them unless they were going to press charges. With that, Paul phoned for a cab and they left the police building for the Homolka home.

Throughout the time Paul, Karla, and Lori remained at the police station, Mitchell and the other officers noted nothing unusual about their behavior, describing them later as being appropriately emotional given the night's tragedy. Before writing his report that morning, Detective Mitchell consulted a medical reference book at headquarters and discovered, as he believed, that gastric acids can, in fact, produce burns when vomited. It appeared to make sense. That was exactly what Mitchell believed had taken place with Tammy.

The autopsy found that Tammy had died after aspirating her own vomit, the fluid entering her lungs and cutting off her breathing and causing cardiac arrest. A few days later, a report from the Center for Forensic Sciences in Toronto revealed that only trace amounts of alcohol had been found in Tammy's stomach. No drugs were found as part of the standard drug test. Why then, would Tammy have vomited? Detective Mitchell, in conversation with the coroner, decided the vomiting had resulted not from the amount that Tammy drank, but from the combination of alcohol and whatever she'd eaten that night. Aside from the angry red burns on the teen's face, there was no sign of any violence on her body. So, Mitchell reasoned, the gastric juices theory seemed to be the most logical explanation for the burns.

Paul and Karla returned from being questioned by the police and were pissed off that they'd been told to take a cab home from the downtown headquarters. Dorothy and Karel were preparing to head out to select a coffin and asked Paul and Karla if they'd come, but they refused to go.

The scene at the funeral home in St. Catharines was chaotic. People were milling about and there were a lot of young people, schoolmates and teammates from the various sports teams that Tammy was involved with. Many were weeping and hugging each other.

At the front of the room reserved for the Homolka funeral was the cherrywood coffin in which Tammy had been laid. Kathy and Alex made their way to the area next to the coffin where they'd seen Paul and where they assumed Karla and the rest of the family would be.

The sight was devastating.

Karel was seated and had a strange, vacant look; Kathy and Alex later wondered if he'd been drinking before his arrival.

Dorothy, Lori, and Karla all had red eyes and pale faces; it was only a matter of time until the tears began again.

But it was Paul who seemed the most visibly affected by Tammy's death.

Alex and Kathy hugged and shook hands with everyone, who thanked them profusely for coming. Paul gave an extra squeeze and led them to the coffin. He reached in and began stroking the dead girl's long, blond hair.

"Isn't she beautiful?" he said, staring at the corpse. "Isn't she just beautiful? . . . Look at her lips. She's an angel. Isn't she an angel?"

Again and again, over and over, as though they were a mantra of sorts, Paul repeated the phrases, lovingly stroking Tammy's hair.

Kathy and Alex nodded uncomfortably. They were shocked that the family had chosen an open-casket arrangement. There was something unnatural about how Tammy looked, and then there were the strange red marks around her nose, mouth, and cheek that the funeral home staff had done their best to obscure with makeup. But despite the pancake mixture, the bruising or burns or whatever they were permeated the makeup, giving the body a strange, almost battered look. Tammy's lips, too, had taken on an unnatural purple hue, adding to the eerie effect.

Throughout the visitation, Paul never left the side of the coffin. At one point Alex and Kathy noticed that he took off his ring and placed it alongside Tammy with a stuffed animal. Often Karla would move beside her fiancé and hold him consolingly, whispering in his ear.

Tammy was wearing her favorite Polo sweatshirt. Beside her, the family had placed a number of the gifts that she was to have received Christmas morning. A portable Walkman also found its way into the coffin, and Karla placed a necklace Paul had given her around her sister's neck.

And there was a letter from Paul and Karla.

The first part was written in Paul's tiny, controlled script on a beige, fine bond card addressed to Tammy Lyn Homolka. On the front of the envelope, in fine ink scroll, was stenciled, MR. AND MRS. PAUL K. BERNARDO.

The letter was dated December 27, 1990, the day of Tammy's funeral.

Dear Tammy,

My dearest little sister, words cannot express the deep sorrow and regret that I now feel. You gave me your love and trusted me like your big brother. We shared a lot of good times and you touched my heart in a way that no one else ever could. I love you Tammy, I always have and will. I miss you so much and my life will never be the same now that you've gone. If I ever caused you any harm or pain, Tammy, please forgive me. I only wanted the best for you. Just for you to be happy and to experience the joys of the world. Please forgive me, Tammy. I'll love you from now till eternity and I'm looking forward to seeing you again once I die.

Love, your brother, Paul.
XOXO

Then, at the bottom of the card, in Karla's distinctive script, her own message:

Dear Tammy. I have so much to say to you that words cannot express. I've talked to you every night and you know how I feel about everything. I won't write everything I want to say, you know it already. I know the card shouldn't be used yet, but I want to give you the thoughts it holds to carry with you. I love you deeply and will hold you in my heart forever.

All my love, your big sister, Karla. XOXO.

P.S. I love and miss you with all my heart. I hope you're happy and loved and in God's hands. I love you so much little sister and can't wait to see you again. All my love to you. Kar.

Paul continued to talk obsessively about how Tammy looked. "How does her hair look? Does her hair look okay?" he asked, over and over.

"He was beside himself," Alex recalls. "Karel, the father of the child, was taking it better than Paul was. Everybody was upset, but nobody more so than Paul. Even Karla was nurturing Paul, because Paul was ready to jump in the casket and hold on to her.''

What confused Alex and Kathy further was the fact that no one would tell them exactly what had happened.

''She aspirated,'' was the answer Paul and Karla gave.

''Well, why? Did she try and commit suicide?'' Alex and Kathy asked in hushed tones.

No, that wasn't it, but neither Paul nor Karla would elaborate.

Among those that visited the funeral home that night were Stan and Lynda Wilson. A nurse, Lynda, too, was immediately struck by the curious markings on Tammy's face. They reminded her of burn marks she'd seen in the hospital, but she couldn't put her finger on exactly where she'd seen them.

She watched with a feeling of awkward embarrassment as Paul fondled Tammy's hair in the coffin. It didn't seem normal, somehow.

Later, Lynda and her colleagues at St. Catharines General would whisper their surprise that Tammy's death had been ruled accidental. Lynda's surprise was based on the fact that it appeared neither Dorothy nor Karel had made any apparent attempt to push the investigation any further. She also factored in Paul's description of how the burns occurred and decided there was something strange about the entire incident. Very strange indeed.

Paul apparently had told no one about the horrible death of his fiancée's baby sister. He called none of his friends or family. And it was only when Gus called the Homolka home to ask if Paul wanted to take off for a few days skiing in Quebec with him and some buddies did a subdued Paul explain quietly what had happened. Paul told Gus he was going to stay and help out as best he could.

Gus immediately called Alex Smirnis's wife, Tina, and told her that Karla's sister had died, leading to some confusion as to whether it was Tammy or Lori. Alex was shopping with Van at the Markville Mall, looking for a black suit for Van, when a call came on the cellular phone one of the brothers was carrying.

It was Boxing Day.

Van called Paul with the cell phone. Paul confirmed that Tammy had indeed died and Van told him he'd be down as soon as he possibly could.

Paul sounded grateful. "I need you. I need my friend here," he said.

Van drove straight to the funeral home on Bunting Drive. He was surprised at the scores of people streaming through for the visitation session.

Paul and Van embraced, and Van felt an unusual coldness in his friend.

"Oh, man," Paul moaned. "Oh, man."

Steve Smirnis was also contacted about the sudden death and came from Youngstown, New York, to the funeral home.

The initial report from Alex's wife was that Tammy—or Lori—had choked to death on a chicken bone.

But Paul explained that Tammy had actually aspirated on her vomit after drinking eggnog.

Paul told about how he been videotaping Karla and the family and the holiday proceedings and at one point he aimed the camera at the unconscious Tammy, pointing out, "There's Tammy, wasted, drunk."

But when she started vomiting, Paul said he dropped the video camera on the coffee table to rush to her assistance. Ironically, the camera kept recording, pointed at the couch where Tammy was lying, Paul told his friend.

Paul told his friends how he repeatedly tried CPR to try to revive her but couldn't.

Later, he showed Van part of the video that he'd begun shooting shortly before the holidays, the last time the three sisters were together. It was during the local Festival of Lights, and Karel and Dorothy had gone across the border to celebrate their wedding anniversary. At one point on the tape, Karel, slouched in a chair, looked up at Paul and said, "Look after my girls." Paul shook his head morosely at that scene, the irony almost too much to bear.

Paul also showed Van a videotape of Tammy sleeping on the couch the night she died. He said the footage of his attempts to revive Tammy were on another tape.

At the crowded funeral home, Van noted an oddly detached look on Karla's face. Beside her, Dorothy seemed barely able to control the flow of tears as the dozens of guests passed, paying their respects, stopping to shake family members' hands or embrace them.

During the visitation, Paul pulled Van aside and made what Van felt was a rather strange request. Earlier, Paul had reached into the casket and placed a ring given to him years before, on one of Tammy's fingers, like a wedding band. Paul then whispered to Van, who owned a matching ring, that he, too, should put the ring inside.

"Do you want to put yours in too?" Paul asked.

"Uh, well, I'll think about it," a perplexed Van responded.

"I thought it was very weird, that he put his ring on her finger and then that he'd ask that I put mine in too," Van recalls.

While Paul performed the ring ceremony, Karla watched, expressionless.

The funeral was held on December 27, 1991. It was massive, the procession seemingly stretching from one end of Hartsell Road to the other. Some people commented on how unusual it was that Karel would have insisted that they all drive in the family van, but perhaps it reminded them of their frequent trips to Tammy's soccer games and other family outings.

As mourners entered the packed Elm Street United Church (a neighbor had arranged for the funeral to take place here since the Homolkas had no affiliation with a specific religious denomination), they were given a red rose, which was then laid on the casket, now closed, as they filed past to pay their last respects.

Paul and the rest of the family, the last to enter the church, moved immediately to the front pew. Again, Paul seemed visibly distressed, perhaps even more so than he'd been during visitation sessions. He had spent hundreds of dollars on a huge, heart-shaped bouquet of red roses, which was set next to the coffin.

At the interment at nearby Victoria Lawn Cemetery, which is a short walk across some open area behind the Homolka home, Paul and Karla were the last to leave Tammy's body, waiting until the tomb was sealed and placed in the ground.

After the funeral, a group of about thirty friends and family returned to the Homolka residence. Again, there was a sense of the surreal as people milled about drinking and eating snacks and sandwiches that neighbors and others had brought.

Alex and Kathy finally found themselves in a quiet space with Paul. They queried him on the marks around Tammy's face. Paul had a ready answer.

He described how Tammy, who was asthmatic, had been drinking earlier in the evening with friends and was drunk and had fallen asleep on the couch. Then she started to throw up and have an asthma attack and aspirated. Karla ran out to dial 911 while Paul dragged her off the couch, and that's where she got the burn marks, from the carpet because he'd dragged her on her face, he explained.

Alex and Kathy listened intently. But there was something about the story that just didn't add up.

"We were, like, why would he drag her on her face? Nothing jibed," Kathy recalls.

It was at that very moment that a peculiar unease set in about their friend. It was something that they couldn't quite put a finger on, but there was definitely something unnerving about Paul and this story.

Nevertheless, Paul and Karla seemed genuinely grateful to have Alex and Kathy there. Paul seemed oddly detached at that point, seeming not to know what to do with himself, rarely leaving Karla's side.

It wasn't until about a month later, the night that Alex got called back to the marines to serve in Desert Storm, that Paul told Alex about how he'd been questioned for hours by the police after Tammy's death and how pissed off he'd been.

A month after that, on January 22, 1991, a senior officer with the Niagara Region Police Department ordered items taken from the Homolka home, including clothing, destroyed even though the case hadn't been formally closed. The final coroner's report wasn't completed by Dr. Rosloski until March 25 of that year. The coroner ruled Tammy's death accidental, even though no one had formally determined what caused the burn marks on her face.

Much later, Constable Weeks would describe his uneasy reaction to the closing of the case. Certain questions remained in his mind, but they were questions he later admitted he never followed up on. His superiors had made all the decisions.

CHAPTER
15

Within days of Tammy's funeral there was a palpable change in the dynamics within the Homolka household. Dorothy and Karel couldn't help but notice that Paul and Karla were never apart, that Paul never seemed to let Karla out of his sight. And Paul seemed to be constantly moping around and talking about Tammy. It was starting to drive everyone crazy.

There was a memorial service planned for Tammy at Sir Winston Churchill High School, and the family had made plans to attend. All but Paul, that is. As they made their way to the school, Dorothy broached the subject of Paul's moving back home, or at least out of the Dundonald Street residence. Karla was shocked. Since quitting his job at Goldfarb, Paul had been living with the Homolkas. The initial plan had been that Paul would live with the Homolkas until he and Karla were married later in 1991. He had no intention of moving back home to Scarborough, and Karla would hear none of that kind of discussion. When she told Paul about the pressure coming from her parents, he, too, became instantly hostile. He complained that they no longer wanted him, no longer considered him part of the family. He was extremely hurt, he said.

Finally, in late January, after Dorothy, Karel, and Lori returned from a lighting trade show in Toronto, the Homolkas got what they wanted. Paul told them he was moving out. But what they didn't bargain for was that Karla had decided to move out, too. There were repeated arguments and discussions.

Paul and Karla stayed in a local Journey's End Hotel for several days before answering an advertisement about a rental house in Port Dalhousie, a picturesque suburb of St. Catharines near the Welland Canal and Lake Ontario. Karla immediately fell in love with her new home and wrote to her friend Debbie Purdie about it and the arguments with her parents:

> Our whole house is done in very neutral shades, (which I love). All of the rooms are white with light grey baseboards and light grey carpeting, except the living room which has a hardwood floor. It sounds boring, but it looks way better than having every room a different color. It's much classier, Deb. . . .
>
> The only things we really need or want are 1. A dustbuster. 2. China. 3. Crystal. 4. Money. As for wedding gifts, please try to let people know that we want money! If they say anything like we don't believe in giving money, tell them to go take a flying fuck! (just kidding) Tell them about the china and crystal. Boy, a maid of honour is a great thing to have. . . . Wedding plans are great except my parents are being assholes. They pulled half of the money out of the wedding saying that they can't afford it. Bull shit. Now Paul and I have to pay for $7,000 to $8,000 of this wedding.
>
> So money is tight, considering we've all of a sudden been hit with this huge bill. . . . Saturday Paul and I just said fuck it—we're doing everything the way we planned and some things even better! Real flowers for everyone, we're paying for the bar, hors d'oeuvres, cocktail party, EVERYTHING! Fuck my parents. They are being so stupid. Only thinking of themselves. My father doesn't even want us to have a wedding anymore. He thinks we should just go to City Hall. Screw that, we're having a good time. If he wants to sit at home and be miserable he's welcome to. He hasn't worked except for one day

since Tammy died. He's wallowing in his own misery and fucking me! . . .

It sounds awful on paper (but I know you'll really see what I'm saying). Tammy always said last year that she wanted a forest green Porsche for her 16th birthday. Now my dad keeps saying "I would have bought it for her, if I'd only known." That's bull. If he really felt like that he'd be paying for my wedding because I could die tomorrow or next year or whenever? He's such a liar. . . .

Paul went to meet some of the owners of the house, who'd spent thousands of dollars renovating it. He provided a list of references and told them he was a free-lance accountant who was about to be married that summer. They were suitably impressed and Paul made arrangements to move into the home in mid-February. The monthly rent was $1,150 and he provided some postdated checks. Throughout the two years Paul Bernardo occupied the home, the landlords never had a complaint from or about him. His rent was always paid on time, in fact usually in advance, and sometimes in cash. He was the perfect tenant.

Van arranged to get a rental truck through his brother, Alex, and he and Paul drove to Paul's Scarborough home to pick up his belongings. Those belongings, including a bureau he'd had since childhood, which would soon bear the carved inscription "Karla is Paul's property." Among the possessions with which Paul wanted to stock his new home were twenty-five full bags of books, including encyclopedias, dictionaries, business books, guides and manuals dealing with dyanetics and positive mental attitude, and a book called *The Art of War*. After dropping off Paul's belongings at the rental house at 57 Bayview Drive, Paul and Van drove to the Homolkas', where Karla's possessions were already neatly lined up outside the side door.

Immediately, the couple adorned their new home with pictures: pictures of Tammy Homolka. Tammy's school photos, her grade eight graduation photos, and others adorned bureaus, Karla's hope chest, end tables, and the walls.

After a full day of moving, Paul suggested that Van stay

overnight. Once Karla had gone to sleep, Paul told Van that he wanted to go to the cemetery to see if anyone had been fooling around with Tammy's grave. Van was incredulous. They'd spent all day moving heavy books and bureaus, Karla's bed, and a spare TV Karel and Dorothy had given them. And what did he mean "fooling around with Tammy's grave?" Van soon realized that Paul was serious. He began insisting they make a trip to the cemetery, because, Paul said, he was afraid someone might have dug up her body to steal the jewelry she was wearing in the casket. Van, who had no interest in a midnight visit to the grave of a dead teen, persuaded Paul that no one would disturb Tammy, and suggested they could go by in daylight.

But if Van thought Paul had forgotten the incident, he was wrong. A few days later Paul again insisted they visit the grave. It was pitch black, but Paul drove straight to the gravestone, got out of the car, and circled the site, kneeling and examining Tammy's grave. "No, no one's touched it," Paul reported when he got back to the car.

When Alex and Kathy heard that their friends were moving into a new place of their own, they imagined it would be similar to the digs they'd chosen, a small apartment in Lewiston. It was tiny, but with help from friends and family, the Fords' new residence was tastefully decorated: the perfect starter apartment for a young couple just beginning their life together.

"So, what did you get? An apartment or a small house?" Alex and Kathy asked.

"No, we got a Cape Cod house. Right in Port Dalhousie," Paul said nonchalantly, knowing his friends would be bowled over by the home.

Sitting on a lot at the corner of Bayview Drive and Christie Street, the tidy pink clapboard house was the epitome of cute. Karla was elated at the new home and talked nonstop about setting up house with her man. Her joy reminded Alex and Kathy of Karla's reaction to becoming engaged. Paul was also enthused. He told Alex he was just biding his time until he actually bought the house outright. He happily led Alex into the basement, where he'd set up a little workshop with tools hanging on the walls and a workbench. He proudly showed off a series of power tools, including a circular saw, some of which had been given to him by his grandfather. Like the rest of the house, the basement was spacious and had been expertly redone. The main furnace area featured at various times a weight bench, exercise cycle, and a stair-climber unit.

Separated by a wall from the main area of their basement was a long, narrow laundry area, including a water heater and twin, old-fashioned concrete washtubs. A root cellar off the end of the basement was perfect for storing vegetables and other perishables.

The main floor was immaculate. There was a spacious living room with a fireplace and two comfy couches. Although there was little in the way of furniture when Paul and Karla first moved in, a large television and stand, matching wood end tables, and armchairs quickly found their way into the home. The extra television set donated by Karel and Dorothy, which required a bang on the top to produce a picture, was relegated to the upstairs bedroom.

Several large, fernlike floor plants gave the home a comfortable feel.

The kitchen, done in black and white tile, was narrow and airy, looking out onto the backyard. Through double French doors was the dining room, with a six-person formal table and matching cabinet. Upstairs, along with the huge master bedroom and twin walk-in closets, was Paul's special room. Later, when he filled it with sound-mixing equipment, microphone, CD player, cassette recorder, and keyboards, he would describe it as his music room, or studio. But in the beginning it was merely his office, a room no one was to enter without his personal consent.

It was the first home Paul had lived in outside the one he shared with his parents in Scarborough, and more recently the Homolka house. Alex and Kathy were impressed, and somewhat incredulous, that their friends could afford such a place. But Paul always seemed to have money, and in early 1991, he seemed to have even more of it.

He's doing well with his business, Karla explained when Kathy brought it up. But as for any more details, Karla was not forthcoming, producing yet another blank area of the puzzle that was Paul and Karla's relationship.

Early on, when the four would go out in the St. Catharines area, Paul would encourage the girls to drive together while he and Alex rode in Alex's Pathfinder, which Paul adored. But not long after they moved to Port Dalhousie, Paul tried to discontinue this practice. It was as though he didn't want Kathy and Karla alone together. The only time that Kathy and Karla seemed to get time alone to chat was when Paul went off to buy drinks at the Late Show or at the Pleasure Dome nightclubs across the border.

Whenever Alex or Kathy called the new home, either Paul answered the phone or there was an answering machine, always bearing Paul's voice. Sometimes Kathy knew Karla was home, but when she asked Kathy why she hadn't answered the phone, Karla would come up with some excuse. Either she'd been in the shower, in the backyard, or somewhere else. Kathy found Karla's explanations annoying, and thought to herself that the house was certainly grand but hardly a country estate where you couldn't hear the phone if you stepped outside!

Alex and Kathy began to conspire to separate Karla from Paul so they could find out what the heck was going on in their friends' lives. "We wanted to know what was going on with them. What was Paul doing? We were saying, he hasn't worked since 1989. We knew that he was doing something. And in the time leading up to the wedding it seemed like they were so disorganized," Alex recalls.

But Alex and Kathy didn't soon make sense of the relationship, or discover anything that shed any light. Karla was busy making wedding plans, so their discussions often focused on the impending marriage.

Then Karla, her mom, and Lisa decided to give Kathy a postwedding shower, since Kathy and Alex had canceled their initial wedding plans in favor of a quick wedding when Alex had been called back into the marines in time for Desert Storm. As the guest of honor, Kathy was seated front and center in the living room of Paul and Karla's house. Because there weren't enough chairs to go around, some of the guests sat on the floor. But no one seemed to mind and the afternoon passed without incident, everyone sipping wine and nibbling on the mountain of food that had been prepared, and laughing at the gifts of lingerie and other marital aids that Kathy unwrapped. Later, because the weather was so nice, the girls moved to the back porch and sat for a time on the deck, everyone commenting on how lovely Paul and Karla's new house was.

In the days leading up to the shower, Lisa visited Karla to help organize and bake. It was the first time she'd seen the new Port Dalhousie digs, and she was suitably impressed as Karla gave her a tour from top to bottom. Although the question went unanswered, Lisa wondered how they could possibly afford the home. She figured Paul was an accountant and he must have known how to save money or get tax breaks to build a little nest egg. Karla went on at length describing plans she and Paul had to buy a dog. Karla was determined to get a show dog, while Paul wanted something that was cool or prestigious. They'd decided pretty much on a Rottweiler, Karla explained, describing the big breed's characteristics and how she'd like to show it on the bustling dog-show circuit in Ontario and New York State. A few weeks later they bought Buddy, a beautiful Rottweiler puppy with a thick, shiny black coat. He cost several thousand dollars, a fact that Paul would often slide into conversation. It was, Lisa thought, in keeping with Paul's constant search for status. Karla, on the other hand, loved the dog and talked about using him in a stud service since he was such a handsome animal. Karla may have wanted a pet, but Paul made sure it was a pet that made a statement.

Karla was clearly excited about her new home and her life with Paul. She bounced around the kitchen making potato skins for her and Lisa. Later, Karla showed off some recipe files she'd collected and they tried to make small iced cakes for the shower. They were a disaster, but the girls laughed and laughed, deciding the guests would just have to do without the little pastries.

For all too brief a moment, Lisa saw again the Karla Homolka she had grown up with and had come to love. She remembered those simple, happy days when she and Karla baked chocolate pancakes in the Homolka kitchen. It was as though a thick curtain had suddenly been lifted and there, underneath it after all, was Karla. But it was a brief glimpse, and Lisa realized later why the curtain had been allowed to ascend: Karla was separate from Paul. She had told friends Paul was going to Toronto to visit his family for a few days. It seemed a little unusual, because Paul didn't get along with his family and rarely mentioned them.

In fact, it was a lie. On the weekend of the shower, Kathy and Alex were driving by Victoria Lawns cemetery, where Tammy was buried. The sight they saw there caused them to pull to the side of the road. They were certain they saw Paul's Nissan amid the headstones and granite memorials. The couple waited in the shade of the tall trees that lined the street that bordered the cemetary, and sure enough, Paul's car pulled out of the driveway. Paul saw Alex and Kathy as he was pulling out. He waved, then pulled up alongside their Pathfinder. The couple noticed that Paul was sporting a great tan and was smiling broadly, obviously in good spirits, "Aren't you supposed to be in Toronto?" they asked.

"Oh, no, I went down to Florida for spring break," Paul said, as though their impromptu conversation, there beneath trees shading a cemetery, was the most natural thing in the world.

"Well, what were you doing?" Alex and Kathy asked.

"Oh, that was my bachelor party. We had a wild bachelor party," Paul explained.

Alex and Kathy were stunned. It wasn't until later that Paul confided he didn't want one of his friends to find out Karla would be alone for a week. Paul claimed he was worried Steve Smirnis was going to move in on her. But the notion that Paul's best friend's brother, who was married, would try to seduce Karla in Paul's absence seem preposterous to Alex and Kathy. Later, however, they learned that Paul even forbade Karla from seeing Alex unless Paul was present. It appeared Paul's paranoia about his friends cut a wide swath.

Paul often bad-mouthed his Scarborough friends to Alex. Van Smirnis, his brother Steve, and the rest of the guys came in for fairly regular bashing. The scenario was always the same: They hadn't done something smart, or they had done something Paul would have done differently had he been there. For Paul, it seemed always to be an exercise in building himself up by tearing others down. Alex realized there was always the potential for Paul to be doing likewise to him, but he somehow felt their relationship was based more on mutual respect. And certainly Paul seemed determined to impress Alex, and often emulated him.

In some ways, Alex wondered whether he was the kind of person Paul strove to be; a marine honor guard, confident, pleasant, popular, all without lording it over other people, a trick Paul never quite seemed to manage. Paul was always quick to show Alex his latest possession, or to describe his latest get-rich-quick scheme. When he bought his videocassette recorder he couldn't wait for Alex to come by to show it off. "Look at this camera. Paid in full," Paul exclaimed proudly, holding the machine aloft. It was a super 8 video, and he was enthralled.

Paul seemed to have a limitless supply of money coming in. And he seemed to spend it as fast as he could get it: a four-track tape recorder with a built-in electronic drum machine to support his plan to have a rap career, exercise equipment— you name it and he bought it. "Well, what in the world are you doing with these things?" a puzzled Alex and Kathy would often ask Paul. And how was he paying for them?

Paul had a ready answer. He'd purchased them on the seedy east side of Buffalo. "I got it real cheap down there."

CHAPTER
16

Within days of Paul and Karla moving into 57 Bayview Drive, Paul and Van launched another attempt at quick money; In February 1991, and from that moment, they formed an underground partnership to smuggle low-cost cigarettes across the border and into Canada. Initially Van's idea, Paul easily agreed to the plan.

For years, Canadians returning from vacations or shopping trips to the United States for more than three days had taken advantage of their duty-free status to legally pick up the maximum allowable two hundred cigarettes when they were crossing from the American border cities of Detroit, Buffalo, Niagara Falls, Port Huron, and other cities and towns into Canada. Picking up cigarettes and booze was a must-do for all Canadians; those who didn't drink or smoke could always pass on the cut-rate savings to an older brother or uncle.

Ironically, most of the cigarettes and booze were manufactured in Canada and exported to the United States, but general increases in so-called "sin" taxes saw Canadians paying more for their own product than the Americans were paying. At one point in the late-1980s, when the Canadian dollar exchange was almost at a par with Canadian currency, Canadians could cross the border and buy the same booze and cigarettes sold in Canada for half price or less. After Canada's federal government added the hated 7 percent goods-and-services tax to almost every purchase, citing the need to slash the mounting national debt, it wasn't only cigarettes and booze but almost every purchase that could be had cheaper in the United States. Shopping mall parking lots in Niagara Falls, Buffalo, Amherst, and Tonawanda, and elsewhere across New York State were packed with cars bearing Ontario plates. It was often joked in American circles that K mart's famous "Welcome K mart shoppers" had been replaced by "Welcome Canadian shoppers." New York State residents, jealous of the apparent wealth of the northern invaders, called them "Northern Dorks." A common joke among waitresses and waiters in Buffalo restaurants was: What is the difference between a Canadian and a canoe? Canoes tip!

At the outset, Van justified his foray into cigarettes by saying he was just providing a service for the smoking population. He asked himself what was so wrong with just bringing cigarettes across the border. Why was that deemed so morally reprehensible when in real terms it was the cigarette manufacturers who were doing the most damage by producing goods that ruined people's lungs, caused cancer, and in many cases, brought on death. Paul never gave a damn about the ethical and moral question over smuggling; he saw it both as a chance to make money and another opportunity to screw the society that hadn't given him what he should have had.

When they started smuggling, Van and Paul were not linked with mobs or gangs. It was their old scam friend Gord who had told Van of the potential involved in cigarette running. All you needed, Gord advised, were some reliable clients. At first, they were fetching cigarettes for Don, a man whom Van had met at his parents' restaurant in Markham. Don made an open-ended deal in which Van and Paul would buy the cigarettes across the border for $10 U.S. and sell them to him in Canada for $25 a carton Canadian. At these prices, Don reasoned, they could make $500 to $600 a week and he could make his cut at the wholesale end. Van mapped out the operation: Paul would buy the cigarettes on the American side and transfer them to hiding places in his Nissan, such as a specially designed speaker box and in the interior side panels; Paul would bring them through the border crossing and re-transfer the cigarettes to Van's truck for the trip to Markham.

It was small stuff, about forty-five to eighty cartons a week. In that first foray, the pals were so bold that they put their cigarette purchases on their credit cards. Because of his clean-cut looks, his nice car, and because he and Van had always thought up a great story as to his whereabouts in the United States, Paul was able to bring the contraband through without any problem.

Small time suddenly turned into big bucks after a month or so, when Don's main client, Johnny, approached Van directly. Johnny, a shrewd-minded contraband entrepreneur who had close links to the Markham chapter of the Paradise Rider bikers, not only offered to pay Van $26 per carton, but he also offered to put up the up-front cash. Johnny immediately asked for two hundred cartons weekly and handed over $4,500 cash for the purchase. Van visited a friend at a bank who exchanged the cash into American funds at a preferential rate without any potential for tracing. Van didn't know what the banker's scheme was and didn't really care. He was getting his action. The pals followed a routine that would become boringly familiar. Van would drive to St. Catharines and give the money to Paul, who in turn would drive to Youngstown, New York, to purchase tax-free cigarettes from Smokin' Joe's outlet. Paul would then drive back across the border and on to Burlington, where, in the most nerve-racking part of the transaction, he would meet Van off Kerr Street in the parking lot of The Keg restaurant. There, under cover of darkness, the two would retrieve the cigarettes from the hiding places and load them into garbage bags and into Van's car. Van and Paul always worried someone would twig that there's something strange about two people exchanging garbage in suburban Oakville late at night. The pair made $1,000 tax-free between them in that first week, the first real money Paul had seen in quite some time. They were not only living on the edge of excitement but were also enjoying drinks, dinners, the most expensive clothes. Who could ask for anything more? Van thought idly. It was perfect timing for Paul, who had arranged to move into the rented house at 57 Bayview Avenue that same month.

As the financial stakes increased, Paul and Van agreed that

their best cover would be if Paul and Karla were to go on the runs together to create the impression of a loving, young middle-class couple returning from a date. When the customs officer asked where they'd been, Paul would answer they'd been for dinner, to a bar, or to a movie, sometimes buying this little thing or that little thing, sometimes not. Karla sometimes wore her sexiest outfits to make sure a male customs guard's eyes would be on her and not probing the car. The explanations and stories evolved over many hours of planning between Van and Paul. Karla did not ask too many questions about the cigarette running, but when it was first explained by Paul and Van her eyes lit up, especially when Paul predicted the volume of money the scheme would produce in the future.

To accommodate the larger loads of cigarettes, Paul and Van needed more hiding spaces. They dismantled the Nissan's interior, hoping to find every little nook and cranny they could hide a carton or even a broken-down carton. Paul measured the two interior compartment spaces by the backseat and found he could get about twenty cartons in each one. Another forty cartons could be stuffed into both the right and left panels of the hatchback. All told, Paul's Nissan could be stuffed with two hundred cartons on each border trip. The rookie smugglers made two trips weekly, which gave them weekly revenue of $2,200 tax free. Because of his biker connections, Johnny could distribute whatever Van and Paul could deliver.

After a time, the smugglers were adept at picking and choosing the most opportune times to cross the border. They avoided what was called "zero hour," between 6 P.M. and 7 P.M., when Canada Customs agents were said to routinely pull over every third car. The intelligence came from a woman who worked at the checkpoints whom Paul had met and befriended. The woman had no idea Paul and Van were smuggling thousands of dollars under her nose, but she offered them safe passage back to Canada if they came through her booth. She also gave them knowledge of selected high-intensity checktimes that often coincided with source tips that big shipments were being brought across. Paul noted his friend's shift schedule and the inspection station she would be working and made a point of driving through her checkpoint. Paul became intimately familiar with the various border systems. He knew, for example, that both Canadian and American customs officers could enter license plate numbers into a shared computer and the information could be recalled at any time. On the first trip of any day, he watched hawk-like through the checkpoint booth's slightly darkened glass to watch if the customs agent was logging his number. He knew if the plate wasn't punched into the system he could make a return run without concern. If, however, the information was entered, he would either have to come up with a viable excuse for the repeated foray or skip the sequel trip.

Initially, Van held all the cards. As long as he kept Johnny and Paul apart then he controlled the price and the profit. Van also figured it was safer for everyone if Paul, the mule, didn't ever meet Johnny, the money man. It also protected him, the middle man, being dumped by Paul and Johnny if they ever met and decided it was best to establish a direct link. One night, however, after Johnny dropped his paying price from $27 to $25 a carton, Paul accused Van of skimming cash off the top. Van arranged a meeting with Johnny at the garage outside Van's parents' restaurant. Johnny showed up at 5 A.M. and assured Paul that Van had been telling the truth.

Paul turned up the volume on his tape deck and laughed: "Face down, ass up, that's the way we like to fuck," the familiar 2 Live Crew rap chant blasted from the speakers. It was a damp evening in March 1991 and Paul, Van, and the boyish Jason were in a carefree mood after just having cleared customs at the Niagara Falls border on their way to Daytona Beach for a celebration of what Van had decided would be Paul's Bachelor Party. Gus had left earlier in his Jeep with two other friends, Dave and Mark, and planned to link up with them at the Marriott.

Van didn't care about the probable $3,000 cost of the party because it would be financed by the bulging cigarette smuggling profits he and Paul had made on the first few border runs. Van thought of this trip more as a hedonistic celebration of great business acumen than a pre-wedding ritual for his old buddy. Van and Paul were keeping their smuggling a secret from even their closest friends, but Jason, only 16, realized something extraordinary was going on between Paul and Van the previous night when Paul arrived at Van's parents' home in the Nissan 240 SX. He noticed scores of cartons of cigarettes in the back of Paul's car.

"Don't ask," cautioned Paul, when Jason's eyes laid on the cigarettes. So he didn't. He thought simply that Paul had laid his hands on some stolen or smuggled cigarettes and had brought them for Van's restaurant. Certainly nothing out of the ordinary.

After loading up whatever space was left in the car with cheap booze, purchased across the border in Niagara Falls, New York, Paul, Van and Jason headed for Florida.

Until this moment, the impressionable Jason hadn't realized just how reckless Paul could be. Paul was outspoken, if not down right rebellious, but was amazed at the breakneck speed Paul maintained on the interstate and at how he wove in and out of traffic without much regard for anything or anybody.

As they flew along the highway at about 100 MPH, Paul urged Jason to videotape him at the wheel. As Jason rolled the camera, Paul gave a running colour commentary on where they were and how fast they were going. Paul led a charmed life; he seemed to believe that he could do anything and get away with it.

As Paul drove on, he and Van talked of the party they would have when they reached Florida. Unlike their other trips, when money was a bit scarce, now they had real cash in their pockets. Like the other years, they schemed about how they would tell unsuspecting women they were not the typical drunken college fraternity boys of Daytona Beach, but successful business entrepreneurs who were on the verge of making it onto Lifestyles of the Rich and Famous. Unlike the previous year, they left their finely-tailored Huge Boss "gigolo" suits behind because there wasn't enough space in the car. This year they would depend on their Ralph Lauren, Nautica and Giorgio Armani casuals. They joked that there were almost as many bottles of after shave in the car as bottles of booze. Paul and Van knew from experience that the type of young women who showed up at Daytona Beach on March break would be suckered by image. Daytona girls, Paul said, were just as interested in getting drunk and getting laid as Daytona guys. Jason slept for eight hours.

They drove all night and most of the next day, arriving at the Marriott Hotel in the late afternoon. Gus, Dave and Mark had seen the threesome arrive and met them at the doors. Within minutes of checking in, Paul and Van had arranged a huge bar in their room and, after washing their bleary eyes, readied themselves for some heavy duty partying. Van felt everything was going fine until Paul suddenly started ranting and raving, screaming obscenities about Jason this and Jason that.

"Hey buddy, what's up?"

"Where the fuck's my jacket. That fucking idiot Jason just took my jacket," Paul shouted, standing before Van clutching Jason's windbreaker. Van couldn't understand why Paul continued his verbal attack over an inexpensive windbreaker.

This was typical of Paul, of course; he wanted everything organized, everything just right, everything Paul's way. He mumbled and grumbled, but ultimately put on Jason's windbreaker to go out that night. He was still fuming as he walked from bar to bar, saying he would have much rather had his own jacket.

They were a curious bunch: Paul, 26, Van, 25 and Jason, sixteen, in one room; Dave, 18, Mark, 19, Gus, 20, in another room. And yet the age difference was hardly noticable because Paul and Van preferred to act like 19 year olds. Paul liked women to think he was younger and often lied about his age. When he hung around with the younger guys, women automatically believed he was younger.

This allowed Paul access to much younger women than if his social group was much his own age. The boys from Lindsay, all of them quite wealthy, thought of Paul not as a role model, but as a fun guy to join for a party. At only age 16, Jason felt that, at the age of 26, Paul should have his shit together much better. What is he doing renting a house when he could be owning a house? Why didn't he try harder for his accounting exam? Still, they all admired Paul for the way he dressed, the car he drove and the way he moved in on girls.

Paul had an uncanny knack of being able to analyse a woman's personality, and change chameleon-like into whatever role he had to play. In all the times Jason watched Paul at work with women, he never heard him use the same line twice. Over the next few days, Paul and Van spun their fictitious yarns of being rich big shots with some of Canada's major corporations. American women, whose idea of Canada essentially consisted of the Toronto Blue Jays, Canadian Club, mounties and eskimos, lapped up almost every lie they told about their social standing in their home country.

On the second or third day in Daytona Beach, Gus, Van and Paul, accompanied by Jason, wore their designer label casuals and took a cab to Club 104, a popular night club on Highway A1A on the beach strip. From previous visits, Paul and Van knew this was where all the American women liked to hang out.

Pretty and perky Alyson, who was in Daytona Beach for a fun weekend with her best friend and nursing colleague Kim and another girl, was returning from the Club 104 washroom when she found Kim dancing with four cute guys. "Wow," Alyson said to herself. "Way to go Kim." She surveyed the four guys: Van, the huge blond guy with the teddy bear grin; Gus, the hairy Mediterranean looking one; Jason, the little boy with the child face; and Paul, the cute blue-eyed blond guy with the infectious love-me smile. She was immediately taken by Paul's looks and charm and was jealous of Kim. It was Paul who had approached Kim and asked her to dance with him, but after a few songs Kim gravitated to Van, which left Paul with Alyson. Alyson admired Paul's dancing as they gyrated together on the dance floor, Paul swivelling his hips unlike any guy she'd ever seen, almost as if he was disjointed. Sweating, heaving bodies crowded the floor, men and women losing themselves in the music, the booze and each other. All around Alyson, guys edged closer to their female partners, rubbing thigh against thigh and buttock to buttock. They had done it to her earlier that night. Yet, unlike the others, Paul kept his distance; he was a perfect gentleman. Alyson was no virgin, nor was she a prude, but she was a modern woman and appreciated a man who showed respect. Alyson felt an intense attraction to Paul; she loved his blue eyes, his boyish grin and his smooth and soft Canadian accent.

Van and Paul smiled at each other when the girls went to the washroom together. They couldn't believe this dual catch. Paul openly salivated to Van about what he would like to do with Alyson's body.

"What about Karla? Van asked Paul above the beat of the dance music.

"Karla who?" asked Paul.

"Karla! Your future wife!" said Van.

"Fuck her," Paul retorted. "She isn't here."

As Karla slept back in Port Dalhousie, Paul and Van played their games of lies with Kim and Alyson. Everybody likes to think they are special, and on this night the Bigger Better Deal move was being played on the unwitting southern girls, who at this stage had no reason to be anything but happy to play along.

"How old are you?" Alyson shouted into Paul's ear above the din of the music.

"Twenty one," he replied.

Alyson looked at the boyish face and thought for a moment he was telling the truth. But she stopped for a moment: this guy had more self-confidence and more control than any 21-year-old she'd ever seen. Besides, where would someone that young get all that money? She didn't believe him. Kim had heard their chatter, and took her own guess.

"I think you're 22. Am I right?"

Paul smiled. He wouldn't say.

Then it was Paul's turn to ask the questions. The girls readily answered they were nurses from Columbia, the capital city of South Carolina, worked bizarre shifts at the Lexington Medical Centre, from 7 A.M. to 3 P.M., or 3 P.M. to 11 P.M., or, worst of all, 11 P.M. to 7 A.M. And they talked of how they didn't have boyfriends and were in Daytona to have some fun for March break, just like everybody else.

"So what do you do for a living in Canada?" asked Alyson, curious to know more about this interesting guy.

"I own my own business."

"What kind of business?"

"Just my own business."

Paul smiled, but he wouldn't elaborate. Alyson felt as if he was teasing her. Obviously, from the way he was throwing money around and from the trendy designer clothes he wore, this guy was a somebody. As they talked, Paul remained vague, if not secretive, about his occupation. Alyson decided not to press him, after all, she knew this relationship would be superficial from start to finish. She sighed: this was a fun weekend. Here was Paul, sexy, charming, funny, and generous. She would dance with him, yes, maybe get drunk with him, maybe go as far as to have casual sex with him, but anything beyond that she would leave to fate.

As the bar closed, Van and Paul followed Kim and Alyson outside and as the girls looked for the Grand Prix their friend had loaned them for the night, Paul called out to her.

"Hey, we don't have our car. Can you give us a ride?"

Kim and Alyson pondered whether they should let the guys ride in the borrowed car, but relented when Paul suggested they could go to the nightclub in the Marriott and then drink their faces off in their room. After a few dances in the nightclub, Paul and Van led their quarry upstairs to the hotel room and soon thereafter the pairs retired to the two beds and tried their best to muffle their clumsy sexual acts. Alyson and Kim felt odd doing these things in the same room, but it was nothing new for their partners.

The next night, Paul and Alyson and Van and Kim were standing in a long lineup outside a popular dance bar for what seemed like hours when a young American man in the lineup made a passing comment to his buddies about how good Alyson looked in her tight top and jeans. Alyson responded by putting one hand behind her head and the other on her hip and smiled, as if posing for a photograph. She returned her eyes to Paul's face to see an angry glare.

"Do you want to be with him, or do you want to be with me," he said firmly, looking her dead in the eyes. "You just have no respect for me. If you want to be with me, you're going to respect me."

Alyson was taken aback. Within a few minutes, she asked Kim to go with her to the bathroom.

"Kim, I don't know what happened to him. He just bit my head off. It was so weird. I like Paul and I want to be with him . . . I was just playing with that guy," she said.

The friends returned to the lineup to see Paul slumped against a railing. Van was getting drinks from the bar, so Kim went off to find him. Paul looked deflated.

"What's wrong Paul?" asked Alyson.

He wouldn't speak and turned his head away. Confused, Alyson pulled away herself. To hell with him, she thought. If he doesn't want to talk to me I'll find somebody else who will.

Then she noticed tears welling in Paul's eyes; one rolled down a cheek and dripped to the ground.

"Paul, what's wrong?"

"I'm thinking about my sister . . .", he said, his words trailing off into his sobbing.

"What about your sister?"

Paul's eyes were now filled with tears. He shook his head, wiped his eyes on a sleeve and sniffed. Alyson, the caring nurse she was, stook closer to him and reached out to touch his shoulder. Paul related the story about his sister, Tammy; who was gone; how she had choked on her vomit in the middle of the night.

"I was down the hall. I heard her. But when I got there it was too late . . . by the time I got there, she died in my arms," Paul cried on her shoulder. "I'm sorry, something made me think of her."

Alyson was almost shaking. No wonder he is upset. She felt a wave of sympathy for this man whom she had slept with but still hardly knew. She didn't know what to say.

As they reached the door, Kim and Van appeared and the four went inside together. Van listened as Paul continued to tell Alyson about his dead sister. Van couldn't comprehend why Paul was relating this morose story about Tammy, especially when passing her off as his own sister. Obviously, Van concluded, Paul's strategy was to bond with Alyson by sharing one of his worst experiences with her. Kim and Alyson were anxious to know more about Tammy's death, so Paul related the entire story of Christmas Eve. Van watched as Kim and Alyson, the nurses who had experienced many people, mostly the elderly, die in their arms, poured out their hearts to Paul. Alyson seemed to completely forget about the jealous outburst outside. In what seemed a few minutes, Paul and she were dancing and drinking and he seemed to get over his sorrow. She felt good she'd helped return him to the world of the living.

The foursome returned to Van and Paul's room for drinks and again they split into separate beds and slept the night. The next morning, as the girls readied to return to Columbia, Paul and Van asked them to return to Daytona Beach the next weekend. The girls passed it off, saying the drive was seven hours and just too far. They left, thinking they would see the last of Paul and Van. That night when Alyson and Kim returned home to their apartment, the telephone rang. It was Paul. He promised to get a separate room if she would come down the next weekend. Alyson liked that idea; she hadn't felt comfortable sleeping with Paul with the others in the same room. He also offered Alyson that on Tuesday night he would drive her back to Columbia in his car and Kim and Van could ride in Kim's car. It sounded fun, and Alyson and Kim agreed they would drive straight to Florida when their night-shift ended Friday and spend Saturday and Sunday nights with their new Canadian boyfriends. Meanwhile in Daytona, Paul and Van were wondering how long they would keep their latest girlfriends, who they'd picked up that day.

"Paul's tickled pink. He's flying through the air like Peter Pan."

Van laughed.

Arriving in Daytona Beach at 7 A.M., Alyson knocked on the hotel room door.

"I can't believe we did this," she said to Kim.

Paul answered with his video camera in his hand. Van and Kim jumped into bed and Paul and Alyson went to their bed. Within a few hours, they were all up, partying as if there was no tomorrow. At one point, Paul and Alyson checked at reception to get a separate room. As Paul tugged a credit card from his wallet, his driver's license fell to the floor. Anxious to find out his real age, Alyson snatched it and read the birthdate.

"Hey, let's see how old you really are," she kidded.

"So you're really 25 . . . why does it bother you so much?" she asked.

He didn't answer, as usual.

While they partied in the main room that day, Van inadvertently mentioned Karla in front of Alyson and Kim.

"So who's Karla?" Alyson quizzed Paul.

"A friend of my dead sister," he responded, a cold expression on his face.

That night, Paul and Alyson left the others and made for their own room. They were no sooner in the room when Paul kissed her hard and forcefully stripped her, completely ignoring the foreplay she had come to expect in intimate situations. She was lying on the bed, naked, expecting that he would mount her and they would experience their first unbridled lovemaking. But it didn't happen. Instead, he told Alyson he wanted anal sex and simultaneously turned her tiny body over. Okay, she said, partly out of curiosity and partly thinking they would do that for a while then move on to something else. She rose to her knees and felt his penis penetrate her anus. At first it hurt, but the pain subsided as this new pleasure swept over her. He moaned, then as he began thrusting told her: "Say you love me!" She ignored him at first, thinking she isn't going to say it if it wasn't true. The thrusting became harder.

"Say you love me!"

Thinking she'd play along with his sex games, she mouthed the words.

"I love you! I love you!"

With each thrust, Paul became rougher and recited his order: "Say you love me. Say you love me. Say you love me . . ."

It was uncomfortable for Alyson. The game was getting out of hand and she wanted him to stop.

"Paul, you are hurting me!"

But when he didn't stop, she wanted to scream.

"Paul, you gotta stop; you gotta quit," she shouted.

He withdrew. Alyson didn't know if her sex partner had reached orgasm, nor did she care, but she wasn't satisfied and was anxious to have him inside her, the normal way. She had driven a long way to be with this guy and she wanted satisfaction. To complete her frustration, Paul rolled over onto his back and closed his eyes. She kissed him and put her head on his chest for a while. Within seconds he was asleep. Alyson couldn't believe Paul didn't even want to curl up with her, feel their bodies together, kiss and perhaps have sex. Fearing she would get the cold shoulder all night, she moved over to the other bed. She was tense but tired. She couldn't believe this was the same man who had made her feel such pleasure the weekend before. She passed into a cautious slumber feeling resentment towards her beautiful yet strange Canadian lover.

When Alyson awoke the next morning, Paul was a sweet as he could possibly be. She thought the night before had been weird, but she didn't want to raise the issue of her frustration at that point. That morning, Paul told Alyson he wanted to videotape her naked.

"Are you crazy?"

He didn't force the issue and Alyson believed he was just teasing.

As promised, Paul drove Alyson and Kim drove Van back to Columbia that Tuesday. Gus and Jason followed in the Jeep.

Gus, Mark, Dave and Jason left for Toronto while Paul and Van spent two more nights at the condo before leaving. At that point, the holiday couples were too bushed from partying to do anything exciting. They exchanged addresses and more telephone numbers and headed north.

On the way home, Paul asked Van: "So what do we tell Karla about these two extra days."

Van had an ample list of possible excuses for the delay: car trouble, lost the map, took the wrong route and on and on. They became lost on Interstate 77 in Tennessee because Paul was driving like the wind trying to make up time and get back for Karla. In West Virginia, a blue Camaro pulled alongside their car in the darkness.

"Hey, this guy wants to race you, Paul."

Paul floored the gas peddle and within seconds the speedometer nudged 110 MPH.

Suddenly, blue flashing lights came on.

"Oh my god it's a cop," Van yelled.

The state trooper came towards the stopped car, gun in hand. He ordered them out of the car and frisked them before handcuffing Paul.

"What's the matter, officer," Paul asked in a demure voice.

"You know what's the matter," the trooper answered.

"You were going 110 MPH, slightly more than the 55 MPH speed limit."

Paul was arrested and took his place in the Camaro and Van followed the unmarked car back to Beckley, West Virginia, where Paul was booked into a cell. An officer told Van he should find some bail money or Paul would spend at least three days in jail.

Deflated at their ill luck, Van went for dinner and by chance ran into a local businessman, who guessed that Van was either in Beckley because he had relatives in town or because he was in some kind of trouble. Van explained the situation. To his surprise, the businessman knew the police officer. Van bought the man dinner, not realizing he not only owned the restaurant but the building it was in. After dinner, the businessman drove Van around town, showing him his developments and the kind of grants Van could get from the state government to set himself up in business in the town. At one point, he even offered Van a job running the restaurant. They ended up at the man's office, where he made a call to a local judge and relayed that Van was willing to pay bail. At 11 P.M. that night, Paul was taken from his cell to a courthouse and freed on minimal bail.

On the way home, Paul told Van the worn and torn jail inmates, both white and black, were betting cigarettes on who would be the first to have Paul's tight ass. Paul tried to back them off by claiming he was pumping iron.

"I was flipping out in there, Paul said.

While driving through Pennsylvania, Paul related to Van his ideas and dreams for a career in rap music.

"Rap music is where it's at, man," he said, telling Van that he should get involved with Paul in creating an all-white rap band, with Van doing some of the singing.

He told of being intrigued at the rap scene, of how it was too pro-black and there was a need for white rappers. In his opinion, blacks were not as smart as whites, and whites were about to take the rap scene by storm. Paul's inspiration was Vanilla Ice, who had made it good in the rap scene and seemed to have girls dripping off each arm. And he did it with minimal talent. They talked for hours about image and potential names and began rapping lyrics as they drove around. They tossed around potential names. Van came up with White Hype, suggesting it was rap's equivalent of Anthony Robbins and Tommy Vu.

As soon as Paul and Van arrived at 57 Bayview Drive, Paul broke open the video camera and showed Karla the videotape of him and Van horsing around with Kim and Alyson and the bikini-clad girls on the beach.

"I gotta show Karla the videotape right here, in front of you, so none of you guys will have anything over me," he said. "I have to show it to her."

"It's okay Paul, really," Van argued.

"No come on, sit down. Watch the tape. I'm going to play it."

The tape showed the group in various stages of drunkeness, horsing around with bikini-clad women, dancing with them, hugging them and kissing them. At one point, the picture showed a couple of bodies twisting against each other under the bedsheets. Paul said nothing, but Van knew it had to be Paul and Alyson. While Paul laughed at his own antics, Karla stared at the TV screen, saying nothing while it played and "thanks, Paul, for showing it to me."

The next night, Paul called Alyson. They talked about going to work and Paul told her they'd see each other again. She thought that would be nice, but didn't think it would really happen. Paul didn't call again, unlike Van, who kept in close contact with Kim. A couple of months later, Kim flew to Buffalo, where Van met her with his brother Steve and they stayed at his house in Niagara Falls, N.Y. Alyson had initially wanted to come to Canada, but decided against it because Paul hadn't called her and on one occasion she'd called him and a girl had answered the telephone. She did reach Paul once, and he told her Karla was his cousin or his sister. Alyson's last words to Kim as she left had been to make sure she retrieved the video that Paul took at Daytona Beach.

Within a day or two of Kim's arrival, Van told Kim they would go over to Paul's house. On the way there, Van confessed to Kim that he and Paul made their living from cigarette smuggling. He also confessed to Kim that Paul's fiancée, Karla, lived with him and had lived with him since February, the month before they had all met in Florida. He told Kim she would likely meet Karla, because wherever Paul was, Karla was sure to be. Kim had known something was fishy with Paul, but she was astounded that Paul could put up such a convincing front. She felt terrible at his betrayal of Alyson. She decided to go along with it to keep the peace with Van, whom she had taken quite a liking to even though she didn't hold out much hope for their long-distance romance.

When Van and Kim pulled up at 57 Bayview Drive, Kim was surprised to see it was close to Lake Ontario and similar in structure to what Paul had described while they were in Florida, except of course for the relatively minor detail that his fiancée also lived there. Paul met them at the door and ushered them in. As Kim glanced around the house she noticed it was immaculately clean, but it was almost devoid of furniture. And suddenly, Karla was before her, a beautiful face with an exquisite smile, dressed casually but still trendy. Paul introduced her as his sister, and, for whatever reason, Karla went along with it. Her first impression of Karla was of someone who was retiring, shy, nervous, but not someone who would be so insecure within herself as to deny her relationship. Within minutes Van and Kim had drinks in their hands. Then came the shot glasses. It was as if the drunkfest of Florida were being repeated all over again, and within an hour or so they were half-bombed.

One of the first items of decor Kim had noticed was the large portrait hanging over the fireplace of a young blonde girl. She assumed this must be Paul's dead sister, but she wasn't quite sure. As the night wore on, she noticed other smaller pictures, one atop the television, others sporadically placed around the house. Karla did not ask Kim anything about Florida and Kim had resolved not to ask Karla about her relationship with Paul.

They were sitting around in a circle on the living room carpet, Kim laughing in disbelief at yet another strange caper Paul and Van were telling her they'd pulled, when Paul suddenly stood up and grabbed the photograph from atop the television. Kim looked at it closer now, realizing the girl was indeed not only very beautiful but very young, perhaps 13 or 14. Paul lifted the bottle of tequila and tipped it into the shot glasses around him.

"A toast to Tammy."

Paul lifted his glass, first Karla, then Van lifted theirs. She followed.

"Tammy!" came the chorus.

Kim looked at Paul as he picked the photograph up with both hands and stared into the girl's eyes. She put his melancholic mood down to the drink. As she watched, his lip quivered as if he were about to cry. He continued talking about Tammy in a monotone dialogue aimed at nobody but himself, telling of her beauty, of how she should never have died. Kim looked at Van, who seemed just as perplexed. An eerie silence set over the room.

CHAPTER
17

As Paul and Karla's wedding approached, they began to rely more and more on Alex and Kathy for help and support. The friends helped bring programs and other wedding accoutrements across the border in Alex's Pathfinder. Kathy helped Karla pick out the wedding dress and veil.

Paul often complained that none of his friends cared about this wedding, that they weren't doing their "duty."

"Everyone had a duty," Alex recalls.

Alex and Kathy were apparently doing their duty, because Paul sometimes praised them indirectly by running down their other friends.

In the weeks before the wedding, Kathy spoke to her parents about wanting to host a get-together for Paul and Karla. Their apartment in Lewiston simply wasn't big enough and there was a pool at the Wilson house, and, well, it would be much more convenient and likely more fun if they could all come out to the Wilson's comfortable home in Niagara-on-the-Lake.

Stan and Lynda agreed without hesitation. They, too, liked a good party and were fond of Karla. Their feelings for Paul were slightly more ambiguous, but they planned with Alex and Kathy how best to host the Jack-and-Jill party for their friends.

Lynda spent several days before the party preparing salads and garnishes. They'd also purchased a nice barbecue and a set of lawn furniture for the young couple, which she and Stan had gone to the trouble of setting up in the garage. They blew up balloons and hung them from the gifts, planning to unveil them by opening the garage door. Both Stan and Lynda were pleased with their preparations and looked forwad to the whole production with great anticipation.

There were about twenty people in the Wilsons' surburban backyard, mingling and chatting, eating food, teasing Paul and Karla about their impending big day. Dorothy and Karel Homolka were also there but seemed to be unnaturally quiet and withdrawn. Lynda initially felt there was some tension between the Homolkas and Paul and Karla, but then she concluded that it was still the aftershocks of losing Tammy and proceeded to chat with Karel and Dorothy briefly.

Also out of sorts that night was Karla, who seemed quiet and withdrawn, even cold.

"That night of any night she looked very pale," Alex recalls. "Very, very distant from everybody. She wasn't her happy, cheery self."

Her mood sparked a number of comments throughout the night, as did the observation that Karla had several nasty bruises on her left arm.

"Oh, those look sore. What happened?" Lynda asked.

Karla dismissed the angry marks by saying that she'd been scratched by a dog at the animal clinic. "It happens all the time," she said. Lynda was skeptical. The bruises ran all up and down Karla's arm.

Both Lisa and Kathy noticed the angry bruises and instantly thought of the bruises they'd seen on Karla's back while she was getting fitted for her wedding dress across the border. Kathy could barely take her eyes off of the marks, which seemed almost to be the shadows of someone's angry grip.

Kathy, too, asked what had happened.

"You know how easily I bruise, Kathy. I was gardening," Karla explained nonchalantly.

There was no further explanation.

Later in the evening as the food was being served, Paul's

friends from Scarborough arrived en masse. There was Gus and Van and Steve and his wife, their friend Arrif, and the whole crew. Instantly, Paul's demeanor changed. He herded the group into a corner of the yard and held court. Clearly he was the leader of the noisy, hyper bunch.

At one point as Lynda ventured near the group, she overheard Paul telling Gus in a fatherly voice, "Someday, you too will have your own sex slave."

She was mortified. Assuming Paul was talking about Karla, she thought it was perhaps the tackiest thing she'd ever heard, especially at a Jack-and-Jill party to celebrate the upcoming wedding.

After the food had been devoured, Alex and Kathy and Stan and Lynda decided it was time to unveil the presents. They gathered the group in front of the garage doors and, using a remote-control opener, slid the door up to reveal the furniture and barbecue arranged as though it were actually in a backyard. There were balloons everywhere. It looked great.

But the response was devastatingly understated. A couple of quiet thank-yous were all the guests of honor were able to muster.

Shortly after, Paul and his friends started getting even rowdier, throwing each other in the pool and yelling loudly. Stan and Lynda, still smarting from Paul and Karla's painfully rude indifference to their guests, figured they'd played good hosts long enough and suggested strongly that the party was over and that they could carry on someplace else if they wanted.

The group left in an orderly fashion and headed back to Paul and Karla's home in Port Dalhousie. There, things proceeded to get pretty much out of hand.

Paul brought Buddy the Rottweiler out of the basement and tied his leash to the back door leading from the tidy kitchen to the backyard so he wouldn't jump on the guests. But as was Buddy's custom when he was excited, he peed on the kitchen floor.

"Karla, clean that mess up," Paul barked.

"Why don't you clean it up, Paul, you're standing right

there," Lisa Stanton asked as she walked by him in the kitchen. "There's a cloth right here."

This was Paul's domain, and it was evident in the way he shouted out orders to his fiancée that the rules of the house had been clearly established and were to be followed without deviation.

Lisa had taken to watching the couple's dynamics closely since hearing the "bitch" nickname over and over and seeing the bruises on her friend's arm.

"Come on, bitch, get these people some drinks," he said at one point.

"Hey, Paul, why don't you do it. You're right there," Lisa suggested, not in an aggressive manner but in a matter-of-fact tone.

"Oh, it's okay, she's already doing it. It's okay," he said, slightly taken aback.

Lisa, who was becoming increasingly angered, snapped back, "Why don't you let her enjoy the party, Paul?"

Looking as though he'd been caught doing something he shouldn't have, Paul became instantly penitent, turning to Karla and giving her a big hug and a kiss. Still, Lisa couldn't help but feel that the show of affection was to placate her, not his soon-to-be bride.

Later, Lisa and Karla were in the kitchen washing shot glasses in a vain attempt to keep up with the heavy drinking that had started shortly after their arrival at the Port Dalhousie home. Even then, Paul's voice could be heard booming out from the living room.

"Karla! We don't have any shot glasses," he'd yell into the kitchen, presumably prompting her to wash faster.

At one point later in the evening, Lisa and Paul were sitting at a table talking and drinking tequila. The fact that she, a girl, could keep up with him in liquor consumption seemed to raise his impression of her as a human being perceptibly.

While it didn't matter a hoot to Lisa whether Paul was impressed or not, it was clear he was.

In another room, the state of Paul and Karla's relationship, always a topic for Karla's friends, was taking on a serious tone as Kathy cornered Steve Smirnis and asked him what he thought of the bruises and how haggard Karla looked.

"What's really going on with these two?" Kathy demanded of Paul's old friend. "Look at the sides of her arms, the backs of her arms! What is going on? You've got to know!" Kathy asked.

The implication of Kathy's question was clear: Did Steve know Paul was beating Karla.

Steve seemed incredulous.

"Oh no, I don't think so. Do you think so?"

"Come on, Steve," an exasperated Kathy said.

"I felt like they were acting stupid and they knew and they wouldn't tell us," she says now. "I always felt that they knew. But he wouldn't say."

Paul decided to impress his guests then, by standing next to Karla and practicing karate kicks inches from her face. Over and over he'd kick, his foot brushing her face. But she never moved a muscle.

"It was really bizarre and we felt really bad for her," Alex recalls, saying Karla didn't enjoy it but that she had "this really synthetic smile, like she was trying to hide it."

It was late when the party broke up and Alex and Kathy headed back across the border to their apartment. As usual, the conversation often drifted back to Paul and Karla and just how perplexing their friends had become.

CHAPTER
18

Paul and Karla were late to their own wedding rehearsal, which was held in the same church in which Alex and Kathy had been married a few short months earlier. Dressed casually, the young people joked around that Paul and Karla weren't coming at all or had eloped or had a bad case of nerves.

The minister, Ian Grieve, was not amused.

When they did finally arrive, they were dressed casually in T-shirts and shorts. When the minister launched into a full-blown explanation of the wedding ceremony, going through each line, describing where each member of the wedding party was to stand and the meaning of the various parts of the service and the serious commitment that was about to be made by Paul and Karla, the couple whispered several jokes and issued more than a handful of audible giggles.

Nevertheless, eveyone agreed to be on their best behavior the following day, and early on the Friday evening the group escaped the church and headed for Paul and Karla's for the traditional post rehearsal party.

Alex and Kathy and Stan and Lynda were among the first to arrive at the couple's Port Dalhousie home. They were aghast to find that virtually no preparations had been made to host a party for thirty or more people, guests who were at that moment on their way.

There were no tablecloths on the table, no cutlery, no evidence of food other than some shish kebab that Karla had made earlier and deposited in the refrigerator.

"There wasn't so much as an ice cube in the house," Lynda Wilson recalls.

Stan was immediately dispatched to a nearby convenience store where he picked up munchies and other supplies. He would be forced to return to the store again before the end of the evening.

While Alex, Kathy, Stan and Lynda, and Debbie Purdie were hastily preparing the refreshments, the first wave of guests began to arrive, including Paul's grandmother and parents, who rolled up in a shiny, new Lincoln Continental Town Car. Van and Alex helped carry Grandma Eastman in her wheelchair to the top of the landing at the front stairs.

Almost immediately, Marilyn Bernardo began braying about some pieces of bronze artwork Paul had hanging in the hallway that she thought belonged to her. Alex recalls that they were pieces that were supposed to date back to the destruction of Pompeii.

"I can still remember Paul's mother yelling at Paul and Paul's grandmother about why she didn't get the two statues of the village of Pompeii," Alex says. "She was a raging lunatic."

Kathy and Alex quickly lit the barbecue to prepare for the shish kebab. It was then that Lynda noticed that Paul had exchanged the barbecue they'd given the couple at the Jack-and-Jill party only a week or so before for a larger model. She was furious!

As Paul and Karla's friends scurried around trying to make the place look presentable Lynda wondered to herself why none of Paul's family was involved in the party's preparations.

Paul's lone contribution to the party he was hosting was to haul a jar of caviar out of a cupboard and dump it on a plate.

"There, not everyone has caviar at their rehersal party!" Paul announced, obviously pleased with himself. But there were no toasts or crackers to complement the delicacy, a detail not lost on Lynda.

Stan and Lynda were run off their feet. They loaded pickles

into dishes; they took drink orders and served drinks to guests. Lynda was still recovering from ankle surgery.

Karel Homolka had positioned himself in a chair in the living room where he could enjoy scotches as quickly as Stan could deliver them.

Although he wasn't too good at actually helping out, Paul was clearly at ease giving instructions. One of the perplexing ones was that no one was to go down to the basement. The basement was off-limits, he said, because it was far too messy for anyone to see.

Within two years it would become all too clear exactly why Paul would make certain none of his guests had any inclination to go rooting around in his messy basement. Luckily for Paul, his friends were more concerned with seeing to it that the rehearsal party went smoothly.

Alex and Kathy were asked to roll and tie the programs for the next day. Although it was something that could have been done weeks earlier, Paul and Karla had left it to the last minute.

As they sat upstairs finishing them, Stan peeked in to see how they were doing, and when he did Alex and Kathy got a wicked idea.

"Nobody's upstairs, are they?" Alex asked.

No, they were alone.

"We should open the door to their office!" he suggested.

The office had always been off-limits. Ever since the couple had moved into the house, Paul had insisted that the door remain closed and that no one could go in. It was full of computers and records and business stuff, he'd explained.

"We were dying to know what was in there. So we opened it up. And this room was a pigsty!"

There were boxes of unopened books from the time of the move four months earlier. There was dust all over the computer, as though no one had ever turned it on. There were candy-bar wrappers and other refuse on the floor.

"It was as if somebody had been living in there. It was gross. It was disgusting," Kathy says.

The group quietly shut the door and finished wrapping the programs.

By midnight the guests had left, including Paul's parents, which produced an almost universal sigh of relief. Paul got out his video camera and the guys began doing mock dance steps, to the delight of the girls. Actually, Alex and Van seemed to have it down pretty well, but then Paul insisted that he help out. The routine soon evolved into his traditional puppet-man dance shuffle, which made everyone giggle quietly.

Paul and Van and some of the other guys began lobbying for a quick trip down the street to the Port Mansion tavern for a last drink. The ladies in Karla's bridal party were going to stay at the house in Port Dalhousie, while Paul's ushers and some invited guests were to stay at a hotel nearby where they'd decorate cars in the morning and dress for the wedding.

Alex was reluctant. He'd had just about enough, thank you. But Paul insisted.

After arriving at the bar, the boys from Scarborough set out in their usual patterns, seeking out and chatting with girls or simply leering at them.

Shortly before 1 A.M. the waitresses called for last orders of drinks. Soon the bar around the wedding party was filled with shots of tequila and B-52s and schnapps and glasses and bottles of beer. Alex figured there had to be $500 worth of booze on the bar.

Paul, obviously in one of his drinking modes, was quaffing shot after shot.

The group emerged from the bar and, not content to call it a night, decided to check out a club in Buffalo, New York. Within a few hundred meters of the Port Mansion, however, the two-car convoy was pulled over at a police spot check. After shining his light around the car, the cop admonished them for not having seat belts on. "Well, guys, put your seat belts on," he said.

The crew made their way to Fort Erie and then decided they'd go to Niagara Falls instead of crossing the border.

Eventually the cavalcade made it to Niagara Falls, where someone popped open the trunk and pulled out some beer and began spraying a guy named Jason McCoby, a friend whom

Paul had met in Florida, as he lay semi-conscious in the back of his car. Jason flew into a rage.

"You're screwing up my car," he screamed, then began spraying Van's car in retaliation, which quickly prompted threats of violence from Van.

The group was near the Falls when suddenly two young girls sauntered by. Paul, not surprisingly, struck up a conversation with them, and soon they were agreeing to go for a ride, one of the girls in each car.

The girl who got in the back with Jason was foulmouthed, cursing and swearing. In the other car, Paul's hands began immediately caressing the other young girl, who didn't seem to mind at all. Soon they were necking.

After driving around for a little while the cars stopped and Paul announced they were all going back to Port Dalhousie.

Alex and Andy Douglas looked at each other.

"That's just not cool," Andy said. Alex agreed. The girls were there. The wedding was only a few hours away. Definitely not cool.

Still, it was Paul's night, and he was the king. So off they went again.

They pulled up to the house and the girls, cigarettes lit, wandered in the front door, Paul close behind. Debbie Purdie and Kathy, decked out in their pajamas, were sleeping downstairs. The lights were flipped on, and within seconds loud music was blasting from Paul's stereo.

Kathy and Debbie were incredulous. "Paul brought back some girls!" they whispered.

"What's he doing?" Kathy asked Alex when they came in.

"Oh, Paul got really hammered," Alex explained.

Karla soon appeared at the top of the stairs. She looked bewildered, as though she couldn't imagine why there were strange women in her living room and a party starting up less than twelve hours before she was to be married.

Kathy began suggesting that the time for partying was over and the time for sleep was now. Paul's Toronto buddy, Arrif Mallick, began berating her.

Soon the Niagara Falls girls began complaining that this

wasn't such a good party after all. Van offered to drive them
back to Niagara Falls, but after getting only part of the way
there, he pulled over and told them to get out because they
were so drunk and bitchy.

Alex got in his truck and drove out to Kathy's parents'
house in Niagara-on-the-Lake. The rest of the guys, save
Paul, headed for the hotel.

Paul was so drunk, or appeared to be so drunk, that he crept
upstairs into his bedroom where Patti, one of the bridesmaids,
was asleep. She awoke and noticed him searching behind the
bureau in what appeared to be a cavity or secret compartment
and withdrawing a bag, the contents of which she couldn't
make out, although the girls later decided it must have been
dope.

Then he left the room, returned with Karla, and sat on the
edge of the bed next to Patti, who continued to pretend that
she was asleep. She could feel him lifting up the hem of her
nightshirt, but Karla interrupted with a stern, "No!"

"Oh, I thought it was you," he said loudly.

"But he knew damn well it wasn't her," Kathy insisted
later.

The fairy tale wedding took place the next day. Paul and
Karla rode in a horse drawn carriage, waving to the friends,
relatives, and local spectators who were captivated by the
regal procession.

The party after the lavish wedding lasted long into the
night. Monday morning, Karel and Dorothy packed Karla,
Paul, and the ubiquitous video camera off to the Buffalo air-
port only to return two weeks later to pick up the newlyweds.
Karla and Paul, tanned from their three-island honeymoon,
chatted excitedly about Hawaii. Dorothy caught them up on
everything that had happened at home while they were away.

"Oh, they identified the body of the girl they found in the
lake," Dorothy mentioned at one point.

"What girl in what lake?" Karla asked quickly.

Dorothy went on to explain that someone had discovered a
dismembered body in Lake Gibson on the very day Paul and
Karla had gotten married. It had taken some time to identify

the girl, but the police had announced it was a missing teen from Burlington named Leslie Mahaffy.

Karla and Paul continued to reminisce about Hawaii.

Not long after their return, Paul and Karla were invited to spend an evening with Alex and Kathy in Lewiston, New York. Alex and Kathy wanted to hear all about the newly-weds' honeymoon and they also had pictures and a video of their own delayed honeymoon in Jamaica which they wanted to show their friends.

Karla and Paul agreed but were, of course, late.

They gave the usual excuse for the delay; there had been a backup at the border. Alex and Kathy knew from experience that if they themselves had been crossing the border it would have been easily accomplished. Paul and Karla always seemed to get delayed at the border.

Nonetheless, the two couples were pleased to see each other after a few weeks' hiatus, Paul and Karla looking splendidly tanned and rested, and they drifted back into their traditional routine. Paul and Alex took off to Topps to pick up party supplies that included beer and some munchies.

When they got back to the Fords' tiny apartment, Paul began drinking at a furious rate. Alex and Kathy knew then that this was to be a drunk night. If there was one thing they'd learned about Paul, it was that nothing was halfway for him. If it was going to be a mellow night, he would be extremely, almost methodically mellow. If he wanted to dance, there would be full-scale, frenetic dancing. And if he was going to drink, which he did often, it was head-on drinking.

Paul and Karla began describing their honeymoon in glowing terms. They talked about how they'd avoided the expensive tourist traps and been adventurous, exploring the tropical island on their own. They caught crabs on the beach and cracked them open on volcanic rock, the surf pounding around them. They ate the crabs in their hotel room. It was all so romantic. Much later Kathy and Alex would learn that the couple was so short of money and food—and accommodations were so expensive—that they ate almost every day in

Pizza Hut and catching crabs was the only way they could enjoy a varied menu.

Paul and Karla looked longingly, lovingly at each other across the room and Karla turned to her friends and gave them the thumbs-up sign and the biggest grin they'd ever seen. It was a grin that said, *Look what I've caught. He's mine.* Paul, too, was grinning, but Alex and Kathy couldn't help but think the grin was somehow more sinister, like that of a cat that's cornered a juicy bird.

Alex and Kathy brought out their camera and the four, as was their routine, began mugging like crazy, making faces, putting rabbit ears behind each other. Paul, who was now well on his way to a resounding drunk, lay on his back on the floor, a giant can of Miller Genuine Draft resting against his pale-blue shorts, his white Hawaiian T-shirt rumpled. He looked up at a laughing Karla, giving her, once again, the thumbs-up.

After the foursome watched a videotape of Alex and Kathy's honeymoon, the drinking continued. But as was Paul's habit when he drank heavily, he began to say things he wouldn't normally say. On this night he began to attack Alex and Kathy's lifestyle in a drunken monologue. He told Alex life was passing him by. "You're living this petty life. You could be doing so much more. And Kathy bosses you around. You shouldn't take that shit. Kathy's holding you back."

His diatribe went on and on. With each passing moment, the good-natured kidding and chiding fell away to reveal a vicious, personal attack.

"These walls are closing in on you, buddy!" Paul continued.

Even Karla, who never opposed her husband in public, tried to take the edge of his tirade.

"Come on, Paul, you shouldn't say that!"

But he wouldn't be restrained.

Alex and Kathy did a slow burn as the attack moved from the comical to the personal.

"Well, Paul, I can't afford a big house like you can," Alex shot back. And soon Alex and Kathy were probing Paul for the source of his income.

"C'mon, Paul, what *do* you do for a living," Kathy began pestering him, determined that he not get away with his ego-driven rant unchallenged.

But Paul kept skirting the issue. "Well, I can't exactly . . . I'm making music tapes for businesses, background tapes."

"There, are you happy?" Karla snapped back, the tension in her voice signaling an end to the conversation. Alex and Kathy knew he was lying, although they didn't know for sure why.

Suddenly Paul blurted out, "Someday I'll tell you all my secrets!"

But nothing more was said.

Many months later, Alex and Kathy would nearly jump out of their skin when they rented the movie *Criminal Law* starring Kevin Bacon. The lead character's name is Martin Thiel, and he's a serial killer. At one point he tells his lawyer, "One day, I'll tell you all my secrets."

As the evening wound down, Alex and Kathy couldn't help but feel that their friendship with Paul and Karla, once so strong and vibrant, had changed somehow. But despite being annoyed at their friends, they realized that Paul was in no condition to drive. They insisted the Bernardos sleep over.

But Paul would have none of it as he staggered out the door, Karla at his heel.

Karla later called to apologize, saying Paul had been out of line. Even Paul seemed contrite, which was unusual for him. Still, he never came right out and acknowledged he'd been extremely rude to his good friends or that he had hurt their feelings.

After that night there was a definite cooling-off period between the two couples. Alex and Kathy were still stung at how brutal their supposed friend had been, even if he was drunk. There was no excuse and they vowed to keep their distance, at least for a while.

But after a time, phone calls became more frequent and the incident, if not forgotten entirely, seemed to be pushed to the side. Still, there was a definite change in their relationship. The invitations to the Port Dalhousie home became less numerous, and if they went out to a New York State nightclub or for dinner, the two couples would meet at the Pleasure Dome or After Hours instead of at either home. Gone, too, were the days the boys and girls hung out separately. Paul seemed more and more determined to keep Karla under his watchful eye.

Part of this evolution in the couples' relationship may have been impacted by changes Alex and Kathy were going through. They decided the Pathfinder was too big and expensive for a newlywed couple just starting off, so they sold it for a significantly less flashy Hyundai.

For Paul, the move was a clear abdication of both style and substance. Alex recalled Paul's berating Steve Smirnis for not having the "things" that Paul felt he should have and thus branding him a loser. For Paul the equation was simple: Alex had traded in status for boring, and he simply couldn't respect that.

Karla also expressed dismay. "Oh, Alex, we loved that truck," she lamented.

One area that Paul still found interesting about Alex, however, was his attachment with the ancient order of the Masons.

Alex had joined the Masons in Washington D.C. Alex's grandfather had been a Mason, and Alex joined the secret fraternity out of a sense of tradition and curiosity. Later, he simply liked to go for the companionship and conversation. Even after he moved north, Alex would still go to local meetings.

Paul had heard Alex talk about the Masons and was intrigued by the secrecy and the mystery that shrouded the group. Often he would examine Alex's intricately designed Mason's ring and press him for details about the order, which Alex was forbidden to discuss. Paul also thought it would be a good way to make business contacts, at which Alex simply rolled his eyes. For Paul, there always had to be an angle.

Alex offered to sponsor Paul at the Seymour Lodge in St. Catharines, a lodge that had a lot of younger General Motors workers. But as it turned out, two local members met Paul and agreed to sponsor him. After he joined, Paul took great delight in performing the secret handshake with Alex. Sometimes the girls would tease them about wanting to see the performance, but Paul was adamant that it was a secret tradition and they should back off.

If Alex and Kathy thought Paul and Karla's marriage might set the couple's relationship on a more even keel, they were mistaken. Paul was still clearly in control and loved to assert that control, often in public. His latest weapon if Karla did something to annoy him was to stop calling her Karla Bernardo and call her by her maiden name, Karla Homolka, or simply Homolka.

This always elicited a whiny "Paul, stop it" from Karla.

"Okay, Karla Homolka," he would respond, knowing it was driving his wife crazy. "Okay, Homolka."

And he'd make a production of disengaging his hand from hers and walking farther ahead or away to the side of the sidewalk.

"Paul! Stop it," Karla would implore until he agreed to take her hand again.

One night at Paul and Karla's, Karla had made a pasta dinner for the two couples. But because she had cut the pasta by hand, the widths of the noodles weren't uniform.

Nonetheless, Alex and Kathy responded to the meal by eating heartily and praising Karla.

"That was a great meal, Karla. Thanks," said Alex, patting his stomach with obvious satisfaction as the four sat around the dining-room table.

"It wasn't too bad, but the noodles were too thick," Paul complained. "Too thick."

"Okay, Paul, why don't you make them next time," Kathy suggested, annoyed but not surprised that Paul would find fault with his wife's cooking.

"Yeah, Paul," Karla piped up. "You need to buy me a pasta maker."

Although Alex didn't realize it at the time, his frequent spur-of-the-moment visits to the house or the animal clinic while he was making business calls drove Paul crazy.

One day a few weeks after Paul and Karla returned from their honeymoon, Alex stopped in at the pet clinic to say hi

to Karla and to tell her he was going to drop in on Paul. Karla
became extremely agitated and insisted on calling Paul first.

Alex waited patiently at the animal clinic counter as she
said hello to Paul. Finally she explained why she'd called.

"Okay, Paul, Alex is here."

And then Karla's face seemed to suddenly drain of color
and emotion. She went totally blank.

"Yeah, he just stopped in to say hi."

More silence.

"Oh, he just wanted to stop in and say hi. He wants to
come over and say hi to you."

"Karla, tell him I'm on my way," Alex said, figuring Paul
was trying to think of an excuse why he shouldn't come by.
And he was out the door.

A few minutes later Alex pulled into the driveway and Paul
answered the door, kind of hip-hop happy, bouncing around.
"Hey, man's what's up, bud?"

Paul was covered in fragments of drywall and plaster dust.
Alex looked around him and saw several holes in the walls of
the house that Paul was apparently trying to repair. One was
at the top of the stairs leading to the basement and there were
two more in the living room.

"What the hell happened?" Alex asked.

"Oh man, I got kind of mad and threw Buddy through the
wall. We were just sort of horsing around," Paul replied, as
though it were the most natural thing in the world for him to
throw his Rottweiler through the walls of his beautiful Cape
Cod home. And sure enough, the holes in the living room
were about five feet up from floor level and looked as though
something heavy had been battered against the wall.

As for the other side, Paul confessed he was trying to move
Buddy's big dog cage downstairs and Karla wasn't helping
him, so he tried to jam it through the opening at the top of
the stairs, ripping into the drywall.

They moved into the kitchen. Paul offered Alex a Coke
from the refrigerator and they sat at the kitchen table chatting.
At no time did Paul leave Alex alone.

It was an extremely hot day, and Paul began to complain
about the air-conditioning system in the house and how it

didn't keep them cool enough and they were sweating like crazy. Alex, who didn't find it particularly hot in the house, looked around the room and noticed that there was paper stuck in the air vents.

"Well, yeah, Paul, that's because you got paper stuck in the vents," he said, having a hard time understanding how this could have escaped Paul's attention.

But Paul clearly knew the paper was there. "Yeah, because it gets so warm upstairs in this house, the air-conditioning doesn't get up there, so I stuffed the vents in this floor to let the cool air get up to the top floor. There's something wrong with the air ducts. They're not put together right."

Paul launched into a tirade about the house and how it wasn't built very well and how he thought he'd like to buy it someday but now had changed his mind and was simply going to rent until they found a nicer home they could buy.

Earlier, Alex had noticed paper in the vents and Paul had explained that it was to keep Buddy's dog food from dropping down the grates. Now it was to facilitate better movement of cool air. Alex shook his head in disbelief.

Alex could barely contain his amazement when Paul led him downstairs to show off a new $1,000 vertical stair climber he'd just purchased. As they descended into the lower level, the temperature began to drop significantly. And by the time they were in Paul's workshop it was downright frosty, as though all the cold air had been trapped below as a result of Paul's innovative air-transfer system.

Later, Alex would tell police it felt like a meat locker.

Late in 1991 or early 1992, Alex stopped by one day and Paul bounded out of the house and without warning whipped out his Eaton's department store bill. "Look! Look! Paid in full! I paid it all off in one shot," he announced. The bill was for an enormous amount, something in the neighborhood of $1,700.

"How'd you manage to do that?" Alex asked.

"I can pay my bills," Paul said smugly, puffing out his chest.

When Alex related the story to Kathy, they half-joked that it seemed Paul was losing his grip on reality to think that it mattered one way or the other to Alex and Kathy whether he paid all of his Eaton's bill or none of it.

Still, it seemed finances were becoming a real problem for Mr. and Mrs. Bernardo. Their home reflected a sense of disarray and confusion even though Paul had always been immaculate in his appearance and demanded the same of his environment, including the way Karla dressed, especially when they went out. But as the couple entered a very frugal period in their marriage and began clipping coupons and growing their own vegetables like latter-day pioneers, their house seemed to fall into further disrepair. Alex and Kathy decided that Paul's seemingly limitless supply of cash must have dried up, at least temporarily.

The patio furniture in the backyard had a covering of mold. There were urine stains on the carpet where Buddy had become excited and had an accident. And there were the holes in the wall from Paul's fits of rage. Even the vegetable garden, which had replaced the exquisitely manicured flower garden, seemed to have a wild, unattended look, adding to the seediness that seemed to overpower the once tidy home.

"Everything's falling apart," Alex later remarked to Kathy.

Karla's phone call came at the worst possible time for Kathy. Lunch where she worked at the Oban restaurant was the busiest time of the day, and she was exhausted. But when Karla called her from the animal clinic, asking if Kathy could rearrange her schedule and have lunch with her the next day, Kathy fought her initial response, which was to be dismissive with her old friend. She hadn't seen much of the newlyweds since that horrible night in their apartment when Paul had been so abusive and mean-spirited, but there was something in Karla's voice, a need, a tone of despair, that made Kathy swallow her feelings of pride and anger. It was the week before Labor Day in 1991.

"Well, I'll have to rearrange my schedule, but sure," Kathy said, hanging up the phone in the historic restaurant's kitchen.

That night, Kathy called Lisa and they talked about the phone call and the meaning behind the sudden urgent luncheon engagement. The girls wondered if Karla was ready to discuss the reality of her relationship with Paul, a relationship they had watched evolve and mutate, becoming something they thought was entirely different from what Karla would have outsiders believe.

The next day Kathy picked Karla up and they drove to Bellamys, a roadhouse-style restaurant a short distance from the Martindale Animal Clinic. Karla was wearing the jeans and top that she'd worn under her white lab jacket at the animal clinic. She was very agitated as they took their seats by the window looking into the parking lot. Karla immediately swore Kathy to secrecy about the lunch.

"You can't tell Paul we met," she said, leaning toward her friend conspiratorially.

She told Kathy there was an investigation at the animal hospital, some sort of external audit, to try to discover the whereabouts of missing drugs. Karla suggested to her friend that a vet at the clinic was responsible, but the explanation sounded too pat, too comfortable, especially given Karla's agitation.

Again Karla swore Kathy to secrecy about the search for the missing drugs.

"You can't tell Paul about that!" she said emphatically.

Clearly Karla was afraid that her husband was going to find out, not only about the investigation but the meeting as well. Kathy was confused at the melodrama but reassured her that she had no intention of telling Paul anything.

Then Karla began describing her life with Paul. It was not, as Karla had long pretended, a storybook romance.

In a quiet voice she described how Paul had been verbally abusing her, how he made her feel small and stupid. How he told her that she was nothing without him, that she was stupid and couldn't make it without him.

Karla talked longingly of wanting to explore different possibilities both professionally and personally. She wanted to go back to school and maybe study child psychology so she could work with kids. She wanted to learn to drive. Paul forbade her doing any of this.

Karla also confirmed what Alex and Kathy had long suspected, that Paul was making money from smuggling cigarettes across the border. She didn't go into great detail about the operation but acknowledged she'd been involved as well.

"What should I do, what should I do?" Karla asked, looking at her longtime friend for easy answers.

"She wanted to do something with her life. She wanted something of her own," Kathy recalls. Although she'd had nagging doubts about Karla and Paul's relationship for months, it didn't lessen the shock of hearing it directly from Karla.

"That's just as bad as physical abuse," said Kathy.

"I know that. I know, I know," Karla replied, shaking her head as though she couldn't believe what she was saying out loud.

"Is he physically abusing you, Karla? Is he hitting you? Tell me now! If he is, we'll get you out of there!" Kathy asked, her memory bringing up images of Karla's bruised arms and the angry marks on her back as she happily tried on her wedding gown in the weeks before the wedding.

"The next thing he'll do is hit you if he's verbally abusing you now," warned Kathy, taking on a tough tone, refusing to let the issue simply die with Karla's lame denial.

For a brief moment, Kathy recognized the fire and determination, and even the stubbornness of the Karla she and the others had come to love and respect a scant few years earlier. And Kathy realized the incredible strength Karla had shown in calling her despite knowing that Paul might find out.

But Kathy sensed there was still something blocking Karla from revealing the whole truth about their relationship, some last wall that could not be broken.

Again she asked if Paul was physically abusing her. Karla denied it. When she asked a third time, Karla lashed out angrily.

"How dare you suggest I would put up with that! I would not put up with that crap!" she insisted. "You know me, Kathy. One time and I'd be out of there."

And as quickly as it had begun, the discussion ended. Kathy paid the bill, feeling somehow that Karla had been too frightened to allow the conversation to move to the next plateau. It had taken extraordinary courage for her to say what she had, and Karla was simply unable to move beyond that.

But as they walked back to the car, it was obvious Kathy had struck a nerve.

While she didn't believe Karla's vigorous denials that Paul was striking her or somehow physically abusing her, Kathy couldn't help but feel at least a small measure of satisfaction and relief that Karla had taken at least the first step toward dealing with what appeared to be an unpleasant domestic situation.

But that feeling of at least a minor breakthrough was short-lived.

A few weekends later, Alex and Kathy saw a smiling Karla and Paul. Karla appeared to be much happier and confided to Kathy quietly that she and Paul had talked things out and that she was going to go back to school and get her license. Kathy smiled thinly and congratulated Karla, embracing her. But it was without feeling, because she knew it was a lie.

"All right, whatever," Kathy said, pulling away, a feeling of despair and even disgust rumbling in her belly.

Although there were still fun times, the two couples saw less and less of each other. 1991 faded into 1992. Paul and Karla continued to act strangely, and Alex and Kathy found their socializing less enjoyable. Most outings were followed by a long period of dissection and introspection as Alex and Kathy analyzed what had become of their friends' peculiar relationship.

During this period in late 1991, Alex would sometimes stop in at Video Joe's, a store Van Smirnis had opened in Youngstown, New York, in the fall. One day, Van and Alex went to pick up some stuff for the video store in Alex's truck and they stopped to get something to eat at a Burger King. Alex began pestering Van about what the hell Paul was doing with his time, asking him how Paul made all his money.

Alex said he figured Paul was smuggling drugs or guns or cigarettes into Canada. Van, without really admitting to any illegal behavior, confirmed that Paul and he were in the same line of business.

Van also admitted that Paul was adamant that he didn't want Alex and Kathy to know what they were doing. Whether this was because he felt Alex was too weak or conscientious to accept his business venture, or whether he felt Kathy might blow the whistle on him remained a secret to Alex and Kathy. Maybe it was simply convenient for Paul to have unknowing American friends in the area to provide a convenient alibi should they ever be caught with whatever it was they were smuggling.

For Kathy, who was trying to obtain a green card and permanent resident status in the U.S., the news was shocking. How could their close friend jeopardize that process by using them as an alibi? Even if they weren't part of the scam, it angered Alex and Kathy, strengthening their resolve to distance themselves from Paul and Karla.

In February 1992, Karla called Kathy asking if they wanted to meet at the Pleasure Dome for Valentine's Day, but Alex and Kathy already had plans and begged off. They hadn't seen the couple in weeks.

Later, they did run into their old friends at a nightclub and discovered that Paul had changed his hairstyle once again. Gone was the closely cropped coiffure that gave Paul his boyish good looks. Instead, there were loopy ringlets that fell rock star–like over his eyes and his hair seemed to have been streaked, giving him a kind of greasy, sinister look.

"He looks so goofy," Kathy decided.

Not long after, there was another chance meeting. In mid-1992, Alex walked into the local Topps grocery store, searching for a short list of supplies. As he turned down the frozen-food aisle, he literally bumped into a grocery buggy pushed by Karla, Paul by her side. All three reacted with surprise.

"Hi," Alex started, but they gave a quick wave and moved on. Karla looked thin and gaunt. Alex stopped and slowly walked on a few steps, puzzled by how briskly they'd moved on. He thought about how they hadn't seen each other in a long time and, how perhaps he should invite them over for a drink. Even if they didn't accept, it was the polite thing to do, Alex figured. He turned, but they were gone. It had only been a few seconds and they were gone.

They must have literally run out of the store, Alex thought, shaking his head. All that was left was the shopping cart full of groceries abandoned in the middle of the aisle. Alex chuckled to himself. On the top of the pile of groceries was a box of Fruit Loops. Figures, he thought to himself.

The next time Alex and Kathy would see Paul, it would be via television and on the front page of every newspaper.

CHAPTER
19

After months of lucrative smuggling, Van had invested in a legitimate video rental store in Youngstown, New York, where his brother Steve now lived with his wife, Bev. It was there Van met and moved in with his future wife, Joanne Fuller. Since Joanne was only seventeen when the two met, her parents didn't like the idea of her dating someone so much older, but they ultimately supported her decisions.

Van did not initially tell Joanne how he made most of his money. But when she began to worry that her boyfriend was selling drugs, he disclosed the cigarette-smuggling scheme he and Paul were operating. Joanne wasn't as comfortable as Karla when making cross-border runs with Van. She far preferred helping Van at the video store.

By the latter part of 1991 Van was grossing an average of over $2,000 weekly at the video store and he considered opening another store with Steve. But the two could never come to terms with how much each would invest in time, effort, and hours. Van loved the video store. It was a clean, honest living. Yet he could not resist the lure of easy money that came with cigarette running. At first, Steve was willing to turn a blind eye to the cigarette transfers in his driveway, but he and Bev dug in their heels in early October and demanded that Paul and Van do their contraband switch elsewhere. That meant the pals had to meet in backstreets and alleyways.

As a Canadian citizen without a work visa, Van could only invest in an American business, not own and operate one himself, so he hired a full-time employee to cover day hours, from 10 A.M. to 6 P.M., just in case the immigration investigators wanted to check out his operation. Either his girlfriend, Joanne, or one of her friends, would cover the evening shift.

Through her friendship with Joanne, Julie had met Paul on one of his many visits to Youngstown. She had developed a strong crush on him and often bemoaned to Joanne the fact that Paul was so cute and "damn it, why does he have to be married?" Not one for holding back her passions, Julie told her pal she would love to receive Paul's affection. Joanne had passed on this juicy tidbit to Van, who shrugged his shoulders. Didn't all the girls like Paul?

Just prior to a dinner date between the two couples, Joanne was starting preparations for the evening meal, exchanging gossip with her friend Julie when Karla called to tell Joanne that Mike Donald, she, and Paul had been drinking heavily. She suggested it wasn't a good idea for Paul to drive across the border while drunk and she invited Van and Joanne to party at 57 Bayview and then stay over for the night. Joanne asked Karla if Julie could come too. Joanne suggested that Julie would likely find Mike cute.

"That's fine," Karla said. "Mike might like that."

It was 9 P.M. when Van, Joanne, and Julie arrived. Karla was visibly drunk, staggering and wobbling around the house with a large vodka and orange juice in her hands, slurring and mumbling her words and giggling. For the past few hours she had been sucking back beer bongs—putting two or more beers and several shots of tequila into a funnel and simply opening the throat and letting gravity slam them into the stomach. Karla would take a beer and a half at a time, a substantial amount for a girl, Paul would remind everyone.

Within seconds, it seemed, the new arrivals had drinks in their hands. As Joanne struggled to relate through Karla's drunken haze the news of the last few days, and Julie and Mike engaged in the awkward conversation of strangers, Van, always the dutiful friend, pulled Paul aside and whispered conspiratorially that the cute Julie had the hots for him. Paul didn't seem surprised.

"I always like to take care of my friends, sexually," Van explained to Paul, giving him a hearty slap on the shoulder.

Van had no twinge of conscience in telling Paul about Julie's fantasy. After what Paul had done with Alyson in March, after the attempted pickups on the eve of his wedding, and after his infidelities with countless other women over the years, Van was under no illusions about the lack of monogamy between Paul and Karla. What the hell, he thought, if Julie wants Paul, he should know about it. Who was he to withhold this information from his best friend? The only roadblock for Paul was Mike, who had taken a fancy to the attractive, albeit immature girl.

Suddenly, without fanfare, Karla stood up straight and announced to her just-arrived guests: "I'm not feeling well. I'm going to bed."

Paul held her as she wobbled up the stairs to the master bedroom to the puzzled goodnights of the four guests. Joanne was surprised. It was so unlike Karla to invite her friends over and then rudely leave them. Van chuckled, wondering whether Karla was really feeling out of sorts or whether her sudden illness was due to Paul's scheming in order to get closer to Julie. Paul disappeared for only a few moments, then went into the dining room, stirring copious amounts of Kaluha, Bailey's Irish Cream, and Cointreau together into a large and potent B-52 as Joanne peeked in to see what he was doing. Paul took one of the drinks to Julie, who slammed it back with him, and then another. As the small talk continued between Mike and Julie and Van and Joanne, Paul zeroed in on his prey. The drinks continued to flow. They wandered around from room to room, chatting, drinking, listening to Paul's CDs, playing with Buddy, their noise seemingly not disturbing Karla's slumber.

Suddenly Mike called out to Van and Joanne: "Hey, they're in the bathroom."

Van, Mike, and Joanne gathered at the closed bathroom door and pressed their ears against it, listening intently for any sounds. They heard two people moaning. It was clear that

Paul and Julie were having sex in the bathroom. Mike could clearly hear Julie's voice: "Oooh, baby, harder, harder." In his drunken state, Van banged on the door and asked what was going on, asked if they were doing it. The continued moans were the couple's only reply. After a second knock, the moaning abated and Julie called out sharply, "Leave us alone!"

She didn't appear to be in any distress. Van and Joanne burst into giggles as the moaning renewed. Mike, however, was disgusted.

He wasn't just mad at having a potential date stolen from him; he was angry that Paul would have such disrespect for his wife.

"Can you believe that guy? His wife is sleeping upstairs." Mike pointed to where Karla was sleeping.

The next twenty or thirty minutes seemed like an eternity. The shocked threesome were still discussing the whys and hows of what was happening and "How could Paul do it?" when the bathroom door opened. Paul appeared first, his expression breaking into a broad grin. Julie remained inside. She was fully dressed but appeared disoriented. In fact, she had vomited everywhere: on the counter, the mirror, the floor. She wandered out, bracing herself on the doorjambs for support. She looked at her friend.

"Joanne, I don't feel well. I don't feel well," she slurred and moaned. She appeared subdued, weak, sick, and grossly intoxicated. Joanne led her into the living room, but as Julie tried to sit down she threw up all over the couch. Joanne led her back to the washroom, where Julie repeated her performance all over the bathroom floor. Joanne eventually led her into the first-floor bedroom. Julie immediately fell asleep.

While Joanne ensured Julie would have a safe slumber, Paul and Van and Mike stood in the kitchen. Paul made for the fridge, and as he poked around for a cold Coors Light he looked up at his pals with a glow on his face.

"I licked every inch of her," he boasted. "I fucked her and fucked her and she just started puking everywhere."

Van noticed that Paul was enjoying recounting the tale, barely containing his giggles. Van and Mike were turned off.

Even in the most loving of relationships, Van thought, sex isn't much fun when your partner is puking all over the floor. He couldn't fathom why Paul continued bragging to Van and Mike about how the younger girl told him how much she wanted him and how she wanted to poison Karla's toothbrush so she could have him all to herself.

Paul tossed Mike an unopened Coors.

"That's not very nice," Van observed.

"Yeah, but it's erotic," Paul said, his voice filled with admiration at Julie's plot.

At this, Mike, still annoyed at Paul's move on his own plans and disgusted at Paul's two-timing, was fit to be tied.

"But your fucking wife's upstairs! You just don't fucking get it, do you? What are you doing, man? Give your head a shake. If you treat Karla like that, why not give her to someone who will treat her a little better."

Paul glared at Mike for a moment, clearly unhappy that Mike was busting the mood.

"Don't you fucking talk like that!" Paul retorted in anger, staring down his younger friend. He abruptly stopped his scolding and curiously picked at his teeth with his fingernails. He held up a pubic hair in front of his face. "There's a fucking trophy!"

The brief humor over, Paul berated Mike again.

"Listen," he demanded, pointing upstairs. "Do you think she cares? She doesn't fucking care; she doesn't give a fuck. She knows. I'll go upstairs and tell her right now!"

Paul scampered up the stairs. Mike thought it best to drop the subject completely.

As night passed into morning, Van and Joanne moved Julie from the spare bed to the couch so they could have the bedroom to themselves. While Julie and Mike were alone on the living-room couch, Julie made a pass at Mike, which, in his partially drunken state, he couldn't refuse. He was wearing jeans and a T-shirt, which she was eager to remove.

"Fuck me up the ass," she pleaded.

Mike was turned off by the hard-core sex scene being played out by a seventeen-year-old girl.

As the combination of alcohol and sex drive took over and

Mike and Julie's bodies rolled in unison on the floor, Julie began calling out Paul's name and moaning.

"Give your head a shake, woman," Mike scolded.

They passed out at around 5 A.M.

Mike and Julie awakened when Van and Joanne tiptoed from the wing bedroom to the living room. Paul quickly joined them. Van and Joanne and Mike were all subdued, wondering what would happen between Paul and Karla after last night's indiscretions. Julie was nursing a whopper hangover and didn't have much to say to anyone. But Paul, dressed in a pair of Buffalo jeans and a T-shirt, surprised everyone when he announced with little fanfare: "Don't worry. I've told Karla everything."

Julie was staring at her hands, apparently embarrassed at what had happened and what was happening right at that moment. When she dared look up, Van caught Paul giving the teenager a knowing wink and a grin.

A few minutes later, Karla walked slowly down the stairs. Joanne watched Karla for any telltale signals. When Karla shuffled into the kitchen and said a reserved but friendly "hello" to the assembled, it was as if Paul had told her he and Julie had stayed up late playing Old Maid and drinking cocoa. If Paul had told Karla about his sexual exploits with Julie, Karla would have surely been raving mad, Joanne mused. He couldn't possibly have told her.

Mike and Julie ventured into St. Catharines to grab a bag of McDonald's breakfast food in an attempt to help everyone cut through their post-alcoholic haze. Inside the house, Joanne asked Paul and Van to clean up the remnants of Julie's vomit from the bathroom. The nauseating mess had been left sitting all night. The friends reluctantly took turns running into the bathroom, holding their breath, and taking wild swipes with cotton rags at the partly dried puke. As the men turned the chore into a game, Karla calmly entered the kitchen and pulled the sliding glass doors closed behind her, separating Joanne and herself from the men. Joanne had never seen Karla do this before. The hurt was now visible in her face. At that moment, Mike and Julie returned with the McDonald's breakfast, their footsteps audible on the porch.

"I want that girl out of the house!" Karla hissed as she began to straighten the kitchen. "You've got to get that girl out of my house. She knew Paul was married! How could she do that, in my own home?"

Joanne didn't think Julie, only seventeen years old, should shoulder all of the blame. In the quietest, most cautious voice she could manage, Joanne looked Karla in the eyes and said what was on her mind.

"But, Karla, what about Paul?"

Karla kept her eyes down as she continued with washing up the dishes and tidying the previous night's mess.

"When you marry someone, you accept their mistakes. You forgive them," Karla explained. Clearly, Karla was directing her anger solely at Julie. Karla saw Julie as the evil seductress. "I can't believe she's in my house right now!" Karla exclaimed.

Mike and Julie brought about forty dollars' worth of McDonald's food into the kitchen and everyone started to rip apart the paper containers to get at the food. The guys talked about cars. Paul had never liked Mike's beat up Nissan Sentra.

"When are you going to get rid of that piece of shit?"

As the men talked, Karla managed to let Joanne know of her demand in a desperate whisper.

"Just get her out of my house. I could kill her!"

The guests settled into their Egg McMuffins and hash browns and sausage and pancakes. Paul and Karla acted as if nothing had happened.

Later that afternoon, Van and Joanne drove with Julie back to Youngstown. The bathroom incident was not discussed.

Several days later, Paul told Van he was going to call Julie soon in New York. Paul made several calls, Julie later complained to Joanne, most of them obscene. Paul described to Julie the sexual adventures he had planned for the two of them, adventures that revolved around bondage and sadomasochistic sex. Julie demanded that Paul stop. Joanne asked Van to step in.

When confronted by Van, Paul vehemently denied making obscene calls. But oddly, the calls ceased.

For weeks, Van and Joanne mulled over the bizarre night at 57 Bayview Drive. Joanne was growing to vehemently dislike Paul. Even Van wondered why Paul would screw a teenage girl under his wife's nose and in front of the ears and eyes of his best friends.

Another incident similar to the "dinner party" at 57 Bayview cemented Joanne's dislike for Paul. In January 1992, the two couples planned an evening outing to Niagara Falls, New York.

Karla's face wore its satisfied-child smile as she handed Joanne the identification card she'd need for the night's trip over the border to the Pleasure Dome, the hedonistic nightclub in Niagara Falls. Joanne chuckled as she rehearsed her nom de guerre for the evening: Karla Homolka, of 61 Dundonald Street in St. Catharines, born May 4, 1970. She giggled when she studied the two-year-old photograph of Karla.

"You look so different, so prudish, so innocent," Joanne said with a chuckle, though she didn't want to make too much fun of Karla's past appearance since Karla's document was her key to fun. It made her twenty-two years old and therefore officially able to go drinking in her home state of New York, where at seventeen years of age Joanne was underage.

As Joanne complimented Karla on the changes her face and hair had gone through in the last couple of years, Paul, Van, and Paul's other buddies, Gus, and Arif, helped themselves to copious amounts of booze from Paul's hutch, sharing jokes and stories. The drinking had started early that night, and everyone but Van and Joanne was blasted. Van had downed five beers and felt a little light-headed, but Joanne was sober, having sipped only a couple of daiquiris because she was pregnant. It was clear to Van now that Paul and Karla were fast becoming alcoholics. The friends hadn't smoked any pot that night, but Paul had proudly showed Van the cannabis plant he was growing with a hydroponic lamp in his basement. To Van's amazement, the plant had grown to about two and half feet. Paul also showed him the bag of weed he'd harvested from a previous plant.

"Holy mackerel!" exclaimed Van. "You've got a green thumb. Even in the basement, you've got a green thumb."

"Hey man, you've got to save money these days. Dope doesn't come that cheap," returned Paul.

All six piled into Van's burgundy 1984 Honda Accord. Van drove with Karla and Joanne squashed together in the passenger's bucket seat. Arif, and Paul were sardined tightly into the backseat. While Joanne liked Karla, she had never liked the way Paul treated his wife. Yet she didn't feel it was her business to intrude, and she reasoned that since Karla was five years older than herself, she surely wouldn't put up with Paul if she wasn't getting something out of the relationship.

The drunken chatter continued back and forth as the partyers drove over the Rainbow Bridge at Niagara Falls to the Pleasure Dome, a gutted and renovated building in the heart of downtown Niagara Falls. The club's patrons are singles seeking their dream partner, that special Mr. or Miss Right, or, if that person doesn't show up, a one-night affair. The dance area itself is a huge warehouse with steel girders spanning the three-story-high ceiling. They are lined with black plastic sheeting that both hides the unsightly roof and shrinks the building's height to achieve more intimacy. The music is pumped to a frightening decibel level. On a Friday or Saturday night, there are so many patrons at Pleasure Dome that the anonymous energy and sexual intimacy these revelers seek is almost guaranteed. When the Pleasure Dome is packed and both sexes pile together on the dance floor like an army of ants, it is hot, vibrant, and mysterious.

As was his custom, Paul hit one of the Pleasure Dome's three bars and bought a round of drinks. Then they headed for the dance floor, sunken three feet from the railing that surrounds it, behind which are the tables. The guys had seen Paul's action in Florida; they knew he was a selfish rogue and would pick up another woman in an instant if Karla weren't there. Having seen Paul's vacation antics, Van didn't put anything past his old pal. Paul and Van stood down on the dance floor as the women danced in their typical twos and threes, shyly ignoring the men who seemed to delight in ogling their bodies. Paul always spent his time close to the dance floor; he often told Van how sitting at the tables or hanging out in the Pleasure Dome's sports bar area, with its pinball machines, video games, and pool tables, was for stiffs who would never pick up girls.

"You have to be right in the middle of the action; get them to notice you," he said.

The six stood at the side of the dance floor within brain-damage distance of the huge speakers. Their bodies jumped in response to the thud of the bass as Public Enemy's techno-pop hit "I Got the Power" thundered out. They could barely hear themselves speak.

"The girls are on the floor. You either talk to them, bump them, or catch their eye," Paul shouted into Van's ear, barely above the din of the music. "The bottom line is to start somewhere."

They danced together by the speakers, all six, with Gus and Arif looking over their shoulders occasionally in the hope they would find a lone female to latch on to. Paul, too, was straying from Karla, dancing with other girls.

"Hey, Paul," Van shouted, his hand over his mouth so his words were hidden from Karla. "What the hell are you doing?"

"I'm trying to get these chicks to dance with us so Gus and Arif can get them," he said. "I have to help my friends."

Because Joanne was pregnant, she tired quickly. She asked Karla to join her for a rest. They raised their backsides up onto the raised floor and dangled their feet over the submerged dance area. Karla seemed tired.

"How's work?" Joanne shouted over to her left, searching for an easy topic that she and Karla could discuss. Karla talked about work, then switched the topic to how Joanne got along so well with her sister Lori.

"It's as if you and Lori are sisters; probably because you are close to Tammy's age," said Karla, sipping her screwdriver.

Van and Paul took a break from dancing. They leaned against the raised floor and sipped their drinks. Paul shouted over, "Hey, where's Karla?" Van thought he had seen the women go to the bathroom, but then he saw Joanne and Karla sitting on the ledge. He pointed them out to Paul. Van could barely hear Paul's words as his eyes stayed transfixed on the women.

"What are they talking about all the time? Like, they have nothing in common. What is my wife telling your wife?"

As Paul walked toward the women, Van thought about how Paul seemed either envious or jealous, as if he had a fear that Joanne would brainwash his gullible wife into looking at him with a different perspective. Van believed that Paul was afraid Joanne would convince Karla of his asshole tendencies; maybe he feared that Joanne would convince Karla to ditch her husband for the night and pick up another guy. Van had noticed that whenever he and Joanne visited 57 Bayview Drive Paul never left Joanne and Karla alone together for more than a few minutes. He thought Paul was being a typical control freak.

Joanne and Karla had talked for about fifteen minutes when suddenly Paul appeared about five yards to Karla's left. Joanne nodded her recognition. Karla looked over at Paul, but then turned her head back to face Joanne. Paul took a sip from his drink, then glared directly at Karla.

"Hey, come here, you fucking bitch," he snarled.

Joanne became angry. "Excuse me, Paul, I'm talking to Karla. And you shouldn't call your wife a bitch," she said as firmly as she could in her soft voice.

Paul became enraged. He flipped out.

"I don't care, I want her over here. She's my fucking wife and if I want her over here, then she comes over here. And you stay the fuck out of my business, stay the fuck out of my marriage."

It was then that Joanne realized Paul wanted total control over Karla. His approach could have been so different; he could have sat down next to her, put his arm around her and whispered in her ear. He wanted her, and he had her, wrapped around his little finger. Earlier in the night he had called Karla fucking stupid; now he'd called her a fucking bitch. It bothered Joanne that whenever Paul spoke to Karla it was without dignity or respect. She couldn't understand why Karla remained silent, obedient, totally under his spell. Repulsed, Jo-anne slid off her perch to the dance floor, put her hands around Van's waist, and hugged him. She told Van of Paul's verbal commands, attributing it all to the obvious abuse.

Van knew it was true, but he didn't know what to do.

An hour or two later, Van set off for the parking garage to get his car. As Joanne and the others waited for Van to pick them up from the sidewalk, Gus began talking with two at-tractive young women who were in a lengthy line for a hot-dog vendor. Arif had discovered that one of the women was interested in philosophy and that the other had majored in philosophy at McMaster University in Hamilton, Ontario. One was an exotic brunette with dark-brown eyes and a dark complexion. She was dressed in skintight black pants and a leather jacket; the other was a cute blue-eyed blonde. One of the women engaged Arif in conversation, and they gloated to themselves about being brilliant thinkers. Van pulled up in the Honda a few yards away, pushed open the doors, and mo-tioned everyone to get in from the cold. Joanne shouted over at the philosopher women in jest.

"I wouldn't bother talking to him. He thinks he's Socrates, but he's a bullshitter."

Then, out of nowhere, Paul butted in, flashing his friendly smile and giving his trendy radio-style voice: "Hey, what's happening?" As Paul began his own intellectual exercise on the women, Arif and Gus were frozen out of the picture.

Joanne had slid into the car's front seat with Karla. Van quickly became impatient: the doors were open and he was freezing his butt off while Paul, Gus, and Arif tried to pick up the two women. Karla and Joanne watched as Paul bla-tantly put the moves on the two women. The brunette touched his cheeks, saying how she thought his dimples were cute.

Karla turned to Joanne, fuming. "Why is he doing this to me? Oh, he's such an asshole. I can't stand it."

Van had seen enough. He got out, walked around the car to Paul, and grabbed him by the shoulder, turning his face to his own. He said quietly, "Hey, buddy, let's go. Your wife is in the car."

"You guys just go. I'll get these girls to drive me back," Paul gushed, and turned back to his conversation.

"No," Van whispered in his ear. "Listen, man, your wife's in the car. We have to go."

By this point, Gus and Arif had bought their hot dogs. They left Van and Paul on the sidewalk, arguing in front of Paul's targets. The women now realized Paul's wife was in the car, and they walked away. Van motioned Paul around the car and physically pushed him into the back door behind the driver's seat.

Karla was sobbing, dabbing her eyes with a tissue. Paul sat in the backseat, pouting, and cursing.

"I had them. I fucking had them. I gave them the address and they were going to come—"

Van cut him off. "Why are you trying to pick them up when your wife's here in the car? Look, she's crying her eyes out."

"Karla doesn't mind," said Paul.

But Karla was wailing loudly now, calling Paul an inconsiderate jerk.

"What do you mean she doesn't mind? Look . . . look at her," Joanne blurted.

Karla was a mess. Her mascara was running down her face; she wiped her eyes with her hands. She turned her shoulder and yelled back at him. "What about Florida?"—referring to Paul's affair with Alyson.

Paul exploded as Van had never seen him explode before.

"What the fuck did your fucking wife tell her? What the fuck is going on? We had no fucking problems until this fucker interfered," he screamed, pointing accusingly at Joanne.

Joanne yelled back at him: "It's all you, Paul!"

Van's hand touched her to be quiet, and he told her to stay cool.

Van was seething now: "You shouldn't have tried to pick up the girls."

"You're fucking stupid," Paul shouted, then he started banging on the back of the seat with his hands and his fists.

"Don't fuck with my marriage," he screamed.

Van's head jolted forward every time Paul hit the headrest. "Don't hit me, Paul. Don't you dare hit me!"

But Paul kept up the shouting and banging for several minutes. Van stopped the car and turned to look Paul in the eyes.

"You fucking stop it right now."

Sensing Van's anger, Paul stopped the beating, opting instead to rip into Joanne's lack of education.

"You, you're so fucking bright you didn't even finish grade twelve," he said.

As Van pulled the Honda to a halt outside 57 Bayview Drive, Karla was still sobbing. She jumped out of the car and bolted into the house.

Van turned to Gus and Arif. "You assholes. Why didn't you stick up for Karla?"

With this, Paul slugged Van's headrest again. It slackened suddenly and tilted to the side. He'd broken it.

Van's head was throbbing from the effects of Paul's assault on the headrest. He had had enough. Paul had tried to screw around on Karla right in front of her eyes, he had belittled Joanne, he had slapped him in the head, and now his headrest was broken. Friend or no friend, brother or no brother, Paul had crossed the line. Van went into a blind rage. He crawled through the two bucket seats and slapped Paul in the head, wrestling him down to the seat. His hands were around Paul's throat for about a minute. He felt like killing him.

Paul wheezed out "Stop" and "I'm sorry, I'm sorry."

Van's temper cooled. Suddenly realizing how far he'd lost it, he let go of his grip and offered to talk.

Paul pulled his clothes and his ego together and got out of the car. "There's nothing much more to talk about."

Van and Joanne talked for a minute and then went into the house, mainly to see if Karla was okay. Paul and Karla were sitting at the top of the stairs, together now, like two lovebirds.

"Sorry, Paul. I guess I got carried away, buddy."

Seemingly out of nowhere, Karla chimed in, "Don't worry, Van. It's all my fault." They talked more, but Paul wasn't in the mood to reconcile.

Paul yelled at Van "Get out of the house."

"Yeah, get out of the house, Van . . . we don't want you here."

The voice was Karla's! Van looked up in disbelief at Karla's words. He looked into her eyes, but she couldn't hold her stare. Instead, she looked down at the carpeted stairs where she sat.

"I argued for you tonight," Van yelled at her. "I stuck up for your honor. I tried to protect you, and now you treat me like shit."

Van turned to Paul. "And you, you're a fucking idiot. I helped you, I got you all of this . . . you wouldn't have had anything here if it wasn't for me setting you up with the cigarettes. How ungrateful can you be. I try to save your marriage and you throw it all back in my face."

Van could have taken it further. He could have reminded Paul about all the things his family had done for Paul when his life was so disorganized. But he didn't, he couldn't. As he and Joanne walked out of the door and toward the Honda he realized that as well as being angry at Paul he was partially feeling sorry for himself. He wondered aloud if he and Paul could continue working the cigarettes strictly as a business, but he shrugged. Not only the smuggling but the entire friendship was in jeopardy.

Van got into the car, shifted his battered headrest and turned to Joanne. "I'm not doing anything more with these idiots. This is madness."

In the spring of 1992, Gus and Arif visited Van in Youngstown, New York. After the usual small talk, the discussion got around to Paul. Van led the charge. His concerns over Paul's apparent disintegration were again growing stronger. Gus and Arif listened intently as Van recalled the Pleasure Dome scene.

"Paul really freaked me out this time, wanting to bring those girls home in front of Karla. You know, he really couldn't give a damn. There's something weird about him. I want to tell you a few things and then you tell me what you think percentage-wise, okay? What do you think the chances are of him being involved with Leslie Mahaffy and Terri Anderson? What do you think the chances are of him being involved in something bizarre in Tammy's death?''

Van sensed both Gus and Arif were uncomfortable with what he was saying, as he was himself, but his suspicions had been nagging at his conscience for over two years and he had to talk about it. ''He told me years ago about wanting to start a female sex-slave farm with young girls and about abducting girls from way back when he was eleven or twelve years old. I've been studying the newspaper about the Scarborough Rapist. The cops say he is an anger retaliatory guy, that he hates his mother . . . You know, Paul is illegitimate and his real dad is the president of some big company in Kitchener. His mother didn't tell him he was illegitimate until he was sixteen years old, and it really freaked him out.''

This was the first time Gus and Arif had heard this story. They were clearly puzzled.

''Look, the cops say the Scarborough Rapist is eighteen to twenty-two years old and is incredibly smart. Paul looks like the profile—Gus, you know that—and he is very smart; he never gets caught at any of the schemes he pulls off. I know he used to hit his girlfriend Carol, and in Florida he tried to use that X-Acto knife on a girl. Did Paul tell you the Metro cops took him in for DNA testing in November 1990? Gus, think about it. The clincher is that the Scarborough rapes stopped once Paul moved out of Scarborough. Now, all of a sudden, young girls are missing and turning up dead in the St. Catharines area, right where Paul lives! So what do you think? Gus, honestly, how would you rate him as a suspect in these cases?''

Gus shrugged his shoulders and offered 25 percent. Arif merely suggested that from the facts, he thought there was a 50 to 60 percent chance. Van offered 99 percent.

''I think I know what I'm talking about.''

Van had hoped he would feel better by getting these concerns off his chest, but he didn't. Paul was his friend, almost his brother. He wanted to erase the suspicions from his mind. But they wouldn't go away.

* * *

A month or so later, Van and Joanne moved back to Canada where Van resumed working for his father at the Brownhill restaurant in Markham. On Friday, May 1, 1992 the day after Kristen French's body was found, Ontario Provincial Police Constable Rob Haney and three other officers sauntered into the Brownhill.

Van had known Rob since Rob was five years old when his parents had brought him into the Smirnis' Stop 14 restaurant. As an adult, Rob ate frequently at the Smirnis' current restaurant where he and Van would often chat.

Now that many were worried a serial killer was on the loose, Van suspected Paul's involvement in the crimes. While Van would eventually take a serious look at the $100,000 reward the *Toronto Sun* was offering for information leading to Kristen French's killer, he was initially sickened by the thought that more innocent girls like Kristen could be murdered.

Joanne had thought Van's suspicions were justified and she had encouraged him to talk to the police. Although Van had recently been charged with smuggling cigarettes, he felt he could trust Rob Haney. He approached the police officer after he had placed an order for lunch.

"I think we should talk about something. It's about a certain case. Have you got time?"

"Yeah, what's on your mind?"

Van motioned Rob to a corner table. "Listen, I don't know if this is going to help, but I have a hunch about a buddy of mine . . . Rob, I don't know . . . it's just off the top of my head, but I'm going to tell you a few things you might want to write down and submit to the proper authorities."

Van told Haney about Paul's background, his address, his subservient wife, his bad temper, his assaults, his fantasy about schoolgirls in pigtails and his love of anal sex.

"And they already have his DNA sample on file as a Scarborough Rapist suspect," said Van, explaining how Paul matched the look and clothing of the "boy next door" in the composite he'd seen in the *Toronto Sun*.

Van had told Haney there was one caveat on his information—he did not want his name linked to the report because he feared Paul would find out he had ratted on him. But he continued to tell Haney about his former best friend.

"He hated his mother. She told him at the age of sixteen that he was illegitimate and he deeply hated her after that. He assaulted a woman in front of me, tried to attack a woman in Florida, again right in front of me."

Van suggested that it wasn't just a coincidence that Bernardo had lived in the Guildwood subdivision just at the time of the Scarborough rapes and that, when the rapes ended, Paul had moved to St. Catharines where the schoolgirl murders then occurred. He pointed out that experts had stated that the Scarborough rapist's attacks had become increasingly violent and that the assailant would probably kill his next victim.

Haney told Van that he had met some Green Ribbon Task Force members only a few weeks earlier and that he would pass along the tip. He later confided in Van that while his superiors at the OPP had been reluctant to take the report, they had eventually done so at Haney's urging. The information was then forwarded to Green Ribbon.

Eleven days later as detectives Brian Nesbitt and Scott Kenney walked up the path towards 57 Bayview Drive they noted the attractive pink Cape Cod house on the corner lot and the serene atmosphere of the streets next to Lake Ontario. It was May 12, 1992, a Tuesday. A tip from Beaverton OPP Constable Rob Haney had sent them to this house to look at a young guy. The tip was one of scores Nesbitt and Kenney had on their caseload. Because he had no criminal record, not even a speeding ticket, Bernardo was given a low rating as a suspect.

After waiting some time, the officers turned to leave when the door suddenly opened and a young blond man invited them inside. The police officers looked around the room for clues as they asked Bernardo some preliminary questions. They saw a tastefully decorated house, nice furniture and a large wedding picture above the fireplace in which stood Bernardo and his beautiful blond wife. When Nesbitt asked Bernardo if he had ever had any involvement with the police, he volunteered that he had been a suspect and he had given samples, but he never heard anything back. They next asked Bernardo where he was on April 16, 1992, the day of Kristen French's abduction. Probably working on his rap album, Bernardo responded. The man looked a little nervous, Nesbitt noted, but nothing out of the ordinary. In all, Nesbitt and Kenney spent twenty minutes in 57 Bayview Drive and left. The next day, Nesbitt was on the telephone to Metro police asking about Bernardo's status. He was told Bernardo had been interviewed in the Scarborough Rapes and that he had given DNA samples willingly, but he was merely one of hundreds what police term "people of interest."

Although Bernardo was never formally cleared by police, Van's tip to Constable Rob Haney about his friend had been noted and filed like the other thousands of tips task force members had worked on.

That same day, or the next day, Nesbitt called Metro police to see if he could learn anything more about suspect Paul Kenneth Bernardo. He was given only basic information on the file and was told that Bernardo was only one of two hundred or so suspects who were tested in the Guildwood area at the height of the rapist's terror. Anything the Metro may have had on Bernardo seemed inconsequential. Nesbitt and Haney filed a report and waited for any subsequent files on Bernardo. Meanwhile, they set about interviewing scores of other suspects that had been assigned to them.

For one reason or another, the link between Bernardo's being a suspect in the Scarborough Rapes and the piece of map showing Scarborough at Kristen's abduction scene was not made. Compared to the hundreds of other suspects in Niagara—the sex attackers, the stalkers, the weirdos—Paul Bernardo didn't seem to rate.

CHAPTER
20

Wherever Paul Bernardo drove in his Nissan 240SX from late 1990 on, it seemed that cassette tapes of 2 Live Crew and other angry rap artists went with him. On the March 1991 trip to Florida, Paul had given himself a great thrill playing the Martinez song at full volume as he drove around in the Nissan or in Gus Drakopoulous's Jeep. He did the same on his return to Canada, pumping up the volume as he drove around St. Catharines, Toronto, or whenever he crossed the border on the cigarette runs.

After the wedding, as the cigarette cash began piling into 57 Bayview Drive at a pace Paul had never imagined, he put together a huge collection of CDs, perhaps up to 300. Many of them were rap CDs. Upstairs in the music room that no one was ever allowed to enter, Paul had an eight-track mixing board, a $4,000 Roland synthesizer, an electronic drum machine, a preediting computer system, and thousands of dollars' worth of recording equipment, including a CD recording unit.

In mid-1991, Paul started recording his own CDs, taking tracks from rap records and mixing them with others. He played his "creations" to Van, telling him all that was missing was his own voice-over. Paul said that he intended to cut an album, combining pirated rap tracks with his own "original" hybrid mix. Without a band and with little musical talent, Paul was trying to become a rap star. Essentially, it was a variation on the motivational-tape scam. Nevertheless, the cuts were truly of professional quality.

As he journeyed deeper into the rap scene, Paul began to dwell on the street-language work of various rap bands: Public Enemy, whose tracks include "Sophisticated Bitch"; Body Count, with song titles such as "Momma's Gotta Die Tonight"; and Ice-T, who performs "Bitches," "Body Count" and "Street Killer." As he mentioned to Van on the return trip from Florida in 1991, Paul believed whites had inherent superiority over blacks and could produce more-sophisticated rap music.

He frequently recorded his rap ideas, music, and lyrics on cassette so he wouldn't forget them. He had a thousand sheets of song lyrics in his music room at 57 Bayview, 105 pages of which were original Paul Bernardo words. His rap lyrics reveal his many insecurities, his deep contempt for women, his vision of himself as a deserving and powerful master. On a sixty-minute tape of concepts and lyrics, his weaknesses show from start to finish.

After rambling some repetitive rap ideas based around "mind your business baby," Paul gets to the meat of the song he envisions: "Jan and Dean, two bitches for every girl, or two girls for every boy, along with love in stereo . . . this bird's in paradise." His voice continues to wander with his mind. In describing how rap music should be written, he refers often to the silver screen: "Look in the movies. Take expressions—the way people say certain words—and then take them out and put them in your songs, man, like something that really hits you, it's like, 'that's cool,' like, 'you wanna see crazy? I'll show you crazy,' like, you know, that type of thing, which is from *Lethal Weapon* . . . take stuff like that."

At the end of this monologue, Karla says only "yeah." She is obviously in the same room, but Paul continues with the talking.

"I like that chorus I just did. Check this chorus out: 'Did you ever get caught, no, never why, because I'm deadly innocent guy du du du du du du du du du du you like that Karla?' "

"Yes I do," chirps Karla.

Paul repeats himself and Karla again offers her support.

"I like that."

Paul follows his lyrical ramblings with an explanation about "Deadly Innocence": " 'Cause that sort of puts a theme to the thing and it establishes street's hard core . . . that's important, okay, important point is street hard-core credibility . . . you know, 'I'm dancing da da da,' you know, "I'm this and that, I'm fucked . . . ,' but I want to come across with a hard-core street credibility . . . 'did you ever get caught?', 'no, never, why?', 'I'm a deadly innocent guy!'."

His talk digresses but then he returns to the street credibility theme and "your hard-core battling the world through your ways of getting your illegal money, or whatever you're doing, um . . . and you use everything, all your feelings and the real-life feelings you all experience, including everything you've experienced, all the smuggling and all the other activities to make a buck on the street, which is important, and that establishes your street credibility."

Paul talks about seeing drop-crotch pants similar to what rap star M. C. Hammer uses in watching a video of the 1964 Walt Disney movie classic Mary Poppins, a part-live part-animation show featuring Julie Andrews as a British nanny. He talks about seeing a video of the rap band Public Enemy and how it relates to the 1931 James Cagney film classic *The Public Enemy*. He talks about an old movie called *Deadly Innocents,* a little-known movie about a female mental patient who escapes to a roadside gas bar and kills people but befriends a young female. The two become lesbian killers.

"That's something, that *Deadly Innocents,*" Paul continues on the tape. "Deadly innocent guy' is a phrase that I want a lot of home boys to start using man, because it's a great thing, and they frutt and they think they can take you on, man, but you're a deadly innocent guy." In his song "Beyond Fear," Bernardo writes, "girlies they motivate, accelerate but never dominate . . . pick them up for dinner when the school is out."

And then Paul launches into an angry tirade: "Like, 'heh, man, you think I'm innocent, but behind this, I'm packing a lot of deadliness. So come at me, man, take your best shot, see what happens to you, pal—you're outta here man. You come at me with your beer, your beer pot belly, you think you're really rough and tough, man; I come back with my Bee Boy hat, looking like I'm thirteen years old, and I'll kick your ass and fucking blow your fucking head off; I'll kill your fucking parents. I'll come after, fucking shoot your girl-friend, and fucking your sister, man. I'll fuck your sister, I'll fuck your girlfriend, I'll shoot the rest of you.' You know that the thing about Deadly Innocence is that we're going to fuck-ing come at them hard as hell, and most Bee Boys are like that: we are tired of these people who want to try and look ugly, to look tough. You know, you want to come at me. I'll fucking kick your ass man, and that's . . . that's the whole image you want to cross, that's what Deadly Innocence is all about, that's the theme of the album.''

His lyrics revolve around sexual fantasy, image, power and domination: ''I'm the solo creep . . . sleep.''

In a song entitled Deep In The Jungle, Bernardo writes: ''Deep in the jungle, a burning desire, deeper and deeper and deeper into her jungle . . . lost in the jungle . . . Stalk like a wolf, and you are my prey, I'll be upon you by the break of day . . . fooled by the innocence, I've paid throughout . . . laughing at your face, got no confession you've got no case. I throw my fist in your face.''

The TV sounds continue on the B side of the tape, and so does Paul.

''Like the Ice T beginning, where he goes, 'yo' man, I do shadda', you know, one of those things. What you do is in the middle of the song, you just have, or at the beginning, you just say, 'yo' pau. what are you frontin' man? What are you packing? Right in there, and you go something like 'Deadly Innocence', you know, something like that, that's kind of like packing Deadly Innocence rather than a piece, because that's all you need, you know, or you need that front of the un-known, the art of secrecy, or something, and the art of decep-tion, okay.''

As he had cheated with almost every aspect of his life, Paul plagiarized the lyrics and styles of real musicians. "In case I forget, there," he appears to say to Karla or the phantom third person, "pick up some Neil Young albums, he's got good lyrics. In case I didn't mention it, I was going to mention something about, you know, jerk-off material and stuff. I don't know if we can mention his songs, but we all used to say it."

"Hello," Karla interjects.

Paul blows into the microphone and responds with "Boring and pointless."

As the music plays, Paul continues to spurt out his ideas: rapping and chanting boring, repetitive chorus sequences based on "hype" and "fuck that shit." Introducing an "original" called "The World Is Yours," Bernardo says it could have an Al Pacino beginning, and goes into a two-person dialogue:

"What do you want, Tony?"

"I want what's coming to me, the world!"

He moves quickly into a title he calls " 'Moving on a Red Light,' which could be a song for sex, or pickup of a girl, um, and also a song like 'boom, I've got your girlfriend, I've got your girl, boom, I've got your girlfriend.' "

Paul liked girlfriends . . . his or anyone else's. New or old, it didn't matter as long as he controlled them.

After six months of separation, Van and Paul naturally drifted back together. In October 1992 Paul, the Smirnis brothers and Gus Drakopoulous headed off to Myrtle Beach, South Carolina, for Andy Douglas' wedding. Paul had phoned Alyson asking to see her, and despite her noncommittal response, Paul had been certain she was still crazy about him. He never did connect with Alyson because, as the boys drove south, they talked about their previous jaunts to Florida and decided to blow off Andy's wedding in favor of a wild party weekend in Daytona Beach.

While Van had phoned Joanne—now several months pregnant—to let her know where he was, neither Alex nor Paul had related the changed plans to their wives. Back in Mark-

ham at Van's parents' house, Joanne noticed she was losing
weight and, feeling sickly, she drove home and checked herself into a hospital in Lewiston, New York. When Tina Smirnis learned her sister-in-law was in the hospital, she phoned
Joanne immediately. While Joanne filled Tina in on her condition, the two engaged in small talk. Tina had spoken with
Alex, but Joanne wondered if Tina still thought Alex was in
South Carolina.

"By chance, Tina, do you know that the guys are in
Florida?"

"What?"

"Yeah, they didn't go to the wedding and they're playing
in Daytona Beach."

Tina's tone of voice betrayed her anger. "Where are they
staying?"

Joanne gave her the number Alex hadn't and after she hung
up with her sister-in-law she wondered if Karla knew where
Paul really was. Before Paul and Van had left for the wedding,
Joanne had offered more than once to visit Karla, but Paul
had brushed Joanne aside, telling her not to worry because
Karla intended to stay with her parents. As the Bernardos'
telephone rang, Joanne prepared herself for Paul's voice on
the answering machine. But Karla answered.

"Oh, I didn't expect to get you; Paul said you were staying
at your parents'."

"Paul said that? I was never planning to stay there."

"Have you heard from Paul?" Joanne tested.

"No."

"Well, he and Van and the others are in Daytona Beach,
not South Carolina."

Karla didn't have a clue that her husband was anywhere
other than where he said he would be. Although Joanne had
expected Karla to react as Tina had, with surprise and anger,
Karla seemed undisturbed. In a monotone voice she simply
asked for the number.

Back in Florida, word reached Paul that Joanne had spoken
with Tina.

"Can't you fucking control your fucking wife?" he berated Van, who quickly realized that Paul was worried Karla would confront him with the trip and find out he had picked up a seventeen-year-old girl named Heather who had easily been sucked into Paul's web. Heather had confided in Van that she was in love with Paul. "There's never been a guy that's had this kind of impact on me," she told Van. "Is this *really* his phone number? Is this *really* his address?"

Van discovered that not only had Paul given Heather his real address, but he had fed her the same tale about his "sisters," Karla and Tammy, that he had fed to Alyson the year before!

Each night during the seven-day trip the guys went out to various bars and nightclubs. One evening after Van and Gus had been partying at the 701 Club they met four girls outside. Gus had drunk too much and was getting sick, but Van nevertheless talked the girls into helping him get Gus back to their hotel room, where they all partied some more. Paul, who had previously been busy with Heather, promptly whipped out his camera and videotaped one of the women who had decided to perform fellatio on two drunken guys.

Van didn't dare touch anyone on this night or during the entire trip for two reasons: he didn't want to cheat on Joanne, and he knew that even if he had wanted to, word would have gotten back to his wife. At worst, Paul would have videotaped his infidelity just as he had filmed everything the previous night. Van was stunned by Paul's growing obsession with videotaping. It seemed his friend craved filming anything and everything that could later be used as some kind of blackmail.

Several weeks after the Andy Douglas wedding fiasco, the gang gathered at 57 Bayview Drive. As usual, everyone was drinking quite heavily except Joanne, who was still pregnant. The men, as they often did, abandoned the women and headed upstairs, where they smoked a joint.

Downstairs, Karla, Joanne, and Lori chatted in the kitchen. Karla steered the conversation to Joanne's pregnancy, just as she had done a few months earlier at Andy's Jack-and-Jill party. It was then that Karla had confided to Joanne her temptation to go off the Pill without telling Paul so that she could get pregnant, a deception Joanne knew would enrage Paul. It seemed that while Paul didn't want a baby just yet, he and Karla did plan to have children. Karla had told her that Paul really wanted to have a girl, and if they did have a daughter, they planned to name her Tammy.

Now Karla lovingly rubbed Joanne's rounded belly, talking dreamily of how much she wanted to have a child. She asked Joanne many of the same questions she'd been asking her for months: What did it feel like to have a baby growing inside? Did Joanne know the sex of the child? How big was the fetus now? Joanne politely answered all Karla's questions, but finally asked one herself: "Well, why don't you and Paul plan to have a baby?"

Karla looked a little mournful. "Paul says we can't afford one right now."

Although the women's discussion ended, the men were having a parallel conversation upstairs. Van, having overheard Karla's earlier chatter about babies, began to chide his buddy. "Well, when are you going to do it? When's Karla going to have a bun in the oven?" he asked.

Paul was unequivocal. "She's too fucking stupid to handle a kid. She'll forget to feed it, and the kid will end up dying. She'll forget to clean it. I tell her where to put the soap and she puts it somewhere else. No way, man."

While Paul clearly felt Karla could not properly care for a child, Van and the others couldn't help but notice how well Karla always tended to her animals.

Downstairs, in a large, glass aquarium Karla had created a home for Spike the iguana. Lime-green, more than two feet in length with a stubby, abnormal tail, he was a fearsome-looking creature. But Karla loved him. A refugee from the pet clinic, Karla felt he was being abused by his owner. When he was brought in, Karla didn't think he was going to live and the owner didn't seem to care one way or the other. After nursing him back to health, Karla brought him home to live in Port Dalhousie. Spike the iguana lived quite comfortably in his aquarium, gazing sullenly at the fish who were his neighbors in a second aquarium.

While the guys were still upstairs, Karla picked Spike up and showed him off to Joanne. But when Joanne reached to pet him, as she would a puppy, Spike snapped, nipping her on the right thumb. Karla was shocked.

"You stupid thing!" she scolded Spike, dropping him back in the aquarium. "I can't believe he did that! He usually likes girls!"

Joanne's thumb was throbbing, and Karla hurried off to get some paper towels to stem the flow of blood from twin puncture marks on the thumb.

By this time the boys had descended from the upper level. Karla told Paul about the incident with Spike and he shooed the girls out of the room, saying they needed to talk about some "guy" stuff.

Karla and Joanne retreated to the kitchen to tend to the wound. Inside the guest bedroom, the "guy" discussion was actually centered around the girl named Heather from Florida. Paul had continued to keep in contact with her, and he was determined to call her again this night. He enjoyed the sensation of her long-distance affection, and he loved the idea of showing off to his pals how this cute, sexy girl could be manipulated even over the phone, from his own home.

While he chatted with Heather he began to tease Spike, poking him and pulling on his little tail. "We nursed you back to health," Paul addressed the iguana after hanging up the phone. "We treated you well. We looked after you, and this is how you treat us?" He continued to talk to the animal, as if scolding a young child. The boys began chuckling. "Do you know how much money I spent on that medicine? I fed you. I washed you. I took you for walks. And you treat me like this. What are you? Stupid?" Paul flicked the sides of the aquarium, then poked his hand inside, daring the animal to defy him. Spike obliged by whipping him with his stubby tail. "Oh yeah!" Paul muttered, squeezing the animal in retaliation. Suddenly Spike snapped again, and this time he caught Paul's index finger in his grasp. Paul screamed and jerked his hand away, tearing the skin more severely. Blood spurted from the cut and flew in the air as Paul waved his hand wildly.

"Keep your hand above your heart," offered Van, mildly stoned and somewhat drunk.

"Karla, the fucking thing bit me!" Paul bellowed, moving out of the bedroom toward the kitchen. "It's your fucking fault! Why'd you ever bring that fucking thing home?" Karla tried to put a bandage on the assaulted finger, but Paul was in such a state that he wouldn't hold still. He alternated between frenzied attempts to wash the cut in the kitchen sink and showing it off to the mildly amused guests. Suddenly, he strode back into the guest room, grabbing the iguana in his left hand. "I'm going to kill you! I'm fucking going to kill you!" He screamed. In a flash, an unrepentant Spike was lying on a cutting board that spanned one of the twin kitchen sinks. Paul grabbed a kitchen knife from a nearby wooden knife block and gave a mighty blow to Spike's head. But the iguana was made of tougher stuff than Paul imagined and survived the initial assault, his stubby tail thrashing wildly.

Van and Joanne watched the carnage from the edge of the dining room. When Paul said he was going to get rid of the animal, they assumed initially he meant to send it back to the clinic. "Don't kill the stupid thing," Van said, trying to placate his enraged, drunken friend. Paul ignored him.

"You fucking thing!" Paul screamed, furious that the animal seemed to be defying him even in its death throes. Three, four thwacks with the knife were needed before the unfortunate Spike's head popped off, landing in the other sink. "I told you I was going to kill you!" Paul said, continuing to address the now headless body, its little legs thrashing, blood flying into the air. Karla, watching horrified from the dining room, burst into tears.

"Paul, don't! Don't! No! No!" she pleaded to no avail.

Instead, Paul strode across the room and grabbed her, leaving an imprint of iguana blood and gore on her shoulder.

Flecks of blood spotted the backs of his hands as well as his tan pants and black T-shirt. "Get a grip!" he said in a menacing voice. "Now, go clean it up!" Then, after a moment, a lightbulb seemed to go on inside Paul's head. He smiled. "No, I want you to skin it!"

Someone picked up on the notion and quipped, "They make good watchbands."

"Try and get the skin off without tearing it," Paul commanded Karla.

And all of a sudden, as though some hidden power switch had been activated, Karla was transformed from a blubbering wreck into a professional animal attendant. She rose from the dining-room chair and pulled an X-Acto-knife from the kitchen drawer and began making incisions. Joanne, who wasn't troubled by the scene, stood next to Karla, watching in fascination. Karla began explaining, as she did for helpers at the animal clinic, what she was doing. She showed Joanne the animal's organs, his liver and heart and his little testicles. Carefully Karla pulled the skin from around his tiny, clawed toes. She laid the organs out as though it were a high-school science project.

"She did a perfect job. She didn't make a single tear," Joanne recalls.

What Karla produced looked like a little green suit that Spike had worn for an evening out. Gone was Karla's distress of a few minutes earlier. "She was really cheery about it. I think she was more excited because it was something Paul couldn't put her down about. It was something she knew how to do," Joanne recalled afterward.

Meanwhile, as Karla operated, the boys stepped onto the back porch and lit up the barbecue. Someone had suggested that iguana is a Chinese delicacy they call "bamboo chicken." Paul made a big show of washing his hands, then grabbed Spike's remains and plopped them onto the barbecue. After some basting with sauce and seasonings, he pulled the meat off the grill. Gus and Joanne refused to try it.

"I don't eat anything I dissected," Joanne explained.

Van tasted a piece. It was rubbery and had a slightly rusty

taste to it. After pretending to enjoy it greatly, he discreetly spit it out into his hand and threw it away. "Hmmm, very good!" he said, much to Paul's delight.

Paul took great pride in eating his kill, like a modern-day caveman, savoring every bite. "Now I'm eating you, you fucker!" he told his former pet and current dinner.

CHAPTER
21

As Mary pulled her car up in front of 57 Bayview Drive she was surprised to see the house in darkness. The Bernardo house on this December night in 1992 was pitch black.

She had arrived shortly before her daughter Jane's eleven o'clock curfew and as Jane emerged from the darkened house and approached the car, it was clear that the teen was crying. The sixteen-year-old walked around the front of the car and opened the back door. As she did, she handed her mother something that had been balled up tightly in her fist. "Here, take this, I don't ever want to see it again," she sobbed. It was a gold necklace—a Christmas present from Paul Bernardo.

Jane first met Karla Homolka when she was twelve years old in the summer of 1988. The tiny, energetic girl loved animals and after looking longingly at the pets lined up in the Number One Pet Centre at the Pen Centre shopping mall, Jane and her mother met one of the store employees, Karla Homolka. Soon, Jane was a regular visitor to the pet store. Once Karla took Jane for a soda in the mall on a break. The younger girl soon found herself talking about Karla at home and occasionally phoning her. Several months later, Karla left the pet store and began working at a veterinary clinic and the contact between Jane and Karla slowly ended.

The relationship resumed, however, in early 1991 when Jane was given an invitation to a wedding shower for Karla. Then fifteen, Jane was ecstatic that Karla had remembered

her after so much time. The shower visit was cancelled, much
to Jane's disappointment, but Karla called and suggested the
two get together for a "girls' night out." They would go for
dinner, do some shopping, and Jane could stay overnight at
57 Bayview. Jane checked with her mother and the sleep-over
was okayed.

The girls had a great time, talking about animals and boys
in whom Jane was interested. It was Friday, June 7, 1991,
three weeks before Karla and Paul's wedding, so they talked
about the wedding plans and how Karla wanted Jane and her
mother to attend.

When they returned to 57 Bayview, Jane asked if it would
be okay if she had a drink. She'd never had alcohol before
and wanted to try it. "We can give you anything you want,"
Karla told Jane, showing her the vast array of liquor in the
dining room cabinet.

Jane settled on peach schnapps and orange juice, which
Karla mixed for her. The two watched the movie *Ghost* on
videocassette although Jane would later say she couldn't recall seeing the popular movie. In fact, Jane couldn't remember much of anything that night. She didn't even remember
waking up the next morning or how she made it downstairs.

She does remember her first meeting with Paul Bernardo,
though. He was sitting at the kitchen table having breakfast
when Jane plunked herself down on the kitchen floor and
promptly vomited. She was so embarrassed. But she couldn't
help herself.

After cleaning herself up in the washroom, she went home
and answered some probing questions from her mother. She
had the flu, Jane explained. And certainly, she felt like she
was going to die. She had never felt that sick. In fact, she felt
so sick she cancelled her participation in a much anticipated
activity the following day.

Although both Jane and her mother attended the couple's
wedding on June 29, Jane was still mortified at how she'd
behaved around the older couple and wrote a letter to that
effect.

Dear Karla and Paul,
Hey you two "Love Birds"! How's married life. congra-
dulations (sic). Thanks so much for inviting me to your

wedding. It meant a lot to me. You guys are the perfect couple. Karla I hope when I get married some day that I find a man like Paul. I mean, I don't know Paul very well but my first impressions were:

—good looking

—sweet

—and seemed to be a very caring person

But there is a lot more, but for some reason I can't really remember what happened that day.

I feel really bad, and embarrassed, of this first time I met Paul. Here I am (or there I was) throwing up all over the place.

I'm sorry Paul and Karla. Hopefully the next time we see each other I will be feeling better. Say hello! to Buddy for me. That sweet, little innocent puppy! You might not think so right now, because of his washroom manners, but deep down I'm sure ya love him.

Hope you have an awesome time in HAWAII

Talk to you later!

Love always and forever.

Jane

Soon Jane was a regular weekend visitor to Paul and Karla's home. The trio would go to dinner, watch movies and order in food. Jane was excited by the attention being paid her by such older, established adults.

Jane's mom was less than thrilled. As the relationship intensified, Jane's mother, uneasy with the age difference between her daughter and the married couple, began to erase messages left by Karla on their answering machine.

A trip the three took to Toronto in August, 1991, turned into an overnight affair when Jane called home to say Paul had too much to drink to drive home. That further strengthened the uncomfortable feelings Mary had toward the Bernardos.

Late that summer, perhaps aware of the suspicions Mary harbored, Paul and Karla invited the single mother to dinner at 57 Bayview. Paul and Karla were the perfect hosts. Paul focused almost all of the conversation on Jane's mom, sitting close to her on the couch, directing comments exclusively at her, engaging her specifically even though Karla and Jane were also present.

"I was treated like an honored guest," Mary later recalled. "I was given 100% attention."

When they all began eating Mary noticed that only when Paul ate, Karla ate. If Paul slowed down, Karla did too. Several times Paul cautioned Karla not to eat so fast, demanding that they eat in unison. As the evening progressed, Paul explained to Mary that they were very fond of Jane.

"He wanted me to know that they had chosen Jane to be a friend of Karla's, that she was worthy of their attention, worthy of their friendship. They had dropped Karla's friends, because they were not good enough for Karla," Mary recalled. "And Jane was the person they saw as the ultimate friend."

Mary was not impressed by Paul's charming ways. She told him directly she was uncomfortable with the relationship and she certainly didn't want Paul buying her daughter presents. "I like to give gifts to my girlfriends and girls," Paul explained innocently.

Not long after, Paul and Karla attended a school event in which Jane was competing. Mary was present as well, and again Paul continued to engage her in conversation, doing his best to charm her.

Mary noted that Paul and Karla rarely approached her together. She couldn't help but feel they were "working" both her daughter and herself. Several times Mary bristled as she watched Paul's hand move lovingly to Jane's back or around her shoulder. She wondered why he wasn't doing that to his wife.

That day, Jane's instructor pulled Mary aside and told her that Jane had approached her in confidence and told her that Paul had been touching her breasts.

Now that Mary's fears were confirmed, she said nothing to her daughter for several days, contemplating how to deal with the situation. Finally, during a workday, she told her colleagues she was going to visit one of Jane's friends and wrote down Paul and Karla's address, in case for some reason she

Paul Bernardo's childhood home in the affluent Guildwood subdivision near Lake Ontario. (Mike Cassese, *Toronto Sun*)

Childhood friend and best man at Paul Bernardo's wedding, Van Smirnis. (*Toronto Sun*)

Paul Bernardo (right) and childhood friend Steve Smirnis are Boy Scouts in the Scarborough suburb of Toronto, Ontario. (*Toronto Sun*)

The police composite drawing that was created with the help of the last Scarborough rapist victim, the only one to get a good look at her assailant's face. When the drawing ran in the *Toronto Sun* May 29, 1990, Bernardo's friends joked about the eerie resemblance. (*Toronto Sun*)

One of dozens of billboards that sprang up throughout Ontario in the summer of 1992. Witnesses who'd been hypnotized led police to believe this was the car used in the abduction of Kristen French April 16, 1992. (Ian MacDonald, *Toronto Sun*)

Paul Bernardo dressed for the 1987 Price Waterhouse Christmas Party in Toronto. By this time the Scarborough rapist has claimed several victims. (*Toronto Sun*)

Sitting beneath a giant picture of their daughter Leslie, Dan and Debbie Mahaffy field questions at a Feb. 20, 1993, press conference, three days after the arrest of Paul Bernardo. (Mark O'Neill, *Toronto Sun*)

Kristen French. This picture was released to the media April 17, the day after her disappearance. (*Toronto Sun*)

Doug French is comforted by a family member as wife Donna looks on during a press conference to appeal to kidnappers to let Kristen go April 20, 1992. (Carlo Allegri, *Toronto Sun*)

Investigators gingerly lift the lifeless hand of Kristen French, April 30, 1992, two weeks after she was abducted on her way home from school. (Bill Sandford, *Toronto Sun*)

Paul Bernardo (middle holding beer can) and Van Smirnis (far right in black) and young friends in Florida, 1989. (*Toronto Sun*)

Paul and Karla, Alex and Kathy Ford, frolic around the Homolka family pool. (*Toronto Sun*)

Alex Ford and Karla Homolka share a dance at Paul and Karla's wedding reception, June 29, 1991, Niagara-on-the-Lake. (*Toronto Sun*)

The tidy Cape Cod-style home occupied by Paul Bernardo and his wife Karla Homolka has a desolate feel to it in late Feb. 1993 shortly after Bernardo was arrested. (Geoff George, *Toronto Sun*)

Tammy Lyn Homolka. This picture adorns her headstone. (Derek Ruttan, *Toronto Sun*)

The gravesite of Tammy Lyn Homolka who died early Christmas Eve 1990. Later, her sister, Karla Homolka, would admit she and fiance Paul Bernardo drugged and sexually assaulted her before she aspirated and died. "You were loved so very much, and now you've gone away. Memories will keep you near. We miss you everyday." is inscribed on the stone. (Derek Ruttan, *Toronto Sun*)

Paul Bernardo and Karla Homolka mug for the camera during a visit to the Lewiston, N.Y., apartment of Alex and Kathy Ford, late summer, 1991. (*Toronto Sun*)

Inspector Vince Bevan, leader of the Green Ribbon Task Force, addresses reporters on Feb. 20, 1993, days after the arrest of Paul Bernardo. Behind him, a giant picture of Kristen French. (Mark O'Neill, *Toronto Sun*)

Police photo of Karla Homolka Jan. 5, 1993, 10 days after being beaten with a flashlight by husband, Paul Bernardo. This photo was taken at St. Catharines General Hospital. (*Toronto Sun*)

Karla Homolka departs for court July 5, 1993. (Veronica Henri, *Toronto Sun*)

Lori Homolka weeps as she and parents Dorothy and Karel leave court after Karla's conviction. (Ken Kerr, *Toronto Sun*)

Paul Bernardo, hands shackled, exits a police transport truck en route to a court appearance in Scarborough on May 13, 1993. (Fred Thornhill, *Toronto Sun*)

The authors; Scott Burnside and Alan Cairns. (Norm Betts, *Toronto Sun*)

didn't return. She drove to Port Dalhousie, backing the car into the driveway.

It seemed to take Paul forever to reach the door when she rang the bell, but finally he did. Buddy was at his side and the Rottweiler made Mary very nervous, especially given the nature of her visit. Paul reluctantly invited Mary into the home but refused to sit down until invited to do so by Mary. They sat on the couch, a pillow between them, Mary's keys still jingling quietly in her hand. Finally, after a few moments of uncomfortable small talk, Mary asked Paul why he was touching her daughter's breasts.

Paul denied any such inappropriate behaviour. "Jane's a friend of Karla's, I would have no reason to do that," Paul explained patiently.

"You're lying," Mary said.

His pleasant demeanour suddenly changed and in a smouldering rage, he led Mary to the door. He told Mary that by the end of the day, Jane would know all about this conversation and that she would also know that she had lost Karla as her best friend. As he spoke, his tone of voice rose. By the time Mary walked to the car and began driving away, he was screaming.

Despite the ugly scene with Paul, Jane insisted on visiting the couple. Mary's mother, fearful of driving an even greater wedge between herself and her daughter, compromised, telling Jane she could only visit on Thursday evenings when the Simpsons were on TV and only if Mary dropped her off and picked her up.

Jane continued to see Paul and Karla on Thursdays with the exception of a few months during which Jane was too busy or preoccupied to keep up the visits, until December 22, 1992, and Jane's tearful exit from an imposingly dark 57 Bayview Drive.

Paul cried. Then Karla. Then tears streamed down Becky's cheeks. Together they cried tears for Tammy; recalling how she looked, how she smiled, how she talked. At 1:35 A.M. on December 24, 1992 the three friends huddled together on the living room floor at 57 Bayview Drive. It was two years almost to the minute of Tammy's death.

Becky missed her childhood friend terribly. For Becky, an only child, Tammy was the sister she never had. But that horrible Christmas Eve Becky learned her best friend had died from an alcohol accident. It hadn't made sense at the time and two things about Tammy's death had always puzzled Becky and her mother, Sharon. A couple of weeks before Christmas, while Becky's mom and her husband repainted Becky's bedroom, Tammy drew crazily on the walls with markers. In one message, Tammy wrote *"Why does my life have to be so screwed up?"* Becky couldn't figure out what this meant. Sure, Tammy had talked about her own set of problems—typical teenage girl problems, but nothing so serious as the words suggested. And it had puzzled Becky to see Tammy lying in her coffin with the bizarre red marks on her face. For two years, Becky had tried and failed to understand Tammy's life and death. In an effort to reunite herself with the Homolka family and make some sense of Tammy's death, the seventeen-year-old had accepted Karla's invitation to a dinner in October. Since then, she had begun to think of Karla and Paul as an older sister and brother.

On the first night Becky visited Paul and Karla, they drank too much booze. They smoked, too, not only cigarettes but marijuana. At one point, Paul threw $5,000 in cash into Becky's lap. She was amazed and concluded the couple was well off because they lived in a nice house, owned a great car and had all that cash. Paul and Karla treated her well that night. Of course, she had known Karla since she was a kid and she and Tammy had often talked about how attractive Paul was and how nice he was to them, especially when he rented movies for everybody to watch. Paul was nice enough to even drive her home that night.

A couple of weeks later, Karla invited Becky to party again and stay overnight. After more drugs and booze, the three slept on the floor. But Becky recalls that night as weird: Paul lay between herself and Karla and for most of the night he pushed his body against Becky's back; she could feel his erection through her clothes. She woke up the next morning with Paul sitting over her, gazing at her. Paul's sexual advances continued. Becky asked him to back off. "I don't want to be doing this to you; you're married to my best friend's sister," she told him.

"I've done this before; I've had other girlfriends and Karla didn't even care," Paul replied. And Karla told Becky quite openly that their love had ended; that they didn't really love each other in June 1991 and should not have even married. Karla told her she and Paul were still friends and that Karla would have no objection if Becky were to date Paul. "Paul is a great guy," she would tell her.

As the friendship continued through November, Paul constantly hugged and kissed Becky who found this relationship confusing, but nonetheless gratifying. One weekend, Paul and Karla offered to take Becky to Toronto shopping because she had never been. While window shopping in the Eaton Centre, Paul bought Becky a pair of $80 Guess jeans and a $30 flannel shirt. A short while later, Paul and Karla offered to take Becky to Toronto for an entire weekend. When she found out about the offer from the older couple, Sharon called Karla: "Karla, why are you doing this for Becky? What are you getting out of it? What is going on?"

"Oh don't worry, Becky is such a special person. We're delighted to take her with us," Karla replied.

Still, Sharon was worried. Becky was acting rebellious at the time and her mom worried her carefree experiences with Karla and Paul would add fuel to the fire. But there were even more pressing concerns. One day, when Paul and Karla came to Becky's house to pick her up, her mother sought reassurance from Paul. "Paul, will you make sure Becky is all right? You know, I've been very worried about her being out at night since Kristen French was murdered. I really don't want anything to happen to Becky."

"Don't worry, everything will be okay." Paul smiled back.

"No harm will come to Becky as long as she's with us," Karla guaranteed.

Becky's mom knew Wendy Lutczyn, a woman who worked as a receptionist at the same animal clinic where Karla was employed. More than once, Sharon spoke with Karla by telephone, asking her if everything was okay with Becky. Karla reassured her time and time again that things were just fine.

In December, the threesome checked into the Royal York Hotel, a five-star Canadian Pacific luxury hotel in the city's downtown. Becky wore her black strapless prom dress to dinner in the revolving restaurant of the CN Tower, a 1,822-foot-tall needlelike structure that dominates the vast Toronto skyline. Later that night they played on the midway rides at the Canadian National Exhibition fair and then returned to the hotel for champagne. Paul paid for it all. Later that night, with Karla passed out in one of the twin beds. Becky climbed into the other bed. To her surprise, Paul joined her.

"Get out, Paul!"

"Why don't you like me? Why don't you love me?" Paul asked with a puppy-dog look on his face.

"Because I don't feel that way," Becky told him, then suggested he should sleep with Karla.

Paul slinked over to Karla's bed. He woke Karla up and repeated his hurt words to Karla: "Becky doesn't like me; Becky doesn't love me . . ."

During the morning, Becky and Paul prowled through the hotel. At one point, Paul set fire to a meal cart. Police and fire trucks came to the hotel. Later, police came to the hotel room door. Paul answered. Becky couldn't believe how cool, calm and collected Paul remained while the officers asked him questions.

She had grown to be a little scared of Paul when he was drinking. It was as if he changed. After the trips to Toronto, Becky always watched how much she drank around Paul and Karla. She wanted to make sure she didn't change too.

On the night of December 23, 1992, she was swept away and embarrassed, by Paul and Karla's apparent Christmas generosity. They had bought her a huge, floppy Gund teddy bear, a white Tasmanian Devil baseball jersey, a Little Mermaid movie poster and a stuffed crab "Sebastian" from the Little Mermaid movie. Paul himself had bought Becky a gold necklace and a gold ankle bracelet.

Becky looked at the paltry Sesame Street book, a figurine

and the stuffed bunny rabbit she had bought Karla for $30 and felt terribly guilty.

The strange visit didn't end when the Christmas gifts were given or even when the tears for Tammy stopped early the next morning. Karla suddenly went upstairs and re-emerged minutes later dressed for bed with a blanket and a pillow in her arms.

"Karla, what are you doing? You should be upstairs," Becky said.

"Oh, I don't feel like sleeping upstairs. I'm going into the wing," she replied, and vanished into the downstairs bedroom.

Becky became confused. She didn't know where to sleep. It was Paul's house. She asked him.

"I guess up in the master bedroom with me," he said.

Becky went upstairs to the bedroom, changed and lay in bed. Paul later joined her. While they talked, Becky asked Paul if Tammy had ever slept with her boyfriend.

"No," Paul responded.

"How do you know that?" Becky inquired. For the next five minutes she tried to prod Paul for answers. "How?"

"Because I slept with her. I was her first," he said.

Becky couldn't believe her ears. "How do you know that?"

"Because I have her bloody underwear to prove it," he said.

Paul told her his sexual attraction to Tammy began when his late sister-in-law was in Grade 7 or 8. At first they just smiled at one another, then their relationship included kidding and hugging. He said they slept together in the summer of 1990. Then Paul had sex with Becky, even though she begged him not to.

After waking that morning, Paul and Karla took Becky home. But that night, they all visited the Homolkas at 61 Dundonald to remember Tammy. At one point, Becky made her way upstairs to Tammy's bedroom. She sat on the bed and cried again. How she missed Tammy. Paul joined her.

"Why did she have to die?" Becky asked Paul.

He gave some mumbo-jumbo answer that wasn't an answer.

Three days later, the night of December 27, Becky and her boyfriend Brian went with Paul and Karla to see the *Muppets' Christmas Carol* movie. Afterwards, they were drinking at 57 Bayview Drive. Paul seemed jealous of Brian and began writing Becky love notes, telling her to leave Brian, that he would "do anything" for her, that she was his "world," telling her that life wasn't worth living without her and implying that suicide was close: "I took a major chance on you. Maybe you took it for granted. But I do know that I'll love you 'til the day I die . . . tomorrow!"

Later that night, as Paul and Brian continued drinking downstairs, Becky and Karla talked in the master bedroom. Karla was now attempting to get Becky to leave Brian. Becky saw the foam mattress near the bed. Becky told Karla that if she didn't love Paul any more she should leave him. Just then, Paul came into the bedroom and overheard what Becky said. He flipped out.

"You're not my friend any more, get out, get out!" he screamed at Becky. He took off his wedding and Masons' rings and threw them out of a window. Becky stormed angrily out of the house, but looked for the rings in the darkness. She found them and slipped them onto the necklace Paul had bought her for Christmas. She returned to the house to find Paul had gone out to find her and was still missing. He returned later, fuming. Becky and Brian were happy to leave when Brian's father arrived to pick them up.

The next day, Karla and Paul showed up at Becky's house, Karla asking for the return of Paul's rings. Her face was red and bruised. Upon seeing Karla this way, Sharon called Wendy Lutczyn, who in November had told her how one day Karla had came into work limping, telling Wendy she had banged her thigh while chasing Buddy around Paul's work bench. Realizing Karla was hurt badly, Wendy related to Sharon how she had kept asking questions and demanding that Karla let her see the injury. Finally, Karla asked Wendy to go into the washroom. She pulled down her vet's scrub pants and showed Wendy a pencil-thick hole in her thigh. It was about a quarter of an inch deep and surrounded by yellow matter. It appeared infected. Karla assured Wendy she had been to a doctor and was taking antibiotics. As Becky's mother and Wendy spoke, they realized something terrible was wrong. Wendy recalled seeing other bruises on Karla, but these, too, had been passed off on playing with Buddy. After hanging up the phone, Wendy disguised her voice and placed an anonymous telephone call to Dorothy Homolka, telling her that Karla was being abused and that she needed help. Wendy didn't say who she was, just in case she was wrong; just in case Karla really had been in a car accident.

On Monday January 4, 1993, the first day back to work after the New Year's vacation, Wendy walked into the animal clinic to find Karla sitting in the back, her back turned. Karla turned around. Her face looked horrible. It was bruised from her eyebrows to her cheekbones, down her neck. One eye was completely bloodshot. Wendy burst into tears as she felt one side of Karla's head to find a mushy dent. This time it wasn't Buddy, Karla explained, but she had been in an accident in a friend's car. She had been to the doctor, of course, and apart from concerns over concussion everything was fine.

"Does your mom know?" ventured Wendy.

"No, I don't want my mom to know," Karla said quickly. "If my mom comes into the clinic, tell her I'm in surgery in the back."

Wendy was shocked. Why wouldn't Karla want her mom to know? Surely her mother should be the first to know. At lunch, Wendy left the clinic and called police, citing apparent abuse. An officer told her there was nothing they could do. Then she called a battered woman's shelter. When she returned to work Karla was still there. They worked together the rest of the day, but at night Wendy called a male friend, Philip, and asked him to call Dorothy Homolka again. Philip promised he would call the Homolka home.

That evening around 5:30 P.M. Dorothy received a strange and disturbing anonymous phone call. An unknown man told Dorothy that she needed to come and see Karla. He said Karla needed someone's help. It was the second such call Dorothy had received in less than a week.

Dorothy never learned who the callers were, but after relaying the nature of the cryptic call to Lori and Karel, all three headed over to 57 Bayview Drive.

The house was dark. After knocking and ringing the doorbell to no avail, the family members immediately drove to a nearby convenience store and called 911. Back at 57 Bayview they waited until two police cars and an ambulance crew arrived.

Dorothy and Karel explained what had happened and there was discussion about forcing their way into the home, but the police said there were no grounds for such action. The Homolkas returned home, still feeling uneasy about what had transpired.

Lori began calling every few minutes to 57 Bayview. Finally Paul answered.

"Can I speak with Karla?" Lori asked.

"What's it worth to you?" Paul asked.

"More than you'll ever know," Lori shot back. Paul summoned Karla to the phone.

The sisters spoke for about ten minutes, but since there seemed to be nothing unusual in her tone of voice or behavior, Lori hung up.

Dorothy still had a nagging feeling of unease. The following day, January 5, 1993, she rearranged her lunch hour at Shaver Hospital and paid an unexpected visit to the Martindale Animal Clinic.

Dorothy couldn't believe her eyes when Karla appeared from the back of the clinic. She was wearing her white lab coat, but both her eyes were deeply blackened and her face was grotesquely swollen. Around her neck were deep, angry bruises that had turned a sickening shade of yellow and brown.

She looked like a raccoon!

"I thought I was going to have a heart attack," Dorothy would say much later. "I shook and I—I just couldn't understand."

Despite the shock of her mother's unexpected visit, Karla remained as upbeat and cheerful as always. Any distress seemed to be born of her mother's emotional response to the severe bruising.

The two headed off to McDonald's for lunch, where Karla tried to explain that she'd been in a car accident. But the story didn't wash: Paul's car hadn't been damaged. Karla explained nonchalantly that she'd been with a friend of Paul's when the accident happened.

But Dorothy would have none of it. She demanded to know what had happened. Finally, breaking down in a torrent of tears, Karla told her mother that Paul had beaten her savagely with a flashlight some ten days earlier.

Dorothy was stunned. The bruises, so sickening, had been healing for more than a week. She shuddered thinking about what her daughter must have looked like immediately after the beating.

Dorothy dropped Karla off at work with the understanding that she, Karel, and Lori would come around that evening to pick her up. And that evening, while Paul was out, the Homolkas returned to 57 Bayview. It was about 9 P.M.

Dorothy noticed then how stiffly Karla was walking, as though every movement was a struggle.

Karla was terrified. She didn't want to leave, she told her family.

Lori, who hadn't seen her sister until this time, was disgusted.

"Bruises everywhere on her body. Disgusting. Disgusting," she said in court later. "I was angry, confused, upset. Angry that she could stay with someone who could do that to a human being."

For almost an hour the family tried to convince Karla that she had to leave the house, and Paul, for good. Karla was frantic.

Finally, Karel physically dragged her and a few belongings out of the house and into their van.

The Homolkas, however, didn't remain at 61 Dundonald long for fear it would be the first place Paul would look for his missing wife. They decided that they would take Karla to a friend of Lori's, Corinna Hannah. Corinna's husband was a Metro Toronto police officer.

While Karel waited at home, the women traveled to Corinna's and called Niagara Regional Police.

Constable Yvette Fleming arrived and took a statement from Karla about the beating. Then Karla was transported to St. Catharines General Hospital.

While she was waiting, Dorothy ran into a friend who asked if the girls were having trouble with their asthma. No, Dorothy explained, Paul had beaten her daughter with a flashlight.

For three days Karla remained in the hospital. She was given a series of painkillers and other medications, and she underwent a battery of tests to determine if there were any fractures or skull damage. Karla was fortunate. She would not suffer additional permanent damage.

Police arrived and took a series of photos, documenting the bruising that covered virtually every inch of her body.

When Karla was ready to leave the hospital, the Homolkas again made arrangements for their daughter to stay somewhere other than a place Paul would expect to find his wife.

Dorothy phoned her brother Calvin Seger and his wife, Patty.

Patty had been out watching a hockey game in the Brampton area on Friday night, January 8, 1993. When she later arrived home, Calvin was on the phone. He had a worried look on his face.

"Can you hold on?" he said into the phone. Cupping the mouthpiece, he told Patty that it was his sister Dorothy and that his niece Karla had been hospitalized following a beating Paul had given her with a flashlight and that she'd left Paul.

Although she'd only met Karla a handful of times since she'd begun dating Calvin in the summer of 1989, Patty was instantly struck with sympathy for Karla.

"Oh, my goodness! How could he do that?" she said.

"Is it all right if Karla comes and stays with us?" Calvin asked.

"Of course. She can stay as long as she wants," Patty answered quickly.

They arranged for Karel and Dorothy to drive Karla to

Brampton, approximately one hour away from St. Catharines, on Sunday the tenth.

After he hung up the phone, Calvin repeated the details of Karla's beating and subsequent hospital stay.

Paul had been leaving messages on the Homolkas' answering machine ever since Karla had left him and Dorothy and Karel were afraid that he might come around and continue to bother Karla.

The next night, Patty was out with a friend at a lingerie party. When the two women returned home Karla, Dorothy, Karel, and Lori were all seated in the living room of their apartment. Patty couldn't believe her eyes.

The bruises on Karla's face were deep and black. There were broken blood vessels in the whites of her eyes, and she could barely move. Later that evening, Patty touched Karla's head and was horrified to feel the lumps and note the areas where her scalp was visible; her hair had apparently been pulled out in clumps. There was a sickening, spongy texture to Karla's scalp. The bruising in her legs and thighs was so severe that when Karla moved it was as if she were crippled with arthritis.

The sight nearly brought Patty to tears, and she had to restrain herself to keep from bawling just at the sight of her niece-in-law.

"What are you guys doing here? I didn't think you were coming until tomorrow," Patty said after introducing her friend.

Dorothy explained that Paul had been calling that afternoon and they felt it was better that Karla leave right away.

Karla, dressed in loose jeans and a white sweater, merely nodded in agreement.

There was a high level of tension in the apartment. For one thing, the families were never particularly close, and here they were imposing on Calvin and Patty. And there was a real fear, at least as far as Dorothy was concerned, that Paul would somehow find out where Karla was.

"He knows a lot of people," Dorothy warned.

"Don't worry, we're the last people Paul would think of," Calvin offered.

Patty nodded. "Karla can stay as long as she wants. And Lori too," she said.

Lori agreed that she'd like to stay for a few days and help Karla recover from her injuries.

Although Karla didn't indicate that she was unhappy to have been moved, she didn't participate in the conversation in any meaningful way, which indicated to Patty that the decision had been made without a great deal of input from Karla.

Dorothy and Karel left for some sort of lighting trade show that Karel was obligated to attend, but they promised to call later. Patty made some chicken noodle soup, but Karla insisted she wasn't hungry and declined.

"We'll give up our water bed for you so it'll be easier for you," Patty told Karla, realizing that a normal mattress would have been as painful as sleeping on a bed of nails for the battered woman.

Karla thanked them and asked if she could take a bath, after which she went to bed. Lori and Calvin and Patty watched a little television but didn't talk about the situation. Lori eventually joined Karla in the water bed, while Calvin and Patty slept on a pullout couch in the living room.

Calvin and Patty lived in condo #130 in the McLaughlin Road complex, one of literally thousands of apartment buildings that mark the horizon around greater Metro Toronto.

Karla and Lori spent some of the following day in their aunt and uncle's apartment complex's hot tub.

Karel and Dorothy were still in the area the following night, and they called and suggested that Karla and Lori spend the night in the hotel with them. In the afternoon the girls joined their parents, but later Karla called Patty at work.

"I want to come back to your place," said the little-girl voice on the other end of the line. "I feel safe at your place. I feel comfortable."

Patty told her she was welcome to come back, and when she and Calvin returned from work, Karla was already there. Lori said she, too, would like to stay, but that she had to get back to work in St. Catharines, and so she left with her parents.

Despite some initial shyness on Karla's part, she and Patty began to chat and Karla's comfort level seemed to rise. At one point Patty told her she felt so bad for Karla after what Paul had done.

"This isn't the first time he did this to me," she explained casually. "He did this on a regular basis."

And thus began discussion of a horrific litany of abuses Karla had suffered at the hands of her husband. With an almost cavalier tone, Karla described her life with Paul.

Her husband seemed to have quite a sensitive sense of smell. He forbade Karla from using traditional cleansing products in their home in Port Dalhousie. He hated the smell, and if he detected—or thought he detected—cleaning smells, he would beat her, Karla said.

Once Karla prepared a dinner for Paul that he thought smelled funny, and he attacked her with the metal stand on which the microwave sat. That time he beat her so viciously that she thought her arm was broken.

"Everything bothered him," Karla explained. "I tried to please him as much as I could. I tried everything."

One of the first times Paul hit her was shortly after they started to date and she said something that set him off. He punched and slapped her and reached across and opened the passenger-side door of the car and pushed her out on the street into a mud puddle, Karla said. She was mortified, not so much at the beating, but that she might have to explain her muddy condition if her parents saw her.

Soon, Paul was using handcuffs and punching and kicking her on a regular basis, Karla said.

Patty and Karla were sitting together on the couch. Patty looked at her niece-in-law and shook her head in wonder as Karla continued to relate the abuse she underwent in her monotone, schoolgirlish voice.

Patty was, needless to say, shocked. Why didn't she leave?

The answer was too complex for Karla to fully explain, at least at this point.

"I loved him too much," Karla said, her eyes tearing.

Paul had apologized over and over that first time for beating her, promising it would never happen again. She believed him. And she didn't want her parents to get involved. She told Patty she felt her parents might be angry at her and blame her for having been beaten.

"No, I could never tell them," Karla concluded.

"But your parents will always be there to help you," Patty said, incredulous at the logic which seemed so clear to Karla. "They're your family. They would help you. . . ."

Karla's eyes began to water and soon she was sobbing. Patty moved closer and hugged her tight, her own eyes tearing.

"It's all right. It's all right. Everything's going to be all right."

The troubling conversation was pushed aside and the pair watched some television.

For those first few days Karla seemed entirely reluctant to eat despite Patty's constant urging. Instead, she asked Patty if she could refill her pain-pill prescription.

In the evenings other stories continued to bubble to the surface. Karla would often return home from the animal clinic in her lab coat and Paul, disgusted at what he said was an overwhelming smell of animals, disinfectant, and veterinary medicines and drugs, would demand she immediately take a shower and clean her clothes.

"You stink!" he'd complain. "Go and have a shower!"

But even though Karla would scrub herself and apply perfume, sometimes Paul could still catch a whiff of something disagreeable for which Karla would be beaten as punishment.

The beatings almost always involved punches, kicks, or attacks with whatever weapon was handy. Karla's upper arms, her legs, her stomach, and her back were less visible to outsiders and therefore bore the brunt of the beatings.

One day at work, after a particularly horrific attack, Karla told Patty she had to pick up a dog that weighed almost a hundred pounds. She said she thought she was going to die, the pain was so excruciating. Still, she said nothing.

Karla explained that Paul really liked oral sex and that she was forced to perform it all the time but that if she didn't do it right he beat her up. One night they were in bed and as she performed oral sex he became displeased. He took the lid off a wine decanter near the bed and bashed her on the base of the spine, numbing Karla's arms and legs.

"Don't do that again," Karla said to her husband. "You'll hurt me!"

"You think I care? I could kill you anytime I wanted to," Paul reportedly responded. "It's only a matter of time before I kill you. And if I do, I'll make it look like an accident."

He told Karla he had no remorse, no conscience, and that he could do anything he wanted to.

Sometimes Paul made Karla sleep in the root cellar. "Beware of night attackers," he'd warn before closing the door on the damp, dark space. Sometimes he'd come down in the middle of the night and brutally attack her or force her to have sex, Karla reported. Sometimes he would let her sleep, knowing that she'd be uncomfortable and worried. All of this occurred, of course, on a night before she'd have to get up first thing in the morning and go to work.

Another time he commanded that Karla go upstairs and not make any noise. She made the bed and suddenly he was there in a rage. "I thought I told you not to make any noise," he screamed before beating her again.

Even at the end, when Paul had left her so visibly beaten that she looked like a raccoon, Karla had returned to work.

At night, now, Patty found sleep eluding her as she thought about Karla's tale. She began to worry more and more about what would happen if Paul did find out where Karla was. What would he do?

Karla shared other stories of her marriage with her aunt Patty. She told her about the other women Paul had dated and had sex with. Sometimes he instructed her to pretend she was his sister if strange women called. Karla agreed, knowing what would happen if she defied her husband.

Often these conversations with Patty were punctuated by a sigh and Karla's refrain that she was happy to be away from Paul.

Patty confided some of the stories to Calvin, who became enraged. He sat Karla at the kitchen table and asked her to draw a map of the Port Dalhousie house, including the doors and exits. He was, he said, going to pay a visit to Paul.

"I'm going to go and teach him a lesson," Calvin announced, grim-faced. "I won't kill him. I'll just hit him on his knees."

Karla seemed neither upset at the prospect nor supportive. She merely completed the map and handed it to Calvin. Finally Patty persuaded Calvin that such a visit would only make matters worse and the subject was dropped.

Calvin had, despite his limited contact with Karla and her family, developed a considerable attachment to Karla. He felt extremely protective of her, and when the frequent calls came from St. Catharines, he always spoke to Dorothy.

During the day, Karla watched TV and relaxed in the hot tub. She slept often and long. At the end of the second week that Karla was Patty and Calvin's houseguest, the bruises had pretty much cleared up.

Karla also talked to friends and her parents on the phone. Patty would note the long-distance charges, sometimes more than $130 a month, and pass those along to Dorothy and Karel, who reimbursed them for the cost. One day, Karla said, she'd phoned Paul. But when she heard his voice on the end of the line she quickly hung up.

Karla told Patty she wanted to phone legal aid to see about getting a divorce as quickly as possible. She found a civil lawyer in St. Catharines, and on several occasions Dorothy would drive the hour or so to Brampton, collect Karla, take her back to the lawyer's office, and then return her to Brampton.

"I just don't want any part of him anymore," Karla explained. "I don't want to get beat up anymore. I just want to get on with my life."

Sometimes Karla would refer to Paul as a "bastard" or "pig" or "son of a bitch," but Patty often got the feeling that she didn't feel anger toward Paul so much as she was merely trying to forget what had happened.

One night at the end of the second week of Karla's stay, Patty suggested to Calvin that Karla had been getting better and might enjoy a night out, perhaps at a local bar. It would be a girls' night out.

Calvin thought that was a good idea.

Patty broached the subject with Karla.

"Your bruises seem to be pretty well healed and we think you should get out. How about going out Friday night to this bar?"

Karla's face lit up like a lightbulb. "Oh good! Great! I've got to buy a new dress. I have nothing to wear," she said, nervous energy bubbling to the surface.

Patty and Karla went to a nearby boutique and Karla picked out a slinky, black, spandex dress that showed off a lot of thigh and hugged Karla's lithe body. Patty couldn't help but think that she herself would never have worn something like that, but it seemed to be what Karla wanted. And Karla was so excited at the prospect of going out that Patty kept her thoughts to herself. Several days later, Dorothy was visiting and they went back to the shop and picked out another black dress. This one left part of Karla's chest exposed; it featured a circular area open and crossed with strips of fabric.

The Sugar Shack is a typical suburban bar at the end of a strip mall in Brampton about a six-dollar cab ride from Patty and Calvin's apartment building. It, like thousands of identical bars in thousands of identical strip malls, serves the exploding suburban housing complexes that have turned Brampton into a giant bedroom community for Metro Toronto. It boasts a 1950s motif with fifties and sixties rock-and-roll music played by a disc jockey.

To say Karla was excited about her first post-beating social adventure would be a tremendous understatement. She talked of little else in the days leading to the outing.

"I can't wait! I love to dance and I love to drink. And I can find some men!" Karla repeated over and over as the night out approached.

Men dominated Karla's thoughts as she and Patty and a friend made their way to the Sugar Shack.

Although apprehensive, Patty, not wanting to be a wet blanket, voiced only mild concern about Karla's seeming determination to find a new man.

"I don't think that's such a good idea," she cautioned,

"You just left a man who beat you with a flashlight. Why do you want to go on out and meet another man?"

"I'm living my life," was Karla's carefree reply.

Karla went on to explain how she and Paul would often go across the border to the Pleasure Dome and he would go off and meet other girls and dance while she was allowed to dance only when Paul wanted her to. Otherwise she had to sit where Paul positioned her and not complain.

As soon as they walked through the door of the Sugar Shack, Karla's eyes darted around the darkened room, searching out prospective partners.

"Wow! Men! This is great! Look at all the men!" Karla said, wide-eyed with excitement, barely able to contain herself.

Patty was concerned. "Karla, relax," she said.

There is a five-dollar cover charge at the Sugar Shack unless you get there before 9 P.M. The girls arrived about 8 P.M. and took up a table near the dance floor and ordered some chicken wings and other bar food. Patty and her friend would stay at the table all night.

Karla, however, was soon up and moving through the bar, making eyes at men, chatting with guys, talking to waiters and bartenders.

All three women would occasionally dance together to fast songs. At about 10 P.M. Karla caught the eye of a tall, gangly man. They smiled back and forth at each other and Karla went over to his table.

"She wasn't shy," recalls Patty as she explains that shortly thereafter the two were gone. It was over an hour until Karla returned, flushed with excitement.

"Karla, where were you? I've been looking all over for you."

"Oh, I was here."

"No, you weren't. Where were you?"

Finally Karla explained she'd been at the other end of the bar in a corner with her new friend making out.

"Karla! You shouldn't be doing that!" Patty said, straining to have her voice heard above the thundering sound system.

Karla became defensive.

"There's nothing wrong. I'm having fun."

Again Patty reminded Karla that she was just getting over a savage beating, but Karla stubbornly ignored her, returning to the table with her new friend.

As closing time approached, Karla returned to the table. She was clearly drunk, having inhaled vodka and orange juices all night. In a little-girl voice, she began asking Patty if she could bring her partner home to the condo.

"Please, Aunt Patty, please. Can I bring him home?"

Patty was incredulous. "No, you can't bring him home."

"Come on, Aunt Patty."

"I don't think so! You're a guest in my home. You can come and go as you please, but you're not bringing anybody home. Calvin would kick your butt."

Like a petulant schoolgirl, Karla returned to where he was waiting a few feet away. "My aunt Patty says you can't come home with us."

He looked over at Patty questioningly, but Patty merely shrugged her shoulders and told Karla that it was time to go.

"Give me five minutes," Karla begged.

Karla and her man exchanged phone numbers and the ladies piled into a cab. It was difficult to figure out which emotion dominated Patty more, incredulousness or just plain disgust. She couldn't understand what motivated Karla to act so flirtatiously.

She told Calvin about the incident. He was also disgusted.

"How can you do that?" he said the next morning.

"You're not my father," she defensively shot back.

The girls had arranged to return to the Sugar Shack the following night, Saturday, but Patty warned Karla that afternoon that she'd better change her tune. Patty had no interest in going to a bar where everyone thought she was hanging around with a sleazebag.

Karla was contrite. She apologized for misbehaving and explained she was just letting off steam.

"Just make sure it doesn't happen again," Patty warned. "You'll be getting a reputation."

The girls returned to the same table they'd occupied the night before, near the shooter bar. Karla sought out her friend but didn't see him. It wasn't too late in the evening when she spied a tall, handsome, blond-haired man in his late twenties wearing a business suit.

"Ooh, look at that guy," Karla said.

She flagged down a passing waiter and pointed at the man. "See that guy? I like him. He's cute. Can you tell him?"

The waiter agreed and passed the information along.

Patty merely stared at her niece-in-law in disbelief. She didn't say anything but merely shook her head.

"What?" Karla said defensively, sensing the unspoken condemnation Patty's look implied.

"Nothing. Nothing," Patty said.

A little while later, Jimmy arrived at the table bearing a single red rose. He handed it to Karla and introduced himself. He was friendly and attractive, made a living as a salesman. Karla asked him to join the girls at their table. Again, Karla was drinking vodka and orange juice at a steady pace.

In what seemed to be an extraordinarily short period of time, Karla was all over the salesman, kissing him and hugging him. They tried to talk, but the music made it all but impossible.

One part of the conversation Patty did catch was Karla's partial confession to Jimmy about her life.

"My life's complicated," Karla said. "Some bad stuff has happened. But you'll find out about it someday."

She went on to describe how she'd been married and that her husband had beaten her with a flashlight.

Jimmy and Karla were sitting close together at the low tables, and they got up often to dance both to fast music and to slow ones. During the slow dances they began to grope each other and kiss passionately. Sometimes Karla would return to Jimmy's table, where he was sitting with a bunch of male friends.

Patty and her friend were all but ignored by Karla for the balance of the evening. Again at closing time, Karla raced up to her aunt and began pleading to be given permission to go home with Jimmy.

"I want to go, I want to go," Karla said. "Jimmy wants me to go home with him! Can I go? Can I go?"

"I don't think it's a good idea," Patty warned. "If you go, I'm going to tell Calvin and you'll be in trouble," she added.

But Karla didn't care. And so Patty and her friend left.

When she got home, Patty explained to Calvin that his niece wasn't coming home and was with some new guy she'd met. He was incredulous.

That Sunday morning, as both Calvin and Patty headed off to work, Patty noticed that Karla was returning home in Jimmy's red Nissan 240SX, the same kind of car that Paul drove.

Patty simply stared. "Did you see who just went by?" she asked Calvin. "That was Karla and Jimmy."

Soon Karla and Jimmy saw each other about once a week, usually for a dinner date. They phoned each other regularly. Jimmy would occasionally call the Seger house, but it was Karla who initiated most of the calls.

About the first night, Karla merely said she and Jimmy had sat up all night talking. Patty didn't press her for details, although she felt talking was hardly what either of them had had in mind. Although Karla would later relate in graphic detail her sexual encounters with Jimmy to her friends, she perhaps felt it was inappropriate to tell Patty, who seemed to have assumed the mantle of surrogate parent.

Patty couldn't help but notice the resemblance Jimmy bore to Paul, both physically and socially. They were both attractive, they drove the same kind of car, and they both liked expensive clothing. Karla insisted she wasn't trying to find a replacement for Paul, but her denial did little to lessen Patty's feeling that Karla still harbored strong feelings for Paul.

Later, when Karla described how Paul had made his money smuggling, Patty wondered why she hadn't bothered to tell police. But Karla explained that that was his living and she didn't want to hurt him any more than she had by leaving him. She wanted a divorce as quickly as possible and she definitely didn't want to face him again, but she didn't want to go out of her way to be hurtful toward him.

Jimmy and Karla would sometimes stay out all night, sometimes until the early-morning hours.

"He's perfect in every way," Karla gushed one time. But Patty didn't press Karla about what made him so perfect.

Karla seemed happy, and she seemed content to have latched on to one partner. Her behavior when she went out with her aunt changed dramatically. She no longer flirted with every available man but was content, it seemed, to have a steady boyfriend.

Karla's newfound happiness caused Patty to soften a bit on the whole Jimmy escapade. But Calvin never reconciled his niece's behavior and continued to give her a hard time about her relationship. He forbade her, for instance, from having Jim over for dinner.

"No way," was all Calvin would say when Karla broached the subject.

"He only wants one thing, and Karla should recognize that," Calvin told Patty.

Apart from her curious social skills, Karla was the ideal houseguest. She cleaned the house voraciously, remarking more than once how nice it was to be able to use regular cleaning products. She did the dishes religiously and became quite angry one night when Patty did the chores.

"That's my job," she insisted.

If the dog happened to piddle on the floor, Karla was on her knees in a flash cleaning up the mess. One night Patty's parents dropped by for a visit and Patty's father couldn't get over how servile Karla was, asking over and over again if she could get anything for him or do anything.

That night, Patty's mom told Karla she was lucky to have escaped from her relationship with Paul when she did.

"The next one might not be so lucky. He could kill someone, you know," she added.

CHAPTER
22

Joanne Smirnis had refused to socialize with Paul and Karla after Andy Douglas's wedding the previous fall. She reiterated to Van her disdain for Paul and his antics; she reminded Van of the insulting night at the Pleasure Dome and told him quite bluntly that she didn't like his being around Paul. Because of Joanne's anger, Van felt uncomfortable even visiting Paul by himself. Sometimes he thought he was doing Paul and Karla a favor by staying away; without him there would be less opportunity for Paul to hit the bars and meet women. So for the first Christmas since they were young boys, Van and Paul neither visited nor exchanged gifts in December 1992.

At the same time, Van and Joanne had been busy: Joanne was now seven months pregnant and was eagerly awaiting the birth of their child. They had also spent the Christmas weeks trying to reconcile their relationship with the Smirnis and Fuller families. Things had improved: Van had worked back at the Brownhill Restaurant since shortly after Steve and Bev had moved from New York to Texas and he had again grown closer to his mother and father; the Fullers were trying to accept Van, with all his spots and blemishes.

In early January, Van received a letter from Revenue Canada asking him to file an income-tax return for the previous year. He needed to know from Paul how they were going to handle a now-defunct side business and who should get write-offs, if any were to be had. He telephoned Paul in the second week of January, opening the conversation by asking how he was doing.

"Terrible," Paul responded in a dour voice.

"Why?"

"I'm separated. Karla left me."

Van could not believe his ears.

"What are you talking about? She left you? Oh my God, that is terrible. Why did she leave you?"

"She just left me. I don't know why . . . she says I hit her."

"Where is she?"

"Back home with her parents, I think."

"Do you want me to get in touch with her? I'll get in touch with her. The Homolkas will talk to me.

"You can't get through to her, Van. I tried that already."

Paul told Van that biker–cum–cigarette dealer Johnny had been to St. Catharines with his girlfriend Linda, and that even Linda had tried to convince Karla to return to Paul, but it hadn't worked. After a few more words, Van told his buddy to hang in and then he hung up the telephone. He called back later that day and the talk was much the same.

That evening, Van turned to Joanne: "He's my friend, I gotta go see him, Jo."

She offered to go along with him.

For once, Van didn't bother calling Paul to tell him they were coming. Under the circumstances, he told Joanne, it likely wouldn't matter. They pulled up to 57 Bayview Drive around 8 or 9 P.M.

The man who answered their knock didn't look much like the Paul of old: he wore a black skull-and-crossbones hat with a black House of Pain T-shirt and Bermuda shorts, and he had double-cross earrings in both ears. He hadn't shaved in many days. His hair was much longer; his bangs were tousled. Joanne thought it weird that Paul would adopt such an extreme look, rap album or no rap album. Paul shook Van's hand, but Joanne shuffled past him with a soft and distant "hi." Joanne was sympathetic to Paul's pain, but deep inside she was happy that Karla had left him. Paul, it seemed, tolerated Joanne because she was Van's wife, and any friendship between the two ended right there.

After Van and Joanne had taken off their coats, Paul pulled Van aside out of earshot of Joanne as she made her way into the living room.

"Come here, I want to ask you something. Did you fucking turn me in for French and Mahaffy?"

"What the heck are you talking about?" asked Van, giving Paul the best puzzled look he could muster.

"Good, I just want to know who my real friends are," said Paul, seemingly satisfied.

While Van and Joanne made themselves at home on the couch, Van clearly remembered his discussion with Constable Rob Haney of the Ontario Provincial Police.

From Paul's comments Van assumed the Green Ribbon investigators had followed up on his tip. The last thing he wanted was for Paul to press him on the matter. He quickly changed the subject.

"So what's going on, buddy? What happened between you and Karla?" Van asked.

"We had arguments, but nothing big . . . she fell down the stairs. She had bruises from falling off the ladder. It's not like I did anything to her . . . Karla is going to say I beat her. She's a liar. She told the people at work she was in a car accident, and that didn't happen, so how can she say now that I beat her?"

As they walked into the kitchen to get drinks, Joanne noticed a pile of dirty dishes in the sink and the filthy countertops. The kitchen had always been spotless; Joanne reasoned that Karla's leaving had obviously been a huge blow.

Paul began washing the dishes while Joanne dried and put them away. As she reached to put the dried dishes in the cupboards, she noticed the neat stacks of plates and Tupperware and the military-like rows of cups and drinking glasses.

"You guys hungry?" Paul said as he finished his chores.

"Yeah, starving," said Van.

Paul reached for a box of frozen burritos from the freezer and tossed a handful into the microwave. As they ate, Paul suddenly ripped into Karla between bites of burritos.

"She's so unorganized. She can't clean. I have to pick everything up after her. She can't even put the soap away after taking a shower. She can't do anything right. She can't even do the laundry. She is so fucking dumb . . . I taught her everything she knows."

Van couldn't believe his ears. Paul was talking about Karla, the same Karla who had idolized him since that lusty night at Howard Johnson's; the same Karla who had boasted about his muscles, his good looks, and his intelligence; the same Karla who had turned a blind eye to the marital indiscretions in Florida and at home; the same Karla who had posed as Paul's sister; the same Karla whose puppy dog–like love for Paul had seen her become his puppet. She had been controlled by Paul, but at the same time she had seemed so happy; it appeared she simply wanted to be controlled by her man and reap the benefits of living with someone who would provide security and take care of business. Van had thought Karla would never leave Paul, that she was hypnotized by his love spell. Why would she suddenly get up and go because she fell down the stairs?

"Have you tried calling her at her parents'?" Van offered.

"Yeah, but she's under the Homolkas' witness assistance program. They won't even let me talk to her. For fuck's sake, she's my wife, they shouldn't interfere. Hey, why don't you call?" He looked at Van.

"I don't see why not," said Van, moving to grab the telephone on the living-room floor. He sat in front of the love seat and the television and called the Homolka home. No one answered. When Joanne called later, Lori answered the telephone. She sounded evasive. Karla was fine, she said, but she couldn't come to the telephone because she wasn't there. As Joanne hung up the telephone, Paul simultaneously blurted "fucking whore."

"She's probably out looking for another guy," Paul continued. "She won't get anybody like me. No one's going to have her after she's been fucking some other guy. I made her what she is. She used to be so fucking ugly. Wait a second, let me to upstairs, I have something I want to show you."

As Paul dashed excitedly up the stairs, Van looked at Joanne.

"Oh brother," he moaned.

They heard the hope chest creak open and then Paul ruffling through it. Noticing a film-development-store package on the coffee table, Joanne quickly peeked inside. There were pictures of Becky in a black dress, similar to the one Karla wore whenever Paul and she went out dancing. Paul and Becky were kissing.

"Oh my God, look at these!" Joanne said to Van, who quickly flipped through the photographs.

"Take some," Joanne said. "Take some. Show them to Rob Haney."

But Van was too nervous. The slamming of the hope-chest lid made up his mind. He replaced the photographs on the table. Paul bounded down the stairs.

"That's how she used to look . . . Look at her," he said, handing Van photographs he recognized were Karla taken five years earlier. Since Van had always considered Karla attractive, he couldn't grasp Paul's point. As if to back up his statement, Paul handed Van and Joanne the latest photographs of Karla, some in her blue and white hooped shirt with white shorts, and others in her black dress. In each she wore her hair long, straight and blonde.

Van calmly passed the photographs back to Paul.

"Paul, why did she leave you?"

Paul was clearly uncomfortable.

"She fell off a ladder and just got sick and tired of me yelling at her. I was yelling 'I hate you, I hate you.' Her mom got to her and said he's no good for you."

"On the phone, you told me you hit her. Did you fucking hit her?"

"Yes, I hit her," Paul responded. "I hit her with the butt end of a flashlight."

"So she didn't fall off the ladder?"

"I can't believe fucking Karla," he continued to rant. "I can get a girl like nothing."

He told Van he had talked with Heather in Florida and she

would be visiting him in a few weeks. Then he paused in deep thought.

"You know, I could go to jail or something for this."

Van decided the situation needed an injection of humor.

"Well, you get free food for six months."

"I ain't going to no fucking jail," responded Paul.

"Well, you hit her, man. You should at least get some counseling."

Paul looked Van in the eyes.

"I don't need fucking counseling," he said, then cleared his throat.

"Karla's not as innocent as you think. Tammy's death was not an accident. I don't know if you know this or not, but Karla's a lesbian and she's not that innocent. Tammy's death wasn't an accident, and I have it on tape to prove it."

Van scratched his head. What would his friend say next?

Paul related that before she left, Karla had searched the garage for certain videotapes but she hadn't found them because he had hidden them elsewhere in the house. The tapes contained scenes of Tammy on the night she died and Karla having sex with another girl.

"You're saying that Tammy's death was not an accident and Karla is a lesbian?" asked an incredulous Van.

"Right," answered Paul. "I got her dying on tape, and I can bring that up in court against Karla because she was negligent and her parents were negligent for allowing her to drink as a minor."

Van and Joanne didn't look at each other but kept their gazes fixed on Paul. Their mild suspicions over the years suddenly boiled to the surface. Joanne didn't believe for one second that Karla was a lesbian. Paul continued to tell them about Tammy, saying he confronted Dorothy at the Shaver Hospital parking lot but she ran away and he chased her to her car. She locked the door, but he shouted through the driver's-side window.

"Do you really think Tammy's death was an accident? Do you really think your daughter didn't have anything to do with her death?" he mimicked himself.

He told them how a frightened Dorothy quickly drove away.

Paul changed the topic as quickly as he had raised it. The three went upstairs to look at the music equipment in his room. Paul described each bit of equipment, telling them what it did and how much it cost, as was his usual manner. He told them his rap album was about ready for release. He was excited at the possibilities and said he planned on approaching Madonna to sponsor him.

As Paul spoke, Van saw a bizarre image. This wasn't the Paul he had known through the 1980s. This was a Paul who had regressed into adolescence. He was acting like a child. As Van looked at the photographs on the music-room wall of some of Tammy's friends, he thought about the guys Paul was hanging around with, guys who were much younger than himself. And he thought about Tammy, about the photographs of her on the end tables and on top of the television, about Paul's constant references to her and about the numerous times Paul had asked Van to visit her grave with him. For some reason, Tammy's death had screwed up Paul's head.

Van and Joanne stayed over that night. At 5 A.M., after talking over Paul's problems through the wee hours with the help of some beer and rye and coke, Paul and Van took off in the Mercedes to Burger King. Paul repeated the story of how he confronted Dorothy in the Shaver parking lot. This time, he laughed.

On Sunday, January 10, 1993, five days after Karla had left the house, Paul Bernardo sat down and spoke into his microcassette tape recorder. With music playing in the background, he spoke to Karla, his normally warm, calm, good-guy voice taken over by a soft, sniffling, sobbing whine tinged with bitterness, anger, and fear.

"When you know you've lost it all and there is no one to turn to, death's welcome mat is the only place you can go. Kar, this one's for you, pal! I don't know what to say. You know, I love you, man. So fucking much. Right now, you know what I'm doing? Holding your wedding picture, looking at you; you're so beautiful. I let you down, you know, I really let you down. I'm sorry, Kar. God, I wish I could make it up to you.''

Paul then spoke about doing the ''honorable thing'' by giving Karla his soul and his ''entire life'' and by setting up something ''real nice'' in an unnamed afterworld.

As the music ended, Paul rambled on to Karla about his love for her.

''You're the best, okay? Don't listen to the crap I said before. You're the best. You're the fucking best, man. You made me so happy, you know. You really did. Like, I really needed love in my life, man, and you gave that to me, and I'm really happy for that, like I treated you like shit near the end and I'm sorry. You're the best fucking thing in the world, Kar, you're the best. I love you. Miss you.''

The soliloquy continued with Paul telling Karla she was ''the most beautiful bride in the world'' and it made him the ''happiest guy.'' He recalled how the sunlight would filter down the corridor and highlight her face. ''You're my princess, you're my queen, you're my everything.''

In the background ''Patience,'' their Guns 'N' Roses wedding song, played while Paul sang along. He stopped suddenly to read Karla a letter he wrote but didn't finish:

''My dearest Karla: It has been five days now. God, it seems like a lifetime; kinda like when Tammy died. I realize now you're never coming back. Fucking kills me, pal. I wish I just could have been given a second chance to make things right again, to make it all better. I could have, you know. I really could have . . .''

His voice trailed off, before it started again, saying he had an important point to make so he had to kill the music. He restarted his oratory, again telling her ''I love you'' over and over again.

''I know you did what you had to do, and I don't blame you for it. In fact, it was the best thing you could have done for me; snapped me out of whatever state I was in; made me realize how much I love you and care for you; how important you are in my life. You are the most special person who ever touched my life, Karla. Yes, even more than Tammy.

''Here's the problem, Kar. I tried to be larger than life, I really did. But see, I didn't try to be average, like the average guy, I tried to be larger. I tried to be the best thing that there ever was, maybe because I needed love, maybe . . . I don't know why. I wanted to get Tammy the forest-green Porsche; I wanted to have your parents on speedboats; I wanted to take care of you and have this huge house with the four children; I wanted to be greater than anything there was and when I didn't reach it I got frustrated and angry and I took it out on you—the person I love the most! Don't hate me for that. Please . . . just please don't hate me for mom's genetics, right, the weak side.''

He sneezed and told her about his cold, about living in a lonely house, a lonely world, for five days; about how he called her name out at night but didn't get an answer. As the tape played on he cried.

''Miss you Karla. I miss you. Anyways, like, we were a good team, you know. We were the best team, you know. We were great, man. United we stand, together we fall. I'm going to fall for us, okay? You keep standing, pal. I gotta go, time's up. I told you that a couple of weeks ago; I knew I was going to go, my time's up. I'm going to go see Tammy.''

He asked her to forget the ''lost times,'' when he wasn't himself, and instead focus on the good times.

''We were the best, man. The envy of everybody. Please remember that. Please remember the good times. There was so many of them. Don't remember this last piece-of-shit fucking action. It wasn't me. I don't know what it was, it just wasn't me, all right? Okay? Babes. Kar. Karly curls. Snuggle bunny. My little rat. Remember that, eh? My little rat? Remember going to the pet shop way back seeing a little rat hiding between your hair?'' But then he returned to his threat of suicide.

''Remember this, okay? Some things are worth dying for, and the only thing worth dying for is you, Karla. I'm going to give you my life, okay? I'm going to give my soul, my energy . . . it's an undying love. I'm taking it with me to the grave. You're my best friend, you were always my best friend. Born a bastard, die a bastard. God, I love you, Kar. I love you so much if you can please forgive me, okay. Please . . . I really wasn't that bad. I really, really wasn't. I just tried too hard; I tried to be macho, too domineering. I thought these were qualities that were important to be successful. But I forgot how to cherish and to love . . . and now you run scared from me. You don't have to run scared no more, okay? Never again, Kar, do you have to be scared.''

He warned her the insurance money wouldn't come through because the policy hadn't been operational for more than two years. She could sell the music equipment and stuff from the house, he said, but he added that he owed ''John'' just over $5,000. After blathering on for a few more minutes, he told her to bury him in the easiest way possible: ''I mean, throw me in a ditch if you want. I know you won't have much money, and I understand there's a lot of things that I could have fucked you guys on, but I chose this option instead because I have an undying love for you and hatred towards myself.''

He started to cry.

''I was saying good-bye to Bud. He's licking me. He knows. Oh, Kar, I had the best honeymoon with you in Hawaii. It was great. I love you so much my tears are falling everywhere, Kar . . . it's five to one Sunday morning. My shrine is built, my pictures are laid . . . my last words, Kar, I love you.''

But they weren't his last words. He kept on talking.

''Kar, if you can ever forgive me for the terror and the hate and the pain that I have caused you I will be eternally grateful. You're my best friend, Kar. The only person in this world I've ever loved is you. I'm going to miss you. I wish I made love to you staring at your face. I wish we had a kid . . .''

He called out the time as he talked, one-fifteen, one-seventeen, then, giving the time at one twenty-five, he told her the first incision was drawing blood.

''Fuck, pal, couldn't you be there once more for me when I called?''

He turned over the tape onto side B, still sobbing and crying as he talked. He whined as he cried out ''Kar'' or ''Karla'' or ''God'' or ''fuck'' close to fifty times in just as many seconds. He told her he had banged the flashlight against his own head. And he asked for a second chance.

"Things would have been so different. Oh, baby. If only you came back to me. Why don't you come back? Jesus Christ, how long, Kar? Don't say forever. You gotta have some fucking compassion? Give me a fucking second chance! Nothing can be over that fast, nothing can go from total submissiveness to "that's it" 'til the end of the world . . . we're right for each other. Better than any other couple in the world. Kar and Paul. Paul and Kar. The best fucking couple. The Teales, man. Kar, we're the winners. We deserve to be together, not apart."

He talked of loving her more than any female on the planet, "one hundred percent, one million percent, plus one."

As he rambled on, Buddy barked a dozen times, as if on cue.

A short while later, he played Guns N' Roses' "November Rain," one of Karla's favorite songs, and as he finished the tape he played it louder.

"You're my princess, okay? I'm your prince. Remember that, okay?"

Six days after taping his threat to commit suicide, Paul turned on the microcassette recorder again and spoke more notes to his estranged wife. He told her about how he was breaking down; he asked Karla to give him a second chance.

"But I guess you don't give second chances. I think I deserve one. I . . . I just don't understand it. I'll never fuck you, you know, in the sense of getting you in trouble. Best I be gone. I know I was bad at the end, but I did some honorable things. I wanted to love you, but I was hurt. No one understood me . . . bad guys like me gotta go. Born a bastard, died the bastard. I'm a bastard, I've always been a bastard, a very bad bastard, very bad person. You're the best. Don't ever believe anything wrong I said wrong about you. Love you, good-bye."

As he signed off in tears, the Platters' "Smoke Gets In Your Eyes" played in the background. It was another of Karla's favorite songs. Within a short time, his voice started again. It still wasn't the end. He talked more.

"Kar, he's coming to get me now. No, the Grim Reaper's coming. I'm afraid. I'm too young to die. You never called. Kar, Kar. Please don't, please don't, please don't. He's outside my car; he's coming for me . . . it's three-ten A.M. I've cried a million tears, Kar. I don't know how to stop."

In early February, Dorothy Homolka received a call from the Metro Sex Assault Squad asking if they could talk with her. They stopped by and asked about Karla and where she was and whether they could talk to her.

Dorothy told them she'd get in touch with her oldest daughter and have Karla phone them. Dorothy then called Karla at Calvin and Patty's to tell them about the inquiry. Initially Karla refused to deal with them.

"I don't want to speak to anybody," she told her mother. Calvin and Patty insisted she do so. Finally Karla agreed that she would call the detectives.

"I'm going to hang up and I'm going to phone them right away," she told her mother.

And she did.

"What do you want?" Karla asked suspiciously of the detective on the other end of the line.

They told her they wanted to ask her some questions.

"Well, I don't really want to talk to you."

Finally Karla relented, but only after she held her hand over the receiver and asked if the police could come do the interview at the apartment. Calvin and Patty nodded, and Karla then insisted that Calvin and Patty be allowed to sit in on any of the questioning. It was agreed.

On Tuesday, February 9, 1993, detectives Ron Whitefield, Mary Lee Metcalfe, and Bruce Smollett of the Metro Toronto sex assault squad arrived at the Segers'.

Patty couldn't help but wonder why Metro police were involved, since the assault against Karla had taken place in St. Catharines.

The officers arrived at about 7 P.M. after Calvin and Patty returned home from work. Calvin and Patty were instructed not to talk during the interview because they were going to tape the proceedings.

As the police started asking preliminary questions about Karla and her background, Smollett took Calvin and Patty into their bedroom and said he was going to fill them in on what was happening. Both stared blankly as he explained that they were looking at arresting Paul for a series of sexual assaults, likely in about three weeks.

For some reason, Patty wasn't at all surprised. It, at least in part, explained why Metro Toronto investigators would want to question Karla.

When they returned to the living room, Calvin sat with Smollett on the red couch, Karla by herself in a love seat, while Patty sat in another armchair. Whitefield and Metcalfe were sitting on the other couch. On the coffee table was a big, broadcast-quality tape recorder.

Whitefield and Metcalfe took turns asking the questions. It seemed to Calvin and Patty that Ron Whitefield seemed less comfortable with the personal questions than Mary Lee Metcalfe.

"Who cuts the hair in your family? What do you use to trim hair?"

Karla answered in short sentences, refusing to elaborate. She sometimes trimmed Paul's hair with regular trimming scissors, she said.

"Does Paul drive any other cars besides the Nissan?"

"No," she answered.

"What types of patterns does Paul like in his clothes? What kinds of clothes does he wear?"

"Polo, things like that."

"Have you ever had occasion to visit Grace Lutheran Church?"

"No."

"Is Paul circumcised?"

"No."

"Have you ever had anal sex?"

"No. Well, we tried it one time, but I didn't like it so we never did it again."

Karla kept fidgeting, clearly uncomfortable with the line of questioning.

"You're doing fine," Mary Lee and the others told Karla.

Patty didn't get it. The questions seemed to have little to do with any kind of rape investigation.

On and on the process continued, the officers compiling background information about Karla's relationship with Paul and asking other curious, less obvious questions.

Finally, around midnight, the officers thanked everyone for their help and left.

Just as they were leaving, Smollett turned to Karla.

"How would you feel if we told you Paul would be arrested in a little while for a series of sexual assaults?"

Karla showed no visible reaction. She merely stared up at them from her perch in the love seat. She shrugged her shoulders.

"We'll be in touch," one of the officers said, and the apartment door closed.

After the officers left, Patty and Calvin were confused. They sensed the police were annoyed with Karla because she offered only one-word answers or seemed not to be able to remember much of what they wanted to know.

An awful pained look suddenly crossed Karla's face, and she began to weep.

"I know what they're after. I know what they're after," Karla sobbed.

"What are you talking about?" Calvin asked.

"I know what they're after," she repeated.

"Tell us what's going on. We're trying to help you. You've got to tell us what's going on," said Calvin, growing steadily impatient and more confused with the bizarre happenings under his own roof.

But Karla merely shook her head. Finally a disgusted Calvin announced he was going to bed.

"The hell with you, then," he said, storming off.

Patty looked across at Karla, who was now lying on the love seat.

"We're only trying to help you. But you've got to tell us what's going on," Patty repeated.

Karla started to mumble about matching pictures.

"I don't understand," Patty said.

Karla asked if Patty remember several years earlier when the *Sun* had run a composite picture of the Scarborough Rapist. Yes, she recalled that.

"That's Paul!"

There was stunned silence.

"It's really serious stuff," Karla said, literally shaking on the love seat.

"Okay, I'm going to ask you a question," Patty started tentatively. "Did Paul kill anyone?"

Karla looked across from her seat and nodded her head yes.

"Did he kill more than one person?"

"Yeah."

Patty began to get a curious sensation of being in a dream that isn't a dream.

"Was one of them Kristen French?" she continued.

"Yeah," Karla responded, the tears now coming more freely.

"Was the other Leslie Mahaffy?"

Again she nodded.

"Oh, my God!" Patty whispered. "This is really bad stuff!"

Then, in no logical or chronological order, Karla started blurting out facts as she thought of them.

"I was forced to do a lot of things, like cut Kristen's hair," Karla confided.

"Was she alive or dead?" Patty asked, hardly able to believe the conversation that was unfolding before her.

"She was dead."

Patty recalled the news reports and the television special that aired shortly after Kristen's body was discovered in the spring of 1992.

"Did you take her from the church?"

"Yeah, Paul told me to roll down the window and call her over to the car," Karla continued.

She described then how Paul exited the car and forced Kristen into the Nissan.

"Why did Paul make you cut her hair?"

"I don't even know," Karla answered, and there was a look that told Patty that perhaps there was no reason for any of what happened.

Karla went on, telling Patty in her tiny voice that Paul had strangled Kristen with a cord. She talked about a video camera and how Paul made her have sex with both girls, videotaping the acts.

Later, Karla said, Paul had told her that he'd use those tapes against her if she ever left him. In fact, the day her mom had come to get her at the animal clinic after the last beating, Karla had searched the home in vain for the tapes. Paul had hidden them somewhere.

"Was Leslie taken from the store?" Patty asked, recalling the media reports that indicated she'd been abducted from a convenience store.

No, Karla explained. Paul had been stalking the neighborhood, driving around looking for young girls, when he ran into Leslie at her house and they'd started talking. She asked if he had a cigarette and he said he had some in the car. Leslie told Paul she'd like one but that she was just going to sit in the passenger side of the car with the door open.

But when Paul got in the driver's side, he reached across with a knife and told her she wasn't going anywhere except with him, Karla explained.

When Paul got Leslie home, he woke Karla up and told her he had a girl and she should come downstairs. Karla told Patty she'd objected, that she'd told Paul what he was doing was wrong, but it didn't matter to him.

He showed her Leslie's I.D. and Karla noted that she was fourteen. Karla went on to describe for Patty how Paul made the two of them have sex and that he'd given Leslie sleeping pills and then strangled her when she was sleeping. He'd had the sleeping pills, cord, and everything all ready in the room. Karla told Patty how she went and got a teddy bear for Leslie and how Leslie begged to be allowed to go home and see her brother. Leslie had vowed not to tell on Paul or say what he looked like.

A little later, after they thought Leslie was dead, she started gasping for air, and that scared Paul and he strangled her again until he was certain she was dead, Karla explained, crying as she unburdened herself.

Patty, for her part, began to fear that the seminal information she'd been given by her niece-in-law might somehow make her culpable in the crimes.

Karla revealed that Paul made her help carry Leslie into the basement and that the next night, when her parents came for dinner, Karla had leapt up and prevented her mother from getting something in the basement.

On the Monday morning after Leslie's murder Karla went to work, and sometime during the day, Paul called to say he'd cut Leslie's body up and was pouring concrete in which he was going to put the body parts.

Karla told Patty she hung up the phone and went to the washroom at the clinic, where she was physically sick and began crying.

Paul picked her up from work and forced her to help dispose of the body, specifically Leslie's torso, which she helped carry from the basement.

The information Karla related about Kristen was less detailed, despite the fact that she'd spent more time in the Port Dalhousie house and her stay there was more recent.

Kristen caused problems for Paul, Karla told her aunt. She wouldn't agree to some of his demands and she told him she'd rather die than do some of the things Paul wanted. At one point while Paul was out of the house, Karla said, Kristen asked her if Paul beat her and she acknowledged that he did. Kristen wanted Karla to help her escape—she even suggested that Karla could take Buddy the dog with her—but Karla was too afraid, she admitted.

Paul showed Kristen a tape made during Leslie Mahaffy's captivity to try and control Kristen," Karla said. "Do you want this to happen to you?" he asked her.

Patty sat numbly as first one hour and then a second passed. "I just couldn't believe what I was hearing. It was awful."

Paul kept saying "We'll never get caught," Karla told Patty.

"You're the first person I've ever told," Karla said, drying her tears. She told Patty how she'd worried that she was pregnant for a while because she hadn't had a period in several months. Toward the end of their relationship Paul told her he wanted to kill again and that he wanted another young girl to use as a sex slave. Only this time, Paul told Karla, he wanted her to kill the girl.

"I knew I couldn't do it," Karla told her aunt.

Patty told Calvin about Karla's confession the next morning. He told her she had to call a lawyer immediately. Karla said she knew of one in Niagara Falls named George Walker. She set up an appointment for a few days later, but neither Calvin nor Patty could drive her. So Calvin called Ron Whitefield of the sex assault squad.

"My niece is involved in something serious," he explained to the detective. "Be patient. You'll know everything. But she's going to see a lawyer."

Calvin then asked if someone could take her to Niagara Falls to see this lawyer, and Whitefield agreed.

Both Calvin and Patty sat with Karla and advised her to tell the truth to George Walker.

At 10 A.M. on the appointed day, Ron Whitefield and Mary Lee Metcalfe drove Karla to Walker's office. At first he didn't believe her story, Karla later explained.

Apparently there was no shortage of nuts who tried to tell lawyers and police they'd killed Kristen French.

But Walker listened to everything Karla had to say, asking her questions which she freely answered.

Finally he agreed to represent her. His first piece of advice was not to tell anyone anything more about this case. She was to have no more conversations with her aunts or uncles, her parents, and especially the police. No one, except him.

This advice came as a bitter disappointment to the two Metro detectives, who assumed Karla was merely getting routine advice before signing a statement about her knowledge of the Scarborough rapes. It was, Karla told her aunt and uncle that night, a very frosty trip back to Brampton. She also told them that she couldn't say anything more.

"Well, I'm tired. I'm going to go to bed," Karla announced. It was 7 P.M.

The next day police were staked out all over the apartment building. A condo manager told Calvin and Patty in confidence that police had rented two units, one on the second and one on the third floor.

Calvin and Patty believed their phone was tapped. Soon they began to recognize strange cars in the visitors' lot, a black Trans Am, a Jeep Cherokee, another blue domestic car. They began to nod in silent acknowledgment when they passed one of these vehicles on the way to or from work or when they walked the dog.

"I felt like I was a criminal," says Patty. "No matter where I went, they were there."

Several times in the ensuing days, Karla was shuffled back and forth to George Walker's office. There were phone calls every day. Calvin drove her one time; Patty's girlfriend from the night at the Sugar Shack drove her another time.

Initially, it didn't dawn on Patty and Calvin that Karla was likely going to be arrested, but once all the police attention started it seemed more and more likely. On several occasions, Patty took time off from work because she was afraid they'd simply come and grab Karla while she was alone in the condo.

Mike Donald made the familiar walk up the stairs to the porch of 57 Bayview Drive on February 13, 1993. As he was about to knock on the front door he noticed that an odd-looking towel had been draped over the tiny viewing window. Paul's Nissan was in the driveway, so Mike knew he was home. The latch clicked and the door opened slowly. Paul didn't drag the door wide open and step out into the light as was his usual style, but instead he stepped back into the darkened hallway and moved to the side and meekly motioned Mike in. It was as if he didn't want neighbors to see him, for only after Mike had stepped inside did Paul close the door behind him. Once Paul came into full view Mike saw the bags under Paul's eyes. His normally perfect hair pointed out in every direction, he hadn't shaved in about eight days and he could have used a shower. After a solemn greeting, Paul motioned Mike into the living room. Mike glanced around him. The ground-floor blinds were all drawn; it was as if Paul had chosen to live in a world of darkness.

"I feel like I'm living in a fishbowl. The neighbors all want to know what I'm doing . . . I don't like them knowing my business," he explained.

It was apparent to Mike that something was very wrong in Paul's life, perhaps even more than just being separated from Karla.

A few days earlier Paul had talked with Mike about the possibility of stealing some cars to get some pocket money. Mike knew Paul was broke, but he didn't think stealing a few cars was the right solution. When Paul had called Mike over earlier in the day, Paul had suggested the telephone was likely tapped. This sounded feasible to Mike, because he thought he had heard a popping sound whenever he used the telephone. Thinking about the tapped telephone and Paul's paranoid re-action at the door, Mike worried that customs snoops might be watching Paul.

Paul started the conversation by reaffirming to Mike that he had to get Karla back. Mike told Paul that if he wanted to fight the assault charge and get Karla back he had to cut his hair, look respectable, get a job, show a willingness to take counseling, tell both the judge and Karla he was wrong for beating her.

"No, I don't think it's going to help if I get a job. Why should I get a job? She should just love me for who I am and not for who I'm trying to be."

Paul became more agitated in his ranting. His frustration turned to anger, and he aimed it at Mike, cursing and swear-ing at his friend and berating him for his not being able to help him. Mike didn't mind hearing what Paul had to say about his screwed-up love life, but he didn't want to be a victim of Paul's transferred wrath.

"Look, I'm here to be a friend. If you freak out at me and be an asshole, I'll leave . . . take a pill. I'm not here to take that kind of abuse," Mike told him.

"Okay, I'm sorry, Mike. I'm sorry."

Paul shook his head.

"You don't understand. It's bigger than it actually is. . . . It's bigger than you'll understand. . . . It's huge!"

Mike wondered if Paul had been running drugs behind his back. He feared for a second that he, too, would be roped into any police roundup. Suddenly, Paul veered in another direction.

"What do you think of Tammy dying?"

"I don't know. Kind of strange, I guess," Mike offered.

"What do you think of a fifteen-year-old girl just dying? Come on, fifteen-year-old girls don't just die! Use your fucking mind. We'd been drinking that night, but Tammy didn't just die—Karla fucking killed her! She pulled the trigger!"

Mike sat there dumbfounded at what his friend was saying.

"And you know what," Paul continued, "I have it on videotape."

"You have it on videotape?"

"Yeah, I should let you watch the tapes sometime. . . . I haven't got it here . . . I've got it off premises . . . you don't stash that in a place of guilt."

Mike regained his composure. He didn't believe what Paul was saying. "You have Karla killing Tammy on videotape?"

"Is it live? Is it Memorex? I have it in fucking living Technicolor!"

Paul told Mike he had many friends in the city and the tape was hidden.

Mike was perplexed by what Paul had said. He remembered what Karla had told him, when he phoned her in an attempt to reconcile the couple, a few weeks earlier, about how he beat her and what a terrible temper Paul possessed. But Mike had passed that off as bitterness on Karla's behalf. Now Paul alleged Karla had killed Tammy. Impossible. He figured these allegations were all part of the typical mudslinging phase of a divorce.

Paul looked Mike directly in the eyes and told him Karla was a lesbian and he had videotapes of Karla having oral sex with other women. Paul said Karla had urged him to have affairs with other women so she could join in and watch the videos later.

"There's some pretty major shit gonna happen if I go down on this assault charge," Paul warned. "If I'm goin' down I'm fuckin' going to sink everybody. She's not getting away looking like the sweet innocent blond girl that everybody thinks she is."

Then Paul switched back to Tammy, asking Mike to recall how Tammy would snuggle up beside both of them as they watched TV in the Homolka home.

"Yeah, I remember," said Mike.

"Karla saw all this and was jealous of Tammy. Karla killed her because she was jealous."

Mike didn't know whether to believe Paul, because he had caught his friend lying in the past.

Paul ended by telling Mike how much he loved Karla. "When you really love somebody you'll do anything to get them back. You'll sink them if you have to, but if they were to come back you know you would love them with all your heart. . . . If she were to come back tomorrow I'd love her with all my heart, wouldn't I? I would just forget everything like nothing happened. But you know, if she doesn't come back, I have no choice. I have to sink her. If I'm going to take the rap, so is she."

Detective constables Brent Symonds from Niagara and Jim Kelly from Metro Toronto walked up the icy wooden steps to 57 Bayview Drive at about 3:30 P.M. Wednesday, February 17, 1993, and arrested Paul Bernardo on allegations he was both the Scarborough Rapist and the Niagara schoolgirl killer. The joint arrest came as much of a surprise to police that day as it did to a stunned public. For more than a week before, Metro and Green Ribbon Task Force officers had quietly worked together in a stressful union after two of the biggest cases in Canada's criminal history collided. Police had already talked with Karla and Bernardo's arrest had been imminent, but before search warrants for 57 Bayview Drive had been signed or the joint forces interview team was fully prepared, Global TV reporter Sue Sgambati forced the police hand after she followed a Metro police detective to the Green Ribbon Task Force's headquarters in Beamsville, north of St.

Catharines. Sgambati had been tipped off that something big was happening and her presence threatened to blow the lid off the Bernardo investigation. There was only one choice: Bernardo would have to be taken down and the evidence would have to fit together later.

The rocky road to the arrest began in mid-January when the forensic sciences centre called Metro police to advise them they would begin DNA testing on samples from the Scarborough Rapist case some two years earlier. The two-year delay in testing was not due to screw-ups, but rather to the reality of a cash-strapped and overburdened and overworked forensics system. Simply put, officials at the Centre for Forensic Sciences had felt in 1990 that it was not feasible for the more than 100 blood and saliva samples taken from rape suspects by Metro to be directly compared to sperm taken from rape victims by state-of-the-art DNA "genetic fingerprinting" analysis. While Metro Toronto would have loved immediate DNA testing on all samples because a match would have meant a probability level of up to one in 30 to 70 billion, the CFS could not accommodate it. At that point, the centre had only just started to apply its DNA program after three years of development. Even then, the application was limited: the centre had only one scientist and one technician qualified to run DNA testing procedures and testing was reserved for higher priorities, specifically murder cases before the courts. Upon receiving the Scarborough Rapist samples, CFS staff had suggested to Metro detectives they should be syphoned through conventional sorology work to reduce the suspect list to a manageable number for DNA testing. Even the sorology testing would take time. The Scarborough Rapist samples were among an estimated 1,600 sex assault and 50,000 general samples submitted yearly in 1990, 1991 and 1992 from Ontario's police departments, coroner's offices, fire departments and defence lawyers. Funding cutbacks and chronic shortages of qualified staff had caused huge sample backlogs at the centre, especially in the biology unit, which, in addition to the fledgling DNA program, handles blood, sperm and saliva testing. Despite its importance to crime-fighting, the centre's $11 million annual budget was frozen through most of the early 1990s.

In January 1993, CFS staff contacted the Metro police squad with the news the sorology testing on the Scarborough Rapist suspects had revealed six possible suspects and that DNA testing on these samples would commence immediately. A week later, Detective Steve Irwin, who at the age of eleven lost his father when Toronto Constable Michael Irwin was shot dead in February 1972 while answering a routine call, learned in a telephone call that forensic sciences had identified a match on the rapes—Paul Kenneth Bernardo.

Irwin, who with Detective John Munro had interviewed Bernardo in November 1990, notified Staff Inspector Steve Marrier, head of the sex assault squad, and within short order the entire squad was briefed of the forensic lab's findings. The Irwin and Munro interview with Bernardo was quickly noted: Bernardo had been extremely cooperative, giving hair, saliva and blood samples. He had even told the two officers about his impending marriage. Further checks revealed Bernardo had moved to the St. Catharines area. As the squad collectively began working on Bernardo's background, more information came to light: in January 1988, a former girlfriend of Bernardo, Carol, had submitted an unofficial report to police through her friend's police sergeant father in which she suggested that her ex-boyfriend of three years could be the Scarborough Rapist. The report, however, had been taken in a coffee shop and lacked detail and made no mention of a key trait Bernardo shared in common with the Scarborough Rapist—a love of anal sex.

In the ensuing days, more conclusive proof came back from the forensic centre. In all, seven tests can be done to compare DNA fragment lengths. In addition to the first test, the second and third tests on Bernardo had came back positive. There was enough evidence for an arrest. In the meantime, the sexual assault squad prepared surveillance on Bernardo to both collect further evidence and ensure that he didn't attack further victims. For whatever reason, nobody bothered to call Niagara police to tell them of the CFS findings and the police surveillance that was about to be launched in Port Dalhousie.

On Wednesday February 3, 1993, the first night of surveillance, a police team had watched Bernardo as he drove his Nissan 240SX up the Queen Elizabeth Way to an Oakville shopping mall, arriving just after 9:30 P.M. He circled the parking lot as the mall closed for the evening, slowing to look at groups of girls and young women as they entered and left the mall.

On Friday February 5, 1993, David Boothby, then-head of Metro Toronto's detective operations and destined to become chief of the 5,500-strong service, telephoned Inspector Vince Bevan asking for a personal meeting the following Monday. Boothby said he had important information to pass on to Bevan, but he would not discuss it on the telephone. On Monday February 8, 1993, five days after Metro Toronto police had started to tail Bernardo, Bevan learned for the first time that Bernardo was a suspect in the Scarborough Rapes. The information rang a bell with Bevan. The piece of map found in the parking lot of Grace Lutheran Church the day of Kristen French's abduction had been of Scarborough. Bevan learned that Metro police had scheduled an interview with Bernardo's estranged wife, Karla Homolka, in Mississauga the following evening.

On Tuesday February 9, 1993, Bevan met with his task force lieutenants in Beamsville and gave them the news. "We have to take a look at this guy," said Bevan. Detective-sergeants Bob Waller of Halton and brothers Steve and Murray MacLeod of Niagara then set about checking out Bernardo's name on the Green Ribbon tip computers and in Niagara Regional police files. Almost immediately they came up with Van Smirnis' tip through Beaverton OPP Constable Rob Haney and the subsequent May 12, 1992, visit to 57 Bayview Drive by detectives Scott Kenney and Brian Nesbitt. Just as they had said in their report, Kenney and Nesbitt now told their superiors nothing had looked out of place with Paul Kenneth Bernardo: he had the nice house in the lovely neighborhood, a wife, a dog, nothing to raise suspicion. And there was no Camaro. Bernardo's file was examined to find a one-

and-a-half-page Metro police report that, after their visit with Bernardo, Kenney and Nesbitt had taken as having all but cleared Bernardo as a suspect in the Scarborough cases. Further checks revealed that Bernardo's ex-wife had filed assault charges against her husband January 6, 1993, while in St. Catharines General Hospital. In order to learn more about Karla, Niagara police pulled the sudden death file on Tammy Homolka. Interviews with Constable David Weeks and Detective Ken Mitchell again raised the question of the red marks evident on Tammy's face at the time of her death. No one ever knew what they were.

By midday Tuesday, some Niagara officers were fuming at their Toronto counterparts. Why wasn't more information contained in the Bernardo file that was requested after the May 12, 1992, interview of Bernardo? Why hadn't Metro police pushed ahead with the DNA testing on Bernardo and other suspects? Why, back in the summer of 1992, had Metro police refused to send representatives to the Green Ribbon Task Force like most other police organizations had done? Why didn't Metro police tell Niagara they were running surveillance operations in their own back yard? And to top it off, the interview slated for that night with Bernardo's ex-wife would not include any officers from the Green Ribbon Task Force. From their perspective, Metro Toronto detectives had simply viewed Bernardo as one of many suspects. And, when it came to forensic testing priorities, who were they to question the experts at the forensics lab? In those early days of stress, relations between Metro and Niagara had gotten off to a shaky start.

That afternoon at a meeting in Toronto, Bevan begged Metro to lay off the arrest until his team could take a closer look at Bernardo in the murders. Metro assured they would give Niagara at least a week or two to put their case together. After Toronto detectives Ron Whitefield, Mary Lee Metcalfe and Detective Sergeant Bruce Smollet had interviewed Karla the night of Tuesday February 9, 1993, and reported she was obviously hiding something, a deal was struck to have the sex assault squad move into Beamsville and work with Niagara on the case.

Shortly after 11 P.M. Thursday, February 11, 1993, Niagara detective sergeants Bob Gillies and Mike Matthew's paid a personal visit to Walker's home. All day long messages had been left for Walker to call Scarborough's head Crown Attorney, Mary Hall, a feisty woman of some fifty or so years whose intense personality both in and out of the courtroom had dubbed her Maximum Mary or Bloody Mary. Whether Hall was simply an aggressive woman, or because people found her difficult, or perhaps because Hall was unquestionably political, some in the legal fraternity didn't much care for her. George Walker was one of them.

The Niagara police duo told Walker face-to-face that they were there not about the rapes but about the homicides of Leslie Mahaffy and Kristen French. They suggested the crown attorney would be willing to negotiate with his client for any assistance in Bernardo's conviction on the murders. Walker, told them they were on the right track with the crown attorney suggestion. Early the next morning, Walker had called Niagara North Crown Attorney Ray Houlahan and negotiations for a plea bargain were underway.

Houlahan forwarded Walker's request to a regional Crown Attorney who in turn passed Walker to the head prosecutors at the Crown Law Office. The decisions in this case would be made at the top.

At about 3:20 P.M. on Thursday, February 11, Van and Joanne arrived at Aurora OPP headquarters to meet with Green Ribbon Task Force detectives at the behest of OPP Constable Rob Haney, who had called them in Markham the day before requesting the meeting. Haney met them inside and introduced Van to task force members Sergeant John Stonehill, Sergeant Peter McEwen and Constable Tom Whiteway. Ten minutes later, Van was separated from Joanne and questioned privately by the three officers in front of Haney. Stonehill told Van Bernardo was one of seven suspects in the French and Mahaffy murders and police were still narrowing down the evidence. He demanded Van's assurance that he would say nothing to Paul about their meeting or the police interest. They were there to talk about Bernardo, but Stonehill began the interview asking Van details about his personal life, about his brothers Steve and Alex, about the video store in Youngstown, about Paul's friends and what cars they drove. In a sure sign that police still sought the elusive off-white Camaro, Stonehill asked if Paul ever borrowed a car from friends. Stonehill asked what Van was doing the previous April, asking specifically the month in which he shut down the video store.

"Middle of June, end of June," said Van.

Did Paul visit, travel back and forth? asked Stonehill.

"No," said Van, omitting to tell the detective about the lucrative cigarette business the two had run for almost a year because it quickly became clear to Van that for some reason everyone—including himself—was a suspect. It also seemed to Van that he was at top of the list.

Getting more nervous by the minute, Van told Stonehill about Mike Donald, Alex Ford and Andy Douglas, telling him that Alex especially would be a great source of information. He explained how Alex had married Karla's best friend, Kathy, and that the couple had often socialized with Paul and Karla until Alex became frustrated at Paul's treatment of his wife's friend.

Van related the story of Paul's abuse of Karla at the Pleasure Dome and how he tried to pick up girls in front of her and how he broke the headrest on his Honda; he told of Paul's past girlfriend, Carol; about the trips to Florida and Paul's picking up of Alyson and his bizarre showing of the videotapes to Karla; about how Paul would first treat his girl like a queen, buy her flowers and chocolates; about how he would talk of having anal intercourse with his girls. Van told Stonehill of how Paul would talk of jumping some girls in the street.

"He used to say 'let's go jump some girl'. I'd say, Paul, it's ridiculous. He'd say, 'no, I'm just joking.' I thought he was joking; I never took it seriously. The only shock was when I saw a picture of the Scarborough Rapist. He looks like him. That is pretty scary." Stonehill had already been apprised of most of Van's suspicions from reading Haney's original report to the Green Ribbon Task Force in May 1992.

The interview ended after almost two hours with Van telling Stonehill about Paul's claims of having Tammy's death on videotape and that Karla was negligent in her sister's death. He still wasn't certain whether they believed him.

Meanwhile, Metro police continued their surveillance of Bernardo. On Friday February 12 at about 1:25 A.M., Bernardo was on the road again, this time cruising the parking lot of a Tim Horton's donut shop in Mississauga. Undercover police teams continued to tail him, watching him pull over beside a Mississauga Transit bus that had stopped to let off passengers on Mississauga Valley Road. He gazed intently at the handful of passengers as they walked from the stop, then sped off. The pattern continued throughout the early hours, making sudden U-turns, circling donut shop parking lots, a 24-hour family restaurant, always watching, but totally unaware that someone was watching him. Later, as he drove south on Hurontario Street in downtown Mississauga, Paul noticed a young woman walking south on the street. He pulled the Nissan 240Sx around in a U-turn and drove by her on the other side of the street. Turning once more, he drove some distance ahead of her, pulled into a sidestreet and flicked off his headlights. The surveillance team watched as the young woman, in her early twenties with dark hair, passed the darkened car, oblivious to both the stalker and the detectives. The Nissan then pulled out, made an innocent-looking pass by the woman and headed home to 57 Bayview Drive. Bernardo pulled the garage door shut at 3 A.M.

Van found himself sitting across from Sergeant John Stonehill again on Saturday, February 13. Stonehill asked Van about Paul's treatment of Karla, about their friends Becky and Jane and about Paul's videotaping peculiarities. They were especially interested in more details regarding exactly what Paul had said about the videotaping of Tammy's death.

Van related to Stonehill how Paul had told him and Joanne that Karla had mistakenly searched the garage rafters for the videotapes when he had hidden them elsewhere in the house. Stonehill would visit Van again two days later asking more questions, including details of Van's cigarette smuggling venture with Bernardo.

That same night, Paul met Gus and Jason at a bar and ran into his old flame, Anna. While Paul and Anna spent the night at 57 Bayview Drive, police were in a panic because they didn't know who Anna was.

After Paul drove Anna to her car the next day, police found themselves behind the Nissan as it made its way to the Upper Canada Mall. Bernardo watched young women coming and going from the large building. As two girls passed the Nissan, Bernardo said something to them, but he shook his head at their response and they moved on. He started the car again, and drove through adjoining streets for six minutes, but then returned to the mall parking lot. Over the next forty-five minutes, Bernardo drove in and out of the mall, circling slowly, looking at young women and girls. On his final circuit of the mall, he parked in the south end and watched a woman walk across the lot.

At 5 P.M., Bernardo left the Newmarket shopping centre and drove to another mall at the west of the city and on to Oakville Place, the scene of his earlier girl-watching escapade. There he followed his usual routine, entering and leaving the mall a number of times. Before leaving the Oakville mall that afternoon, Bernardo pulled up in front of the Toys Я Us store and watched young girls enter and leave.

Despite police differences, the net was starting to close during the early afternoon of Wednesday February 17, 1993, when Vince Bevan and Steve Marrier burst into the room where the interview team were laying down their tactics of what they should ask Bernardo after his arrest.

"Get your suit on; he's going to be arrested now," said Bevan, referring to the hi-tech ear devices the interview team would wear while interrogating Bernardo. Steve Irwin resisted, saying the team wasn't ready.

"That's too bad," countered Bevan. "You're going. Get your suits on."

* * *

Early that evening, Niagara regional Sergeant Gary Beaulieu and Metro Toronto Detective Steve Irwin sat in a Halton police interrogation room across from the most heinous suspect they had ever faced in their careers. This was the man both officers had spent so much of their careers tracking. Finally, here he was; they were face-to-face with Paul Bernardo. Unknown to Bernardo, twenty or so police officers and criminal profile specialists watched his every twitch and listened to his every word on a closed-circuit television set, among them Ron McKay of the RCMP, Chuck Wagner of the FBI in Buffalo, New York, and Peter Collins, the head of forensics at the Clarke Institute in Toronto and the contract psychologist to Metro police. Bernardo sat slumped in a chair as the interview began. In other circumstances he might have admired Beaulieu and Irwin, both known for their immaculate dress sense; both exceptionally well mannered. But they weren't there to be his friend. They knew it and he knew it.

The officers wasted no time in letting Bernardo know he was toast. They knew about Leslie; they knew about Kristen. And he knew about Leslie and Kristen didn't he? And Tammy? What about Tammy? Right off the bat, they left him with the impression that Karla had talked. He was barraged with comments like "She's going to sink you! She'll cut a deal and take you for everything!" Bernardo sat, slightly hunched. This was perhaps his darkest hour, and yet he looked cocky, defiant. He didn't say much at all, except for interjecting with something like "I didn't do it" and "I don't know what you're talking about" and "I wasn't there." He almost let his guard down and lost his nerve once, when Beaulieu reminisced about the dead schoolgirls and Tammy. But he regained his composure and returned to the brick wall. Deny, deny, deny.

One officer who witnessed the interview would later read the lyrics from Bernardo's Deadly Innocence rap concept and suddenly understand that Bernardo had long prepared for that moment: "You got no confession, you got no case."

The interview went on for hours. At some point, Bernardo made some mention of a lawyer, but it was vague. The two cops, helped here and there by the profilers, did their best in an attempt to break him down. Finally, Bernardo pointedly asked to talk with his lawyer. His request was so bold that it couldn't be ignored.

That afternoon Patty and Karla had been out shopping. As they returned to the underground parking lot of the condo complex, Karla literally turned white and began to whimper.

"What is it, Karla?"

"Listen," she said, turning up the radio.

It was a news report announcing the arrest of a suspect in the Scarborough Rapes and perhaps the Schoolgirl Murders, as the abduction and killing of Leslie Mahaffy and Kristen French had become known in the press.

They rushed up to the condo and flicked on the TV. The story was everywhere.

"Oh my God!" said Karla as the footage of Paul being led out of their house in Port Dalhousie was shown over and over. As the TV cameras followed police removing Buddy the dog from the home, Karla really started to cry.

Patty was a bit bewildered.

"You'll be okay. Your dog Buddy will be fine," Patty said, comforting Karla.

They flicked from channel to channel. It seemed the news was on every channel. But Karla wanted to watch it all anyway. At one point there was a close-up of a wreath on the front door and Karla became incensed.

"That's mine. I made that. That's my house. How could they plaster it all over television like that?"

Patty and Calvin warned Karla that night that it was likely she would be arrested next, that it seemed inevitable and Karla needed to prepare herself for that eventuality.

Karla nodded. But she was a nervous wreck, shaking and sobbing at the thought.

She had continued to take painkillers even after the bruises had faded, and she turned to those with renewed vigor in the days after Paul's arrest.

She also began drinking more heavily, asking Patty to pick up liter after liter of red wine. The mixture of wine and pain pills sparked a significant concern for her in Patty and Calvin.

They began to wonder if Karla would be around long enough to be arrested.

Four days after his last visit to Bayview Drive, Mike Donald returned home at 6:15 P.M. after driving his girlfriend to work.

"Did you hear the good news?" his mom asked as he entered the house and made himself comfortable.

"No, what?"

"They caught that guy that killed Kristen French . . . and they think he also killed Leslie Mahaffy."

Thank God, Mike thought to himself. He had been concerned for his niece and nephew, who were the same age as Kristen French.

His mom continued: "He lived in Port Dalhousie. I think his name was, um, Bob . . ."

Mike's mind drifted. Who did he know in Port Dalhousie?

"I don't know his last name, a Spanish name, I think. Anyway, Bob, and he lived on Bayview . . ."

Mike started. He moved toward his mother.

"It wasn't . . . his first name wasn't Paul, was it?"

"Yes, Paul. He has an Italian name or a Spanish name."

"Not Paul Bernardo?"

Mike's mom smiled. "Yes, that's it. Paul Bernardo on Bayview. How did you know . . ." Her words trailed off as she saw the look of horror on her son's face.

"Oh, it's not your friend, Paul, is it?"

"Yeah, it's my friend Paul."

Mike moved to the telephone and called the Green Ribbon Task Force.

"Hi, could you tell me the name of the guy who was arrested in the Kristen French murder?"

A female operator brushed him off, told him she couldn't say anything.

"Whether you can tell me or not, if it was Paul Bernardo I have something to tell you."

The operator's voice sang with recognition. "Do you know him?"

"I'm one of his closest friends. He told me some things a

couple of days ago that your officers should know . . . about Karla's sister, Tammy.''

Mike was put on hold, and within a minute he was on the speakerphone with Vince Bevan.

"Hello, Mike. It's a good thing you called us, because we were just about to send someone around to talk with you. Don't leave the house. We'll be right there."

Mike now understood what Paul had meant when he said "it" was bigger than "it" actually seemed; this is what he meant when he said it was huge. Mike wondered if he should call a lawyer before speaking with the police. He let it pass. He was totally innocent and didn't have anything to fear. He just hoped he could help.

Constable Scott Kenney and Sergeant Brian Nesbitt didn't waste any time at Mike's house.

"At this point you're a suspect and only you can change our minds," Nesbitt said to him.

Sergeant John Stonehill gave Van the news of Bernardo's arrest at around 8 P.M. outside Van's parents' home in Markham. In yet another interview, Stonehill and McEwen asked Van about Bernardo's reaction to the composite of the Scarborough Rapist back in May, 1990. Stonehill then asked Van if he had called the police.

"I did think of it," Van responded, "but I just didn't think Paul would ever really do that."

Van also told police that Paul said the DNA tests had cleared him. The proof it had seemed, was that the police hadn't arrested him.

After Stonehill left, Van tried to come to grips with what this all would mean for the rest of his life. How would he get through the ensuing decades with the albatross around his neck of having been Paul Bernardo's best friend?

On the afternoon of February 17, Lisa Stanton was at her boyfriend's apartment when a friend called her to say Paul Bernardo had been arrested in the rapes and killings of Leslie Mahaffy and Kristen French. Lisa quickly turned on the television and saw Paul and Karla's house. Crowds were already starting to gather near the tidy Cape Cod bungalow, now draped in distinctive yellow plastic police tape.

Although she was dumbfounded, Lisa had an odd feeling that the police had indeed arrested the right man, that Paul Bernardo had killed those young girls, and that he had raped other women. As had often been the case in the weeks since she had learned of Karla's beating, Lisa thought of her friend and wondered just what her life had been like behind that impenetrable shell of happiness and devotion.

Lisa immediately called Alex and Kathy, but they weren't home. She left an urgent message that they should call as soon as they could.

When Alex and Kathy returned from a night out, the light on the couple's answering machine was flashing like crazy. It was chock-full of messages from family and friends. They all bore the same explosive information.

Kathy collapsed on the bed. Alex merely stopped and thought. "It figures that it's Paul," he said, marveling at how little disbelief he felt at the stunning news.

Kathy's mother, Lynda Wilson, was sitting at her desk at St. Catharines Hospital when she heard about Paul's arrest. She reacted not with shock but with suspicion. She thought back to the Jack-and-Jill party she'd hosted for Paul and Karla and remembered the sight of all those young, jousting men who'd gathered in a corner of her backyard, whispering furtively. She wondered who among them had been part of the murderous scheme; she was certain one of them was the second suspect police were still watching.

The night of February 17, 1993, Barry Fox had been out and returned home about 11 P.M. His wife, Cindy, was watching the news in their comfortable Bayview/York Mills home and remarked about a breaking news story involving the Scarborough rapes and the murders of Kristen French and Leslie Mahaffy.

The suspect's name was Paul Bernardo, she said.

The criminal lawyer stopped. Oddly enough he had two clients named Paul Bernardo. But there'd been no phone calls, no frantic pages, so he shrugged his shoulders and went to bed.

Shortly after 3 A.M. on February 18, Fox was roused from a deep sleep by his 24-hour answering service. It was a Metro police officer named Campbell, advising him that one of his clients had been arrested and charged with a series of sexual assaults. Fox thought he heard him mention the Scarborough Rapist but it was, after all, the middle of the night.

Campbell turned the phone over to the steady voice of Paul Bernardo.

"I've been charged. I'd like to see you," he said. He also mentioned that he had no money and that he'd need Fox to take the case on through the province's Legal Aid Plan.

Fox told him he'd come down soon and hung up.

Barry Fox remembered the first time he met Paul Barnardo six weeks earlier, shortly after the January 5 assault on Karla. A stocky man with a balding pate and curly black hair that fell to his shoulders, Fox handles between twenty and twenty-five clients a month. He had represented drug dealers, smugglers, murderers and rapists in his time.

Fox had known Van Smirnis from several years earlier when Van was being investigated for one of his quasi-illegal computer ventures. After the assault on Karla, Van had suggested Paul talk to Barry, or another lawyer he was familiar with through the biker gang they'd supplied with thousands of cartons of contraband cigarettes.

Paul met with both lawyers and told Barry that he wanted to retain him. "I don't like that other guy's cardboard suit," he had said. Fox, an immaculate dresser, whose tastes run to Hugo Boss and Armani, didn't know whether his new client was joking or not. He didn't seem to be.

Paul had arrived in Fox's Scarborough office to discuss the assault on his wife. He was clean shaven and his bleached blond hair was tidy despite the odd little curls that had been fastidiously worked into the hairdo. He sat in Barry's comfortable leather chair while Barry sat across a broad desk in a worn high-backed wooden chair.

They talked briefly about the assault with a weapon charges. As is Barry's practice, he never asked if Paul was guilty but merely asked him to explain what it was the police accused him of doing. They chatted for no more than thirty minutes, and when Paul left, he seemed calm, cool, casual.

Fox didn't hear from him again until the phone call in the early-morning hours of February 18. Although he had had every intention of going back to sleep, he kept thinking about the call. Suddenly, his accountant client was out of money. He'd been charged with some sort of sexual assaults, and worse, Barry knew the officer who called was connected to Toronto's Sexual Assault Squad, which gave him a nagging sense that there was something more than a routine case at hand.

At about 4 A.M. Barry arrived at 41 Division where Paul was being held overnight until his first court appearance. The building at the corner of Birchmount Road and Eglinton Avenue was eerily quiet. Barry recognized the officers at the reception area when he walked in and they acknowledged him. It seemed to take a little longer than usual to get Barry into the prisoners' area, but he chalked that up to the hour.

Finally, he was ushered into a long narrow room with about half a dozen spartan holding cells. Paul Bernardo was standing, waiting, clad only in a pair of dark briefs. He seemed to be neither agitated about his incarceration nor despondent. He didn't weep. He didn't hang his head in shame.

Barry asked his standard set of questions.

"Why are you here? What do you think is going on? What did the police say you did?"

For ten minutes Paul lucidly recounted the allegations facing him: that he was the notorious Scarborough Rapist as well as the murderer of Kristen French and Leslie Mahaffy. He was, Barry thought later, almost too lucid.

At no time did they discuss guilt or innocence.

Although Paul's first appearance in court lasted less than a minute, security was unusually tight at Scarborough courts. The tiny courtroom was jammed with the press and the curious, each of whom was searched before they entered.

Bernardo, clad in a black t-shirt and grey sweatpants, his hands cuffed behind his back, stood impassively as he remanded until March 2. No plea was entered and the reading of forty-five sex-related charges was waived. While the appearance was fleeting, it lasted long enough to start one of the many Bernardo rumours: that he developed an erection during the hearing.

Outside the grey, single-level court building, several reporters and photographers. including Mike Cassese and Ray Smith of the *Toronto Sun*, cautiously discussed what they believed they'd seen. One said he was sure he'd seen Bernardo look down at his sweatpants and shrug his shoulders as though an erection was as natural as blinking.

For his part, Barry said he had no knowledge of any unexplained penile movement during the hearing.

After the brief court appearance, Bernardo was moved to the Metro East Detention Centre, an oddly shaped, red brick structure just south of the court building. To the uninitiated, Metro East looks like many of the factories and industrial complexes surrounding it. Even with its razor wire and tower, it blends into the industrial scenery.

Barry's first order of business was to talk to the local Crown Attorney, Mary Hall. Barry told her he wanted an outline or synopsis of the case against his client since he had only the information the press had provided him about the allegations.

"I have nothing for you," Hall apparently told Barry.

Someone within the court system had tipped reporters to the ironic fact that Paul's father, Ken, had only a week before Paul's arrest been convicted of sexual assault for attacks dating back to the early 1960s. Even more ironically, Ken was to appear in Scarborough courts for sentencing the same day as Paul's next court appearance. Luckily, there would be separate courtrooms for the Bernardos although there was much joking among police and reporters that a special Bernardo courtroom could be designated.

The media, which had set up camp outside the Sir Raymond Drive address as soon as word of Paul's arrest began to circulate late Wednesday afternoon, continued to pester Ken, Marilyn and David, who was once again living at home.

Ken acknowledged his son had been charged but said he'd had no contact with Paul and had no idea whether he could have been involved in the French/Mahaffy murders.

Marilyn, who seemed to waver unsteadily between chatting amicably with media and slamming the door, described herself as "an old-fashioned woman" who has been "kept out of those problems."

She said she'd end up in the "psychiatric ward in the hospital" if both son and husband were to land behind bars. She acknowledged Paul and the family had been estranged for several years. Marilyn explained to Joe Warmington of the *Sun*, the "tiff" had come at the wedding.

"All I said is I don't want to be a bitchy mother-in-law. I said I didn't like pheasant. That's all it was—big deal!"

A day later she would tell Warmington jokingly that she wanted to put cannons on the roof with which to disperse the bothersome media. "It's been absolutely the worst time of my life," she told the reporter. "It's just awful. I didn't do anything wrong."

Marilyn said she was on medication to calm her nerves but even when she went to the drug store she was followed by photographers. "What do they want to take pictures of me for?"

After harassing phone calls and constant traffic slowing and stopping in front of the house, sometimes shining lights in through the window, they'd asked for police protection, Marilyn said.

"I'm just fed up and tired and sick. I haven't been getting any sleep."

Ken, in his usual verbose way, nodded agreement. "Yeah, it's been embarrassing, what would you expect?"

On Friday, February 19, Fox announced he was going to seek a bail hearing within the week. He wanted the officer in charge present to give information on each of the alleged assaults. Fox was quite sure that if he could pull off the hearing, he had a good chance of getting Paul out on bail, since he didn't think there was much evidence against his client. Fox also spoke to the lead investigator on the murder investigation, Inspector Vince Bevan. While the murder charges were being bandied about in the press, they still hadn't been laid. Nor would they be for almost three months. Nonetheless, Bevan offered to begin disclosure on the case.

"Do you want them on computer disc or hard copy?" Bevan asked. Fox wasn't sure. "Well, do you have a warehouse?" Bevan asked. Because that's how much room he'd need if he wanted the hard copy. But despite Bevan's bravado, the police, at that time, had virtually nothing. The following day, Fox had a very different conversation with the Crown Attorney on the case, Ray Houlahan, who told him that they wouldn't be sending any information just yet. In reality, the promised murder charges had been put on hold indefinitely. It was a curious turnabout for the police, one which indicated something had gone awry.

On Thursday evening February 18, Niagara Region Chief John Shoveller announced through a press release his personal congratulations to the investigators who'd worked on the case with the task force, and to the members of Metro's Sex Assault Squad. He praised the working relationship and cooperation between the two units. He also announced that two murder charges were to be laid against Paul Bernardo that night. But that wasn't the case, and a day later, Shoveller issued a cryptic press release that indicated the charges had been put on hold and that they would answer no more questions from the media. It was a curious reaction from police, who had earlier held several press conferences, including one with the girls' families in attendance, to discuss the case.

In Barry Fox's office, the phone was ringing off the hook. There were literally dozens of calls from the media. Not just Canadian media, but reporters from throughout the United States, Great Britain and beyond. There were also calls from people who knew Paul. Several women phoned in tears, saying that Paul couldn't possibly have committed the crimes he was accused of.

Then there were the calls from his clients. Hours after the news hit the radio and newspapers that Fox was representing Paul Bernardo, he was fired by a dozen clients who feared Fox wouldn't have enough time for their files or that judges would suddenly begin to dislike Barry. Some wondered how he could defend someone like Bernardo.

They needn't have worried. Early Friday morning, during one of several visits to the Metro East Detention Centre,

Barry Fox and Paul had a conversation that led them to dissolve their working relationship. "We had a falling out. There was a conflict," is all Fox will say on the matter.

There were several conflicts. One of them was the fact he represented Van Smirnis on a smuggling charge and learned that Van was likely to be a Crown witness against Paul. He learned this when Van called to say he wanted to apply for the various rewards being offered for the arrest of the people responsible for the deaths of Kristen French and Leslie Mahaffy.

Fox adamantly recalls that at no point did Paul ever discuss or describe any videotapes that might have been secreted away in the Port Dalhousie home.

CHAPTER
23

On February 18, 1993, Alex and Kathy made the three-hour trip to St. Catharines from their new home outside of Syracuse, New York.

"Karla must not have known," Kathy said when she read the newspaper clippings that reported that police were watching a second suspect. They recalled Karla telling them their house was haunted and that the noises coming from the basement were their ghosts, and it reaffirmed in their mind that Paul had developed an elaborate means of keeping Karla in the dark about his deranged activities.

"You see, she couldn't have known," Kathy repeated as they made their way to St. Catharines.

"He wouldn't have told Karla what he was doing because he wouldn't have trusted her," added Alex. "Paul knew Karla's work schedule. He could have worked around it. Karla couldn't have known."

Even though Karla was staying with her uncle and aunt at this point, Alex, Kathy, and Lisa visited the Homolkas. Dorothy quickly ushered them downstairs so they wouldn't be rushed by reporters who hung around the quiet street like birds on a telephone wire.

Karel was drinking heavily and appeared to be somewhere between complete unconsciousness and boozy introspection. The blinds were drawn, adding to the dreary, oppressive mood. It reminded Alex of the scene in the Homolka basement after Tammy's death. Everyone stared blankly into his own private space.

The Homolkas had taped all of the news reports from the night before and were watching them repeatedly. Sometimes they would chuckle at some piece of information like one report that Karla had a brother. But mostly they sat in stony silence watching the images flickering away on the screen. It was an odd tableau. Even though they were players in the drama unfolding in the newspapers and on every television station, they turned to the media as though it were an event about which they knew nothing.

One television clip that received constant exposure was one of Paul being led into the Metro East Detention Centre in Scarborough, his head almost entirely obscured by the hood of his green duffle coat. His hands manacled behind his back, surrounded by officers, he was led like a calf to market.

"I loved that jacket he had on," Lori said absently.

The phone rang off the hook and the guests took turns with the rest of the family answering the calls, almost all of which were from reporters. The conversations were brief. No comment. Click.

Someone joked that if anyone had to go upstairs he had better watch out for the Sue Sgambati Mobile, a reference to Global Television reporter Sue Sgambati, who'd broken the story of the arrest the previous afternoon. And sure enough, at the first hint of motion behind the sheer curtains in the living room, the glaring white light from television cameras and the frantic popping of still photographers' flashes would light up the neighborhood.

Still, in the basement bunker, there seemed an almost obsessive desire to hear what was being said about them on the outside. One news show broadcast a segment of video taken at Paul and Karla's wedding, and Karel remarked that it must have been sold to the television station by an uncle and aunt who'd just announced they were going on a month's vacation. At one point, they debated who the second suspect was. The papers had reported that police were watching another suspect, who presented no danger to the public while under constant surveillance. In the Homolka basement, they discussed a television special broadcast after the disappearance of Kristen French that had indicated there were two male suspects.

"With the weight of the concrete they moved, it has to be some other man," someone remarked.

"I bet it's Van," another voice suggested.

"No, no, but maybe Gus or someone else from Paul's circle of friends in Toronto," someone else offered. Karla's name never entered the discussion.

Someone asked what was going to happen to Karla, and Dorothy said she'd be charged. Lisa assumed it would be for a minor offense like concealing evidence or harboring a fugitive. "Damn, she's going to be in a lot of trouble," Lisa said. "Why didn't she tell?" But the question hung awkwardly without an answer before slowly evaporating, replaced by even more questions.

Dorothy and Karel described their utter surprise that Paul had been beating Karla. "We had no idea," they said repeatedly. "We just didn't know."

"What about the bruises, though?" Kathy asked.

"Well, she always had a good excuse," Dorothy explained.

Kathy and Alex talked about their suspicions over the past year or so. They believed something was terrible wrong with the relationship. And Karel and Dorothy asked the same question Alex and Kathy had tortured themselves with: "Why didn't you tell us what you thought was happening?"

"Would you have believed us?" asked Kathy. "And how do you bring up your suspicions?"

Finally, Kathy asked if she thought Paul might have had anything to do with Tammy's death. "Didn't you wonder?" she asked.

Lisa looked at her friend with a mixture of shock and admiration. It was a question that had crept into her subconscious almost from the moment that she'd learned of the arrest, but she hadn't had the courage to bring it up with Karla's family.

The question made Dorothy and Karel recoil in horror. "It was just an accident," said Dorothy. Clearly, she had reached the saturation point. "No! This is enough! I've had enough! I can't deal with any more!" And rather than discuss the subject any further, she left the room.

Lori, on the other hand, seemed to rise to the occasion even as her parents seemed to crumble. She told Alex and Kathy and Lisa how she thought there was something weird and that maybe they should tell someone. She admitted she'd thought they might have been doing cocaine in the basement the night Tammy died, because of the odd burn marks on her face.

Karel sank deeper into his chair. He blamed himself for not protecting his eldest daughter better. He recalled with sad irony how he had once asked Paul to look after his three girls.

Within hours of Paul Bernardo's arrest, the province's Chief Coroner, Dr. Jim Young, announced that he had re-opened the investigation into Tammy Homolka's death given the circumstances and charges facing Paul Bernardo.

While the Homolkas visited with Karla's friends, Niagara police heard surprising reports about their suspect. Late Saturday evening March 28, 1992, two weeks before Kristen French's abduction, police were told, St. Catharines resident Lori Lazurak picked up her sister, Tania, from work at Brock University in St. Catharines. The sisters drove to their regular evening coffee haunt, Robin's Donuts, at the corner of Lakeport and Lakeshore roads in north St. Catharines. The slim and attractive sisters, both in their mid 20s with long, blonde hair, always sat at their favorite window table of the practical one-storey donut shop and talked for hours. As they drank their coffee that night, the window was only a few feet to the side.

Around midnight, Tania noticed a gold-colored sports car drive slowly past the window. A short time later, the car drove slowly by again, then again, then again, then again. Each time it drove in the same direction and then disappeared around a bend in front of the store. The Lazuraks continued their chat and put the odd sports car out of their minds.

Suddenly, only a few feet away from them in the lower part of the glass window, they saw a video camera lens. It stayed there for about half a minute then disappeared. They thought it weird, but seeing no harm had been done they continued to talk and drink coffee. About fifteen minutes later, the video camera had returned to the window. This time they could see a man's hair. It was long and spiky.

At 2:30 A.M., with their sisterly chatter ended and sleep calling them, Lori and Tania left the donut shop. As they drove away in Lori's car, they saw the gold sports car in a tiny strip mall parking lot across the street. It was empty. They drove home, but just as Tania was about to get out of the car and walk to her house she noticed the gold sports car drive by with its lights off. Scared, Tania jumped back into Lori's car. Lori drove around the block. They returned to find the sports car parked four houses away. The car was clean and shiny, but the license plate was extremely dirty and could barely be seen in the darkness. Lori jotted down a partial license number of 660 NF. . . . Tania recalled 660 MAN. The sisters drove around the block one more time and the sports car left. Tania reported the odd incident to Niagara Regional Police March 29, 1992. For their own safety, the sisters vowed to each other they would keep their eyes open for the gold sports car.

Police officers who took the Lazuraks' statements shook their heads in disbelief when the sisters told them that just before 6 P.M. on Saturday April 18, 1992—two days after Kristen French went missing—Lori was driving westbound on the Martindale Road bridge across the Queen Elizabeth Way when the gold sports car passed her in the opposite direction. Lori had been watching for the car for more than two weeks. Determined to get a license plate number, she plucked up her courage and followed it to Main Street in the Port Dalhousie residential area. She tried to note the license plate through a grey-tinted plastic cover. She believed it read 660 HFM. As the sports car turned in to the quiet residential streets along Lake Ontario, Lori tried to keep up with it, but after about thirty seconds on Bayview Drive the car suddenly vanished. Lori drove around the area for ten minutes trying to find it again, but she couldn't. That night she filed more information with Niagara police about the March 28, 1992 donut shop stalker, telling them the gold sports car had tinted windows. None of the police officers involved in the Lazurak complaint matched the gold sports car with the beige Camaro sought in Kristen French's kidnapping. Paul Bernardo's license plate number was 660 HFH.

In another report, Rachel Farron of St. Catharines told how she was driving along deserted St. Catharines streets at about 2 A.M. one morning in July of 1991 when she noticed a car that had passed her had then made a quick U-turn on a red light and begun following her. Farron, twenty-one, 5-foot-3 and 128 pounds, became frightened and decided to return to her boyfriend's house, thinking at best, her stalker would flee when she pulled up to his house. Instead, she changed her mind and drove home. The car followed but when she drove into her driveway on Meredith Street it passed by without stopping.

A week later, she was driving on a city street late at night when she noticed the stalker sports car in a turn lane. She noted the make, a gold Nissan 240SX, and the license plate, 660 HFH. Hoping to avoid the car, she turned right, in the opposite direction, but she looked in her rear view mirror to see the Nissan in subtle pursuit. This time, Farron drove to her boyfriend's house, but when she arrived it was in darkness. Petrified with fear, Farron ducked under the dashboard. The Nissan drove by. Thinking all was clear, Farron started up her car and drove to the video store where her boyfriend worked. Suddenly, the Nissan was in her rear mirror. Farron parked her car alongside the video store; the Nissan driver had the audacity to park right beside her car. Her boyfriend wasn't there, so she struck up casual conversation with the owner. After ten minutes, the Nissan left. She talked to the owner for another twenty minutes. There was no sign of the Nissan when she walked to her car and sunk behind the wheel, but as she pulled away, the Nissan was right behind her. Again, she drove to her boyfriend's; again he wasn't home. She parked the car in the driveway, locked the doors and stayed inside.

The boyfriend didn't come home until 4:30 A.M. Farron nervously rushed up to him and told him about the sports car. They turned to see the Nissan driver standing in the bushes only two houses away. The boyfriend gave chase. They found the car around a nearby street corner, but there was no sign of its owner. They backtracked to the bushes, but as they did, the Nissan started up and roared away.

They told a passing police officer about the incident and gave him the license number. Using the license retrieval system, he told them the license came back to Paul Kenneth Bernardo. Nobody had ever heard of him. He sure wasn't a local boy. A week later, the boyfriend and some friends saw the Nissan at a donut store on Ontario Street. The driver had blond, curly hair. Farron's complaint to police apparently had ended with the officer telling them the stalker's name.

Shortly before Paul's arrest, Lisa had written a number of comforting letters to Karla assuring her old friend that if she needed company or support, her friends were behind her. Alex and Kathy had made numerous trips to see Karla as well.

"Call anytime," Lisa wrote.

Later, she got a letter from Karla during her seven-week stay in Toronto where she underwent a barrage of psychiatric/psychological tests. She described how the medication she was taking made her hands shake like crazy. She never referred to being beaten by her husband or to any of the charges he faced, instead saying only: "I'm getting the help that I need."

She went on to write about how much she missed Buddy and how concerned she was because of a fire in the veterinary clinic where he'd been taken after Paul's arrest. Karla was also in contact by phone and letter with Alex and Kathy. Several days after their first visit, Karla called Alex and Kathy in Skaneateles to tell them how happy she was to learn that they'd come by to visit, even though she wasn't home. It meant a lot to her family, she said. More important, Karla wanted Alex and Kathy to come back to visit when she returned home, sometime in March.

Not surprisingly, the news of Paul's arrest spread with blinding speed throughout Shaver Hospital, where Dorothy Homolka worked. The hospital was abuzz with the news. Some reacted with shock and anger. Karla had baby-sat for many of the nurses, and the implications were obvious.

"That could have been my kid!" was a common refrain.

Dorothy took little time off work. As she'd explained after Tammy's death, she needed to get out of the house, even though she must have known virtually every coworker in the hospital was talking about her and her daughter. She remained nonplussed, however, carrying on as if nothing had happened. If she talked at all, it was to reinforce that Karla had been horribly victimized.

On the Friday following Paul's arrest, Dorothy's coworkers noticed she appeared upset. Police had begun searching the Port Dalhousie home. Dorothy was weeping, and a coworker offered to drive her home. When they got there, the woman offered to stop by the local grocery store to pick up some coffee and other supplies, to which Dorothy thankfully agreed.

The hospital administration also supported the notion of Karla as victim, bringing in an expert to describe the psychological condition known as battered wife syndrome to concerned employees.

Several times in the week following Paul's arrest, Dorothy and Karel visited their daughter, always bringing a supply of red wine, which Karla drank steadily during the daytime.

"Listen, if you're going to drink, you're going to eat," Patty would say. But Karla was childlike in her obstinance. She refused to eat, seemingly more content to be merely loaded.

Despite her renewed depression, Karla honored George Walker's command that she not talk about any aspect of the case or the negotiations she'd entered. Patty and Calvin didn't press her on the issue.

Unlike other members of the Homolka family, as soon as they read that there was a second suspect, Calvin and Patty realized that suspect was living in their home.

Several days after the arrest, when the *Toronto Sun* newspaper purchased and printed Paul and Karla's wedding pictures, Jimmy called Karla to say he was sorry and that he was sympathetic to what had happened to her. But soon thereafter their relationship cooled dramatically, as far as Jimmy was concerned. They spoke occasionally and Karla later wrote to him but her letters went unanswered.

About that time, a neighbor in Brampton recognized Karla from the pictures and called the press, which soon set up camp, trying to talk to or get pictures of Karla and her aunt and uncle.

Finally, Dorothy and Karel decided that since everyone knew where Karla now was, she might as well come back to St. Catharines. On February 24, they came and got Karla. Patty was home sick that day and was napping when Dorothy and Karel arrived. Karla crept into Patty's room and hugged her, crying.

Karla thanked her for everything, but mostly for being a good friend. Patty, too, began to cry.

Later there was a card in Karla's script: "Thank you for being supportive of me. I love you very much. Thanks for letting me stay, I wish I could have stayed longer."

Calvin was steadfast in his support of Karla and the Homolkas, who viewed their daughter as a victim. Patty, however, found herself asking more and more questions. "There's only so much someone can make you do," she argued.

As February gave way to March, Dorothy talked freely about the negotiations between Karla's lawyer and the prosecuting Crown attorneys. She acknowledged Karla was going to have to go to jail, but only for twelve years. And she was going to get a chance to go to college, something she'd always wanted to do!

According to some coworkers, Dorothy confided that the time leading up to Karla's trial had not been an easy one in the Homolka house. With both Karla and Karel at home, drinking heavily, there was considerable tension and she was glad to go to work each day to avoid it.

In mid-March, Karla returned home after her psychiatric assessments. Kathy made another trip home to St. Catharines, determined to see her friend. She and Alex circled the block several times looking for the ubiquitous media, but seeing only a man in a nondescript car who they assumed was Karla's police protector, they parked a few houses away from the Homolkas'.

Again they walked the familiar steps to the semidetached home. Lori met them at the door. Peeking around the corner from the kitchen was Karla, a bottle of Piat d'Or white wine in her hands. She broke into a smile and rushed down the steps to embrace Kathy.

"I'm so happy to see you. I'm so glad you came. You're my best friend!" Karla said, holding Kathy tight. Kathy smiled. Despite the sadness of the situation, she couldn't help but think with relief that the old Karla seemed to be standing in the kitchen, not the stranger she'd watched move into Karla's body.

It was obvious that Karla didn't want her parents around. While Alex chatted with Dorothy and Karel, Karla led Kathy upstairs. She told Kathy about the medication she was on, and how awful she felt. She told her about how she'd been sloshing back the booze since 8 A.M. and how most of the alcohol in the house was gone. Kathy found that hard to believe, given the vast caches of liquor she knew were normally stashed away in the Homolka home.

Within minutes they were upstairs in Tammy's room. Buddy the dog was with them. When Karla had moved out of the house in early 1991, Lori had moved into her older sister's downstairs room, so when Karla moved back home, Tammy's room was the only one available. All of Karla's stuff was there—clothes, knickknacks, shoes, suitcases, boxes. It was obvious these were the belongings she'd grabbed in her frenzied escape from her Port Dalhousie home. Karla showed off the nice clothes neighbors, relatives, and friends had bought or given her. Everybody, it seemed, wanted to help Karla.

"Thank God you're not pregnant, Karla!" Kathy blurted out, not meaning for it to sound as harsh as it did. Buddy flopped his massive head on Kathy's lap and wagged his tail. She could barely move with the weight of his giant head.

Karla screwed her face up and nodded sadly.

"Yeah, me too. Paul said if he'd ever had a girl he would have had sex with her," Karla confided.

Kathy was aghast.

Karla turned to Kathy and gave her an inquiring look. "What do you think happened?" It was as if Karla was searching for answers different from those she was painfully aware of, as though Kathy could tell her something to ease the pain. Or maybe she was just testing her old friend.

Kathy hesitated, then spoke: "I know you knew something was going on. Maybe you knew more than I believe, but that's okay. I understand because you're a victim."

Karla hugged her, backed off, and looked her straight in the eye. "You and Alex will be the first people I talk to, I promise."

"Tell me . . ." Kathy started.

"I can't. I can't. I'm sworn not to say anything," Karla said. "But if you want to ask me things, I'll tell you if I can."

Kathy wondered for a few minutes, then asked, "How did you live through all that?"

"I just shut down."

"Why did you leave?" Kathy asked.

"Because he was going to do it again. He wanted more," Karla explained. "That's why he bought that old blue car, the second car."

But Kathy heard the hollow ring of a lie in the answer. "That doesn't jibe. Your mother had to drag you out of there," Kathy muttered to herself.

Karla told how the female Niagara Regional Police officer who'd helped take her statement about the disappearance of the girls told her they weren't after her.

" 'We're not here to get you, we need you to get him,' " Karla said, recounting the conversation. " 'You're innocent. You're the victim.' "

Clearly, those words had become a kind of mantra to Karla.

Still, Karla admitted she hadn't told the whole story about what had happened, at least not initially. Because she was afraid of going to jail herself, she told them only about Paul's involvement, insisting she hadn't known what was going on and that she learned everything only after the acts had been completed.

Four or five times police questioned her, but she refused to acknowledge that she knew anything more. Finally, she told

Kathy, her lawyer George Walker told her police had only enough evidence to charge Paul with second-degree murder, so Karla agreed to tell the whole story. She told Kathy she was afraid Paul might get off.

She described how, during the hunt for Kristen French's killers, she and her family would be having dinner or chatting and the topic would come up. They would discuss different theories about who might be responsible. Paul always loved those conversations and participated with great earnestness, only to laugh himself silly when he and Karla were alone.

The night the CHCH television special aired describing the FBI profile, Paul and Karla watched the show in their bedroom, and Paul literally danced with glee, Karla told her mesmerized friend. "He just thought it was the funniest thing. 'Ha, Ha, Ha, they'll never get me,' he kept saying over and over," Karla recalled, running her hands through her blonde hair. "All I can tell you, Kathy, is that there's a deal," she stammered. Then, in a completely different tone she half moaned, half sighed. "I can't believe this is happening to me. It's like a bad dream."

Karla went on to describe how police had insisted that she keep a journal, that she try to remember all of the things that had happened to her from the moment she met Paul. She reached for the book and opened to a page and began reading to Kathy. She described how Paul had tried to make her have sex with Buddy, the dog, but that neither she nor the animal had cooperated.

Karla confided that Paul had threatened to kill her entire family, that one night he'd gone over to the Homolkas' and broken a downstairs window, then reported back to Karla. "There, you see that broken window? I could have killed your whole family. I was that close," Paul reportedly said to his wife.

Kathy shuddered. The enormity of her friend's confessions washed over her, overwhelming her. Yet she knew then that her friend needed help. And if she hadn't been able to reach out for help in the past, she seemed to be reaching now, and Kathy was determined to be there for Karla. Karla went on, telling Kathy about shopping at Topps and how Paul would

count out loud as they made their rounds with the cart—
"that's one, that's two, that's three ... ," counting out transgressions of his personal code of conduct. Perhaps Karla
hadn't asked if a particular brand of cereal was acceptable or
she ignored a comment or walked too far ahead. Regardless,
when they returned to the car in the parking lot, Paul would
produce the long-handled flashlight and bludgeon her legs
with a corresponding number of blows.

As Karla recited a litany of brutality and savagery, she did
so as though reading from a grade-school primer. Kathy
thought for a moment back to the conversations about the
handcuffs and the matter-of-fact tone in which Karla had described those events early on in her relationship with Paul.
She was now using that same tone of voice to report on even
more horrific acts; her voice still betrayed nothing.

"I was numb. It was just unbelievable," Kathy recalls.

Curiously, Kristen French and Leslie Mahaffy never entered the discussion. The focus was always on Karla and what
was happening to her. "But what about the girls? We're so
sick of not knowing what's going on!" Kathy exclaimed.

"I can't tell you, I'm not allowed," Karla said. "But I
want to tell you everything, though. Myself. When this is
done. I think you guys deserve that because you're the only
ones who stuck by me."

Although Karla wouldn't disobey the orders her lawyer and
presumably police had imposed on her not to discuss the
crimes, Kathy and Alex later talked about how they felt Karla
was clearly afraid the details would come out and she
wouldn't be able to put her spin on them. She was also clearly
fearful that they would abandon her. Again and again she
thanked them for coming to visit and for sticking by her.

Undeterred, Kathy brought up the subject of Tammy.

"About Tammy. I think Paul did something to her."

"I can't believe how much you guys know, how much you
found out," Karla said, with a hint of incredulity.

"So what made him change from rapes to murders?"
asked Kathy, feeling as if she was on a roll. She wanted the
truth from her friend. It was a painful conversation, but she
needed to hear the truth.

Karla sighed. "That's one incident. Look, Kathy, I'm sure you can figure it all out."

She said again, "Kathy, you and Alex will be the first to know. I'll speak with you first. You were there, you deserve it."

Even before the dramatic arrest, police officials were planning for what they knew would be a critical search of the home on Bayview Drive. Detective Constable Mike Kershaw of the identification unit had been trying to line up a battery of experts to help or guide them as they tried to link the deaths of two schoolgirls to Paul Bernardo.

By the time the news of the arrest was public, Kershaw had spoken to chemists and biologists at the Centre For Forensic Sciences in Toronto, forensic experts from the OPP and Metro Toronto police. "We were very concerned about this scene, dealing with Leslie Mahaffy, twenty months old, and Kristen French, ten months old. The normal crime scene comes to us after a matter of minutes or hours. Normally there is a body there, a gun or a knife. Evidence is fairly fresh. We realized getting blood, hair and fibre from this scene would be a difficult task," Kershaw said much later at Paul's trial.

At 7 P.M. the identification team entered 57 Bayview Drive. Throughout their research, officers wore airpacks borrowed from the St. Catharines fire department. Their bodies were covered from head to toe by white laboratory treatment suits and hair covers. The team moved in and out of the home looking like something out of a science fiction movie. Kershaw led the group, taking initial still photographs and video to record exactly where everything was when they started.

For the following ten weeks, through at least two extensions of the original warrant, a team of officers combed the home. In the garage, the first significant discovery was made: it was a six-inch-long, green-handled hunting style knife that Kershaw found while poking through the insulation in the rafters. As he worked, the knife fell out, handle first, coming to rest next to a wooden support beam. In the downstairs guest bedroom, police came across a patchwork quilt made of a lively combination of yellow, green blue and white stripes and tiny floral patterns. On one section they noted a peculiar reddish/brown stain and sent it to the CFS for testing. It was later confirmed to be blood believed to have come from Leslie Mahaffy. In a desk drawer in the master bedroom, police found a test tube with a black rubber stopper. Inside was a blue-coloured liquid with flecks of something in it. It was later shown to contain the sleeping medication Halcion. Police were also surprised to discover a distinct repair mark on the west wall of the master bedroom. After removing the repaired drywall, they discovered it was directly behind the electrical outlet in the washroom. The view afforded a perfect look at the toilet and sink area.

Under the couple's double bed a stun gun, an empty cherry Coke bottle and some industrial style headphones were found. Also on the floor near the bed was a Compendium of Pharmaceuticals and Specialties, a thick blue volume outlining a vast array of drugs, their manufacturers and their properties and side effects.

In the walk-in closet belonging to Karla, police discovered a pair of handcuffs.

In Paul's meticulous closet, among the rows of business suits, ties and button-down collar shirts, police discovered a mottled section of carpet. The sample, sent to the CFS, revealed vomit stains from Kristen French.

In the living room, forensic experts sifted through the ashes in the fireplace as well as the ash repository in the basement. They discovered a series of staples similar to those that are used to hold large cardboard boxes together, boxes similar to the ones that at one time encased Leslie Mahaffy's body, boxes similar to the ones folded neatly in the garage at 57 Bayview Drive.

Traces of metal and gold were also found in the fireplace although there was no conclusive evidence as to the material's origin.

A host of tools and equipment stored in the basement were also examined, including a rubber mallet.

Bernardo's car, a Nissan, revealed black paint marks around a frayed section of the front passenger seat, as though something very heavy had split the fabric. Police later took pictures of the car loaded with twelve 66-pound bags of concrete from Beaver Lumber to prove that the car could accommodate the amount needed to encase Leslie Mahaffy.

After an initial visual search, they brought in a 500-watt quartz light that helped highlight unseen hair and fibre samples. They also used an ultra violet radiation light, with a 125-watt blue light bulb, which fluoresces hair, fibre and body fluids. A luma light, a blue-green light that also lights up hair, fibre, body fluids and fingerprints, as well as portable laser lights and an infra red monitoring system also made their way into the home. A chemical fuming was performed to define fingerprints. Any identified fingerprint ridges were photographed and then removed from the wall. But by the time the search ended, they had discovered only fourteen identifiable prints in the house. None belonged to Leslie Mahaffy or Kristen French.

The team either swept or vacuumed all floor surfaces using sophisticated equipment, then cut all the carpet into pieces and packed them off to the CFS where they underwent special light examination for blood. They also examined between the tongues and grooves of the hardwood floors for samples. The hardwood near the patio door, the tiles in the kitchen and foyer, were methodically examined but revealed very little.

Police did discover two spots of blood on the basement floor. Cracks in the concrete floor were chiselled out to make sure no samples were trapped there and entire sections near the spots were removed. They examined the fruit cellar board by board, looking for hair, fibers and blood. A series of chemical tests were used on surfaces to determine if there were blood traces. The chemicals can identify samples as small as parts per million yet yielded nothing except a number of false alarms which merely added to the problems for investigators.

Tucked between the bed and the bedside table they found a copy of Bret Easton Ellis' controversial novel, *American Psycho*. Prosecutors would later argue that Paul Bernardo read the much publicized fictional account of a Wall St. stockbroker turned serial killer as his "bible."

Paul Bernardo shared the same initials and, at the time of the books' release, was the same age as the novel's protagonist, Patrick Bateman. Like Bernardo, Bateman and his colleagues wore all the yuppie designer-brand clothes—Armani, Ralph Lauren, Hugo Boss, Nautica. The Lauren line pops up one hundred times in the book. Karla had bought Paul an imitation Rolex; Bateman had a Rolex. Bateman kept his healthy skin glow by going to tanning salons; so did Bernardo.

In a review of the novel, Halton Regional Police Const. Mike Demeester noted that Bateman's girlfriend, Evelyn, is blond and attractive, in many ways like Karla. Upon leaving the office at night, Demeester noted, Bateman transcends into a dark netherworld, where he kills both men and women, especially women. And like Bateman, Bernardo's rape dialogue centered on woman hating obscenities such as "fucking whore" and "bitch."

Scenes from the book depict Bateman's sadistic view of women. He clearly sees them solely as objects:

"Idly, I wonder if Evelyn would sleep with another woman if I brought one over to her brownstone and, if I insisted, whether they'd let me watch the two of them get it on. If they'd let me direct, tell them what to do, position them under hot, halogen lamps. Probably not; the odds don't look good. But what if I forced her at gunpoint? Threatened to cut them both up, maybe, if they didn't comply?"

Depraved sex acts degenerate and the gratuitous sex and violence increase as the novel progresses. Bateman also ponders sawing the head off a female character, Torri, commenting on how "weightless" the body part felt.

Bateman also talks of videotaping his sadistic escapades: "I set up the Sony palm-sized Handycam so I can film all of what follows. Once it's placed on its stand and running on automatic, with a pair of scissors . . . I occasionally stab at her breasts, accidentally slicing off one of her nipples . . ."

Among the thirty-six books and magazines found at the Bernardo home, many of which contained scenes of horror and crime, police also discovered a copy of *Perfect Victim.* The true crime book chronicles the abduction in 1977 of Colleen Stan, and her subsequent seven year confinement and sado-masochistic torture by Cameron and Janice Hooker.

Although the books would later be deemed inadmissible in court unless it could be proved that the kidnapping of Leslie Mahaffy and Kristen French came as a direct result of the book, prosecutors noted from a sales receipt found inside *American Psycho* that it was bought two months prior to Leslie Mahaffy's abduction. They argued the book was "almost a blueprint or pattern for this man to follow."

On April 30, 1993, seventy-one days after they entered, police ended their search. Kershaw said he was confident every area of the house and every item within had been examined. The only thing they could have done, he said, "would be to actually tear down the house, demolish the home. We didn't have the legal authority to do that."

Eight other Green Ribbon Task Force members went through the house one last time, but found nothing of significance. They knew from discussions with Van Smirnis and Mike Donald that Paul had bragged about videotapes showing Tammy's death. A few days later Paul Bernardo's lawyer at the time, Ken Murray, received permission from police to remove some of his client's personal things. Murray was in the house a matter of hours. The exercise equipment was removed, the television set, the couch, the hope chest, some bottles of perfume and a package: material that would dramatically alter the course of the case.

Every few days after Karla returned to St. Catharines, Lisa called or visited. But one day in mid-May she called and Lori answered the phone. There was a distressing edge to her voice. "Here, you'd better talk to my mom," she said quickly.

In a moment Dorothy's voice was on the line. "What have you heard, Lisa?"

"What? Nothing . . ." Lisa responded, puzzled by the mysterious conversation.

"Oh, well, things are happening today," Dorothy said without really explaining. "It sounds worse than it is."

Lisa hung up and raced to the television and radio to find out what Dorothy's cryptic comments meant. Karla Homolka had been charged with manslaughter in the deaths of Leslie Mahaffy and Kristen French.

Still, Lisa couldn't accept that her friend had actually participated in any meaningful way. And she assumed Karla would plead not guilty and that, given the litany of abuses she'd suffered at Paul's hands, be acquitted, or at the very least serve a short term.

On Tuesday, May 18, 1993, more than thirteen weeks after Paul Bernardo's arrest, Karla Homolka appeared in St. Catharines court on her first appearance. Photographers waiting outside the courthouse snapped Karla arriving in a burgundy minivan that wheeled into the secured and restricted underground parking lot. Everyone in the packed courthouse waited. All except police were puzzled and wanted to know what had happened and what would happen.

Karla walked briskly into the courtroom just before 4:17 P.M., looking straight ahead with a frown on her face and taking tiny, quick nervous steps. Her straw-blond hair was clipped back, nicely framing her suntanned face. She wore a black blazer and a black and red and white plaid kilt, giving her the appearance of a teenage schoolgirl. Karla nodded to her lawyer, George Walker, as she took her seat beside him at the front of court.

A pin drop could have been heard in that deathly silent court. At 4:21 P.M., Murray Segal, a plea-bargain specialist from the Criminal Law Office of the Ministry of the Attorney General, took his seat at the prosecutor's table. Karla looked horribly unhappy with her lot as she waited. It looked as if she was about to burst into tears. Karel Homolka did cry as he, Dorothy and Lori watched Karla.

Within seconds of the justice of the peace entering the court, Walker had stood up and said he would be seeking bail. Citing section 517 of the Criminal Code of Canada, Walker asked that the evidence not be published or broadcast until either the preliminary hearing, guilty verdict, or acquittal. As soon as the justice of the peace gave approval, the court clerk read an indictment showing that Karla would be charged with two counts of manslaughter in the Leslie Mahaffy and Kristen

French murders. Walker asked for trial by judge alone. He said Karla would waive the preliminary inquiry. Segal read in only the briefest of facts: first, that Paul Bernardo allegedly abducted Leslie Mahaffy and brought her to the couple's home. Leslie was unlawfully confined, assaulted and sexually assaulted, and strangled in the presence of Karla, and then Bernardo enlisted Karla's help to dump Leslie's body parts after her dismemberment; second, that Paul and Karla abducted Kristen French and that she was sexually assaulted and strangled by Paul Bernardo in Karla's presence. Karla also joined in the task of removing and dumping Kristen's body.

The court agreed to release Karla Homolka on bail, provided it was given a $110,000 surety, which Dorothy and Karel gave by putting up their home at 61 Dundonald Street. She also agreed to live with her parents, or another relative approved by Inspector Bevan, and report to Bevan each day between 9 A.M. and 4 P.M. Karla was also ordered not to talk with any witness, not to leave her residence without notifying her police surveillance team, to abstain from drugs or alcohol, and appear in court as required. She was also ordered to be accessible to whatever psychiatric treatment doctors required. Walker made the point to the court that "Mr. Bernardo was the leader and the dominant party in this horrific conflict." The court appearance ended with Karla and her family going out the side door at 4:42 P.M. Outside court, Walker said he was not in a position to talk about any plea or whether Karla would appear at Bernardo's trial, nor would he discuss the question regarding Tammy Homolka that everyone now pondered: Did Paul Bernardo and Karla Homolka have anything to do with the younger girl's death?

Karla's waiver of her right to a preliminary hearing meant her case was to go directly to trial. A date of June 28 was set for the trial to begin. St. Catharines was abuzz with anticipation at the first chance to find out what had happened and who was involved. They were to be sorely disappointed.

CHAPTER
24

The weekend before Karla left for prison the Homolkas held an open-house party, a kind of going-away bash for their eldest daughter. Alex and Kathy were sitting in the backyard, the June sun baking them. They noticed that Karla's usually tanned, unblemished legs were lumpy and disfigured.

"Oh, that's from where Paul used to hit me with the flashlight," Karla explained from behind sunglasses and a sun hat, a feeble attempt to disguise herself from the photographers and cameramen beyond their backyard fence. Her hand moved to another point above the kneecap on her bumpy, scarred right leg. "Here's where he stabbed me with a screwdriver."

Karla's face was puffy, and Alex and Kathy wondered if it was merely the medication stew they knew she was ingesting daily, or if Paul had actually left her with some sort of permanent brain damage. Alex and Kathy recalled other poolside visits and shuddered. This was not the same attractive, vibrant young woman of those earlier years.

Throughout the weekend, neighbors stopped by with food and small gifts for Karla.

Alex began reading a copy of a manual sent by the Kingston Prison for Women. Although her trial wasn't quite over, everyone knew Karla was going to jail. They weren't sure for how long, but everyone knew it was going to happen.

Alex read aloud from the booklet. It described what kind

of women were incarcerated in the prison and what crimes they'd committed. It described the prison routine, what the cell accommodations were like, what prisoners could bring to prison, what they couldn't. It described the university courses available through correspondence and the in-prison courses and programs that were available.

"Hey, it's like half summer-camp primer and half university course guide," Alex joked, making Karla and Kathy and some of the other guests giggle shamefully. He went on, kidding Karla about what kind of fine, upstanding citizens her new neighbors and cellmates might be.

"Gee, look, Karla, they've even got women who kill their husbands. There's a group for that," Alex announced.

"Ooh, I think I could have gotten into that club if I'd acted sooner," Karla jokingly responded.

They laughed about the media too, still camped out behind the Homolkas' backyard fence. The family and guests had made a kind of game of it all, holding up tinfoil and pieces of metal in the hope of beaming the sun's rays directly into the probing lenses of the cameras. It had been a long time since Kathy or Alex had heard Karla offer a sincere laugh.

Karla went on to explain that as soon as she got done with prison, she was going to return to Brampton. And for a moment, Alex and Kathy got the feeling that this imminent voyage to Kingston was merely a side trip, a momentary inconvenience for Karla.

As they sat alone, Kathy took Karla by the arms and told her she'd never turn her away. Karla was clearly relieved. Kathy sensed that of all the things in the world Karla needed now, it was her friends she needed most. Karla put her head down and quietly predicted, "When my friends find out what really happened, I'll lose a lot of people."

The stark implications of the comment weren't lost on Alex or Kathy.

There was a carnival-like atmosphere outside the St. Catharines courthouse on the first day of Karla's trial, June 28, 1993. Spectators and reporters lined up before dawn hoping to get seats. Reporters who had followed the case since Kristen French's abduction noticed a startling change in the public attitude to the media: instead of dumping over the Toronto media for their alleged exploitation of beloved Kristen's death, the locals seemed fully supportive of the media attempt to keep the court open. The Toronto media—the *Toronto Sun,* the *Toronto Star,* Thomson newspapers, and the Canadian Broadcasting Corporation were paying for the mutually advantageous plea. It was widely assumed that the defense team would request a publication ban on Karla Homolka's trial details in order for Paul Bernardo to have a fair trial, a request the public did not want granted.

The gossip outside the courthouse halted abruptly at 7:30 A.M., when St. Catharines court services manager Pat Clarke told an assembled crowd of over one hundred that the media should form one line and the public another. Over fifty reporters checked in with the clerk and made their way by elevators and stairs to Courtroom 10, a sizable jury courtroom on the fourth floor. When reporters were allowed into the courtroom just after 9 A.M., they found Karla in the defendant's box. Her family sat in the first row of pews on the right-hand side of the court. An entire row of seats behind them was empty to avert any contact with the public.

Karla sat impassively, wearing a green jacket over a one piece green dress that seemed oversized and somehow too broad for her slender shoulders. On her feet were black shoes with a slight heel. Unlike her court appearance a month earlier, when she wore a schoolgirl's tartan kilt and blazer, Karla now looked somewhat matronly. Yet her clothes were out of place with the false eyelashes, deep-red lipstick, and heavily caked foundation on her face. If she was matronly, then she was a matronly Lolita.

At the front of the court, directly in front of the judge's chair, sat Crown attorney Murray Segal, a plea-bargain specialist with the Ontario government's Crown Law Office, accompanied by Niagara Crown attorney Ray Houlahan and assistant Crown attorney Gregg Barnett. The local Crowns each had laptop computers in front of them on the desks. To their left sat George Walker, Homolka's lawyer. To his left, at a separate table, sat two case associates of Ken Murray:

Tim Breen, an eloquent constitutional lawyer who worked with the Rosen Fleming law firm in Toronto, and Murray's junior counsel, Carolyn MacDonald. Still farther to the left, sitting along a hastily arranged line of tables and seats, was a battery of lawyers representing various media outlets.

Karla barely moved her head. At 10:27 A.M. on June 28, 1993, Judge Francis Kovacs strode into court from his chambers. What was to become one of the most controversial—if not notorious—trials in Canadian legal history was under way.

Charges against two or more accused in connection with one crime are not uncommon in Canadian courts. In this case, Karla Homolka had clearly struck a plea bargain in the past few months and in return would tell about Paul Bernardo at his trial. Normally, the defense team would opt for a ban on publication of details from a co-accused's trial to protect a fair trial for their client, especially a jury matter. The law aims to protect the jury pool from hearing information about the case prior to hearing facts read into court. Similarly, a publication ban can be imposed if an accused is facing trial on other matters.

The dynamics of the Homolka-Bernardo case, however, were different from anything Canadian courts had ever seen. The usual roles had been reversed: instead of wanting evidence from the Homolka trial muzzled, Bernardo sought a full-blown open trial; the Crown, on the other hand, led the charge to have severe restrictions placed on Canadian journalists and have the public and American reporters kicked out of court altogether. American reporters, the Crown said, could not be trusted to obey Ontario's publication bans. Similarly, the public could not be stopped from giving information to American reporters. Homolka's lawyer, George Walker, also wanted the court shut down. Neither the Crown, nor Homolka, nor Bernardo, had exclusive purview over the disposition of the trial, but instead the decision rested with the court; it would be a decision between balancing Bernardo's fair trial rights and the right to freedom of speech and open justice.

Segal, who led off the parade of legal eagles, pleaded to hear details of Homolka's trial out of the public realm until after Bernardo's trials ended. In a rambling submission that took four hours, Segal also threw in some emotional curves, saying certain press reports could cause psychological harm to the victims' families and students at various high schools in St. Catharines. He gave the court letters from high-school principals, medical reports of the French and Mahaffy families, and a letter from one of their neighbors.

The court's first obligation, Segal said, was to the Crown and Karla Homolka: "We are the only true parties in litigation." The Crown had a "significant role in maintaining the integrity of the court process . . . and ensuring, from its vantage point, that administration of justice is properly served," Segal told Kovacs, stressing that the Crown's viewpoint should supersede that of Bernardo, the media, and the public because of overall societal interest. He said that previous appeal precedents demanded the "obligation of the court is to protect its own process."

The dour courtroom atmosphere changed when Tim Breen took the floor as an intervenor on behalf of Bernardo and attacked Segal's points. He warned of the inherent evil that can result from the state's monopoly on legal affairs. He noted a delicious irony of Segal's position: "How can a party whose object is to put my client in jail for the rest of his life say in another proceeding we're looking out for his interests?"

He also noted the difficulty of arguing against the Crown's motion when no formal disclosure had been given the defense on the murder charges. He said the defense had "no idea" of what details would be read into court and the full extent of Karla's cooperation with the authorities.

Breen noted that police had released details about Bernardo from the day of his arrest but had refused to answer any questions about Homolka's involvement. The press, he charged, fueled by carefully orchestrated information leaks by the police, continued to portray Karla Homolka as a victim and Paul Bernardo as the perpetrator. Breen argued that a publication ban would further skew the public perception against his client, whereas an open court would level out the playing field.

As court ended for the day and Karla left the witness box,

Lori rose to meet her sister. Karla offered a slight smile and slipped her right arm around Lori's thin waist, and Lori draped her left arm over Karla's shoulder, and the two walked off into the safety of the jury room. Despite everything, this show of support was an incredibly touching moment.

Media lawyers made their pitch for an open court the next day, with *Toronto Star* lawyer Bert Bruser quarterbacking the offense for all media intervenors, arguing that the public has a right to witness all court proceedings, but if "ever there was a case where the public needs to know about what has transpired, what is going on, this is the case." Bruser specifically keyed in on Breen's speculation about a plea bargain and pointed out: "The only people, as far as I see, who want to keep the details secret, or have a publication ban, are the people who are making the deal." He closed by saying the ban was not "temporary" and for a few weeks' duration, but a ban that would last years.

As the day ended, Kovacs went through the arguments and, without giving a formal ruling, made it obvious what it would be when he turned aside Bruser's warning of lengthy delays by saying the court would make every effort to bring Bernardo to trial as quickly as possible. He adjourned Wednesday afternoon and promised to make a ruling the next Monday, July 5.

Karla sat in the prisoner's dock that Monday in a beige two-piece suit, her blond hair swept back and held in a bun with a barrette. She showed the first signs of animation, peering over at her family, staring, as if she were about to burst into tears.

Adjusting the wire-rim glasses over his nose, Kovacs began his ruling in his nasal monotone. While he accepted Bernardo's right to control the conduct of his defense, he said that a fair trial is "not only an individual interest, or the right of an accused, but a societal interest." The Crown's viewpoint, he said, is legitimate, notwithstanding Bernardo's objection. Opening up Homolka's trial would be a "dangerous path for the court to follow," he said. Kovacs reminded the court that Bernardo was presumed innocent until found guilty, and evidence could be tendered at Homolka's trial that may not be admissible at his trial. "This would not protect the court process," he said.

To a silent court, Kovacs ruled that the Canadian media, on proof of accreditation, may be admitted, but the public, the American and any other foreign media, and book writer Stephen Williams would be denied entry. He ruled that it would be contempt of court for any journalist present to relay banned information to a member of the foreign media. He went on to say that publication of any circumstances of the deaths of any persons referred to during the trial, and in fact anything but the following trial details, were forbidden: the contents of the indictment; the facts of a conviction and joint submissions for sentencing; the duration of the sentence imposed; the court's reasoning under "prosecutorial discretion" and "the principals of sentencing." The Kovacs ban was the most sweeping in Canadian legal history, and the media quickly realized that they would only be able to report the scantiest details about what would happen the next day.

On July 6, 1993, Karla sat rigid in the prisoner's box in a tight-fitting navy-blue suit, her face devoid of feeling. The Homolka family sat in their usual pew up front. Lori's anxiety showed as she chewed at her fingernails; Karel wore his usual look of resigned despair; the usual cold, detached expression could be seen beneath the foundation and the blush Dorothy had caked onto her puffy, sleepless face. On the other side of the court, the Frenches sat in the first pew with a bevy of relatives around them. Dan and Debbie Mahaffy were also at the front of the court. As the fifty-five or so reporters and court artists took their places, a clutch of black-gowned lawyers pored through stacks of files and papers on three separate tables in front of Judge Francis Kovacs's chair.

Kovacs finally made his way into court at 10:50 A.M. He apologized for the delay, saying he had met with staff to emphasize confidentiality.

This was an early indicator of the publication ban's sieve-like loopholes.

Shortly before 11 A.M., Kovacs had the court clerk read the indictment, after which George Walker motioned Karla to her feet and slid slowly over to the prisoner's box and stood in front of her. She stood in demure silence as first the Leslie Mahaffy manslaughter indictment was read and the plea question asked.

"Guilty," she said on Walker's coaxing, her soft, almost inaudible voice straining to say the word.

It was as if Karla had to reach even deeper for her response to the Kristen French manslaughter indictment, but somehow she found it.

"Guilty," she whispered in a pitiful little-girl voice.

After a few preliminary statements, Segal stood at the prosecutor's podium and cleared his throat. Without much warning, he started reading the much-awaited facts, at least enough facts to satisfy the court. After brief preamble about the lives and character of Kristen French and Leslie Mahaffy, Segal said both girls were "totally innocent victims to predatory conduct and had the misfortune of being in the wrong place at the wrong time." Then Segal stated that the court would hear facts "surrounding her criminal liability in the death of her younger sister, Tammy Homolka."

A collective gasp came from the journalism ranks. While most everyone in the media knew that Paul and Karla were with Tammy when she died, only those reporters closest to the case knew some of the details.

After a fifty-five-minute recess, court resumed to hear the victim-impact statements of the families. Kovacs gave no indication that after the statements were read he would protect them with a permanent court seal to stop the media from using them, an order sought by the French and Mahaffy families.

Segal told Kovacs that both he and Walker had agreed on a joint submission of a twelve-year sentence on each manslaughter count. Based on what Karla told police, Segal continued, she could have been charged with murder, but the Crown had exercised its prerogative to enter manslaughter charges.

"In this respect the Crown has taken into consideration the accused's past and future assistance. The facts read in are necessarily abbreviated given that this is a guilty plea and that a party to the offenses is yet to be tried.''

But for Karla's cooperation with police, he added, the total truth might never have been known.

''In presenting manslaughter charges the Crown has also considered her admission that she did not personally cause death in the sense of stopping the breath of Leslie Mahaffy and Kristen French, yet at the same time the accused contributed to their deaths by aiding, by supporting, by condoning, by callously observing as these young women met those violent deaths.''

But for Karla's admissions, Segal said, the Crown might not be able to prove the circumstances of Tammy Homolka's death.

Segal said he also considered Karla's age, crime-free record, Bernardo's abuse, her secondary role, and the fact that she would be ''marked forever.'' Psychiatric assessment showed, he said, that without Bernardo as her master she would be unlikely to reoffend.

Segal then asked Kovacs to sentence Homolka to twelve years on each manslaughter count. Those reporters in court familiar with the Canadian parole system recoiled in horror at the thought this woman who had done such horrible, unforgivable acts as Segal had described could possibly be free in four years and almost certainly free in eight years. The parole system, based on amendments in the Corrections and Conditional Release Act, allows unescorted temporary absences after one-sixth of a sentence, day parole after one-sixth but not six months earlier than the one-third mark, full parole at one-third, and mandatory release after two-thirds. Karla's first full-parole hearing would be in January 1997. Furthermore, the informed realized, most of her sentence would likely be served in a minimum-security prison the Correctional Services Canada had earmarked for the city of Kitchener, about seventy miles west of Toronto.

After a break, Kovacs returned to court at 4:30 P.M. He told the press that he would tell them what could and could not be reported. Kovacs revealed he had conducted pretrial conferences with Walker and Segal and his assistant, Michel Fairburn. This only fueled media speculation that Kovacs and the lawyers had given themselves ample time to draw the lines in this case.

After reading the facts in the murders and explaining that Homolka had admitted involvement in Tammy's death but had immunity from charges, Kovacs turned his attention to Homolka's situation.

"From about six months after their meeting, Paul Bernardo commenced a systematic, physical, and psychological abuse of the accused, according to the report of Dr. Arndt. The beatings escalated. He strangled her, threw knives at her, hit her with firewood, hit her with his shoes and finally with a flashlight. He stabbed her with a screwdriver, pulled handfuls of hair from her head, punched her, kicked her, and raped her. He pushed her down stairs. On one occasion her foot was punctured when he pushed her onto a board with a rusty nail. He systematically made her feel unworthy and cut the contact with her family down."

Kovacs related how the emergency-room doctor told Dr. Arndt the injuries Homolka received in the January 1993 beating were "the worst case of wife assault that he had seen." The day before that, Kovacs continued, Bernardo handcuffed Homolka's hands behind her back and tied her legs together with the same electrical cord he used to kill the other victims. Then he put her in the same root cellar where he had kept Mahaffy and French.

During her psychiatric hospital care from March 4 to April 23, 1993, Kovacs noted, Homolka required massive doses of medication to even begin calming her. In his report of May 28, 1993, psychologist Dr. Malcolm concluded: "She knew what was happening but she felt totally helpless and unable to act in her own defence or in anyone else's defence. She was in my opinion paralysed with fear and in that state she became obedient and self-serving." Homolka, he said, is a "passive, non-violent person" who even in her extremity could not attack Bernardo in a "final attempt to protect herself from what seemed certain death." Kovacs noted that Dr. Arndt's report of May 30, 1993, concluded that despite the "rather horrendous events" Homolka is not a danger unless she is in contact with Bernardo or someone like him. "In my opinion, Karla requires lengthy psychiatric care, that is for a number of years with medication and initially hospitalization in order to allow her to recover from the very severe emotional scars that have been inflicted on her."

Homolka's actions in the Kristen French abduction and slaying, the Leslie Mahaffy killing, and her sister Tammy's death were "monstrous and depraved," said Kovacs, adding that her careful attempt to cover up her sister's death and eliminate evidence in the French and Mahaffy murders shows "the consciousness of evil thought processes." He paused, peering out at the stunned court over his round-lensed glasses. He moved on, saying how Homolka had had her self-esteem destroyed through harsh beatings.

The maximum sentence for manslaughter is life, Kovacs said, with the sentence reserved for the worst offense committed by the worst offender. Homolka had committed the worst crimes; however, she was not the worst offender because she had no criminal record, cooperated with police, and pleaded guilty, thus avoiding additional trauma to the victims' families. The paramount consideration in a case of such violence is to deter others, Kovacs said.

"It is the court's responsibility to be objective and to consider the very special circumstances of this case and this accused. There are serious unsolved crimes, here and elsewhere. There can be no room for error in the successful prosecution of the offender for the safety of the community, whoever that offender may be, and I ask that no inferences may be drawn from my remarks in that instance."

When it was all done, reporters filed out of the room shaking their heads. All this horror, this barbarism, this drama, this truth, and yet the laws forbade all but reporting of the skimpiest details. As Judge Kovacs left the back door to get into his shiny car, the crowd turned its anger on him, booing him and calling him names. By then, radio had carried the news of Karla's sentence over the airwaves and a crowd of about one hundred to two hundred protesters had assembled outside the court's rear door. A phalanx of uniformed Niagara

Regional Police officers closed ranks around Judge Kovacs and escorted his car through the crowd.

The ban notwithstanding, it wouldn't be long before the American media and the Canadian public heard the essence of what had happened. Kovacs's order seemed to forget the time-tested will of the people and modern technology such as personal computers, fax machines, and satellite television.

CHAPTER
25

Within short order, Paul Bernardo quickly realized that day-to-day life at the Metro East Detention Centre would be a far cry from the flamboyant, playboy lifestyle he had enjoyed for much of his adult life. Jail officials purposely put Paul in the fifth and last cell in the L-shaped second-floor special-needs unit in order to best isolate him from other prisoners. His claustrophobic cell was a dour place. There was a tiny stainless-steel bathroom unit featuring a toilet with a little flusher handle and a hand sink. There were no towel racks, so in order to dry his damp towels Paul draped them from the upper level of the concrete bunk bed or from the air vent. A couple of steps from the bunk bed and in front of the cell's only barred window, a stool was built into the cell floor and a table and shelf unit was anchored to the wall.

As in all the cells at Metro East, Paul's window was four feet high by three feet wide, with three bars and four thick panels of unbreakable glass. During day hours, the guards illuminated its darkest corners by manipulating a table-mounted light from an outside control panel. After the 11 P.M. lights-out call, a dim night-light posted above the toilet brightened the cells. Every twenty minutes, guards checked the inmates by looking through a six-inch-by-one-foot clear-plastic screen. The checks are mandated to prevent suicide attempts, a safeguard designed primarily to deter lawsuits.

Looking outside from their cells, other inmates could view

the comings and goings in the jail's parking lot, but Paul's view was limited to the adjacent brick walls of the three-story C-block and a small portion of the sky. He could look out of the window only if he sat on the table with his back against the wall. In those early days of captivity, Paul sat there for three or four hours at a time, staring at the bricks and the other cell windows and gazing off into the clear winter skies. He seemed comfortable there, but he would learn to hate the table perch during Karla's manslaughter trial, when C-block inmates would write obscene messages on their windows with toothpaste, in reverse so Paul and all the other inmates in his unit could read them.

Paul had a hard time with these blatant messages. He was often overheard muttering and spluttering obscenities at the toothpaste-graffiti artists.

Most inmates could view a wall-mounted color television screen by getting on their knees and peering through the waist-height one-foot-by-six-inch plastic food hatch in the cell door. But because Paul's cell was at too much of an angle, he couldn't view the screen and had to be content with sound only.

In order to ensure his safety, Paul was given different lunch, yard, and visiting hours than other inmates; whenever he was moved from his cell the unfamiliar call of "all runners hold" went up through the institution. This meant that all inmates had to cease whatever they were doing, hatches and windows were closed, and guards had to pay special attention to all prisoners in their care as three guards and a supervisor formed a diamond shape around Paul and moved him to the yard or to the visiting area. After a while the order was resented by prisoners and guards alike, because they knew only one man, Paul Bernardo—allegedly one of the worst of the worst sexual predators Canada had ever known—was causing this universal intrusion.

Paul's first nights at Metro East saw him routinely teased by guards who were eager to capture a piece of the excitement over his arrest. Prior to Paul's tenancy, any guard in the jail could visit the special-needs unit without hindrance. And visit they did, peering through the viewing plastic at the Boy Next

Door turned serial killer. Some of the more cavalier types among Paul's jailors took great delight in banging on his door and calling him names. But in his typical manipulative way, Paul whined to supervisors, in person and through his lawyers, about guard behavior. Before long he was filing official complaint forms against several guards, charging that his rights under the Canadian Charter of Rights and Freedoms had been breached.

Other inmates, most of whom were hardened criminals awaiting trial yet again, would shout through their meal hatches: "Hey, Paul, you've got to expect this . . . you've got to be strong . . . you can't always be running and complaining."

One imprisoned killer who was kept in a cell beside Paul for a few weeks loved to bug Paul; he needled him about his baby face, his flabby body, and his penchant for young girls.

"Hey, Paul. Can I borrow your flashlight?"

"Hey, Paul. Can I borrow your chain saw?"

"Hey, Paul. You're sick in the head, man."

More than once Paul was reduced to tears and silence. The other prisoner let out a chuckle. It amused him that he'd scored direct hits on the yuppie smart-ass. He and the other cons viewed Paul as a wimp; a skinny little guy whose head would bob nervously around whenever he walked. The tough guys in Metro East believed they could easily kick his flabby ass in a fight.

Paul routinely turned his nose up at the jail food, which was slid through the food hatch on Styrofoam plates and eaten with plastic spoons. In his first few months of captivity he lost twenty-five pounds owing to his lack of appetite. From the beginning, he feared someone was trying to poison him. When he did eat, the meal cart would pass by his cell and Paul would take his pick of numerous plates. No poison was ever discovered, but unknown to Paul, it was rumored that inmates who had prepared the meals had spit on the food and flicked their nasal mucus into it, as had some of the guards.

Whenever Paul's story came on the television news, the other prisoners would hoot and holler. They would spare Paul no mercy, yelling; "Hey, here's Hollywood; here's the big superstar. Hey, Mr. Hollywood, you're on the screen."

"Hey, I want to hear this. It's on TV, eh?" Paul would cry out, asking the inmates to keep quiet.

Similarly, Paul would get agitated when prisoners spoke during an animated episode of *The Simpsons*. Whenever CITY-TV's Electric Circus was on, Paul would comment on how he could dance better than the guys gyrating on the stage, viciously cutting up the on-screen dancers in the process.

"I should be out there making the videos. I can do better than that; look at that jerk . . ."

"Hey, at least the guy's out there dancing; it's better than what we're doing," another inmate would respond.

"But if I was out there, I'd be doing way better," he responded.

Even after he was charged with the most heinous murders in Canadian history, and even when confronted with almost certain imprisonment for the rest of his life, Paul Bernardo had to assert that he was better than everybody else. He similarly bragged about finishing college, about being an accountant, and about all the material items he'd had in the past few years.

"I had a nice car; I had a 240SX. A nice house. Nice clothes. Nice babes."

"Whatever, Paul," his fellow jailbirds would respond. "What have you got now?" The only babe he had now, they chided, were the two palm sisters and five-finger Mary.

One night the television was tuned in to the movie *Roxanne* and actress Darryl Hannah came on the screen. Paul was able to see a portion of it as he knelt in his cell floor and peered out of the plastic hatch.

"Oh, she reminds me so much of my wife," Paul said wistfully.

He talked about Karla often, sharing fantasies with his fellow inmates, talking about touching her skin, her twenty-six-inch waist, and her hard body, but then he would quickly break off the conversation as if he had shared too much of his past, too much of his fantasy.

With the exception of his frequent complaints to guards,

the only time Paul talked with anyone at length was when he summoned the chaplain after Karla had served him divorce papers. They chatted for about thirty minutes. Inmates noted a change in him after that; he moped around in his cell, very quiet; he wouldn't take his yard times. Some wondered if Paul did, in fact, love Karla. One night some of the cons were chattering idly when Paul suddenly interrupted from his perch on the table by the window. "A few nights before I was busted, I was in my house, watching a clock. I remember feeling that I was never going to see that clock again. . . . A couple of days later, boom, they stormed the house . . . he trailed off into silence.

For days, weeks, and months after Karla Homolka's trial, everyone speculated about her plea-bargain deal. As Bernardo's lawyer Ken Murray continued to insist in media scrums at Paul's court appearances that prosecutors had made "a deal with the devil," those who made the deal had no option but to remain silent. Knowing that talking to the media would be a career-ending move, police officers and prosecutors consoled themselves by painting various scenarios on how things would have been so different if they had chosen not to negotiate with George Walker.

Most didn't blame the media and the public for being angry; after all, they didn't have all the facts to make an objective judgment. It wasn't as if authorities had rushed into the deal, but the public didn't know that.

The deal began to come together even before Paul Bernardo's arrest. As Walker offered his client's full cooperation for blanket immunity, prosecutors at 720 Bay Street and Green Ribbon Task Force leaders put their heads together to consider the alternatives. At that point, there wasn't even enough evidence to put a search warrant together on 57 Bayview Drive to obtain evidence in the schoolgirl murders. After Paul's premature arrest, police interviewed Calvin and Patty Seger and were given the story of Karla's confession. At that point, Paul was charged with the Scarborough rapes but was merely under arrest for the murders. Given Karla's admissions to the Segers of involvement in the murders, prosecutors felt they could probably make a charge of second-degree murder stick.

Paul Bernardo was another story. Anything Karla said to the Segers about him was hearsay evidence, so their testimony would be inadmissible in court against him. Everyone involved in the negotiations believed, given the Scarborough evidence and FBI case models, that Paul was the sexual sadist and predator and Karla his follower. When Casey Hill drew up the search warrants with assistant Michel Fairburn in the days after Paul's arrest, he based the police request on Karla's information and on Paul's arrest in the Scarborough rapes, then added FBI profiling information on how rapists escalate into sex killers. Hill was confident of gaining approval to search the house, but he expected a battle to make it hold up if it were challenged in court.

Prosecutors had to be careful in their dealings with Karla. If they were to charge her, she would remain silent, or in police parlance "dummy up." If this happened, they would be left with only Calvin and Patty's testimony, which would assuredly be inadmissible against Paul, and whatever evidence came out of the house. Forensics experts had already warned them not to expect too much from crimes that were committed ten and twenty months earlier.

Around the time of Paul's arrest, George Walker's demand for blanket immunity slipped to five years and then ten years. It was at the ten-year offer that the details regarding Tammy Homolka were put on the table by Walker. Most police officers on the Green Ribbon Task Force and the Metro Sex Assault squad would have taken the five-year offer just to get Paul. There was general consensus that Paul was the threat; Karla, might be many bizarre and nasty things, they thought, but she would probably pose no danger whatsoever if she were released after a short prison stay. Paul, on the other hand, was allegedly one of the most dangerous criminals in Canada. The stakes were high and everyone knew it.

As forensics specialists used all the latest gadgets and gizmos and went through the house with a fine-tooth comb, Walker had Karla admitted to Northwestern General Hospital in Toronto, not for any treatment in particular but just to make sure that his client was in full control of her faculties and was capable of giving full statements to police. It wasn't until mid-April that Karla was able to tell Karel and Dorothy Homolka what had actually happened to their darling youngest daughter, Tammy. Too afraid to talk about it in person, Karla opted to have her and her family members gather at Walker's office and together read copies of a letter of explanation she had written while in the hospital.

When the search warrants expired at the end of April, it was clear to authorities that they would have to deal with Karla. The evidence that came from the house wasn't enough to ensure the first-degree murder conviction on Paul that everybody so desperately wanted. On May 5, 1993, Walker and Segal met to go over a draft proposal for the deal. The fine tuning was done over the next week, and on May 12, 1993, Walker and Karla signed the deal in front of his associate, Jeff Hatfield.

Over the next few days an army of police officers, prosecutors and support staff descended on a Whitby, Ontario hotel to take down an unsworn preliminary statement from Karla. If her statement went to the satisfaction of prosecutors, then the deal was on. Karla gave her evidence to Niagara police Sergeant Bob Gillies and Metro's Mary Lee Metcalfe on May 14, 1993, as a backup team of interviewers, stenographers, and support staff listened and recorded in an adjacent hotel room and a prosecutor and police team monitored the event in a third room. Segal, watching the interview on a closed-circuit television in another hotel room with Inspector Vince Bevan, Detective Sergeants Steve and Murray MacLeod, and Sergeant Gary Beaulieu, was more than satisfied with what he heard. The deal was on.

The next day, May 15, Gillies and Metcalfe took Karla's first videotaped and audiotaped statements under oath. As they asked the questions, they confronted Karla with two black-and-white photographs taken from VHS videotapes they found during the search of the home. One clip showed a short segment of three-way sex in a hotel room; another showed Karla having oral sex with an unidentified young girl whose face was mostly blurred. Karla had the impression that police had seized all the videotapes. She told them everything: the trip to Atlantic City and the three-way sex they had with a prostitute; the kidnappings, confining, the videotaped sex acts, and the murders of both Leslie Mahaffy and Kristen French and the disposal of their bodies; the drugging and rape death of Tammy and the recruiting of both Jane and Becky. She also told of Paul's bragging that he allegedly raped a young female rower on Henley Island, near St. Catharines, at 6 A.M. in the summer of 1991. For some reason, she didn't tell Gillies and Metcalfe that she and Paul had drugged her friend Jane.

During the interviews, Karla told of her limited knowledge of Paul's violent sexual history; that Paul had told her he was a rapist and that in one case he had tied a girl to a fence by the neck with a black electrical cord. Karla said that Paul claimed to have raped forty women and had started his attacks at age nineteen. She continued giving statements for the next few days. Her testimony was solid evidence against Paul, but there was still nothing to put him directly in 57 Bayview Drive at the same time the victims were there. Paul was still protected by reasonable doubt. There were also major concerns about the stability of the search warrants.

On June 17, 1993, only eleven days before her trial was due to begin, Karla accompanied Niagara police officers on a tour of the body-disposal sites and on a walk-through of 57 Bayview Drive. Much of the information she gave that day had been covered in her interviews, but as she walked around the master bedroom, she stopped at Paul's closet and told her police escorts, "That's where Kristen threw up." While most of the carpet throughout the house had been rolled up and removed for testing, the little piece in the closet had been untouched. Within days forensic specialists had removed it for testing. In the meantime, Karla appeared in court and was sentenced to twelve years in prison as had been agreed on by Walker and Segal.

Evidence from the house was even more disappointing than the forensic types had warned. Tests on four hundred pieces of hair, fiber and other items that came out of the house proved inconclusive. Leslie Mahaffy could be placed in the house because of the DNA match with the blood on a blanket. Because of Karla's statements, police tracked down a return slip of twelve bags of Kwik–Mix brand ready-mix cement to a Beaver Lumber store in St. Catharines. The store also revealed that earlier that day Paul had bought ten bags of cement. Forensic tests matched paint in the house with black paint that had been sprayed on the block containing the head to hide protruding hair. There were deep gouges in the basement stairs where Karla said Paul had carried the blocks upstairs. Potential matches with Kristen French's hair type would, with Karla's testimony, perhaps prove only that she was in the house. All in all, it looked as if it would come down to Karla's word against Paul's.

There was great rejoicing when test results on the closet carpet came back months later. DNA tests proved not only that the vomit was Kristen French's but that it contained sperm that matched the DNA of samples Paul gave in the Scarborough Rapist investigation. For the first time, independent evidence linked Paul directly to having sex with one of his alleged teenage victims. Prosecutors knew the evidence was important, but they had no idea that the evidence would set off a chain of events that would bring forth evidence beyond their wildest dreams.

In September 1994, the Crown team prosecuting Paul Bernardo received a package that sent them into wild fits of excitement. The package, delivered by noted Toronto lawyer Clayton Ruby, who was acting on behalf of Paul's new lawyer, John Rosen, consisted of six 8mm tapes. The tapes showed hours of graphic sexual torture and pornography featuring Tammy Homolka, Leslie Mahaffy, Kristen French, and several unknown teenage girls. There were videotaped images of girls being stalked, one of whom had also been taped undressing, through her bedroom window. Prominent in most of the tapes—and most important, the ones involving the murdered schoolgirls—were Paul and Karla.

This one critical piece of evidence turned the case around for the Crown. Instead of having nervously to rely almost solely on the testimony of a convicted accomplice, they now had a solid case against the accused. The tapes were numbingly horrific. They were capable of dragging Paul Bernardo down and out of sight.

There was only one slight hitch in the euphoria that swept the prosecution team. Where the hell had the tapes come from? They knew the tapes had most recently been in the possession of Paul's longtime lawyer, Ken Murray. But where the hell had he gotten them?

When police searching the home had not been able to locate the tapes that first Van Smirnis, then Mike Donald, and then Karla had told them existed, they decided that Paul had secreted the tapes somewhere off the property of 57 Bayview Drive. They assumed the ten weeks of intensive searching by police was thorough and absolutely complete.

Wasn't it?

Ken Murray had discovered otherwise.

A former Crown attorney who'd turned to private practice, Murray was tall and lanky with a balding head and full, drooping mustache. His quick wit and amiable manner—not to mention his willingness to give a quick television clip sharing the ''deal with the devil''—quickly made him a favorite of the media corps covering the case.

Sometime in mid-February 1993, Murray had been driving toward Peterborough, east of Toronto, when someone who knew the Bernardo family called him on his cell phone. The caller explained that Paul Bernardo had been charged with the Scarborough rapes and was also being accused of killing Kristen French and Leslie Mahaffy.

Was he interested in the case?

Naturally, he was. But when he found out that Barry Fox had already been retained to represent Paul, Murray called Fox to tell him that he, too, had received a call about the case but would beg off. That became a moot point as Fox was dismissed by Paul less than a week after his arrest. Murray took over.

There were whispers of surprise throughout the legal community. Most observers felt that Paul Bernardo would attract some of the best-known lawyers in the country given the profile of the case. Even if the defense was going to be paid at the publicly funded Legal Aid rate, the case would still be worth its weight in publicity gold.

But here was Ken Murray, who operated out of a small, nondescript office in Newmarket, north of Toronto, and whose clientele was made up mostly of drug dealers and other small-time hoods, suddenly handling what the police were calling the crime of the century.

Joining Murray on the defense team was associate Carolyn MacDonald, who'd become a tenant in Murray's office after she passed the bar a few years earlier. When MacDonald, a bright, energetic woman, received the call from Murray that they'd landed the biggest criminal case in the country, she was vacationing in Utah. She thought it was a joke and hung up on her colleague.

Murray called back and insisted it was true. MacDonald returned within days as his junior.

The case, needless to say, was enormous. Initially they were dealing only with the Scarborough indictment (forty-five sex-related charges), but always the specter of the Mahaffy and French murders waited in the wings.

At one point in the Scarborough courts, a judge asked Murray if perhaps he had bitten off more than he could chew, to which Murray answered:

"No one knew how big the dinner was when we sat down at the table."

Paul Bernardo was a compulsive note-taker and letter-writer. He constantly sent messages to his attorneys. And so when he gave Carolyn MacDonald another sealed envelope in late April 1993 and asked her to give it to Ken Murray, she thought it was nothing out of the ordinary.

In fact, Murray might not have opened the letter at all had he not been late and lost as he motored toward St. Catharines and 57 Bayview Drive on May 6, 1993. He opened the envelope hoping it contained directions to the home where he was to meet with the defense team and the home's owners. After an extraordinarily long ten-week search of the home by police, Murray and the defense team were being given limited access to pick up any of their client's property that hadn't been tagged and seized as possible evidence.

That day in the bright spring sunshine Murray joined Carolyn MacDonald and assistant Kim Doyle along with the Delaneys, the owners of the home. Uniformed police monitored the situation from the street, but since they had temporarily relinquished control of the home, they had no legal right to be inside until Murray and the others had finished.

The lawyer had contacted several former clients with vans and pickup trucks and arranged to meet them later that evening so he could move some of the larger furnishings and boxes out of the house as inconspicuously as possible.

In the interim, Murray showed his colleagues the curious note from his client. It was actually more like a treasure map showing the upstairs bathroom and a series of recessed lights in the ceiling, just below the attic rafters. The note instructed Murray that if they did get access to the house, he might want to look up inside one particular pot light. If the police hadn't found them, Paul suggested the items he'd secreted there might be of value to the defense cause.

After touring through the rest of the house with the Delaneys, the owners were politely asked to leave so the defense team could have some privacy.

Murray, MacDonald, and Doyle ascended the stairs to the upstairs washroom. As soon as they entered, it became clear that the pot lights had all been examined. The circular lighting units, which should have been flush with the ceiling, were all hanging loose, or had been remounted haphazardly.

Murray clambered up onto the vanity, one foot on the toilet, and pulled the designated light down, searching blindly with his hand.

Suddenly his hand struck something hard.

Murray gingerly withdrew six 8mm videotape cassettes. The three legal associates stared at each other in disbelief. For a few moments there was silence as all three stared at the tapes. They were literally shaking.

Their first thought was that for some reason someone was trying to set them up by leaving the tapes where they could easily be found.

There was no reason anyone would do that, but the suspicion overwhelmed them. Later that afternoon of May 6, 1993,

Paul Bernardo phoned Murray's office and was patched through to Murray, who was still at 57 Bayview.

Paul wanted to know how things had gone and asked about several items in the house, including his train set. The Delaneys witnessed the call.

Later, the call would receive much attention, as police and Crown officials assumed Paul had been directing his lawyer to the tapes at that point. Because of this, rumors that the tapes had somehow been hidden in the train set, at the bottom of cereal boxes, or in a bus locker began to circulate.

Paranoia ruled for several weeks in the defense-team offices as they put in a new security system. One night it was discovered that the system had been breached and it appeared that someone had entered the Newmarket office, although nothing was taken.

Several times subsequently, the defense team hired an investigator to sweep their phone lines to make sure they weren't tapped.

After the tapes were secured, Paul's next instructions for his lawyer were that Murray not examine the tapes until after the murder charges were formally filed.

Those charges were filed May 19, 1993. Murray then finally viewed the horrible evidence and realized just what kind of explosive items he'd carried out of the house that day in his briefcase.

As Paul's scheduled preliminary hearing approached in the spring of 1994, Deputy Minister Michael Code, the second-ranking member of the Attorney General's ministry and the man who pulled the strings throughout the Paul Bernardo affair, began phoning Murray's office, cryptically asking about a potential "pub ban" during the preliminary hearing.

A preliminary hearing, while not mandated by law, is common practice in Canadian criminal matters and acts as sort of a dress rehearsal for the trial, ensuring that the Crown's evidence is sufficient to warrant a trial and giving the defense a chance to hear and see the witnesses to be called against a client. The hearings, while open, are normally subject to a publication ban and as a result are rarely covered by the media.

But this was no ordinary case, and there was great concern, given the sievelike leaks that followed Karla's trial, that American media would ignore Canadian trial laws and report the critical information revealed at the preliminary hearing, including the testimony of the Crown's key witness, Karla Homolka. Code wanted the courtroom closed to the media and public.

But Murray, who'd vigorously opposed the publication ban at Karla's trial, refused to budge on the issue. He was, after all, the man who'd coined the much-quoted "deal with the devil." His position was that the public should have heard about the whole affair from the beginning and he certainly wasn't going to jump on the bandwagon to close down the court process even further.

Without Murray's support, Code knew he couldn't get the hearing closed. So Code engineered the next-best thing. He ordered, under the signature of then Attorney General Marion Boyd, a preferred indictment. The rarely used legal option allows for a preliminary hearing to be scuttled and for an accused to be moved straight to trial.

Part of the direct indictment included a guarantee that the defense team would be given access to witnesses. That guarantee was buried in material passed along to the defense team. And it was only after making special arrangements that they were able to interview Karla at the Prison for Women for more than a week that July. And even then, the interviews were conducted with Niagara Region Crown attorney Ray Houlahan overseeing the proceedings and interrupting on Karla's behalf when he felt the questions were becoming too sensitive.

The first solid effort to come up with a guilty plea that both sides could live with came on May 2, 1994, a Monday, in St. Catharines when Crown Regional Director Leo McGuigan suggested they meet in Ray Houlahan's office, even though the local Crown attorney wasn't there and from all reports wasn't aware of the meeting.

Michel Fairburn, who had helped to put together the search warrant for the Crown, was also present, as were Carolyn

MacDonald and Ken Murray. They talked about the trial in general, then McGuigan cut to the chase.

"Isn't there any way we can resolve this thing?"

"What do you mean?" Murray asked.

"Is there a plea?" McGuigan wanted to know.

"Well, give me something I can take to my client," Murray responded.

From there the discussion moved to the Scarborough sexual-assault charges. No one, it seemed, knew what was happening with them. While Paul never conceded culpability in the Scarborough rapes, Murray and his team knew these charges could not be ignored and that a guilty verdict on the rapes would all but insure that Paul would spend the rest of his life in jail.

"We can't do anything without Scarborough," Murray announced.

The meeting lasted almost two hours. But little did Murray or MacDonald know that at that very moment, Michael Code was trying to reach Murray at his Newmarket office to tell him that Attorney General Boyd had just signed another preferred indictment, this time on the Scarborough charges, thus eliminating another preliminary hearing and another opportunity for Murray to question Karla on the stand.

Murray was paged by his office with the news. He was livid, feeling he'd been set up by McGuigan and the others, who had feigned ignorance of what was happening with the rapes.

"How can we put together a deal when this kind of crap is going on?" Murray asked.

There was universal shoulder shrugging. No one knew, Fairburn told him.

Within days, meetings resumed in an effort to try to hammer out some plea arrangement. Murray met once again in Brampton with McGuigan and the regional head of Crown attorneys, Jim Treleavan.

In much the same way the autoworkers hammer out a contract, a tentative deal was presented to Murray after this series of back-and-forth meetings. Paul would plead guilty to first-degree murder for Kristen's death, second-degree for

Leslie's. He would also plead guilty to a handful of the Scarborough rape charges, namely those involving the most vocal complainants, plus the most obvious cases in terms of the forensic evidence.

Paul would then be sentenced to life in prison with no chance of parole for twenty-five years on the first-degree murder charge. In Canada, unlike the United States, prisoners can receive only one life term with a twenty-five-year parole eligibility. The rape charges would carry a sentence of fifteen years less a day, which he would serve concurrently with the murder sentence.

In exchange, Paul would be offered a name change and his choice of federal institutions, although Murray pointed out that Paul had already tried the name-change thing and it hadn't worked. Prosecutors would agree not to ask for a dangerous-offender label on the rape charges or bring any witnesses or evidence should Paul attempt a judicial review of his parole eligibility after fifteen years, after which he'd have served the full amount of the rape sentences.

Murray said he would take the issue to his client. Within a week or so there were more meetings, this time involving Jerry Wiley, the senior Crown for Metro Toronto, and Casey Hill, who'd helped do the search warrant of the Bernardo home, as well as Leo McGuigan.

The deal continued to be discussed until the end of June. It was, all agreed, the best deal Paul Bernardo would ever get.

But Paul wasn't impressed. He still wanted Karla on the stand, and he was growing more and more enamored with the image of himself taking the stand and somehow freeing himself with his vast intelligence and charm. It was rumored that his comment was, "I want the bitch on the stand," or something to that effect.

Paul would ultimately take the stand in his own defense. But he would do so without Ken Murray in his corner.

In August 1994, after a series of interviews with Karla and a subsequent vacation, Ken Murray met with Michel Fairburn, Vince Bevan and Ray Houlahan in St. Catharines to tell them he was getting off the case. The group was stunned.

Houlahan immediately assumed it was because he had

failed to sell his client on the deal. But it went further than that.

The original defense strategy had been simple enough: Paul insisted that his wife was a bisexual who got off on kinky sex and that she had played a significant role in the crimes. Paul, as he would throughout, steadfastly insisted that he was not present when either girl died. And the tapes did not offer any direct evidence to disprove this claim.

For Murray, the tapes were merely another piece of ammunition, albeit a cannon-size piece. Early on, his client hadn't asked him to alter the tapes and wasn't denying he'd been in the house during the crimes. There was no obligation, as far as the defense team was concerned, to turn the tapes over to the Crown, even though it was clear they would have wanted desperately to see them.

If things went according to plan, the tapes would be used only as background material on which Murray would cross-examine the Crown's chief witness, Karla Homolka.

If the disclosure given to the defense at the time was accurate, the Crown's case was flimsy at best, relying almost entirely on Karla's testimony. And Murray knew the tapes had the potential to blow Karla's story out of the water.

Problems surfaced, however, in early July 1994, when a DNA sample linked Kristen to Paul's sperm and a vomit stain in the upstairs closet. At that point, it became fairly clear that the defense would have to enter the tapes if Paul Bernardo had any chance at all. He would have to take the stand to explain his side of the tapes.

The problem was that Paul didn't want to stick to the defense strategy. He had his own ideas about his role on the stand. A defense attorney is ethically restricted from putting a client on the stand if there's reason to believe the client will perjure himself. Thus, if Paul was determined to get on the stand and suggest, for instance, that Karla was directing the tapes and punching the girls when the tapes showed otherwise, Murray couldn't allow that to happen.

Paul was determined, however, to get on the stand. Murray suggested that new counsel should be found. Paul agreed but demanded that the tapes not be given to the new defense counsel. He did not want to create a similar problem that might impede his performance on the stand.

At that point Ken Murray retained the highly respected lawyer, Austin Cooper, who in turn contacted the Law Society of Upper Canada, the governing body of Canadian lawyers. A special panel of three senior benchers—Paul Copeland, Colin Campbell, and Earl Levy—listened to Murray's explanation of the situation and immediately advised him to hand the tapes directly to trial judge Patrick LeSage, the province's Associate Chief Justice, a man who'd been handpicked by the Chief Justice, Roy McMurtry, to handle the high-profile case.

There was no indication from the Law Society at the time that Murray had breached any ethical or legal guidelines in his handling of the case.

For months leading up to Ken Murray's removal as the lawyer of record, top-notch criminal trial lawyer John Rosen had indicated, through associate Tim Breen, who had handled the publication-ban argument at Karla's trial, and who was living with Carolyn MacDonald, that he'd likely get a chance to become involved in the case if there was an opportunity.

When Murray returned from his vacation in July, he called Rosen about taking over the case and provided Rosen with a detailed synopsis of the videotapes.

In late August, Murray met with Judge LeSage. John Rosen, Carolyn MacDonald, and Crown attorneys James Stewart, Shawn Porter, Ray Houlahan, Greg Barnett, and Michel Fairburn were present when Murray explained that he needed to be taken off the record.

Normally, a lawyer being taken off the record from a criminal case has to swear out an affidavit explaining his reasons, but Murray argued that if he did that he'd be breaching lawyer/client privilege as well as impairing his former client's right to a fair trial. As well, there was the potential that he might become a witness in the trial itself once the tapes were handed over, and any affidavit could be used by the defense in cross-examination. So it was decided that there would be no affidavit.

Publicly, Murray explained that he was simply overwhelmed by the workload connected with the case. Rosen, part of a successful Toronto firm, offered far greater resources than the lone-wolf Murray could muster.

Privately, the reason was more clear-cut: attorney/client breakdown.

But even though the Law Society's advice to turn the package over to Judge LeSage had been crystal clear, Rosen intervened, telling LeSage that as far as he was concerned the package was defense material and should remain defense material.

At that point, LeSage, the Crown, and police were not aware of the contents of the package. They only knew what the *Toronto Sun* reported regarding the nature of the items that were being so mysteriously referred to in court. All they knew was that it was big, very big.

LeSage agreed to hand the package over to Rosen and his lawyer, Clayton Ruby, provided that they agreed not to alter them in any way. But several weeks later, while the Crown's office considered executing a search warrant to retrieve the package, Ruby returned them of his own accord.

The Crown finally had the last, critical piece of evidence they needed—even if they weren't at all sure where it had come from.

In court, Rosen likened viewing the tapes to opening Pandora's Box.

In the weeks after John Rosen took over the case from Ken Murray's team, plea-bargain possibilities for Paul resurfaced. Paul's sadistic actions on the videotapes meant that conviction of homicide was almost guaranteed. But given that Karla's appearances might turn the jury against her and soil the Crown's case, those at 720 Bay Street let word drift to Rosen that they might be able to cut a deal if terms were right. Rosen, however, steadfastly refused to accept any offer that involved pleading a client guilty to first-degree murder.

"Never in my career have I pleaded a client guilty to first-degree, and I'm not about to start," Rosen told one official. He made it be known that he needed something he could sell to Paul; he needed a break.

Realizing no deal would fly without the support of the Mahaffy and French families, prosecutors stood aside as Rosen negotiated directly with lawyer Tim Danson, a constitutional and victims'-rights specialist who had attempted to help the victims' families keep the videos from being played in court.

It is rare, if not unheard of, for a defense lawyer to get into direct plea negotiations with victims' families. The Crown would have the final say on whether a deal would be accepted. Later, the French and Mahaffy families revealed that Danson did not ask for or receive any payment from them. However they did set up a fund to help pay for his disbursements.

At a pretrial motion hearing in Toronto in October, a possible plea-bargain was discussed. It offered that if Paul Bernardo plead guilty to two counts of second-degree murder, in return he would get parole eligibility after twenty years. Rosen declined this, saying he had to get Paul under the fifteen-year eligibility mark. There was an unofficial clause attached to Rosen's counteroffer: If the plea was accepted, there would be no appeal and the French and Mahaffy families would never have to worry about the videotapes surfacing. The families, he offered, would have closure. Clearly, Rosen was playing hardball on his client's behalf.

The families turned down the possible plea bargain in November or December. When Danson filed a motion to block a public screening of the videotapes, he found himself not only opposing the media, who wanted the videotapes played in open court on principle, but also Bernardo, who, through his lawyers John Rosen and Tony Bryant, sought a public screening to ensure his fair trial.

CHAPTER
26

For most murder trials, the sheriff's office in metropolitan Toronto calls perhaps two hundred people of the city's 2,000,000 inhabitants from which to select a jury. But when it came time to select a jury for Paul Bernardo's double first-degree murder trial in May 1995, a staggering fifteen hundred people were called. The panel was so large that they had to be marshaled into a giant ballroom at the Colony Hotel across the corner from Toronto's main court building at 361 University Avenue.

Trial judge Patrick LeSage, the province's associate Chief Justice, had already decided that the trial would be moved from St. Catharines, where it would normally have been held. LeSage believed there had simply been too much media attention and the crimes had affected the local communities too deeply to allow for the likelihood of a fair trial in St. Catharines.

There was tremendous speculation that finding a jury to try Paul Bernardo would be the most difficult aspect of the entire trial. The case had received so much media attention, both nationally and internationally, many believed that even in Canada's largest metropolitan center, it would be nearly impossible to find twelve people who hadn't already convicted Paul Bernardo in their minds.

But within a week the twelve had been chosen. Virtually none of the 250 or so that were questioned before the twelve were found said he or she had been influenced by the media at all. The eight-man, four-woman jury was older on average than most; the youngest juror was thirty-four years old. They seemed a dutiful bunch, and as the trial wore on, they could be seen walking at lunch breaks en masse, roaring with laughter and joking with the court officials assigned to the trial. Unlike some American murder trial juries, Paul Bernardo's jurors would not be sequestered for the duration of the sensational trial.

Through the most emotional evidence and the most graphic videotape, the jury would betray next to no emotion. And each day they would greet LeSage with a cheery "Good morning."

There were many reasons Toronto, and specifically 361 University Avenue, was selected as the trial site. The imposing sandstone seven story building has tremendous security provisions both externally and internally, meaning Paul and Karla would be able to enter and exit the building without threat of attack or fear of escape. The building was fitted with airport-style electronic security equipment to check the hundreds of media and spectators expected to attend the trial.

The court building is close to hotels, benefiting the prosecution and its team and as well as investigators, who occupied an entire floor of the Colony Hotel, where they worked late into the night on a daily basis preparing witnesses and going over the next day's testimony. The defense team occupied two small anterooms on the sixth floor adjacent to Courtroom 6-1, where the trial was held. Sometimes reporters, other lawyers, friends, and family would crowd into the small, windowless rooms to chat or engage in friendly, off-the-record discussion of the day's proceedings. Courtroom 6-1 is a sprawling, cavernlike room that can accommodate some 210 spectators in three banks of seats.

The courtroom had been modified to assist in the presentation of the evidence; this included the installation of video monitors for the jury that couldn't be seen by the public. Upright monitors were installed in the prisoner's box, the witness stand, on the lawyers' tables, and in front of Judge LeSage's elevated seat at the head of the courtroom. There was also a high-tech overhead projector on which hundreds of exhibits would be shown and a bank of computerized video-playback equipment that allowed for frame by frame movement of videotape.

At the head of the spectator's wooden bench seats in the main body of the court, on the other side of a low wooden railing past which no members of the public were allowed to venture, was the prisoner's box, surrounded on three sides by clear, bulletproof glass, a feature in many Canadian courts. That box would be Paul's temporary home for almost four months. The box's tiny video monitor was set low in the box, and as the tapes recounting the agony inflicted on Kristen French and Leslie Mahaffy were played for the jury over and over, Paul would look down, completely devoid of emotion, sometimes arching one eyebrow. Sometimes he adopted a casual pose, his left arm resting on the wooden frame of the box, fingers touching his temple or chin as he looked quizzically at a witness or the jury.

A few feet away, at the front of the right bank of seats, sat the French and Mahaffy families and their supporters. Throughout the trial, whenever any graphic videotape evidence was played, regardless of whether it involved the two schoolgirls, they would stand in unison and leave the court. On several occasions John Rosen objected to their departure, complaining that they were trying to influence the jury.

As the trial date loomed, outside 361 University Avenue unprecedented arrangements were being made to accommodate the massive media corps that would soon arrive. Scaffolding was erected along Armoury Street, across from the courthouse, on which the national television networks would do their nightly live hits, stand-ups, and interviews. Perpendicular to the tangle of girders and cables, on Centre Street, was a string of portable trailers. Inside these trailers were editing suites, fax machines, banks of telephones, and other broadcast equipment. Network staff tried to brighten the drab exterior of what became known as "Camp Bernardo" by securing flower boxes and other decorations to the trailers. But often vandals left a more lasting impression, spray-painting the trailers on a number of occasions with the names

"French" and "Mahaffy" and anti-media slogans. Never had a Canadian trial attracted such attention and spawned such a physical presence.

In a black suit jacket and dark, printed tie, Paul stood in the witness box staring without emotion at the jury as they were formally presented with the case by the court registrar on Thursday, May 18, 1995. "Let us look upon the accused and harken to his charge," the registrar said, following the traditional form of Canadian jury trials.

The court registrar then read out the charges facing Paul Bernardo: two counts of first-degree murder, two counts of aggravated sexual assault, two counts of forcible confinement, two counts of kidnapping, and one count of performing an indignity on a human body. "And harken to the evidence," the registrar concluded.

As the registrar spoke, Paul continued to stand, casually surveying the men and women who would decide his fate. It was as though he was sizing each one up, perhaps selecting one on whom he could concentrate, whom he could somehow influence with his piercing blue eyes. But the jurors seemed nonplussed, staring back before returning their attention to the charges and the task at hand.

For a public who had been denied access to information revealed at Karla Homolka's trial almost two years earlier, the day-long opening address by lead prosecutor Ray Houlahan was a relentless avalanche of sexual degradation, brutality, and murder. In painstaking detail, Houlahan laid out the Crown's case from beginning to end. Rarely moving his voice beyond a gravelly monotone, Houlahan described the Crown's belief that Paul had first dominated Karla, reducing her to a compliant victim through systematic physical and mental abuse, then used her to exploit his sexual fantasies in the rape of Tammy Homolka, a rape in which Karla participated. Unable to shake free of Paul's violent control and scared he would reveal her role in Tammy's death to her parents, Karla then took part in the rapes and murders of Kristen French and Leslie Mahaffy, Houlahan insisted.

Houlahan ended his stunning remarks by describing in graphic detail the videotaped rapes of the schoolgirls, providing a gruesome frame-by-frame depiction of the torture of the girls. He asked the jury to consider who was directing the action on the tapes, who was beating the girls, who was deriving sexual pleasure from the attacks. It certainly wasn't what Kristen, Leslie, or Karla, Houlahan told the jury. This was clearly Paul Bernardo's show. And the Crown was determined to prove it.

The Crown's case began by calling friends of Leslie Mahaffy to the stand, those who had seen the teen on that fateful night in June 1991. These witnesses were followed quickly by men who found Mahaffy's concrete-encased body parts in Lake Gibson and experts who described the various weights and forensic findings.

The case moved quickly to the testimony of Donna French, who fought back tears as she described the morning of April 16, 1992, the last day she saw her daughter alive. Friends testified to seeing the pretty schoolgirl walking home in the rain, and there was testimony of a struggle in the parking lot of Grace Lutheran Church. Finally, Roger Boyer described his grisly discovery of Kristen French's body on #1 Sideroad on April 30.

More than two dozen witnesses paraded through the witness box, and only occasionally did the defense team ask anything more than a few cursory questions. Their plan of attack was clear: They were prepared to accept the Crown's version of much of what had transpired. They were merely biding their time, waiting for the Crown's main witness. They were waiting for Karla Homolka.

Rosen did take the opportunity to cross-examine Karla's mother, Dorothy, giving the jury a taste for what lay ahead when Karla finally took the stand. In direct contrast to the plodding style of Houlahan and the team of prosecutors who directed the various witnesses, Rosen was quick and disarmingly friendly.

Dorothy looked bewildered as Rosen peppered her with questions about the significant opportunities Karla had to escape the brutal relationship in which the Crown asserted Karla had been ensnared. He forced Dorothy to acknowledge that Karla had never complained about her relationship with

Paul and that even when they went to rescue her from 57 Bayview in January 1993, Karla had to be physically removed by her father. By the end of Rosen's onslaught, Dorothy was merely nodding her head, agreeing with virtually every statement he made, including his assertion that Karel liked to call her "bitch" in front of the children.

During the second week of the trial, the Crown introduced the controversial videotape evidence that had been overlooked by police during the ten-week search of 57 Bayview Drive. The tapes had created a firestorm of controversy, not only because they were evidence missed by police, but because there had been attempts by the victims' families to seal the tapes and limit their use in court. Only lawyers, court officials, and the jury should see and hear the tapes, the families' attorney, Tim Danson, argued.

The *Toronto Sun*, the *Toronto Star*, the *Globe and Mail*, and the Canadian Broadcasting Corporation, challenged the families' bid, arguing that blocking evidence would breach basic rights upheld in the Canadian Charter of Rights and Freedoms—specifically, the right to a free press and an open court system. In the weeks leading up to the trial, this debate had taken on a life of its own beyond the issue of Paul Bernardo's guilt or innocence. Danson tried to use public pressure to force the media to back off on its stand, suggesting that the media was interested only in ratings and selling newspapers. He submitted volumes of material to Judge LeSage suggesting that his clients' psychological well-being hung in the balance and intimated that an already unstable Debbie Mahaffy might be driven to suicide if the tapes were shown in open court. The arguments led the public to believe that the media wanted to reproduce the tapes, show them on the evening news, and print still pictures of the girls being tortured, none of which was true but which certainly helped swing public opinion solidly behind the families.

Nevertheless, as he would do throughout the trial, Judge LeSage found a balance that would recognize the plight of the families and the needs of the press. He ruled that the tapes be shown only to the jury and legal counsel and, of course, the accused. But he refused to kick people out of his courtroom or to stop everyone else from hearing the audio portion of the tapes.

Most of the segments were played three times so the jury could first watch and then follow along with printed transcripts before finally noting specific items shown by Staff Sergeant Gary Beaulieu, who was part of a team of six investigators who had spent almost a thousand man-hours watching the tapes over and over while preparing the transcripts.

For the most part, the families chose not to listen to the girls' ordeal. Only Debbie Mahaffy remained during the searing videotape evidence involving her daughter, Leslie. In spite of strong urgings from a number of people, especially the full-time victims' counselor who worked with the families, often sitting next to them in court, Debbie returned to the crowded courtroom as the anguished cries of her daughter were heard from the videotape made by Paul and Karla.

Debbie was a woman who had been torn apart by the abduction, murder, and subsequent dismemberment of her daughter. The cries heard on tape, among the last sounds made by her daughter, left her crumpled on the shoulder of a friend, almost unable to rise when court broke. Long after the day's proceedings had ended, Debbie still had to be helped from the building. So obvious was her torment that when police asked photographers from the Toronto dailies, The *Toronto Star* and the *Toronto Sun*, to back off as they led Debbie to the Colony Hotel, the photographers agreed, an unusual show of restraint.

The tapes, in and of themselves, were powerful evidence of Paul Bernardo's sexual depravity, and occasionally jurors would glance over at Paul during a particularly horrifying moment. But Paul spent much of the time closely watching his handiwork or scribbling meticulous notes in the leather legal binder given to him by co-defense counsel Tony Bryant.

However, the tapes merely provided the backdrop for the Crown's main witness. Karla Homolka would be able to take the jury into the master bedroom at 57 Bayview Drive. She would walk the jury through the kidnappings, the sexual torture, and ultimately the murder of Leslie Mahaffy and Kristen

French. If the jury believed her amazing evidence, she was going to drive the stake through Paul Bernardo's heart.

The following passages were composed directly from court testimony given at the trial of Paul Bernardo in Toronto during July and August, 1995.

Karla Homolka was tinier than anyone had expected as she made her way, waiflike, to the witness box for her long-awaited appearance in Courtroom 6-1. A female court officer held her firmly by her left arm, but no one needed to worry about the Crown's star witness fleeing. Just after 10 A.M. on Monday, June 19, 1995, more than two years after striking a deal with prosecutors, Karla Homolka was finally about to live up to her end of the bargain and tell the truth as she saw it. She climbed a couple of stairs, fixed a tiny microphone to the lapel of her taupe-colored jacket, and for the briefest moments glanced awkwardly at Paul Bernardo. Then she focused her eyes firmly on the prosecuting Crown attorney, Ray Houlahan; she would not take them off him for the rest of the day.

Sitting in the prisoner's box, Paul glanced at his ex-wife with calm disinterest, looking up from his legal notepad only briefly as the woman who had made a deal that could put him in prison for the rest of his life prepared herself to testify.

Judge LeSage, in an unusual move, cautioned the jury about weighing the evidence they were about to hear. Karla was, after all, a convicted accomplice in the murders of two young schoolgirls. Sometimes, LeSage said, accomplices minimize their own involvement while maximizing the role of partners. Spectators who had lined up outside the courthouse during the middle of the previous night, craned their necks for a better look at the enigmatic Karla. Houlahan asked Karla to identify the person who killed Leslie Mahaffy and Kristen French. The words had barely left his lips when Karla turned her gaze toward Paul, raised her left arm, and excitedly pointed a finger.

"It was Paul," she said, her voice girlish but resolute.

How did she know? Houlahan asked.

"I was in the same room, watching," Karla replied with a quiver.

Karla went on to chronicle her obsessive love affair with Paul, her "indescribable infatuation" with the man who would become her husband, the man who would rape her sister and murder two young schoolgirls. Houlahan led Karla through her memories of a happy childhood. She said her parents had a solid marriage and a loving relationship. Yes, Karel sometimes called Dorothy a "bitch," she said, but it was all in fun. The revelation that Karla, as a teenager, had harbored desires of becoming a police officer was greeted with ill-concealed giggles and guffaws from the crowded courtroom.

Then came Karla's description of her fateful meeting with Paul Bernardo, October 17, 1987, a one-in-a-million encounter. Earlier in the evening, she and Debbie Purdie, sharing a room for their weekend pet-store employees' convention, had been out dancing and drinking at a local nightclub. Two men agreed to give them a ride back to Howard Johnson's and invited themselves up to the girls' room. When they wouldn't leave, Debbie stole out on the pretext of getting ice and asked their pet-store's manager, Kristy Maan, to kick the two men out. Still giddy, the girls sought room service. It was closed. As they settled into a window table at the hotel restaurant two different men, Paul and Van, arrived.

As Karla described Paul—his magnetism, his charm, his almost supernatural ability to attract women—he glanced periodically up from the box. She described how they'd made love that first night, and how, somehow, she knew then and there she was destined to marry Paul. At Houlahan's prodding, Karla described the evolution of the passionate love affair between herself, the naive seventeen-year-old high-school student, and Paul, the worldly twenty-three-year-old accounting student.

She said she invited Paul to St. Catharines the weekend following their initial meeting. Soon he was traveling two or three times a weekend to see his new girlfriend. The meetings usually led to sex, whether in Paul's Capri in a secluded lovers' lane near Lake Gibson, or on Karla's bedroom floor while friends and family chatted away and watched television in the adjoining basement recreation room. Karla told of being treated like a princess in those first few months; Paul wined and dined her, opened car doors, bought her flowers. His respectful treatment of her parents prompted them to invite him to spend weekend nights on the couch instead of making the long, lonely drive home to Scarborough. Within weeks, Karla said, her devotion to Paul was so entrenched that she happily abandoned her wardrobe, her hairstyle, even the places she frequented after school, and her friends. It was a trade-off, Karla explained, since Paul agreed to cut back on his own socializing, even though later she learned he hadn't curtailed much of anything in his own life, including other women.

Karla admitted that in those heady first months of new courtship, Paul was mostly affectionate toward her. He even came up with pet names for her, like "Little Rat," a name he started using after he came into the Number One Pet Centre one day and watched a pet rat crawl through Karla's hair. He called her "Princess," and she referred to him, in some of the dozens of letters and cards she wrote, as her "Prince."

Karla didn't know that Paul had named his first love, Nadine Brammer, "Princess" back when he was sixteen years old.

Soon Paul told Karla that he wanted her to be the aggressor, to initiate their sexual activity, not just respond. Determined to please Paul in every way, Karla said she began sending him suggestive letters and cards.

Karla said her first Christmas with Paul was a memorable one. He bought her a $300 Christmas dress, a gold chain, and an expensive stuffed animal named Bunky, among other presents. She was ecstatic.

"He just totally swept me off my feet," she recalled.

Among the Christmas gifts the seventeen-year-old delivered to Paul was a coupon that read: *"This coupon promises that Karla Leanne Homolka will perform sick and perverted acts upon Paul Kenneth Bernardo. These acts may be chosen by the recipient of the coupon. This coupon expires Jan. 2, 1988."*

The coupon, Karla told the court, referred to her grudging acknowledgment that she would perform oral sex on Paul, something he demanded almost immediately after they met. At first, Karla was scared and refused, until he insisted.

"He said, 'Yes, you're going to do it' type of thing, so I did it," Karla told the jury.

From then on, oral sex became Paul's preferred act. He would get angry if she didn't swallow his sperm.

Paul also asked Karla to demean herself during sex: "My name is Karla, I'm seventeen years old, I'm your little cock-sucker, I'm your little slut, I'm your little cunt." The litany was repeated over and over during sex. Karla was also asked to denounce her old boyfriend, Doug, saying she hated him. Paul would not allow Karla to remain friends with Doug.

In the late spring or early summer of 1988, Paul told Karla he wanted to have anal intercourse. "He told me that because I wasn't a virgin this would be a good way to make up for it. And that he had never done it before, either, so this was something we could do together that we hadn't done with anybody else," Karla explained, talking so quickly that the court reporter couldn't keep up. Anal sex seemed very important to Paul, Karla said—slowing her delivery—so she did it. She admitted that even after fellatio and anal intercourse became regular items on Paul and Karla's sexual menu, Paul still seemed dissatisfied. She said he asked her to role-play other women during sex.

Karla acquiesced to virtually every demand, but there was always something that seemed to bother Paul about his girl-friend. Karla struggled to correct those imperfections. Often, that meant apologizing either in writing, on the phone, or in person, sometimes all three.

"I was always apologizing to him for various things. I would do something and he would get angry. It would happen all the time. I would buy cards, like 'I'm sorry' cards. I actually used to buy them in advance 'cause I knew I would use them."

Of the more than five hundred cards, letters, and notes recovered by police after Paul's arrest, the vast majority chronicled Karla's desperate bid to make her older boyfriend happier. In a January 7, 1988, letter, apparently written after she described her previous sexual history with Doug, Karla wrote this mournful letter:

Dear Paul,

I feel I must write this letter, although I have said it all over the phone. I am so sorry for what I have done. I hate myself. I know I don't deserve it, but I am begging for another chance. I wish you could find it in your heart to love me again. Hearing you say "I don't love you anymore" was one of the worst moments in my life. Then there was "I don't want you." I only pray I won't hear the final "I'm breaking up with you." I love you so much, and I wish to God you could believe me. I know I don't have the right to ask you to. I guess I've really screwed things up. The best person—the only person I ever loved—in my life and I deceived and hurt him. I hate myself for that. Part of me wants you to let me go. Oh you deserve someone perfect—someone who is truly yours. But there are no perfect people in this world. You may find your virgin, but there will be something wrong with her. I know many—no—all of the girls have said this to you but nobody will ever love you as much or as intensely or as deeply as I do. After you there could never be anyone else. You are such an incredible man, no one else can come close. I couldn't even attempt to find someone to replace you. And I won't. You have captured my heart, my life—and it will be yours forever. I am telling you the truth. I wish to God I wasn't such a stupid idiot. I'll pay for the rest of my life for what I've done. If you can find the slightest bit of love or forgiveness, please hold onto it. We can rebuild our relationship. I can be the perfect girlfriend if I only try hard enough. Please, please give me another chance to.

Thinking of you in another girl's arms tears my heart in two. I want to die when I imagine my life without you. Whatever could I do or be without you by my side? I need you so much. You told me that coming clean now would be much better than having you find out later. I only thank God I told you now. If this is better, I hate to think what it would have been like later. In the past I might have thought I wished that I hadn't told you. Not now.

Four days later, Karla wrote to Paul:

"I love you, I love you, I love you with all my heart. You're the best, you big, bad businessman, you."

Karla explained matter-of-factly that Paul liked Karla to refer to him as a "big, bad businessman" because he liked to think of himself as a ruthless, successful executive.

Karla testified that one weekend in the fall of 1988, she visited 21 Sir Raymond Drive with Paul while his parents were away for the weekend. Karla said she lied to her parents, telling them Ken and Marilyn Bernardo would be home. She insisted that once she was there, Paul begged her to let him take sexually explicit Polaroid photographs. "He said that, you know, it would be okay, that nobody would ever see them and there was nothing wrong with it and he really wanted to do it. I figured, well, if he really wants this and I am going to marry him anyway, then there wasn't anything wrong with it. And I agreed. He told me it wasn't a big deal," she said. She posed naked, kneeling on the bed so Paul could photograph her face and her breasts; she knelt on all fours so Paul could capture her vagina and buttocks; she lay on the bed with her hands tied and a gag over her mouth; lay on her back, whipped cream on her crotch, nipples, and her mouth. And, ultimately, she let Paul photograph her as he inserted a wine bottle into her vagina. Paul put the camera on automatic and took photographs of Karla smiling while fellating him. In another, Paul put a black electrical cord around Karla's throat and held a knife to her neck, pulling on the cord in strangulation.

As Karla described the photographs, each picture flashed up on the monitors. Karel Homolka left the courtroom at the first hint of the degrading spectacle. Dorothy and Lori Homolka remained, staring steadfastly at the floor. Without emotion, Karla explained that she was "looking happy for the camera. I was also partially happy at the time, I believe."

Karla told the court that it wasn't long after the Polaroid photos were taken that Paul had Karla buy a dog's chain and choke collar, not for a dog, but for her to wear during sex. She said Paul told her that his choke fantasy was "important to him and it wouldn't hurt anybody." So she went along with it.

"I would be on my hands and knees with the collar around my throat and he would be pulling it while he had intercourse with me. It was tight. Sometimes I had to ask him to let up because I couldn't breathe," she said. She explained that he would climax in this position, whereas he wouldn't in others. For Karla, the bizarre sex twists were simply part of maintaining the most important thing in her life—her relationship with Paul. Whatever he needed or wanted, she fulfilled.

On April 27, 1988, Karla wrote:

Dear Paul,
    Hi honey. I just called you but nobody's home, at least nobody answered. Where are you? Who are you with? What are you doing? These are the questions burning in my mind. I want to talk to you so badly (and much more than that, I want to see you). I ache to be with you. It is Wednesday at 9:16 p.m. Just think—if this were any other normal week we would be together right now. How I wish we were. Guess what? My parents are going to a dance tomorrow night. They'll be going for a long time. Want to come over and play. I know, I know. We have to learn to work together as well as play together. How does a 50-50 mixture sound to you? Okay, 60-40 (work to play?). Sounds good to me! Please say yes. Please. Please. Please. Please! I'm on my knees begging, begging in the way you love most. You know, there's only one short week left for you to enjoy your cute little 17-year-old girlfriend! Better take advantage of it (and her) while you can. And how can you resist your cute, cuddly furry little creature, your adorable little rat, your sweet little Karla Curls, your very own little fantasy, your lov-

ing princess, calling to you, begging on her hands and knees to come and spend a scant few hours with her? You can't, can you? I didn't think so. You know what I love? Having you make love to me on my bedroom floor. With my parents in the next room. Having you ram it inside me, making me gasp for air. Having us united spiritually and physically as one. You turn me on so much, Paul. Just thinking about you and your perfect body excites me so I can hardly stand it. Oh your strong chest, your muscular arms, your beautifully shaped legs, your hard flat stomach, and Snuffles, oh Snuffles. The pleasure I get from touching, from licking, from sucking Snuffles is indescribable. I love it when you shoot in my mouth. I want to swallow every drop and then some. And seeing you in your suit does incredible things to me. The power you wield over me is indescribable. Sometimes when you come directly from work and we sit on the couch together I have to use every ounce of my strength to keep from ripping off my clothes, from begging you to have mercy on me and make love to me. You make me so horny. There's just something about you. Paul, when you caress my face and my body you send shivers up and down my spine. My whole body tingles with your touch. How can I love you so much? I do love you such an incredible amount, an amount I never thought possible. In fact, the words I love you don't even come close to expressing my full feelings for you. With you in my life I feel complete. I feel whole. With you by my side, I know that nothing can go wrong. You have done so much for me Paul—you have taught me what love really is. You have opened my eyes to a new way of thinking and being. I am so happy to be. I love you, Karla XOX."

Karla said Paul first hit her in the summer of 1988 while driving on Highway 406 to their lovers' lane parking spot on Lake Gibson. During an argument, he slapped Karla on the face with an open hand. He immediately pulled over to the side of the road and started crying, Karla recounted, saying he hadn't wanted to hit her. Karla felt guilty, she said, believing it was all her fault.

That August, while driving to Florida for a vacation, she said Paul hit her during an argument over directions. On the return trip, they stopped over at New York City. She testified that as Paul showered in their hotel room, he asked Karla to videotape him.

"I went into the bathroom. It was all steamy and hot. I had the camera in my hands. He told me to open the shower curtain, but I only had one hand on the camera and I was afraid to do that because I only have little hands and I was afraid to drop the camera. He started yelling and screaming at me and he threw it from one hand to the next, saying, 'Look, it is not dropping.' But then it dropped, bounced on his foot, and fell to the ground and broke. Then he got really mad and started punching me and kicking me and beating me up, mostly on my back, arms, about mostly on my back, I think."

Still, there was no thought of leaving her man.

"For the most part he was treating me nicely and I was blaming myself. I took partial blame for it because I didn't do what he asked, I did not open the shower curtain. And he treated me well in other ways," Karla explained. "He used to tell me the reason I looked the way I did was because of him. He told me I was nothing without him and he would call me names, like slut, bitch, cunt, things like that. He made me feel I was totally dependent on him."

According to Karla's testimony, the abuse started in earnest in the fall of 1990, although there was no medical evidence to back up her allegations. Karla hid the abuse from her friends and family, she explained, because she still loved Paul. Besides, Paul had told her time and time again never to air her dirty laundry to friends, because they would remember it a long time after she had forgotten.

One early evening on a weeknight in November, Karla testified that she was in bed at her parents' house when she heard a knock on her bedroom window. It was Paul. He motioned her outside but indicated she wasn't to tell anyone he was there. Once inside Paul's brand-new Nissan 240SX, she said Paul nervously told her he had just been questioned by the

Toronto police in connection with the Scarborough rapes. He had voluntarily given them blood, hair, and saliva samples.

With that, court broke for the day.

When Karla returned to the stand for her second day of testimony, she was dressed primly in a navy-blue blazer and skirt, white blouse, and sensible black shoes. Her golden hair bounced behind her in the short escorted walk from the entrance door to the witness box, but without makeup, her face looked wan. As soon as she hit the stand, she gingerly picked up the tiny microphone and clipped it on the lapel of her blazer. In a flat, emotionless monotone, Karla continued to recount the twisted descent of her relationship with Paul and the extraordinary lengths to which she went to maintain it.

On October 17, 1988, the couple's first anniversary, Karla wrote:

> *Dear Paul, On October 17th, 1987, the most important event in my life occurred in a hotel restaurant in Scarborough. I met you. You have enriched my life beyond belief. You've opened my eyes to attitudes and ideas I was previously blind to, shown me wonderful places and taken my heart for your very own. You have allowed me to participate in the most beautiful experience two people can . . . To my big, bad, businessman, my prince, my hero, my honey, sweetheart, fantasy, sir . . ."*

The letter ended with what became a regular sign-off:

> *. . . from your honey boo bear, your princess, creature, little rat, Karly Curls, sweetie, little cocksucker, little cunt, little slut.*

Karla described the first time Paul mentioned sex with other women, in the summer of 1990. "He indicated to me that it was okay for a man to have more than one sexual partner. But it wasn't okay for a woman to have more than one partner," Karla recalled. What did she think of this suggestion? Houlahan wanted to know. "I didn't agree with that at all. I believed in being faithful with the person you loved."

It was also during this summer that Paul began to talk to his fiancée about his attraction to her little sister, Tammy. One afternoon in July, there was a get-together at the Homolka home. The wine and beer ran out, so Paul volunteered to get more. Tammy said she wanted to go too. The two left in Paul's Nissan. They did not return for almost six hours. Paul explained their absence saying they had crossed to the United States to pick up supplies.

"I was wondering where they were," Karla said.

Karla said it was around this same time that Paul decided he'd be pleased if Karla started pretending she was Tammy during sex. Again, Houlahan asked how she felt.

"Well, I stupidly still loved him at that point and I wanted to make him happy. He was threatening me. He wanted me to do these things and I did them," Karla said, faltering slightly. To play out the fantasy, Karla would sometimes wear Tammy's clothes and follow a definite script.

"He would have me say, 'My name is Tammy. I'm fifteen years old, I'm your virgin, I love you and I want to marry you,' during sex."

A court official, sensing some distress, handed Karla a tissue. She quietly tucked it in her lap; only later did she reach for another, dabbing quickly at her eyes one at a time.

Later that fall, Paul demanded that Karla assist him in breaking the ultimate taboo; he wanted sex with Tammy.

"I didn't want him to do it at all. I was totally against the idea," Karla insisted. But he continued to badger and threaten her, she said, promising it would only be once, would take only a few minutes, then everything would return to normal. He promised there would be no more violence, Karla said.

On November 26, 1990, Karla wrote to Paul.

Please accept my apology even though actions speak leader than words and my actions haven't been great. I swear things will change. Just remember how much we loved each other, Paul. I know we'll get through this. All my love Karla, your princess XOX.

Karla couldn't recall for certain, but she said the letter may have referred to Paul's sexual desire for Tammy.

While the couple had not set a date for the assault on Tammy, Karla explained that they began to plan in advance because, Karla said, Paul figured the only way to pull off the attack was to make sure Tammy was drugged and sleeping. Paul instructed Karla to find out what they should use for the deed. Karla studied a compendium of pharmaceuticals she'd taken from the animal clinic. Later, she phoned a Big V Pharmacy across the street from the Martindale Animal Clinic and lied about needing Halcion sleeping pills for the clinic. She also took a brown bottle of liquid anesthetic Halothane from the clinic, the drug used on animals, to ensure that Tammy wouldn't wake up during the rape. Karla had seen Halothane administered at the clinic by a machine that regulates the flow of oxygen. Nonetheless, she figured a small amount of the drug on a cloth would do the trick.

Paul also told her he wanted to videotape the event, so the two purchased a camcorder from an Eaton's department store. The purchase was made on Karla's credit card, because Paul could get no credit after his May 1990 bankruptcy. A few days before Christmas, Paul announced that they would rape Tammy. She said he later abandoned the plan without explanation.

Finally, late on December 23, 1990, Paul and Karla were sitting in the rec room at 61 Dundonald Street in the late afternoon when Paul leaned over and whispered to his fiancée.

"I believe he said to me, 'You know, this is the day that I want to do this. It would be a great Christmas present for me,' " Karla recalled. "I cried and I begged him not to do it and he said, 'No, we're doing it,' and that was it."

Because the Halcion had to be placed in either food or drink, Paul began smashing the pills in the basement, using a hammer. Hearing the pounding from the kitchen, Dorothy asked what the racket was about. Paul and Karla then went for a drive and crushed the pills in the car.

After returning to 61 Dundonald in time for Dorothy's macaroni-and-cheese dinner, Paul started videotaping the family, and both he and Karla made drinks, including rum and eggnog for Tammy. Paul put the ground-up pills in the eggnog. Karla said she warned him not to use any more than five pills, but she had no idea how many he used. Tammy downed the eggnog and began sipping on other drinks, sampling Paul's Rusty Nail, champagne, and daiquiris. She seemed to be slurring her words a bit, but she wasn't too sleepy, Karla said. Because Paul was impatient, Karla explained, he mixed another Halcion-laced cocktail, this time putting the sleeping potion in orange juice.

Paul, Karla, and Tammy went to the basement to watch a movie and the others went to bed. When Tammy finally dozed off in the basement, Paul told Karla to poke her to see if she was really out. Karla gingerly touched her sister's shoulder. There was no reaction. Karla retrieved the Halothane from its hiding spot in the basement washroom cupboard, soaked a cloth, and held it to Tammy's face.

Her voice shaking, Karla described how Paul undressed Tammy, unbuttoning her shirt and pulling down her pants. Her sister was wearing cut-off track pants and a shirt, but Karla couldn't remember whether Tammy wore a bra or underwear. Paul videotaped while he pulled his pants down and began having vaginal sex with Tammy. Despite an earlier promise, Karla said, Paul refused to wear a condom.

"I begged him to wear a condom. He had agreed to previously because I was afraid Tammy would get pregnant. And he just told me to shut up."

Karla said that while Paul raped Tammy, she held the Halothane to her sister's nose again. Paul told her to use more to make sure Tammy stayed unconscious. Then she said Paul ordered Karla to take off her clothes. That hadn't been part of the original plan, but Karla obeyed anyway. When Paul told her he wanted her to suck Tammy's breasts, Karla said, she did.

Later, Houlahan guided Karla through the videotaped attack on Tammy, in which Karla's attempts to get Paul to wear a condom are met with one "shut up" after another. Paul is seen having anal and vaginal sex with Tammy, then Karla performs oral and digital sex on her sleeping sister. The conversation between Paul and Karla is in hushed whispers.

Paul: "Will you blow me?"

Karla: "Yes."

Paul: "Suck on her breasts. Now. Suck!"

Karla: "Hurry up, please."

Paul: "*(Inaudible)* . . . tongue out."

Paul: "You're not doing it."

Karla: "I am so."

As Karla balked at Paul's insistence that she perform oral sex on Tammy, Paul pushed her head down.

"I was crying. I felt absolutely horrible, I felt guilty and scared," Karla told Houlahan, dabbing at her eyes with a tissue, biting her bottom lip nervously, sometimes closing her eyes as though that would help make the words come easier.

Paul: "Do it. Lick her cunt. Lick it up. Lick it clean. Lick it clean."

Karla: "I am."

Paul: "Put your fingers inside."

Karla: "No, I can't."

Paul: "Do it. Do it now. Quick. Right now."

Karla: "No, I can't."

Paul: "Do it now."

Karla: "No."

Paul: "Do it now, quick. Right now. Right inside. Three fingers. Right inside."

Karla: "No."

Paul: "Taste it. Put it in. Put it inside. Taste it. Taste it. Inside . . . inside and taste it. Quick."

Karla: "No."

Paul: "Inside. Deep. Deep."

Karla: "I did."

Paul: "Inside? Taste good?"

Karla: "Fucking disgusting!"

Paul: "Taste good?"

Karla: "No."

Paul: "Lick her cunt."

Karla: "No, I did."

Her responses enraged Paul.

"He shut the video camera off and hit me in the head with his hand. Just on the head," she said. And then Karla gave the explanation she would use to justify her actions on all the other videotapes shown in court: "He never let me forget that I had ruined his only videotape of Tammy, and he constantly beat me for it. Right up to the time I left him, whenever he made a videotape I smiled and acted happy so I wouldn't ruin another videotape and give him another excuse to beat me," Karla asserted.

Later, when Paul wanted to videotape sex acts with Kristen and Leslie and others, Karla claimed she always made sure she was smiling so he wouldn't beat her again. "This is the only videotape in existence that shows my true feelings," she said with confidence.

She testified that when Paul stopped the assault and shut off the camera. "He said, 'I don't know, I just felt like I should stop.' And he sat down beside her."

Within minutes, Tammy had vomited and stopped breathing. Karla grabbed Tammy by the waist and turned her upside down as she had done at the clinic when trying to clear aspirating animals' stomachs. Paul tried frantically to revive her with mouth-to-mouth resuscitation, Karla said, while she called 911.

"She wasn't breathing and the lights had been dimmed in the rec room and I wasn't thinking straight and I said to Paul, we have to get more light," Karla said.

So they dragged her, into her bedroom where the light was on. Later, Karla noticed the obvious burnlike mark on Tammy's face but assumed it was a rug burn. Houlahan asked if there was other material applied to Tammy's face, some sort of cleaning agent or chemical, but Karla said no.

While they waited for emergency crews to arrive, Karla said they hurriedly dressed Tammy and then Paul instructed Karla to clean up. She dumped the rest of the Halothane down the drain and took the pill bottle and the Halothane-soaked cloth and hid it behind some shelves in the laundry room. The video camera, still containing the sex tape, was moved to Karla's room. After police arrived, she said Paul took the tape and hid it behind some of Dorothy's pickle jars.

Tammy, with a tube in her mouth, was transported to the hospital. Dorothy and Karel followed. Police told Paul, Karla, and Lori to stay at home. Shortly after, a police officer took the phone call telling them that Tammy had died.

"The three of us started crying, and I couldn't believe it was true. And Paul started banging his head against the wall. I was totally devastated. And I blame myself for not being able to . . . to be strong enough to tell him no," Karla said, for the first time her voice betraying a hint of emotion.

Later, Karla said, she went down to the laundry room and began washing the blankets on which Tammy had vomited. "It sounds really stupid, but all that I could think about was that my mommy was going to be mad at me and I wanted to clean up," Karla said. "It wasn't my intention to destroy evidence when I cleaned those [blankets]. It was my intention to destroy evidence when I hid everything else."

Paul, Lori, and Karla were taken to police headquarters in St. Catharines, where they were interviewed separately. Karla concocted a story police believed. At no point did she mention the sex, the drugs, or the video camera. "I didn't want to incriminate myself or Paul," she said.

And she certainly didn't tell her parents what had happened, either. "I didn't want them to hate me. I thought for sure they'd hate me forever."

After their release, the trio hailed a cab and returned to 61 Dundonald. Karel paid for it. Karla testified that they immediately returned to the basement, where Paul searched for the videotape he had tossed into hiding. She explained that, initially, he couldn't find it and assumed the police had found it. In a second, more intense search, however, he found the tape. Paul quickly watched the tape in the viewfinder. Turning to Karla, he said, "It's a good thing they didn't find this, because we'd be screwed."

When the couple moved into 57 Bayview Drive a month later, Paul hid the tape in the rafters of the garage. "He told me that if anything happened to him or if the police ever came around and were really serious, I should destroy it," Karla said.

Houlahan suggested to Karla that the attack on Tammy,

and her subsequent death, would never have taken place without her assistance.

"I don't believe so," she said, closing her eyes and biting her bottom lip. "I feel absolutely terrible."

Despite her apparent anguish, Karla stayed calm, showing no more than a brief glimpse of pain. The composure she maintained during her nine days of direct examination prompted heated debate: Was Karla burying a burden of grief and anguish that was beyond the realm of normal comprehension, or was she simply a coldhearted, soulless psychopath?

When Tammy was buried on December 27, 1990, Paul and Karla put letters in the casket with other gifts. Karla said she also cut three locks of hair from Tammy's head as a keepsake for her family, for herself, and, of course, for Paul.

After Tammy's death, Karla went on to say, the frequency and severity of Paul's beatings increased dramatically. She testified that he would often threaten to tell her parents or police about what happened with Tammy, saying she'd go to jail forever and her family would hate her.

"Totally trapped. I felt like I had to do whatever Paul said because he had this major, horrible thing to hang over my head. I didn't feel like I had a choice. And he knew it."

Nevertheless, between January 12 and 16, 1991, while Dorothy and Karel were away at a convention in Toronto, Paul and Karla recorded two bizarre sex clips in which Karla appears to play an assertive role. In the first tape, as the couple lies naked on the basement floor at 61 Dundonald, Karla describes various sex acts she'd like to help Paul perform, including the kidnapping and raping of virgins. "If you want to do it fifty more times, we'll do it fifty times more," Karla coos to her betrothed. They could abduct young girls every weekend in the summer, Karla offers on tape, because it's easier to find virgins when it's warmer. She will go with him, if he wants, she says, or she'll stay at home and both prepare for the sex that will follow and the cleanup afterward.

The tape also reveals Karla describing how "proud" she was of Paul when he raped Tammy and how "horny" the event had made her. Karla explained that Paul scripted her dialogue. Nevertheless her voice and her thoughts sound genuine. "I love it when you took her virginity. I love it when you put Snuffles up her ass," Karla tells him.

Paul asks Karla how she felt as she watched the Tammy rape.

"I felt proud. I felt happy," Karla says, with adoration in her voice.

Paul: "What else?"

Karla: "I felt horny. It is my mission in life to make you feel good."

At this, Paul turns to the camera and says, "This is why I am going to marry her."

At Paul's urging, Karla says she had fun with Tammy and she learned that "we like little girls: I like you to fuck them. If you're gonna fuck them, then I'm gonna lick them."

Paul: "When do you want me to fuck them?"

Karla: "When?"

Paul: "What age?"

Karla: "Thirteen."

Paul: "Why?"

Karla: "'Cause it'll make you happy."

Paul: "But why thirteen?"

Karla: "That is a good age, I guess."

Paul: "Because why?"

Karla: "They'll still be virgins."

Paul: "So what are you saying?"

Karla: "I'm saying I think you should fuck them and take their virginity . . . because you should break their hymens with Snuffles. They are our children and I think you should make them ours even more."

Paul: "I think you're right. You're absolutely right."

Without showing emotion, Karla watched the tape on her private video monitor in the witness box.

"One thing I want to make clear is that the things that I'm saying on this tape are not things that I put into his head," Karla declared emphatically. "It was very typical of normal sex at that time between us. I'm saying things that he wants me to say. Talking about fantasies of his. Raping little girls. Things of that nature," Karla explained. "What I said was not true.

I was trying to make him happy and make up for poor performance on the original tape.''

At one point, Karla rubs a single red rose on Paul's genitals, saying they would later put it on Tammy's grave. Then Karla removes several pairs of Tammy's underwear from a brown paper bag and masturbates Paul with the garments. Karla also refers to Paul's having brought a young girl to the Dundonald Street home a few days earlier.

The second portion of the tape, filmed in Tammy's bedroom, features Karla dressed in Tammy's clothes pretending to be her dead sister while having sex with Paul. It opens with a pan of Tammy's room.

Paul: "Here's my baby's room."

Karla: "Tammy-Lyn Homolka's room."

Paul: "This is where I used to fuck my wife-to-be. Think of Tammy. I'd look at her outside this window. She was in the pool. Of course, the blind is broken, thanks to moi, so I could watch her change. Fucking love this girl so much. My little virgin girl. There's her closet, and her typewriter and the mirror she used to change in. And her water bed."

The camera shows Tammy's clothes still hanging in the closet; her teddy bears and rag dolls are still propped up on the pillow.

Two wallet-sized photographs of Tammy appear before the camera lens. Karla says she'll get the bigger photo, and a five-by-seven-inch photograph of Tammy appears.

"Okay, there's my baby right there. . . . There is my little virgin there. Tammy-Lyn Homolka, fucked only by me. Broke her hymen and everything. I wish I still had it today, Kar. . . . Wish I still had her. I think part of the blood is on that white thing that was there, I know that."

The sequence is broken. When it restarts, the camera is stationary and the water bed fills the viewfinder. Paul is naked and sinks into the water bed. Karla appears over him, dressed in a black shirt and gray checked skirt.

"Hi, Tammy!"

Karla crawls on top of him, squats on his midriff, and gives his face a deep, passionate kiss.

"Hi, Paul! You know, this is her favorite outfit," says

Karla. But then her voice changes into a higher, softer pitch. She mimics Tammy's voice.

Karla: "I am your little virgin. I'm glad Karla doesn't know about us. She'll never know."

Paul: "She knows I'm bad, but she doesn't know that I do all these things."

Karla: "I didn't know she knew anything. Does she know that I was your virgin?"

Paul: "Yes."

Karla: "That you broke my hymen with Snuffles? Does she know that you made me bleed, that you were the first boy to ever enter this body? Does she know that?"

At Karla's request, Paul turns over onto his knees and she feverishly performs anilingus. He turns his head to look at the video camera dispassionately. As Karla licks, Paul looks at photographs of Tammy. Between licks, Karla talks about how Paul used to masturbate near Tammy's head while she slept.

Again in Tammy's voice, Karla says, "I'm your little pervert. I love you so much. You make me so horny, coming inside me. Tell me you love me."

"I love you, Tammy," Paul responds.

Paul lumbers over to the side of the bed. Karla kneels on the floor.

"Suck me, Tammy!" he says, laughing.

Karla asks Paul if it is enjoyable.

"Better than Karla, that's for sure," he says.

"I love Paul. Paul Bernardo. Paul Kenneth Bernardo. I love you so much," she says in a little girl's voice.

When it comes, his orgasm doesn't last long and appears to give little satisfaction.

"Oh, Tammy. I love you."

There is silence. He pats her on the head and slumps his own head to the right.

"I love you, Paul," Karla sobs.

He gets up to switch off the camera, leaving Karla on her knees. In what seems to be an instinctive move, she smiles and waves at the camera.

Once Paul and Karla moved out of 61 Dundonald and into 57 Bayview, any thoughts she had of telling her friends about the reality of her relationship vanished, Karla explained, because Paul routinely read her mail and would know if she'd told anyone that anything was less than wonderful in her relationship. She said that as soon as they moved in together, Paul's brutality worsened. Sometimes he would beat her without warning; other times he warned her to "be ready for nightly terrorist attacks."

One night, while she was sleeping on the floor beside the bed, Karla told the court, Paul savagely kicked her because she had fallen asleep while he was still awake.

"I slept on the floor for most of our marriage," Karla explained. "When we first moved in together we would sleep together in a queen-size bed. He didn't think the bed was big enough. He would wake me up in the middle of the night and say, 'Kar, can you go on the floor?'" Karla said.

Finally she moved onto the floor full-time, using a sleeping bag. Karla testified that Paul later bought a foam mattress pad for the bed, but he didn't like it because the sheets didn't fit properly. Having no more use for the pad, he passed it on for Karla to use on the floor.

Karla rarely missed work, even though Paul often demanded she stay up late with him—more often than not, drinking heavily.

"He doesn't like being alone very much at all," she testified.

Day after day, with only a few hours' sleep, Karla would drag herself to work and come home at night to face the same routine. Within weeks of the move, she said, Paul also demanded that Karla see her doctor about getting a second Halcion prescription, "just in case."

Later, Karla testified, Paul joined a Masonic lodge to help cultivate his public image of being an upstanding young man. She said he liked to portray the illusion of having the perfect home, wife, dog, everything, and that he even demanded they go shopping together, so that others would observe their youthful good looks and their apparent happiness.

Karla described for the court how on a warm June night two weeks before their wedding, Paul set out to capture his own fantasy.

Telling Karla he was off to "see some friends," Paul left 57 Bayview Drive at 11 P.M. Friday, June 14, 1991. She said that as he left, he told Karla he would take some things with him: the hunting knife in the camouflage sheath that he kept hidden in the garage rafters; twine kept in the kitchen cupboard beside Buddy's food and puppy toys; a pair of panty hose taken from Karla's drawer.

"Just in case," Paul told his fiancée.

Perhaps five hours later, sometime between 3 and 4 A.M., Karla said she was roused from slumber by Paul.

"Kar, be quiet. There's a girl in the house."

Still groggy from sleep, Karla testified she didn't exactly know what Paul was talking about. Had he picked up a barfly, or had he used the rape kit and brought himself home the sex slave that he'd spoken of so often, so longingly?

Paul didn't elaborate.

"Be quiet and stay upstairs," he commanded.

So she stayed upstairs, she said, and soon fell back asleep.

A few hours later, an ecstatic Paul reentered the bedroom. Karla explained that Paul told her he had kidnapped and raped a girl who was now in their guest bedroom. Karla testified that Paul told her the girl was blindfolded and hadn't seen the outside or the inside of the house. Again, he told Karla to stay upstairs and remain quiet. Then he left his fiancée to be alone with his victim.

He was, Karla told the court, very happy.

In the same quiet, even voice the jury, the media, and spectators had come to expect, Karla recounted how she heard Buddy whining from down in the basement. She feared if she didn't let the dog out the blindfolded girl would hear him, and that would give police more information on her captors. Karla crept down the stairs and into the basement, putting Buddy's leash and collar on so the rambunctious dog wouldn't go bounding off in search of Paul.

Tiptoeing silently up the basement stairs, she opened the back door and let Buddy out into the yard. Through it all, the guest bedroom door was closed tight. Still fearing Buddy would make noise, Karla got his food and water bowls, called the dog in from the yard, and took him with her to the upstairs bedroom. As she lay in her bed upstairs, Karla said she became concerned the girl might grab the telephone in the guest bedroom and call for help.

But she did nothing to act on those worries, and for the rest of the day she kept Buddy quiet; she told a stunned courtroom she may have read a book. Around 6 P.M., when Karla said she went down to the kitchen and ate, Paul waltzed out of the guest bedroom and into the living room, and related how he had kidnapped the girl.

She claimed that he told her he was in a backyard in Burlington when he saw a girl standing outside her back door, that she saw him and asked what he was doing. Paul told her he was going to break into the house next door and asked why she was out at that hour. She had missed curfew, her parents had locked her out, and she was scared to wake them. The girl asked him for a cigarette. Paul said he had some in the car. They walked to the Nissan. He suggested she get in and they smoke together. The girl was leery of Paul and said she would get into the car but wouldn't close the door. Karla testified that Paul told her that as soon as she was in the car, Paul brought out the knife and told the girl to shut the door. Then he blindfolded her.

"Did anybody see you?" Karla said she asked Paul who responded "No, don't worry. Nobody saw me."

Karla said Paul told her he was taking the girl to the master bedroom, and that because he hadn't decided whether Karla should be involved, she stayed downstairs. She said Paul instructed her to take the telephone-answering machine from the living room to the guest bedroom and set it up to take incoming calls, and to disconnect all the other phones in the house.

Karla told the court that a few hours later, around 9 P.M., Paul came downstairs and told Karla to go up. She said he instructed her not to talk and that when she walked into the master bedroom she saw the girl sitting on the floor, her back to the hope chest. She said Leslie Mahaffy was dressed in the same clothes she had seen the girl wearing downstairs when Paul had led her out of the guest room, and that she still had Paul's red designer sweater wrapped around her head for a blindfold. Paul told Karla to make some mixed drinks. She couldn't remember how the booze got upstairs.

"We were all sitting on the floor. I found out the girl's name was Leslie," Karla recalled. The girl appeared drunk. It also seemed as if she didn't want to be there and "she was off in another place in her mind," Karla said.

In a gentle tone, Paul asked Leslie a series of questions, which she answered in a trembling, slurred voice, Karla said. She was fourteen, in ninth grade at school, and liked to be with friends. She talked about her little brother, Ryan, and how close she was to him and how she wanted very much to see him again.

In the front row of the courtroom, directly behind Houlahan, Debbie and Dan Mahaffy sat with friends and a court counselor. Clutching a tissue, Debbie sobbed through most of Karla's description of Leslie's abduction and captivity, leaning her head on the shoulder of a woman friend to her left.

Karla told the court that she didn't speak to Leslie but whispered her questions into Paul's ear, which he then repeated to the blindfolded girl.

The teen said she had been to a wake that night for some friends who died in a car crash. Karla said that Paul asked Leslie which radio station she liked and when she replied CFNY, Paul tuned the clock radio to the Toronto-based alternative-rock station.

"How would you feel about having sex with two people?" Karla said Paul asked. Leslie became very upset and started crying and shaking.

Karla testified that Paul then asked Leslie how she would feel if the third person was a woman.

At this, Leslie appeared relieved, as if she believed that if a woman was there, no harm could come to her, Karla said quietly from the witness box, the irony not lost on her. She further explained that at Paul's command, Leslie stripped down to her bra and panties while Paul judged her body, saying it was "pretty good" except for her stomach, which Paul said was a little potlike. When Paul asked Karla what she thought, Karla testified that she just nodded.

Karla assured the court that the blindfold remained on Leslie's face and that Paul told her to tell him if it began to slip, because if it did, and she saw him, then he would have to kill her.

Soon, Paul wanted three-way sex, Karla said. He had already videotaped Leslie urinating and showering, at one point demanding menacingly that she flatulate for him. "Give me a big fart. I want a big fart out of there. I want something really, really good, you see, 'cause otherwise I'll kill you . . . ," Paul growled.

In one ninety-second clip, Leslie is seen on the guest-room bed, naked except for the blindfold. Her face is shown, her lips obviously swollen. Bernardo tells her to touch her body sensually, including her breasts and her vagina.

At one point he removes the blindfold and focuses on her face.

"Keep doing that. I like that sound. Who is your favorite guy right now?" asks Paul in a calm and gentle voice.

"I don't know," says Leslie, her voice trembling.

"Who's your favorite guy? I think you know who I want you to say," he asks again.

"I want you," she says.

After a few more words are spoken, Paul's voice barks out an order. "Keep your eyes shut . . . tight!"

He turned on the video camera again. In the background, CFNY played David Bowie, R.E.M., Bob Marley.

The camera was propped up on a chair, taping the three-some.

In Karla's first appearance on the tape, Paul tells Leslie her sexual performance is being judged.

"You're doing a good job, Leslie, a real good job. . . . You're in my good books," Paul says encouragingly on the tapes.

But seconds later he reminds her again that she has to make him feel good. "I'm judging you right now, okay? These next two hours are going to determine what I do to you. Okay, right now you are scoring perfect."

The final video segment was filmed sometime after midnight on Saturday, almost twenty-four hours after Leslie's abduction. Karla was operating the camera.

As Paul has vaginal sex with Leslie, her hands are bound behind her back and her ankles are also bound. She cries out loudly, in obvious pain, as Paul forces his penis into her anus as punishment because she couldn't defecate. Leslie pleads for her freedom.

Leslie: "Just let me go. I won't ever say anything about you."

Paul: "Is this teaching you?"

Leslie: "Uh-huh. This is teaching me. I learned."

Paul: "What is it teaching you?"

Leslie: "I'll never tell. I'll never double-cross you. I'll never double-cross you."

Paul: "Are you sure?"

Leslie: "I will not, ever . . . I want to see my family and my brother and my friends, and please . . ."

Paul: "Let me fuck you. I'm going to fuck you. . . . I want your ass up in the air."

Plainly visible in that sequence is a knife and a black electrical cord, the same knife Karla told police Paul used to control his victims and the same type of cord Karla said he used to strangle both schoolgirls.

With the horrible pleas of Leslie Mahaffy echoing through the grim pews of Courtroom 6-1, Houlahan asked Karla whom Leslie was calling.

"It would have to be to me," Karla said, her voice cracking slightly. "I didn't feel like I was able to help her, because I was too afraid of Paul."

The words sounded hollow as they hung in the crowded courtroom. Karla added, "I find it very difficult to put my feelings into words, because putting them into words trivializes the whole thing."

Around 1 or 2 A.M. that Sunday morning, with Leslie still on her hands and knees in front of the hope chest, Karla testified that Paul told her it was time to decide what to do with his sex slave. She said he asked the blindfolded teenager what she could recall about his car and that a terrified Leslie said she couldn't remember anything about the car's interior but that the license-plate number had a three in it even though it didn't.

Leslie, perhaps sensing that a critical juncture in her ordeal was near, begged for her life and promised she would never tell a soul.

But, said Karla, Paul didn't believe Leslie. Karla told the court that he thought Leslie was lying and that he angrily beat the bound girl on her back and shoulders while Leslie cried, tucking her chin to her chest, as if cringing to escape her tormentor.

Again, Leslie promised not to tell.

"How are you going to explain this to your family?" Karla said Paul asked the girl.

"I'll just tell them I was with a friend," she whimpered. "I want to go home and see my little brother."

Karla alleged that Paul stopped his questioning and took Karla aside. With Leslie still bound on the carpet behind them, Karla said Paul told her that Leslie could identify him if freed, so she would have to be killed.

Karla said he reminded her that he had been questioned by police in Scarborough and that he had given samples of his hair and blood and saliva to police and was afraid if he let Leslie go that samples on Leslie could be matched with the Scarborough ones.

"I asked him to reconsider, and he said to me, 'Would you rather I go to jail for twenty-five years? She can identify me, and do you want me to go to jail?' And I said, 'No,' and he said he was going to kill her. I asked him if we could please give her a sleeping pill, so at least she wouldn't be awake when he killed her, because I didn't want her to feel any pain," Karla said, betraying no emotion.

An anguished wail came from the front of the otherwise silent courtroom.

"How kind of you," muttered Debbie Mahaffy, her body wracked with sobs, her words trailing off into nothingness.

Karla could not remember who gave Leslie the Halcion that was brought from the washroom cabinet. After taking the drug in a drink, Leslie was still scared, so Karla grabbed Bunky, the white teddy bear Paul had given Karla on their first Christmas together, and put it in Leslie's arms.

"It's okay," Karla whispered.

These were the only words Karla spoke to Leslie, who, despite this hollow comfort, cried until sleep overcame her. As Leslie lay on the floor, Karla said, Paul kneeled over the unconscious girl with the black electrical cord he must have brought from the basement.

From the witness stand, Karla used her own hands to demonstrate how Paul wrapped the cord around one wrist, then the other wrist, and then wrapped it tight around Leslie's throat. She was still unconscious as he pulled tight. Karla said she turned her head until he was finished.

"I was panicking and he told me to calm down. He seemed shaken, and I asked him, you know, 'What now? What are we going to do?' He said, 'Just calm down.' "

At that moment, a gasp of air came from Leslie's stilled, limp body.

"She was blue. . . . Paul and I both jumped, and I was just freaking at that point, and he went back and he strangled her again. . . . He did it the same way, but it was more intense what he did. . . . He told me that even if she hadn't been strangled the second time, that if she had lived she probably would have had brain damage because of lack of oxygen to her brain," Karla recalled.

She said Paul pulled the cord tight for seven minutes this time to make sure she was dead.

"What are we going to do?" a shaken Karla asked.

She testified that Paul responded, "We're not going to make any decision tonight, 'cause we're both tired, and if we do anything now we'll do something stupid."

Then she said that he wrapped Leslie's body in a blanket and put it in the root cellar, explaining that they would deal with the problem the next day.

The next day, however, was Father's Day. Dorothy and Karel Homolka visited 57 Bayview between 12 noon and 3 P.M. Before they left their home, Karla called her mother and asked if she would bring some chicken when she visited, saying Paul had been too busy to take her out to buy it herself and now she was feeling a touch of bronchitis coming on.

As Karla prepared the dinner, her mother noticed they needed potatoes. She headed for the basement stairs and the root cellar. Karla jumped between her mother and the steps and told her to relax and she would get the potatoes. In a flash she was down the stairs and up again, potatoes in hand.

The afternoon conversation focused on the wedding, only two weeks away. Her parents left around 8 or 9 P.M.

Karla told the court that once the Homolkas had gone, Paul told Karla he had a great plan for Leslie's body. He wanted to put the corpse in concrete so it would never be found, but to do that he would have to dismember the body and encase the parts in small blocks that could be easily carried to a dump site.

"He told me he wanted me to help him do it. I told him, 'No,' I couldn't do that. He said, 'Yes, you can, and if I want you to you will.' I told him I couldn't do it. And then it was just over for the evening," Karla told the court.

On Monday morning, Karla got up early, put on her makeup and casual work clothes, and at about 7:45 A.M., following her daily routine, caught the bus that would take her to the Martindale Animal Clinic. She didn't call Paul all day.

Paul arrived at the clinic just before 6 P.M. He drove the quickest route home. Barely a word was spoken between the two.

They were almost home when Karla testified that Paul turned to her and said, "It's done."

"What do you mean, it's done?" Karla said she asked, knowing in her heart what he meant.

"It's done," she said he repeated.

"I knew he had dismembered the body and put it in concrete," Karla told the court.

Once in the house, Karla said Paul took her downstairs to the basement workshop because he wanted to show her his handiwork. It was darker than usual, she said because Paul had placed towels over the small windows. At the far end of the room stood nine or ten corrugated cardboard boxes—some of the same boxes she and Paul had used to move into the house a few months earlier—filled with wet cement. One box stood apart from the others in size. She saw the plastic bucket she used for washing the floors, its inner walls caked with dried concrete. They went upstairs and sat facing each other across the dining-room table.

"He was pretty quiet and seemed to be kind of shaken by the whole thing," Karla said. "I asked him if he wanted something to eat. He said he didn't want to eat meat for a long time. He talked about what he had done, about dismembering the body; he told me that he had cut the body into ten pieces. He told me that he couldn't believe how light [the head] was and he had just plopped it in concrete. He was just talking in a very dead sort of tone . . . he was laughing and joking about it. I believe he told me he did it with the saw. I don't know if he told me at that time it was the circular saw or not. . . . He told me that he had put black paint on one of the blocks, the one containing the head, because some of the hair was sticking out and he wanted to make it less noticeable."

Karla said Paul told her that he would dump the concrete blocks into Lake Gibson, the same secluded lake where he and Karla had had sex in their early dating days. She told the court that he added he would need her for cover, because it would be less suspicious for a guy and a girl to be at the lake than for a strange guy to be there by himself.

On either Tuesday or Wednesday, Karla couldn't recall which day, she went to work and when Paul picked her up at night he told her he had two of the smaller cement blocks in the hatchback and that he had already tossed the five smallest blocks into the lake earlier that day, burning the cardboard boxes in which the blocks had been formed in the fireplace at home. She said he told her that she would have to help him toss the two small blocks that remained into the lake and then return to the house to pick up the large torso block he had left there.

The pair drove to Lake Gibson and Paul dumped the two smaller blocks, while Karla stood lookout, but even then, she said, Paul became angry with her for shutting the hatch on the Nissan too loudly.

Despite the fact that the block containing Leslie's torso weighed more than two hundred pounds, Karla said Paul didn't ask for help in carrying the block up the basement stairs. Instead, she said she opened all the doors between the basement and the car, while Paul carried the torso block in front of him, up the stairs, through the kitchen, and into the garage area. When Karla noticed a plastic garbage bag wrapped around it she said Paul told her it was leaking fluids and he didn't want to have to clean anything up off the floor.

She told the court that he carried the block out onto the narrow landing in the garage, laid it down, and then eased it into the reclined front seat of the waiting Nissan, angling it forward so that part of the block sat on the floor and part on the seat. Karla slipped into the backseat through Paul's side, and again they drove to Lake Gibson.

Karla said that this time Paul chose a different location, a bridge on Faywell Road that crossed a fast-flowing stretch of the DeCew reservoir pond that adjoins Lake Gibson. There she said they dumped the last of Leslie Mahaffy's remains into the water.

Later that night, Karla said Paul directed Karla to clean everywhere Leslie had been in the house. She recalled that he told her to vacuum the rooms, especially the guest bedroom, and to wash down the walls and wash all the sheets Leslie had touched. She explained that Paul planned to burn the vacuum bags and the plastic bag used to contain the torso-block drippings. At one point Karla said she suggested that Paul dispose of the black electrical cord, but Paul dismissed her, saying he was going to keep it.

"I didn't think it was a good idea to have the murder weapon in the house," Karla explained.

Karla also cleaned the interior of the car, wiping it down to try to remove all fingerprints.

After Leslie's death, the physical, emotional, and sexual abuse escalated to even new levels, Karla told the court.

"He told me that I would be an ugly bride because I had bruises and nobody would think I was pretty."

"I didn't want to get married," Karla insisted to Houlahan, to a whispered chorus of chuckles from journalists and spectators. But, "because Paul had the incident with Tammy to hold over my head and now he had the incident with Leslie to hang over my head,'' Karla said she didn't feel she had a choice in the matter.

In a rare interruption, Judge LeSage pushed his wire-rimmed glasses from his nose and asked Karla in his gentle way if Paul wouldn't have had as much—if not more—to lose from telling anyone about Tammy.

Karla nodded up to LeSage and, referring to him as "Your Honor" as she did at all times, she politely explained that the main threat involved Paul telling not police but her parents about Tammy, and that "they would be in this horrible bind . . . like, what should we do? Do we tell people what our daughter's done? I didn't want my parents to know. I was terrified. It's very difficult to explain, but that's how I felt, Your Honor."

As for Paul's thoughts on marriage, she explained to the court that "He said that if we were married, then I couldn't be forced to testify against him. "At one point, he said to me that if he ever got caught that he would tell police that he forced me to do it and he would go to jail for a few years and write a book, and because a criminal can't profit from their crimes, he would have me sell it and that's what I would live off of," Karla said.

Still, most of all Karla asserted, Paul believed he'd never be caught. "He'd gotten away with so much, there was no reason to believe he'd ever be caught."

And so they were married in their lavish ceremony less than two weeks after murdering Leslie Mahaffy and throwing her body parts into Lake Gibson.

The jury was shown segments of video shot at the ceremony and reception, including a speech by Paul in which he thanked his new parents, the Homolkas, for their help in ensuring that the relationship survived. Sitting a few rows behind Paul in the courtroom, the normally stoic Dorothy broke down and both she and Karel sobbed at the memory. This was the first time Dorothy was seen to shed a tear during either her daughter's trial or her former son-in-law's trial. As the wedding video images flickered onto the public monitors, a scruffy young man in jeans stood up at the rear and yelled out the words that many thought but dared not say:

"That's nice, but you're still both murderers," he bellowed, pointing an accusatory finger at both Paul and Karla. As he continued his rant, he scolded Paul for his "smug face."

"You killed all three of them," he yelled. "And you, your sister," he said, focusing on Karla. "Make a deal with your lawyer and be out in a year!"

When guards came, the man put his arms in the air and was escorted out without further incident. During the entire outburst, Paul didn't even bat an eyelid; when order had been restored, Karla continued with her testimony, apparently unfazed.

On their wedding night, Karla said, they returned to their hotel room and opened some gifts. Then Paul wanted fellatio, or as Karla related Paul's request, "Suck my dick!"

"It's our wedding night, don't you want to make love?" Karla asked.

When he said he didn't, Karla obliged her new husband with fellatio, saying the words she knew would please him as she did.

Even her treasured Hawaiian honeymoon turned out to be a "honeymoon from hell," Karla told the court. On one of the three islands they visited, Karla dropped the camera because she had too many things in her hand. She said Paul was furious and beat her on the head and buttocks with his hands, pulling out chunks of her hair. She said he kicked her and then he whacked her with a pair of industrial-style headphones that he had brought along because he needed them to sleep at night. The force cracked the headphones, which sent him on an even greater spiral of rage.

"They cut my scalp and there was blood everywhere," Karla said.

Still, one video scene from the trip belies Karla's story of abuse and terror. While staring out at a glorious Pacific Ocean sunset, Karla videotaped a loving soliloquy while Paul showered for dinner.

"The beauty of the ocean, and the beach, and everything here doesn't even come close to the love I feel for you. I love you sweetheart," Karla says in a dreamy voice.

The explanation was simple, Karla told the court. It was a sort of preemptive strike, telling Paul something he wanted to hear in an attempt to reduce future beatings. In a phrase she would repeat several times in her testimony, Karla said she was "a lot better off with him happy than with him angry."

If it was the honeymoon from hell, it certainly wasn't portrayed as such when they returned to Canada. "I didn't tell anybody about the bad parts of any part of our relationship. They thought it was great. I told them we had a great time and I didn't tell them anything bad," Karla explained matter-of-factly.

One element of their vacation that Karla said made a lasting impression was Paul's discovery of a nightly turndown service at Mauii Marriott. Hotel staff would turn down the bed, leaving behind a seashell or chocolate on the guests' pillows. Paul decided Karla should start leaving him nightly notes for when he went to bed.

"So I started putting little notes on his pillow. They were all talking about how great he was and how much I loved him, things like that," Karla explained.

The pillow notes were left virtually every night until January 1993, when Karla left Paul. And as Karla wrote them, pack rat Paul saved them, storing each little note away in his desk.

The affectionate tone of the turndown service and nightly love notes hides the violence and terror that dominated the marriage, Karla insisted. In October 1991, Karla visited her regular doctor, Dr. Valerie Jaeger in Welland, complaining of severe back problems. She said she'd been horseback riding and the horse had stumbled, wrenching her back. She needed pain medication. The horse incident was true, but Karla didn't tell Dr. Jaeger that afterward Paul had knocked her down and kicked her many times in the back.

In March 1992, Karla returned to Dr. Jaeger, this time with sore ribs. Karla said she dismissed the aches and bruises in the usual way, blaming the animals at the clinic, disguising Paul's beating her with his fists. Later, it was revealed she had a cracked rib.

Also in March 1992, Karla visited a walk-in clinic in St.

Catharines with a broken finger. This time she explained that her dog had accidentally bitten her, but in truth, she said Paul had beaten her again. On this occasion, Karla had locked herself in the downstairs bathroom, but Paul told her that if she didn't open the door it would be even worse. She opened the door to a hail of punches to the head and upper body. As she tried to shield her face, a punch smashed her finger.

"He called me a stupid idiot for putting my hands on top of my head to protect myself," Karla told the court.

When Paul tired of hitting her with his fists or feet, she said he turned to an arsenal of common household objects: firewood, dress shoes, a flashlight, car keys, the top of a lead crystal wine decanter.

"All kinds of things," a deadpan Karla reported. "Anything that was within reach, he would hit me with it."

Paul would frequently whip her as well. She explained how she would be forced to strip naked and kneel on the floor, saying, "Please whip me, sir, I deserve to be whipped." She was to stare straight ahead as Paul circled her menacingly. At random he would strike her with the belt or kick her.

"If I turned to look, I was punished for that."

Karla testified that Paul's violence exploded for the least of reasons. If Karla didn't turn off the water tap tightly enough, he would punish her. If she didn't rush to answer the door quickly enough, there would be hell to pay.

The car was a favorite beating place, because it was confined and Karla could never get far enough away from Paul. Typically, he would whack her head, face, and thighs with a long-handled flashlight. He also took delight in slapping and punching Karla in the face and pulling at her hair.

"There was hair all over the car," she said. "He would punch me on the temple, and when he did that the whole side of my face would swell up and it would look like I had something in my cheek."

Karla told the court that Paul's drinking became worse, but no amount of alcohol dulled the pain for Karla. Paul often told Karla to stay up late drinking, watching TV or having sex, she said. He didn't like to be alone much, Karla explained. To avoid severe hangovers, Karla secretly mixed her own weak drinks. But Paul caught on and began testing her drinks for potency. Then she poured the alcohol in last to make it taste stronger to the sip than it really was. Again, Paul caught on. He made her mix the drinks in front of him.

Paul talked of his dreams to build his own home in the country. A luxurious estate, but with a difference: The home would be equipped with a soundproofed dungeon in which he could keep sex slaves. It was a project he discussed "very frequently," Karla said.

And how did she respond to such a bizarre plan? Houlahan wanted to know.

"I didn't say much of anything. I didn't disagree with him in any way. I was careful not to," Karla said.

With wedding vows still fresh in their memories, Karla said Paul decided he would introduce Karla to his well-practiced ritual of stalking women. "He had told me at some point that he used to do this without me. Once we were married and he knew that he had me under his total control, he decided that I should go with him," Karla explained.

A nice-looking young woman made for good cover, she said Paul explained. He instructed Karla to wear her hair in a ponytail and to wear nondescript clothing and then they would head out in the car. They traveled all over the Niagara Peninsula and beyond, to the lakefront cities of Hamilton, Mississauga, Burlington, even as far as Toronto.

"He would drive in the car, and he would look around and get me to look around, and look for young women," Karla explained.

Young women driving their cars, girls walking along the street, girls going to their cars in parking lots—Paul was interested in all women. Typically, they had to be young, lithe, and have long hair. If he saw a girl he fancied in a car, he would turn and follow her home. If that happened, Paul would sometimes get out of the Nissan and try to catch a glimpse of his quarry disrobing through a bedroom window. If he could watch from the car, Paul would instruct Karla to look away and he would masturbate, she said. But more than anything, Karla testified, Paul was waiting for the opportunity to grab a girl and bring her home as his sex slave. Paul, she said, fre-

quently took his knife in its camouflage sheath and his ny-
lons, presumably to place over his head during an abduction.

Karla told the court about one night when they cruised the
parking lot at the Pen Centre mall in St. Catharines. She said
Paul saw a woman he liked getting into her car. The couple
followed her car outside the city and through the countryside
to the small community of Fonthill. She said Paul told her of
his plan: they would put a nail under her car tire in the parking
lot so her tire would go flat by the time she hit the secluded
rural roads, then they would follow in the Nissan, and seeing
her in distress, they would stop to offer their help changing
the tire or offer the cell phone in the Nissan.

"And he would get her in the car and that would be it,
bring her back to the house," Karla explained. "I didn't
argue."

Karla also testified that one night, after telling Karla about
the latest girl he had been watching undress, Paul drove to a
home in St. Catharines. She said the girl worked as a waitress
at the Red Hot Chili Pepper restaurant in downtown St. Catharines and that he had followed her home from work. At one
point he videotaped the girl undressing from her backyard.
The girl had no idea she was in Paul's sights until police told
her she was on one of the videotapes Ken Murray had handed
over.

Some time later, Paul and Karla were in the Red Hot Chili
Pepper drinking with Mike Donald and his girlfriend when
Paul pointed out a young woman getting drinks for customers. Karla saw she had long, curly reddish-auburn hair and
appeared to be in her early twenties.

"That's the one I've been watching change," she said Paul
whispered to her.

Karla also testified that Paul later told her he'd learned the
woman's parents were going away, and he talked about breaking into her house and raping and killing her. There was no
talk about definite plans, just idle chatter. One night, friends
arrived unexpectedly. Paul angrily confided to Karla later that
he'd planned that very night to carry out his murderous plan.
The woman moved away, Paul told her later.

Although some of the women Paul had been stalking were adults, Karla made it clear he had not lost his penchant for young girls.

Jane was a cute prepubescent girl when Karla first met her at the Number One Pet Centre in 1986 or 1987. Her mother would bring her in to look at the animals. Young Jane liked Karla; she even asked her mom to get Karla to baby-sit her in those days and they would often talk on the telephone about animals.

When Paul first came on the scene, Karla lost touch with Jane just as she lost touch with everyone else. The friendship, however, would be rekindled when Paul told Karla he was tired of their relationship and he wanted a virgin girlfriend. Jane fit the bill perfectly. Karla testified that she agreed to deliver her on a platter to Paul, because she "wanted him to find somebody else and leave me alone." After the engagement, Karla called Jane with the happy news. The fifteen-year-old couldn't get to Karla's shower, but Paul told Karla to call her over to the house and talk to her as often as possible. She was to tell Jane the love between Paul and her was finished and that their relationship was more like that of a brother and sister. She was to secretly push Jane towards Paul. At that point, Karla was twenty-one, Paul, twenty-five.

"Paul kept telling me, 'Call her, call her, call her,' " Karla emphasized to the court.

Just before the wedding, Jane was a frequent visitor at 57 Bayview Drive. She enjoyed playing with Buddy and going out for meals. Paul showered the young girl with lavish gifts, such as clothes, stuffed animals, and jewelry. One weekend, they stayed at the Hilton in Toronto, ate in the revolving CN Tower restaurant, and went to the Canadian National Exhibition fairgrounds.

"He was basically wining and dining her like he did with me," Karla explained. The wining and dining, however, was done with Karla by their side.

In May 1993, when Karla gave her statements to police, she revealed that Paul had sexually assaulted Jane, perhaps in 1991, but she did not mention her own involvement. While searching the house in the winter and spring of 1993, police found a short video clip of Karla having oral sex with a girl or young woman who wasn't either Kristen French or Leslie Mahaffy. In August 1993, the *Toronto Sun* revealed the existence of the tape. Perhaps the story prompted police to visit Karla in the Prison for Women in September 1993 with a still photo from the short clip.

Karla appeared confused in court as she testified that her first recollection of being involved in the Jane attack came during a dream after police left. The dream was about Kristen French, she said, but the victim bore Jane's face.

"I was very confused," she admitted. Later, she said, she talked to a prison psychiatrist about the dream.

Karla admitted on the stand that she was so worried about the Jane videotape that she sent her lawyer, George Walker, a letter in October 1993 and told him she didn't want to face further charges and she would cooperate fully with police. In December 1993, Karla said in a police statement that she recalled giving Jane Halcion-laced drinks and that Paul instructed her to lie beside the sleeping teen while Paul sexually assaulted the girl. She also recalled a moment frighteningly similar to Tammy's death, in which Jane appeared to stop breathing after she was given Halothane. Karla recalled calling 911, but Paul called out that Jane was okay and he had just panicked. She canceled the call.

The full extent of the sex assault would not come to light until fall 1994, when Paul's lawyer, Ken Murray, quit the case and the videotapes appeared. Even when Houlahan had the brief segment played, Karla could not recall wiggling her hips burlesque-style at the camera and performing oral and finger sex on the unconscious Jane. Karla could not even recall inserting Jane's limp fingers in her own vagina.

"I can't explain it. I don't remember this happened," Karla said, her voice never losing the flat quality that had marked most of her testimony. "I can't believe I actually did that . . . I'm not saying I didn't, I just can't believe I actually did it."

After meetings between George Walker and government officials, it was decided on June 15 or 16, in the middle of Paul's trial just before Karla's testimony, that no additional charges would be leveled against Karla. Some journalists complained that a strong case could be made for charging Karla with sexual assault. Clearly, they said, she had purposely lied. Anticipating a similar defense accusation, Houlahan asked Karla if she had any reason to lie about Jane. She said she didn't and cited the incriminating information she had already revealed about much more serious matters—namely, the Tammy Homolka, Leslie Mahaffy, and Kristen French deaths.

"I have told the truth from the beginning," she said.

Comments like these seemed to burn the ears of the defense team, who more and more dreamed of their date with Karla.

In spite of everything—the whippings, the kicks, the hair-pulling and smashes to the temple with the flashlight—in spite of Karla's repeated testimony that she hated and feared her husband, she still craved a simple good-night kiss. The sentiment was laid bare in dozens of love notes and letters in the form of postscripts begging Paul to kiss her.

Karla had a ready answer for the apparent inconsistency. Because she couldn't leave Paul and he wouldn't let her go, Karla said, she figured the next-best thing was to try to convince him to act as if he loved her. If she could convince him of his love, then maybe he wouldn't need to do anything else, Karla explained.

"I either wanted to be totally away from him or I wanted him to love me."

There were, of course, dozens of other letters written during the period following Leslie's murder.

Dear Paul,
I love you so much. Once we were an unbeatable team. You and me against the world. Best friends to the end. You used to ask me, "Who's your buddy, who's your pal, who's your best friend?" I want our love back. People think we're the perfect couple. We are we've just gotten sidetracked. Even though we have our problems I am still so much in love with you. I want us to put our arms around each other and fall in love all over again. Some

*couples are meant to be and we're one of those . . . Let's
try to have a fairytale marriage like we were meant to.*

Some of the notes Karla left were merely to let Paul know
her whereabouts and what time it was. If she came home from
work and he was sleeping or out, she would leave a note explaining where she was, even if she was just taking a nap in
the guest bedroom.

It was, she said, what was expected of her.

"I felt like I always had to account for every second of the
time I spent away from him."

Some journalists who heard the pathetic letters admitted a
new understanding of Karla. Some even felt sympathy for the
young woman. But for most, the sentiment was short-lived.

CHAPTER
27

On a rainy Thursday in April, Karla took the bus to work as usual. Because veterinarian Dr. Patty Weir did not work at the clinic Thursday afternoons, there were no appointments and very few telephone inquiries, so Karla and the receptionist would not work on alternate Thursday afternoons. On Thursday, April 16, 1992, Karla left the Martindale clinic at noon and took the bus to the downtown St. Catharines library, a few yards from police headquarters. She didn't return to 57 Bayview Drive until around 2:30 P.M.

When she walked in the door, Paul was furious, Karla told the court.

"Why didn't you come right home? You knew we were going out to look for a girl today," he said angrily.

Karla said Paul had talked to her about joining him on stalking expeditions on Thursday afternoons, saying it would be a good time to find young girls, especially young virgin schoolgirls walking the streets on their way home from school.

Paul ordered her to get changed, which she did, dressing simply, as Paul had decreed. Paul, too, dressed in clothes that would not attract attention; blue jeans and a nondescript shirt.

For weeks, Paul had talked over and over to Karla about his kidnapping plan, and as they drove out in the rain at about 2:45 P.M., he made her repeat it over and over again, "because he thought I would screw it up,'' Karla said, interrupting her recollection.

Paul had his hunting knife between the driver's seat and the center console, Karla said, and they drove down Main Street, through the commercial section of Port Dalhousie, along Lakeshore Road, and up Linwell Road. They passed dozens of teenagers as they made their way home from Lakeport Secondary School and the neighboring Roman Catholic secondary school, Holy Cross.

A few minutes after Paul drove through the traffic lights at Lake Street and continued east on Linwell Road, Karla said he noticed a young girl walking west on the street's north sidewalk. She was approaching the adjoining parking lots of the Giles Presbyterian Church and the Grace Lutheran Church.

''She was on the same side of the street, on the sidewalk. Paul saw her and he said that he liked her. And he turned around. And he drove past her again to make sure she was what he wanted,'' Karla recalled. ''Then he turned around and again drove into the church parking lot, because he thought she would walk by the church. There was a big tree there. As soon as he saw the tree he was really happy; he said that would provide a good cover. He was very, very excited. I just felt totally dead inside. He told me to stay calm and make sure that I got her over to the car. So she started walking on, still on the sidewalk.''

Karla told the court that Paul had pulled the Nissan 240SX into the Grace Lutheran Church parking lot with the passenger's door facing the road, about ten yards from where the girl would walk by. As the pretty teen passed, Karla rolled down the window.

''Excuse me! Can you give me directions?'' she called out.

''Yes,'' replied the girl, walking over to the car.

''Could you tell me where the Pen Centre is?'' asked Karla.

The girl began to explain through the open window. Karla said she knew she had to get out of the car if she was to lure her into the trap. ''Wait,'' Karla said, cutting off the girl in midsentence. "I'm really bad at directions. Can you show me on the map?"

Karla picked up a map inside the car. Paul had told her it didn't matter what map she used, because by the time this girl realized it wasn't a St. Catharines map in her hands it would be too late, Karla said. Only partially out of the door, Karla began to open the map, spreading half over the roof and resting the other half on top of the open door. The girl stood in the open car door trying to make sense of a map of Toronto. As the girl strained her eyes toward the map trying to find a landmark, Karla stepped aside from the door in order to let Paul come up behind the schoolgirl with a knife in his hand.

"He said something like 'You're coming with us,' and that was my signal. He had told me before that when he said that I should get in the backseat of the car. He said he would have more control over her in the front seat, so I got in the backseat. I can't recall which side of the vehicle I got in . . . I got in the car quickly. He tried to push her in the car. She fought back, but she didn't scream, she just called him a bastard. He just pushed her into the car and closed the door. As he came around he told me to hold her down, so I quickly grabbed hold of her hair. She wasn't fighting at that point. Once she was in the car she didn't fight anymore," Karla said.

Karla testified that Paul got into the car and told their captive not to say a word.

"I have a knife and I'll use it," he said in his quiet voice.

The girl's head rested on the center console. Karla held her hair. Kristen now lay limp and whimpered. Paul drove slowly out of the church parking lot and turned west onto Linwell Road. Karla said Paul had told her many times that if you're doing something illegal you should always follow all the traffic rules, since it would be stupid to get caught for something big because of a simple traffic violation.

Asked by Houlahan if she knew what was going to happen to Kristen French when they picked her up, Karla nodded, looking straight at the prosecutor.

"I knew she had to be killed, because I knew that she was going to see both of our faces in the car. And also because of what had happened to Leslie Mahaffy; she had been killed because Paul thought she could identify him.''

Once safely at 57 Bayview Drive, Karla hid all of the phones save one in the master bedroom closet. Paul would later berate her for choosing that hiding place and move them to the guest bedroom, she said.

Karla recalled that Paul warned the girl to ''be quiet and do what I say.''

Following the pattern of Leslie's captivity, Karla said Paul demanded that he be given some time alone with his sex toy. Karla said she didn't object as Paul took the girl upstairs.

''I was scared somebody had seen what had gone on, and I was just waiting for the police to come to the house. I felt very guilty. I couldn't believe it,'' Karla said. ''When Tammy first died I started to feel very numb, and when Leslie was kidnapped and in her house I started to feel even number. When Kristen was in our house, I was even more so. It is hard to explain, but it is feeling number inside because I wasn't, didn't want to be there, and I was feeling extremely bad about what we were doing. It is the body's way of protecting itself. Everything numbs right out.''

Several hours later, she explained, Paul told her to come upstairs. Karla entered the master bedroom to find the girl sitting on the floor, crying. She wasn't blindfolded, but she was still wearing a white turtleneck sweater and green kilt. Seeing blood on the turtleneck, Paul examined the girl's shoulder and found a superficial knife wound, presumably inflicted by Paul's knife during the struggle to push her into the car. As Paul put a Band-Aid on the wound he apologized, telling the girl he was sorry and that he didn't mean to do it.

Paul asked the girl what her name was, but she gave a phony one. The couple didn't learn her true identity until they heard a news broadcast about the abducted schoolgirl.

Karla said that as they sat, Paul encouraged drinking. Karla brought some alcohol from the dining-room bar, but she thinks Paul may have already had some in the bedroom.

Although he had the latest sex slave in his house, Paul told Karla he was uneasy about the abduction she said because he knew now that one of Kristen's shoes had been left behind and that police had a crime scene, a starting point from which to work. She said Paul believed he saw something else lying on the wet asphalt as he left the parking lot, but he could not identify what it may have been.

Karla joined Kristen on the floor. Paul sat too. Encouraged by Paul, Kristen talked about herself: She was fifteen years old; she had several brothers and sisters; she had been a rower, but had quit because of back problems; she wanted to be a veterinarian or a lawyer; she had a boyfriend named Elton Wade; she had a dog; she was supposed to be a brides-maid in a summer wedding.

It wasn't long before Paul became bored with the talk and wanted the sex to begin, Karla said. She recalled that Paul told Kristen he expected her to do everything she was told to do, and if she did, Paul told her, she could go home. Kristen's clothes came off: the white turtleneck, the green plaid kilt, the green tights, the University of Georgetown Hoyas boxer shorts, the black bra, and the white underwear. She also wore a Mickey Mouse wristwatch and a gold chain with three charms on it. On one finger was a ring with the initial *E*, Elton's ring.

"I've never been a hundred percent positive of what exactly occurred [and] when [it occurred], but I believe on Thursday . . . Paul had vaginal intercourse with Kristen. He had her on her hands and knees with her back arched, having intercourse from behind. He told her to arch her back. If she didn't arch her back, he would punch it until it was arched. He had Kristen perform cunnilingus on me and me perform cunnilingus on Kristen. He told us both what to do." Most of the sex took place on the bed, but Karla can't remember what happened where.

It didn't take long for Kristen to catch on to what Karla said Paul's sexual fantasies were about.

"He told her what he wanted her to say, that she was a slut and a bitch and that she was his Holy Cross sex slave and that he was the king and the master and everything else like that. And she quickly learned what she had to do and she did it."

When Paul told her to drink, she drank, although she had a difficult time drinking his prescribed amounts of alcohol

Karla admitted. When Paul told her to treat him like "the king," she did.

Karla also unquestioningly did as Paul said, serving his drinks on a silver platter and joining in the sex with Kristen. "I knew from past experience that if I didn't do what he told me to do I would get beaten and have to do it anyway. It was not a case of saying 'no' and just taking the beating. It was a case of taking the beating and doing it anyway."

At one point Paul told Kristen he would give her an opportunity to escape, Karla said. She said he placed the knife on the floor between them and told her to grab it, stab him, and run away. Kristen refused.

Some of the sex was videotaped, some was not. Karla said she was not aware that Paul had videotaped Kristen urinating until police showed her the videotapes at the Prison for Women in February 1995.

One segment, presumably shot on Thursday afternoon in the upstairs washroom, lasts one minute. Kristen is seen sitting on the toilet wearing a white cloth blindfold.

Karla also testified she'd never seen the portion of videotape involving Paul and Kristen during the initial Thursday-night bedroom scene where Paul scripts Kristen on how to be a sex slave. The segment lasts almost seven minutes and is shot in the master bedroom. In the background, loud rap music by the rapper Ice-T is heard. Kristen French is heard crying. The white blindfold is still visible. Kristen is seated, in part, in front of the hope chest on the floor. There is a wine bottle and a silver serving tray seen nearby.

Bernardo: I want you to lean back, there's a chest there to lean on. I want you to pull down all your clothes, and your leotards, lift up your skirt and show me your cunt, okay.

Bernardo: Okay?

French: Is it okay?

Bernardo: Keep going, you're doing good.

Bernardo: I'm happy, that's what you want right?

French: Uhuh.

Bernardo: Tell me you want me to be happy.

French: I want you to be happy.

Bernardo: So maybe you can go home later.

French: Okay.

Bernardo: Yeah. You know what I want you to do, have a drink.

Bernardo: Now make me happy right, don't make me mad.

French: I won't.

Bernardo: Okay. Be good to me no matter what.

French: Sure.

Bernardo: Make me happy, do it nice, okay.

French: Watch the drink.

Karla testified that Paul told her later that night that he had raped Kristen while she was downstairs. Later, after Kristen was forced to do more sex acts at Paul's direction, Karla said she had obediently joined in. Kristen continued to follow Paul's scripting, at one point telling him she loved him nineteen times in a row while performing oral sex.

Late that Thursday night, Paul and Karla went to bed, but Karla said that just beforehand, Paul gave Kristen Halcion sleeping pills to make sure she didn't wake up in the middle of the night. Karla isn't sure whether Kristen slept on the bed with Paul or was kept in the closet all night. Karla believes she herself slept on the floor at the side of the bed, which by that time in their marriage was where she always slept.

On Good Friday, Paul and Karla awoke late. Karla said Kristen was allowed to watch updates on her kidnapping on the bedroom television. She was ordered by Paul to stay in the master bedroom. She could leave to go to the upstairs washroom, as long as either Paul or Karla accompanied her. Once, Paul took Kristen into the music room and played his rap tapes. Karla recalled that Kristen acted as if she was "totally bored with the whole thing. It was almost as if he was trying to impress her but she just didn't care."

The sex continued, Karla said. Kristen essentially did what she was told, but the first time Paul told Kristen to say she hated her boyfriend, Elton, she resisted Karla recalled.

"But he hit her and made her do it," Karla told the court.

Around suppertime, Paul told Karla to leave the master bedroom so he could be alone with Kristen and have sex with her. Karla said she went downstairs and cooked some chicken for the threesome to eat. Whenever she went downstairs she would check the messages on the answering machine to make sure they didn't miss any important calls and that nobody was inviting themselves for a quick visit.

Within a short time, Paul called Karla back upstairs. She took the cooked chicken with her, but Kristen did not want to eat. She said Paul asked his sex slave whether there was anything special she wanted and Kristen suggested she wouldn't mind a McDonald's pizza, because she had not tried it.

Before he left to get her some, Paul handcuffed Kristen and tied her feet together, Karla testified, either with a black electrical cord or a rope, and put her in the master-bedroom closet. He made sure Kristen was comfortable and left her lying with her head on a pillow, Karla told the court.

Paul went downstairs and came back with a rubber mallet that his grandfather, Gerald Eastman, had given him along with many other tools.

"He told me to stay in the room and to guard Kristen and if somebody came to the house and she started screaming that I should hit her with it," Karla continued.

While Paul purchased the fast food and rented some movies, Karla, the rubber mallet at her side, talked with Kristen. Although it did not come out at Paul's trial, Karla told police that the captive schoolgirl talked about Elton and how she really loved him. And, Karla would claim, Kristen asked Karla if Paul hit her all the time. When Karla told Kristen the beatings were constant, Kristen told Karla she knew the abduction and rapes were not her idea.

"Why do you stay?" Kristen asked.

"You don't understand," Karla said.

Karla thought about letting Kristen go, but she couldn't.

"First of all, I was scared, because I was so involved in it, and second of all, all I could picture was the two of us walking down the stairs and Paul coming in and freaking and killing."

Paul returned within a half hour with two McDonald's pizzas and two videos: *Angel Heart*, an odd film noir, and *Criminal Law*, about a serial killer named Martin Thiel IV, Paul's fictional namesake.

Paul untied Kristen in the closet and then everyone ate supper, Karla said.

On the bedroom television that night, Kristen watched her father, Doug, in an emotional television interview telling her "not to worry, that they would find her, and to be strong and something like that," Karla testified.

"She cried. She got really upset. And she said she was sure that somebody had seen what had happened and she was sure that the police were going to come and see her. Karla said Paul told her that if somebody had seen what had happened they would have been here a long time ago; he also decided she shouldn't watch the news anymore because he didn't want her getting upset."

The routine for Kristen became clear early in the teen's captivity, Karla said. If she was good and cooperated with Paul's demands, "Paul told her she could go home." If she didn't, she would be beaten.

Karla believes it was Saturday that Paul became angry at Kristen when she wouldn't open her mouth wide enough during fellatio; he kept telling her she wasn't performing properly, so he beat her on the back.

"He punched her really hard and I couldn't stand to look, so I looked away," Karla testified.

As he had the night before, Paul asked Kristen if there was anything special she would like for supper. She opted for chicken. After tying up Kristen and putting her in the same master-bedroom closet, Paul left in the car, Karla told the court.

"I was supposed to guard her again. I had the mallet again and I had the same instructions: If someone else came and she screamed, I was supposed to hit her."

From Videoflicks, Paul drove to the Swiss Chalet restaurant at 285 Geneva Street, only a few blocks from Kristen's house. He bought two half chickens with fries and an extra small fries with extra sauce. He handed over a $100 bill for the $18.06 food order. He also rented *Shattered*, a movie about a woman who kills in order to save her love affair, and picked up a Saturday *St. Catharines Standard* to read about the latest in the police investigation into Kristen's abduction.

While Paul was gone, Karla said, she again thought of freeing Kristen, but she was too afraid.

After supper, Karla and Kristen made a pornographic tape for Paul. Afterward, Kristen had a Jacuzzi bath in the upstairs washroom while Karla showered downstairs.

Karla said Paul's next fantasy was for the girls to dress in schoolgirl uniforms and put on perfumes. He decided there should be a contest of sorts; whoever put on the nicest perfume would not have to have anal sex with him. Karla passed over the perfume bottles to Kristen, and they each chose one.

"Paul judged us and he said that Kristen was the winner because she had the nicest perfume, but he said he owed his wife preferential treatment and that he would have anal sex with Kristen."

Karla and Kristen went into the master bedroom, Kristen wearing her green kilt and Karla wearing the schoolgirl outfit Paul had had her wear on numerous occasions in the past.

"He had us both kneel down on the floor on our hands and knees, side by side, and we arched our backs, and he had vaginal sex with her, and vaginal sex with me, and then he had anal intercourse with her. She found it painful. She cried and made it clear it was painful, but she tried to cooperate. . . . He ejaculated . . . and I could tell from his reaction that he was very happy," Karla testified.

Paul then told Karla and Kristen that he wanted them to do a "little porno movie" in which they had to "act like we were lesbians and we liked each other and we wanted to have sex with each other. We were told to touch each other and kiss each other," Karla said.

Paul, however, was not pleased with some of Karla's responses on the tape she told the court.

"Kristen said something to me, like 'Have you done this often?' Something like that, and I made the mistake of saying 'No.' Paul got very angry and he later hit me; he wanted me to say 'yes,' that I had done this before. I ruined another videotape . . . he told me I had ruined another videotape."

At one point Houlahan asked Karla if she ever derived any sexual pleasure from her encounters with Kristen. The former veterinary assistant screwed her face up in disgust and rubbed at her eyes.

"Never," she said emphatically. "Because I'm not a lesbian, don't like women, and don't enjoy having sex with people against their will.''

Although Kristen tried her best to please Paul, presumably in the belief that he would honor his word and let her go, Karla said the teen grew defiant late on Saturday evening.

"I believe I first noticed on Saturday night, later Saturday night, she was performing fellatio on him and he was getting really angry because she kept on dropping his penis. He was hitting her and hitting her and she wasn't crying. She gave this look, she just had this look on her face, like I'm totally sick of this whole thing and I'm not going to do it anymore,'' Karla said. ''He threatened to kill her. He said something like 'Three drops and you're out.' Before that she had tried everything that he told her to do.''

But Paul did find a reason to punch Kristen, not once, not twice, but several times, many of which are recorded on the tape. Kristen could not keep up with Paul's demands to both fellate him aggressively while at the same time speaking his ''you're the king'' and ''I'm the little cocksucker'' script. Midway through the clip Paul's face becomes contorted and he hits Kristen because she isn't talking enough.

"He said, 'Suck for your life, you bitch,' meaning that if she didn't perform that was going to be it, because she had been told if she did everything she had been told to do she would be allowed to go home.''

Paul threatened a number of times to kill Kristen. On the tape, when Paul's penis slips out of Kristen's mouth again and again, Paul comments ''Three drops and you're out.'' On another occasion when Kristen annoys him, Paul calls out, ''Give me the knife; I'll kill her now.''

Paul slaps Kristen in this segment, and Karla, who was operating the camera, explained to the court that she turned it off because she ''couldn't stand to watch what he was doing and I didn't want to record. He hit her some more and he told her, like, he was really mad at her.''

At one point, Paul took Kristen to the Jacuzzi and threatened to urinate and defecate on her because she'd called him a bastard during the kidnapping.

Paul's sadistic tendencies are obvious in this clip. First he tells Kristen to apologize, but no matter what she says, it's not enough. Throughout, he makes Kristen feel she is the one at fault.

Paul: "Why'd you call me a bastard?"

Kristen: "I was scared."

Paul: "So, why'd you do it?"

Kristen: "I don't know. I'm sorry."

Paul: "Who the fuck do you think you are?"

Kristen: "Pardon me?"

Paul: "Who the fuck do you think you are?"

Kristen: "I couldn't help myself."

Paul: "Yeah, but you did call me a bastard."

Kristen: "I'm sorry."

Paul: "All I did was tell you to turn and smile."

As the tape continues, Paul becomes annoyed because he cannot urinate on Kristen because of his erection. He blames her, of course. Then he has Kristen beg him to urinate and defecate on her. His orders appeared to confuse, humiliate, and break her down.

Although she wasn't in the washroom scene, Karla was reminded of her own experiences with Paul. Paul would sometimes ejaculate on Karla's face, she said. And at one point, after Kristen's murder, he demanded that Karla eat his feces.

"He was angry at me for something. I can't remember for what. We were upstairs. He told me that he wanted me to eat a piece of his feces and I resisted and he told me, basically, 'You're going to do it.' "

Karla said she knew she'd be beaten and would have to do Paul's bidding anyway. Paul defecated, alone, and brought Karla into the bathroom.

"So I asked him if it would be all right if I wrapped it up," she said, and he agreed. "So I did it and I swallowed it."

Throughout Karla's recounting of Kristen's ordeal, Doug and Donna French sat stoically in either the first or second row, as though determined to deny Paul and Karla any degree of satisfaction either might realize from having them break down. Doug's solid arm was often wrapped comfortingly around his wife's shoulder as she dabbed at her eyes with a tissue. Occasionally he would glance to his left at Paul, who sat disinterestedly in the prisoner's box. Their grief, as it had been throughout the case, was a private, fiercely protected one.

The three awoke midmorning on Easter Sunday. Karla said she knew Kristen would die that day.

"Paul and I had to go to my parents that evening for Easter dinner." Karla explained, as though it was the most natural thing in the world to execute a teenage sex toy in order to visit family for a holiday celebration.

At some point the couple had discussed just what they were going to do with Kristen, Karla went on. Paul wanted to keep her longer, but Karla said she discouraged him.

"I told him that we should go to my parents' house to establish an alibi. And he agreed," Karla said with apparent ease, acknowledging that if she wasn't the executioner then she had determined the time of death.

The three began drinking but as the morning wore on Kristen became more and more defiant Karla said. She recalled that Paul wanted her to perform fellatio on him, which she did, but Kristen refused to follow his scripting.

"She acted like she didn't care," Karla said. "She said that some things are worth dying for."

Paul's response to Kristen's defiant statement was "Oh yeah? You really think so?" Karla said. He then retrieved a videocassette, which he put into the camcorder, and played. A portion of the tape showed Leslie Mahaffy saying her name.

Paul asked Kristen if she knew who Leslie Mahaffy was. Kristen acknowledged that she did.

"She didn't get all scared or anything, but she started to cooperate more," Karla said.

Later, Kristen was tied at the ankles with a black electrical cord Paul brought from the basement, although Karla couldn't remember what time he brought it up.

Kristen's hands were cuffed behind her back and she was placed on her knees in front of the hope chest in the master bedroom, she said. Paul got a wine bottle out, "and he told me to put it in her vagina and he said something like, 'Ram it really hard, she called me a bastard,' " Karla recalled for a sickened audience.

"I put it in her vagina. I moved it in and out but I didn't ram it like he told me to. He took over and did it himself."

After violating Kristen with the wine bottle, Paul had vaginal and anal intercourse with her while she remained in the same position, Karla recalled. That session was the final videotape of Kristen. At the beginning of the tape, Kristen smiles and waves at the camera. There is a mark on Kristen's left ankle and her right wrist, presumably from the handcuffs and cord that restrained her throughout her captivity.

Kristen is being punished with sexual pain for calling Paul a "bastard" and an "asshole." He makes her apologize over and over again before combining his sexual punishment with the schoolgirl fantasy and his "I am the king" routine.

Paul: "Who am I?"

Kristen: "My master, you're my master and I'm very sorry. I didn't mean to call you the things I did. I had no right and I should be punished for doing that."

Paul: "Who wants me?"

Kristen: "Pardon me?"

Paul: "Who wants me?"

Kristen: "Oh, all the girls at Holy Cross want you."

Paul: "Would you like me to fuck you . . . at your school?

Kristen: "Yes, I'd like you to fuck every girl in my school you think is pretty. As long as it makes you feel good. I'm really sorry. I know I shouldn't have done it. And I'm glad you're punishing me for it. 'Cause I had no right to do it, right? I'm really sorry, master. You deserve a lot better than me. You deserve all the girls at my school. All of them. Owwww."

Kristen cries out in pain at Paul's sudden penetration. Then she continues the dialogue she's been told to repeat over and over again: "All the girls at my school want to fuck you 'cause you're the most powerful man in the world. And you're the most sexiest man in the world. And they'd never say anything to bother you. 'Cause they're not bitches like I am. I'm glad you're punishing me for what I did. I am really sorry, master. But it's good that you're getting me back. If you went to my school all the girls would line up to have you.

Paul interjects with a gruff ''Fucking bitch.''

Kristen continues: You're so much in control of everything, and that's good. Nobody can overpower you, nobody. I'm really sorry for what I said. I shouldn't of said it . . . 'cause you're the king. You're the master.''

Finally, Paul has an orgasm.

Paul then shuts the camera down. Karla said she announced she was going to go downstairs and take a shower. About twenty minutes later she returned to the master bedroom. She can't recall whether Kristen had been untied, but within an hour the schoolgirl was back in her previous position, bound at the feet, her hands cuffed behind her back, kneeling in front of the hope chest.

This time Paul placed a black electrical cord around Kristen's neck. He raped her vaginally and anally. As he knelt behind Kristen, he started talking about dying.

''She started talking to him and she was really calm . . . just talking. And he just cut her off in the middle of a word,'' Karla recalled for a stunned court. The cord was looped around both of his hands, ''and he just pulled it tight and just cut her right off in the middle of what she was saying. He held it really tight.''

Karla was standing sort of behind the two, watching as Paul squeezed Kristen's breath from her body. She said he calmly turned to her and said he had to hold the cord tight for seven minutes so she wouldn't revive as Leslie had.

''And he looked at the digital clock and counted off the time,'' Karla said.

As he strangled Kristen French to death, she also said Paul turned to his wife and told her it wouldn't hurt; that he had once been strangled during karate, and that it had engendered a euphoric feeling.

''I was standing behind them. And I looked at him. I couldn't believe that it was happening. It sounds really stupid. I was standing there and I couldn't believe it. I felt absolutely terrible. It's so difficult to put feelings into words because it totally trivializes it,'' Karla explained, her quiet monotone giving an eerie quality to her testimony.

After seven minutes had passed, Paul loosened the ligature, untied Kristen, and removed the handcuffs, placing her limp body on her side in the fetal position on the floor of the master bedroom, Karla recalled.

Both Karla and Paul went downstairs, leaving the corpse, she said. Paul went to have a shower while Karla blow-dried her hair.

The couple then drove across the city to have Easter dinner with Karla's parents.

As they drove, Paul was extremely happy. He turned to Karla and told her she was the best wife, ''that he was very happy,'' Karla said.

After spending the balance of the day chatting and eating at 61 Dundonald, the couple returned to 57 Bayview Drive around 9 P.M.

''I didn't want to go. I wanted to stay there as long as we possibly could. I didn't want to go back to the house,'' Karla recalled. But Paul insisted they leave, and finally they did.

Once home Karla said, Paul declared that he wanted to dispose of the body as soon as possible but that he didn't want to be caught driving around in the middle of the night. Rigor mortis had begun to set in on Kristen's body. Paul joked that it was a good thing he'd put her on her side or else they'd have never been able to get her body in the hatchback of the Nissan, Karla told court.

He then instructed Karla to cut Kristen's long, dark hair, because he didn't want it to pick up carpet fibers. Using a pair of gray-handled scissors, Karla clipped the hair where the body lay in front of the hope chest. They then disrobed the body and put it in the Jacuzzi, where Paul told Karla to wash it to remove fingerprints, seminal fluid, and fiber traces. They both wore gloves when handling the body.

Karla used a douche to remove any fluids from Kristen's vagina and anus. She had bought the douche prior to the kidnapping.

''He said it was the least that I could do since he was the one who'd actually killed her,'' Karla said.

Karla testified that Kristen's necklace and ring were burned in the fireplace, as was her clothing, including the victim's fashionable black leather and suede jacket. Paul took the band of the Mickey Mouse watch and burned it. He then smashed the face and threw the bits out along Seventh Street Lough in St. Catharines.

About 10 P.M. that night, they left the house with the body in the back of the Nissan and drove straight to Burlington.

"He told me that he decided that he wanted to put the body in Burlington close to where Leslie was buried because he wanted to confuse the police into believing the killer came from Burlington," Karla explained.

They drove to a desolate area with brush to the side, Karla said. She had never been there before. She explained how they pulled off to the right side of the road and together carried the body off into the brush a short distance before letting the body roll out onto the ground. They kept the blanket. Karla ran back to the car while Paul lingered. He covered the body with a few branches, an act that had been a last-minute thought, Karla testified he told her.

Paul told Karla he wanted police to find the body right away, but in the days that followed there were no news reports. "He kept saying, 'What's going on? Why haven't they found it?'" Karla said.

After disposing of Kristen's body, Paul felt nothing could touch him, that he was totally invincible. Karla said she felt even more numbed: "Very, very guilty and ashamed, and I just wanted to die."

"We had a lot of sleeping pills in the house, and at one point I told Paul I couldn't live like this and I wanted to take some of those pills and he stopped me and later took those pills someplace else."

She thought often about killing herself, she said.

"I hated myself and I hated Paul."

Karla came home from work on Tuesday, May 12, 1992, to find Paul in an ecstatic mood. Paul excitedly told her how two Niagara police officers had come to the house and had asked what he had been doing April 16, 1992, the day Kristen was abducted. "He said he was upstairs, sleeping, and he heard a knock at the door and looked out the window to see two men standing there," Karla told the court, her narration building to the moment when she would leave her husband. "Right away, he knew they were police officers and he knew why they were there—to question him about Kristen. He thought about it: Should he go answer the door or not," Karla recounted. "He decided to go talk to them, because if he didn't they would come back and it would give him time to think about it and get nervous. He went downstairs and opened the front door just as the officers were leaving. He called out, 'Hi, guys! Can I help you?' They came back to the door and he invited them in. They asked him questions."

Paul told Karla that as soon as the officers walked through the door and into the spacious living room, their eyes focused on the handsome, framed wedding picture above the fireplace. Paul believed the photographs threw the officers off the scent: They simply couldn't believe a nice, young married couple could be involved in something so heinous.

"He said that he got through the interview like he was cool as a cucumber and it went off really well and he felt very proud of himself," Karla testified.

Paul related a series of strategies he'd recalled to avoid looking nervous during the brief police visit: He always looked them in the eyes; he put his fingers together so they wouldn't shake; he didn't swing his legs. All these gestures helped him appear confident.

A short time after the police visit, Karla said Paul talked with her about kidnapping and raping another girl.

"Aren't you afraid to get caught?" Karla asked.

She said his response was, "Don't you realize? I'll never get caught!"

On Thursday, June 18, 1992, Karla and Paul were shopping and smuggling in Niagara Falls, New York. During an angry fit, Karla said Paul punched her on the top of the head and cracked the stone insert in his Masonic Lodge ring.

"We had an argument about something and he was really angry at me and told me not to speak to him until he told me

I could. I did what I was told and didn't talk to him and tried to avoid him, and this went on for four days.''

For those nights, Karla gave up her place on the mattress beside her husband's bed and slept in the guest bedroom. She didn't even write him any adoring pillow notes.

''I was very pleased to do that, I didn't want to talk to him or give him pillow notes or have anything to do with it.''

But on the fourth day of silence, Karla became afraid their estrangement would go on and on and Paul would become more and more angry because she hadn't talked with him. She wrote him a note asking: ''Can't we make up?'' The note was left on Paul's bed. She was asleep when Paul burst into the guest room.

''He was really angry with me. He had a note he had written and threw it at me. It said he would never be there for me, that he was never going to support me, and that I was there for cover and cover alone. Then he took the note from me, saying it was silly he gave me the note, and said he would never let me use that against him,'' Karla said.

After reading newspaper accounts of the exhumation of Leslie's body by detectives on the Kristen French murder task force the same day as the ring incident, Paul forbade Karla to speak about either Kristen or Leslie unless Paul brought it up or unless it was when Karla pretended to be either Leslie or Kristen in one of their sex fantasies. Obviously, Paul thought, police would compare forensic findings from the bodies of both dead girls. The following Saturday or Sunday, Paul ranted and raged at Karla because she hadn't talked to him and hadn't left him pillow notes, she said.

Sunday, the day Paul and Karla normally drove across St. Catharines for supper at the Homolka house, Karla awoke in the morning and gingerly asked Paul if he would be joining her.

''What do you think?'' he replied.

''I figured because we had been arguing and he hated me so much, that meant he wasn't coming. I made the mistake of phoning my father and saying Paul was either sick or tired and would he come and pick me up,'' Karla said.

As soon as Karla hung up the telephone, she remembered, Paul called out, asking her to go upstairs and cut his hair.

"My dad's on his way over and he'll be over here in a few minutes," she told him.

She said his voice was incredulous: "You called your dad?"

"Yes."

Before she knew what happened, Karla said. Paul bounded downstairs and kicked and punched her, holding her up against the wall. She screamed in fear.

"I cannot believe you called your father," he bellowed.

She said Paul then ran upstairs to the master bedroom and returned to the top of the stairs with armfuls of her clothes. He began throwing them down the stairs.

"When your father gets here, tell him to take you away and don't ever come back," he screamed. Then he ran downstairs and laid a beating on her again, she told the court.

"I heard my dad come to the front door. I was thrilled, because this was my opportunity to leave. I had wanted to leave for so long, but he wouldn't let me go. I was crying because I was hurt, but I was also crying because I wanted to leave; I was crying because I was happy," Karla explained, though the words seemed to ring false.

On the telephone, Karla had told her father not to knock on the front door because it would wake up her sleeping husband. As Paul ranted on, walking up the stairs, Karel Homolka knocked on the rear door. Karla was crying when she opened the door. She told her inquiring father that she was leaving Paul. He took her back to 61 Dundonald Street, where Dorothy Homolka seemed pleased that her daughter was coming home.

"I decided that I would get my clothes that day. My mom and dad drove me back to pick them up. We went to the front door and it was chain-locked; we went to the back door and it was chain-locked; then we went back into the van and called Paul on my dad's cell phone. The answering machine was on. Next thing I knew the door opened. My mom was with me. We went into the house, went upstairs, and started to bring my clothes down. My dad was waiting in the van."

Paul was seated on the master-bedroom floor, liquor bottles scattered around him. He seemed drunk to Karla. Normally, alcohol had such little effect on him. As Paul drank more, Karla and her mother walked upstairs and brought down more clothes, Karla said. Karla was at the bottom of the stairs with the final load when Paul called down, "Kar, I want to talk to you."

"I didn't want to go upstairs, but I did," she said. "He and I were upstairs in the master bedroom and my mom was downstairs. He was nice to me at first; I felt like we were having a real conversation for once."

Karla said Paul's tone suddenly changed when he threatened her. "Do you know what I could do to you right now? Do you know where your parents are right now? I could wreck your life right now. I could show them the tape and show them what you did to your sister!" he hissed.

And with that, Karla told him she would stay. She went downstairs, told her mother they had made up, grabbed her clothes, and took them back upstairs.

Perhaps uneasy about the whirlwind break up and reconciliation, Karel and Dorothy remained for dinner and Karla said she begged Lori to drop in as well. But despite pouring drinks into Paul all night, the rage building in him revealed itself moments after her family left 57 Bayview, she said.

"Paul burst in and started punching me in the head and back and shoulders and stomach and anywhere else he could get me, saying "I can't believe you. You actually tried to leave me.' And he was screaming and I was screaming and he went to the dresser and picked up a book and threw it at me and it hit me on the face."

When Paul's fists landed in her body she heard cracking noises. There were bruises all over her body and a hard, red lump under her eye.

Paul and Karla were among the estimated one million people who watched the televised special *The Abduction of Kristen French* the night of Tuesday, July 21, 1992. Included in the show was a reenactment of what police believe were Kristen's last steps and an FBI profile compiled by agent Gregg Mc-

Crary. On the program, police revealed for the first time that witnesses saw two men at the abduction scene. Karla told the court that after watching the show, Paul jumped up and replayed a videotape recording he had made. He chuckled throughout the program, pointing out error after error.

"He said they've got the wrong car; they've got it wrong, saying it was two men; they've got parts of the FBI profile wrong; he said specifically that the dominant male worked with his hands, he said, 'Wrong, I don't work with my hands,' he said, 'Wrong,' 'Wrong', 'Wrong' to everything. He was very happy." Karla recalled.

The same month, Paul decided he and Karla would spend twelve days on a Florida trip. Paul resumed beating Karla on the way to Florida, she said, hitting her with his fists and with the plastic flashlight. Once in Florida, they spent time in Daytona Beach and in Orlando. Among their many cigarette money–financed purchases was a stun gun that carried an electrical force that could incapacitate a person's muscles for twenty minutes. She said Paul told her he wanted the gun to use on future rape victims; instead of using physical force to subdue them, he would zap them with the 80,000-volt stun gun. The self-defense gadget is considered a weapon in Canada and it is illegal to sell or possess it.

While at Fantasy Island amusement park, Paul took a liking to a female employee with long hair and fantasized about raping and killing her Karla testified. He found out her name, and one day he followed her home from work.

Karla said Paul told her the girl would be an easy target if they could get her to stop on the isolated stretch of road she traveled between work and home, and then he thought up a plan. He would travel ahead of the girl and feign a breakdown with the Nissan 240SX. Karla would stand at the side of the road and flag down the approaching young woman. Using one scheme or another, they would get the girl into the Nissan; if they couldn't get her into the Nissan by trickery, they would force her in at knifepoint.

For one reason or another, Paul didn't carry out the plan.

In one videotape clip taken in Florida, Karla comes out of the hotel-room washroom area wearing only a white bra and panties. She removes the bra, showing tan lines around her breasts, then she removes her undergarments. Paul asks her what she likes doing best. "Showing off," she says. Then she says she likes "pleasing her man" and licking little girls. She proceeds to touch and fondle her genitals while doing a gyrating stripper-style dance. She smiles constantly throughout the entire performance.

While driving back to Canada, Paul stopped the car to purchase gas. They used the gas-station bathrooms. The women's unit was occupied and the men's unit was empty. Paul motioned Karla into the men's bathroom, but then left to pay the attendant or buy something. She tried to lock the door, but the lock was broken. While Karla washed her hands a man unwittingly opened the door. Paul saw the entire episode as he paid for the gas. When Karla returned to the car, she said he was angry. As he drove off, he told Karla she had earned punishment points.

"He started saying things like I was a 'tease' and a 'show-off' and I 'didn't lock the door on purpose' and I 'wanted the guy to walk in on me.' He got the flashlight, beat me over the head with it, and grabbed my hair. He grabbed my head, smashed it against the window, the door, the center console, pulling hair out of my head and hitting me the whole time. Finally, he stopped. . . . My head was pounding and very sore."

As they drove on Paul told Karla it was all her fault, but he also told her how she could make it up.

"He said the only way he would ever love me again would be if we went to Atlantic City and hired a prostitute and I did stuff with her—things of a sexual nature. I said 'Okay,' 'cause I wanted him to stop hitting me."

Karla reminded Paul that she had to be at work the next day, Monday August 17, 1992, and that they should keep driving until they reached St. Catharines. But Karla said Paul made up a story that Karla could use as an excuse for being late. Karla would claim they were driving through terrible weather when a car hit the wheelwell of the Nissan and caused driving problems. She called the animal clinic from Atlantic City and left a message for her boss that she would be a day or two late.

In Atlantic City, they booked a room at the Trump Plaza Hotel, Paul's choice. Before they went out for dinner and their search for a hooker, Karla said Paul decided he would secretly videotape the night's expected sex. He set the video camera in his suitcase, stood it in a corner of the room, and put a dress shirt over the top to camouflage it. She revealed that he planned to start the camera with a remote control once he had brought the prostitute back to the room. The viewfinder showed the entire length and breadth of the king-size bed. After having dinner in a French restaurant, Paul drove around the seaboard gambling city's seedy streets looking for a hooker Karla said, but when Paul asked her to pick her prostitute, and she did, it didn't work out. Paul picked the second prostitute, a small-framed blonde named Michelle Banks, who used the street pseudonym of Shelly, Karla said. Shelly said she didn't usually perform with couples because the only time she tried to do it her clients became embroiled in a big argument.

Aided by Karla, Paul persuaded Banks to get in the car. Back at the hotel, Paul and Shelly struck up the deal: $300 for an hour of three-way sex with no oral-vaginal contacts and no kissing. The three had sex. Karla recalled that the prostitute pointed out the many bruises on her body and remarked with surprise that she had more bruises than herself, "a working girl." According to Karla the sex lasted about forty-five minutes, with Paul having erection problems, not only because, in his words, he was used to "more submissive" women, but also because the condoms kept falling off his penis.

At the end of the video clip which was shown in court, Banks becomes frustrated with the arrangement and pulls away from the couple. What is not shown on video is Karla's claim that as Banks went to the washroom before leaving, Paul followed and watched her urinate.

Karla returned home to find that the clinic's answering machine had malfunctioned, so she had to offer Paul's bad weather and traffic story. She lost two days of pay.

Throughout the summer, Karla hid her body bruises from friends and relatives. Whenever she and Paul would go to her parents' house, which was most Sundays, she would wear clothing to hide the bruises. Facial bruises were covered with makeup. She attributed a black eye from one beating to either Buddy's boisterousness or a run-in with one of the animals at work—the usual excuse for her plethora of bruises.

Karla said Paul seemed to enjoy making his wife perform stripteases like the Florida hotel-room performance. Karla often performed similar acts for Paul outside 57 Bayview Drive. She told the court that Paul ordered her on a regular basis to dance naked in the backyard outside the house late at night while he watched from the window and masturbated. When the late-night stripping moved to the front yard, she said it became a tricky proposition because she had to both strip and make sure nobody saw her. Each time she would dance for five minutes. The lawn dancing lasted through the summer and into the chill of fall.

On one smuggling trip, Paul had parked the Nissan 240SX in a Topps store parking lot on Niagara Falls Boulevard in Niagara Falls, New York, so he could break down the cigarette cases and store them in the Nissan's side panels, Karla said. As Paul replaced the passenger-door panel by turning a screw with a screwdriver, Karla recalled that he became very angry and hit Karla in the leg. She said he had somehow forgotten that he had a screwdriver in his hand.

The screwdriver had gone clean through Karla's denim jeans and deep into her thigh.

She said Paul told her not to move her leg.

There was blood, and Karla could feel pain. By the time she got home she could hardly walk. As usual, Karla didn't seek medical attention. She felt she didn't need it because she had already received her tetanus shot for her work duties.

Karla testified that throughout the fall, the abuse got worse. She recalled that one of Paul's favorite scare tactics was to pull kitchen knives from the wooden block on the kitchen counter and throw them at Karla. He threw one knife at her head, another at her torso, she said. When one knife hit the door and left a mark, Karla said Paul became angry and said she had made him mark the door. He threw the knives at her feet, held them at her throat, said he was going to kill her if she didn't do what he wanted.

She also told the court that late one fall night in the living room after drinking heavily, Paul fondled his hunting knife, looked at Karla, and asked her if she wanted to die. His voice was odd, quiet, different, Karla said.

Paul demanded she drink a shot glass of vodka or he would kill her, Karla testified.

She also said that in order to torment her, Paul would sometimes flick off the basement light and hold the door shut on her when she went down to do the laundry.

"He would shut the light off and hold the door shut and tell me that Leslie was going to come and get me. It usually lasted about five or ten minutes. I would try to open the door and he would be laughing and telling me that she was going to come and get me and she was down there and things like that."

On another occasion, Karla said her husband forced her to sleep in the root cellar where Leslie's body had lain before it had been dismembered.

"He was angry at me for something, so he brought me downstairs and made me sleep in the root cellar, right beside where Leslie's body was kept."

The 80,000 volt stun gun was never used on a sex victim, Karla said, but one evening around Christmas, 1992, Paul told her he would zap her with the gun. She recalled how he pressed the button to form an electric current between the two probes and then chased her around the house with an evil laugh.

When she ran, screaming, from the back door to escape Paul, she said he locked the door. She stood, shivering, in only her track pants and a T-shirt and socks. She cleared a little spot on the edge of the deck so she could sit in the snow. She said Paul threw her a sweatshirt and a pair of socks before letting her in some time later.

She testified that even the most banal events, like trips to the store, became marathon terror sessions for Karla. Whenever she did something that went against what Paul wanted or liked, Paul would tally the transgressions for future punishment, she explained.

"Instead of punishing me right there, he would say, well, that will cost you five, or that will cost you ten, or whatever. That would mean five hits with the flashlight or five punches or slaps or whatever. This would happen all the time we were out in public. He would actually do it when we got back to the car. When he said these things to me, I would get really nervous, because I knew what would be coming, and I continued to make these mistakes. He would say, 'That just earned you five,' or 'ten,' and he was laughing. But it wasn't funny."

Paul was out driving one day when he saw Tammy's best friend, Becky. Karla recalled his commenting on how Becky had "really grown up" and that he wanted to have sex with her. A relative of Becky's worked at the animal clinic and Paul encouraged Karla to call Becky and invite her over. She did. After a few visits to 57 Bayview Drive, Karla said she was instructed to explain the same scenario she had with Jane, that Paul and she weren't really lovers anymore and that Becky could be with Paul if she wanted.

Karla told Becky that she and Paul were still good friends, so it would be okay to kiss Paul in her presence; she would simply look the other way. Becky was only seventeen years old.

"So Paul, he wined and dined her. Bought her all kinds of things, gave her money, took the both of us to Toronto, to the CN Tower, for dinner, and we stayed at the Royal York [Hotel]. And the whole time I tried to do my job and let her know that she should have a relationship with him." Karla told the jury.

Paul chose the exclusive and historic Royal York Hotel because he wanted to impress Becky, Karla said, explaining that the night they stayed there, Paul began working on the seventeen-year-old the way he knew best.

"I was pretending to be sleeping. There were two beds and I was in one with Paul. We were not sleeping at this point—I was sleeping in bed tenuously. She was in the other bed. She didn't want to sleep with him. He complained all night, 'Becky doesn't love me. Why doesn't Becky sleep with me,' but she didn't—she didn't want to. I couldn't sleep all night for the two of them laughing and giggling. I heard a fire alarm. They came back. I pretended I had woken up. They told me they had set a little fire in a meal cart or something. It was just a prank. I believe Becky told me security had seen them and obviously knew what they looked like. Paul told me what to say to them, answer the door, and again, be his cover; act like I didn't know anything, that nobody left the room that night, and pretended we'd been sleeping and that's it. I did exactly what I was told to do. I gave my story and they left."

Karla said that at the same time that Paul trained his sights on Becky, Jane reappeared on the scene. She began talking about a boy she liked at high school, which drove Paul crazy since he wanted the teen for himself.

Jane and Becky had never met, but Karla said that in his attempts to win the love of both, Paul would try to play each off against the other. Karla would tell Jane that Becky had been over the weekend before and it had been a great time.

"He wanted to make them jealous, but it didn't seem to work." she testified. The entire scenario frustrated Paul, she said, because he was used to getting his way.

"He was acting like I'd never seen him before," Karla said, not like the confident guy who had it all. "He was acting desperate."

An anguished Paul would analyze everything that happened with Jane and Becky, Karla said, trying to figure out ways to get them to fall for him. He questioned Karla about how they should be proceeding, blaming her for his scheme's failure.

"I was blamed for it all. I was desperate to make her like him. Finally it ended and I left him shortly after that point."

At Christmas, he showered both girls with gifts, she said.

"He went out and bought them all kinds of gifts. This was normal: Both got stuffed animals. Gund; they each got a watch; each got a necklace; Becky got another stuffed animal, a poster, a gold ankle bracelet, a shirt. I cannot remember what else Jane received, but they both received a lot of expensive gifts. That was his way; he did the same thing to me. He thought he could buy people. He wanted to impress them.

They were young girls, and this was a great way to impress them.''

"But it didn't work," Karla said. "And he got angry about that too.''

Just before Christmas, Becky came over one night. Karla said she knew Paul was upset with his failed plan. Becky and Karla were upstairs in the master bedroom, talking. Becky saw the foam mattress on the floor by the bed and asked why it was there. Karla told Becky that she and Paul were just friends, not husband and wife. Karla said Becky then began crying. "It's not supposed to be this way.''

"It is this way," replied Karla.

Then she told Becky again that it would be okay if she wanted to date Paul. And again, Becky said she didn't want it. Karla went downstairs and told Paul it was over, that Becky wasn't interested in him at all. Karla said Paul went upstairs and a short while later he came down.

"I don't know what you were talking about, but things are fine," said Paul.

Becky came down shortly after. The three went out for dinner that night. Karla recalled that hardly anybody talked, and that Paul took Becky home that night. Later, she said he told her that he and Becky had had sex and that Becky had wanted it, even though she was teasing him and saying 'No, no, no.'

On Sunday, December 27, 1992, Paul had to deliver a load of cigarettes to smuggling partner Johnny, who had recently opened a restaurant north of Toronto. Johnny invited Karla and Paul for a drink. Karla tried to get out of the trip, because she said she knew that being in the car with Paul meant being hit with the flashlight. But there was no way out. Paul said it would be impolite for them not to go. Karla was off work for a week and had no handy excuse. About thirty minutes into the ninety-minute trip, Karla said, Paul hit her a few times with the flashlight, on the head, on the shoulder. They finally arrived at Johnny's, dropped off the cigarettes, and went to the bar for drinks. On the way home, Karla fell asleep in the car.

She woke up to find Paul driving through a residential area. "Where are we?" she asked Paul.

"In Mississauga, following a girl," she said he replied.

"Oh, okay," said Karla before falling back to sleep.

Karla recalled that Paul then parked the car and told her he was going to watch the girl undress.

"He came back and told me he had masturbated. The words he normally used were "jerk off,' but he may have said 'got off.' I was always unsure of what to do, because he told me beforehand that he always wanted me to hug him, to express affection to him. He told me not to hug him after he had already masturbated. But [this time] he got angry and said, 'Why aren't you hugging me?' So he picked up the flashlight, hit me on my head, my back, my shoulder, and continued to beat me over and over again. He was driving down the QEW (Queen Elizabeth Way) and doing this at the same time."

When they arrived home, Karla was dazed and in agony. Her head began to swell. She took the dog out and heated up pizza for Paul. She said he demanded she sit at the table and eat with him. At first Paul was nice, but then he said, "Why am I being nice to you?" When she went to bed, Karla took some pain medication. She needed as much sleep as she could get because she had to get up early the next day, not to go to work, because she was on vacation for Christmas week, but to take the garbage out. As she took the painkillers she looked at herself in the mirror. The left side of her head was swollen and was starting to turn black and blue; one eye was swelling shut.

Upon waking the next morning, Monday, she looked in the mirror again to see that the swelling and bruising had spread to the middle of her face.

Karla remembered Paul's response when he awoke: "Holy shit, you look like shit."

She said he then decided not to hit Karla in the head for a while because he didn't want anybody to see the results of his beating. But that didn't stop him from hitting Karla in other areas, she added. He still beat her throughout the day, targeting her back and shoulders. He jumped on her feet she admitted.

By Tuesday, the bruising had spread across her face. Her entire head was swollen. One eye was completely closed.

"I looked like I was deformed or something," Karla told the court.

Later that week, Becky and her friend Joe came over. Becky had called Karla after an argument with her mother, Karla said.

"Paul said, 'Get her over here, get her over here.' He wanted her to move in with us."

Karla called Becky back with the invitation, but Becky told her the matter had been settled. Karla said Paul told her to get Becky over anyway; the girl came, but she brought her friend Joe. Karla gave Becky and Joe the same excuse she would later give her colleagues at work to explain the massive bruising and swelling: She said she had been in a car accident.

"She was very cold when she came over. Her and I spent time talking. It was mostly Paul and Joe in the dining room drinking; we were all together for long periods. Paul was talking to Becky and she was being really cold and quiet. He got a piece of paper and started writing love notes," Karla said.

"I love u forever, Becky. Love Paul."

"Whatever, love, Becky," she replied on paper.

"I took a major chance on you!! You maybe took it for granted. I don't know but I do know that I'll love you until I die . . . tomorrow," Paul threatened.

"What do you mean tomorrow? I don't think so babe. You ain't never gonna die. At least I hope not. You'll probably outlive me, man. Becky."

"Becky, I fuckin' love you, why do you constantly hurt me? I'll fuckin' die for you. You don't understand, you are my fuckin' world babes, you are you fuckin' are . . . forever . . . I wanna die, Paul death. Paul death . . . ahhrg."

"At some point he was upset and angry and went upstairs," Karla recalled. "Becky and I were both up there. He took off his wedding ring and Masonic ring and said he was going to throw them out the window. Becky said don't do that. He said he didn't want them anymore. Becky picked them up and put them on the chain around her neck.''

Becky became angry at Paul's antics, Karla said, and left the house. Paul went out to find her, but couldn't. Karla recalled that she returned on her own, and when Joe's father came to pick him up, Becky left with him. Karla knew that Paul called Becky on the telephone again and again that night, "saying all kinds of stuff, saying he loved her," but she hung up many times and he finally got the message.

"In the morning we drove to Becky's house to get his rings. He told me to knock on her door to get them from her. I had to tell her she wasn't making Paul happy, so she wasn't making me happy, so we couldn't be friends anymore."

On New Year's Eve, 1992, Paul, Gus, and Arif were to go to the Pleasure Dome. Expecting the guys from Toronto to arrive at any minute, Paul told Karla to hide in the closet until they left because he didn't want them to see her bruises. She did.

Karla spent New Year's Eve and most of New Year's Day by herself. She was sleeping on the bed when Paul returned in the early afternoon, announcing that he was going on a ski trip in Quebec with Gus and the others for a couple of days.

"That's great," she said.

"You know, Kar, things have been really rough the last little while, but when I come back things will be better," she remembers Paul telling her.

Before he left he gave her a hug.

"I was incredibly stupid and I half believed him, because I wanted to believe him so badly."

Paul returned the night of Sunday, January 3, 1993, at around 10 or 11 P.M. just as Johnny phoned them. Karla told Johnny that Paul had just arrived and would return his call. When Paul came to the door, Karla recalled hugging him and telling him Johnny had just called and that she had told him Paul had just arrived. She said an angry look crossed Paul's face when he asked, "Why did you tell him that?"

"Because you just pulled up—"

The words were barely out of her mouth when Paul

punched her under the right eye, she said. It took her a while to regain her composure.

"Things are never going to change, are they?" she said.

"No. Things are never going to change because you're never going to change," he barked.

On Monday, January 4, 1993, Karla was supposed to go to work but was still severely bruised. She said Paul didn't want anyone to see her bruised, but since she had already taken a week off from work she went back, telling coworkers the fictitious story of a car accident.

That morning, staff members saw she was in a lot of pain and had a hard time picking up animals and restraining them. While everyone at work was out for lunch, Karla looked up the telephone number for the battered women's shelter in St. Catharines. She called but was incapable of speaking.

"I couldn't say anything, so I hung up. I didn't know what to say and couldn't say the words, so I hung up. I was too scared."

After work, Paul drove by to pick her up. They had to smuggle that day. She said he became angry because she hadn't covered up the bruises well enough. She recalled that on the way across the border he hit her more with the flashlight, this time on the thighs. She said he hit her more on the way back, and that she knew Paul was growing more and more angry, hitting her for any reason.

"I didn't talk enough, or I talked too much, whatever. Whatever reason came into his head, he would use it."

Upon their return to 57 Bayview Drive, Lori called Karla on the phone. They talked for a short time.

Karla testified that that night, Paul told Karla that at some point before 12:30 A.M. she should expect anal sex and she should be ready for it. Karla went to the guest room, where she had slept since Paul's return from Montreal. It was 12:45 A.M. and she said she was reading, when Paul came in the door.

"He gave me one of my black dresses, a short tight black dress, and told me to put it on, and I did. He came back and he had handcuffs and the black electrical cord, the same cord that he used to strangle Kristen and Leslie with. . . . He had a chisel as well. He told me to get on my hands and knees. He tied my feet together with a cord; he handcuffed my hands behind my back and gagged me with something; he put one of the cords around my neck and told me to put my face in the pillow," Karla said. "He looped the cord around my neck and told me to arch my back, and if I screamed or resisted he would kill me. I didn't resist, I didn't scream; I arched my back like I was told, I couldn't breathe because I had my face in the pillow. . . . I could see the chisel beside me."

She said Paul then had pulled the black electrical cord tight around her neck. She could feel it. She could barely breathe, because she was gagged and her face was stuffed into the pillow. She recalled that he finally let her move her head to one side and that, finally, he ejaculated in her anus. When he untied her and released the handcuffs, Karla said he told his wife she should be thankful he was so nice to her.

"So I said, 'Thank you for being so nice to me, sir; thank you for treating me so well, sir.' And he left."

On Tuesday, January 5, 1993, Karla went to work again. It was lunchtime and she was getting ready to go to the store when, suddenly, her mother appeared. Karla knew her mother was shocked by her daughter's appearance. They talked over lunch. Karla told her mother she would call that night after Paul left.

Paul picked Karla up from work again for another smuggling run. Again he was angry that Karla's bruises were visible, and again he punished her for this transgression by hitting her on the thighs with the flashlight. She cried as they approached the border crossing at the bridge into New York.

"Stop crying and clean yourself up," Karla said Paul ordered after his assault on her had ended.

After buying the cigarettes, Paul hid them in the car. Then he drove to a drugstore and bought a few groceries as a cover for the smuggling trip.

"He didn't want me in the store ruining his image. He didn't want his bruised wife accompanying him," Karla testified.

Paul returned from the store with fifteen to twenty jugs of spring water.

Karla remembered that on the trip home, Paul hit her thighs some more with the flashlight. He even told Karla to take off her coat because he didn't want her to have any padding on her legs to soften the blows, she said. She took off the coat and testified that he pounded her on the legs. At 57 Bayview Drive, Paul ordered her to carry the water to the basement root cellar and store it where Leslie's body had once been kept Karla said. After packing the cigarettes, Paul left, but not before he told Karla exactly how to clean the house.

"I called my family. I spoke to my mother and father and sister Lori. They came over. While I was waiting I started doing what was on the list. I was washing dishes, trying to complete my chores for the evening."

Even after her family arrived, Karla decided she would stay with Paul. She was too scared to do otherwise.

"For most of the conversation my intention was not to leave, because I was terrified to leave and I was sure he would kill me if I left. Eventually I did leave. I looked for the video-tapes. I looked in the rafters in the garage, where Paul told me they were kept, and I also looked in the hideaway, which was the crawl space in his music room. . . . I found the hunting knife in the rafters in the garage."

But she couldn't find the incriminating tapes.

At first Karla went to her parents' house, but she stayed there only ten minutes. She knew that was the first place Paul would look for her. She found sanctuary in Lori's friend's house. Karla called the animal clinic and told her coworkers she was quitting, because she knew Paul would try to come after her at the clinic. Constable Yvette Fleming of the Niagara Regional Police arrived and took Karla to the hospital. Karla gave her a statement.

Karla spent three days in hospital after leaving Paul on January 5, 1993. She was treated for pain and given a much-needed iron supplement. She was given X rays and a CAT scan, none of which indicated any long-term physical problems as a result of the final beating.

After she left the hospital, Karla was taken to Calvin and Patty Seger's apartment in Brampton. She felt safe there. It was as though she'd been given a new lease on life, Karla told the court. And she celebrated her freedom from Paul by shopping for new clothes, calling friends, and going out dancing with Patty Seger.

Karla's first contact with police was February 9, 1993, at Calvin and Patty's. After the police left Karla spoke with her uncle and aunt, and the next day, on February 10, she called a lawyer, George Walker, in Niagara Falls.

Walker's wife had come into the animal clinic and Karla had read about him in the paper and decided he would be a good person to help her, Karla told the court.

Karla made an appointment for February 11, 1993, with Walker and explained, at least in part, what she had become involved with.

"I instructed him that I wanted this issue resolved as soon as possible and to go ahead and do whatever he thought was best and speak to the Crown," Karla said.

Two days later, on February 13, Karla again met with Walker. There, the initial document that would ultimately lead to Karla Homolka's plea bargain was drafted in George Walker's handwriting and signed by Karla.

The document instructed the lawyer to proceed with negotiations with senior officials with the Ministry of the Attorney General. The most important clause in the document was the line indicating that Karla was "desirous of obtaining blanket immunity against prosecution for any offense alleged to have been committed by me, or any offenses that I am alleged to be a party to, or an accessory to . . ."

The blanket immunity was Walker's idea, Karla explained as though she hadn't thought of the concept at all.

On February 17, 1993, Paul was arrested.

Meetings continued with Walker until, finally, on February 26, 1993, Karla was back in Walker's office, where she signed another document authorizing her lawyer to continue to plea-bargain a resolution with Murray Segal the Attorney General's plea-bargain specialist. She acknowledged that she would be truthful and frank in cooperation with police regarding the French and Mahaffy investigations and any other crime she had knowledge of.

The document went on to acknowledge that Karla would

have to testify against Paul and that a record of her participation and cooperation would be forwarded by the authorities to the parole officials when it came time for Karla's release hearings.

In exchange, Karla was to be sentenced to a ten-year term for manslaughter.

The signing was witnessed by Karla's parents. But the agreement never went into effect, because a few weeks later on, March 5, 1993, Karla checked into Northwestern General Hospital at the suggestion of her lawyer, where for seven weeks she underwent a series of psychological and psychiatric tests, administered by doctors Hans Arnt and Allen Long.

Several times during her prolonged hospital stay, Walker visited Karla. Karla acknowledged her involvement in Tammy's death, writing a letter to Lori and her parents explaining what had happened. That information was also passed on to Walker and the Crown officials working on the plea-bargain deal. The ten-year deal was now off the table, replaced by the twelve-year sentence Karla ultimately agreed to.

On May 7, 1993, Karla was back in Walker's office, where she signed what would be the final plea arrangement, settling for a twelve-year term in exchange for total cooperation. If at any point it was determined that Karla had in fact caused the death of any of the girls, the deal would be null and void and interviews done to that point could be used against her in a prosecution.

Among the clauses in Karla's deal was one in which she agreed not to give any interviews to the media, nor attempt to make any money from her crimes through books, movies, or interviews.

It was a deal that was sanctioned by the families of both Kristen French and Leslie Mahaffy.

On May 14, 1993, police began the first of dozens of interviews with Karla, most of which were audio- and videotaped.

The statements continued May 15, 16, and 17. The first series of interviews with Karla ran a total of eighteen hours.

On May 18, 1993, dressed in a schoolgirl kilt and white top, Karla was taken to police headquarters and formally charged with manslaughter. She was released after her parents put up $100,000 bail.

In the time leading up to her trial, Karla remained at home, although she spent three days—May 28, 29, and 30—back at Northwestern General Hospital in Toronto battling depression and stress.

Before her trial began on June 28, Karla continued with police interviews. On June 17, she and members of the Green Ribbon task force drove throughout the area in a van pointing out various sites connected with the murders, including the locations where the two bodies had been discarded, where the circular saw housing had been thrown near Lake Gibson, and where Karla remembered the Mickey Mouse Watch had been discarded.

Less than a month after moving into the Prison for Women in Kingston, Karla filed for divorce from Paul with the help of St. Catharines lawyer Virginia Workman.

On February 25, 1994, Karla's divorce was granted on the grounds of separation, the most common grounds cited in Canadian divorce proceedings.

A year later, during the week of February 20, 1995, Karla was shown the series of videotapes that had come into the Crown's possession in the fall of 1994. Through the winter and spring of 1995, Karla said there had been consistent contact with the Crown and police.

From the moment Karla arrived at Kingston's Prison for Women, the country's only federal correctional institution, she has been kept under close scrutiny. Her new home is in administrative segregation, where she is kept safely apart from the women in the general prison population.

"It's a place where I live for my own protection," Karla says.

Karla explains that for twenty-three hours a day she is kept in a lockup area. She is allowed into a ten-by-twelve room with TV, although she also has a TV in her room, a standard privilege in segregation. Karla is allowed yard duty for one hour a day in a fenced-in tarmac. She must eat with plastic utensils in her cell.

Between the many interviews with police, Karla began taking a correspondence course of study through Queen's University in Kingston and is majoring in sociology. At the time of her testimony in Paul Bernardo's trial, she was in her second year of study.

"Prison is not nearly punishment enough for what I've done. The real punishment is having to live with the guilt and the shame for the rest of my life. And never being able to make it up.

"But it's a lot better than living with Paul," Karla said. She doesn't have to worry about getting beaten up every day. "I have a lot more freedom in prison than I ever had with him."

And with that, after almost nine days of emotional, stunning testimony, Karla Homolka finished her direct examination. But she and her handlers knew well that the most difficult task lay around the corner: the face-to-face duel with the formidable defense counsel John Rosen.

CHAPTER
28

O n July 4, 1995, as Americans celebrated their Independence Day and Canadians returned from their Canada Day holiday weekend, the most dramatic fireworks in Canadian criminal trial history were about to ignite.

The spark was Paul Bernardo's lawyer John Rosen, defending Paul courtesy of the Ontario Legal Aid Plan's deep pockets. Warm green eyes that dominate a delightfully gentle face combined with an affable manner and a gregarious personality to disguise Rosen's legal brilliance, his burning passion, and a bred-in-the-bone love of legal trench warfare.

When the Bernardo case fell into his lap upon Ken Murray's withdrawal, the fifty-year-old Rosen said it was "just another murder case." But as the trial approached he began working out every morning, losing weight, as though he were a boxer in training for a championship bout.

As he stood impatiently at the front of a packed courtroom awaiting his turn with Karla, Rosen fairly bounced up and down with anticipation. He was keenly aware of the surrogate-watchdog status that had been conferred on him by a mistrustful public and media.

It was of the accused killer's lawyer that reporters asked the questions nobody else would answer. In the absence of any independent barometer of truth, Rosen would have to do. Rosen, known for starting his questioning in dramatic fashion, was determined not to disappoint. In spite of all his pro-testing, this was not just another murder trial.

Karla nervously fidgeted with her lapel microphone in the witness box as Rosen paced back and forth waiting for the anticipatory courtroom murmer to settle.

Rosen strode quickly to the witness box then, whirled on his left heel, and in a whirl of black robes came to a standstill directly to Karla's left, almost touching her. For a moment he stood deathly still. His eyes looked over the crowded court-room, then his right hand suddenly shot up in front of Karla's face.

"I'm going to show you a picture. Can you tell me who is in that picture?" Rosen demanded.

"My sister, Tammy," Karla said trancelike, her eyes averted from the photograph.

"Your sister Tammy, alive," said Rosen.

He lowered the picture and thrust another in her face. "Can you tell us who that is?"

"My sister, Tammy," Karla answered, clearly taken aback at the sudden intrusiveness of Rosen's assault.

"Your sister Tammy, in the morgue, with a red stain on her face, dead! Isn't it?" Rosen growled.

A loud gasp issued from the crowded courtroom at Rosen's audacity.

"Yes," Karla blurted, clearly unsettled.

"You saw her like that, didn't you?"

"She wasn't that bad when I saw her," Karla sniffed.

Rosen launched into a tirade about how Karla drugged Tammy, sexually assaulted her, and dragged her across the floor in a feeble attempt to save her from the lethal drugs.

"That's a picture you can't possibly forget, isn't that right?" asked Rosen.

"That's correct," Karla answered, her eyes lowered in shame.

"I would have thought that from December 24, 1990, to January 1993, those pictures, that nightmare, would have bothered your conscience every living moment of your exis-tence," Rosen offered.

"It did!" she said.

"It did, did it?" asked Rosen, his voice mocking.

"Yes, it did!" pouted Karla. Rosen took the morgue photo away and replaced it among the half dozen or so he carried in his left hand. Suddenly, another photograph was shoved rudely before Karla.

"See that picture? See the girl on the left?"

"It's Leslie Erin Mahaffy," Karla said in a subdued voice.

"Leslie Mahaffy, alive!" said Rosen. After another exchange, another photo.

"You know what that is?" Rosen asked.

Karla may have wanted to turn away, but there was no escape from the courtroom, no escape from Rosen, who moved, if possible, even closer. She cringed, cast her eyes away to the right. Then, seeing no refuge, her eyes fixed downward.

She whispered a softened "Yes."

"It's the torso of Leslie Mahaffy after it came out of the cement. It is lying in the water, decomposed. You participated in that, didn't you? You would have thought that would have bothered your conscience and driven you to do something about it in June 1991," said Rosen.

Regaining some composure, Karla barked back defiantly, "Yes, and I did do something about it."

At this, the unflappable Rosen gave a dramatic sigh, then, after his eyes rolled quickly across the jury, he looked into the astounded gallery again.

"Yes, you did. And we'll get to what you did in a minute." He then showed her similar photographs of Kristen French. Again he questioned her about her conscience.

Why didn't Karla disclose the killings in early January 1993 when interviewed by Niagara Police Constable Yvette Fleming? Why didn't Karla call police from Calvin and Patty Seger's home when she was safely hidden from Paul? Why didn't she confess her nightmare to St. Catharines lawyer Virginia Workman when seeking a divorce January 23, 1993?

Karla replied that she was terrified of Paul.

"Paul didn't know where you were," mused Rosen. "Besides, Paul has everything to lose and nothing to gain . . . if you tell a police officer, 'I was beaten, I was abused, I was bludgeoned; he's the bad guy; he's the rapist'—he loses everything if you do that. He's not gonna call police and say, 'Have I got a story to tell you about my wife!' "

Karla's voice dropped in tone and volume. "I was obviously not thinking straight, or none of this would have happened."

But wasn't it true that after police tried to contact her in early February, Karla put them off and instead went dancing and drinking at the Sugar Shack nightclub in Brampton, where she met Jimmy? Rosen asked. And after a second meeting and sex with him, Rosen said, Karla "coolly and collectively" got her thoughts together and waited to see what police would ask at their prearranged interview the following Monday, February 9, 1993.

"That's not right," she shot back.

When police did arrive at the Seger home, Rosen said, and "asked you about your sister, Tammy, you looked them right in the eye, and without the blink of an eye you told them the same thing you told the constable on December 24, 1990— that Tammy had too much to drink, vomited, and died, didn't you?"

Lawyer George Walker's attempt to get blanket immunity became Rosen's next target. Karla steadfastly denied that she had sought blanket immunity, saying she instructed Walker to get "the best deal he could." Rosen kept up the assault, trying to goad Karla into reacting by hammering away at the fact that at the end of Paul's trial she would be immune from further prosecution.

Karla took the bait. "I'm not the one who actually did the killing. I didn't do it and I'm in prison serving my sentence."

"Long sentence, isn't it?" Rosen quipped.

"No, it isn't," Karla replied, perhaps realizing she'd been caught.

Rosen then had Karla tell the jury about her parole eligibility: She would be eligible for unescorted temporary absences as of July 6, 1995, only two days away; day parole, January 6, 1997; full parole July 6, 1997. Rosen trotted out that a Prison for Women psychiatrist had already judged Karla "ready for parole and the sooner she is out the better."

Rosen alleged that Karla didn't tell police about the murders until she was "guaranteed a deal you could live with . . . from January 1993 you held your silence until you were looked after."

"I followed Mr. Walker's advice," snapped Karla.

Rosen shrugged and sighed. "Isn't that what this was all about?"

Then he mimicked Karla's voice. " 'It's not me; I didn't do it; I was forced to do it.' "

"I don't know what you're asking."

"Your position, as I understand it," said Rosen, "is that whatever you did, whatever involvement you had in these offenses is because you were brutalized, terrorized, and controlled by your husband Paul Bernardo."

Karla measured her words. "I wouldn't put it in those simple terms. You have to understand, from the beginning he started to exercise the control and domination over me. You have to understand how I got to the point I got to, how I got so terrorized and how I let him control me so much. You can't just look at the offense and that's it!"

"You have to look at the relationship, right?" asked Rosen.

"Definitely," said Karla.

"Well," Rosen said cockily, knowing his plan to maneuver Karla to this point had worked like a charm. "Let's just do that."

Rosen planned to expose Karla's infatuation with Paul and explore what he felt was her love of the passionate and kinky sex they shared. He also sought to reveal Karla's hell bent desire to marry Paul. If he could first prove that Karla was an equal sex partner, and secondly that Karla, not Paul, drove the relationship down the aisle to the altar on June 29, 1991, then there was a chance he could get the jury to start to wonder about the many vague areas of Karla's testimony, especially the parts involving Tammy and Jane. If he could punch holes in her credibility in these areas, then the jury might be all ears by the time he explained Paul's version of how Leslie Mahaffy and Kristen French died.

Canadian cross-examination rules, which allow any question to be asked of a witness, favored Rosen. While prosecutors could only introduce evidence against Paul that was relative to who actually murdered the girls or to Karla and Paul's relationship, it was open season on Karla for Rosen. Rosen knew, however, that it was ultimately Paul Bernardo who would be judged. He could turn Karla inside out, but it wouldn't matter if he couldn't create a reasonable doubt in the jury's mind about who'd actually killed those two girls.

Karla's relationship with Paul, Rosen began, was founded on sex and was thereafter driven by Karla's "desperate desire" to marry a good catch and a man with whom she was sexually compatible.

Karla's face contorted in misunderstanding. It wasn't that simple; she liked Paul for more than just sex.

Following that answer, Rosen returned to the now well-documented beginning of Paul and Karla's sexual relationship at Howard Johnson's on October 17, 1987.

Rosen then assailed Karla for having sex with Paul that first night and then in her bedroom the following weekend with Van and Kathy in the next room. "Not only did you have sex," Rosen offered, "but you used your handcuffs to tie yourself up on your bed so you could have sex, with your friends in the next room."

Karla couldn't recall the handcuffs, but she admitted that she and Paul had sex every night they were together in the first six weeks.

Rosen then began to discuss the five hundred or so cards, letters, and notes Karla had written Paul in their more than five years together. Prosecutors had picked through the cards for evidence of abuse; now Rosen offered the cards that either talked about sex or portrayed Karla in a negative light. In the first month, Karla had sent Paul a half-dozen cards, many of them containing sexual innuendo. On one side of a card dated Thursday, November 12, 1987, Karla wrote: "Dear Paul, How I miss you . . . I like you a lot, I care for you. I'm really starting to fall for you, etcetera, I can't wait to cuddle. Love Karla." And on the other side she wrote: "Don't believe that's all I want to do with you for a second!"

The next day, Karla sent a card to Paul bearing the pre-printed verse "Roses are red, violets are blue, there's nothing move fun, than a pervert like you."

A week later Karla sent two more cards, one of them bearing the preprinted message "You're a vulgar, disgusting sex maniac" on the cover and "I like that in a man" on the inside.

On Wednesday, December 2, 1987, Karla admitted, she attended the Price Waterhouse Christmas party with Paul at the Howard Johnson's hotel where they met. To celebrate their meeting, they had sex in a stairwell.

The cards continued through New Year 1988, with Karla giving Paul a card each time he arrived in St. Catharines and each time he left. The letters and notes indicate that within a couple of months Karla willingly gave Paul carte-blanche approval to ask for and do anything he wanted.

Karla told Rosen that it was Paul who sought the sex talk, Paul who wanted Karla to be more sexually aggressive.

On October 17, 1988, Karla wrote Paul a card celebrating their one-year anniversary in which she thanked him "for the best year of my life." This was the twelfth anniversary card she had sent Paul; eleven previous cards had been given, one for each successive month of the relationship.

On November 28, 1988, came an anniversary card for a year to the day on which Karla had told Paul she loved him. In July 1989, Karla wrote Paul a letter inviting him to her house while her parents were away, offering "good eating, oral sex, mass kissing, and, of course, good old fashioned fucking."

Around the same time, she sent a card. "You are cordially invited to . . . fuck the shit out of me."

In contrast to the X-rated sex messages, Karla would put her own imprint on the cards: ink hearts colored with red wax crayon; little animal stickers, each one saying love words from Karla to Paul; drawings of happy faces and sad faces. No matter what she may or may not have done, it was clear from her cards that Karla had a pitiful, pathetic, needy obsession with Paul. Its genus seemed to lie more within her own troubled psyche than solely in Paul's charm or magnetism.

"You were madly, passionately, desperate for this man over here to be part of your life," Rosen attacked again.

"Yes, I was passionately in love with him and, yes, I

wanted him to be part of my life, and I have never denied that!" she said.

"You're the one who could have said no at any time, but you kept saying 'yes' and 'yes,' " said Rosen.

Rosen pushed Karla repeatedly on why, if Paul was abusing her so much, she did not tell her parents or her friends. He noted that there were so many opportunities for discreet talks while Paul was away, back in Scarborough.

On August 27, 1989, while Paul was philandering in Florida on his twenty-fifth birthday, Karla wrote Paul many messages. One offered an "x-rated gift certificate" that promised a "quickie, plain fucking, fancy fucking, movies, picture taking . . ."

Karla wrote to her friend Debbie Purdie telling of her plans to celebrate Paul's birthday upon his return: twenty ten dollar bills shaped into flowers; a Rolex watch Paul had picked out at a native store in New York; a lobster, steak, and oyster dinner.

Rosen noted another letter in which Karla sent Debbie Purdie claws taken from a cat during a declawing operation at the Thorold Veterinarian center, where Karla worked at the end of 1989.

In another letter, Karla pinned a severed puppy tail to a hand-drawn picture of a dog. The veterinarian had chopped the tail from a four-day-old schnauzer puppy. Normally the claws and tails were thrown away, but Karla saw this as fun between two animal lovers. "Show your friends. God, they must think I'm sick. Hmmmm, how am I going to top this one?"

From the time Paul slipped the engagement ring onto her finger in December 1989, Rosen said, Karla became obsessed with marrying her lover. Again, he said, her letters show it all. She wrote about the engagement party, invitations, a shower, the wedding party, and other matrimonial concerns in letters to Debbie Purdie.

In June 1990, Rosen suggested, Karla's preoccupation with marriage should have changed when Paul told her he would like to have sex with other women.

"I did not want my parents to know that anything was

wrong in my relationship. A lot of women go through this. It is not something unusual for a woman to go through the type of a relationship and still think they love them,'' Karla said.

How could she not confide her angst in either her parents, her sister, her doctor, or friends? asked Rosen, noting Paul was the stranger and lived out of town.

''You don't have to be physically isolated to be emotionally isolated,'' Karla replied. I was ashamed I was in this situation, but I still loved him. At this point I still wanted to be with him. Now I feel stupid, now knowing how wrong I was.''

Rosen moved to the summer of 1990, when, Karla testified, Paul first mentioned having three-way sex with Tammy. That July, during a party at the Homolka family house, Tammy and Paul left to get more booze. They should have taken twenty minutes but did not return for almost six hours. Rosen asked Karla if it hadn't crossed her mind that her ''pubescent little sister'' Tammy was being molested by Paul or had made a pass at him.

''It never crossed my mind that Tammy was doing anything wrong with Paul,'' Karla said emphatically.

''You looked your boyfriend of almost three years in the eye and knew something had happened between him and your little sister, didn't you?'' said Rosen, suggesting that Paul and Tammy had fooled around.

''I knew nothing,'' Karla said.

Why then, Rosen asked, did Karla refer to Paul's having sex with Tammy in ''the summer'' in the videotape she made with Paul only three weeks after Tammy's death?

Karla said it was all part of Paul's fantasy.

And why, Rosen asked, did Karla not do something that summer when Paul began their ''pillow talk discussions of Paul having sex with Tammy?

''I would have thought at this point you would have sprung out of bed and said, wait a minute, what are you talking about here? You're not touching my baby sister! That would have been the right reaction, wouldn't it?''

''Yes,'' said Karla.

''But you didn't do it!''

''No.''

"Instead, what you did was say that 'If my little sister thinks playing with fire isn't going to get her burned, I'll show her what this is all about,' " said Rosen.

"You're dead wrong," Karla said sternly.

Rosen alleged that on another day Karla ground Valium pills into her "famous spaghetti sauce" and fed it to Tammy so that Paul could rape the teenager while she was unconscious.

"That's not true!" Karla stated defiantly.

The pattern that would dominate the almost seven days Rosen had Karla on the stand was clearly established. Apart from Rosen's stunning opening, which seemed to set Karla back on her heels, she had proven herself to be tough as nails. Whenever Rosen made a statement that she disagreed with, she spoke up loud and clear. Sometimes it appeared as though Karla was enjoying the sparring, the matching of wits with Rosen, grinning when he sometimes made a joke about his lack of hair or something.

Whether it was part of Rosen's initial strategy or merely a fortunate by-product, the obvious question became: Where was this strong, defiant young woman when teenage girls were being murdered in her bedroom?

In the fall of 1990, when Karla contends that Paul pressured her to let him have sex with Tammy. Rosen noted that her letters showed "not a word, not a hint, not a suggestion that there is trouble in paradise . . . not a hint that your sister is in any jeopardy."

"I didn't believe she was in any jeopardy," said Karla.

"You didn't? And yet there was pressure from your boyfriend to have sex, if not more sex, with your sister?"

"I didn't believe her life or physical well-being were in jeopardy," responded Karla.

"Never mind her life. Do you still understand, Miss Homolka, that her personal security was in jeopardy, her integrity as a woman was in jeopardy? Do you not understand that what was being planned and being discussed was the rape and assault of your little sister?"

"I have never not understood that," Karla answered.

"Yet you did nothing to stop it and everything to help it," said Rosen.

"I felt totally terrorized. I did not feel I had a choice . . . I wish to God I had of, and I have to live with that every single day for the rest of my life."

Yet despite her protests of despair and remorse, in December 1990 Karla wrote Debbie Purdie telling her excitedly about "two absolutely wonderful events: marriage and a dog," referring to Paul's agreement that after their marriage—still six months away—they would get a puppy.

"And within twenty days your sister's dead!" Rosen said.

As he continued his probing into the Tammy issue, Karla became flummoxed; often her wan face would contort, even turn a little red. It was clearly hard going for the stellar witness. In her testimony, Karla said Paul had planned to have sex with the unconscious Tammy only once and that would last only five minutes. She agreed with Rosen that from her extensive sexual history with Paul, she knew he often needed up to two hours of stimulation to achieve orgasm. Rosen also noted that there was no objection on Karla's part when Paul told her to undress in the videotape. Rosen again pushed at Karla, trying to get her to admit she wanted sex with Paul and her sister, but she would not budge.

"You don't seem to understand the level of fear," Karla said. "When you're afraid, you don't question every little thing."

When Rosen suggested that Karla's comment of "fucking disgusting" in the video of Tammy's rape was expressed out of physical disgust over the fact her sister was menstruating, and not from inherent moral disgust, Karla shot back that it was "a lie."

Rosen had co-defense counsel Tony Bryant roll the video footage of Tammy's assault for the jury on monitors, asking Karla to step off the witness stand so she could get a closer look. She stood only a few feet away from Rosen.

"Surprise, surprise, she's wearing some sort of a sanitary napkin," Rosen pointed to the screen. "Look, look there."

"I never saw one," Karla said indignantly.

"What? Were you blind?" Rosen asked.

"No, I was not blind. I wasn't looking," Karla shot back.

Rosen finally seemed to crack the tough-as-nails veneer when he pressed Karla on the night of Tammy's death. Karla sobbed quietly in the witness box as Rosen recalled how, in the early hours of Christmas Eve after Tammy died, she lied to Constable David Weeks and then signed a false statement for Detective Ken Mitchell.

"I didn't want my family to know," Karla explained.

"Your family?" Rosen said incredulously. "Weren't you thinking of your dead sister?"

Rosen moved to the sex-fantasy tape filmed several weeks after Tammy's death. He noted that in the opening of the schoolgirl-rape fantasy video, Karla is on her back, legs spread with a smile on her face, saying "I get so horny when my husband is with me." There is no direction from Paul, he concluded.

"I'm trying to make a good videotape," Karla responded.

Advancing the tape to where Karla tells Paul that a surprise awaits him upstairs—the prelude to the clip in which Karla dresses in Tammy's clothes and pretends to be her dead sister during sex—Rosen asked Karla to think about how she could say this only eighteen days or so after she watched her sister being buried. At the end of the clip, Rosen noted, Karla seems to lead the action when she grabs Paul as he walks naked toward the camera to turn it off prior to going upstairs.

"And you would have us believe you were just playacting on this video?"

"It's the truth . . . I was playacting," Karla said.

"Well, you're quite the actress," said Rosen.

Rosen's relentless assault against Karla continued throughout the first week. To the quiet glee of the pathos-hungry media and sometimes to uproarious laughter from the audience, Rosen bombarded Karla's illogical situation with logical questions. Why, for example, did she let Paul pick her up after Tammy's January 18, 1991, memorial and stay that night at the Relax Inn in Burlington? Did she have sex with Paul that night? Karla's vague answer led Rosen to ask, "What? You and Paul Bernardo in a hotel room and you didn't have sex?"

Laughter rippled through the packed court. It was around that time that the court clerk began his daily demand that spectators refrain from comment or laughter during the proceedings.

Rosen seized on Karla's wedding planner, noting the meticulous entries and how enthralled Karla seemed to have been with her plans to marry Paul. The diary shows Karla's fixation with photographs, shoes, wedding dress, attendants' dresses, honeymoon reservations, stationery, invitations, confetti cards.

When Rosen noted that there is no mention of Tammy's death, burial, memorial, or her January 1 birthday, Karla said sternly that it was a wedding planner and not a daily diary.

Karla was so thrilled at moving in with Paul—the man she claims to have hated—that she couldn't wait to tell her friends, Rosen charged.

In a January 24, 1991, letter to Debbie Purdie, Karla wrote: " 'Hi. I finally have some good news in my life. (It seems as if there's been an unhappiness forever even though it's only one month today).' And that's the last we hear of Tammy," Rosen reminded Karla before continuing to read. " 'Paul and I are moving in together! Yes Deb, we are going to live in sin! We got a beautiful house in Port Dalhousie, right near the lake . . .' "

In a February 19, 1991, letter to Debbie Purdie, Karla gave her friend advice: "Never feel guilty" about taking, because "the world will screw you in every way it can, so take as much as you can while you can." She follows with mercenary requests for wedding gifts, asking for a Dustbuster, china, crystal, and money. Then she goes into a vitriolic rant over her parents' cutting half their donation to Karla and Paul's wedding. She calls her parents "assholes," her father "a liar," and exclaims, "Fuck my parents. They are being so stupid. Only thinking of themselves."

As Paul and Van meandered back from Daytona Beach in March 1991, with stops at Alyson and Kim's apartment in Columbia, South Carolina, Karla made several telephone calls to both the Marriott Hotel in Daytona Beach, Florida, and to Paul's car phone. On March 18, 1991, Rosen noted,

Karla sent Paul a card in which she wrote: "Yay! My honey bunny's home! Let's never be that far apart for that long or any length of time, again. I love you so much and I'm glad you're home."

Rosen noted Karla's trademark stickers of bears, an octopus, champagne popping, and a guy on a surfboard with little quotes from each sticker. That night, Rosen said, Karla became rip-roaring drunk when she learned of the threat Alyson posed to her relationship. Instead of giving Karla a card for her twenty-first birthday, May 4, 1991, Paul told her he was infatuated with Alyson and they should not marry.

"That is the most ridiculous thing I've ever heard," Karla jabbed back.

With that, Rosen read the letter aloud:

Dear Paul,
You hate me. You say you want to go out with other girls after you've left me. You say I make you sick. You tell me to pack and leave. You tell me to eat shit and die etc. etc. etc. You have every reason to tell me these things. I am the no good fucking idiot. I don't know how to show you my love and respect. You think I have no respect. I make so many huge mistakes. I am stupid. I am probably really stupid in saying this, but I'll say it anyway. I think that if we truly loved each other, the way we thought we did, we would have been able to overcome anything. I don't care how big the mistakes are, or how many times they are made. I think (but I mean to remember here that I am stupid, therefore what I think doesn't matter) that in all probability that we should overcome it. I have screwed things up so much that the love that should be there isn't. It's not supposed to be like this. You aren't supposed to say things that hurt me. I'm not supposed to say things that hurt you (I know they don't hurt anymore because you don't care anymore). I can say I'll change until hell freezes over, but I haven't yet, so why expect that I will now? I desperately want to—I want us to—be happy like we used to, but I think you hurt me too much for that to ever happen.

Rosen's eyes came up from the letter. It appeared, Rosen suggested, that it was Paul who wanted to leave and Karla who was begging to get him back.

"I wanted him to leave me alone. If he wouldn't do that, I wanted him to stop sexually and emotionally abusing me," Karla replied.

Rosen noted that despite Karla's protesting that she hated Paul and lived in constant fear, the wedding plans marched on in the spring and early summer of 1991.

Rosen moved on to Jane, whom Karla first met at the Pet Centre. Rosen asked Karla what reason she would possibly have to get in contact with Jane, other than to set her up for Paul.

"You had nothing in common to discuss or socialize about, isn't that right?"

"No, that's not right," said Karla.

"So what did you talk about?" Rosen chuckled. "The Blue Jays?"

"The pet store, animals, mutual friends. We talked about all kinds of things," Karla offered, unfazed.

Rosen said Jane was "a little kinky three-way sex" peace offering to Paul after the rift over Alyson.

Again, Karla denied the suggestion.

Rosen then alleged that Karla and Paul had twice sexually assaulted Jane, once on the videotape, which he believed was June 7, 1991, and then again on August 11, 1991, when a 911 call was made from 57 Bayview Drive to emergency crews asking for assistance with a person who had stopped breathing.

"I don't believe that it happened twice at all," said Karla.

But Rosen proved her wrong. He noted that in a video sequence Karla shot of Jane playing with Buddy, Jane wore a white "Oxford Hall" sweatshirt. Underneath was a yellow T-shirt. Both garments were visible in the sex videotape. Rosen also noted that as Jane played with Buddy in the regular tape, Karla suggested watching the movie *Ghost*. Rosen produced a rental receipt from a St. Catharines video store that showed Paul had rented the movie on June 7, 1991.

"You watched the [sex] tape on other occasions with Mr. Bernardo, didn't you, Miss Homolka?"

"No, I didn't; you're very wrong," Karla replied.

"You watched it, and you enjoyed it, and you got a big laugh out of it because it's part of the kinky sex you were into," said Rosen.

"That's a lie," Karla shot back.

Rosen noted that on the side of the 8mm tape with the Tammy and Jane clips was one of Karla's trademark title stickers that she put on all her cards and letters. "Just as you signed your feelings on cards, after watching the tape you put your mark, that little heart, as if you'd just signed your name to this video," said Rosen.

"No, that's not true," said Karla, adding that Paul put the sticker on the tape at 61 Dundonald Street rather than inviting a potential viewing by her parents or Lori by writing "Tammy" on it.

As court broke for the weekend after four days of cross-examination, it was obvious things had gone well for Rosen.

Meanwhile, the dapper man with the schoolboy face sat quietly in the defendant's box. The alleged multiple rapist from Scarborough, an alleged rapist in Mississauga, an alleged rapist on Henley Island, the alleged rapist of two teenage girls in his house, the alleged beater and sodomist of girlfriends, the man prosecutors said directed the videotaped sex and, ultimately, killed Leslie Mahaffy and Kristen French, was almost a forgotten person.

But Rosen's greatest task lay ahead. Even if he could reduce Karla to tears, Rosen still had to sell the jury on Paul's version of events.

When the cross-examination resumed, Rosen immediately launched into Karla's testimony around the confinement, rape, and murder of Leslie Mahaffy, suggesting to Karla that she enjoyed the tableaux of sex the captive girl supplied. Rosen noted that in one of the videotapes Karla was "smiling, eyes wide, tongue out, licking in anticipation of performing oral sex" on the girl. Karla repeated that she was trying to make a good videotape so Paul wouldn't beat her.

"You tell us that," Rosen challenged.

"And every time you ask me I will keep telling you that," Karla said, showing newfound combativeness.

"If that's not believed, all of this could be taken to be one of the natural, happy moments in the life of Karla Homolka," said Rosen.

"I'm overacting," said Karla.

"Or acting natural," Rosen threw in.

"That's not natural," Karla said of her video smile.

As the two continued to joust over Karla's sex smiles, Debbie Mahaffy sobbed quietly in the front row, just a head's turn from the jury. Earlier, Rosen had warned them he was about to play the videotapes. Donna French had left, but Debbie had stayed, as if tormenting herself for locking her daughter out of the house on June 14, 1991. It was as if that by tormenting and punishing herself somehow, Debbie felt she would somehow heal.

Rosen suggested that it was Paul who wanted to drop Leslie Mahaffy off in Burlington drugged, drunk, and blindfolded. It was Paul who felt Leslie would be unable to identify her captors or where they lived. But when Paul was in the garage putting gas into the Nissan, Rosen said, Karla killed her by kneeling on her back and pushing her head into a pillow until she suffocated.

"That's when you decided she had to die, isn't it?"

"No, that's not right," Karla shot back in defense. "Nobody kneeled on her back. Paul strangled her with a black electrical cord."

Rosen didn't stop. "You had just as much motive to want the girl to die," he said, his voice rising almost an octave as he strode back and forth in front of the jury.

"I didn't want her to die," Karla calmly replied. "What you are putting to me is a lie."

Moving quickly, Rosen turned to the dismemberment.

"You were there when he cut her up, weren't you?"

"No, that's a lie."

Rosen said it was nearly impossible for Paul to dismember Leslie's body, buy ten bags of concrete, buy another twelve bags of concrete, mix the concrete, set the body parts, return the unused concrete, and then pick Karla up from work in eight hours, as she insisted.

"That's what happened," Karla said.

"But there wasn't enough time," said Rosen, implying it would have taken two people to do so much, beginning perhaps on Sunday evening.

"There was enough time, because that's what happened," said Karla.

Rosen went as far as to suggest that Paul cut the body and passed the parts to Karla, who then put them in the concrete.

"No, that's wrong. What you are suggesting is a lie," Karla said, eyeing down her adversary with a phrase that was repeated over and over during the seven days she faced Rosen.

Although Karla was certainly confused and perhaps had a selective memory about the letters, Tammy, Jane, and her desire to marry Paul, she had been unshakably smooth on the Leslie Mahaffy details. Rosen, on the other hand, looked shaken; he hadn't controlled the testimony as he had in the first week. He could make all the allegations in the world, but if Karla continued to respond with "that's a lie" and "that's not what happened" and "Paul knows that's true," then in the eyes of the jury she would become a stronger and stronger witness.

Wednesday of the second week of Karla's testimony saw Rosen move to the wedding. Again, Karla's letters and videotape footage seemed to reveal that the horror of rape and murder had been forgotten in her absorption in her marriage fantasy.

Try as she would to tell the jury she hated Paul and didn't want to marry him, it didn't seem to fit. Rosen played a videotape of the wedding rehearsal the night of June 28, 1991. In it, Karla stares moon-eyed at her fiancé; even when Paul isn't looking at Karla, her adoring eyes fix on his face. She is also seen laughing, giggling, stealing glances at Paul here and there as a happy bride-to-be is wont to do.

Rosen then played a videotape of a romantic sunset Karla had taken from the balcony of an oceanfront hotel room in Hawaii while they were on their honeymoon. As the sun sets on the horizon, Karla's voice is heard to say, "The beauty of the ocean, this beach, of everything here, doesn't even come close to equaling the love I feel for you. I love you, sweetheart."

Rosen suggested that this love message was more the truth of the honeymoon, not the "honeymoon from hell" with its attendant beatings that Karla had described.

"Paul knows what happened," she fired back.

Rosen bristled. Time and again Karla had fallen back on statements like that: "Paul knows what happened," "Ask Paul," "Paul knows."

Twice Rosen responded that at the appropriate time, they would in fact ask Paul just what had happened. It was the first inkling the jury and the public had that Paul Bernardo might actually take the stand. The assumption had been that Paul's defense would rest solely on Rosen's ability to tear apart Karla's credibility. But it now seemed there would be one final star witness before the trial ended.

Rosen appeared tired as he turned his sights to April 16, 1992, the day of Kristen's abduction. Rosen began his attack by reminding Karla that she took half a day from work and visited the downtown St. Catharines library before she went home that day.

"You're living with someone you hate, and who is talking about abducting a girl right off the street, and yet you don't rush into the police station and say, "I'm living with a maniac and you've got to stop him before somebody else gets hurt'?"

"No," Karla replied. Untypically, she offered no further explanation.

Rosen offered that after Karla came home in the afternoon, she and Paul decided to go shopping at the Grantham Plaza. Karla interjected that the plan was to kidnap a girl, not go shopping.

Karla, Rosen said, preferred tall, thin, dark-haired girls, and when she saw Kristen French she said, "That's the one I like." After that, Paul turned the car around to take a look.

"What you're suggesting is totally wrong," said Karla, shaking her head slightly as if in disgust.

It did not happen as Karla told police, Rosen suggested. If

it had, why didn't she refuse to take part in a kidnapping, just as she had refused to help Paul dismember Leslie's body?

"I would have gotten beaten. . . . It wasn't a matter of saying 'no' and getting beaten, it was a matter of saying 'no,' getting beaten, and have it happen anyway," she said tersely.

"You could have jumped out of the car and ran like hell," said Rosen.

"I wish I had done that, but I couldn't," she replied.

He asked her why she couldn't just sit in the car and let Kristen walk on by.

"That's not the way it works, Mr. Rosen, not with Paul."

Karla denied Rosen's suggestion that it was she who pulled Kristen into the car by the hair. Karla reiterated that Paul forced Kristen into the car; Kristen had stopped fighting, Karla said, when she grabbed her hair to keep her down.

On Thursday, Rosen focused mainly on the videotape footage of Kristen's rape, which Karla said happened on Sunday, April 19, 1992, an hour before Paul strangled the schoolgirl with the black electrical cord. It was the only sex video clip, Rosen noted, that Karla could pin down to a time and a date. There was no evidence, he said, other than her testimony, to prove the clip was taken Sunday. Then he gave his own scenario of Kristen's death. At around 6 P.M., Rosen said, Paul left 57 Bayview Drive to get take-out food, leaving Karla to guard Kristen with a rubber mallet, as Karla had testified. But Rosen contradicted Karla's testimony that Kristen was kept tied up in the closet, he claimed she was tied to a handle on the hope chest with an electrical cord looped around her neck. While Paul was away, Rosen said, Kristen became upset when she saw a televised newscast in which her father told her to escape.

Kristen, he said, tried to escape, and in the ensuing struggle Karla hit her with the mallet. In the frenzy, he said, Kristen twisted on the noose and strangled herself.

"That's a total lie," offered Karla. "I've never hit anybody in my life, Mr. Rosen."

When Paul came home, Rosen said, Kristen was "dead on the floor."

"No, that's a lie," she said glibly.

On Karla's twenty-second birthday—within weeks of Kristen's murder and days after Roger Boyer discovered her body—the couple exchanged loving cards.

"This must have been a terrible nightmare to you," he said sarcastically.

"Yes, it was," Karla answered.

Rosen shook his head in disgust. "This business about hating this marriage and hating Paul Bernardo, it really is nonsense, isn't it?"

Karla insisted she did hate her husband.

"If that was true, the last thing in the world you would want is to produce offspring of this marriage," he said, producing a May 8 letter to Debbie Purdie in which Karla wrote:

Also now, I'll finally tell you what Paul is doing. He's making a rap record. He is doing extremely well. His raps are amazing and it won't be longer than a few months until he gets a contract. That's why we can't have kids yet. It may hamper his contract to have kids. So as soon as he signs, I'm getting pregnant. I can't wait. I'll let you know as things develop.

From the moment of Kristen's death until she fled on January 5, 1993, Rosen said in an almost quiet voice, Karla had many opportunities to find the tapes and destroy them.

"You may think that's correct. But I didn't feel that way," she answered quietly. She still feared that Paul would kill her or her family. "I felt like I was in a tunnel and could not see either side of me."

Unless he had been in the same situation, Karla said to her inquisitor, he would never be able to understand what she was going through.

Rosen sighed. "All of these letters and cards make your conduct hard to explain."

Karla agreed. "It is very difficult for me to make people understand. Some people understand."

"Those are my questions," Rosen said, closing his legal binder and heading for his seat beside Tony Bryant and legal assistant Kim Doyle.

No one person in the room had expected such a sudden end to the cross-examination. It seemed premature; it seemed there should be more. In all, Karla had been on the stand sixteen days, nine giving testimony and seven in cross-examination. All that remained was Ray Houlahan's redirect examination.

Later, a frustrated Rosen would lament his inability to deliver the knockout punch to the Crown's main witness. There were openings, he said, but they closed quickly because Karla was so stubborn, so unwilling to bend on anything. Even when she was caught in inconsistencies, she acknowledged them as if to say, "So what?"

Lost in all the drama was the fact that Rosen hardly ever referred to Karla's initial statements of May, 1993—statements made before police had the videotapes, the reference being that her story from that moment on remained consistent. Karla's dramatic testimony ended on Friday, with Houlahan asking only a handful of questions. Karla reiterated at several points that it was Paul who drove the rapes and murders and it was because of her fear of Paul that she kept a happy public face.

After Judge LeSage excused the jury at the end of the day, Paul stared blankly at the woman who had been his lover, his wife, his accomplice; the woman whose testimony had probably sent him to prison for the rest of his life. As he stared, Karla's eyes looked up to meet his gaze for five or six seconds, then fell to her hands. Her eyes rose again and focused on Paul. The stare held longer this time. Then Karla's eyes switched to her parents, sitting in the second row, just behind the glass that shielded Paul. A show of concern crossed their faces, Karel almost in tears. Karla leaned forward in the witness stand, as if to embrace them.

But then it was time to go. She had fulfilled her part of the deal with the authorities. Now all she had to do was serve her prison time. She bounced off the stand, passed through a door and into the room beyond.

Paul rose. After guards placed handcuffs on his wrists, he shuffled out of court. Karla was gone, but he would be back.

CHAPTER
29

There seemed to be a palpable change in the courtroom atmosphere after Karla returned to her *Sesame Street* bedsheets and Disney posters at the Prison for Women. The flow of the trial became jerky, with frequent breaks and legal wrangling.

It had been clear from John Rosen's broad hints that, barring something unforeseen, Paul would take the stand. The shift in defense strategy threw the trial schedule out of whack, and instead of the expected finish by the end of July, Judge LeSage told the jury he thought it would more likely be the end of August before they were released from their duties. As promised, he let them have almost two weeks off at the end of July so their entire summer wouldn't be lost.

LeSage and the legal teams and a handful of reporters stuck around for almost three days of legal motions regarding stalking evidence, the "Deadly Innocence" lyrics, and just what was going to be allowed as far as psychiatric evidence was concerned. Those motions were followed by a week of holidays, although for the legal teams on both sides of the issue, there was little rest.

Rosen, Bryant, and Doyle spent long days at the Metro East Detention Centre trying to get Paul into some sort of shape to take the stand. It was a difficult task, given Paul's personality. Rosen was doing his best to prepare his client to give a very narrow version of what had happened, to tell his story, not to argue his case as if on the defensive. Crown prosecutors would be able to cross-examine Paul only on the things he'd testified to, and Rosen had to make sure he didn't allow his client to open up great holes that the prosecution could exploit.

Yet Paul, filled with ideas of conspiracy and wild theories on how he could escape his legal destiny, proved a difficult witness to prepare.

For hours on end, the defense team sat in the small, plexi-glass-walled room at Metro East, watching as Paul ate his lunch and then his dinner. By the end of the week, the entire team looked as though they'd been put through a wringer—and they hadn't even gotten their boy on the stand yet.

When the trial resumed in Courtroom 6-1 on July 31, the Crown's case was clearly winding down. The most critical witness left was Carol, Paul's former Scarborough girlfriend. She entered the courtroom, not through the public gallery like all the other witnesses, but through the rear door by which the jury had entered. The only other witness to enter in that manner had been Karla.

Almost immediately after the attractive twenty-seven-year-old with the luxuriant dark hair took the stand, Donna French began to weep. The girl's resemblance to Kristen was overwhelming. Carol smiled at Crown attorney Lesley Baldwin as Paul examined his longtime lover with his trademark emotionless, almost puzzled expression.

[The following passages are composed from courtroom testimony at Paul Bernardo's trial in Toronto during July and August 1995.]

Judge LeSage had been very clear concerning just what Carol could testify about: one night during which Paul used a ligature around her neck during sex. But anything else from their three year relationship would be too prejudicial.

Carol, it appeared, wanted to say more.

When Baldwin asked her to describe their relationship as boyfriend and girlfriend, the registered nurse, who still lived at home with her parents in Scarborough, spat out, "I was his little servant girl. His play toy."

As she shifted nervously in the witness box, Carol began stealing angry glances at Paul. Baldwin asked her to describe an incident during the summer of 1986, when she was eighteen years old and a petite 105 pounds.

Her words came out in a rush.

They had gone parking in Paul's white Capri behind a factory parking lot. It was night.

"He demanded me to go to the back of the car and get down on my knees," she said.

Paul pushed her down with his open hand in the middle of her back. "Now arch your back," he commanded.

She did as she was told, arching her back, her face pushed into the side of the burgundy interior. Her arms were down in front of her.

Paul's voice was cold, Carol told the jury, struggling to fight back tears but keeping her voice strong and brusque with bitterness. He gave her simple, harsh commands, she said. Suddenly Paul produced some twine from somewhere in the car, a piece about two feet in length.

"And he put it around my neck. And he got pissed off at my hair and kept going, 'Fucking hair.' "

Paul pulled at her head, yanking it back so he could get the twine fixed around her throat. Carol motioned with her own head how he'd pulled at her.

"He took the rope and he placed it around my neck and pulled it back. He used two hands," she said in a halting voice.

The rope was prickly, and she could feel it irritating the skin on her neck. He pulled it tight, but not enough to cut off her breathing. As he pulled on the rope and then her long hair, Paul pulled her clothing away and penetrated her, first vaginally and then anally.

It didn't take long, she said. Once Paul knew you were in discomfort, that you were experiencing pain, he would cry out that he was coming and he would ejaculate, she told the jury.

However, there was no pleasure in the act for Carol.

"It hurt and I was uncomfortable and sweaty, and I felt like I had to go to the washroom all the time," she told the court. "I was looking at the carpet, focusing on the carpet, and saying, 'It will be over soon and I won't have to deal with it. I'll just please him and make him happy, and if he's happy I'll survive it and just go on and face the next day.' "

The choking was accompanied by dialogue from Paul.

"He kept saying he was the king and I was his little servant girl and I deserved what I was getting," Carol said, bitterness and anger seeming to rise off her like a vapor. "Yeah, I'm great, I'm the best, I'm the king, you're my little servant girl," she said, mimicking her lover and tormentor.

The entire episode lasted perhaps fifteen minutes, she said. After, Paul was extremely happy. He got back in the front seat and turned on the radio and began grooving to the tunes.

"As if nothing had happened," Carol said incredulously.

Paul had turned to her. "You look like shit. Why don't you put on some makeup. And stop crying," he had commanded. And she did. "It was just like nothing had happened. He was happy. I was, like, what just happened to me?"

John Rosen stood up to cross-examine his client's accuser. He asked her about how she met Paul. She said she and Steve Smirnis had been on a double date with Paul and another girl and they'd switched partners.

"Paul kept playing with my hair in the backseat and trying to get my attention," Carol explained.

That was August 16, 1984. The sex Carol had described to the jury took place more than a year before she and Paul finally broke up, hadn't it? Rosen asked.

"Correct. It just got worse and worse," Carol spat out.

Rosen bristled at the additional information offered by the witness.

"That wasn't my question. Just listen to my question, all right?"

Paul had picked her up the night of the choking incident at her home, where she was living with her parents, was that correct? Rosen wanted to know.

Again Carol gave unwanted elaboration. Yes, Paul had picked her up at home. He often did. And if he ever thought

Carol's parents looked angry or upset when he arrived, Paul became extremely angry, Carol offered. The implication was clear: The abuse was a regular element of their relationship. Rosen angrily warned her again that she was merely to answer the specific questions he asked.

Wasn't it true that Carol and Paul had gone straight to the parking lot that night, just as they had many times before and would continue to do after the incident? Rosen asked.

"Yes," she admitted.

And Paul only grabbed her hair and held the rope for a few minutes? Rosen asked.

"No, it took longer than that. He liked it when you were in pain," Carol offered again, enraging Rosen with her disregard for his questions.

"But then he took you home, right?" Rosen asked.

"Yes, because he got off and he was happy."

Shaking his head in disgust, Rosen ended his questions and Carol left the courtroom through the same door by which she had entered, turning to glare one last time at her old lover.

For weeks, the jury had heard and seen the mysterious Jane, the young woman whom Paul and Karla had drugged into unconsciousness and sexually assaulted in a scene startlingly similar to that which led to Tammy Homolka's death.

They'd heard about the frantic 911 call when she appeared to have stopped breathing in August 1991. And they heard the unlikely story of how Karla recalled the bizarre sexual trysts only after she began serving her prison term.

Finally, as the trial was winding down, they heard from Jane herself.

As the Crown prepared to call her to the stand, a lawyer for Jane's family approached Judge LeSage and asked that the public be cleared from court for her testimony. Her emotional psyche was so fragile, the attorney argued, that the idea that a member of the public might recognize her was enough to send Jane into a spiral of anxiety and despair that might lead to suicide.

Even though the media was already forbidden from printing her name or otherwise identifying Jane, she was still terrified at the thought of testifying, the lawyer argued. LeSage agreed with the lawyer and banished the public from the courtroom, while allowing accredited journalists to remain.

As Carol and Karla had previously done, Jane Doe entered the court from the rear door. She was startlingly tiny, with long dark-blond hair. Although she gave her age as nineteen, her fragility and innocent countenance left the impression that Jane was still very much a child.

In a quiet, wavering voice, Jane recounted meeting Karla in the Pen Centre and then resuming their relationship just prior to the couple's wedding. She recalled the first night she spent at the house, or at least as much as she could. It was the first time she'd ever drunk alcohol, she explained. Jane went on to describe how she looked up to Karla as an older sister, the one she never had.

"Karla was very important to me," Jane told the court. "I could talk with her about anything . . . boyfriends, stuff like that."

When she visited, Jane would help Karla in the kitchen, preparing meals, setting the table, enjoying the sense that she was helping.

Her relationship with Paul, however, was very different, Jane said quietly.

"He was doing stuff that I didn't agree with."

The "stuff" included taking Jane into the guest bedroom downstairs on a regular basis. Paul would merely say to Karla that Jane and he needed to talk and they would disappear. Once in the bedroom, he would ask the fifteen-year-old girl to perform oral sex on him. She didn't want to, she told the court, but Paul explained that if Jane wanted Karla to be happy, the best way to ensure that was to keep Paul happy.

"And I wanted to keep Karla happy," Jane explained tearfully.

In late August 1991, the three traveled to Toronto, where they went shopping at the Eaton Centre. There Paul bought Jane a number of gifts, including a pair of jeans. They stayed at the Hilton and went to the CN Tower for dinner.

When they returned to the hotel, Karla went to sleep in

one bed, while Jane was on a second bed. Paul ordered a pornographic movie on television and then moved into bed with her, Jane said. He began stroking her over her clothing.

"I told him that I didn't like it, that I felt it was wrong," Jane told the court. "He stopped then and got on the floor."

Although Jane was performing oral sex on a more or less regular basis—whenever Paul wanted—he still wanted more. He wanted to have intercourse with Jane, who at that time believed she was a virgin since she had not seen or been made aware of the videotaped assault on her which the court had now viewed.

"He came up and just said, 'Will you have sex with me or will you make love to me.' " she said. "I said, 'No.' "

"He was married and I was a virgin, and I just didn't think it was right."

Paul, undaunted, continued to press her to go to bed with him, Jane said. One night the two stayed awake the entire night in front of the fireplace as Paul tried to convince her. He then made Jane promise that he would be the first, which she did. The conversations bothered Jane greatly, mostly because she was afraid Karla might find out what was going on and she desperately wanted the friendship to survive in spite of Paul's behavior. But Karla never seemed to show any kind of concern about seeing Jane and Paul kissing or when they left to go into the guest bedroom.

One night the three were sitting in the living room and Paul scribbled a note and passed it to Jane.

"I want to fuck (make love) to you all night. You drive me fuckin' crazy. Your love for life, Paul. XOXO."

Jane was incredulous. Paul's wife was sitting right there, smiling away as if nothing was going on.

Jane goes on to testify that one day her mother confronted Paul about fondling Jane. Later, she received an angry call from Paul demanding to know what was going on.

"He was very upset and said I should have told the truth, that I wanted him to touch my breasts," she said.

But Jane, too, was angry, she said, "because I didn't like the stuff he was doing to me. And I told him that."

But angry or not, the three continued to see each other whenever her mother would allow it. Sometimes Paul would pick Jane up from school and they would drive around until it was time to pick up Karla from work. Jane acknowledged that she never brought any of her young friends over to 57 Bayview Drive because she wanted Paul and Karla to herself. It made her feel good to be treated as an equal by much older people.

At one point, the three went on a day trip to Toronto to see a play, *The Phantom of the Opera*. They had champagne and Paul bought Jane and Karla T-shirts and a program. During the show, Paul reached over and guided Jane's hand to his crotch. She quickly removed it, she said, afraid, as always, that Karla would see.

After a break in the relationship that lasted through late 1991 and early 1992, Jane resumed visiting the Bernardo home. One night they began talking about Tammy Homolka. Although Jane hadn't known Karla's little sister, she became upset and started crying. "I felt she didn't deserve for her sister to die."

Karla, too, began to weep, and finally Paul was sobbing as well. Jane fled upstairs to the master bedroom, where Paul joined her, asking why she was so upset. Then his voice took on a strange tone.

"He said something like, 'What's it like to see the light? What's it like to die?' I thought he was comparing me to Tammy, and he said, 'Someday you'll understand.'"

The relationship began to unravel during late 1992. As Christmas approached, Jane was visiting one night and Paul suggested that the three look at the lights he'd just strung off the deck in the backyard. Karla pointed out that one of the lights had burned out and Paul went into a rage, telling her to shut up.

When they went back inside, Karla suggested that Paul was upset and really needed a kiss and a hug from Jane. "It felt like she was pushing me on him. It was weird," Jane told the court.

Later, on December 22, Jane visited again. They exchanged gifts, and among those given to Jane was a Gund stuffed animal named Big Trouble and an expensive gold chain. It was, said Paul, a present a boyfriend would give his girlfriend.

That night, Paul was drinking quite heavily and smoking marijuana or hashish. Later, while Karla was on the phone with her mother, Paul gave Jane a long, passionate kiss right in front of Karla. Then Paul disappeared upstairs into his music room while Jane, upset at what had happened, waited to talk with Karla. When Karla hung up the phone, she told her young friend that it was okay, that she knew that Jane was in love with Paul.

"I told her, 'I don't like Paul. The only reason I've ever come over is for you,' " Jane explained.

But Karla was not moved. In fact, she became annoyed and told Jane that she needed to talk to Paul about this, that their conversation had never happened.

Confused and angry, Jane stormed into the music room and told Paul she didn't ever want to see him again.

Paul exploded. He began screaming at Jane, telling her she was worthless and didn't deserve to live. He called her names. But as she turned to leave, he softened, telling her that she could make it up to him, that everything would be forgotten if she went to bed with him.

Jane descended the stairs with Paul at her heels, continuing to berate her. Teary-eyed, Jane sat silently on the couch with Karla. Paul picked up a picture of Jane that she'd given to Paul and Karla as a present and threw it across the living room. Then he picked up Karla and proceed to carry her upstairs.

"Karla, are you mad at me?" Jane asked before Karla disappeared from view.

"Well, I'm just a little bit upset at you," Karla responded.

And then she was gone. Paul turned out the lights, leaving Jane alone in the darkness. She could see him standing at the top of the stairs. But he said nothing, merely staring down at her as though his anger and disgust had left him speechless.

For forty-five minutes, until Jane's mother arrived, the two remained frozen in this bizarre dance.

Finally, as she was leaving, Jane asked Paul if he wanted his necklace back.

"No, keep it," he said.

In the end, the Crown's case just seemed to fizzle out, as though someone had thrown a bucket of cold water on a roaring campfire.

After the emotional testimony of Carol and Jane and Jane's mother, weary jurors watched in seeming disbelief as a parade of Beaver Lumber employees marched to the stand to tell about how they couldn't remember whether Paul Bernardo had ever been in their store, even though the defense had already acknowledged that Paul had purchased concrete there.

Then a series of Karla's coworkers and friends went to the stand as well. All described seeing bruises at various times on Karla's arms and back. Without exception, they recounted how Karla had downplayed the marks as the result of the hazards of work or of frolicking with Buddy.

Perhaps the most significant witness among that group was Wendy Lutczyn. She was the one who made the initial call to the Homolkas over Christmas 1992 when she'd seen Karla's racoonlike eyes and angry bruises. She had also maintained a steady correspondence with the convicted schoolgirl killer, a correspondence that the defense pointed out had carried on until within days of Lutczyn's testimony. Much of the letter writing seemed to focus on Karla's efforts to win Lutczyn over to the Crown theory of battered wife syndrome as the explanation for her behavior. She sent Wendy books and articles that discussed the syndrome. As with the earlier letters to Alex and Kathy from prison, the message was obvious—here are some things you can do to understand me.

> *Dear Wendy,*
>   *This is a difficult letter for me to write because I'm not sure that you'll take it the right way . . .*
>   *I want you to know that more than anyone, I under-*

stand your feelings about our friendship. I know your family hates me. I know your friends hate me. I know you remember the good person you saw in me when we worked together. I know you saw the results of his beatings. I know you're feeling all kinds of conflicting emotions and I understand. If I could only tell you my side, perhaps it will make it easier for you. One day I will tell you. If you still want to hear. You will have a much greater understanding when you hear my testimony at trial—I promise you.

In the meantime, something that may help you a bit is a wonderful book that I can't find any fault with—The Battered Woman by Lenore Warker . . .

Anyway, please write & let me know what you think about everything I've said.

By the way—Dr. Hatcher is a Godsend.

> *Love,*
> *Karla*

The Crown wanted desperately to be able to call expert witnesses to describe their take on Karla Homolka. But the defense argued just as strongly that the trial wasn't about Karla Homolka but Paul Bernardo. Judge LeSage agreed and allowed only hypothetical evidence from London, Ontario, specialist Dr. Peter Jaffe and San Francisco–based trauma expert Dr. Chris Hatcher.

After several scheduling gaffes that left the jury sent home for partial days and excused for entire days, the Crown called its last witness, a last-minute addition to their witness list: Niagara Region Police diver Bill Wiley.

Less than a week before he was called to the stand, Wiley had discovered a saw blade along with some women's jewelry in a channel between Lake Gibson and Lake Moody, a few hundred meters from where the saw housing had been found during a search of the lake a year earlier.

The Crown team was excited. Even though the jewelry wasn't connected to the case, they felt certain the blade was the one used to dismember Leslie Mahaffy.

In court that morning, August 14, they scurried around before the jury was brought in, placing the blade on a model saw previously entered as an exhibit. Without warning, assistant Crown attorney Greg Barnett bent and plugged the saw in. The roaring sound erupted in the courtroom, shattering quiet precourt conversations.

In the front row, Debbie Mahaffy, taken totally by surprise, shot out of her seat with a terrible moan. For a woman who could barely look at the saw, the sound was a shocking precursor to that day's proceedings. She wept openly, her head leaning on the shoulder of a disgusted court counselor.

The Crown rested its case later that day.

[*The following passages are composed directly from court testimony in Paul Bernardo's trial in Toronto during July and August 1995.*]

On Tuesday, August 15, the defense opened its case. As he had before his cross-examination of Karla, veteran defense attorney John Rosen paced uneasily in front of the empty jury box as he waited for them to enter.

With a disarming smile, he told the jury that in many areas the case was simple. All you have to do is put in the tapes and press Play and the entire case is laid out, he said—with the exception of who actually killed Leslie and Kristen.

In each case, only three people were in the house, Rosen continued. In each case, one of those people is dead. The jury has heard from the second person—Karla.

"The only other person who can tell you what happened in the house . . . is Paul Bernardo," Rosen said. "Why not just call the witness and hear what he has to say?" Rosen asked rhetorically. "And that's what I intend to do."

"Members of the jury, I call to the stand Paul Bernardo."

Journalists and spectators, many of whom had stood in line through the night to get a glimpse of the accused serial killer, craned their necks as he moved the short distance from the prisoner's box to the witness box.

Wearing a black jacket, white shirt, and patterned tie, Paul stood in the box as he would throughout his testimony, fixing the same microphone to his tie that his ex-wife had fixed to her jacket weeks earlier.

Rosen played several sex assaults from the videotapes. He asked Paul if he'd strangled them to death with a black electrical cord, as his ex-wife had earlier suggested.

"No, sir," Paul said in a clear, high voice.

"What do you say, Mr. Bernardo, what do you now say about all the other things that you have done as shown in these videos and that we've heard for the last several weeks from all these other witnesses? What do you say about that?" Rosen asked.

Paul turned directly to the jury, his arm pointed at them for emphasis, as though he were a politician making a speech or a televangelist beginning a sermon.

"People. I know I've done some really terrible things, I know that. And I've caused a lot of sadness and sorrow to a lot of people, and I'm really sorry for that and I know I deserve to be punished. But I didn't kill these girls."

"Let's find out what did happen," Rosen said.

And they were off.

From that moment on that Tuesday morning it was clear that John Rosen was not going to belabor his client's testimony. They began at breakneck speed, recounting the night Paul had kidnapped Leslie Mahaffy and then tracking back in time to the initial stages of Paul and Karla's relationship.

"I thought she was a really different person. And I liked that, at the time. I thought she was really strong-willed, independent, and a little weird," Paul said.

The weekend following their October 17, 1987, meeting, when Paul and Van visited Karla in St. Catharines, and after seeing the movie *Prince of Darkness*, Paul said, he and Karla had sex in her bedroom while Van and Kathy were in the rec room next door.

"She had some handcuffs. She had some handcuffs on the posts of her bed. And the first thing that she wanted me to do was to handcuff her behind her back. And she told me I could do anything with her. And she was the prisoner, and stuff like that," Paul said.

Every weekend he would visit, Paul explained, his eyes fixed on the jury, and every weekend they would have sex.

"It was worth the drive down," he said, shrugging his shoulders.

The relationship evolved, and Paul admitted he continued to date other girls, although he never told Karla. In the summer of 1990, during a party at the Homolkas', he and Tammy went to the States to buy alcohol.

"We got some McDonald's and we ended up going to the Niagara Gorge. And we ended up eating. What happened, we got really drunk, we ended up kissing and touching, and we didn't end up returning home until later that night," Paul explained.

"Well, when I came back, Karla was really upset. And we went down to our bedroom and she started accusing me of fooling around with Tammy. Well, I originally denied it and then I finally fessed up and said, 'Yeah, I did.' And she was jealous about it. And she started to goof around and say, you know, 'Tammy wouldn't know what to do with Snuffles if she had it,' Paul told the jury.

"The discussions led to talk about Karla and me having sex with Tammy to teach her what sex was like. And we couldn't do it consensually because we didn't think that she would want to, you know, come in with us."

So, Paul said, they decided to drug her and have sex with her anyway.

Only, it wasn't in December as Karla and the Crown insisted, he told the twelve people who would decide his fate. It was much earlier, in the summer of 1990.

Karla made pasta for her sister, Paul explained, and "she ground up a lot of Valium and put it into Tammy's spaghetti sauce.

"When Tammy went down, I pulled down Tammy's pants and I entered her, and I was in her for about a minute and Karla was there watching, and as soon as I finished Tammy started to wake up, so we both went out of the room."

That wasn't all, though, Paul told the jury, his voice never going above or below a normal speech pattern.

"Unfortunately, we thought it was really neat and we

wanted to do it again, so we started to try and put the Valium into the drinks of Tammy and her friends when they came over.''

But Tammy and the girls found the drinks bitter and wouldn't finish them, foiling the couple's plans, he claimed.

To fill in the sexual void, Paul said they did other things, including watching Tammy change from outside her bedroom window. He would also creep into her room while she was sleeping and masturbate on her pillow.

''And Karla would be in the doorway watching,'' he told the jury.

They then set about devising a more comprehensive plan to drug and rape Tammy again, this time using Halothane and Halcion, Paul said. It worked, he said, but when the time came to perform oral sex on her sister, Karla balked.

''She noticed that Tammy was on her period, and she didn't want to perform it. And I thought it was no big deal because I had done that before, so I forced her to do it. I was all excited in the situation, and we didn't have much time, so . . .''

Of course, Tammy died, in spite of the couple's efforts to revive her. Tammy's death, Paul said, forged his and Karla's relationship on a level that no one else could understand.

''We were like soul mates, we were really, really close. And what we did is we just bonded together, and every time we're together, what we would do, we had sex.''

Not only did they have sex, they talked about sex, Paul explained, and the kind of sex they invariably talked about was kinky, three-way sex.

Within weeks of Tammy's death, Paul said, he brought a hitchhiker home while Dorothy and Karel Homolka were out of town.

''When this girl was in the car, what I did is I threw my jacket over and then I blindfolded her. When I came to the Homolkas' residence, Karla was in the living room and I brought the girl in and I motioned for Karla to come downstairs. And we went down into Karla's bedroom, and I proceeded to rape the girl.''

As he described the act with the unknown girl, Paul's voice never wavered, he never looked away from the jury.

"It was supposed to be for three-way sex. But what happened at the time was . . . the girl, she wasn't compliant, she started fighting, and arguing and complaining and not wanting to do the sex acts," Paul recalled. Karla was scared of the woman's defiance and refused to participate.

Paul denied that he forced Karla to leave her parents' home in February, 1991, as she had testified. He did acknowledge, however, that they argued frequently when they moved into 57 Bayview Drive and that many of those arguments centered around Tammy's death.

But as with much of their relationship he said, the arguments were resolved through sex—either discussion of sexual fantasies involving others, or acting out fantasies together.

When he returned from Daytona Beach in the spring of 1991, Paul said, he met a girl named Alyson with whom he developed a relationship. They called back and forth, and he told Karla he had feelings for this new woman.

"And Karla was really upset about it, and just because of what everything happened with Tammy, I wasn't sure, you know, whether or not I wanted to get married at the time," Paul said.

But they did ultimately get married, Paul explained, and the reconciliation was forged on twisted sex. In this case, he said, they conspired to ensnare Jane in their sexual web.

A week or so after the first drugging and rape of Jane, Paul said, that he was out transferring cigarettes to Van and Steve when he decided to stop off in Burlington on the way back to St. Catharines to steal some license plates to aid in smuggling. By pure chance, he said, he drove into the neighborhood of Keller Court.

"I got out of my car to get a plate, and as soon as I got out, Leslie Mahaffy was coming around the corner at the time," Paul explained.

He ran between some houses, but Leslie Mahaffy ended up in the backyard next to where he was. He watched as she tried the doors of her house. They appeared to be locked. After waiting a few moments, he moved and literally bumped into the teen.

"I didn't know what to say to her, so I said I was breaking into the house next door. And she thought that was cool. And she said she was locked out of her house, and she asked me for a cigarette."

Paul admitted that he thought Leslie was attractive and that he thought it would be good to bring her home for three-way sex, just as Karla had earlier lured Jane into their home. As they walked toward the Nissan to get a cigarette, Paul said he took his long-sleeved hooded sweatshirt and wrapped it over Leslie's head and told her to shut up. He forced her into the car and drove her to 57 Bayview.

Contradicting Karla's testimony, Paul said, he woke her up to tell her about the kidnapping, and she followed him downstairs and watched as he videotaped the blindfolded teen identifying herself.

Apart from minor details, Paul's recollection of the events during Leslie's twenty-four-hour captivity more or less matched Karla's—until he got around to discussing the final video segments.

Paul said that in the last, horrible segment, when he anally rapes Leslie despite her screams for mercy, it was the first time she'd ever been tied up or restrained.

"We thought it would be a good scene for the videotape to have her tied up," Paul explained, taking on an almost professional countenance, lecturing on the finer points of sexual videotaping.

He testified that he'd earlier brought up from the basement a length of black electrical cord with which to bind his captive, but it was too long and too bulky to work with, so he threw it aside and instead used twine. The cord is seen underneath Leslie in the video.

"After that last act, I—I'd had enough. I mean, Leslie was screaming. And it was like, okay, I've had enough," Paul said.

So Karla and Paul discussed what they were going to do, and Paul testified he wanted to drop Leslie off in Burlington near her home. Karla was upset, Paul said, worried that Leslie had seen him well enough to give police a good identification. "She had concerns about my sample that I gave to Metro. And I told her that, you know, Metro is different from Burlington Police and I thought there was no chance of them finding us because we're in St. Catharines, which is a different city. I basically told her, you know, listen, if anyone ever came back it's our word against hers, there's two of us and she's a runaway, and who says she didn't come over consensually," Paul explained.

At that comment Debbie Mahaffy, who'd been sitting quietly, moaned out loud.

Paul continued. They decided that they'd drug her, so she wouldn't get a look at his license plate when he dropped her off. He said they dressed her, gave her a pillow and Bunky the stuffed animal, and she went to sleep.

Paul said he left the upstairs bedroom and cleared a path to the car so he could carry her down. While downstairs, Paul related, he noticed that the car needed some gas and he poured some in from a container he kept in the garage for the lawn mower. He then had a shower and returned to the master bedroom. Leslie appeared to be in the same position he'd left her, Paul said.

"Then I went over to Leslie to pick her up, and when I turned her over, I noticed she wasn't breathing," he said.

Paul told the court that he checked her pulse and listened for a heartbeat, and there was nothing.

"Leslie is not breathing," he said he told his fiancée.

Then, he said, he started pushing on her chest and blowing into her mouth.

"It's too late, she's dead," Karla said, according to Paul.

When he asked Karla what happened, he said she told him the Halcion and alcohol must have been too much for her.

The couple grabbed each other and began crying, Paul said.

But why, asked Rosen, would they possibly have been upset. After all, Paul had kidnapped the girl literally out of her own backyard. And then he and Karla had tied her up and raped her.

"Why do you now find this upsetting?" Rosen asked, the

jury, Judge LeSage, even the Crown team waiting for his response.

"Well, what we did was for sex, that's all it was supposed to be for. It shouldn't have cost the girl her life," Paul said. Although he was answering Rosen's question, his response was directed straight at the jury.

"We were pretty much hysterical. We thought of calling 911, but we had a problem in that we couldn't explain why the girl was here. So we didn't."

The following day, Father's Day, the Homolkas came to visit. After they left, Paul said, he and Karla decided that the body should be placed in cement and thrown in the lake so no one would ever find it. It was Paul who decided that the body should be dismembered, pointing out to Karla that one block containing the body would be so heavy that they could never lift it. Paul said Karla suggested that, given her experience at the animal clinic, she would wield the saw and cut up the body.

"And I said no, because it was a big power saw and I didn't want her to get hurt," Paul explained.

It was still Sunday night when they decided they should get the job over with, Paul told the jury, knowing that his version differed dramatically from the one told by Karla some weeks earlier. Still standing, he allowed his gaze to run from juror to juror, occasionally flitting back to Rosen as he clinically discussed how he and his fiancée cut up a fourteen-year-old girl in their basement after celebrating Father's Day.

First, he said, they cut off Mahaffy's clothing with some scissors. He then rigged a tarp into a tentlike structure to restrict the spread of blood and gore in the basement, and he covered the floor with newspapers. Paul then disappeared under the tarp, and with his grandfather's circular saw cut up Leslie Mahaffy's body, handing the parts to Karla, who washed them down in the sink and placed them in a garbage bag and stored them in the root cellar.

The entire process took an hour and a half, Paul said.

The next morning, Paul drove Karla to work, then went in search of cardboard boxes in which to pour the cement. By the time he picked Karla up from work that afternoon, he said, the job was done.

Although the cleaning up Paul described was similar to Karla's recollection, there were some minor variances. Paul said they discarded the bloody tarps and newspapers in the garbage disposal at the animal clinic, for which Karla had a key.

As for the electrical cord that Karla insisted Paul used to kill Mahaffy, Paul said he threw it out along with the twine that had been used to bind her.

It was, of course, only a matter of days from the time the blocks containing Leslie Mahaffy were dumped into Lake Gibson to the couple's wedding. Paul said they tried to block out the memory and carry on as usual.

He said the couple's bizarre sex life continued to thrive.

"We kept the fantasies going. We kept talking about three-way sex. We kept checking out girls and videotaping girls," Paul told Rosen.

Rosen asked Paul about earlier testimony from Carol, his longtime Scarborough girlfriend.

Paul matter-of-factly described their "consensual" relationship.

"She was my girlfriend and I was her boyfriend," he explained. Part of their sexual life, he said, involved placing a rope around her neck "just when I would penetrate her, like I was riding her."

At this point Paul used his hands to show how he would loop the rope around Carol's neck, and he gave his hips a brief, mock thrust to illustrate the riding motion. "Then I stopped doing it. She said it hurt and I never used it again," Paul said, his calm, even voice a stunning contrast to the angry, bitter woman who'd described being violated in the back of Paul's car.

Later in the summer of 1991, Paul said he and Karla decided to subdue Jane once again. Only this time, when Karla applied the Halothane, he said, the teen stopped breathing. Paul began trying to revive her while Karla called 911. Of course, Jane was revived and didn't realize until much later any of what had befallen her at the hands of her friends.

But, Paul said, the incident scared him.

"I had totally had it at that point and I said, 'No more Halothane. No more Halcion, ever again. We're never ever going to touch the stuff again.'"

So he explained that they tried to trap Jane in what she would believe was a consensual relationship.

On April 16, 1992, Paul said, he and Karla were going shopping in the Lakeport Road area, not far from their home.

"And as we were driving along we were checking out the girls that were walking along, making comments about them, and Karla said, 'How about we grab one for the weekend? You know, well, for the night.' And I was like, yeah, you know. We were just joking around, and it wasn't really a serious thing until we saw Kristen, and Karla said that she really liked her and that she was hot. We turned around and went into the parking lot, and Karla said she would ask her to look over at the map."

There was, Paul said, no plan. Notwithstanding Karla's evidence, there was no discussion of getting a girl, of how they would do it, of what would be done or said. Nothing like that, Paul said.

"Like I said, we were just driving out, and we were making comments, and it just happened. Before we knew it, we were actually doing it."

In the front row of the courtroom, Donna and Doug French sat motionless, staring straight ahead at the man who was describing the kidnapping and sexual torture of their daughter. But as though they were determined to deny him the satisfaction of seeing them break down, they remained steely-eyed.

Paul explained that he happened to have the knife with him in the car because it was a precaution taken on the couple's smuggling runs to the U.S. Still, that didn't entirely explain why Paul insists he didn't have a knife when he kidnapped Leslie Mahaffy.

They lured Kristen to the car, although she struggled desperately at first, Paul said. During the struggle, Karla was knocked down and Kristen was nicked with the knife in the shoulder. But eventually Kristen was subdued and driven to 57 Bayview Drive.

"Well, I guess I am going to ask you the hard question," Rosen said, watching his client. "I don't understand. Why did you do this? Why did you just pick this girl off the street and kidnap her? What was going on?"

Paul nodded as the question was being asked. If there was criticism that Karla had appeared scripted by the Crown, there was certainly ample evidence that Paul, too, had been well-coached by his legal handlers.

"At that time, Karla and me had evolved so much in our sexual life, so much fantasy, and actual events had happened and we were drinking a lot, I was drinking almost every day, and we used drugs at that time, and we were basically out of control."

Again the answer was directed at the jurors, as though the courtroom was empty except for them.

Initially Kristen was blindfolded, and Paul insisted that their intention was to let Kristen go later that night, even though she might have had a good look at them during the parking lot struggle.

But then he said the blindfold fell off and it was decided she would stay indefinitely.

"So I told Kristen that instead of staying for the one night, I told her she was going to stay for a few days and then she was going home," Paul explained.

Rosen asked Paul what he wanted to do to Kristen after the blindfold loosened. "I thought she was going to go home at some time, but I wasn't sure when," Paul said.

"What do you mean by that, that you weren't sure when?" Rosen asked, his voice carrying an incredulous edge even though he was questioning his own client.

"I never decided on anything. I just . . . the blindfold was off, she's staying, and that was . . . wasn't sure how long, what . . . you know, if we would ever let her go. I wasn't sure," Paul stammered, for the first time.

Paul described going out for dinner on Friday night, after tying Kristen with a black electrical cord to a center partition in his walk-in closet, the cord looped around her neck.

There were he said, multiple sex acts. And at one point, Paul admitted, he began striking Kristen. He'd never struck Leslie, but Kristen was much more defiant.

"Well, what happened is that the first two times that she performed fellatio she did it really well, and when she didn't, I just thought she was messing around and to be noncompliant. By the time the fourth time came, I just thought that she's just messing around and being noncompliant, so I struck her," Paul said.

He insisted he never struck her in the head or the face, although the videotapes later showed otherwise.

On the first night, Kristen was handcuffed and slept in the closet. The second night, Paul said, she joined him and Karla in bed.

"Why?" Rosen asked.

"Our fantasy was to have three people together, and to love each other, and everyone to be happy, and that's the world we lived in," Paul said, again his voice barren of emotion as he described this utopian sex world he and, presumably, Karla were determined to create.

On Saturday evening, Paul left 57 Bayview to get take-out Swiss Chalet chicken for dinner. This time he tied Kristen by the neck to one end of the hope chest, he said.

"When I came home I pulled my car into the garage and Karla was in the living room and she was crying," Paul recalled. "Well, the first thing she said was that Kristen tried to escape. And I basically ran upstairs, and that's when I saw Kristen, and she was dead."

She was, Paul said, still attached to the hope chest, her hands still cuffed behind her back, her legs untied.

"The ligature was tight around her neck at this point, just squeezing right in there," Paul said, motioning to his throat with both hands. "And there was blood around her mouth and the hair was over her face."

"I said, 'Oh my God, what happened?' " Paul said.

Karla, he said, told him that Kristen had asked to go to the washroom, and that as she untied her legs, she tried to escape.

As she related the story, Karla began to weep and hugged him, Paul said. And then he too, began to weep.

They talked about what to do with the body, but dismembering was immediately ruled out, Paul insisted.

"The last thing I was going to do was cut anyone up again," he said. "Because that was one of the most disgusting, horrible things I've ever done."

They dumped the body that night, Saturday—not Sunday, which is when Karla insists the murder took place. Paul claimed not to have any knowledge that Kristen's final resting place would be within several kilometers of Leslie Mahaffy's grave site. It wasn't until seeing the television special on the murders that the couple realized the irony of the location they'd chosen to dump Kristen's body, Paul said.

The marriage went pretty much downhill from that point, Paul admitted. He felt a lot of remorse and anger over what had happened to Tammy, he said, and the couple argued about that often. Sometimes he struck her, he conceded.

The most violent beating took place on December 27, the anniversary of Tammy's funeral; Paul said he struck Karla in the head several times with a flashlight. Earlier in the evening he'd pulled the tapes down from their hiding place in the garage and watched the Tammy segment.

On January 4, 1993, he beat Karla again during a smuggling run. The next day she was gone.

Paul said he immediately moved the tapes, because he feared Karla would come back and take them and destroy them or take them to the police. So he shoved them inside one of the recessed potlights in the upstairs bathroom.

Rosen wanted to know why he didn't destroy the tapes himself, and why, indeed, he'd ever watch them again.

"I was a chronic saver," he explained. "I couldn't bring it in myself to throw them out. It was the last memory of these girls' lives. They were such a significant part to our life, events in our life. And we would watch them to remember."

In the front row, Donna French bowed her head in disbelief.

Rosen asked his client if he thought about what had happened to him in the more than two years since he'd been arrested.

Again, Paul nodded even as the question was being posed.

"When I look back on how our life went and how our sexual fantasies went and how they hurt so many people, I can't believe it. I can't believe it's the same person."

Paul's direct testimony lasted less than three hours. And despite the fact that the prosecuting team had speculated almost from the trial's outset that Paul would take the stand, lead Crown attorney Ray Houlahan seemed to be caught off guard when he began his cross-examination of the accused on the afternoon of August 15.

Houlahan initially stumbled through his questions, jumping from topic to topic, often using incorrect information or crowing that he'd caught Paul in a fabrication when in fact he'd merely misunderstood Paul's answers. It was a rocky start to what was a critical part of the Crown's case. Outside court, journalists and others close to the case rolled their collective eyes.

Over the following days, however, Houlahan recovered and began focusing on specific areas of the murders and abductions, methodically taking Paul through the sex tapes, the most powerful piece of evidence at his disposal. He was aided in no small part by assistant Crown attorney Lesley Baldwin, who sat near Houlahan's lectern, scribbling furiously on yellow lined paper, handing him note after note.

Houlahan suddenly began to exploit cracks in Paul's cocky, self-assured demeanor, often forcing him to read the brutal, degrading dialogue from the transcripts of the videotapes.

Paul, who remained standing for the six days he was on the stand, explained to Houlahan that he and Karla were equal partners with a seemingly unquenchable appetite for kinky, three-way sex. But Houlahan pointed again and again to the tapes where it apparently was Paul, and Paul alone, receiving sexual gratification and meting out punishment to the captive schoolgirls.

It didn't matter what it looked like, Paul explained, Karla was happy.

"Karla enjoyed watching me having sex with other

women. I enjoyed Karla watching me have sex with other women. I enjoyed sex with other women. We both enjoyed having sex with other women," Paul said. "Karla was very happy with our sex life."

Yet in one videotaped scene during which Paul anally and then vaginally rapes a screaming Leslie Mahaffy, he is the only one who looks over at the camera and smiles broadly.

"I think I smile just before she starts screaming," Paul explained impassively. "I was enjoying myself, sir," he said. But, he added, he had stopped when Leslie began crying.

"I'd had enough."

"You'd had enough, all right. That's why you killed her," Houlahan insisted angrily. "You were finished with her."

"No," Paul responded. "She was going home."

Later, when shown videotaped segments of a sobbing Kristen French telling Paul she loves him, repeating the phrase twenty-six times in a row, Paul insisted it was the adoration and affection that turned him on, not the infliction of pain as Houlahan suggested.

"I don't believe it was the pain, sir. I believe it was the sexual act, and the 'I love you' part," he said.

But why, then, would he want to videotape himself urinating on Kristen's face and trying desperately to defecate on her? Houlahan asked. Furthermore, Houlahan bluntly pointed out, Paul had a noticeable erection during the scene, which he complained to Kristen made it difficult for him to urinate.

"Obviously, looking back, I had a problem with sexuality. For me to explain now, I don't think I really can. But I think down the road, I'm going to have to be seeking professional help," Paul said, straight-faced.

A ripple of derisive laughter echoed through the courtroom at what many believed was the most understated comment of the trial.

As his stint on the stand wore on, Paul's demeanor changed dramatically. During the first days he'd been coolly analytical, almost professorial as he demonstrated how he'd walked the cement blocks containing Leslie Mahaffy's body parts to the basement steps, or animatedly explained how Karla's story about Kristen seeing a video clip of a captive Leslie Mahaffy wasn't technologically possible.

But, perhaps feeling he was giving the wrong impression, an apparently new Paul showed up for Day 5, Monday, August 21. Gone was the gesturing, the wild facial contortions, the eye-rolling. He was subdued and almost pensive when faced with his deeds, or as he liked to remind Houlahan over and over, Karla's accusations of his misdeeds.

For hours during her testimony, Karla had related a litany of physical and sexual perversions she was forced to endure at her husband's hands and feet and anything else he could bash her with. But when Houlahan asked Paul about these incidents, he categorically denied all of them with the exception of the final assault that landed Karla in the hospital in early January 1993.

Paul insisted that Karla was trying to redefine the history of their relationship and paint herself as a complete victim. Her testimony was "bizarre," Paul concluded. But as the day wore on, many believed it was his explanation of incidents and scenarios that took on a bizarre quality.

In response to Karla's description of being beaten in the General Motors parking lot and pushed into a mud puddle, Paul denied the incident ever happened but said it sounded an awful lot like a scene out of the movie *Wall Street.*

Paul also flatly denied Karla's assertion that Paul would often count transgressions during shopping trips and then deliver a like number of blows with the flashlight in the car.

"No way would you do a thing like that, eh?" Houlahan asked sarcastically.

"Not with Karla, sir. She's trying to redefine the whole relationship," Paul answered.

Paul told the court that Karla's recollections of the June 1992 fight that nearly resulted in Paul's kicking Karla out of the house was grossly distorted. He claimed that Karla marched through the house with Dorothy while he cried his eyes out.

Paul denied that he ever told Karla he was keeping her around for "cover" in case the police became interested in him again. "That's ridiculous. She was my wife; we were in love," he said.

In July 1992, Karla told the court that Paul beat her so badly there was hemorrhaging in her eyes. But Paul said her eye problems might have been caused by the pollution in Lake Ontario or some sand that got blown into Karla's eyes.

"A lot of dogs come to her clinic that played in the water, Lake Ontario water, and they have the same red-eye," Paul explained matter-of-factly.

Paul also had an explanation for stabbing Karla with a screwdriver while on a smuggling run. Karla said he stabbed her in a rage, forgetting that the screwdriver was in his hand. Paul said he was trying to take a screw out of the passenger-side door panel and he slipped, stabbing his wife above the knee.

"I freaked out," he told the court.

Paul also refuted Karla's testimony that he systematically isolated her from her friends.

"At no time did I ever isolate Karla from anybody. I am the one that didn't have the job. If there was anyone who was isolated it was me, but I am not crying victim," he said defensively.

Paul acknowledged that he did take Karla on trips to look for girls, but he denied it was for his enjoyment. Rather, he said, it was in the hopes he could spot a girl changing so he could videotape the act for both he and Karla to watch later during sex. He denied that these trips were merely an opportunity to engage in public masturbation.

"The camera would be very jerky," he said, straight-faced. "If you were holding the camera, you couldn't be masturbating at the same time."

Karla's eerie story of the final night she spent with Paul, of how he placed her in the same positions the abducted girls had been placed in prior to their murders, and of how he placed the same electrical cord around her neck, was denied by Paul.

"She had no reason to feel that she was the next victim?" Houlahan asked, incredulous.

"That's right, sir, she had no reason," Paul said.

"More blarney, right?" Houlahan asked, sarcasm dripping from the comment.

"Yes, sir, unfortunately there's a lot," he answered.

"We're not hearing any from you, of course," Houlahan shot back.

"No, sir," Paul answered.

Houlahan appeared surprised by Paul's new, meek appearance.

"What's this 'yes sir,' 'no sir,' 'three bags full, sir'? That's not the real you, is it?" he asked.

Judge LeSage interceded before Paul could respond.

Paul also explained why the court had never seen a card from him to Karla offering an apology, even though literally dozens had been entered as evidence showing Karla begging forgiveness or offering apology on top of apology.

"I apologized to Karla verbally. I'm a guy. I just didn't write a lot of cards," he said.

The only attempt at personal introspection appears to have been when he recorded the so-called suicide audiotapes in January, shortly before his arrest and after Karla had left him, Houlahan said. And even then, the prosecutor charged, that was in the hope of luring Karla back to their home because she knew so much that could incriminate Paul.

Paul denied that, saying, "At that time, it was a broken heart. This was not something to be mailed or sent, just something I was going to leave her, because I was going to kill myself."

Then, during this, the fifth day of his cross-examination, Paul made a comment that everyone, including Paul, knew was out of line as soon as he said it.

When asked to explain a video clip in which he is stimulating his own nipple while raping Kristen and being fondled by Karla in the area of his scrotum, Paul replied, "I did that quite frequently. I picked that one up from Tammy Homolka when I watched her masturbate one night," Paul said in his trademark, emotionally flat voice.

In Courtroom 6-1's second row, Dorothy and Lori Homolka bowed their heads in disbelief.

Houlahan was incensed.

"Is that right? You demean that poor young girl by saying that," he barked.

"I apologize if I demeaned her," Paul said quickly, as though he'd crossed some imaginary line.

But Houlahan pressed on.

"So Tammy taught you? She taught the king, the master?" he asked sarcastically.

"No, sir," Paul answered contritely. "I shouldn't have said that. It was very inappropriate."

"But you said that," Houlahan continued. "That sums you up, doesn't it? That shows your true colors, doesn't it?"

"It's inappropriate," Paul answered again, emotionless.

But despite his protests and apologies, Paul referred to the incident again only seconds later.

Paul's account of Leslie's mysterious death while he was getting gas in the car seemed far-fetched, but it was Kristen French's abduction that he could never fully explain. According to Paul, the couple's initial plan was to keep Kristen for one night and one night only, but when her blindfold fell off, he told Houlahan, they decided they'd have to keep her. Houlahan hammered away at this point, continually returning to it to ask again: Just how did Paul think he was going to be able to hide this girl, alive, inside his house, and for how long?

Was he planning to keep her indefinitely, until she grew old? Houlahan wanted to know.

That was an option, Paul claimed, since he wasn't working. But, he admitted, he continued to tell Kristen that she was going to be able to go home, even though he'd already decided she couldn't leave because she'd seen them and could identify the house and the car. She had even come to know Karla's name. "Not a very common name in a small city like St. Catharines," Houlahan pointed out. It was a dilemma Paul claimed he never really had to come to grips with, because Kristen died while he was out picking up Swiss Chalet chicken.

But Houlahan pointed to the final videotaped segments as proof that, as Karla had testified, Kristen's fate had been sealed the moment he walked up to the Nissan in the parking lot of Grace Lutheran Church.

During the final segment, moments before Karla testified that Paul strangled Kristen, Paul calls Karla a "fucking idiot," to which Kristen responds, "I don't know how your wife can stand to be around you. . . ."

"Shut up, okay?" Paul is heard commanding on the tape segment.

Houlahan seized on the comment.

"What we have here, by Kristen saying these words, is an independent judge of your character, isn't that right?"

"Not necessarily, sir. I don't understand the motive," he said, implying that Kristen was merely trying to curry favor with Karla in the hope of setting one captor against the other.

Paul did acknowledge, however, that he was "being a jerk" when he called his wife a fucking idiot.

The final videotaped segment shows Paul raping Kristen while Karla also performs sexual acts on her husband. But Paul cannot seem to maintain an erection, driving him into a fury, demanding that Kristen "suck for your life, bitch."

"Kristen's use as a sex slave is rapidly diminishing. She can no longer get you hard," Houlahan charged.

"I disagree," Paul said.

But Houlahan insisted that Paul's demeanor on tape had changed, that he'd grown dissatisfied with his toy. He wouldn't even let her go to the washroom, Houlahan pointed out disgustedly.

"She's finished. Her life is nearly finished. You're finished with her, aren't you?" Houlahan said.

Always unflappable, Paul denied that. But Houlahan had made his point. As the last video segment abruptly ends Paul orders Karla to shut off the camera. As both Karla and then Paul testified, Kristen would die within the next hour.

At about 3:30 P.M. on Thursday, August 31, the jury rose to deliberate the charges against Paul Bernardo.

While they were in the jury room, police and reporters placed bets as to how long it would be until their release. The standing joke had been that they would refuse to leave the jury box, so certain observers were of a guilty verdict. But day became night as reporters sat and sprawled across the sixth floor landing doing crossword puzzles, reading novels, tensely awaiting the jury's decision.

Finally, at about 9:00 P.M., Judge LeSage reconvened the legal teams and told them the jury would retire for the night. Minutes later, a series of black limousines ferried the jurors to a downtown hotel where they spent the night in rooms denuded of television, newspapers and radios. Court constables were assigned to the jurors to make sure there was no contact with the outside world. At 9:00 A.M. the following day they were hard at it again. As the morning wore on there, concern rippled through those awaiting the verdict. Perhaps the jury did not feel everything was as cut-and-dried as those waiting in the wings believed.

Shortly before noon, word spread through the courthouse that the jury was ready to come back.

Dorothy, Karel and Lori Homolka were the first of the family members to enter court. Dorothy choked back tears as she held Lori's hand.

The French and Mahaffy families took their places in the first two rows. Donna French turned, her eyes red, and embraced Debbie Mahaffy. Kristen's brother, Darren, and Leslie's brother, Ryan, both bore striking resemblance to their sisters. Darren, a year older than Kristen, stared defiantly at Paul as he was led into court, his hands cuffed behind his back.

But Paul, dressed in his olive green jacket and patterned tie, seemed oblivious. His face portrayed nothing.

The muted conversations ended and silence enveloped the courtroom when Judge LeSage entered, and moments later, the jury filed in. Most jurors had changed from the casual outfits they had worn the previous evening to more formal clothes.

The registrar instructed Paul to stand just as he had when the charges had first been read aloud at the outset of his trial some fifteen weeks earlier. His attorneys, John Rosen and Tony Bryant, stood at his side. Paul looked at the jury foreman with a blank stare. Nine times the registrar asked what the verdict was. Nine times the foreman answered in a clear voice: "guilty." Guilty as charged.

Paul Bernardo portrayed not a flicker of emotion. At that moment he seemed to mirror more than ever Patrick Bateman of the novel *American Psycho,* a man who had "all the characteristics of a human being—flesh, blood, skin, hair—but (whose) depersonalization was so intense, had gone so deep, that the normal ability to feel compassion had been eradicated."

While everyone in the courtroom felt compassion for the families of the slain teens as they continued to hold each other and weep quietly, Paul Bernardo seemed not only devoid of compassion, but of any human feeling.

Two rows behind Paul, Dorothy leaned on her daughter, Lori, and sobbed. Karel rested his arm comfortingly around his wife's shoulders.

There was no other sound in the courtroom. No cheers. No cries of anguish. Nothing but silence.

Judge LeSage ignored Paul and turned his attention to the jury. He thanked them for a job well done under trying circumstances.

"No single judge ever brings to bear on the issues, the wisdom, the experience, the knowledge that the twelve of you collectively have," LeSage said. He told them the entire country owed them a debt of gratitude. "Thank you, thank you so much," he said warmly.

And at 12:30 P.M. the jury walked out of Courtroom 6-1 for the last time.

LeSage then asked Paul to stand again and informed him that his conviction on both counts of first-degree murder, the most serious charge in the Canadian criminal code, carried an automatic life sentence with no chance of parole for twenty-five years.

He thanked the legal teams and the media, and the trial was over.

As court security moved to replace Paul's handcuffs, Staff Sergeant Steve MacLeod turned to Paul and gave him a big thumbs up signal. It was the same motion Paul had used on the videotapes showing one of the final sexual assaults on Leslie.

Television and radio stations had interrupted regular programming with live news of the verdict. On highways, vehicles flashed their lights and honked their horns to mark the decision.

Outside the courtroom Karel, Dorothy and Lori Homolka avoided the throng of cameramen and reporters who followed them. Karel said little, but he did offer that the guilty verdict had vindicated his eldest daughter.

Assistant Crown Attorney Lesley Baldwin, trailed by reporters to the Colony Hotel which hosted the prosecution headquarters, stepped into the lobby. Thrusting her hands triumphantly in the air, she called out jubilantly, "It's over!"

Surrounded by dozens of reporters and cameras, Rosen said he would suggest to his client that he appeal the conviction based on concerns he had with Judge LeSage's instructions to the jury. The veteran lawyer was quick to denounce any suggestion that the jury's verdict vindicated the Crown and the deal they had cut with Karla.

"This verdict represents the jury's opinion of the guilt or the innocence of Mr. Bernardo based on the evidence that they heard and nothing more. I think that if the jury could speak, some, if not all of them would tell you that they have personal opinions about the deal made with Karla Homolka that differs from the Crown's opinion. I'm sure this jury would have preferred to have both of them sitting in the box together so that they could judge both of them . . . rather than having (the decision) made by bureaucrats ahead of time," Rosen said.

Often criticized by his own people as being aloof and unapproachable, Inspector Vince Bevan was gracious, knowing perhaps that in the coming months his entire operation would come under scrutiny with an internal probe and public inquiry.

He was, he said, "very, very proud" of the Task Force members. "If there is any credit that flows from a job well done in this trial, then we all share in that. If there is any blame or criticism, that blame and criticism is mine alone,'' he said.

The normally cool Bevan appeared shaken with emotion when he spoke of the families.

''This verdict does nothing to bring back those girls. Each of these girls would be nineteen years old today,'' he said, his voice breaking. ''We miss them and we would rather that they were here. I hope they were watching this trial and I hope now they can rest in peace.''

The fathers of the slain girls bore the dreadful task of trying to sum up their families' feelings and, as Christie Blatchford of the *Toronto Sun* noted, gave everyone a brief glimpse into the empty days that stretched ahead for these people.

Dan Mahaffy graciously thanked those who had supported them, both friends and strangers.

''The intensity of the overwhelming pain and strong emotions have once again swept us, rendering it impossible for us to adequately talk about the verdict, the death of Leslie and what this moment really means to us. Only the trial is over. Leslie is still not coming home.'' He then embraced Ryan, his only remaining child, and turned to Debbie.

Doug French, perhaps in anticipation of this moment, had slipped a turquoise T-shirt over his white dress shirt and tie when the verdict was delivered. On it was written *in memory of Kristen.*

''It's been over three years since our daughter was taken from us. It's a difficult and painful time, but finally today, with the guilty verdict, especially the guilty verdict of first-degree murder of our daughter, there is some sort of closure. While it can't return our daughter to us, we have the satisfaction of seeing this perpetrator punished,'' he said, his gravelly voice almost a whisper.

Reading from a hand-written statement, Doug looked briefly to the sky.

''Finally, and as always, our final words are for our daughter with the trial over: ''Kristie, you can't be hurt anymore. We love you.''

Minutes later, hundreds of spectators jeered and hollered as the police transport carrying Paul Bernardo to jail left the courthouse for the last time.

CHAPTER
30

Although women's-abuse specialist Dr. Peter Jaffe of London, Ontario, testified for Crown prosecutors at Paul Bernardo's trial, Judge LeSage did not allow him to give the jury his opinion on what had happened to Karla Homolka. Jaffe could only testify about battered woman's syndrome in general and hypothetical terms. In short, Jaffe's testimony didn't help anyone understand what had happened to Karla specifically. At times during his testimony, LeSage became most agitated, reminding Crown prosecutors that Paul Bernardo was on trial for the schoolgirl murders, not Karla.

At the request of Crown prosecutors, Jaffe, who had studied abused women and children for almost twenty years, and his London Family Court Clinic associate, Melikie Joseph, a social worker, interviewed Karla for ten hours in the Prison for Women during two visits in August and September 1994. He also interviewed Karel and Dorothy Homolka and Karla's surviving sister, Lori. He conducted psychological testing on Karla, analyzed information from thirteen police interviews, read transcripts of five days of Ken Murray and Carolyn MacDonald's cross-examination interviews in the Prison for Women, read the statements of Karla's friends, and reviewed transcripts of Bernardo's suicide tapes and the rap tape "Deadly Innocence." Reports from Karla's prison psychiatrist, Dr. Roy Brown, and counselor Jan Heney were also used. There was no direct access to Paul Bernardo.

In a report dated December 8, 1994, Jaffe wrote that Karla "exhibits all the signs and symptoms of a young women who has been extremely traumatized by an abusive relationship . . . she fits all the criteria for battered woman's syndrome. In our views, she was groomed, by Mr. Bernardo, to become involved in increasingly bizarre and dangerous behaviour that was harmful to herself and others."

Karla was "extremely vulnerable" to Paul Bernardo at the time of their meeting "due to the difference in power and status" between them, Jaffe wrote, specifically the differences in age, accumulated life experiences, finances, education, independence, and physical size. It is significant, he said, that Karla was "captivated" by Paul Bernardo during her late adolescence, a crucial period of her development. The rapid changes in her life would make her vulnerable to Paul's tactics.

Jaffe believes that Pauls' emotional abuse of Karla occurred early in the relationship and continued with daily frequency. She was made to feel unattractive, stupid, inadequate, and unable to survive in the world without Paul. He held such total control over Karla's thoughts that she was "afraid to even hold a contrary point of view." Jaffe acknowledged that physical abuse was rare early in the relationship, but when it did happen, he noted, Karla was "stunned" and because of Paul's apologies believed he had not intended to hurt her.

As the abuse escalated and Paul's coercion tactics became more intense and sophisticated, wrote Jaffe, Karla gradually accepted his demands for nude photographs and anal sex. She would make more attempts to please him, thus becoming more accepting of his negative portrayal of her.

Karla wasn't the only Homolka who was hoodwinked into believing Paul was a good man, Jaffe wrote.

"In fact, Mr. Bernardo was able to elicit Mr. Homolka's trust fairly quickly. In spite of his tendency to be over-protective of his daughters, he no longer insisted on a curfew."

And as the Homolkas began to call Paul their "weekend son," Jaffe said, Karla began to pity him for his own family difficulties and wanted to welcome him into her own family.

In the summer of 1990, Jaffe noted, after his incessant berating of Karla for not retaining her virgin status for him, Paul told her he wanted sex with her virginal sister Tammy. Paul described Tammy "in terms of being the younger, prettier and virginal version" of Karla, Jaffe said. His interest in sex with Tammy further reinforced Karla's feelings of inadequacy, Jaffe wrote. After Tammy died, Karla was blamed by Paul for Tammy's death "because Mr. Bernardo believed that if Ms. Homolka had been everything he desired in a woman, he would not have wanted to have sex with Tammy." After Tammy's death, Jaffe said, Karla felt trapped. She also feared that Paul would carry out his threats to have her entire family killed and "make it look like an accident." Her biggest fear was that her role in Tammy's death would be revealed.

During the rape and murder of Leslie Mahaffy, Jaffe wrote, "Ms. Homolka felt helpless about her ability to protect Leslie from harm. Ms. Homolka attempted to voice objections to Mr. Bernardo's sadistic demands; however, she felt she was under his control. Afterwards, she had no alternative but to marry Bernardo because she feared failing to do so would result in revelations around Tammy."

At the time of Kristen French's kidnapping, rape, and murder, Jaffe wrote, "Ms. Homolka believes that she had totally surrendered to his dominance." Karla told Jaffe that she developed emotions for Kristen and felt empathy for her, but viewed herself as "too weak a person to free Kristen" when Paul twice left the house for food.

"We considered whether or not she was fabricating or exaggerating the extent of abuse she suffered, simply to minimize her role in the deaths of Tammy, Leslie and Kristen," Jaffe wrote. Upon a review of all the records, it was found "she was able to consistently give detailed accounts of the abuse, which involved not only physical and sexual abuse, but also psychological abuse."

"While a finding of truthfulness can only be made by a judge and jury, we would indicate that Ms. Homolka's reports are consistent with other abused women who have lived with extreme levels of violence . . . her inability to disclose the abuse to her family, friends and even medical authorities is understandable in light of her fear of Mr. Bernardo, and her belief that he had the power to destroy her entire family, as threatened . . . Ms. Homolka's sense of powerlessness and awe of Mr. Bernardo's power was reinforced by his ability to cover up and get away with the alleged murders of Tammy, Leslie and Kristen.''

Some women who have faced extreme and repeated violence, Jaffe said, feel that their only escape from their tormentor is to kill him.

''According to Miss Homolka, killing Mr. Bernardo was not a consideration. Despite the fact that her physical and psychological well being was in imminent danger, she still did not believe she had the capacity to kill, but wished for his death through some accident, like a motor vehicle collision. These feelings are consistent with the feelings of battered women trapped by extreme violence.''

Karla, Jaffe concluded, represents an ''extreme form of the battered woman's syndrome.'' The syndrome refers to the violence and the impact it has, including fear, anxiety, depression, and a sense of hopelessness. Extensive research has shown that women also blame themselves for all the problems. Karla, Jaffe notes, was led to believe that if she were a virgin Paul would not have needed to have her perform sexual acts such as anal intercourse.

Jaffe said Karla's self-esteem and self-identification has been increasingly eroded and then redefined by Paul. She perceived that she could never escape. At times, her hopelessness and feelings of disempowerment caused her to think about suicide, Jaffe noted, but she couldn't kill herself because it would inflict further pain on her parents. Whenever Karla resisted Paul's domination, he would abuse and torment her, and the resistance quickly dissipated. Karla told Jaffe that she had to assert control over her own thoughts because of her belief that Paul could read her mind.

''She viewed Mr. Bernardo as the most powerful person in her life and she was clearly justified in her fear of him,'' said Jaffe, noting that Karla was aware that Paul had escaped detection as a rapist and in Tammy's death. She had also seen him disguise his sinister behavior and project the image of a handsome, intelligent, and caring person.

Karla told Jaffe that the only way she could survive was to "shut her mind down." This phenomenon of dissociation is characteristic of battered women, as well as child sexual abuse and rape victims, Jaffe noted. File materials from the Prison for Women show that on one occasion a "potentially explosive" incident occurred in the confinement area where Karla was held. Through the screaming and shouting, Karla kept on sleeping "without so much as a flinch." Jaffe interpreted her actions as "shutting out" or "dissociating" from a threatening situation.

Jaffe likened Karla's reality to that of captives in concentration camps. Because the captors have such extreme power over the victims, the victim perceives the captor as the "supreme authority" over life and will try to appease if only to survive. The phenomenon sees the victim continually lose power to the captor.

Brainwashing was also undertaken on Karla, said Jaffe, noting that Karla was routinely isolated, deprived of sleep, plied with alcohol, and psychologically tormented. This fits with the battered-woman's-syndrome experiences at the London clinic.

While Karla's sense of self-esteem and self-worth were totally destroyed by Paul, Jaffe wrote, her "earlier socialization and solid family background shaped her earlier adolescence to think of herself in terms of being a strong, independent and capable young lady. Since the time of her physical and somewhat psychological departure from Mr. Bernardo, she describes herself 'almost 100 per cent better' and views herself in terms of being seventeen years old again. . . . Ms. Homolka will need considerable therapy and close supervision for many years to come. On one hand she presents herself as a naive, optimistic young woman who wants to start her life over again as if she was 17. On the other hand, she is emotionally fragile and forever traumatized by her victimization and the victimization of Tammy, Leslie and Kristen."

Jaffe noted that intellectual and personality testing put her in the top 2 percent of the population. A mental-health test showed she still had "a high degree of disturbance, consistent with an abused woman and a woman suffering from post-traumatic stress disorder.''

"The significant elements of her profile relate to her extreme anxiety," with nightmares and flashbacks, and "anger that fluctuates between self-blame and hostility" at Paul Bernardo for not only killing Tammy, Kristen and Leslie but destroying her own life.

In addition to Jaffe's testimony, prosecutors offered assessments by other forensic experts, including kidnap and homicide expert Dr. Chris Hatcher of San Francisco and Canadian specialists Dr. Stephen Hucker and Dr. Angus McDonald. But as he had with Jaffe, Judge LeSage would now allow the witnesses to tell the jury their full conclusions.

In his report, Hatcher noted that Paul Bernardo systematically planned and carried out his sexual takeover of the victims and it continued for years without any mistakes. Prior to Karla, Hatcher noted, Paul was obsessed with his girlfriends' virginity and typically used anal intercourse as a means of establishing a bond. By the time he met Karla, Hatcher said, Paul's experience with sexual assaults was enough for him to dominate her.

From a six-hour interview and various psycholocial tests, Hatcher concluded that Karla "had an intense need to be in a romantic relationship with a male who could project and maintain an image of dominance over others and financial/personal/family success in life."

In one psychological test, Karla was evaluated thus: "feelings of depression, loneliness and isolation may have typified extended periods of her life, although she is not inclined to play up these troublesome moods. Her underlying tension and emotional upset are present in disturbing mixtures of anxiety, sadness and guilt. Her insecurity and her fear of abandonment account for what may appear to be a quiet, accepting and benign attitude towards life's difficulties. Apart from her infrequent outbursts, she is conciliatory, placating, and even ingratiating. She hopes to evoke nurturance and protection by assuming a dejected and self-denying manner, by expressing self-doubt, by communicating the need for assurance and direction, and by displaying a desire to submit and comply. By subordinating personal desires, and submitting at times to abuse and intimidation, she hopes to avoid what she fears most—total abandonment.''

Karla, Hatcher said, found the initial relationship with Bernardo exciting and emotionally intense and thought it her best opportunity to obtain a much-wanted lifestyle.

Evidence of Paul Bernardo's fantasies are found in his rap lyrics, Hatcher said, citing Pauls' lyrics on ''The World Is Yours'': ''The world is yours, the illusion has become real, and the more real it becomes, the more desperately they want it, the world is yours, the illusion has become real, ideal, how does it feel, go it at a steal, you're the big wheel, Paul Jason Tale, the world is yours in totality, the illusion has become reality.''

Karla accepted Paul's various abuses ''as part of a price to be paid in order to maintain the image to herself and to the world of a successful, happy couple,'' Hatcher said, adding that she believed her survival and the survival of the relationship would depend upon her cooperation in acting out Paul's sex fantasies.

Although Hucker did not interview either Paul or Karla, he concluded that the evidence suggests Paul is a sexual sadist and demonstrated this before he met Karla.

McDonald, who interviewed Karla Homolka for about six hours on May 13 and 14, 1995, and observed her during court testimony, said it is impossible to give any diagnoses on Karla's sexual deviancy because she is unable or unwilling to admit she has any. He suggested that her behavior ''cannot be explained solely on the basis of intimidation or abuse'' from Paul. McDonald noted that Karla's ''relatively aggressive presentation at times does not seem consistent with the view of her as a fearful, terribly dominated individual, lacking the spine to stand up for yourself. Some of this (new found?) feistiness could be reactive to her growing realization that her earlier lack of backbone led her into an untenable, even life-threatening set of circumstances.'' He concluded: ''Karla Homolka remains something of a diagnostic mystery. Despite her ability to present herself very well, there is a moral vacuity in her which is difficult if not impossible to explain.''

Judge LeSage would not allow expert evidence tending to show that Karla was a compliant victim of a sexual sadist, because it had not been proven that Paul is a sexual sadist. Under the rules of court, Paul would have to put his ''character at issue'' before the Crown could introduce evidence of sexual sadism. Prosecutors argued that the videotapes clearly show that Paul is a sexual sadist and experts are not needed to corroborate this finding. LeSage also noted that some reports were based on information that was not introduced at trial—for example, the ''Deadly Innocence'' tapes and the evidence from a series of rapes. ''Evidence that the accused may be [a serial rapist] is highly prejudicial and inadmissible,'' LeSage ruled. Much of Hatcher's report, he said, focused on Paul Bernardo's character and was not admissible. LeSage added that the issue at trial is whether Paul Bernardo or Karla Homolka killed Leslie Mahaffy and Kristen French. The experts could talk about battered-spouse syndrome and post-traumatic stress disorder, LeSage ruled, but only in a hypothetical manner. He reminded the jury that Karla had given sixteen days of testimony on abuse and had been ''a most bright, articulate and responsive witness.'' Given hypothetical situations about the syndromes, LeSage said, the jury can ''confidently assess the testimony of Homolka.''

Although not unique, cases of man-and-wife killing teams are exceedingly rare. To better help understand what may have happened between Paul Bernardo and Karla Homolka, the authors looked at the studies of former Federal Bureau of Investigation agent Roy Hazelwood, a behavioral sciences expert with the FBI in Quantico, Virginia, for seventeen years until his retirement in January 1994. Hazelwood, a bright, articulate, and religious man who was a military policeman for eleven years before joining the FBI, has helped hundreds of police departments in more than 3,000 homicides and up to 5,000 rape cases. He has also pioneered field research in the strange phenomenon of what are called ''compliant victims'' of sexual sadists—in other words, the wives and girlfriends of serial rapists and killers.

Along with about two hundred police officers, mental-health professionals, and social workers, the authors attended a conference organized by the California-based Specialized Training Services, Inc., at the Hotel Plaza II on Thursday, September 21–22, 1994 in which Hazelwood gave a formal presentation on sexual sadists and their compliant victims. Later, Hazelwood gave the authors a rare personal interview. He would not talk specifics about the Bernardo/Homolka case, because FBI profilers were involved in it and at the time it was still before the courts. However, he openly talked about his studies of serial rapists and killers and their female companions. His research on the women—although only a limited number of women were studied—is the most extensive work in this new field.

To understand the women, Hazelwood said, you have to start with the man who controls them. The serial killers and rapists are not the ignorant, stupid, ugly, miscreant oafs our imagination tells us they should be, he warns; most are intelligent, witty, and charming. "We've fallen into a trap: We expect to see someone with a bad eye, with green teeth, preferably with a couple missing."

In almost all the sex killings Hazelwood has studied, the killer inflicts severe pain on his victim, mostly through sex, before he kills them. Hazelwood believes the human sex drive functions on 10 percent innate biological reproductive drive, 20 percent physiological stimuli, and 70 percent psychosexual or sensory experience. The third component, he offers, explains why some sex criminals are attracted to children, different types of clothing, inanimate objects, and such. While the sex drive might be strong in the killer, the motivation for the sex crime is not in sex, Hazelwood said. The FBI has seen rape victims as young as two hours, he went on, the oldest being ninety-eight years. Hazelwood quoted a 1977 study by Groth, Burgess, and Holmstrom in which the researchers ascertained that the underlying motivation for these crimes is a quest for power, anger, or a combination of both. Sexual assault, they said, services nonsexual needs.

"From the motivation come complementary fantasies. These fantasies begin to be acted out," said Hazelwood.

In one interview Hazelwood had with a sex killer, he asked the man to say what he told his victims during rape. The man told Hazelwood he expressed his innermost anger. Hazelwood asked him what he meant. "I told her she's a no-good fucking cunt," the killer replied.

"They hate their moms, we hear that repeatedly," said Hazelwood, adding that it is not uncommon for a sexual sadist to be illegitimate and this fact "certainly plays a role" in their behavior. They can understand love from an intellectual standpoint, but emotionally they have no knowledge of the feelings associated with love. For some, their previous attempts to show emotion was met with brutality and punishment.

Hazelwood reported in a joint article with noted psychiatrist Dr. Park Elliott Dietz and social worker Dr. Janet Warren that one sadist defined his affliction as follows: "The wish to inflict pain on others is not the essence of sadism. One essential impulse: to have complete mastery over another person, to make him/her a helpless object of our will, to become the absolute ruler over her, to become her God, to do with her as one pleases. To humiliate her, to enslave her, are means to this end, and the most important radical aim is to make her suffer, since there is no greater power over another person than that of inflicting pain on her to force her to undergo suffering without her being able to defend herself. The pleasure in the complete domination over another person is the very essence of the sadistic drive." The sadist who wrote these words, Hazelwood noted, had planned to build a residence with a built-in sadomasochistic "play area," or dungeon, and an incinerator so he could get rid of evidence.

Many sex killers choose prostitutes as victims solely because of easy opportunity. A prostitute will do anything and go anywhere with anybody. But unlike the still-at-large Green River killer, Britain's Yorkshire Ripper, and Rochester's Arthur Shawcross, notorious American serial killer Ted Bundy stayed away from the easy-to-get prostitutes because they were far beneath his fantasy. Bundy, whose intelligence could never help him overcome the rage he felt at being illegitimate and raised in a lower class, targeted college women because he could never acquire and dominate them in real life. Bundy used some well-planned ruses—including a cast on his arm and crutches—to gain sympathy from his intended victims and thus lure them into an unnatural closeness with him. Bundy, Hazelwood said, was not only a psychopath but also suffered from narcissism and delusions of grandeur.

The most violent rapists, Hazelwood said, are the killers who fit either into the categories of the anger-retaliatory rapist or the anger-excitation rapist. The first category includes rapists who use excessive violence in their attacks solely to punish and degrade women. The anger-retaliatory rapist typically has an explosive temper, is impulsive, often has a bad credit record, and is involved in domestic violence. The anger-excitation rapist wants to get total domination and conrol over his victims; to cause physical and emotional pain to his prey. This type of rapist is "a true sexual sadist," said Hazelwood. He is not sexually aroused by pain, but uses sex as a tool to elicit the suffering of his victim. Typically, Hazelwood said, sexual sadists are always psychopaths who feel no shame, no empathy, no remorse, no anxiety, although they "fake it" very well.

Hazelwood said a sexual-sadist rapist will drive "miles and miles" seeking out his prey. For example, one of the Hillside Stranglers, Ken Bianchi, logged an average of 250 miles in eight hours while working as a security guard in a segment of a Washington State city that was only twenty-five square miles.

Hazelwood has interviewed fifteen women who were in relationships with sexual sadists involved in serial rapes and serial murders. Four of the women helped their husbands commit murder. One helped her husband kill ten other women. All fifteen women who found themselves snared in the perverse web of sexual sadists shared normal middle-class to upper-middle-class backgrounds and were of average or better intelligence. They worked as a bank employee, a fire systems engineer, a business owner, an insurance broker, a nurse, a retail clerk, and in other respectable professions. One woman, Elaine, was street-savvy enough to earn $65,000 a year, but at home she was completely submissive to her sadistic husband. One weekend, Elaine was bound like a mummy with adhesive tape and every hour on the hour her sadist husband would stand her up and knock her down, just for his fun. Realizing, finally, that her husband was going to kill her, she hopped out of the house when her husband left. Later, when she was unwrapped of tape and asked by police if she wished to press charges, Elaine said, "I just want to go home."

Before their involvement with the sadists, only one of the fifteen women had prior sadomasochistic experience, and only soft bondage at that. Similarly, only one woman had received psychiatric treatment, one had a criminal past (stealing a tube of lipstick at age fourteen), one had been an alcoholic, and one had abused drugs. Afterward, they were all addicted to alcohol and drugs and all except one is now in mental-health care, not because she is better, Hazelwood said, but because she denies everything and refuses treatment. All the victims suffered from low self-esteem and a lack of confidence prior to having met their sadistic masters.

It has become apparent to Hazelwood that the women described not only the same types of extreme emotional, physical, and sexual abuse, but also a common process of transformation through which each became the compliant appendage of her sexually sadistic partner. Hazelwood and his colleagues have now established five definitive steps that occur when a sexual sadist is successful at taking over a woman's will.

First, it appears that sexual sadists develop an innate ability to identify a naive, passive, and vulnerable woman. All the women told Hazelwood they were feeling depressed about themselves when they met the sadist. In turn, Hazelwood concluded, the sadist has the ability to exploit the women's vulnerability and manipulate them into scenarios that would meet the sadist's need for dominance, control, and sadistic sex. He chooses "nice" women, perhaps because they are easier to degrade and humiliate.

Second, the sadist charms his chosen target into loving him, acting as if he is considerate, daring, unselfish, attentive.

He gives them spontaneous gifts and constantly attends to their desires. The sadists seduce the women with romance. Hazelwood learned that all the women rapidly fell in love with the men. The sadist continues heaping his affections on the woman until he manipulates her into gratifying his sexual desires. Then he cultivates the woman's genuine affection before going on to the third step.

Third, the sadist persuades the woman to engage in sex far beyond her normal sexual repertoire. After starting the relationship with hardly any sexual experience, the woman is introduced to bondage, fellatio, dildos, anal intercourse, and sex photography, Hazelwood noted. The sadist then uses positive reinforcement, telling his woman he likes what she is doing, or negative reinforcement—he pouts or rejects with the ultimate aim of securing continued sexual compliance. Over time, what begins as infrequent sexual behavior becomes routine. There is a breaking down of the old values and isolation from the woman's family and the norms the woman identifies with. What was once abnormal behavior becomes normal. Typically, the woman's family is unaware of the changes and the problems in the relationship. The friends notice the changes, especially the control, said Hazelwood, but they rarely interfere because there is no direct evidence and they fear intruding in a relationship that on the surface appears to be happy.

Fourth, after he has shaped the woman's sexual behavior, the sadist sets about isolating her from her friends. At first it starts out as possessiveness and jealousy. Any activity that does not center on the sadist is sharply criticized. Said Hazelwood: "Restrictive measures were used so that the world of these women became increasingly circumscribed and their circle of confidants eventually dissipated." Sometimes these measures are subtly orchestrated. One man, he noted, convinced his wife they could afford her to have only $1.50 a day for lunch. Gradually she became socially isolated. The women become totally dependent on the sadist; they have been conditioned to such a degree that they need the affection and connection and will do anything to maintain it.

In the fifth and ultimate step, the woman is transformed to

become the object of the sadist's physical and psychological punishment.

"Having met, seduced, and transformed a nice woman into a sexually compliant and totally dependent individual, the sadist has validated his theory of women. The woman is now a subservient, inferior being who has allowed herself to be re-created sexually and has participated in sexual acts that no decent woman would engage in, thereby confirming she is a 'bitch' and deserving of punishment.''

Hazelwood noted common abuse patterns in the 15 compliant victims: 15 told of regular beatings; 15 were held captive; 14 were subjected to bondage; 14 were recorded, videotaped, or photographed during sexual acts; 14 were verbally abused; 12 were verbally scripted; 10 were bitten, and 8 were whipped. Six victims reported ligature strangulation during sex.

In the Toronto seminar, Hazelwood played a videotape interview with a woman who was seventeen when she met a thirty-five-year-old man. The women recalled that after only four days of dating the man asked her to marry him. The naive teen agreed, and six weeks later they were married. She had believed his talk of having been a police officer and a military man before he became a restaurant owner and a house owner, but later found he had lied and lied and lied. She told how her husband's mom used to call him the "bastard child.'' He had been the reason why his mother married his father against her desire, and that's why his mother never showed him any love. Her goal at marriage was to please him.

"Everything I did, I did to try and be the perfect wife, not be what all those other women weren't,'' she said.

At first he was a caring sexual partner, but after three months that changed. The teenage wife was housecleaning one day when she found a suitcase full of torture magazines in his special room, a room that had knives and guns and machine-gun belts and other war paraphernalia on the walls. He saw her open the case and became quite angry.

"He was full of rage . . . he said the stuff I found was all part of a fantasy he enjoyed. He had a death fantasy he liked to carry out. He said if I didn't participate, he'd go somewhere else and find someone who would.''

Her husband's games started out with capture, struggle, torture, and rape. Then he turned to demeaning her verbally: "He called me a pig; he called me a cunt; he called me a bitch.''

He scripted her to plead for her life: "Please don't kill me, master; I don't want to die.'' In a talk with the authors, Hazelwood noted that during the interview the woman had "a flat affect, with no visible emotion, which is very common in women like her who have gone through such a traumatic experience. She has been conditioned not to register any emotion or feelings.''

Of the cases Hazelwood has dealt with, the women ultimately told the police of the sadist's crimes and their own role in them and were able to plea-bargain prison terms of between five and fifteen years.

There are certain inherent problems with getting the case ready and the witness ready, Hazelwood told the authors. The woman has made a plea, and she's involved with the offender. The natural reaction of the public is to become angry with what's happened, because they don't understand the rules of evidence and other matters. The bottom line for police in many of these cases is What can we prove without her? She is often the only person privy to what really happened.

"The defense, of course, is that she's lying. That's very difficult to overcome,'' said Hazelwood.

The average person, Hazelwood said, does not understand why the woman acted in the ways she did, because "they are not in that person's position. They are unaware of the conditioning that has led to that point.'' Suggestions that the women are evil are "not true,'' he maintains.

"It's not that they don't appreciate the value of life. It's not that they don't have feelings. They're unable to make decisions. They've been conditioned to the point that they don't have any choice. . . . It's sad, it's really sad.''

Hazelwood said there are many women in our society who have the potential to be exploited but who are not.

CHAPTER
31

Sometimes the phone rings at 61 Dundonald Street and an angry voice threatens to kill Karel or Dorothy or Lori, and, of course, Karla. Sometimes the phone rings and it's a woman who says that she, too, is ensnared in an abusive relationship and can, in some small way, understand what Karla went through, and indeed what the entire Homolka clan has endured.

Throughout Karla's captivity, the Homolkas have visited her in the Prison for Women's "little houses" many times, driving the four hours or so up Highway 401, sometimes with eldest daughter Lori, sometimes with Buddy the rottweiler. Karla, it seems, has a great affection for Buddy, perhaps because it is the pet she always wanted, perhaps because the dog experienced the same sadism she did. Acquaintances of the Homolkas say Dorothy has told them that Karla sends the dog treats from prison, not to mention the packages of used underwear she sends so the dog will remember her by the smell of her body.

Dorothy Homolka told the authors that each day they beat themselves up wondering how they could have been so blind to their daughter's reality. Could they have seen something? Could they have done anything? Might they have stopped the destruction of two of their three daughters?

On the days they attended Paul Bernardo's trial, during Karla's testimony, Paul's testimony, or, in the case of Lori and Dorothy, to testify themselves, they went through excruciating pain as the puzzlement of Paul and Karla's private lives played out in newspapers and on television sets and on the dreaded sex videotapes that were played over and over for the jury to see and the spectators to hear. It is little wonder that Dorothy and Lori covered their ears while the audio sections of the rape videotapes were played.

Sometimes Dorothy and Karel Homolka found themselves on the court's television monitors, such as when the videotape of the younger couple's wedding was played; or when Paul's videotape of his surprise visit, along with Karla, Tammy, and Lori, to a Niagara Falls, New York, hotel on Dorothy and Karel's wedding anniversary in Christmas 1990, was shown to the court, or when the court saw the night of the videotaping at 61 Dundonald Street, when Tammy died. Etched on their minds are the videotaped images, especially at moments like the one in the hotel room on the elder Homolkas' anniversary, when Karel raised his glass to Paul's video camera and says, "Okay, Mr. Bernardo, take care of my daughters!"

"I've cried over that so many times . . . I can't believe we were so stupid," offers Dorothy.

Through Paul's testimony, Dorothy sat stone-faced as the man she used to call her "weekend son" told the jury and millions of Canadians how Karel used to jokingly call her "bitch" and "slutface" and how, according to Paul, it was Dorothy and Karel who taught him how to smuggle.

This horrible courtroom invasion into their privacy—however necessary it may have been for the purposes of the trial—mirrors the problems the family has faced in St. Catharines. They were treated like circus animals, their comings and goings picked apart and ridiculed. They are criticized for anything they do, or for what they don't do. Even at Zehr's department store, where Lori works as a cashier, some customers have complained to management that they shouldn't have "someone like that" employed at the store.

And still, the Homolkas stand behind their daughter in her darkest days. Despite what happened to Tammy, it appears they will be behind Karla forever.

From the start of their nightmare, Dorothy and Karel have avoided reporters like the plague.

Karel Homolka told the authors that he wanted simply to fade away following Paul Bernardo's conviction. More power to him and his family if such a dream can become a reality.

But then, every time the phone rings, the nightmare keeps flooding back. There is no escape.

The truth of the matter is that this story is not going away. And, as with all such complex, emotional events, what gives this story its life are the questions. Always the questions.

Strangely, or perhaps not so strangely since he is a man and men are invariably more violent than women, there are fewer questions surrounding Paul Bernardo. There is little doubt he is a sexual sadist and a psychopath.

There is evidence of his penchant for narcissism, voyeurism, and exhibitionism in his own court statements as well as in the videotapes found in his home. Some behavioral experts would also claim that his avid interest in having sex with drugged adolescent girls shows tendencies of necrophilia. In a chart that maps out the characteristic acts of thirty psychopathic sex murderers compiled by the FBI, Paul's behavior matched nineteen out of a total of twenty-two recorded acts, behavior that represents the work of the worst sexual sadists in North America.

It is clear from the testimony of his longtime girlfriend, Carol, and the observations of his best friend Van Smirnis, that Paul Bernardo drew great pleasure from sexual perversion and power. It is clear from the recollections of those who knew him that Paul Bernardo had a seemingly unending capacity to lie and mislead.

When the authors assessed Paul with the Psychopathy Checklist of Dr. Robert Hare, a guide used by psychologists across North America to identify psychopaths, Paul scored 33 out of a possible 40. Based on FBI studies, Paul also fits the typical profile of a serial sex killer.

As so many sexual sadists tend to be, Paul Bernardo is a psychopath. During his time in court, he exhibited nothing in the way of traditional emotion. He appeared puzzled whenever Crown attorney Ray Houlahan confronted him with the

558   Scott Burnside and Alan Cairns

moral aspects of his forced sex. He described cutting up Leslie Mahaffy's body as clinically as he would have analyzed a
balance sheet at Price Waterhouse.

For all his dreadful sickness, Paul Bernardo is the easy one
to figure out, the one to whom a label can be quickly affixed.
And the jury obviously felt the same way. He will serve a life
term for his acts, as he should.

But the troubling, nagging question—what if Karla was
lying?—will remain. What if Karla, not Paul, killed those
girls? Karla Homolka will forever be the great enigma, the
troubling wild card in this brutally tragic game.

The jury, weighing the significant evidence before it, chose
to believe Karla, at least insofar as who was most likely to
have killed Kristen French and Leslie Mahaffy. They chose
to reject Paul's explanation that the two schoolgirls met their
deaths during those brief moments when he left them alone
with Karla Homolka.

But ultimately, the public will never know what really happened in the tidy Cape Cod home at the corner of Christie
Street and Bayview Drive in Port Dalhousie. Karla, sentenced
to a maximum twelve-year term, proves most troubling to
those who view her tale of Paul's horrific abuse with skepti-
cism.

Strangely, Karla Homolka's harshest critics seem to be
women. Perhaps she receives such severe judgment because
she herself is a woman who contributed in no small way to
the deaths of three young girls and the assault of several others. Perhaps it's because many fear that by hiding behind the
cloak of the battered woman, she may have outfoxed everyone in order to literally get away with murder.

Imagine, if you can, the reaction had Paul Bernardo advanced a psychological defense based on a dysfunctional
family life.

However, if Karla Homolka's story is taken at face value,
there is little doubt that she is someone to be pitied. Not necessarily absolved, but pitied. Paul Bernardo was the second
man to know Karla sexually. Compare her desperate declara-
tions of love and devotion, almost from the moment they met,
to Paul's narcissistic writings in his lyrics. Her only interest,

it seems, was to please him; his only interest was in power, violence, and degradation.

The crucial question, then, is whether Karla Homolka sold her soul for the promise of that Cape Cod home, the handsome husband, and the rottweiler puppy; whether that dream was worthy anything, even the deaths of three young girls, one of whom was her sister. It's a notion that suggests mental illness. Yet, when one considers her character at age seventeen, prior to her meeting Paul, Karla does not even register a trickle on either the Antisocial Personality Disorder criteria or the Hare's Psychopathy Checklist scale.

Some investigators and others close to the case have theorized that Paul Bernardo and Karla Homolka were merely two evil entities drawn together by some great, malevolent force. While an interesting theory, it leaves too much to chance.

If Karla Homolka had been unable to attend that pet-store managers' convention in October 1987, would Paul Bernardo merely have found another compliant companion, another killing partner? Certainly, there seemed to be no shortage of attractive women with bewilderingly low self-esteem who offered themselves willingly to the would-be accountant and rap musician.

Still, one gets the feeling that Paul and Karla together formed an incomparable bond, becoming more than their individual parts would have indicated. If Paul Bernardo was a fire of evil and hatred, then Karla Homolka seemed to be the accelerant that fanned the fire to an even greater frenzy.

By her very actions, Karla Homolka proved true all of Paul Bernardo's twisted beliefs about himself and women. Paul Bernardo thought he was the king, and Karla licked his feet and offered up her sister as proof that he was. Paul Bernardo believed that women were bitches, sluts, whores, and Karla Homolka told him over and over again that she was just that.

Beyond the central figures themselves, controversy will almost certainly follow the various police and government bodies ensnared in this case. Questions will be asked about Carol's discussion with her friend's father, a Metro Police officer, about Paul's behavior. The 1990 tip from Alex and Tina Smirnis that led police to Paul's doorstep, prompting the collection of a blood sample from Paul, also continues to provoke controversy, as does Van Smirnis's May 2, 1992, tip to OPP Constable Rob Haney. Were Niagara police given enough information by Metro police regarding Paul Bernardo, and subsequently did they do a good enough interview with him when they visited his home May 12, 1992? Why didn't Niagara police at that time link Paul with the death, only seventeen months earlier, of Tammy Homolka, whose face bore the strange red marks noticed by so many? Indeed, Jim Cairns announced before Paul's trial that there would be an inquest which would probe the original handling of Tammy Homolka's case.

If police had not trusted witness accounts of the abductor's car being a Camaro and instead broadcast an unidentified two-door sports car, would the likes of stalking victims Lori Lazurak and Rachel Farron have come forward with more formal tips, or would the 44,000 tips on Camaros simply have swollen to 440,000 tips on assorted two-door sports cars?

In addition, there is the twenty-six months it took the DNA sample from Paul to pass through the cash-strapped and understaffed laboratories of the Centre for Forensic Sciences in Toronto. It could be argued that if the CFS had given a greater priority to the sample, the lives of Leslie Mahaffy and Kristen French might have been saved.

Of course, all criticism comes from looking through the thin end of the telescope. Unencumbered by the literally thousands of tips that crossed the desks of Metro and Green Ribbon investigators, there is now a clarity that facilitates criticism. In reality, police started with victims who, in the case of the Scarborough Rapist, hadn't seen their assailant, and, in the cases of Leslie and Kristen, were deceased. From there investigators struggled to identify potential suspects from among Southern Ontario's seven million inhabitants. On the surface, hundreds—if not thousands—of these people appeared to have more potential to rape and murder than did Paul and his beautiful wife Karla.

Who would have thought that such a handsome man, such a beautiful woman, such a perfect couple, would have been wrapped up in something so sinister? They destroy the stereotype of evil that many, including police, cling to, and this explains, in some way, the tremendous attention the case has garnered.

In the end, authorities clearly had no option but to make a deal with Karla. While a longer sentence of sixteen to eighteen years might have been more palatable to a public hungry for justice, it's doubtful it would have meant more truthful testimony. In the long run, would a longer sentence have offered more protection to society or merely keep a shattered woman imprisoned at massive taxpayer expense?

The publication ban, however, is a different bureaucratic animal. The ban almost single-handedly ensured that this sensational case became even more sensational. There is little doubt that facets of the plea bargain and the reasons for sentencing Karla Homolka could have been released to the public without endangering Paul Bernardo's right to a fair trial. It is a fact that despite the massive media coverage and numerous ban breaches, a trial jury was found in Toronto with very little effort. The belief that the jury can make an objective decision based on the evidence they hear at trial is, of course, at the root of the Canadian judicial system.

Many believed the Kovacs ban was a gross insult to the intelligence of the Canadian public.

But all of these issues pale when compared to the discovery of the sex tapes. If the tapes had been discovered during the ten-week search of 57 Bayview Drive, the deal with Karla Homolka would be a moot point. Faced with the searing images on those tapes, Karla Homolka would in all likelihood have been content to plead out to second-degree murder. Had the tapes been found, the length and cost of the Paul Bernardo case would have been dramatically reduced.

As for the people portrayed within this book, they, too, are paying a price.

From the public viewpoint, the victims are easily identifiable: Doug and Donna French; Dan and Debbie Mahaffy, and their families and friends. These people, of course, have suffered what no human being should ever suffer.

But the list of those whose lives have been changed forever by this case goes much deeper.

562 Scott Burnside and Alan Cairns

Consider, too, Karel and Dorothy and Lori Homolka. What tortured thoughts exist under their roof? Many people ask how the Homolkas can stand by Karla after what she did to the schoolgirls and to their own daughter, Tammy. Dorothy Homolka's response is "Any parent should know what the answer is."

The answer lies not only in the innate love parents have for their children but most certainly in the guilt they must feel for their part in allowing the relationship between Karla and Paul to prosper. Wasn't it the Homolkas who allowed their "weekend son" to stay over? Wasn't it the Homolkas who entrusted all three of their daughters to Paul Bernardo? Wasn't it the Homolkas who financed the lavish 1991 wedding.

According to Dorothy Homolka, the family feels it has been treated like "accomplices instead of victims." People forget, she laments, that through this tragedy they, too, lost a dear, innocent daughter. In addition, they must live with the fact that another daughter helped kill her.

At another level, hardly a day passes that Van Smirnis doesn't think about the man who was his best friend for twenty-five years and then turned out to be a serial killer. The old friends, the old places, are part of another man's live now as Van tries to rebuild his tattered identity with his wife Joanne and their young daughter.

In a quiet New York State town, Alex and Kathy Ford raise their own child, trying to come to grips with a past that included Canada's most infamous couple. They dare not view their own wedding video for fear of seeing Paul and Karla walking hand in hand as part of the wedding party. The foam board on which the wedding guests signed their names and wrote congratulatory messages will be forever stained with the names of Paul and Karla.

Patty Seger is now separated from Karla's uncle, Calvin.

In Scarborough, Ken and Marilyn Bernardo continue to live together at 21 Sir Raymond Drive, closing their eyes to the facts of their son's behavior just as they did throughout their marriage. Ken has suffered many consequences as a result of his conviction on the sex-related charge back in February.

The victim of about twenty years ago cannot be named to protect her identity.

The Bernardo's did not attend court, says Ken, because Paul was concerned for their safety. It is more likely that Paul did not want them in court because, in his warped mind, they are an embarrassment to him, a sentiment he voiced to friends time and time again.

On the outskirts of a Northern Ontario city, Paul's sister Debbie lives a life estranged from her parents. When contacted to help with this book, Debbie refused to give an interview, saying her life is hell. And it is. Her son, David, who was eleven years old at the time of Paul's trial, had great difficulty after this mother's separation from Glen Yandeau. Police officers who have many times been called to Debbie's house to quell David's fury find him "uncontrollable." If he is not taken out tied to a stretcher he will fight them from the house to the cruiser. Debbie's daughter, Samantha, on the other hand, eight years old at the time of the trial, recently complained to her mom about a baby-sitter's actions.

Somewhere in Kitchener, Ontario, a businessman lives with the secret that his sexual affair around Christmas 1963 resulted in a child who is not only illegitimate, but a bastard, a child named Paul Bernardo. The alleged father did not cooperate with police and has not returned numerous telephone calls made by the authors.

As for Karla Homolka she will remain in prison segregation, probably until her release. There is little doubt that if she were put into the prison's general population she would be killed, or severely injured. Karla Homolka will be moved from the archaic Prison for Women to the less restrictive Kitchener Women's Prison upon its completion, which is slated for 1996.

There is no death sentence in Canada, but Paul Bernardo will likely spend the rest of his life isolated in a private cell in a high-security prison. Upon his conviction, Paul was dispatched to a special wing at the Kingston Penitentiary, where a special plexiglass-fronted cell has been built, much like the one that houses Hannibal Lecter in one of Paul's favorite movies *The Silence of the Lambs.* Any other arrangement would mean a death sentence.

From his small, barred window, Paul can see the towers of the Prison for Women, only a few hundred yards away. He is so near, but so far from, his ex-wife, his former slave, his accomplice, and the woman whose testimony brought his sick fantasies crashing to the ground. Never again will Paul Bernardo terrorize teenage girls and young women. In prison, everyone knows who he is and what he did and what he could do again. In prison, deadly innocence goes nowhere.

ABOUT THE AUTHORS

SCOTT BURNSIDE has been a journalist for over a decade. After earning Bachelors Degrees in both Journalism and Education, he served as a reporter for the *Windsor Star*, where he covered City Hall and was the principle writer/reporter for two award-winning series. In his three years at the *Toronto Sun*, Burnside has covered the major stories of the day, including the Kristen French murder investigation. He is the recipient of numerous awards for outstanding journalism, among them: The 1994 Edward Dunlop Award for Spot Reporting; The 1991 Southam President's Award; The 1991 Western Ontario Newspaper Award and the 1990 National Newspaper Award.

ALAN CAIRNS began his career in journalism as a reporter and photographer for the *Windsor Star*, where he covered municipal politics, agriculture, labor and news events, eventually serving as their police reporter. After working briefly for the *Hamilton Spectator*, he joined the *Toronto Sun* as a general reporter. He left his post as Assistant City Editor to cover the Kristen French/Leslie Mahaffy murder probe and the subsequent cases against Karla Homolka and Paul Bernardo. Specializing in prison and parole reporting, he has written numerous feature stories on multiple murder cases. Cairns has been distinguished by a number of awards, including the 1994 Jamie Westcott Award for Crime Reporting and the 1993 Edward Dunlop award for Investigative Reporting. He is a two time recipient of the Western Ontario News Award for Spot News, first in 1983 and again in 1988.